Visual Database Systems 3

IFIP – The International Federation for Information Processing

IFIP was founded in 1960 under the auspices of UNESCO, following the First World Computer Congress held in Paris the previous year. An umbrella organization for societies working in information processing, IFIP's aim is two-fold: to support information processing within its member countries and to encourage technology transfer to developing nations. As its mission statement clearly states,

> IFIP's mission is to be the leading, truly international, apolitical organization which encourages and assists in the development, exploitation and application of information technology for the benefit of all people.

IFIP is a non-profitmaking organization, run almost solely by 2500 volunteers. It operates through a number of technical committees, which organize events and publications. IFIP's events range from an international congress to local seminars, but the most important are:

- the IFIP World Computer Congress, held every second year;
- open conferences;
- working conferences.

The flagship event is the IFIP World Computer Congress, at which both invited and contributed papers are presented. Contributed papers are rigorously refereed and the rejection rate is high.

As with the Congress, participation in the open conferences is open to all and papers may be invited or submitted. Again, submitted papers are stringently refereed.

The working conferences are structured differently. They are usually run by a working group and attendance is small and by invitation only. Their purpose is to create an atmosphere conducive to innovation and development. Refereeing is less rigorous and papers are subjected to extensive group discussion.

Publications arising from IFIP events vary. The papers presented at the IFIP World Computer Congress and at open conferences are published as conference proceedings, while the results of the working conferences are often published as collections of selected and edited papers.

Any national society whose primary activity is in information may apply to become a full member of IFIP, although full membership is restricted to one society per country. Full members are entitled to vote at the annual General Assembly, National societies preferring a less committed involvement may apply for associate or corresponding membership. Associate members enjoy the same benefits as full members, but without voting rights. Corresponding members are not represented in IFIP bodies. Affiliated membership is open to non-national societies, and individual and honorary membership schemes are also offered.

Visual Database Systems 3

Visual information management

Proceedings of the third IFIP 2.6 working conference on visual database systems, 1995

Edited by

Stefano Spaccapietra
Swiss Federal Institute of Technology
Lausanne
Switzerland

and

Ramesh Jain
University of California
San Diego
USA

SPRINGER-SCIENCE+BUSINESS MEDIA, B.V.

First edition 1995

Originally published by Chapman & Hall in 1995
MyCopy version of the original edition 1995

DOI 10.1007/978-0-387-34905-3

A catalogue record for this book is available from the British Library

Printed on permanent acid-free text paper, manufactured in accordance with ANSI/NISO Z39.48-1992 and ANSI/NISO Z39.48-1984 (Permanence of Paper).
www.springer.com/mycopy

In memoriam Elöd Knuth

It is with deep sorrow that we have heard of the decease of Professor Elöd Knuth on December 25, 1992. Professor Knuth, who was with the Computer and Automation Institute of the Hungarian Academy of Sciences, had organized the Second IFIP 2.6 Working Conference on Visual Database Systems in Budapest in October 1991.

Given the economic hardships of Hungary shortly after the fall of the iron curtain, his success in assembling a scientifically demanding program, arranging a pleasant conference, and editing the proceedings in a timely fashion, all with very little help from outside, demand our greatest respect. As participants in the series of Conferences on Visual Database Systems we owe him very much.

For the 1991 Program Committee
Lutz M. Wegner

CONTENTS

PREFACE

Both the way we look at data, through a DBMS, and the nature of data we ask a DBMS to manage have drastically evolved over the last decade, moving from text to images (and to sound to a lesser extent). Visual representations are used extensively within new user interfaces. Powerful visual approaches are being experimented for data manipulation, including the investigation of three-dimensional display techniques. Similarly, sophisticated data visualization techniques are dramatically improving the understanding of the information extracted from a database. On the other hand, more and more applications use images as basic data or to enhance the quality and richness of data manipulation services. Image management has opened a wide area of new research topics in image understanding and analysis.

The IFIP 2.6 Working Group on Databases strongly believes that a significant mutual enrichment is possible by confronting ideas, concepts and techniques supporting the work of researcher and practitioners in the two areas of visual interfaces to DBMS and DBMS management of visual data. For this reason, IFIP 2.6 has launched a series of conferences on Visual Database Systems. The first one has been held in Tokyo, 1989. VDB-2 was held in Budapest, 1991. This conference is the third in the series. As the preceding editions, the conference addresses researchers and practitioners active or interested in user interfaces, human-computer communication, knowledge representation and management, image processing and understanding, multimedia database techniques and computer vision.

Based on the call for papers, we received 44 submissions, approximately two thirds in the area of visual interfaces and one third in the area of visual data management. Such a number is currently typical for focused conferences like VDB-3. Less typical is the fact that the average quality of the submissions was remarkably good, resulting in the acceptance of 24 of them, whose reviews by three members of the Program Committee resulted in good scores. Geographically speaking, submissions were quite widespread, coming from Germany, Italy, France, UK, Sweden, USA, Chile, Singapore, Korea, Japan, Australia. A great thank to all authors, whose dedication made this conference possible.

We were happy to be able to complement the accepted papers with an invited talk by one of the most prestigious figures in visualization, Prof. Ben Shneiderman, and with a panel lead by Prof. Tiziana Catarci to explore new metaphors for visualization. Prototypes demonstrations and a poster session were also arranged, to welcome delegates with a whole set of opportunities to get acquainted with the most recent advances in the areas covered by the conference.

We would like to thank all program committee members and external referees for the time they have dedicated to a careful evaluation of the submissions.
We are also very grateful to the Conference Chair, Prof. S.K. Chang, for his support in the preparation of the conference. Many many thanks are due to Dr. Yves Dennebouy, Organizing Committee Chair, who has been solving so many practical problems and issues since the announcement of the conference, and to Mrs. Marlyse Taric and Emmanuel Buff for the many hours they have spent in secretarial support.

At last, we would like to forward a very warm welcome to the delegates, hoping that they will find this event stimulating and beneficial to their future activities. We are looking forward to see them back at VDB-4.

Stefano Spaccapietra　　　　Ramesh Jain

Program Co-Chairs

The Working Group on Data Bases of the International Federation for Information Processing

Prof. Dr. E. J. Neuhold
GMD-IPSI
Dolivostrasse 15, 64293 Darmstadt, Germany
Phone: ++49/6151/869-802
Fax: ++49/6151/869-818
e-mail: neuhold@darmstadt.gmd.de

The International Federation for Information Processing (IFIP) was founded in the late fifties as a federation of computer related professional associations like ACM, IEEE Computer Society, GI or AFCET.

It currently has 41 members and has given itself a technical substructure of 14 Technical Committees. The second of those Committees (TC-2) contains nine working groups all closely related to programming or programming specifications.

The Working Group (WG 2.6) as the sixth of the groups in TC-2 is concerned with many of the aspects encountered in today's databases.

It has been involved from its inception (1974) with all aspects of data modelling and database models. WG 2.6 has organized a number of working conferences on data models and five working conferences on data semantics (DS-1 to DS-5). All of the proceedings of these conferences have been published in the IFIP series of Elsevier/North-Holland Publishing Company. In these conferences you will find discussions on the benefits of relational versus network data models. Also many approaches to represent the data structures and their semantics with models like the Entity Relation-ship Model, the Semantic Data Model, NIAM, the Binary Data Model, etc.

Over the last few years the Working Group has extended its scope to include databases that contain visual and multimedia data but also towards the visualization of data models, data, and information. The present proceedings contain the papers delivered of the third Visual Database Systems Working Conference (VDB-3) organized by the Working Group.

Formally the Working Group 2.6 on Database has the following scopes and aims:

Aim:
To assess the different approaches to knowledge representation, their practical relevance, and their architectural requirements with respect to database systems.

Scope:
Formalisms and architectures exist for expressing and capturing knowledge for the purpose of its representation and manipulation in information bases. Knowledge representation formalisms and their associated languages require formal semantically rich descriptions of all aspects of a knowledge-based system.

Its current membership stands as:
Prof. Dr. E.J. Neuhold, Chairman
Prof. S. Spaccapietra, Secretary

P. Apers, NL	W. Kent, USA	T.B. Steel, Jr., USA
R. de Caluwe, B	W. Klas, D	R. Studer, D
O. de Troyer, NL	R. Meersman, B	K.-Y. Whang, K
T. Dillon, AUS	M. Papazoglou, AUS	G. Wiederhold, USA
K. Dittrich, CH	C. Piprani, CDN	T.U. Zahle, DK
H.-D. Ehrich, D	A. Pirotte, B	
E.D. Falkenberg, NL	F. Saltor, E	
H. Kangassalo, SF	M.H. Scholl, D	

If you like to join (you would first become an observer, later possibly a member) please contact the group's chairman Erich J. Neuhold (e-mail: neuhold@darmstadt.gmd.de).

Chapman & Hall has now become the official publisher of IFIP and the current proceedings are the first one of the WG 2.6 Working Conferences published by them. We are very thankful for the excellent work they have been doing.

I would also like to thank S. K. Chang as General Chair and Ramesh Jain and Stefano Spaccapietra, who as Program Chairmen and editors of the proceedings have made these proceedings possible and have contributed manyfold to the success of the conference.

CONFERENCE ORGANIZATION

Conference Chair:

S. K. Chang, University of Pittsburgh, USA

Program Co-Chairs:

Stefano Spaccapietra - EPF Lausanne, Switzerland
Ramesh Jain - University of California at San Diego, USA

Program Committee

Dave Abel, Australia
Christian Breiteneder, Austria
Tiziana Catarci, Italy
Max J. Egenhofer, USA
William I. Grosky, USA
Hannu Kangassalo, Finland
Stefano Levialdi, Italy
Pericles Loucopoulos, UK
Yoshifumi Masunaga, Japan
Alberto Mendelzon, Canada
Wayne Niblack, USA
Haran Samet, USA
Peter Scheuermann, USA
Stephen W. Smoliar, Singapore
Daniel Thalmann, Switzerland
Kyu-Young Whang, Korea
Marie-France Barthet, France
Alfonso F. Cardenas, USA
Richard Cooper, UK
Amarnath Gupta, India
Tosiyasu L. Kunii, Japan
Robert Laurini, France
Tom D.C. Little, USA
Rajiv Mahrotra, USA
Robert Meersman, The Netherlands
Erich Neuhold, Germany
Jan Paredaens, Belgium
Masao Sakauchi, Japan
Arnold Smeulders, The Netherlands
John Stasko, USA
Agnes Voisard, Germany
C. Thomas Wu, USA

Organizing Chair:

Dr. Yves Dennebouy
EPFL-DI-LBD
CH 1015 Lausanne
Switzerland
fax: +41 21 693 51 95
email: dennebouy@di.epfl.ch

External Referees

Gulrukh Ahanger
Carel van den Berg
Subhash Bhalla
Sanjiv Bhatia
Pedja Bigdnavich
Alberto Del Bimbo
Hans-Dieter Boecker
P. Bottoni
Mark Cameron
Gisli R. Hjaltason
Pat Kelly
Richard Potter
Andy Tai
Ulrich Thiel
Jae-Dong Yang

INTRODUCTION

Shi-Kuo Chang
Department of Computer Science, University of Pittsburgh
Pittsburgh, USA, Tel 412-624-8423, Fax 412-624-8465, E-mail chang@cs.pitt.edu

The theme of the two previous IFIP Conferences on Visual Database Systems was on the description and management of image data. The third Conference on Visual Database Systems has a dual theme: the management of visual data and the visual management of data. Therefore the scope of this conference is broader and addresses two important and related areas of research. Indeed, both research areas have reached a certain level of maturity, so that the researchers are now prepared to address some important issues. Let us first examine these two areas separately, and then look at the common issue.

For the visual management of data, the first important question is: "What are the appropriate visualization techniques?" The British economist Schumacher wrote a book, "Small is Beautiful - Economics as if people mattered", in which he proposed *appropriate technologies* that are suitable to the people and to the environment. These days we are overwhelmed by the multimedia hype. Maybe we should also paraphrase Schumacher, "Small is Beautiful - Visualization as if people mattered", and ask: what are the appropriate visualization techniques that are suitable to the users and effective in the solution of real world problems?

The second important question is: "Can the visualization techniques scale up?" Especially for very large databases, a brute-force approach to visualization can lead to a massive amount of details, which may be even worse than the raw data themselves. Can visualization techniques scale up and how?

The last and most pressing question is: "How to perform experiments to prove appropriateness and scalability?" In other words, what experiments should be done, to convince people that visualization of very large databases can increase productivity?

For the management of visual data, which includes graphics, images, video and animation sequences, we can also pose the following questions.

The first question is: "What are the appropriate indexing techniques?" Many indexing techniques have been developed for image data, graphics data, and more recently video data. Some techniques are appropriate for predetermined queries, and some for arbitrary queries. Some take into consideration the temporal aspects, and the others consider mainly spatial information. A comprehensive classification and evaluation of these indexing techniques is yet to be made.

The second question is: "Can these indexing techniques scale up?" Large scale experiments need to be performed, to validate the different proposed approaches.

Finally, for both the management of visual data and the visual management of data, a common issue can be phrased as the following question: "How and when to switch among different paradigms?" As an example, Ben Shneidermann's recent work clearly demonstrates the desirability of a principled approach in providing visualization paradigms to the end user. In the management of visual data, the guided switch between spatial and temporal domains may be of fundamental importance. Although time and space may have similar mathematical structures, the techniques and pragmatics in the management of temporal and spatial information may be quite different.

It is a pleasure to note that papers in this proceedings have addressed many aspects of the above described issues, reporting on important new results, especially in the area of visualization, which may impact the related issues in the management of visual data in the years to come.

INVITED PAPER

1

Starfield visualization with interactive smooth zooming

*N. K. Jog† and B. Shneiderman**
Human Computer Interaction Lab, Institute for Systems Research
University of Maryland, College Park MD 20742-3255, USA
phone: 1-301-405-2680
fax: 1-301-405-6707
e-mail: ninad@visix.com, ben@cs.umd.edu

† Current address: Visix Software, Inc. Reston, VA 22091.
** Department of Computer Science*

Abstract

This paper discusses the design and implementation of interactive smooth zooming of a starfield display (which is a visualization of a multi-attribute database) and introduces the zoom bar, a new widget for zooming and panning. Whereas traditional zoom techniques are based on zooming towards or away from a focal point, this paper introduces a novel approach based on zooming towards or away from a fixed line.

Starfield displays plot items from a database as small selectable glyphs using two of the ordinal attributes of the data as the variables along the display axes. One way of filtering this visual information is by changing the range of displayed values on either of the display axes. If this is done incrementally and smoothly, the starfield display appears to zoom in and out, and users can track the motion of the glyphs without getting disoriented by sudden, large changes in context.

Keywords

starfield display, smooth zooming, animation, zoom bar, dynamic queries, information visualization, focal line

1 INTRODUCTION

Exploring large multi-attribute databases is greatly facilitated by presenting information visually. Then users can dynamically query the database using filtering tools that cause continuous visual updates at a rate of at least 15 frames per second (Carr 1994). Such dynamic query applications typically encode multi-attribute database items as dots or colored rectangles on a two-dimensional scattergram, called a starfield display, with ordinal attributes of the items laid out along the axes.

Geographic applications arise as natural candidates for dynamic queries by representing latitude and longitude along the axes, making the starfield display a map of locations. Other databases exploit the starfield display by mapping two ordinal attributes along the axes and using a third to color code the dots. Additional attributes can be controlled by widgets such as sliders and buttons.

Many applications can employ Visual Information Seeking (VIS) principles (Ahlberg 1994a, Shneiderman 1994, Robertson 1993) to facilitate rapid information browsing and empower users to find patterns and exceptions at a glance. VIS principles encompass direct manipulation, rapid query filtering using sliders and buttons, immediate and continuous visual updates of results, tight coupling i.e. interrelating query components to preserve display invariants and zooming the starfield display to reduce clutter. The users begin with an overview, zoom in on areas of interest, filter out unwanted items and then get details on demand.

Unlike traditional applications such as image browsers that do zooming in large fixed stages, zooming a starfield display should be incremental and flicker-free so that users can track the motion of each rectangle. This gives users a feeling of flying through the data instead of getting disoriented by sudden large changes in view. As Bederson and Hollan affirm in their work on Pad++ sketchpad (Bederson 1994), zooming should be a first-class interaction technique. This paper deals with the design and implementation of zooming on a prototype dynamic queries application, the Film Finder (Ahlberg 1994a).

Whereas zooming an arbitrary image in real time necessitates computations at every pixel, zooming a starfield display is a simpler problem because computations have to be done only for the colored rectangles - not for the background - and there are just hundreds to thousands of rectangles as opposed to a million pixels.

2 PROTOTYPE APPLICATION

2.1 Film Finder

The prototype application that we used as a substrate was the Film Finder (Figures 1 to 3), which is a visualization of a database of two thousand movies. Each film has multiple attributes such as title, director, year of release, popularity, the lists of actors and actresses, length in minutes, category (drama, comedy, horror, etc.) and rating.

The starfield display is formed by plotting each film as a small colored rectangle, with its popularity (scale 1 to 10, where 10 = most popular) on the y axis and the year of release (1920 through 1993) on the x-axis. Therefore recent popular movies appear at the top right of the starfield display. Categories are color coded, so that dramas appear as red rectangles, musicals as yellow, etc. The database is static and has more recent movies than old ones i.e. the distribution of data is non-uniform.

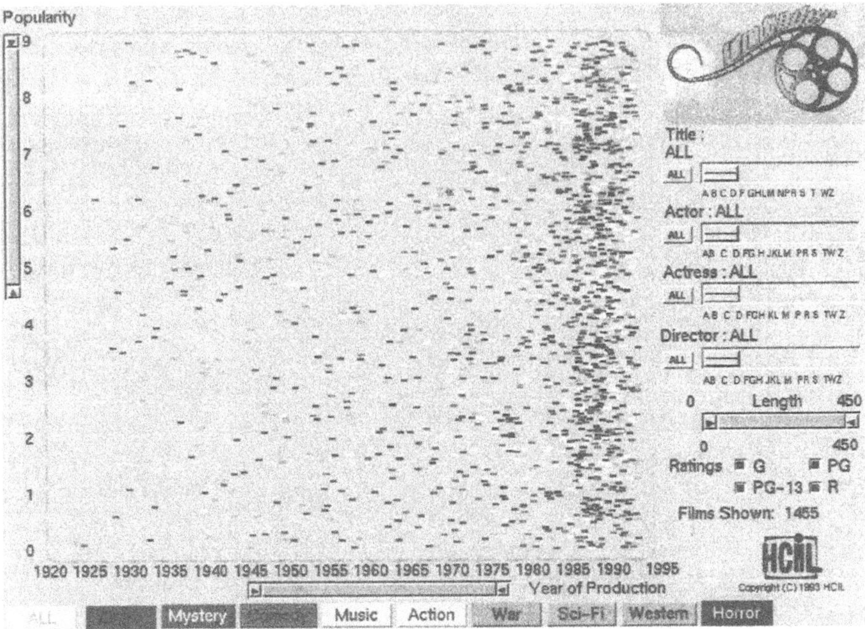

Figure 1 The Film Finder with a fully zoomed-out view, showing films 1920 onwards.

Clicking on a rectangle pops up an information card that lists the attributes of the selected film and shows a still picture from it. The number of rectangles that appear in the starfield display can be controlled by selecting attributes of the films (e.g. show just dramas) or by changing the scale on the x and y axes (e.g. show films made between 1940 and 1970).

These query filters are implemented using widgets such as toggles for category and rating; Alpha Sliders (Ahlberg 1994b) for the title, actors, actresses, director; a range selection slider (Carr 1994) for movie length and a new widget called the zoom bar for varying the scale on the x and y display axes.

2.2 Global and local effects of varying attributes

We distinguish query filters that have local effects and those whose effects are global. For example filters such as an Alpha Slider for selecting the name of an actor affect a small number of display rectangles compared with the total number of films in the database, whereas category toggles have a global effect both in terms of the large number of films they affect and the large display area over which these changes take place.

Since a zooming action changes the scale on one of the display axes, forcing a redisplay of all rectangles, the scale change filter is a global-effect filter. The classification of attributes as global-effect and local-effect ones is highly application-dependent. For example if a query such as "Display all films whose directors' names begin with B" were to be supported, the director would be classified as a global-effect attribute. Because changes to global-effect attributes take a longer time to render, special data storage and access techniques were designed to speed up the display refresh rate.

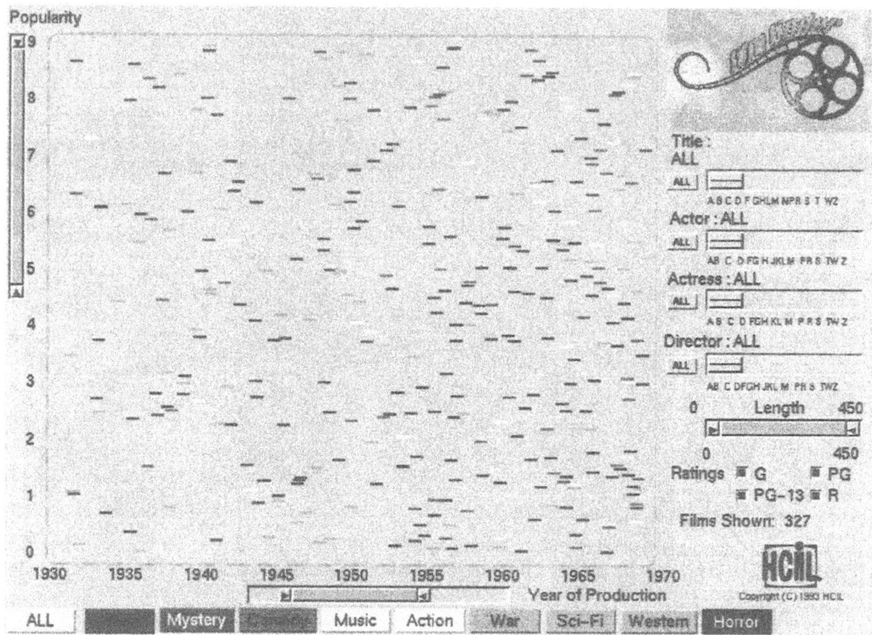

Figure 2 A partially zoomed-in view showing films from 1930 to 1970.

3 THE ZOOMING MECHANISM

Zooming is done by changing the range of attributes on either axis individually, e.g., when the upper limit of years is continuously decreased from 1993 to 1960, the scale on the x-axis keeps increasing. Rectangles representing recently-made movies keep leaving the display and the ones that are within the range grow in size and move so that the display range occupies the entire width of the starfield, looking like a patterned rubber mat getting stretched.

On the other hand, varying any of the non-axis attributes such as category or film length causes rectangles to drop out of the starfield or get added to it, but there is no scaling or movement involved.

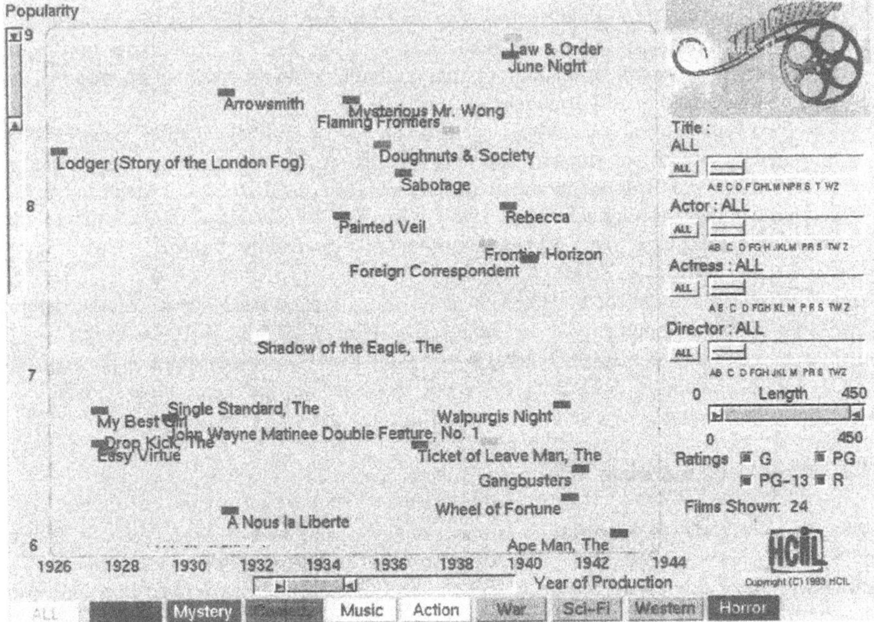

Figure 3 A zoomed-in view showing films from 1926 to 1944.

3.1 A taxonomy of zooming methods

An image can be zoomed continuously or in discrete steps. Zooming in discrete steps is employed when substantial computations are involved in drawing the new view (e.g. zooming an arbitrary picture), or when there is nothing to be gained by doing a continuous zoom, as in changing the view size of text in a desktop publishing application.

Continuous zooming is important to give the user a feel of flying through a space, such as a world of three dimensional graphical objects as in virtual reality applications, or in an information visualization like a starfield display. This allows users to get more detail in areas of intense interest and preserve the sense of location in the surrounding items.

Since continuous zooming requires rapid redrawings, the image must consist of simple objects that can be hierarchically structured. It is difficult to do it on an arbitrary image. Another way of classifying zooming is based on the effects it has over the entire image.

- Some zooming methods typically use a lens that can be moved over an image. The magnified portion appears within the lens boundaries or in a separate window, while the rest of the image stays undistorted. In either case, there is a sharp discontinuity at the boundaries, so users need to mentally integrate the two views. Ghostview, an X-Window application for viewing postscript files uses such a lens, as does the Magic Lens (Bier 1994).

- With a fisheye lens (Sarkar 1992), the selected object is magnified the most, and surrounding objects are progressively diminished in size, giving a perspective view that retains both the focus and the context. Fisheye views free the user of the burden of mentally integrating two discontinuous pictures, but they always retain all the information on the screen, making it look cluttered.
- The third type of zooming changes the scale on one or all of the display axes, causing information to leave or enter the viewing area. It changes the amount of information viewed within the focus area without changing the focus area size, and is identified as the canonical *adjust* operation in (Rao 1994). This has the advantage of uncluttering the screen, but if it is done in big discrete jumps, the user can feel disoriented.

Any of these three zoom methods can be done either continuously or in discrete jumps depending upon the complexity of the image. The FilmFinder uses the third of the above methods in a continuous manner. Figures 1 to 3 show three successive views of the starfield display when zooming is done along the x-axis by decreasing the upper range boundary of the films' year of release.

3.2 Purpose of zooming

Zooming an information visualization display can have twin purposes. When used on images or hierarchy-oriented diagrams such as network node-link diagrams (Schaeffer 1992), successive views can reveal previously hidden detail. For example, each node in a node-link diagram of a network may function as an icon of a sub network, so that zooming in would reveal the details of the sub network as another node-link diagram one rung lower in the hierarchy of networks - what is termed semantic zooming (Bederson 1994). This use of zooming is akin to magnifying an image at a selected point.

The other use of zooming is to reduce visual clutter by filtering out data points that lie outside the new zoom range. The Film Finder uses zooming to achieve the latter effect. Due to zooming, rectangles that overlapped partially in the zoomed out view get spread apart, making it easier to click on them.

To make the zooming seem more realistic, rectangles change size as they are zoomed, but the change is bounded to prevent them from shrinking into nothingness or growing to occupy a large part of the screen. It is also easier to select a larger rectangle than a smaller one, and the amount of zoom can be gauged by looking at the size of the rectangles.

Zooming is trickier to do than panning:

- Panned objects translate by the same amount without changing in size but zoomed objects change size and also move by different amounts depending upon their distance from the focus. This means that zooming exacts more extensive geometrical recomputations than panning.
- The amount of translation of each zoomed rectangle in either the x or y direction is a function of both the current range boundaries, making it impractical to precompute increments and store in a lookup table.

4 A NEW WIDGET FOR ZOOMING

4.1 The zoom bar

Existing zoom widgets such as interactive lens tools are suited for applications where zooming takes place in jumps over small image areas, but they don't work when zooming is continuous over the entire screen and is triggered by changes to a range boundary.

Initiating a zoom using a mouse button works when we wish to zoom towards or away from a fixed point, but the interface is not obvious to the user - there is no on-screen widget to provide a visual cue. Another disadvantage of this method is that there is no feedback to users about the degree of zooming in the current display.

We tried using a pair of buttons for increasing and decreasing each range boundary, but the use of these buttons proved confusing to users. Not only were they unsure of whether a button decreased or increased a boundary, but it was also hard for them to see the link between changing a range boundary and the concomitant zooming effect.

We overcame this deficiency by developing a new widget called the zoom bar, shown in Figure 4, which is a slider with three thumbs. The two extreme thumbs are used to adjust range boundaries. When the right thumb is moved, the upper range boundary is increased or decreased, causing a zoom out or a zoom in by changing the scale on the corresponding display axis. Similarly, the left thumb controls the lower range.

The middle thumb is used to pan over the display range. Its size varies according to the positions of the left and right thumbs, thus changing the width of the window that pans over the data.

Figure 4 The zoom bar. The viewing range is varied by sliding either of the two thumbs. Panning is done using the middle thumb.

The middle thumb has a minimum width, which means that the left and right thumbs can come close together by no more than a specified separation. This separation defines the maximum zoom in of the view. When the two thumbs are at the opposite ends of the slider, the view is fully zoomed out and the middle button is disabled. The scale of each of the x and y display axes is varied individually by its own zoom bar.

When the zoom bar is clicked in the channel on a position other than the thumb, the thumb closest to the clicked point snaps to that location. This causes a jump in one of the range values and results in discrete zooming.

4.2 Strengths and Weaknesses

The zoom bar is intuitive and easy to use because of its similarity with a scrollbar. It occupies a small rectangular area, saving on precious screen space and its operation is rapid because of its small size. The zoom bar also provides clear feedback of the degree of zooming in the current display. It is well suited for both continuous and discrete zooming as well as for panning (sliding a fixed range over the data). However, its scope is restricted to one display dimension at a time.

5 A MODEL FOR ZOOMING

The single-axis-at-a-time-zooming of the prototype application cannot be described in terms of a camera using a focal point. This section describes an alternative model.

While traditional continuous zoom techniques give users the impression of flying perpendicular to a plane (the starfield display plane) towards a fixed point, our novel zooming technique gives the impression of a rubber carpet getting stretched and contracted with the user being a fixed distance away from it. This fundamental difference arises because our zooming scheme provides for independently alterable zoom factors for the x and y axes.

These different zooming techniques can be described as the view seen through a camera which has a variable focal length and whose position can be changed.

Traditional zoom techniques employ one of two possible schemes. Either the camera stays at a fixed place and the focal length changes over time (as in a movie camera), or the camera's field of view remains fixed and the camera moves towards or away from a fixed point. If either case were used in a starfield display, rectangles would appear to move away from the focal point in all directions during zooming in, and appear to converge toward the focal point during zoom out as shown in Figure 5.

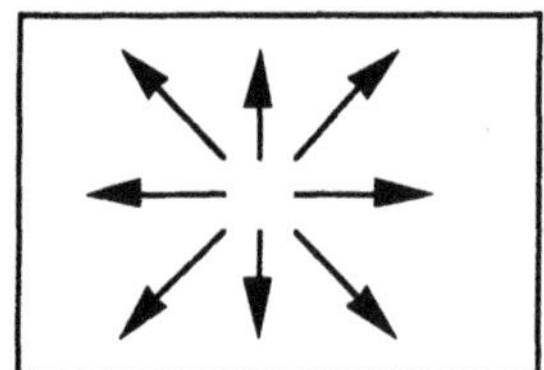

Figure 5 Zooming in causes rectangles to move radially outward from the focal point.

In contrast, zooming in the FilmFinder is done independently in the x and y directions, so there is no single focal point. Instead, there is a *focal line* corresponding to the range boundary that remains fixed. This line could be any of the four sides of the starfield display.

For example, if zooming is done in the horizontal direction and the upper range is increased, the focal line is the left side of the display. Rectangles that lie close to the left boundary move by very small amounts compared with the ones near the right boundary, though all rectangles shrink by the same amount.

As the range increases, rectangles enter the viewing range from the right and start moving leftwards. Figure 6 shows this behavior. In other words, rectangles flatten as they move toward the focal line and elongate as they move away from it.

If a traditional zooming technique with a user-defined focal point of interest is used in the absence of an additional overview screen, the user may feel lost even if the zooming is smooth. However, when the individual-axis zooming of this paper is used, the user's view is always firmly anchored to one of the sides of the starfield display. We conjecture that this leads to a better grasp of location and thereby improved user satisfaction.

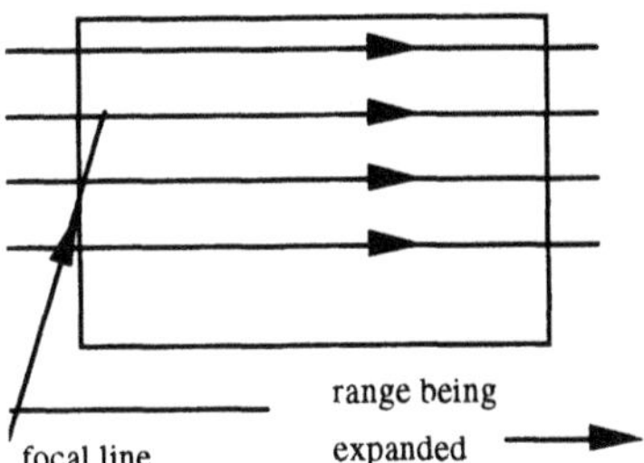

Figure 6 Zooming along x-axis. Arrows show motion of rectangle.

6 IMPLEMENTATION

The Film Finder has been implemented on a Sun SPARC using Galaxy/C, a cross-platform application environment developed by Visix Software (Visix 1994). It can be ported to several platforms - from a slow DOS machine running Windows to a fast Sun, so it becomes imperative to seek software speedups and optimizations to get a rapid display refresh rate instead of relying solely on the use of faster hardware.

Galaxy's object-oriented constructs were used to build customized widgets and other parts of the program. The film data is in flat-file format, taken from the Internet. The entire data is read into a linear array and sorted by several other attributes like length, actors, etc. Each of the individual sorted lists contains pointers (indices) to the linear-array database i.e. the set of all the records are always in the linear array in the order in which they were read in.

6.1 Attaining Smooth Zooming

The following strategies were used to attain smooth zooming.

- **Efficient storage** The items from the database are stored in an array and direct indexing based on the attribute values is used to access them.
- **Rapid access** Items that are being displayed are cached into a contiguous array, so when the display range changes, searches are limited to a smaller subset of items.
- **Double buffering** Successive frames are composed off-screen and dumped onto the display, thereby eliminating the flicker caused by an erase and redraw operation pair.
- **Increased axis resolution** The display positions of item rectangles in successive frames are placed close together so that the animation appears smooth.

7 CONCLUSIONS AND FUTURE WORK

This paper discussed the design and implementation of a smooth zooming mechanism in a dynamic queries application, presented a taxonomy of zooming methods and introduced the zoom bar, an intuitive and rapid widget to facilitates zooming and panning. Smooth zooming of items in a database visualization was achieved by reducing the data access and display bottlenecks.

Zooming can be made faster and smoother by extending the above techniques. When the screen has a large number of rectangles, draw just half of them alternately, as done in the X-Window application xgas. The buffering technique can be varied: instead of erasing and redrawing rectangles on the buffer, an updated image of the union of the old and new areas of each rectangle can be copied onto the buffer.

An important challenge is to find an upper limit on the number of rectangles that can be displayed before the illusion of zooming fails, and to get a concrete measure of the maximum speed of the rectangles (say 1 cm. per second) that can be tolerated.

A more challenging problem is to visualize a database containing 50 000 items. Such a visualization can be made by displaying a small number of representative rectangles (Keim 1993) and zooming in to reveal the hidden ones - using zooming for its traditional purpose of revealing more detail. Handling such huge amounts of data would necessitate the use of linked data structures like k-d trees, range trees or quadtrees (Samet 1990).

A 3-D display of rectangles might be an appealing alternative, but there's the danger of items obscuring each other and of the user getting lost in the "star-tank".

Although the zoom bar is an adequate tool, an alternative tool like a resizable rectangle roving over a miniature overview of the starfield display would permit both zooming and panning over both axes to be done with the same widget.

Another goal is a flexible starfield widget that can visualize many databases. Such a visualization would determine the type of each attribute (integer, string, etc.) and display the corresponding proper widget for controlling it (such as an ordinary slider or an Alpha Slider, etc.)

8 ACKNOWLEDGMENTS

We thank Christopher Ahlberg for implementing the initial version of the FilmFinder, and for his suggestions and review of the paper; Bruce Chih-Lung Lin for identifying efficient storage and access techniques, Andries van Dam, John Hughes and Marko Teittinen for helping define zooming with the camera model and David Mount for helpful suggestions.

Thanks are also due to Richard Chimera for numerous suggestions, to Richard Potter for his review and to Visix Software Inc. for providing us their cross-platform application environment, *Galaxy*. Thanks to Teresa Casey and Ara Kotchian for helping with the images. Finally, we thank the Institute for Systems Research for their support. This research was supported by grants from the National Science Foundation, NSFD CDR-8803012 and NSF EEC 94-02384.

9 REFERENCES

Ahlberg, C. and Shneiderman, B. (1994a) Visual Information Seeking: Tight Coupling of Dynamic Query Filters with Starfield Displays. *Proceedings.of CHI* . ACM, New York. 313-7.

Ahlberg, C. and Shneiderman, B. (1994b) The AlphaSlider: A Compact and Rapid Selector. *Proceedings of CHI*. ACM, New York. 365-72.

Bederson, B. and Hollan, J. (1994) Pad++: A Zooming Graphical Interface for Exploring Alternate Interface Physics. *Proc.eedings of UIST*. ACM, New York.

Bier, E., Stone, M., Fishkin, K., Buxton, W. and Baudel, T. (1994) A Taxonomy of See-Through Tools. *Proc.eedings of CHI*. ACM, New York. 306-12.

Carr, D., Jog, N., Kumar, H., Teittinen, M., Chimera, R. and Ahlberg, C. (1994) The HCIL Widgets: Motivation, Specification, Development and Use. *CAR-TR-734* University of Maryland, College Park.

Foley, J., van Dam, A., Feiner, S. and Hughes, J. (1990)*Computer Graphics, Principles and Practice.* 2nd edition, Addison Wesley, Reading, MA.

Jain, V. and Shneiderman, B. (1994) Data Structures for Dynamic Queries: An Analytical and Experimental Evaluation. *Proceedngs of the Conference on Advanced Visual Interfaces.* ACM, New York. 1-11.

Keim, D., Kriegel, H. and Seidl, T. (1993) Visual Feedback in Querying Large Databases. *Proceedings of IEEE Visualization*. 158-65.

Rao, R. and Card, S. (1994) The Table Lens: Merging Graphical and Symbolic Representations in an Interactive Focus + Context Visualization for Tabular Information. *Proceedings of CHI.* ACM, New York. 318-22.

Robertson, G., Card, S. and Mackinlay, J. (1993) Information Visualization Using 3-D Interactive Animation. *Communications of the ACM* .**36**, Number 4. 57-71.

Samet, H. (1990)*The Design and Analysis of Spatial Data Structures.* Addison Wesley, Reading, MA.

Sarkar, M. and Brown, M. (1992) Graphical Fisheye Views of Graphs. *Proceedings of CHI.* ACM, New York. 83-91.

Schaeffer, D., Zuo, Z., Bartram, L., Dill, J., Dubs, S., Greenberg, S. and Roseman, M. (1992) Comparing Fisheye and Full-Zoom Techniques for Navigation of Hierarchially Clustered Networks.. *Research Report # 92/491/29.* University of Calgary.

Shneiderman, B. (1994) Dynamic Queries for Visual Information Seeking. *IEEE Software.* **11**, Number 6, 70-7.

Visix Software, Inc. (1994) *Galaxy Application Environment* documentation. Visix Software, Inc. Reston, VA.

10 BIOGRAPHIES

Ninad Jog received his B.S. in computer engineering from the University of Bombay, India in 1990, ranking first in the university, and his M.S. in Electrical Engineering from the University of Maryland in 1995, where he worked as a Research Assistant at the Human-Computer Interaction Lab.

He is currently working as a Software Engineer with Visix Software, Inc., Reston, Virginia. His primary interests are in graphical user interfaces, object-oriented programming and parallel programming.

Ben Shneiderman is a professor of computer science, head of the Human-Computer Interaction Laboratory, and a member of the Institute for Systems Research, all at the University of Maryland at College Park. He organizes an annual satellite television presentation, "User Interface Strategies", and is the author of several books, including *Designing the User Interface: Strategies for Effective Human-Computer Interaction* (Addison-Wesley, 1992).

He received a PhD in computer science from the State University of New York at Stony Brook.

PART ONE

Querying by Content

2

Querying Multimedia Data from Multiple Repositories by Content: the Garlic[1] Project

W. F. Cody, L. M. Haas, W. Niblack, M. Arya, M. J. Carey, R. Fagin, M. Flickner, D. Lee, D. Petkovic, P. M. Schwarz, J. Thomas, M. Tork Roth, J. H. Williams and E. L. Wimmers
IBM Almaden Research Center
650 Harry Road
San Jose, California 95120-6099
(408) 927-1740, fax (408) 927-4121
e-mail: cody at almaden.ibm.com or laura at almaden.ibm.com

Abstract

We describe Garlic, an object-oriented multimedia middleware query system. Garlic enables existing data management components, such as a relational database or a full text search engine, to be integrated into an extensible information management system that presents a common interface and user access tools. We focus in this paper on how QBIC, an image retrieval system that provides content-based image queries, can be integrated into Garlic. This results in a system in which a single query can combine visual and nonvisual data using type-specific search techniques, enabling a new breed of multimedia applications

Keywords

Multimedia Database, Heterogeneous Databases, Image Database, Query By Content

1 INTRODUCTION

Many applications today require access to a broad range of datatypes. A patient's medical folder contains MRI scans (image), lab reports (text), doctors' dictated notes (audio), and address and insurance information (record-oriented database data). A geographic information system needs maps, satellite images, and data about roads, buildings, and populations. In many of these areas, specialized software has emerged to allow key datatypes to be queried efficiently, or to support type-specific predicates. For example, there are special systems for fingerprint recognition, for finding specific molecular structures, and to locate areas that overlap or that contain a specific object on a map. The expanding role of multimedia data in many other application domains has sim-

1. Garlic is not an acronym. Most members of the team really like garlic, and enjoy our laboratory's proximity to the Gilroy garlic fields!

ilarly resulted in special purpose systems that provide content based search of their data. Since multimedia data is largely visual and hard to describe precisely, it will be increasingly important to support content based searches that can be specified visually "by example" and that allow for degrees of similarity in the answer set.

The increasing diversity of datatypes and the need for special-purpose data servers is occurring even in traditional application areas like insurance (e.g., to manage videos of damaged property), catalog sales (e.g., to manage collections of photos for product spreads) and advertising (e.g., to manage shots of magazine ads). In these traditional applications, this new data must be managed in coordination with the large amounts of business data and text data that are already managed by a variety of information systems. In the current environment, developing a multimedia application requires the developer to deal with different interfaces for several different data systems, while worrying about how to locate the right system to handle each part of the query, how to optimize the accesses to the various data systems and how to combine the results into a meaningful form for the user. All these tasks are inhibitors to the creation of modern multimedia applications that exploit the rich data environment we live in.

Garlic is an object-oriented multimedia middleware system that is designed to address this problem. Garlic allows existing data management components, such as a relational DBMS, a full text search engine, or an image retrieval system, to be integrated into an extensible information management system. Applications can access any of the data in the underlying data sources through a common, nonprocedural interface, and can exploit the specialized query capabilities of those sources. A single query can access data in several repositories, using the type-specific predicates they support. Garlic also provides a powerful query/browse application that includes type-specific query interfaces in a uniform query framework.

In this paper, we show how Garlic enables applications that need content-based search of visual (and nonvisual) data stored in separate specialized servers. The paper is organized as follows. In the next section, we describe related work. An overview of Garlic is given in Section 3. Section 4 shows how visual data can be incorporated into Garlic. It introduces an image retrieval system supporting content-based image queries (QBIC), describes the steps and the decisions involved in integrating QBIC into Garlic, and then shows how queries combining visual and nonvisual predicates can be processed. At the end of this section we briefly describe a Query/Browse application and show how it allows visual data to be browsed and queried in conjunction with other data reachable through Garlic (Section 4.4). We summarize our contributions and discuss future work in Section 5.

2 RELATED WORK

The multimedia area is expanding at a rapid pace. It includes work on hypermedia systems, specialized servers (e.g., video servers), image and document management tools, interactive games, authoring tools, scripting languages, and so forth. In the personal computer industry, a large number of small-scale multimedia software packages and products have emerged due to the availability and affordability of CD-ROM technology. Several companies are offering "multimedia database" products. These products combine the functionality of a DBMS (typically based on a relational or object-oriented model) with the ability to store images, text, audio, and even short video clips. These systems store and manage all their data, and typically provide keyword search for pre-annotated multimedia data. It is not clear that these systems can scale to large volumes of data.

Mainline database vendors have only recently started to pay attention to multimedia data. The Illustra object-relational DBMS (Ubell, 1994) provides media-specific class libraries (DataBlades(tm)) for storing and managing multimedia data. IBM, Sybase, Oracle and others can store image, video and text in their databases, but support for searching these types by content is just starting to appear. IBM's new UltiMedia Manager is the first product to offer content-based image query (based on QBIC (Niblack, et. al., 1993) technology) in conjunction with standard relational search. Garlic differs from these systems in that it aims to leverage existing intelligent repositories, such as text and image management systems, rather than requiring all multimedia data to be stored within and searched by a single DBMS. Garlic's open approach should enable it to take advantage of continuing advances in multimedia storage and search technology. It should also be more effective for legacy environments, where multimedia data collections (such as document or image libraries) and business data already exist in forms that cannot easily be migrated into a new DBMS.

Content-based retrieval of data is highly type-specific. Years of research have produced a solid technology base for content-based retrieval of documents through the use of various text indexing and search techniques (Salton, 1989). Similarly, simple spatial searches are well-supported by today's geographic information systems ((ESRI, 1990), (TYDAC, 1990), e.g.). Image content-based retrieval of visual data is still in its infancy. Although a few specialized commercial applications exist (such as fingerprint matching systems), most content-based image retrieval systems are research prototypes. Some examples, which focus on interesting feature and model indexing techniques, include (Pentland, et.al., 1994), (Kato, et.al., 1992), (Swain, et.al., 1991), and (Grosky and Mehotra, 1990). Further, with the exception of simple approaches like attaching attributes to spatial objects, or associating user-provided keywords with images, these component search technologies remain largely isolated from one another.

In the database community, much research has been done on heterogeneous distributed database systems (also known as multidatabase systems). These systems aim to enable applications that span multiple DBMS. Surveys of the relevant work can be found in (Elmagarmid, et.al., 1990) and (Hsiao, 1992). Commercial middleware products now exist for providing uniform access to data in multiple databases, relational and otherwise, and to structured files, usually through the provision of a unified relational schema. Models with object-oriented features have been employed in projects such as (Rosenberg, 1982), (Connors, et.al., 1991), (Fang, et.al., 1993) and others. What distinguishes Garlic from these efforts is its focus on providing an object-oriented view of data residing not only in databases and record-based files, but also in a wide variety of media-specific data repositories with specialized search facilities. With the exception of the Papyrus (Connors, et.al., 1991) and Pegasus (Shan, 1993) projects at HP Labs, we are aware of no other efforts that have tried to address the problems involved in supporting heterogeneous, multimedia applications.

3 GARLIC OVERVIEW

Figure 1 depicts the overall architecture of the Garlic system (Carey, et.al., 1995). At the leaves of the figure are a number of data repositories containing the data that Garlic is intended to integrate. Examples of potential data repositories include relational and non-relational database systems, file systems, document managers, image managers, and video servers. Repositories will vary widely in their ability to support content-based search, from a video server which can simply retrieve by video name, to a relational DBMS with its powerful query language. While Garlic will accommodate (i.e., provide access to) more limited servers, we are particularly interested in enabling a richer style of query for a broader range of datatypes. Thus we focus on repositories that provide content-based querying of multimedia datatypes, and on the technology needed to incorporate them into Garlic, in such a way as to exploit their special abilities.

One special repository shown in Figure 1 is the Garlic complex object repository. This repository, provided with Garlic, is used to hold the complex objects that most Garlic applications need to relate together legacy information from different systems, or to create new multimedia objects. For example, an advertising agency that had information about its clients in a relational database, stills of ads in an image server, video clips on a video server and financial reports in a document manager might build Garlic complex objects representing the ad campaigns to link all of this information together.

Above each repository is a repository wrapper. A repository wrapper serves two purposes. First, it exports to Garlic a description of the data types and collections of data that live in that underlying repository. This description is basically a schema for that repository instance, expressed in the Garlic Data Model (Carey, et.al., 1995) (a variant of the ODMG-93 object model (Cattell, et.al., 1994)). It also describes to Garlic the search capabilities of this repository type -- what predicates it supports. Second, the wrapper translates data access and manipulation requests (i.e., queries) from Garlic's internal protocols to the repository's native protocol. Initially, wrappers will have to be created by hand; eventually, we plan to provide tools to ease the task of wrapper generation.

Query processing and data manipulation services, especially for queries where the target data resides in more than one repository, are provided by the Garlic Query Services and Runtime System component shown in Figure 1. This component presents Garlic applications with a unified, object-oriented view of the data accessible by Garlic. This view may be a simple union of all of the repository wrapper schemas, or it may involve subsetting or restructuring of those schemas. Garlic Query Services processes users' and applications' queries, updates and method invocation requests against this view. Queries, expressed in an object-oriented extension of SQL called GQL, are broken into pieces, each of which can be handled by a single wrapper. This process relies on Garlic metadata that describes both the unified Garlic schema and the individual wrapper schemas. The subqueries are initiated by the Garlic Runtime System and the results are combined and returned to the user.

Garlic applications interact with the Query Services and Runtime System through Garlic's ob-

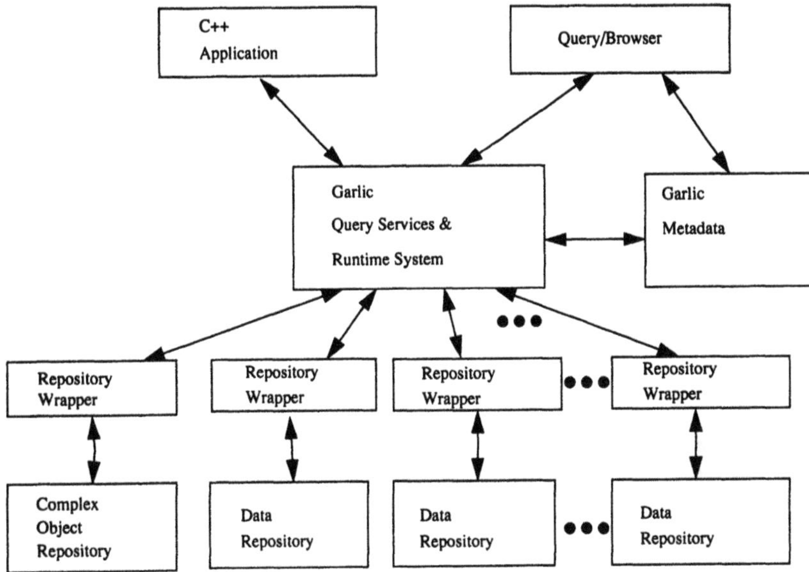

Figure 1. Garlic System Architecture

ject query language and a C++ application programming interface (API). One particularly important application, which is also shown in Figure 1, is the Garlic Query/Browser. This component of Garlic will provide end users of the system with a friendly, graphical interface that supports interactive browsing, navigation, and querying of Garlic databases.

4 QUERYING VISUAL DATA IN GARLIC

In this section, we focus on how queries involving visual data can be handled in Garlic. We start by describing one particular image repository that we are integrating; the QBIC repository provides the ability to search for images by various visual characteristics such as color, texture or layout. We then discuss the design of a wrapper for this repository. Once a wrapper is defined, it is possible to query data in this repository through Garlic. The advantage of Garlic, however, is its ability to handle queries spanning data in visual and other repositories. We illustrate this with an example involving three repositories. Finally, we describe the Garlic query/browser application, and show how it could be used in the same example.

4.1 Query by content of image data -- the QBIC repository

QBIC (Niblack, et.al., 1993) is a research prototype image retrieval system that uses the content of images as the basis of queries. The content used by QBIC includes the colors, textures, shapes, and locations of user-specified objects (e.g., a person, flower, etc.) or areas (e.g., the sky area) in images, and/or the overall distribution and placement of colors, textures, and edges in an image as a whole. Queries are posed graphically/visually, by drawing, sketching, or selecting examples of what is desired. A sample QBIC query is "Find images with a generally green background that have a red, round object in the upper left corner", where the image predicates (red, round, ...) are specified graphically using color wheels and drawing tools, by selecting samples, and so on.

QBIC is a stand-alone system. It has two main components, database population, which prepares a collection of images for query, and database query. Each component has its own user interface and engine. In this section, we describe these two components, and in the next, consider the issues involved in making QBIC's collections and query function accessible to Garlic.

4.1.1 QBIC database population

The QBIC database population step is a one-time process that prepares images for later query. The images are loaded or imported into the system, and several utility operations are performed -- preparing a reduced 100x100 "thumbnail", converting each image to a common system palette and storing available text information. An optional but important step is "object/area identification" in which objects or areas in an image -- a car, a person, swatch of background texture -- are identified. This may be done manually, semi-automatically, or fully automatically, depending on the nature of the images and the objects they contain. For unconstrained natural scenes and general photo clip art, objects are usually identified manually by outlining with a mouse, or by using semi-automatic tools such as flood-fill algorithms for foreground/background identification, or spline-based edge tracking to refine a rough user outline. Automatic methods such as background removal can be used in constrained cases such as images of museum artifacts on generally uniform backgrounds, or images of industrial/commercial parts in a fixed position and under controlled lighting. In any case, the result of object/area identification is a set of outlines or, more generally, bit masks (to allow for disconnected and overlapping areas) defining objects and areas in the images.

For each object/area and for each image as a whole, a set of numeric features are computed that characterize properties of image content. These features are listed in Table 1, and described briefly below.

TABLE 1. QBIC Features

Objects	Images
Average color	Average color
Histogram color	Histogram color
Texture	Texture
Shape	Positional edges (sketch)
Location	Positional color (draw/paint)

Average and Histogram Color: QBIC computes the average Munsell (Miyahara, et.al., 1988) coordinates of each object and image, plus a k element color histogram (k is typically 64 or 256) that gives the percentage of the pixels in each object/image in each of the k colors.

Texture: QBIC's texture features are based on modified versions of the coarseness, contrast, and directionality features proposed in (Tamura, et.al., 1978). Coarseness measures the scale of the texture (pebbles vs. boulders), contrast describes the vividness of the pattern, and directionality describes whether or not the image has a favored direction or is isotropic (grass versus a smooth object).

Shape: QBIC has used several different sets of shape features. One is based on a combination of area, circularity, eccentricity, major axis orientation and a set of algebraic moment invariants. A second is the turning angles or tangent vectors around the perimeter of an object, computed from smooth splines fit to the perimeter. The result is a list of 64 values of turning angle. All shapes are assumed to be non-occluded planar shapes allowing each shape to be represented as a binary image.

Location: The location features are the x and y centroid of the object.

Positional edge (sketch): QBIC implements an image retrieval method similar to the one described in (Hirata, et.al., 1992) and (Kato, et.al., 1992) that allows images to be retrieved based on a rough user sketch. The feature needed to support this retrieval consists of a reduced resolution edge map of each image. QBIC computes a set of edges using a Canny edge operator, and then reduces this to a 64 x 64 edge map, giving the data on which the retrieval by sketch is performed.

Positional color (draw): Positional color or "draw" features are computed by partitioning the image into a number of roughly square grid cells and, for the pixels in each grid cell, computing a set of features. The features computed are average color, a partial color histogram that captures the main colors, and a set of texture parameters. The set of computed features, one for each grid cell, is the draw feature for the entire image.

4.1.2 QBIC image query

Once the set of features for objects and images has been computed, queries may be run. Queries are initiated by a user in an interactive session by graphically specifying a set of image and object properties and requesting images "like" the query specification. For example, images may be requested that contain objects whose color is similar to the color of an indicated object, or a color selected from a color wheel. Full image queries are based on the global set of color and texture features occurring in an image. For example, images may be retrieved that are globally similar, in terms of color and/or texture, to a given image, or, using a menu-based color or texture "picker", a user can select a set of colors and textures and request images containing them in selected proportions. Sample pickers for various features are shown in Plates 1 and 2.

All retrievals on image features are based on similarity, not exact match, and similarity functions are used for each feature or feature set. Most of the similarity functions are based on weighted Euclidean distance in the corresponding feature space (e.g. three dimensional average Munsell color, three dimensional texture, or 20 dimensional shape). Special similarity measures are used for histogram color, turning angle shape, sketch and positional color, as described in (Niblack, et.al., 1993). These measures can be used individually or in a weighted combination. Also, "multi-queries" can be formed, querying on multiple objects, each with multiple properties, and on multiple image attributes, as in a query for an image with a red, round object, a green fish-shaped object, and a blue background.

Example queries are shown in Plates 1, 2, 3 and 4. In all cases, the returned results are ranked, and are shown in order with the best result in the leftmost position, next best in the next position, and so on. Each image returned is displayed as a reduced "thumbnail". The thumbnails are active menu buttons that can be clicked on to give a list of options. The options include: initiate the query "Find images like this one", display the similarity value of this image to the query image, display the (larger) full scale image, place the image in a holding area for later processing, or perform a user defined image operation or comparison.

4.2 Wrapping a QBIC repository

In this section we show how QBIC can be integrated into Garlic. The goal of this integration is to enable applications to exploit QBIC's special facilities for image search in conjunction with other kinds of search on other types of data. So far, we have not thought about integrating QBIC's database population component. Thus, in this section we discuss integration of the two pieces of the database query component of QBIC: the query formation interface and the query engine.

QBIC's specialized query engine was developed as a stand alone system with its own user interface for querying image data. This architecture is similar to many systems on the market which provide content-based querying of particular datatypes (e.g., text, images, maps, molecular structures). In an increasing number of these systems however, (e.g., Lotus Notes, Excalibur's Electronic File System) the search engine is accessible through a published application programming interface (API), making integration as a repository feasible. On the other hand, the query formation interface is not usually accessible through an API. These systems can either be integrated into Garlic as a monolith, with no exploitation of Garlic's ability to provide cross repository queries or to integrate and synchronize presentation of results; or, the callable search engine can be integrated as a repository and other user interfaces exploited for query formation. One drawback of this latter approach is the loss of the familiar user-interface that a particular system provides. However, we believe the benefits of a closer integration with Garlic (and consistency of user interface when accessing multiple similar repositories) will outweigh the costs for most users/applications that need Garlic functionality. Thus, we are trying to borrow or develop good general query interfaces for specific types, including image.

The QBIC query formation interface, unlike other systems, has provided tools to specify queries on rather general purpose image properties. We'd like, therefore, to take advantage of this generality by integrating this interface with the Garlic Query/Browser (section 4.4) as the basis for our general image query interface. Furthermore, the QBIC search engine will be "wrapped" so that it presents itself to Garlic as an image database manager with an object-oriented schema. In the next two subsections we discuss some of the issues involved and choices made in this integration process.

4.2.1 Integrating the QBIC query formation interface

The QBIC pickers provide intuitively appealing and general mechanisms for users to specify colors, textures, and other image features. To make these pickers available to the Query/Browser, we have encapsulated the QBIC query formation interface with a socket protocol that enables them to be invoked by Garlic and to exchange query specifications in a form permitting them to be combined into a full Garlic query. The query formation features interact with the user in the same way they currently do in the QBIC system.

Secondly, to enable these pickers to be used to query both QBIC and non-QBIC image databases, it must be possible to use the same query specification to query different repositories having different computations for the same feature (e.g., different shape feature vectors for the same shape). Thus, QBIC pickers do not return a feature vector but capture the user specification in a small, say 100 x 100, image which can be input to the feature computation functions in another image database supporting query by content for the same feature. This also eliminates the need for client machines to have implementations for potentially expensive feature computations. The cost is that "image literals" must now be handled by Garlic's Query Services. These literals will be carefully passed "around" the system in order to minimize copying and query cost. (Similar mechanisms are used to handle long fields in relational databases today (Lehman and Lindsay, 1989)).

Another requirement is that it must be possible to integrate the resulting image query within the complete user query being built by the Query/Browser. The QBIC query formation functions will therefore capture the logical expression of the user's query in a text form with references to the image literals discussed above. The text form will be a subset of the Garlic Query Language which can be pieced into the full GQL query that the Query/Browser will submit to Garlic Query Services.

The thumbnails available from QBIC in response to an image query will be displayed by the query/browser using the image display tools available at the client. They will therefore appear integrated with data returned by other repositories in response to the user's full query (Plate 6). If selected, the thumbnails are then expanded into the full image and presented in a separate window.

4.2.2 Wrapping the QBIC query engine

Typical information servers, whether general purpose or domain specific (e.g., Lotus Notes, Excalibur's Electronic Filing System or ACR/NEMA DICOM Medical Image Servers), organize the data they manage under a schema that presents a model of that data to the user. Document systems compose a document from pages and then organize the documents into folders, filedrawers, cabinets, etc. Medical image servers organize tomographic images into series, series into studies and studies into sections of a patient folder. Although instances of these data objects and data collections can be added, the object and collection types in each schema are fixed by the underlying system. Furthermore, the systems support several levels of search capability through a published API. We believe this model of an information server is representative of an increasing segment of the information server market. Trends in industry standardization of domain-specific data models and in marketplace standardization of general purpose information and data management systems will further support this model. Therefore, most repository wrappers in Garlic will bridge the gap between Garlic's object-oriented model and a fixed schema in a similar modeling discipline.

However, QBIC is a research prototype, and does not have a published data schema or APIs. Instead of describing the data stored, QBIC's file-based data organization is oriented around handling image and feature vector data structures. To integrate QBIC into Garlic so that Garlic can exploit QBIC's data and search capability, the QBIC wrapper must present an object-oriented schema to Garlic, and be able to map this schema down to the file structures and call interfaces currently provided by the QBIC search engine. It is a virtue of Garlic's architecture that even in this case integration is possible.

The query engine wrapper has two parts: a model of the data in QBIC and of the predicates QBIC can apply, and code that translates between GQL queries and QBIC's call interfaces and returns results to Garlic. The model for QBIC's image data must express the relationships between base images (scenes that have outlined objects in them), their thumbnails, and outlined objects within the images. Although these data objects are stored as bitfiles or as records in data files in QBIC, the QBIC wrapper provides Garlic with a more integrated view. This view allows navigational access from one object to its related objects through the Query/Browser, the use of image feature queries over particular collections in a type safe manner and the incorporation of QBIC data (as Garlic objects) into Garlic complex objects (e.g., advertising campaigns) without copying the large data objects into Garlic.

Interface definitions satisfying these requirements are given in Figure 2. There are three key interfaces (classes), one for full QBIC scenes (*QBICScene*), one for outlined objects within a scene (*OutlinedObjects*), and the third containing the actual image (*BasePixelImage*). A *QBICScene* has pointers to the raw image and a thumbnail (both instances of *BasePixelImage*). It also has a set of pointers to objects outlined in that scene. These objects are represented by the *OutlinedObjects* interface. Each outlined object has a pointer to a thumbnail of that outlined object within the image. *OutlinedObjects* also point back to the *QBICScene* they occur in. Finally, the *BasePixelImage* class provides exactly the information needed to interpret the image bits faithfully, including width, height, and pixel size. Appropriate methods are provided with each interface definition to allow searching and manipulation of these classes. These interface definitions shield Garlic users from the details of how QBIC keeps track of which image features have been computed for a given scene, or a given object. It also hides the actual feature values. All of these are managed by the QBIC repository, but are only accessible to Garlic through the interface methods.

The interface definitions are exported by the wrapper and copied into Garlic structures used by Metadata Services to record schema information. They are used by Garlic Query Services during

```
interface QBICScene : persistent {
     relationship BasePixelImage original_image;
     relationship BasePixelImage original_image_thumbnail;
     relationship set <OutlinedObjects> scene_objects
                         inverse OutlinedObjects::original_scene;
     fuzzybool match_image (QBICScene image_srch_arg);
     void QBdisplay();
      ...
}
interface OutlinedObjects : persistent {
     relationship BasePixelImage original_obj_thumbnail;
     attribute int[2] upperleft;
     relationship BasePixelImage objectmask;
     relationship QBICScene original_scene inverse QBICScene::scene_objects;
     void QBdisplay();
      ...
}
interface BasePixelImage : persistent {
     attribute int image_width;
     attribute int image_height;
     attribute int pel_depth;
     attribute float pel_physical_size
     attribute int total_image_size
     attribute char[total_image_size] image_pels;
     BasePixelImage getimage();
      ...
}
```

Figure 2. A Wrapper Schema for QBIC

query compilation (e.g, to ensure type safe queries) and by users and applications to examine the objects available in a Garlic database. The wrapper also exports a set of named collections. These collections are assigned identifiers by Garlic upon import and the wrapper is responsible for maintaining mappings between these identifiers and the underlying repository entities. For instance, if it is desired to make a set of *QBICScenes*, called *Wilderness_Shots*, available to advertisers, a QBIC server will register the directory containing the feature data and thumbnail files to Garlic as a collection during the wrapper registration process. QBIC will guarantee that the same set of features is computed for each *Wilderness_Shot* scene. Therefore, any feature-based search of the *Wilderness_Shot* collection can be assumed to be exhaustive by the user. The QBIC wrapper will map a Garlic *OID* (i.e. an object identifier understood by Garlic) for the *Wilderness_Shot* collection into a reference to this directory, and will map method invocations, such as the *match_image* search predicate, into the appropriate calls against the control file structures in the QBIC search engine.

The second part of the wrapper handles queries. The QBIC wrapper is passed that part of a user's query that applies to collections that are exported by QBIC. A feature of QBIC is that searches can be performed against lists of images that are subsets of the exported collections, or against an entire collection. This allows Garlic Query Services considerable flexibility in choosing how to execute a query (Section 4.3).The query fragment sent to QBIC is represented by an abstract parse tree that has all references to Garlic objects bound to unique identifiers which the wrapper can map to underlying repository entities. Any literals needed to evaluate the query (e.g., a sketch to be matched) will also be passed. The wrapper creates an iterator, which provides the answer set (in a relevance sorted order created by QBIC) to Garlic's Runtime System. After mapping the Garlic subquery into QBIC entities and function calls, the wrapper relies on the client/server mechanisms provided by QBIC, e.g., socket calls, to remotely execute the appropriate search and return the answer set. The answer set contains identifiers that can be mapped to Garlic *OIDs*, can be filtered and/or can have methods applied to them.

4.3 Queries over visual (and other) data

Once a wrapper is defined for QBIC, QBIC data can be queried through Garlic. But the power of Garlic lies in its ability to answer queries that span multiple data types in multiple repositories. In this section we will show how queries in Garlic can combine predicates over visual and other data. To illustrate how queries are processed, we need both wrapper schemas for each repository and a global Garlic schema. We complete this set of schemas for a simple subset of our advertising example. We assume that in addition to a QBIC repository with images from magazine ads, the agen-

```
class Document {
        ....
public:
     char* title;
     char* text;
     Date date;
     int matches(char* search_expr);
}
```

```
make_doc_db /financial/documents
add_doc /financial/report1.text
add_doc /financial/report2.text
....
```

Figure 3. Text Repository Contents

cy also has a text repository that stores financial reports for each campaign. The contents of this repository and the commands to create it are indicated in C++ notation in Figure 3. Suppose that the agency wants to correlate their reports with the magazine ads. They can use Garlic complex objects to do this. The wrapper schemas for the text repository and for the complex objects managed by the Garlic complex object repository are given in Figure 4. (The wrapper for the QBIC repository was shown in Figure 2). Notice that the text wrapper renames the *title* attribute of *Document* to *campaign*, based on the wrapper designer's knowledge of the actual documents being stored. Also, note that there is no magic involving complex objects. Once the complex object schema is defined, the complex object repository must be populated. In some cases this can be done through a query, but in our example this would have to be done by hand (unless there were some information in the document to identify the associated images, or vice versa). Finally, one possible Garlic schema for this example is given in Figure 5. This schema promotes the *campaign* attribute of the report into the *Campaign* objects themselves, so that *Campaigns* now have a name, a set of magazine ads, and a report.

The Garlic Query Language extends SQL with additional constructs for traversing paths com-

```
interface Document(extent Document): persistent {
     attribute String campaign;
     attribute Date date;
     attribute String text;
     fuzzybool matches(String search_expr);
     void QBdisplay();
}
```

Figure 4. (a): Text Wrapper Schema

```
interface Campaign (extent Campaign): persistent {
     attribute String campaign_name;
     relationship Set<QBICScene> magazine_ads;
     relationship Document report;
}
```

Figure 4.(b): Complex Object Repository Schema

posed of inter-object relationships, for querying collection-valued attributes of objects, and for invoking methods within queries. These extensions are similar to those of other recent object query language proposals (e.g., (Bancilhon, et.al., 1989), (Kim, 1989), (Dar, et.al., 1992)), including the ongoing efforts of the SQL-3 committee (Kulkarni, 1994). To get a flavor of these extensions, consider the following query, written against the Garlic schema of Figure 5:[2]

```
interface Campaign (extent Campaign): persistent {
     attribute String campaign_name;
     relationship Set<Scene> mag_ads;
     relationship Document report;
}
interface Document (extent Document): persistent {
     attribute String campaign;
     attribute Date date;
     attribute String text;
     fuzzybool matches(in String search_expr);
     void QBdisplay();
         ....
}
interface Scene(extent Scene): persistent {
     void QBdisplay();
     fuzzybool match_image(in Scene image_arg);
         ....
}
     ...
```

Figure 5. Global Garlic Schema

> **select** C.campaign_name, C.report, C.mag_ads
> **from** Campaign C, C.mag_ads A
> **where** (C.report.date > "1989") **and**
>   A.match_image(SKETCH) > .5

This query finds the campaigns and the associated report and magazine ads for those campaigns that ran since 1989 and which had a magazine ad that resembled a particular image (for ex-

2. We are still working out the exact details of our SQL extensions. This example is provided to give the reader a feeling for what we intend, and should not be taken too literally!

ample, a user-drawn sketch). This would be useful for those situations in which the ad executive remembers roughly what a particular ad looked like and when it was run, but not the details of the campaign. The query illustrates several of Garlic's object-oriented SQL extensions. First, it contains a number of path expressions. Second, it contains an invocation of the *match_image*() method of the *Scene* object. This method passes QBIC a literal representing the sketch in an appropriate form for QBIC (this may have been produced visually by a sketch picker), and returns a number indicating the "goodness" of the match. Finally, *C.mag_ads* in the **select** clause illustrates the retrieval of an unflattened set.

To answer this query, Garlic first translates it into an internal representation which reflects the query's semantics. Each operation is then re-written in terms of the underlying wrapper schemas, using the Garlic metadata. Next, Garlic decomposes the query into a plan containing a number of smaller queries, each of which can be answered by a single repository. The plan also specifies how the results of each subquery should be combined to form the final answer. For example, one possible plan for our query would be to ask the text wrapper for the Garlic *OIDs* of reports written after 1989, then ask the complex object repository for the *OIDs* of the magazine ads associated with these reports, then probe QBIC with the list of ad *OIDs* to see if those ads match the sketch sufficiently closely, and finally, get the report title (campaign name) associated with the document *OID* of the surviving campaigns. Other plans are certainly possible, and it would be up to the optimizer to choose among them based on its estimates of cost.

In Garlic's distributed environment the issue of optimization is very important. The amount of work that each server does in order to handle its part of the overall query can vary greatly, from efficient range searches on a primary key in a relational database, to the costly computation of feature vectors followed by the computation of an expensive distance measure against an entire collection of images in QBIC. Ideally, Garlic would sequence the data system accesses in order to exploit parallelism and the special functions that a server provides (e.g., relevance sorted answer sets) while minimizing potentially wasted time and expense at the servers and in the Garlic system itself. Optimization will require the specification and use of several new pieces of information. We need computational models of feature calculations and distance measures in order to distinquish between the costs of different feature predicates applied within QBIC. Selectivity factors that can aid in predicting the amount of data returned by a similarity query are also needed. Finally, models must be created that can reflect the existence of special purpose indexing structures, e.g., multi-dimensional indexes for feature vectors, in their estimates of a similarity query's cost. These will all be captured in the descriptive part of a repository wrapper for use by Garlic's Query Services. In addition, Garlic will maintain information on processor speeds, I/O rates and communication costs for its installed servers and networks, in the tradition of relational optimizers.

It is the responsibility of each repository wrapper to convert its individual subplan into a form the underlying repository can understand -- either one or more queries in that repository's query language, or a sequence of calls to its native search API. The wrappers will execute their subplans in a demand-driven fashion under the control of the Garlic runtime system, returning a stream of values to Garlic for any final processing.

This final processing may involve joins, projections or restrictions, as in any middleware database system. However, Garlic has an additional challenge: to reconcile the different query semantics of its various repositories. While in database management systems data items are returned if and only if predicates are true, QBIC and other repositories managing multimedia data return data items in order of "closeness" to a given predicate. We are currently developing a set of SQL extensions and query processing algorithms to support queries that involve both exact and approximate search criteria. This work involves introducing into SQL the notion of graded sets, in which each object is assigned a number between 0 and 1 for each atomic predicate; this number represents the degree to which the object fulfills the predicate, with 1 representing a perfect match. Boolean combinations of predicates can then be handled using the rules for combining predicates in fuzzy logic (Zimmermann, 1990). To enable query writers to specify the desired semantics, GQL permits the specification of the number of matching results to be returned and whether or not rank-ordering (rather than an attribute-based sort order, or an arbitrary order) is desired for the query's result set. We are also devising new query processing algorithms that will produce the best N results efficiently, without materializing every intermediate result item that matches to any degree at all.

4.4 Visual Query/Browse in Garlic

The purpose of the Garlic Query/Browser component is to provide end users of the system with an easy and highly visual way to access and manipulate the data in a Garlic database, as the typical end user will not normally want to write GQL queries. As its name implies, the Query/Browser will provide support for two basic data access functions, namely querying and browsing. However, unlike existing interfaces to databases, the Query/Browser will allow users to move back and forth seamlessly between querying and browsing activities, using queries to identify interesting subsets of the database, browsing the subset, querying the contents of a set-valued attribute of a particularly interesting object in the subset, and so on.

The Query/Browser will support exploration of a Garlic database by allowing users to browse through the contents of Garlic collections (via next/previous buttons or scrolling) and to traverse relationships by clicking on (selecting) objects' reference attributes. When multiple related objects are being simultaneously displayed, synchronous browsing will be implied (*a la* (Motro, et.al., 1988), (Agrawal, et.al., 1990)). To illustrate these points, we'll walk through a short scenario using screens generated by our current prototype system. Consider what an advertising executive might do to find the campaign she wants without writing any GQL. She might start by just browsing through campaigns. Plates 5a and 5b show the screen after she has chosen to browse the *Ad_Campaign* collection, resulting in the display of the first campaign object called the "Warp-NTheNuns" campaign. Selecting *ad* will show images of the ads (5c), using *Scene*'s *QBdisplay* method. Clicking *next* on the *Ad_Campaigns0.ad* window would browse through the ads for this campaign. *Next* in the *Ad_Campaigns0* window will move to the next campaign (5d), and the ads related to that campaign.

The Query/Browser will support querying via a "query-by-graphical-example" paradigm, extending the well-known query-by-example paradigm (Zloof, 1977) for use in formulating queries over an object database. Suppose our account exec, tired of browsing, decides to specify a query similar to that discussed above (section 4.3) but simplified to conserve space and exposition. She wants to find campaign information for those campaigns of products selling above a certain price and having an ad photo that is mostly white. She clicks on the query button ("?" see Plate 5b) of the *Ad_Campaigns0* window, and then clicks on the fields she wishes to restrict (Plate 6a). In Plate 6b, she has specified a predicate on the *price* of the product (*price* > $18,000) and in Plate 6c she will click on the *adimage* field to initiate the QBIC query formation tools. This enables access to QBIC picker windows just like those shown in Plates 1-4, which she will use to specify a query for an image that is mostly white. When she's done specifying predicates, she selects the *GO!* button (Plate 6a) to cause the query to execute. The first set of results presenting product data and illustrated ad information is shown in Plates 6d and 6e. She can then browse the results with the query's constraints remaining active until explicitly cleared.

In addition to smoothly combining querying and browsing, the Garlic Query/Browser will also provide other useful features for exploring and manipulating the contents of a heterogeneous multimedia data collection. First, the objects on the display at any given time will be active objects -- the Query/Browser will remember their Garlic identities and will provide a graphical means of obtaining a list of their available methods and requesting that one of the methods be applied to the object of interest (prompting for method arguments if needed). Second, clicking on "query" followed by a multimedia (e.g., image, audio, video, or text) attribute of a displayed object will result in the display of a type-specific picker (or set of pickers) to support the construction of a media-specific predicate on that attribute of the object, as discussed in Section 4.2.1. The Query/Browser will contain a number of such pickers to support the graphical specification of content-based multimedia predicates. In time, the Query/Browser will become still more sophisticated, supporting the graphical definition of end-user views. Ultimately, we believe that good support for customizing the browser's behavior with respect to a given Garlic database and Garlic user may lead to a new paradigm for visual application development, at least for applications of a "browsy" (i.e., navigational) nature.

5 CONCLUSIONS AND FUTURE WORK

We have presented an overview of the Garlic project at the IBM Almaden Research Center, the goal of which is to build a heterogeneous multimedia information system (MMIS) capable of integrating data from a variety of traditional and non-traditional data repositories, and allowing query by content of any type of data. We described the overall architecture for the system, which is based on repositories, repository wrappers, and the use of an object-oriented data model and query language to provide a uniform view of the disparate data types and data sources that can contribute data to a Garlic database. As we explained, a significant focus of the project is support for repositories that provide media-specific query capabilities. We described QBIC, a system that provides query by image content, and showed how QBIC could be integrated into Garlic so that queries might range over data in this and other repositories simultaneously. We also described exploratory access to Garlic by end users via the Garlic Query/Browser.

The Garlic project was initiated in early 1994. Early in 1995 a first "prototype" system reached a stage of development to enable a first round of internal demos. This system was used to generate the screen shots in section 4. and is being used to solicit feedback from various local groups. The repositories included in this system are: a.) DB2 Client/Server on RS/6000 machines; b.) The ObjectStore object-oriented database from Object Design Incorporated; and c.) a QBIC repository. We are currently using this system to explore the nature of wrappers, to experiment with algorithms and design approaches for query translation and processing, and to test the efficacy of the query/browser as an end-user window into a collection of multimedia data.

In the longer term, we expect the Garlic project to lead us into new research in many dimensions, including object-oriented and middleware query processing technologies, extensibility for highly heterogeneous, data-intensive environments, database user interfaces and application development approaches, and integration of exact- and approximate-matching semantics for multimedia query languages. There are also many interesting, type-specific issues, such as what predicates should be supported on image and video data, how to index multimedia information, how to support similarity-based search and relevance feedback, and what the appropriate user interfaces are for querying particular media types. We believe that significant challenges exist in each of these areas, and that solutions must be found to meet the emerging demand for large-scale multimedia data management.

6 ACKNOWLEDGMENTS

We would like to thank Rakesh Agrawal for his input in the start-up phase of the Garlic project; he contributed significantly to our vision for both the project as a whole and the query/browser in particular. John McPherson and Ashok Chandra have been particularly supportive of our efforts throughout; we thank them for their encouragement and many suggestions. Many others contributed to the definition of the Garlic project, including: Kurt Shoens, K.C. Lee, Jerry Kiernan, Peter Yanker, Harpreet Sawhney, David Steele, Byron Dom and Markus Tresch.

7 REFERENCES

R. Agrawal, N. Gehani, And J. Srinivasan, "OdeView: The Graphical Interface to Ode", Proc. ACM SIGMOD Conference, Atlantic City, NJ, May 1990.

F. Bancilhon, S. Cluet, and C. Delobel, "A Query Language for the O2 Object-Oriented Database System", Proc. DBPL Conference, Salishan Lodge, Oregon, June 1989

R. Cattell, ed., "The Object Database Standard: ODMG-93 (Release 1.1)", Morgan Kaufmann Publishers, San Francisco, CA, 1994.

M. Carey, P. Schwarz, L. Haas, et al., "Towards Heterogeneous Multimedia Information Systems: The Garlic Approach," RIDE-DOM '95, Taiwan 3/95. (5th Int'l Workshop on Research Issues in Data Engineering: Distributed Object Management.)

T. Conners, W. Hasan, C. Kolovson, M. Neimat, D. Schneider, and K. Wilkinson, "The Papyrus Integrated Data Server", Proc. 1st PDIS Conference, Miami Beach, FL, December 1991

S. Dar, N. Gehani, and H. Jagadish, "CQL++: A SQL for a C++ Based Object-Oriented DBMS", Proc. EDBT Conference, Vienna, Austria, 1992.

A. Elmagarmid and C. Pu, eds., Special Issue on Heterogeneous Databases, ACM Comp. Surveys 22(3), September 1990.

ESRI Inc, Understanding GIS -- The ARC/INFO Method, (1990)

D. Fang, S. Ghandeharizadeh, D. McLeod, and A. Si, "The Design, Implementation, and Evaluation of an Object-Based Sharing Mechanism for Federated Database Systems", Proc. IEEE Conf. on Data Eng., Vienna, Austria, April 1993..

W.Grosky and R. Mehrotra, "Index-Based Object Recognition in Pictorial Data Management," Computer Vision, Graphics and Image Processing, 52, 416-436 (1990)

K. Hirata and T. Kato, "Query by Visual Example", Advances in Database Technology EDBT '92, Third International Conference on Extending Database Technology, Springer-Verlag, Vienna, Austria, March 1992

D. Hsiao, "Federated Databases and Systems: Part I -- A Tutorial on Their Data Sharing", VLDB Journal 1(1), July 1992.

T. Kato, T. Kurita, N. Otsu and K. Hirata, "A Sketch Retrieval Method for Full Color Image Database", International Conference on Pattern Recognition (ICPR), IAPR, The Hague, The Netherlands, pp. 530--533, September 1992

W. Kim, "A Model of Queries for Object-Oriented Databases", Proc. VLDB Conference, Amsterdam, the Netherlands, August 1989.

K. Kulkarni, "Object-Oriented Extensions in SQL3: A Status Report", Proc. ACM SIGMOD Conf, Minneapolis, MN, May 1994.

T.J. Lehman and B.Lindsay,"The Starburst Long Field Manager," VLDB Conference Proceedings, Amsterdam, Aug., 1989 pp. 375-383.

M. Miyahara and Y. Yoshida, "Math. Transform of *(R,G,B)* Color Data to Munsell *(H,V,C)* Color Data", Vis. Comm. and Image Proc., SPIE, Vol. 1001, pp. 650-657, 1988.

A. Motro, A. D'Atri, and L. Tarantino, "The Design of KIVIEW: An Object-Oriented Browser", Proc. 2nd Int'l. Expert Database Systems Conference, Tysons Corner, VA, April 1988.

W. Niblack, R. Barber, W. Equitz, M. Flickner, E. Glasman, D. Petkovic, and P. Yanker: "The QBIC Project: Querying Images by Content Using Color, Texture and Shape", Proc. SPIE, San Jose, CA, February 1993.

A. Pentland, R. Pickard, and S. Scarloff, MIT Media Lab: "Photobook: Tools for Content Based Manipulation of Image Databases", Proc. SPIE, San Jose, CA, 1994

R. Rosenberg and T. Landers, "An Overview of MULTIBASE", in Distributed Databases, H. Schneider, ed., North-Holland Publishers, New York, NY, 1982.

G. Salton, "Automatic Text Processing: The Transformation, Analysis, and Retrieval of Information by Computer", Addison-Wesley Publishers, 1989

M. Shan, "Pegasus Architecture and Design Principles", Proc. 1993 ACM SIGMOD Conference, Washington, DC, May 1993

M. J. Swain and D. H. Ballard", "Color Indexing", International Journal of Computer Vision, 7:1, pp. 11-32, 1991.

H. Tamura, S. Mori and T. Yamawaki, "Texture Features Corresponding to Visual Perception", IEEE Transactions on Systems, Man, and Cybernetics, SMC-8:6, pp. 460-473, 1978.

TYDAC Technologies, "SPANS: SPatial ANalysis System", (1990)

M. Ubell, "The Montage Extensible Datablade Architecture", Proc. ACM SIGMOD Conference, Minneapolis, MN, May 1994.

H. J. Zimmermann, Fuzzy Set Theory and its Applications, Kluwer Academic Publishers, Boston, MA, 1990

M. Zloof, "Query-By-Example: A Data Base Language", IBM Systems Journal 16(4), 1977.

3

Representing concave objects using Virtual Images

T. Arndt, G. Petraglia, M. Sebillo and G. Tortora
Dipartimento di Informatica ed Applicazioni
University of Salerno
I-84081 Baronissi, Salerno, Italy
Tel. +39(0)89 965333 Fax +39(0)89 965328
e-mail: jentor@udsab.dia.unisa.it

Abstract

Recent research in the design of image database systems emphasizes the necessity of defining an indexing methodology which is not based on form features but rather on invariant numerical, topological or geometrical characteristics of the images. In this paper, we concentrate on the spatial data and relationships which represent the most important method for recognizing images. In particular, we focus on iconic indexing methodologies based on order theory and symbolic projections and we address the problem of ambiguity arising from the description of concave objects with these representations. Towards this end, we extend the cutting mechanism of the 2D C-string iconic index to perform cutting lines whenever a concave point (split point) might lead to ambiguity during the reconstruction process. The iconic index obtained according to this set of rules can be managed by the Atomic Relation Extraction Method to derive the corresponding virtual images which represent the normalized pictorial information.

Keywords

Iconic indexing, spatial reasoning, image data model, content-based query

1 INTRODUCTION

In designing image database systems, to obtain a representation which is independent of the user's point of view (and therefore more flexible), it is necessary to define an indexing methodology which is not based on form features but on invariant numerical, topological or geometrical characteristics of the images.

With this observation in mind, the most attractive approach takes into account the requirement of a unified framework for image representation, indexing, visualization and for spatial reasoning (Chang, 1988). Conventional data models are not particularly suitable for pictorial information because of the complex nature of images. Images incorporate a huge amount of information. In particular, it is possible to distinguish explicit information concerning the objects contained in the image, and implicit information, such as that concerning the relative positions of the objects in the image. It is also essential to decide which features should be stored. Generally speaking, the data can be classified as non-spatial, spatial and graphical, i.e. attribute-based information, implicit information, and information used mainly for display, respectively.

We concentrate on the spatial data and relationships which represent the most important method for discriminating among the images. In particular, we focus on the iconic indexing methodologies based on order theory and symbolic projections and we address the problem of ambiguity arising from the description of concave objects with these representations.

An image can be described by an iconic index which is constructed by projecting the objects along a chosen system of axes. Then, by applying the spatial operators according to the relations existing between the projections, the index is obtained and the representation of the visual content of the image is derived. However, when a concave object has to be represented, the concavity point (*split point* (Jungert, 1993)) recognized according to an axis, can cause ambiguity during the reconstruction process since the position of the objects cannot be uniquely derived from the index.

This paper aims to avoid the ambiguity arising from the split point incorporated in the 2D C-string knowledge structure (Lee, 1990). In particular, we extend the cutting mechanism of this iconic index by introducing further cutting lines whenever a split point of a concave object might produce ambiguity.

The rest of this paper is organized as follows. In Section 2, we review iconic indexing methodologies. The definition of a virtual image is given and the normalized (with respect to reversing and rotation) iconic indexing approach is recalled. In Section 3 we propose a representation of images with concave objects by virtual images. The representation inherits the properties of the normalized iconic indexing methodology. Conclusions are given in Section 4.

2 ICONIC INDEXING METHODOLOGIES

In order to describe the kinds of spatial objects present in an image and to determine what their particular properties are, it is necessary to introduce a spatial data model. A spatial data model is a formulation of the spatial concepts used to organize and structure human perception of the space (Egenhofer, 1991). The role of a spatial data model is similar to the conceptual schema in the 3-schema view of traditional databases. Without such a formal framework it would be impossible to investigate and discuss the formalization of spatial relationships, because it may vary considerably depending on the data model selected.

A compact and exhaustive way of managing spatial relationships is to apply mathematical order theory (Egenhofer, 1991). The formalism on which our data model is based is the segmentation of the plane with respect to a system of axes, called *symbolic projection*. Symbolic projections translate exact metric information into a qualitative form and allow reasoning about the spatial relationships among objects in a 2-D plane. In particular, an image can be described by an iconic symbolic representation (Tanimoto, 1976). This iconic representation is itself an image used as an index which preserves the visual information and allows different levels of abstraction and management (Chang, 1992), (Tanimoto, 1976). The Query-by-Pictorial-Example (QPE) approach introduced by Chang and Fu (Chang, 1980), is a methodology in which the objects and the spatial relations among them in the image to be retrieved are expressed by a symbolic image which serves as the query and which is matched against the images in the database. Thus, the query contains both explicit and implicit information, since the query itself is a symbolic picture.

In successive works the QPE approach has been further developed. In IIDS a pictorial query is converted into 2-D strings and an image is retrieved by matching the iconic indexes (Chang, 1988). The problem of pictorial information retrieval then is reduced to the problem of 2-D subsequence matching (Chang, 1987).

However, the 2-D string iconic index is not sufficient to give a complete description of the spatial knowledge for complex images since every object is considered as a point, thus, an image with many objects with complex sizes and shapes may not be completely described.

In order to describe more accurately the spatial relations, Chang and Jungert (Chang, 1991) extended the idea of symbolic projections by introducing the cutting mechanism concept and defining the generalized 2D string (2D G-string) knowledge structure for pictorial databases. In order to establish the relations among the objects in terms of spatial operators, they partition the real image by drawing cutting lines at the beginning and ending points of the overlapping objects, thereby decomposing the image into many smaller subpictures.

A more efficient cutting mechanism has been introduced by Lee and Hsu in the knowledge structure of 2D C-string (Lee, 1990), where they introduced the concept of dominating object. The 2D C-string uses a cutting line only at the ending point of the dominating object. The spatial operators used in the 2D C-string representation are shown in Table 1.

Table 1 The definition of 2D C-string spatial operators

<table>
<tr><th>Notation</th><th>Meaning</th><th>Condition</th></tr>
<tr><td>A<B</td><td>A disjoins B</td><td>end(A)<begin(B)</td></tr>
<tr><td>A=B</td><td>A is the same as B</td><td>begin(A)=begin(B)
end(A)=end(B)</td></tr>
<tr><td>A|B</td><td>A is edge to edge with B</td><td>end(A)=begin(B)</td></tr>
<tr><td>A%B</td><td>A and B have not the same bound and A contains B</td><td>begin(A)<begin
(B)
end(A)>end(B)</td></tr>
<tr><td>A[B</td><td>A and B have the same begin bound and A contains B</td><td>begin(A)=begin(B)
end(A)>end(B)</td></tr>
<tr><td>A]B</td><td>A and B have the same end bound and A contains B</td><td>begin(A)<begin(B)
end(A)=end(B)</td></tr>
<tr><td>A/B</td><td>A is partly overlapping with B</td><td>begin(A)<begin(B)
<end(A)<end(B)</td></tr>
</table>

As an example, for the picture in Figure 1 the cutting mechanism uses two lines in the x-direction (Figure 1(a)) and no line in the y-direction (Figure 1(b)).

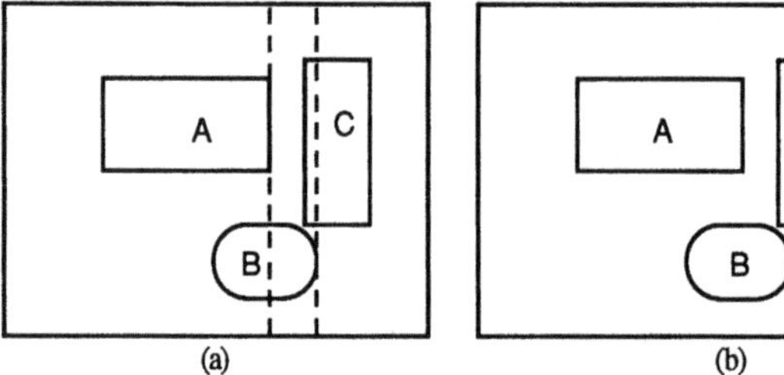

Figure 1 The 2D C-string cutting mechanism.

The corresponding 2D C-string representation (u, v) is
u: A] B | B] C | C
v: B | C % A

2.1 Normalized iconic indexing

It has been shown that symbolic projections are suitable for powerful spatial reasoning, as well as topological relations (Egenhofer, 1991). However, unlike topological relations, which are invariant under topological or geometrical transformations, symbolic projections depend on the orientation of the objects, i.e., the relative spatial positioning and ordering of objects in 2-D space is preserved. Thus, a spatial relation A *op* B differs from B *op* A and it is possible to recognize of the specific spatial arrangement of two objects.

On the other hand, the conventional methodologies based on orthogonal projections do not lead to two identical indexes for an image and its transformation (e.g. reverse, rotation), even though their visual content is essentially the same. In such cases, an iconic index like those discussed earlier is not sufficient to guarantee that the solution to a query is complete, since pictorial information is positional information.

In (Petraglia, 1994) this problem is faced by introducing a normalized indexing methodology based on virtual images. The aim of this indexing methodology is to satisfy the previously stated requirements. In particular, the limitation of the reversing problem is overcome by defining a transformation law which allows one to obtain the index of a reverse image starting from the index of the original one. Moreover, in order to obtain rotation invariance, the rotational iconic index 2-R string is introduced. A system of polar axes whose origin, the rotation center, coincides with the centroid of a chosen object (Petraglia, 1993), is used. As with the 2D C-string, the 2-R string is obtained by a cutting mechanism. Here, however, the cutting lines along the x- and y-direction are replaced by circles having the rotation center as center, and radial segments around the rotation center, i.e. cutting lines along the ring-direction (c-direction) and sector-direction (s-direction), respectively. Consequently, every spatial relation and operator is described in terms of conditions over the beginning point and the ending point along the s-direction and the c-direction.

In order to make our discussion concrete, let us recall the definitions of virtual image and normalized virtual image on which the normalization process is based (Petraglia, 1994).

Definition 1

The virtual image P associated with an image is a pair (Ob, Rs) where
$Ob = \{ob_1,...., ob_n\}$ is a set of objects;
$Rs = (Rs_u, Rs_v)$ is a pair of sets of the form: $\{r(p_i, p_w) \mid r \text{ is a spatial operator}, p_i, p_w \in Ob\}$.
Each $r(p_i, p_w)$ in Rs_u (resp. Rs_v) represents the spatial relation, called *atomic relation*, holding between the objects p_i and p_w along the projections of a chosen system of axes.

Definition 2

A normalized virtual image can be defined as a pair (NOb, NRs) where
$NOb = \{ob_1,...., ob_n\}$ is a set of objects;
$NRs = ((Rs_c, Rs_s), (u,v))$ where
(Rs_c, Rs_s) is the pair of sets of atomic relations corresponding to the 2-R string, and (u, v) is the 2-D string over the centroids.

In order to derive the virtual image corresponding to an image, the Atomic Relation Extraction Method (AREM) is introduced, which allows us to obtain all the spatial relations among the objects, starting from an iconic index extracted according to a chosen system of axes (Petraglia, 1993).

For sake of clarity, in the following, AREM methodology is described with respect to the Cartesian system.

Given objects A and B where A is the dominating object, let $\{A_1,.., A_n\}$ and $\{B_1,.., B_m\}$ be the sets of their subparts derived from the cutting mechanism of the 2D C-string. The spatial relations holding between (A_1, B_1), (A_n, B_m), and (A_n, B_1) are called characteristic relations, while the subparts A_1, B_1, A_n and B_m are called the characteristic subparts.

Table 2 describes the correspondence between the characteristic relations of two objects A and B and the relations holding between their borders.

Table 2 The characteristic relations and the corresponding conditions on the borders

<table>
<tr><th>Condition on the borders</th><th>Condition on the characteristic subparts</th></tr>
<tr><td>begin(A) < begin(B)</td><td>A1 < B1 or A1] B1 or A1 % B1 or A1 | B1</td></tr>
<tr><td>end(A) > end(B)</td><td>Bm < An or An [Bm or Bm | An or An % Bm</td></tr>
<tr><td>end(A) = end(B)</td><td>An] Bm or Bm] An or An = Bm</td></tr>
<tr><td>begin(A) = begin(B)</td><td>A1 [B1 or B1 [A1 or A1 = B1</td></tr>
<tr><td>end(A) = begin(B)</td><td>An | B1</td></tr>
<tr><td>end(A) < begin(B)</td><td>An < B1</td></tr>
<tr><td>end(A) < end(B)</td><td>An < Bm or An | Bm or Bm [An or Bm % An</td></tr>
<tr><td>end(A) > begin(B)</td><td>B1 < An or An] B1 or An = B1 or An % B1 or
B1 | An or An [B1 or B1 [An or B1 % An or
B1] An</td></tr>
</table>

Then, given a 2D C-string for a picture *f*, AREM produces a virtual image, i.e., a description of the picture *f* in terms of objects and atomic relations. AREM uses the spatial operators defined in Table 1 and consists of three steps:
(1) starting from the 2D C-string index, all the objects and the subparts are numbered in a progressive way, deriving the indexed 2D C-string;
(2) all the binary spatial relations are derived from the indexed 2D C-string using the picture algebra laws (Lee, 1991);
(3) starting from the binary spatial relations over the characteristic subparts obtained from the second step, the atomic relations are derived according to Table 2.

3 HANDLING CONCAVE OBJECTS

The interest in using normalized virtual image as an iconic index is motivated by the possibility of exploiting conventional database methodologies for the complete solution of pictorial queries, since the virtual image representation is independent of any indexing method and provides a virtual description of the image.

In this section, we focus on the cases where the reconstruction process is not unique. An iconic index should satisfy the properties of compactness, constructability and reconstructability, i.e., an image and its iconic index should be uniquely related. The aim of this section is to manage the problems arising when the property of reconstructability is not satisfied.

In particular, we distinguish two different ambiguous cases. We deal with the ambiguity which derives from physical features of the represented objects and we analyze the situation where the ambiguity is dependent on the choice made to describe the pictorial information. That is, we deal with objects with irregular shapes (concave objects) where the ambiguity is due to the nature of the objects, apart from the representation used to describe them. We also consider objects which have regular shapes but may lead to ambiguity due to their spatial arrangement.

We note that the normalized virtual image describes the visual content of an image in terms of objects and spatial relations among them independent of any orientation, since the 2-R string can be extracted with the respect to the centroid of each object and the positional information is given by the 2-D string with respect to the orientation used to store the image in the Image Database. Then, the presence of several independent systems of axes allows one to derive different representations which contain complementary information; i.e. the normalized pictorial information is the result of these representations and derives from the analysis of the spatial arrangement of the objects along both axes of specific selected systems.

The result of this orientation independence assures the possibility of deriving unique representations even if the atomic relations, which describe the spatial arrangements of the objects, imply ambiguity during the reconstruction process. When the ambiguity arises from the spatial arrangement of the objects and from the choice of a particular point of view, moving the point of view to another rotation center eliminates the ambiguity, since the analysis of the complementary information which is in the normalized virtual image gives enough information to overcome the previous ambiguity.

As an example, consider the pictures in Figure 2. The pictures are described by the same iconic index with respect to the Cartesian system, thereby introducing ambiguity during the reconstruction process:

u: A<B%C
v: B%C<A

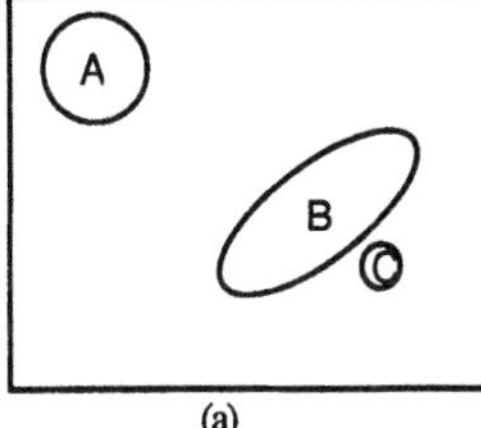

(a)

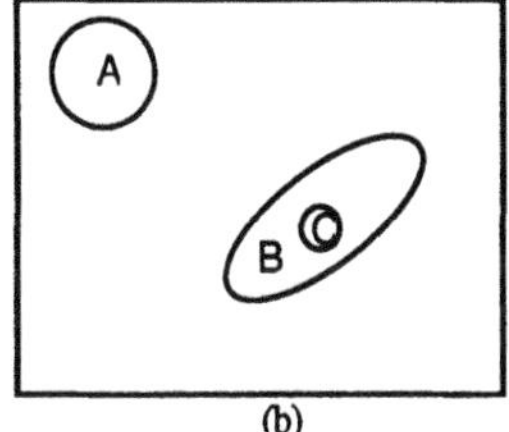

(b)

Figure 2 Pictures that lead ambiguous reconstruction processes.

The corresponding normalized virtual images (NOb, NRs), where the rotation centers correspond to the centroid of the object A are:

Figure 2a):

NOb = {A, B, C};

NRs = ((Rs_c, Rs_s), (u,v)) = ((Rs_c={B<C}, Rs_s={B%C}), (A<B<C, C<B<A)).

Figure 2b):

NOb = {A, B, C};

NRs = ((Rs_c, Rs_s), (u,v)) = ((Rs_c={B%C}, Rs_s={B%C}), (A<B=C, C=B<A)).

Then, by analyzing the normalized virtual images, it is possible to recognize the exact spatial arrangement of the objects, since the positional information is derived from the 2-D string indexes and the relative positioning of the objects is contained in the virtual images, which can be obtained according to the rotation center of each object.

We now concentrate on concave objects and their representations. In particular, to satisfy the requirement of a uniquely reconstructable index we introduce a solution which is based on the AREM methodology and extends the 2D C-string cutting mechanism by determining further conditions to fix cutting lines. In fact, it is necessary to use the AREM methodology since the normalized virtual image does not solve the ambiguity arising from the presence of concave objects.

As an example, consider the images of Figure 3, where the rotation center corresponds to the centroid of the object C. The projections of the beginning points and the ending points of the objects are drawn along the c-direction, where the split point is recognized. Both pictures are described by the same set of atomic relations along the c- and s-direction and their corresponding iconic index is:

c: A%B
s: A%B.

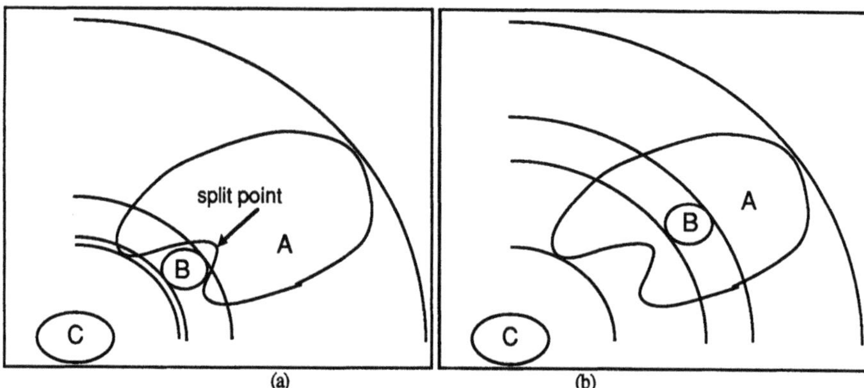

Figure 3 The projections of the objects along the c-direction.

Obviously, this representation is ambiguous, since the property of reconstructability is not satisfied: it is not possible to recognize the position of object B with respect to the split point of object A since this information is not contained in the index. In order to represent concave objects uniquely, it is necessary that the index contains information about split points to determine the spatial arrangement of the objects exactly.

To this aim we distinguish the two situations depicted in Figure 3 and extend the 2D C-string cutting mechanism by introducing cutting lines to be performed whenever a split point produces ambiguity in the reconstruction process. In particular, we recover the *empty space* object of the 2D G-string mechanism (Chang, 1991), (Jungert, 1993), which plays an important role in discriminating between the two cases represented in Figure 3.

Basically, the algorithm of the cutting mechanism of the normalized iconic indexing is defined as follows, where the conditions are checked both in the c- and s-direction.

Let I be an image made up of two objects A and B, where A is a concave object, then

1) if split_point(A) < end(B) < end(A) or begin(A) < begin(B) < split_point(A), then A is partitioned by the cutting lines projected with respect to the beginning point and the ending point of the object B. The iconic index corresponding to the derived subpicture could contain the empty space object *e*;

2) otherwise the 2D C-string cutting mechanism is applied.

As an example, let us consider the pictures in Figure 3, again. The corresponding cutting lines along c-direction are shown in Figure 4(a) and 4(b). In particular, the picture 4(a) is segmented according to the extended cutting mechanism, since condition 1) is satisfied. The corresponding iconic index is:

c: A|AeB]A|A

s: A%B

On the contrary, the picture 4(b) needs no cutting lines and the iconic index is:

c: A%B
s: A%B

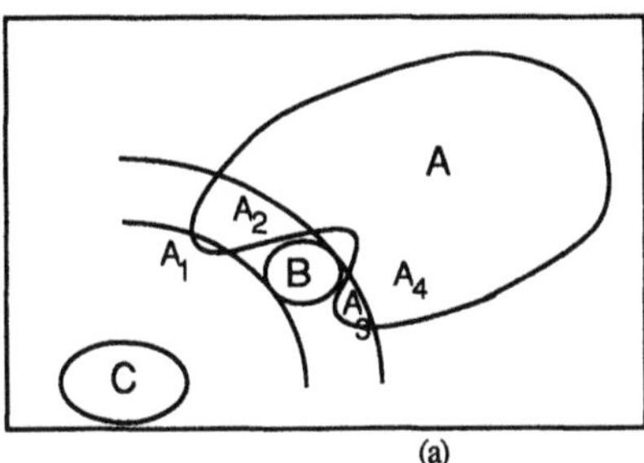

(a)

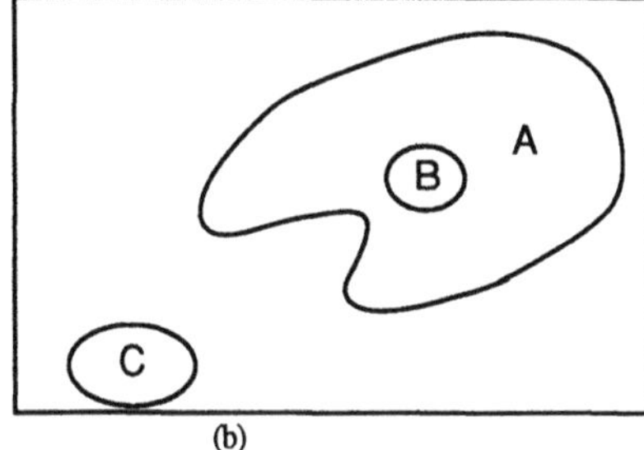

(b)

Figure 4 The cutting mechanism applied to the pictures of Figure 3 along the c-direction.

By applying the Atomic Relation Extraction Method, the corresponding virtual images are obtained. In particular, the picture 4(a) is represented by the following set of binary relations according to the c-direction:
$\{A_1|A_2, A_1<A_3, A_1<A_4, A_1|B_1, A_1|e, A_2]A_3, A_2|A_4, A_2=B_1, A_2=e, B_1=e, e]A_3, B_1]A_3, B_1|A_4, e|A_4, A_3|A_4\}$.

Then, by collecting the characteristic relations, the following set of atomic relations are derived: {A%B, A%e, B=e}.

Therefore, the virtual image corresponding to the picture 4(a) is:
P = (Ob, Rs) where Ob = {A, B} and Rs = (Rs_c, Rs_s) = ({A%B, A%e, B=e}, {A%B});
while the virtual image corresponding to the picture 4(b) is:
P = (Ob, Rs) where Ob = {A, B} and Rs = (Rs_c, Rs_s) = ({A%B}, {A%B}).

Note that each spatial arrangement where the first condition in the algorithm above is not satisfied, is covered by the 2D C-string mechanism, completely. As a matter of fact, Figure 5 describes two possible spatial arrangements along the c-direction, which do not satisfy the first condition. In particular, the image of Figure 5(a) requires a cutting line at the ending point of the object B, since B is dominating with respect to the object A. The corresponding iconic index is:

c: B]A|A
s: A%B

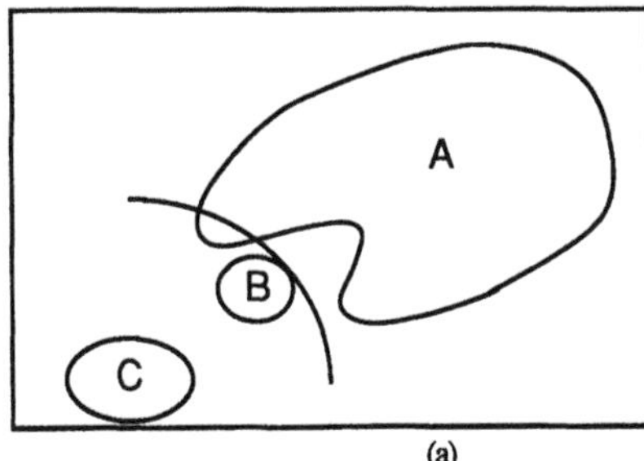

(a)

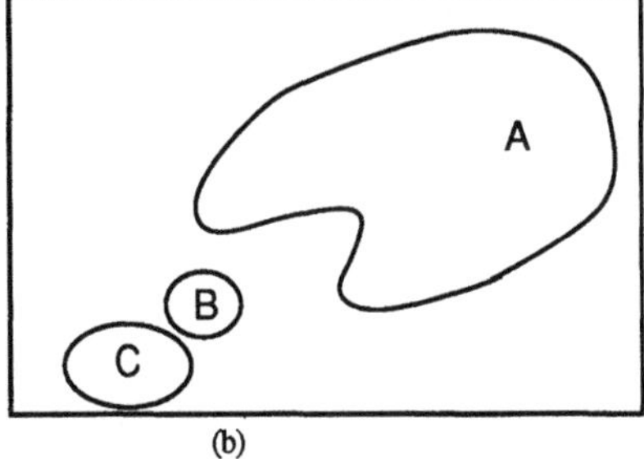

(b)

Figure 5 Two spatial arrangements which do not satisfy the first condition.

On the contrary, the image of Figure 5(b) does not require any cutting line, since B is totally disjoint from A. The corresponding iconic index is:

c: B<A

s: A%B

In these cases no ambiguity arises during the reconstruction process, since the indexes describe the spatial arrangements of the objects A and B uniquely.

4 CONCLUSIONS

In this paper we have shown how the concept of virtual image may be extended to handle the case of images with concave objects. Previous approaches led to ambiguity. We are currently implementing a prototype image database system which will incorporate the methodology described in this paper.

5 REFERENCES

Chang, N.S. and Fu, K.S. (1980) Query-by-pictorial example. *IEEE Trans. on Software Engineering*, **6**, 519-24.

Chang, S.K. and Hsu, A. (1992) Image information systems: Where do we go from here?. *IEEE Transaction on Knowledge and Data Engineering*, **4**, 431-42.

Chang, S.K. and Jungert, E. (1991) Pictorial data management based upon the theory of symbolic projections.*Journal of Visual Languages and Computing*, **2**, 195-215.

Chang, S.K. Shi, Q.Y. and Yan C.W.(1987) Iconic indexing by 2-D string. *IEEE Trans. Pattern Anal. Machine Intell.*, **9**, 413-28.

Chang, S.K. Yan, C.W., Dimitroff, D.C. and Arndt, T. (1988) An intelligent image database system. *IEEE Trans. on Software Engineering*, **14**, 681-88.

Egenhofer, M. and Franzosa R.(1991) Point-set topological spatial relations. *Intern. Journ. of Geographical Information Systems*, **5**, 161-74.

Jungert, E. and Chang, S.K. (1993) An image algebra for pictorial data manipulation. *CVGIP: Image Understanding*, **58**, 147-60.

Lee, S.Y. and Hsu, F.J.(1990) 2D C-string: A new spatial knowledge representation for image database systems. *Pattern Recognition* , **23**, 1077-88.

Lee, S.Y. and Hsu, F.J. (1991) Picture algebra for spatial reasoning of iconic images represented in 2D C-string. *Pattern Recognition Letters* , **12**, 425-35.

Petraglia, G. Sebillo M. Tucci M. and Tortora G.(1993) Towards normalized iconic indexing, in *Proceedings of the 1993 IEEE Symposium on Visual Language*, Bergen, Norway, Aug. 24-27, 392-4.

Petraglia, G. Sebillo M. Tucci M. and Tortora G.(1994) Rotation invariant iconic indexing for image database retrieval, in *Progress in Image Analysis and Processing III* (ed. S. Impedovo), World Scientific.

Petraglia, G. Sebillo M. Tucci M. and Tortora G.(1994) Virtual images for spatial reasoning in image databases. Submitted for publication.

Tanimoto, S.L. (1976) An iconic symbolic data structuring scheme. *Pattern Recognition and Artificial Intelligence*, 452-71.

6 BIOGRAPHY

Timothy Arndt received the B.S. degree in mathematics and computer science from Purdue University in 1984, the M.S. degree in computer science from the University of Florida in 1985 and the Ph.D. in computer science from the University of Pittsburgh in 1990.

He is currently Assistant Professor of Data Bases at the University of Benevento. He has been Assistant Professor at the Southwest Texas State University in San Marcos and at Lamar University in Beaumont, expert technician at the University of Salerno, research assistant at the University of Pittsburgh, teaching assistant at the University of Florida and summer intern at the Software Technology Program of the Microelectronics and Computer Technology Corporation.

His research interests include image processing, image database indexing, picture matching on parallel architectures, multimedia database systems, computer networks and software engineering.

Gennaro Petraglia is Professor at the University of Salerno. He published more than 20 papers in international journals, books, and conference proceedings, in the area of databases and knowledge bases.
His research interests include also distributed multimedia databases and telematics.

Monica Sebillo received the Laurea degree in Computer Science from the University of Salerno, Italy, in 1992. She is currently a Ph Student in Applied Mathematics and Computer Science at the University of Naples.

Her reserch interests include image database indexing, multimedia databases, distributed databases.

Genoveffa Tortora received the Laurea degree in Computer Science from the University of Salerno, Italy in 1978.

She was a Research Associate and Teaching Assistant at the University of Salerno from 1978 to 1988. From 1989 to 1990 she was Associate Professor and then Professor at the Department of Computer Science at the University of Salerno.

Her research interests include software development environments, visual languages and pictorial information systems. She coedited two books, and chaired the *Fourth International Conference on Software Engineering and Knowledge Engineering*. She is a Senior Member of the IEEE Computer Society and is on the editorial board of the *International Journal of Software Engineering and Knowledge Engineering* .

4

Feature–index–based similar shape retrieval

R. Mehrotra
Departement of Mathematics and Computer Science
University of Missouri–St. Louis
8001 Natural Bridge Road
St. Louis, MO 63121, USA rajiv@arch.umsl.edu

J. Gary
Department of Computer Science
University of Kentucky
Lexington, KY 40506, USA jgary@ms.uky.edu

Abstract

Efficient retrieval of images containing matching (or similar) shapes is an important problem in image database management. A few shape similarity-based image retrieval techniques have been reported in the literature. Most of these techniques are designed to deal only with images of rigid objects and cannot easily handle shape similarity-based retrieval of images of articulated objects (i.e., objects with one or more joints with movable components). Some of these techniques are incapable of handling images of overlapping and touching objects. In this paper, a new feature-index-based shape similarity-based image retrieval technique, which is capable of handling images of rigid as well as articulated objects, is proposed. The proposed technique can also retrieve images of overlapping and touching objects that satisfy the query constraints. In this approach structural components of a shape called features are represented as points in a multidimensional space. Any multidimensional point access index structure can be used to organize shape features. Given a query shape or image, a query shape feature is selected and similar (or matching) shape features belonging to images in the database are found by searching the feature index structure. If the query shape and a stored shape containing any of the retrieved matching features are found to be similar (or satisfy similarity constraints), the stored shape is included in the response to the query.

Keywords

image database, content-based retrieval, feature indexing, shape similarity retrieval

1 INTRODUCTION

With recent advances in computer technologies, numerous new application areas requiring management of pictorial data have evolved. Efficient management of pictorial data is required in areas including meteorology, medical, space exploration, manufacturing, entertainment, education, and defense. In these, and other, application areas large and constantly growing repositories of images are available. But such image repositories and of little use due to the lack of techniques for image retrieval based on their content or semantics. In recent years, there has be an ever increasing interest in developing content–based image retrieval techniques.

Similarity of two images can be defined by general image characteristics such as intensity, color, texture, etc. (Faloutsos, 1993, Barber, 1993), in terms of spatial relationships among image objects (Chang, 1987), or in terms of the shapes present in the images. This paper is concerned with the problem of **shape similarity based retrieval**. In shape similarity based image retrieval, stored images that satisfy the specified shape similarity constraints with respect to a query image are required to be retrieved from the database. In simple terms, shape similarity-based image retrieval can be stated as follows:

Given a shape similarity measure, retrieve (or select) all images containing shapes similar to one or more shapes present in the query image.

The focus of this paper is on image databases of two-dimensional (2D) (i.e., flat or almost flat) objects/shapes[1]. Two types of 2D objects are usually found:

1. **Rigid objects** - These objects have a single rigid component (or link).

2. **Articulated objects** - These objects are made up of two or more rigid components called *links* joined by movable *joints* (rotating or sliding). Examples of articulated objects include a pair of scissors, a pair of pliers, etc.

An ideal shape similarity-based retrieval method must be general enough to handle images of articulated as well as rigid objects. Furthermore, in an uncontrolled environment, objects may overlap and touch each other. Such cases result in complex shapes (or images) caused by the occlusion or overlapping of the object. An ideal shape retrieval techniques must be flexible enough to handle images with overlapping or touching objects (referred to as *complex images*) as well as images of isolated shapes (referred to as *simple images*.

Existing shape similarity-based image retrieval techniques can be broadly classified into two classes. Techniques belonging to one of these classes rely on specially designed index structures for shape retrieval whereas the techniques in the other class utilize existing point access methods or spatial access methods.

Grosky and Mehrotra (Grosky, 1989, 1990, 1992) proposed a technique which represents

[1]The terms object and shape are used interchangeably in this paper.

a shape in terms of local structural features of its boundary. They proposed a specialized index structure based on the m–way search tree to organize boundary components of shapes stored in the image database. This technique can handle images of occluded and touching objects, but the index structure is very complex.

Jagadish's technique (Jagadish, 1991) represents a shape in terms of the properties of a fixed number of largest size rectangles from the set of rectangles that cover the shape. A shape is represented as a point in a multidimensional space and therefore any multidimensional point access method (PAM) (Nievergelt, 1984, Robinson, 1981), Seeger, 1987) can be used for indexing. The shape representation utilized in this techniques is suitable only for isolated shapes and therefore it cannot handle images with occluded or touching objects.

Recently, Mehrotra and Gary (Mehrotra, 1993, Gary, 1993) proposed an approach which combines the strength of the above two techniques while overcoming some of their weaknesses. Their approach represents an object in terms of its local structural boundary features. Each structural feature is represented as a point in a multidimensional space. Thus, any existing multidimensional PAM can be used to build a feature index to efficiently organize the structural features of all the stored shapes or images. This approach is capable of dealing with images of overlapping and touching objects.

In Mehrotra-Grosky's and Mehrotra-Gary's techniques, for a given a query image, a query feature (i.e., a structural boundary component of the query shape) is selected from the query image and the matching features are found by searching the index structure. Associated with each feature in the index is a list of (parent-shape, feature-location) pairs, which tells where and in which shape that feature occurs. The lists associated with the matching features are used to retrieve the shapes that satisfy the specified similarity criteria.

A very few computer vision researchers have considered the problem of recognition of articulated objects. Beinglass and Wolfson (1991) describe a generalized Hough transform approach. Their approach is similar to the one presented here, but uses a "voting" procedure in generation of hypotheses. Lowe (1991) describes the use of least squares model fitting for parameterized models to images. This approach is quite flexible and may have application in pose estimation once hypotheses have been identified, but is too time consuming for an interactive query session in a large database.

Most existing approaches of similar shape retrieval lack the capability of dealing with articulated objects in a simple way in the context of a large database. One possible way to handle articulated shape retrieval using these methods is to automatically generate a sufficiently large number of shapes corresponding to different relative positions of the components of a query shape. Then for each generated shape, similar shapes can be retrieved. Obviously, this approach is impractical due to its very high time requirement. An alternative approach, which is adopted in this work, is to employ a general transformation invariant shape representation method which can represent both the rigid as well the articulated object in the same way. In this paper, a general and flexible shape similarity-based retrieval approach is proposed. This approach represents an articulated shape in terms of its rigid components and articulation points. Each rigid component is represented in terms of its boundary components which are in turn represented as points in a multidimensional space. The proposed technique is described in the following sections. Some experimental results are also presented to demonstrate its performance.

2 FEATURE BASED SIMILARITY RETRIEVAL

Three primary issues to be considered in designing a shape similarity based image retrieval system are shape representation, similarity measure, and index design. The symbolic shape representation should be flexible enough to allow retrieval of isolated images and images with overlapping or touching parts. The representation should also be general enough to handle rigid and articulated shapes. The similarity measure should be consistent with human interpretation and efficiently computed. It is also advantageous for the similarity measure to be a metric. Together, the representation and similarity measure should lend themselves to a efficient range search method to facilitate retrieval of similar or matching shapes. A specially designed index could be constructed, or existing indexing techniques could be used.

2.1 Iconic index construction

Each shape to be stored in the database is first processed to obtain the shape boundary. Points on the boundary with maximal local curvature are chosen as **interest points**. The details of this process are not addressed in this paper. A variety of techniques have been developed for the robust identification of interest points (Tsang, 1994, Wuescher, 1991). The object is thus represented as an ordered sequence of interest points. We define a feature to be a collection of a few adjacent interest points. In other words, a feature represents a boundary segment and the shape is a set of boundary segments. We have experimented with 4, 5, and 6 interest point per feature. Each feature is encoded to make it scale, rotation, and translation invariant, and entered into the index structure. The steps involved in index construction are illustrated in figure 1.

2.1.1 Feature encoding

Given a set of n interest points, a pair is chosen to form a basis vector. A coordinate system is defined with this vector as a unit vector along the x axis. All other interest points in the feature are transformed to this coordinate system. Figure 1 illustrates this transformation. This form of encoding is essentially arbitrary; any pair of points could form the basis vector, or indeed all pairs could be used. In our experiments, we select only adjacent interest points for feature encoding. The vector $F = (x_1, y_1, \ldots, x_n, y_n)$ where (x_i, y_i) is the normalized coordinate of the ith interest point in that feature, is used as a key in the index structure. Each feature is characterized by the transformation used to encode the interest points. This is represented as an attribute vector $P = (S, T_x, T_y, A)$ where S is the scale, or length of the basis vector, T_x and T_y are the translation parameters, or location of the tail of the basis vector, and A is the angle the basis vector forms with the x axis. Thus a feature of n interest points is represented as a point in $2n + 4$ dimensional

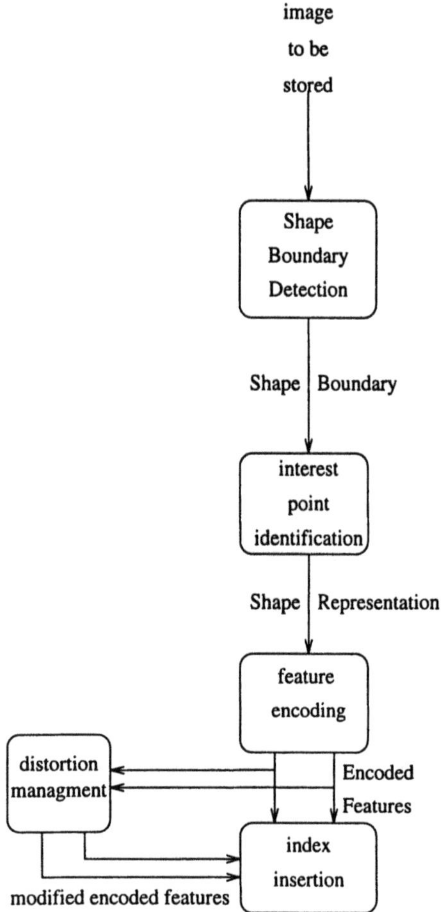

Figure 1: Index Construction

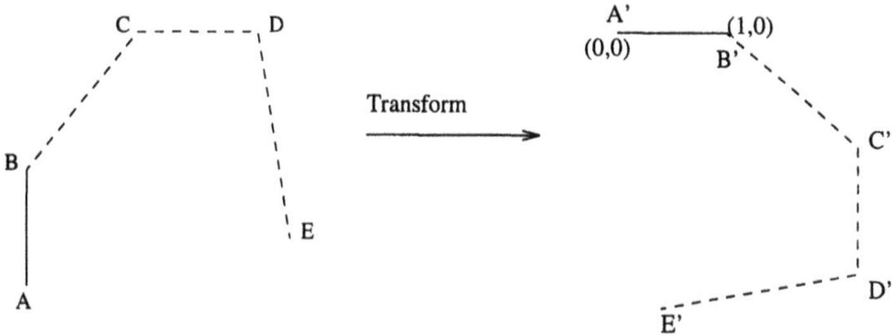

Figure 2: Feature Encoding Example

space. The Euclidean distance between two points is used as a measure of the similarity of the corresponding boundary features.

2.1.2 Shape representation

A rigid shape with m interest points is represented by a set of boundary features $(F_1, \ldots, F_m)$, its object identifier, and its model type (rigid). A feature is generated for each set of n adjacent interest points. For example, if a shape was represented by interest points $(I_1, \ldots, I_m)$, where $I_i = (x_i, y_i)$ and feature size was chosen to be four, then $F_1 = (x_1, y_1, x_2, y_2, x_3, y_3, x_4, y_4)$,$F_2 = (x_2, y_2, x_3, y_3, x_4, y_4, x_5, y_5), \ldots, F_m = (x_m, y_m, x_1, y_1, x_2, y_2, x_3, y_3)$. Each boundary feature is defined by its transformation parameter set, P. An articulated object with n components is represented by a collection of its rigid components $(C_i, \ldots, C_n)$, its object id, and its model type (articulated). The representation of a rigid component of an articulated shape is similar to that of a rigid object, but is augmented with a list of articulation point locations (in the normalized coordinate system) and the identifiers of components associated with those articulation points. A rigid component C with m interest points of an articulated object is represented by a set of boundary features $(F_1, \ldots, F_m)$, a set of articulation points $((x_1, y_1), \ldots, (x_n, y_n))$ where n is the number of articulation points on the component, and identifiers for the components $(id_1, \ldots, id_n)$, that share each articulation point.

2.1.3 Index structure

The encoded vectors representing the boundary features are used to form a feature index for the shape database. The similarity between two features is defined as the Euclidean distance between the two vectors. Given this structure and similarity measure, our index can take the form of any multi–dimensional point access method (PAM). Several such data structures have been designed to be used with large databases on external storage and to support range searches. These structures are generally hierarchical. The encoded feature vectors serve as the key values and associated with each leaf of the index structure is a list where each node stores information about where and in what shape this feature appears. Specifically, for features of rigid shapes, the node consists of a (transformation parameters, object identifier) tuple. Articulated shape features have an entry for each articulation point in that component in the form of a (transformation parameters, object identifier, articulation point location, sibling component identifiers) tuple, where sibling components are the ones that share the articulation points. The list associated with a feature is used to generate a set of hypotheses regarding shapes in the image database that may satisfy shape similarity constraints with respect to a given query shape. In principal, the transformation parameters could be made part of the feature vector and used in the index search, but doing so would increase the dimension of the search space and reduce the efficiency of the search if the query is intended to ignore their values. Our focus is on finding features of similar shape independent of transformation parameters to hypothesize a set of possibly similar objects (objects that contain similar features). Hypothesized shapes may be rejected if they fail to meet similarity constraints or specified restrictions on transformation parameters.

2.2 Query processing

Processing shape similarity queries involves three phases, query feature selection, hypothesis generation, and hypothesis verification. The system selects a feature from the query shape using criteria designed to maximize the chances for a successful search. The index is then searched for features similar in shape to the selected feature. The tolerance on similarity is specified in the query and since the similarity measure is Euclidean distance, a range search is performed on the index. For each feature found to be similar in the search, each object where the feature is present is added to the set of hypotheses. The set of hypotheses contains shapes which have some feature similar in shape to the query feature. The verification phase then attempts to reject those shapes that are not globally similar in shape to the query shape. We describe the details of these phases below and illustrate the steps involved in figure 3.

2.2.1 Query feature selection

There are a few issues to be considered in selection of a feature from the query shape for searching. We wish to minimize the amount of time spent searching, so we should attempt to choose a feature that has a good chance of generating all valid hypotheses.

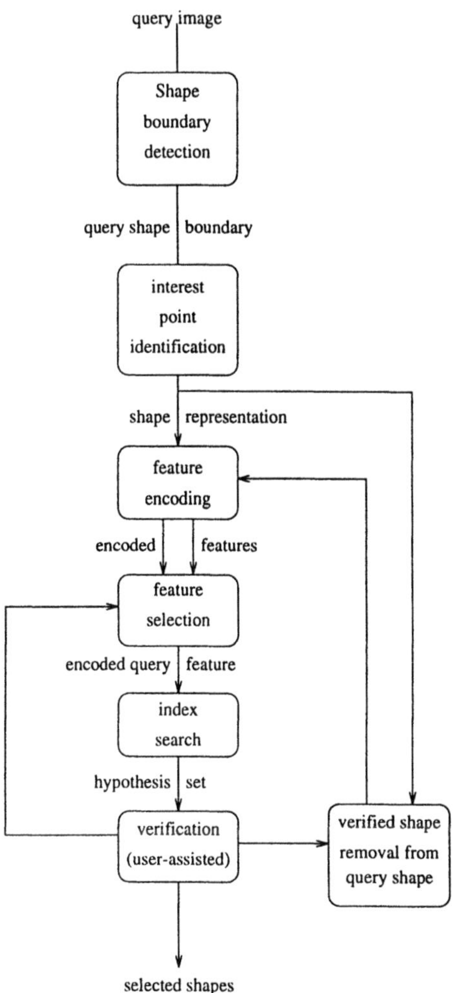

Figure 3: Query Processing

We also prefer features that are less sensitive to noise and distortion in the input image.

It should be noted that, for our feature representation, the intersection of articulated components (or occluding objects in general) will most likely produce an interest point, since the overlap should produce a well defined corner point. This interest point will cause a concave angle in the boundary representation, except in the unlikely case of two corners of the overlapping objects coinciding. It seems reasonable to choose only interest points that do not form concave angles in the boundary. Unfortunately, it is not always possible to find n adjacent interest points with no concave angles.

The problem of distortion in an input image is partially accounted for by adjusting the tolerance on similarity during the search. It should also be noted that small basis vectors will magnify errors more than large basis vectors. Distortion in an input image could also produce false interest points, but such points should form shallow angles in the boundary. We therefore prefer interest points with sharp corners to reduce the likelihood that a false interest point is present. Distortion effects are discussed in greater detail section 2.2.4.

In summary, we want to choose features with large basis vectors, sharp angles, and, preferably, no concave angles. To select a query feature, the length of each line segment in the feature is normalized by dividing by the length of the longest segment, and each angle is normalized by dividing by the size of the largest angle. We then define a measure of the quality of the feature: $R_i = L_i/A_i$, where L_i is the average normalized segment length for feature i, and A_i is the average normalized angle for feature i. Our initial query feature will be i where R_i is maximized over all i. The selected feature should be the one least likely to be involved in an overlap of components or objects or to contain a false interest point. Its encoding should also be least sensitive to noise in the input image. If the selected query feature fails, the next best feature is used for searching the feature index.

2.2.2 Index Search and Hypothesis Generation

For a given query feature, the index is searched to produce a set of hypotheses, that is, a set of shapes that have a feature similar in shape to the query feature. The details of the search procedure are of course dependent on the PAM being used, but in general a range search is required. The query may specify a tolerance on the similarity measure, which may be 0 if an exact match is required. Each feature found during the search will have an associated list of objects where the feature occurs. These objects may be either rigid, or components of articulated objects. These objects form the set of hypotheses that are passed on to the verification step.

2.2.3 Hypothesis verification

If the set of hypotheses is small, then the user may elect to review the set manually and skip the verification stage. In cases where the hypothesis set is large, hypotheses of rigid objects or components of articulated objects may be verified or rejected by overlaying the hypothesized shape (suitably transformed to input query coordinates) over the query shape and analyzing the amount of overlap between the two shapes. The transformation parameters are computed by minimizing the distance between the query interest points and the hypothesis interest points in the matched features. This is a non-linear optimization problem, which in general form is a complex and time consuming problem. However, we have a good initial approximation to the minimum by computing the transformation parameters necessary to exactly overlay the basis vectors from the matched features. In addition, the dimensionality of the problem is only 4 (rotation, scale, and translation in x and y) and we only require tolerance to a pixel. Under these conditions it is possible to find a good approximation to the transformation parameters giving minimum distance by using the 'Downhill Simplex method,' (Press, 1988)

If the query shape is from an image that contains overlapping or touching parts, then the shapes may not have similar boundaries, but the hypothesized shape should be contained within the boundary of the query shape. A database shape whose boundary overlap with the query shape exceed a user specified threshold is added to the selection set. At this point, the user may intervene in the selection process to eliminate hypotheses from the selection set that are judged to be poor. If a hypothesis is validated by the user, then interest points in the input image that correspond to that shape are removed from consideration and the process begins again using the remaining interest points to generate a new query feature in an attempt to locate other shapes in the input image. This process continues until there are no longer sufficient interest points to make a valid feature or the user elects to terminate the process.

If multiple components of an articulated object are hypothesized, then the relative orientation of the components can give strong evidence of a match by determining if the articulation points of the components are sufficiently close to one another. The transformation parameters that were calculated to minimize the distance between feature interest points are applied to the articulation point of each respective component. If the components are truly present in the query image, then the transformed articulation point of one component should lie very close to the transformed articulation point of the other component in the query coordinate system. Components that agree, within some tolerance, on the location of their common articulation point, are assumed to be connected about the articulation point, and the articulated object is added to the selection set. It should also be noted that multiple components of one articulated object that are present in a query image should have little difference in the scaling factor needed to map them into the image coordinate system. It is also possible to determine the relative orientation of the components of the articulated object by comparing the rotation parameters of each component.

2.2.4 Handling distortion effects

Distortion in a query image may manifest itself in three ways. Interest points may be displaced from their ideal positions, false interest points may be introduced, and legitimate interest points could vanish. The problem of displaced interest points is addressed directly

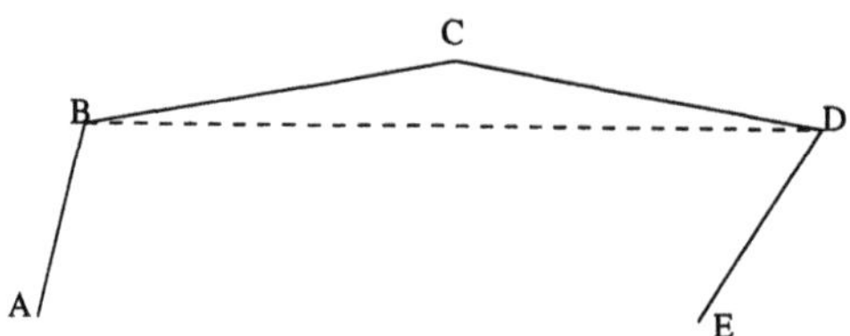

Figure 4: Removal of a feature point determined to be distortion sensitive

by our encoding mechanism and search procedure. Features are encoded as n-dimensional vectors, and a displaced interest point will have a proportional displacement effect on the encoded feature vector. The search process looks for feature vectors within a user–specified range of the query feature vector, so displaced interest points are not likely to cause a failure of the search criteria unless the displacement is very large. They will cause a reduction in the confidence level of the match, but the search tolerance can be increased at will to account for any amount of interest point displacement.

The problem of false interest points is addressed by the query feature selection process. A false interest point is likely to form a shallow angle with its adjacent interest points. The query feature selection algorithm explicitly attempts to avoid shallow angles for exactly this reason.

Missing interest points require a different approach entirely. There is no way to determine where an interest point should have been by examining the input query image only. We address this problem by doing some additional work on the shape boundaries as they are being added to the database. In addition to encoding the features found in the shape boundaries, the angles formed by each interest point are examined, and if sufficiently shallow they are flagged as likely to be missed during query shape analysis if present in an input image. In other words, interest points that are most likely to vanish during query shape processing are identified in the database construction phase. These interest points are then removed from the boundary and the resulting shape is encoded and entered into the index. This is illustrated in figure 2. This is done in addition to the normal case of considering all interest points.

3 PROTOTYPE SYSTEM

A prototype system has been implemented to test the performance of the proposed approach. A database consisting of 101 rigid shapes and 6 articulated shapes, with 2 components each was used for experimental purposes. A KD–Btree (Robinson, 1981) is used as the index structure. The KD–Btree is one of the earliest and most primitive point access methods, so we expect that more sophisticated PAMs (Buddy Trees (Seeger, 1987), Grid Files (Nievergelt (1984), etc.) would yield better performance. Indices were created using

4 Dimensional Index (2210 features)			
Tolerance	0.15	0.30	0.45
Total Seeks	4292	7985	12240
Average seeks per search	37.54	70.66	108.32
Average hyp. per search	3.72	14.72	33.01

6 Dimensional Index (2316 features)			
Tolerance	0.15	0.30	0.45
Total Seeks	4004	7850	12154
Average seeks per search	35.43	69.47	107.56
Average hyps. per search	1.43	4.19	9.49

8 Dimensional Index (2421 features)			
Tolerance	0.15	0.30	0.45
Total Seeks	4441	8807	13625
Average seeks per search	39.30	77.94	120.58
Average hyps. per search	1.13	1.88	3.94

Table 1: Search Results

4, 5, and 6 interest points per feature. The three indices contained, respectively, 2210, 2316, and 2421 features (including distorted features).

A performance experiment was conducted by applying the query feature selection algorithm to each of the original shapes present in the database. This test was performed on each of the three indices and at three levels of tolerance in the range search. The results are summarized in table 1. It is noted that the dimensionality had little effect on the number of disk seeks. The higher dimensional cases (more interest points per feature) produced fewer false hypothesis. This is unsurprising as a greater portion of the object is encoded in each feature. Increasing the search tolerance increases the number of false hypothesis and number of seeks, but high tolerance may be required if query images are highly distorted. The tolerance of 0.45 on the 4-dimensional case is clearly too high, however, as almost one third of the shapes in the database are hypothesized on the average.

The prototype system also has a GUI interface written using the XWindow system. Screen shots from this interface illustrate the matching process. A few sample query results are presented in figures 5, 6, 7, and 8. In figure 5, a scissors shape is supplied as an input query (displayed on the left hand side of the figure). Note that this is an articulated object, but the input query contains no information about individual components or articulation point. A feature is selected from the handle (bold lines in figure) and a search of the database produces the correct component (displayed on right hand side of the figure). Actually, in this case, 2 hypotheses were found during the index search. That

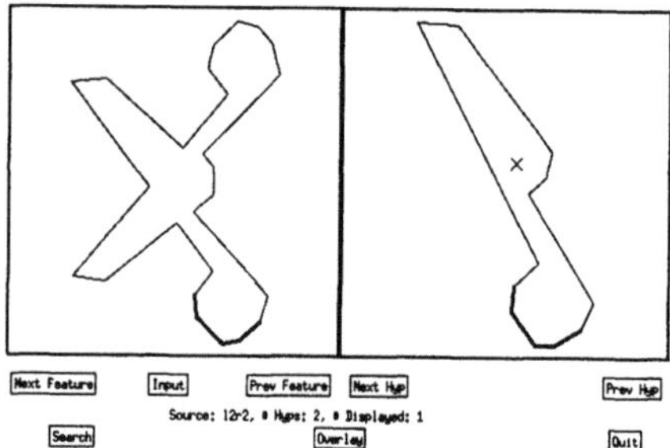

Figure 5: Good Feature Match

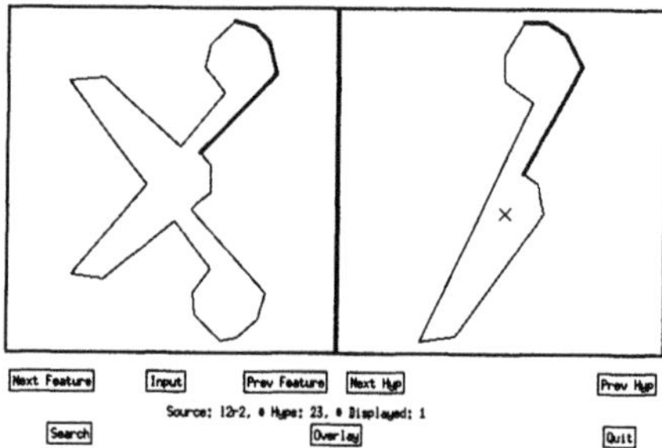

Figure 6: Second Component Match

is, the database contains two features that are within the user's tolerance level of similarity. One hypothesis is displayed with the similar feature highlighted and the user may view other hypothesized shapes by selecting the 'Next Hyp' and 'Prev Hyp' button. Note the 'X' that marks the position of the articulation point in the hypothesis. Subsequently the interest points associated with the matched component would be removed from consideration and a feature is selected from the interest points remaining in the query shape. Another search of the index would find the other component (figure 6) and the system finds that they agree on the location of the point of articulation to within a few pixels.

To illustrate the problem of bad query feature choice, examine figure 7. The input shape is similar to the shapes from figure 5 and 6, but the scissors are in a more open postion. Here a feature has been chosen with interest points that are from different components of the articulated object. A match is found in the index for that feature. The matched feature has a fairly high error value, indicating that it is not very similar to the query feature. A lower setting on the tolerance level would prevent this specific hypothesis from being generated, but the possibility of matches like this remain. Verification processes, either automated or user-assisted, would eliminated this hypothesis from consideration.

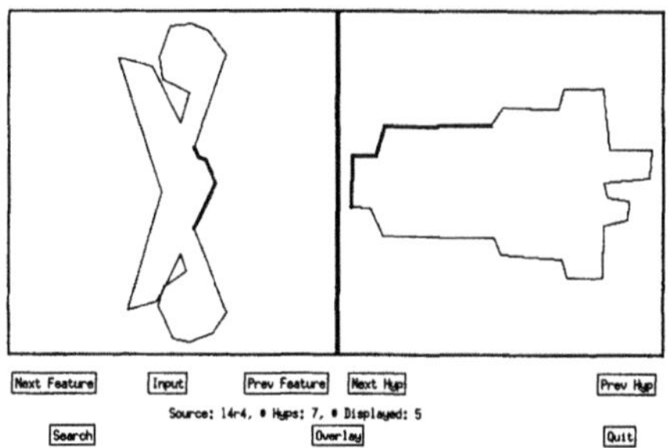

Figure 7: Bad Feature Selection

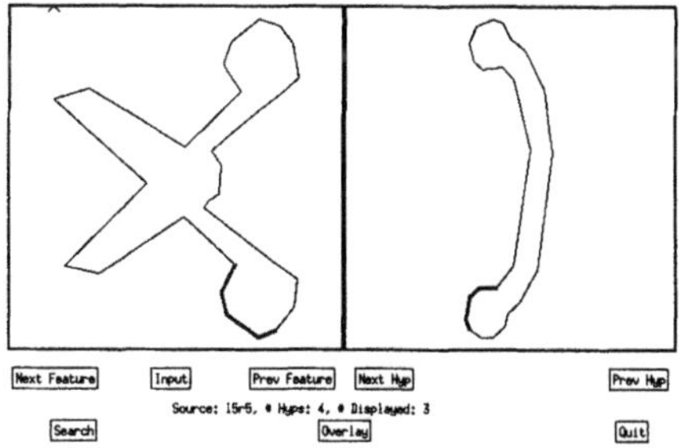

Figure 8: Good Feature, Bad Match

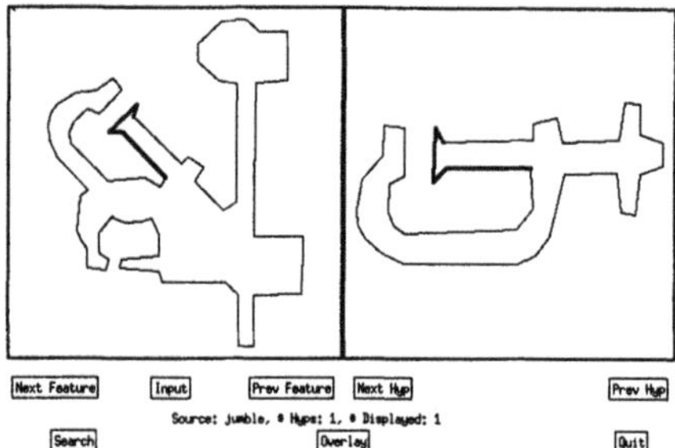

Figure 9:

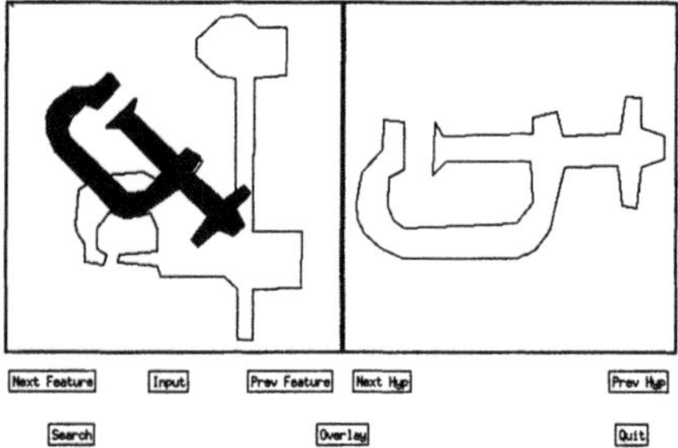

Figure 10:

It is of course possible to find similar features even without having an unacceptable query feature choice. Figure 8 shows a match for a feature, but the shape it matches is not globally similar in shape to the scissors. In general it is not possible to avoid these cases altogether, but the verification stage can automatically reject many bad hypotheses and the user can manually decide to reject others.

To illistrate some additional features of the prototype system, consider figure 9. Here the query image consists of several objects from our database that are overlapping. The feature chosen by the program has been rejected by the user who may interactively specify a query feature by selecting the "Next Feature" and "Prev Feature" buttons. The user then selected the "Search" button to generate hypotheses. A single hypothesis was found and is shown on the right hand side of the window. In figure 10, the user has selected the "Overlay" button to see how well the hypothesis matches the query after suitable translation, rotation, and scaling.

Figure 11 shows a feature choice that generates many hypotheses (the error tolerance was set pretty high in testing). The first hypothesis seems to be reasonable. In figure 12, the user has selected the "Next Hyp" button to display an alternative hypothesis.

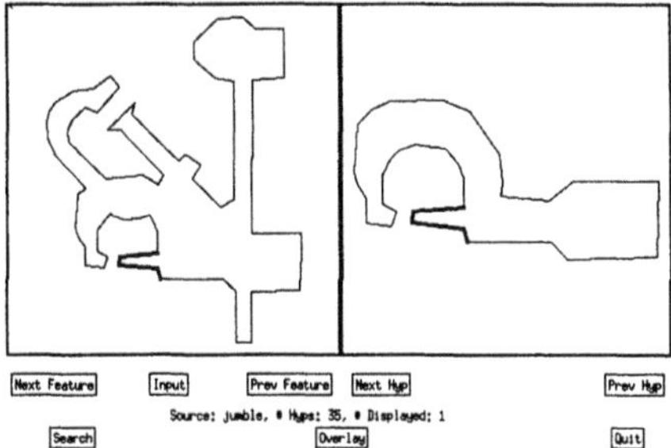

Figure 11:

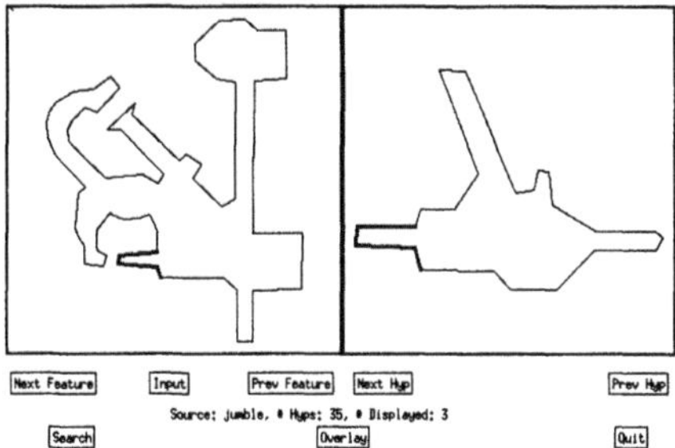

Figure 12:

If desired, the "Prev Hyp" button allows the user to move backward through the list of hypotheses. The hypothesis list is sorted in increasing order of error, so the best one appears first. The poor hypothesis is overlaid on the query shape in figure 13.

The prototype also allows the user to interactively sketch a shape to be used as a query. In figure 14, a shape was sketched with the intention of being similar to the hypothesis of figures 12 and 13. Notice that a match did occur and the overlay illustrated in figure 15 shows a high degree of global similarity.

4 CONCLUSIONS

Existing techniques for shape similarity based retrieval in image databases are limited to rigid shapes. Our proposed iconic index structure is general enough to handle articulated shapes as well as rigid shapes and flexible enough to handle retrieval of isolated shapes as well as overlapping or touching shapes. A prototype system presented and performance analysis reveal it to be efficient and effective. We are continuing to evaluate performance of various point access methods with different sized image databases and other shape representations and similarity measures. We are also investigating the extension of the

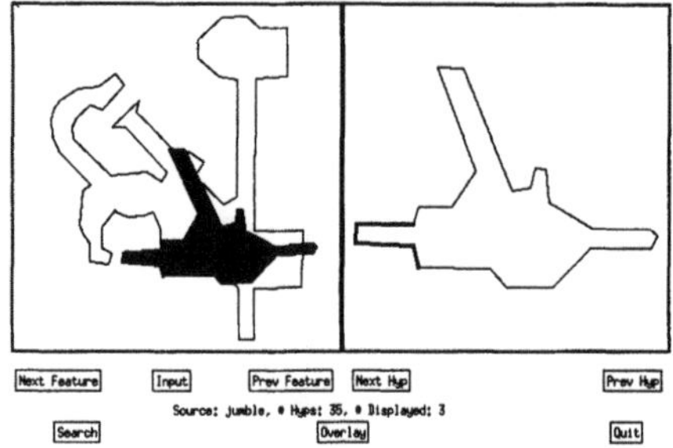

Figure 13:

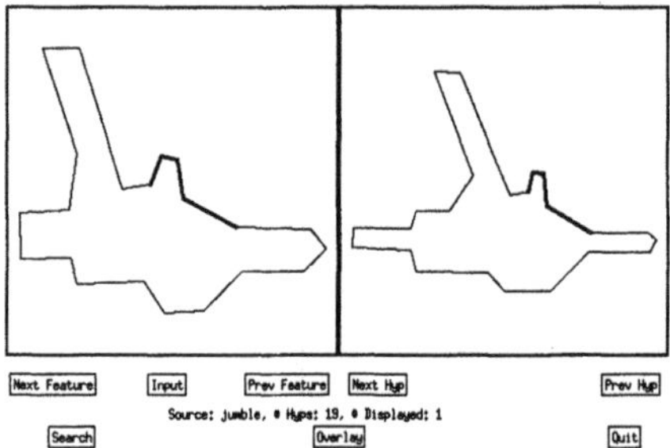

Figure 14:

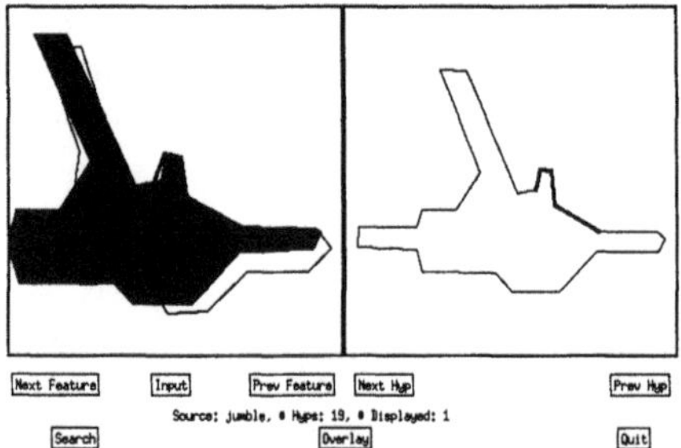

Figure 15:

technique to 3 dimensional shapes.

5 ACKNOWLEDGMENTS

This project was supported in part by NASA-Langley Research Center Grant NAG-1-1276, by the Biomedical Research Support Grant BRSG SO7 RRO7114-21 of the National Institute of Health

6 REFERENCES

Chang, S. K. and Yan, C. W.(1987) Iconic Indexing of 2D Strings. *IEEE Transactions on Pattern Analysis and Machine Intelligence*, **9(3)**, 413–428

Barber, R. , Equitz, W. , Faloutsos, C. , Flickner, M. , Niblack, W. , Petkovic, D. , and Yanker, P. (1993) Query by Content for Large On–Line Image Collections. *Research Report RJ 9408 (82660)*, IBM Research Division.

Beinglass, A. and Wolfson, H. (1991) Articulated Object Recognition, or: How to Generalize the Generalized Hough Transform, *Proceedings of the 1991 IEEE Computer Society Conference on Computer Vision and Pattern Recognition,*, Lhaina, Maui, Hawaii, 461–465.

Faloutsos, C. , Flickner, M. , Niblack, W. , Petkovic, D. , Equitz, W. , and Barber, R. (1993) Efficient and Effective Querying by Image Content. *Research Report RJ 9453 (83074)*, IBM Research Division.

Gary, J. E . and Mehrotra, R. (1993) Shape Similarity-Based Retrieval Using a Structural Feature Index. *Information Systems*, **18(7)**, 525–537.

Grosky, W. I. and Mehrotra, R. (1990) Index-Based Object Recognition in Pictorial Data Management. *Computer Vision, Graphics, and Image Processing* **52(3)**, 416–436.

Grosky, W. I. , Neo, P. , and Mehrotra, R. (1989) An Iconic Index for Model-Based Matching. *Proceedings of the Fifth International Conference on Data Engineering*, Los Angeles, California, 180–187.

Grosky, W. I. , Neo, P. , and Mehrotra, R. (1992) A Pictorial Index Mechanism for Model-Based Matching. *Data and Knowledge Engineering*, **8**, 309–327.

Jagadish, H. V. (1991) A Retrieval Technique for Similar Shapes. *Proceedings of the ACM SIGMOD International Conference on the Management of Data*, Denver Colorado, 208–217.

Lowe, D. G. (1991) Fitting Parameterized Three-Dimensional Models to Image. *IEEE Transactions on Pattern Analysis and Machine Intelligence,* **13(5)**, 441–450.

Mehrotra R. and Gary J. E. (1993), Feature-Based Retrieval of Similar Shapes. *Proceeding of the Nineth International Conference on Data Engineering*, Vienna, Austria, 108–115.

Nievergelt, J. , Hinterberger, H. , and Sevcik, K. C .(1984) The Grid File: An Adaptable Symmetric Multikey File Structure. *ACM Transactions on Database Systems*, **9(1)**, 38–71.

Press, William H. (1988) *Numerical Recipes in C.* Cambridge University Press.

Robinson, J. T. (1981) K-D-B-tree: A Search Structure for Large Multidimensional Dynamic Indices. *Proc. ACM SIGMOD Conference on the Management of Data*, Ann Arbor, Michigan, 10–18.

Seeger, B. and Kriegel, H. P. (1987) The Buddy Tree: An Efficient and Robust Access Method for Spatial Database Systems. *Proc. 16th International Conference on Very Large Databases*, Brighton, U.K., 590–601.

Tsang, W. M. , Yuen, P .C. , and Lam, F. K. (1994) Detection of Dominant Points on an Object Boundary: a Discontinuity Approach. *Image and Vision Computing*, **12(9)**, 547–557.

Wuescher, D. M. and Boyer, K. L. (1991) Robust Contour Decompositions using a Constant Curvature Criterion. *IEEE Transactions on Pattern Analysis and Machine Intelligence*, **13(1)**, 41–51.

7 BIOGRAPHY

Rajiv Mehrotra received a B. Tech degree in Electrical Engineering from Kanpur University, India, in 1977, an M. Tech degree in Electrical Engineering from the Indian Institute of Technology, Kanpur, India, in 1979, an M. A. and a Ph. D. in Computer Science from Wayne State University, Detroit, Michigan, in 1983 and 1986, respectively.

Dr. Mehrotra is currently an Associate Professor in the Department of Mathematics and Computer Science of the University of Missouri-St. Louis. His prior employments include faculty positions at University of Kentucky, Lexington, KY (Associate Professor of Computer Science and Electrical Engineering, 1990-94) and University of South Florida, Tampa, Florida (Assistant Professor of Computer Science and Computer Engineering(1986-90).

His current research interests include multimedia information management systems and visual information procesing and management. He was a co-guest editor (with B. P. Berra, F. Golshani, and O. Sheng) of a special section of IEEE Transactions on Knowledge and Data Engineering on **Multimedia Information Systems (August 1993).** He coedited (with M. R. Varanasi) a reprint collection entitled "Multirobot Systems," published by the IEEE Computer Society Press. He was a co-guest editor (with W. I. Grosky) of a special issue of *IEEE Computer* on Image Database Management (December 1989).

Dr. Mehrotra is a senior member of IEEE and a member of ACM.

James Gary received a B. A. in Physics and Mathematics from Indiana University, Bloomington, Indiana in 1982 and an M. S. in Computer Studies from North Carolina

State University, Raleigh, North Carolina in 1985. He is currently pursuing a Ph. D. in Computer Science at the University of Kentucky, Lexington, Kentucky.

Mr. Gary has worked as an instructor at Winston Salem State University in North Carolina and at the University of Kentucky. He will be joining the Mathematical Sciences faculty at Cameron University in Lawton, Oklahoma in the Fall of 1995. His research interests include Image Databases, Computer Graphics, Image Processing, Programming Languages, and Computer Vision.

PART TWO

Visual Languages Assessment

5

Diagrammatic Vs Textual Query Languages: A Comparative Experiment

T. Catarci and G. Santucci
Dipartimento di Informatica e Sistemistica
Università degli Studi di Roma "La Sapienza"
Via Salaria, 113 - 00198 Roma, Italy
(catarci/santucci)@infokit.dis.uniroma1.it

Abstract

The significance of usability as one of the most important system characteristics is widely recognized in all the application fields, including databases. This also implies the involvement of the user in the activities of design and testing of any interface. However, very few studies aiming at validating the usability of a system have been proposed in the database field, in contrast to many other computer science areas. In this paper we present an experiment comparing, from the point of view of the ease-of-use, a novel visual query language, namely QBD*, against a well-known traditional textual language such as SQL. The results of the experiment confirmed the superiority of the QBD* approach, which is based on a conceptual data model, closer to the user view of the reality than the relational model, a visual representation of such a model, more attractive and graspable than a textual list of table names, and direct manipulation commands, having a syntax much more easier than the SQL one.

1 INTRODUCTION

Several classes of users, both professionals and naives, need to be able to access databases for extracting meaningful information. The traditional interaction style with databases relies on using textual query languages, such as SQL (Date 1987). This kind of language is hard to use by non-programmers. Thus, alternative query modalities have been proposed in the literature, often based on using visual representations and direct manipulation interaction mechanisms (see (Batini et al. 1991) for a survey of visual query languages, and (Shneiderman 1983) for the definition of direct manipulation). All the proposed approaches emphasize in principle the role of the final user in the design life-cycle of the query systems. Also, the significance of usability as one of the most important system characteristics is widely recognized ((Nielsen 1993, Bevan Macleod 1993), see also a recent panel on user interfaces at VLDB'94 (Spaccapietra 1994)). However, very few studies aiming at testing and validating the usability of a system have been proposed in the database field.

(Reisner 1988) is an interesting paper recalling the majority of the experiments done on the ease of use of traditional query languages, mainly SQL and QBE. Other earlier surveys on experiments are (Shneiderman 1978, Shneiderman 1980, Thomas 1977), and a recent one is reported in (Ahlberg Williamson Shneiderman 1993). A common goal of such experiments is to provide a quantitative estimate of the ease of use. The general approach in order to do this is:

1. define precisely what one is to measure;

2. develop a task for users to perform;
3. measure relevant parameters of user performance (i.e. error rate, time to complete a task, etc.).

Unfortunately, measuring ease of use is not as precise as measuring the quantity of a substance in a physics experiment, it involves cognitive activities and is determined by a large number of variables. To capture at least some aspects of ease of use, experimenters have developed a number of different tasks (Reisner 1988). The most common are query writing tasks, in which subjects are given questions in natural language and asked to write the corresponding query language statements. The tasks can be used in different kind of tests to capture different facets of ease of use. Two different classes of experiments have been reported in the literature: one aiming at evaluating the ease of use of a single language, the other aiming at establishing which is the easiest to use among two or more languages.

Our approach falls in the second category. We performed a series of experiments in order to compare, based on their usability, QBD*, a diagrammatic query language developed in our Department (Angelaccio Catarci Santucci 1990a; Angelaccio Catarci Santucci 1990b) and SQL. Analogously to previous experiments, also in our case the task was query writing, and the actual usage experiment was preceded by a teaching period, not part of the variables observed in the experiment. We tried to make as many of the conditions of the experimentation of the two languages the same as we reasonably could (i.e., teaching method, exam questions, exam procedure, method of scoring). We also examined some background information about the various users in order to divide them into equivalence classes and to assign to each language the same set of classes. This is commonly done in experiments to determine whether factors other than the one being measured might influence the experiment results.

It is worth noting that, as far as we know, this is the first rigorous study of comparison between a visual query language and a well-known traditional language, such as SQL. The results of the experiment confirmed our belief (see (Catarci et al. 1994)) that a visual approach is particularly suited for medium and naive users, and for certain types of queries.

The paper is organized as follows. Section 2 provides a short description of the QBD* system (we assume the reader familiar with SQL). Section 3 introduces the evaluation techniques that have been adopted in the experiment. Section 4 describes the experimental framework and reports the numerical results. In Section 5 a discussion of these results is presented. Finally, conclusions are drawn in Section 6.

2 QBD*

The QBD* (Query By Diagram) system is a visual query system based on a diagrammatic representation of the Entity Relationship schema (Chen 1976) describing the underlying (relational) database. It balances a high expressive power with a noticeable facility of use. Concerning the expressive power, it has been proved to be relationally complete; moreover it includes a significant class of recursive queries (transitive closure) and handles an extension of the relational algebra set-oriented operators that we call *generalized set-oriented operators* (Santucci Sottile 1993). Through those operators it is possible to compute set-oriented operations on any pair of relational tables sharing the same identifier. The ease of use has been reached through a fully graphical environment. In that environment the user interacts with the system mainly with a mouse-like device, using the keyboard only when necessary. To increase the friendliness of the system a set of *helping facilities* has been devised. Among them, the most important ones are top down browsing and schema transformation. The former allows for browsing a library of top-down refinements documenting an ER schema at different levels of abstraction. While browsing through the top-down schemata, the user can easily locate the fundamental concepts and links. Top-down browsing may be also used to locate the subschema of interest. The schema transformation allows for converting a schema into a new version closer to the query. As an example it is possible to collapse a path in the schema giving rise to a new concept or to replace an ISA relationship with the child entity.

Nevertheless, the helping facilities of QBD* have not been posed at the user disposal in the experiments. In order to equate it with SQL, the user interacted with the query module only.

The general structure of the QBD* query is based on the location of a distinguishing concept, called *main concept* (entity or relationship), that can be seen as the entry point of one or more subqueries; these subqueries express possible navigations from the main concept to other concepts in the schema. The attributes belonging to each subquery are determined by the following strategy: the attributes of the main concept are automatically considered (unless explicitly deleted by the user), while the other ones are shown in the result only if requested by the user. The presence of a main concept associates a type with each subquery: as an example, if the main entity is the entity person, the result of the query will be a set of persons (possibly enriched with attributes coming from other concepts), no matter what kind of subsequent operations the user performs to specify it.

The subqueries can be combined together by applying several set-oriented operators on two or more subqueries derived from the same entity. The structure of the involved subqueries being, in general, different, it is impossible to perform simple set-oriented operations, and a more general approach is needed (see (Santucci Sottile 1993) for the specific solution adopted within QBD*).

Once the main concept has been selected, two different types of primitives are available for navigating in the schema. The first one allows the user to follow existing paths on the schema (see Figure 1); the other one (see Figure 2), is used for comparing two concepts by building a new path (relationship) on the schema. Comparison conditions, as well as generic conditions on the attributes, are expressed by means of a simple window mechanism including a suitable set of icons. Roughly speaking, we can say that a path on the schema corresponds to an ordered sequence of natural joins[1] among the pairs <entity, relationship> constituting the path, followed by a final selection and projection. The explicit presence of relationships releases the user from the need of looking for concepts like "foreign keys" and the system can perform in the right way the join operations. On the other hand, comparing two concepts via a new relationship corresponds to a theta-join between the two involved entities, and it is up to the user the specification of the theta-condition.

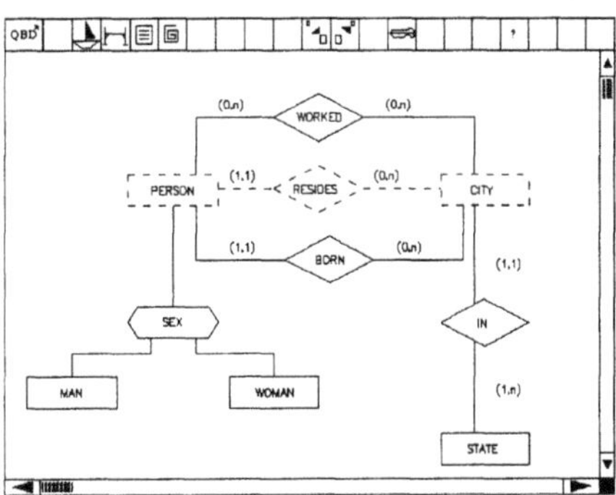

Figure 1 Schema navigation through existing paths.

Queries involving transitive closure are expressed by a visual approach similar to the one in Figure 2b, the difference being the pre-selection of a particular icon, which signals the

[1] We mean here the natural join and theta-join operators as defined in relational algebra (Codd 1972).

beginning of a recursive session. However because of standard SQL does not support recursion, this kind of queries has not been included in the experiments.

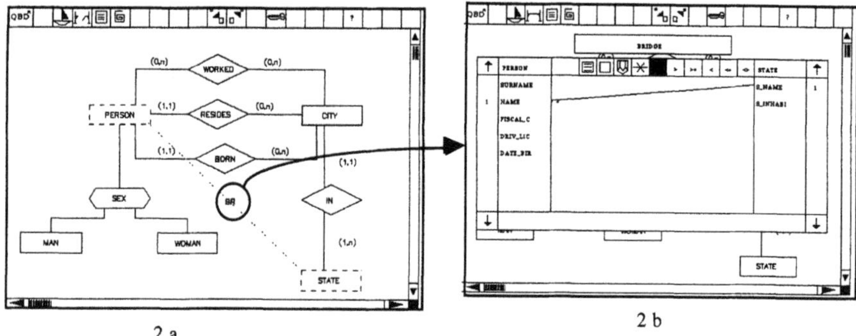

Figure 2 Schema navigation through the building of a new relationship (2a) on the basis of attribute comparisons (2b).

3 EVALUATION TECHNIQUE

Recently, a lot of emphasis has been placed on evaluation techniques, since there are several reasons to evaluate software. People involved in developing software products are interested in evaluations to assist them in making design decisions and to determine whether or not the products achieve the quality measure that must be met. Individuals, who buy the software because they want to use it, need to evaluate the software before purchasing it to check whether it answers key question about usability measures. Even if there is some similarity in the various evaluations, since they are all looking to answer whether the system adequately meets the needs of the user, the above interests are not served by a single evaluation technique. On the contrary, a variety of techniques have been proposed.

The first requirements in order to design a system evaluation are to assess the evaluation purpose, what is being evaluated, who the evaluation is for and, finally, what one hopes to gain. In our case the purpose of the evaluation is to compare two different query systems (a visual one and a traditional one) in order to understand which one is the most easy to use by different user classes. In other words, we are trying to compare the *usability* of the two systems.

Several different definitions of usability exist (Miller 1971; Shackel Richardson 1991; ISO 1991 ISO 1993; Badre 1993; Maissel et al. 1993). In particular, in MUSiC (Maissel et al. 1993) a very comprehensive definition of usability is given as "the extent to which a product can be used with efficiency, effectiveness and satisfaction by specific users to achieve specific goals in specific environments". From this point of view, the usability is the quality of interaction between the user and the overall system. It can be evaluated by measuring three factors: 1) effectiveness, i.e. the extent to which the intended goals of the system can be achieved; 2) efficiency, i.e. the time, the money, the mental effort spent to achieve these goals; 3) satisfaction, i.e. how much the users feel themselves comfortable using the system. It is worth noting that the usability depends on the overall system, i.e. the context, which consists of the types of users, the characteristics of the tasks, the equipment (hardware, software and materials) and the physical and organizational (e.g. the working practices) environment.

The elements that make up the quality of interaction need in general to be measured. Since the quality of interaction depends on the context of use, there is no general rule for how measures can be combined. Usually we will have to provide at least one measure for each element of the quality of interaction. In our experiments we aimed at measuring the effectiveness and the efficiency of the query systems. The effectiveness has been evaluated by relating the goals or subgoals of using the system to the accuracy and completeness with which these goals can be achieved. In our case the main goal is to extract information from the database by asking queries and the accuracy in achieving such a goal has been measured in terms of the user correctness rate when writing such queries.

Measures of efficiency relate the level of effectiveness achieved at the expense of some resources, like mental and physical effort, time, financial cost, etc. In principle, we can consider both the user and the organization point of view, while for our experiment purposes we have measured only the former in terms of time spent carrying out the task. In the latter, we could measure the economic efficiency as the effectiveness in relation to the total cost, which is the labor costs of the user's time, the cost of both resources and equipment used, and the cost of any training required by the user.

Moreover, other kinds of measures can be evaluated. Measures of satisfaction describe the comfort and acceptability of the overall system used by people. Some measures are related to the need to quantify learnability and flexibility, which can be assessed by measuring effectiveness, efficiency and satisfaction across a range of contexts. The learnability of a product may be measured by comparing the usability of a product handled by one user, keeping in mind his/her knowledge and experience. The flexibility of a product handled by users to carry out different tasks can be assessed by measuring usability in different contexts.

The method we adopted in order to measure the effectiveness and efficiency of the systems was the so-called *observational evaluation*, one of the most well known methods for evaluating usability (Macleod 1992; Bevan Macleod 1993). Such a method involves real users that are observed when interacting with the system and offers a broad evaluation of usability. We may either apply the observational evaluation by direct observation or record the interaction between users and system. The recording (done by video camera) is more valuable, since it allows to store a lot of information, for examples the critical points during the interaction (when the user has to consult the manual, when and where s/he is blocked, etc.), the time a user spends to perform a task, the mistakes a user makes, and so on. However, it is also very expensive, not for setting up the equipment, but for the time required to analyze the recorded data. For this reason we preferred to rely on a very careful direct observation.

4 THE EXPERIMENT FRAMEWORK

The goal of this section is to describe the overall experiment framework, i.e., the involved users, the queries we chose, the training the users were given, and the experiment results.

4.1 The Sample Users

The subjects involved in the experiment were undergraduate students, secretaries and professionals for a total of 102 people. They were classified in three categories:

1) Naive users, i.e., persons having little or no knowledge about computer science, for an amount of 56 people;
2) Intermediate users, i.e., persons having a general knowledge about computer science but naive about databases, for an amount of 30 people;
3) Expert users, i.e., persons having a precise knowledge about databases, for an amount of 16 people.

The subjects were assigned to one of two groups: one involved in QBD* tests, the other one in the SQL tests. Each group was composed by 28 naive users, 15 intermediates, and 8 experts. We tried to make the groups as homogeneous as we could in terms of relevant subjects' characteristics, such as educational level, background preparation, employment, sex, and age.

It is worth noting that most subjects were naive users, being the QBD* environment mainly thought for non experts. Nevertheless, in order to get results also on intermediate and expert users, we analyzed the performance of each category separately, as explained in Section 4.4.

4.2 The Query Classes

The users were expected to answer queries of increasing complexity. At this aim we defined a metric for evaluating the complexity of the queries. Note that here we are not dealing with the expressive power of the queries: with the word complexity we mean the mental effort required to the user to compute the query.

After a discussion involving several experts in query languages, we assigned an initial weight to each relational operator and we used such weights to compute the complexity of a set of queries, slightly adjusting the initial weights on the basis of the total score we got for the measured queries. In this phase, looking at the SQL query structure, we decided to add additional weights taking into account the increase of complexity for the presence of subqueries. The weight is proportional to the subquery depth. In Figure 3 the correspondence among relational operators and weights is shown.

Operator	Weight
Identity/Projection in a (Sub)query	$n^{1.5}$ (n=depth level)
Renaming	3
Selection	$n^{1.2}$ (n=number of conditions)
Complement	1.5
Self join	3.5
Natural join	1.5
Theta join	1.5

Figure 3 Adopted weights in measuring query complexity.

In Figure 4 we show two examples of the application of the above metrics.

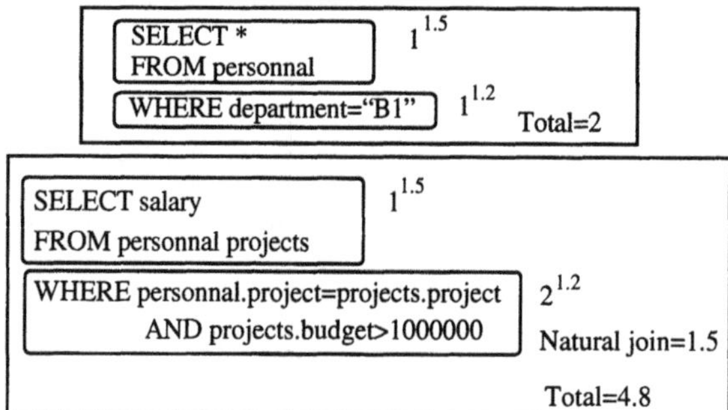

Figure 4 Evaluation of two sample queries.

The strategy we adopted for evaluating the query complexity is based on the expertise of the people asked for designating the weights rather than on a formal approach. Nevertheless, the results we got are quite reasonable and do not affect, directly, the comparison between the two environments. In fact, we used the introduced metric to determine three sets of six queries, of low, medium, and high complexity and the QBD* and SQL sets of users were asked to answer the same sets of queries. Moreover the experiment gave us a significant feedback on the goodness of our metric: the more the query weight increased, the more the users took a large time and made a high number of mistakes in computing them (see Section 4.4). In general, we conjecture that there is a significant relationship between the independent variables, user skill and query classes, and the visual query language used.

More precisely, the naive users (SQL+QBD*) were exposed only to the low complexity set of queries, the intermediate users were exposed to the low and medium complexity sets, the expert users were exposed to all the queries.

Each set of queries was composed by six queries. In particular, the low complexity queries consisted of selections on single relational tables (single entities in QBD*), with selection conditions as follows: simple positive (queries D1, D2, D3), simple negative (D5), multiple in conjunction (D6), multiple in disjunction (D4). The medium complexity queries comprised join operations (path navigations in QBD*) with different join and selection conditions. Queries D1 and D3 were simple equijoins involving two relational tables, D2 was a join with a simple positive selection condition on the join result. Queries D4 and D5 were similar to D2, but with a negative condition. Finally, D6 was the only query of this group containing a join on three relational tables. High complexity queries comprehended both set operations and complex joins. In particular, D1 was a join among several tables; D2, D3, D4, D5 involved set operations with growing complexity conditions; D6 contained a self-join.

4.3 The Learning Phase

Our goal was to compare the effectiveness and the efficiency of the two approaches to query formulation, i.e., a textual declarative language against a graphical query language, discarding each aspect involving the learning time of the two environments. Following this guideline we set up two exhaustive courses about the two environments, giving to the users all the time they were needing to study them.

The SQL course was about the relational model and the SQL language, the QBD* course was about the Entity-Relationship model and the usage of the QBD* environment. In this way the users were totally acquainted with the query language, the underlying model, and, in the QBD* case, also with the environment implementation. In this way, during the final test, they were free of concentrating exclusively on the query formulation.

From a technical point of view, courses were set on a PC based environment and arranged in a self-learning fashion. Each user was provided with a floppy containing her/his course and was left free to study it. Several check points insured us of the correct learning of the subjects.

4.4 The Experiment Results

For each group of users, naives, intermediates, and experts, we measured the number of errors plus the time spent in formulating the query. Thus, the independent variables in the experiment were the type of query language, the users' skill, and the class of queries; the dependent variables were the time in seconds to complete a query and the accuracy of query completion.

In this section we report the Figures summarizing the whole experiment, a more detailed discussion about its results is in the next section. For each group of users we report the results obtained for the corresponding classes of queries (low complexity for naive users, low and medium for intermediate users, low, medium and high for the experts). Figure 5 shows the results outcoming from the SQL user groups while Figure 6 is concerned with the results of the

QBD* groups, were the number of correctly completed queries is expressed as a percentage (out of 100) and the answering time is the average time.

SQL		Low complexity		Medium complexity		High complexity	
	Query #	Right answer	Time (sec)	Right answer	Time (sec)	Right answer	Time (sec)
Naive	D1	99	74	-	-	-	-
Users	D2	96	67	-	-	-	-
	D3	78	88	-	-	-	-
	D4	98	100	-	-	-	-
	D5	93	120	-	-	-	-
	D6	84	145	-	-	-	-
Intermediate	D1	97	50	93	70	-	-
Users	D2	87	40	57	110	-	-
	D3	71	39	68	170	-	-
	D4	95	52	93	130	-	-
	D5	91	70	91	107	-	-
	D6	82	63	70	226	-	-
Expert	D1	100	36	100	102	100	270
Users	D2	100	42	100	84	64	165
	D3	87	36	73	108	100	108
	D4	100	42	100	70	26	183
	D5	100	48	100	126	94	162
	D6	96	57	93	180	92	126

Figure 5 SQL users' results.

5 DISCUSSION

The hypothesis that a graphical query language would perform better than SQL was confirmed by the experiment results.

In Figure 7 we show the comparison of SQL and QBD* in terms of average time (left side) and correct answers (right side) of the low complexity queries per user group. Referring to SQL it is interesting to note that the naive users performed better than the intermediate ones. This is probably due to the fact that the intermediate users were mainly acquainted with some types of procedural languages, then it was difficult for them to learn a declarative language such as SQL. Moreover, they felt themselves confident in solving so easy questions, as a consequence they did not put enough attention in doing it. On the other hand, the naive users were completely unaware of programming techniques, so their mind was free of influences in learning a certain kind of language. Furthermore, even expert users did errors in simple questions. Such errors were mainly due to the need of remembering table names and using a precise syntax. This confirms our believes that even experts can profit from a more flexible query language.

QBD*		Low complexity		Medium complexity		High complexity	
	Query #	Right answer	Time (sec)	Right answer	Time (sec)	Right answer	Time (sec)
Naive	D1	100	26	-	-	-	-
Users	D2	100	40	-	-	-	-
	D3	100	51	-	-	-	-
	D4	83	82	-	-	-	-
	D5	86	80	-	-	-	-
	D6	95	100	-	-	-	-
Intermediate	D1	100	18	100	49	-	-
Users	D2	100	28	100	50	-	-
	D3	100	47	100	49	-	-
	D4	100	52	100	54	-	-
	D5	100	52	100	90	-	-
	D6	100	61	87	122	-	-
Expert	D1	100	17	100	50	100	125
Users	D2	100	27	100	48	100	62
	D3	100	45	100	50	87	90
	D4	100	48	100	52	50	143
	D5	100	51	100	91	87	126
	D6	100	57	87	128	76	136

Figure 6 QBD* users' results

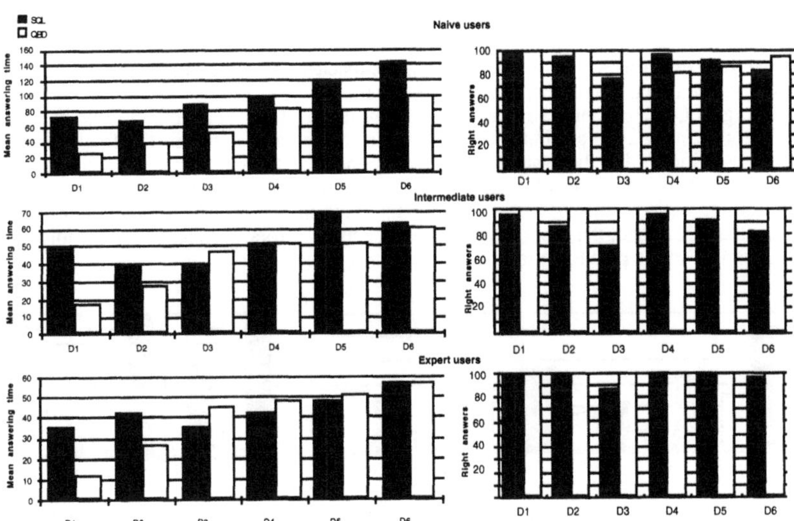

Figure 7 Mean answering times and percentage of correctly completed queries for low complexity queries

Referring to QBD*, we noticed that the fourth query, involving the use of the "OR" connective between the selection conditions, gave the most of the problems to the users. This is certainly due to the fact that the system makes use of some default assumptions that can be modified by the user. In this case the default consisted in considering all the selection conditions in conjunction. This means that if the user is interested in using the "AND" connective s/he does not need to specify it, while he should do it for the "OR", but s/he probably tends to forget this different treatment of the two connectives. We noticed that, in general, the use of the default does not help the user, on the contrary, it introduces more error possibilities.

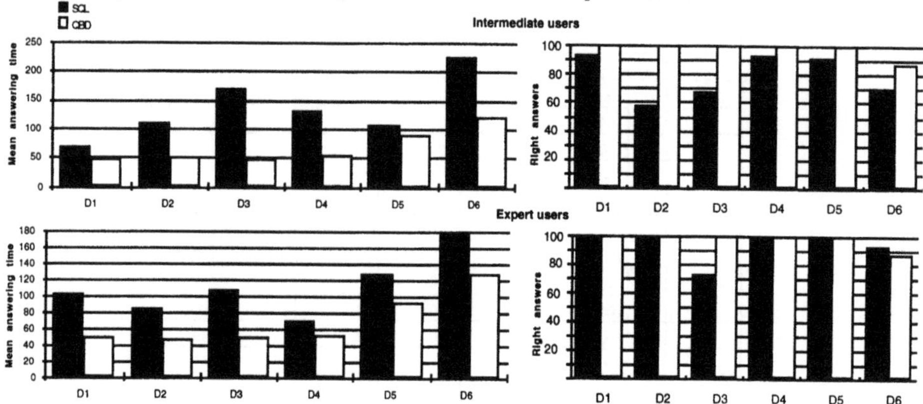

Figure 8 Mean answering times and percentage of correctly completed queries for medium complexity queries

In Figure 8 we show the comparison of SQL and QBD* for medium complexity queries. As for the SQL users, this set of queries gave the expected results, in the sense that the more experts were the users, the more they performed well.

Referring to QBD* we noticed that in the last question (D6) both intermediate and expert users forgot to include the attributes not belonging to the main entity in the final result. We recall (see Section 2) that the system automatically includes the main concept attributes in the final result, while the attributes of the other concepts selected along the path have to be explicitly added. Again, we note that having some default rules in the system behavior confuses the users. On the other hand, the users never did "conceptual" errors, such as a wrong choice of the main concept or of the path to be followed.

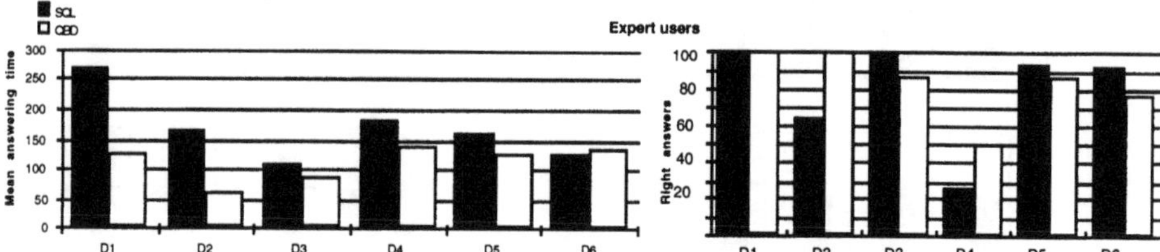

Figure 9 Mean answering times and percentage of correctly completed queries for high complexity queries.

In Figure 9 we show the comparison of SQL and QBD* for high complexity queries. SQL users, even if experts, did not gain great results for this kind of queries. In particular, they found very difficult the use of the self-join in query D6. Also, the time results were particularly bad compared with the performance of the expert users in simple and intermediate queries.

QBD* users had a main problem in understanding the correct way of composing subqueries through the set operators. It is worth noting that for this last set of queries the differences in performance between the two query languages were significantly reduced, meaning that the main advantage in using a direct manipulation, graphical query language is in composing simple and intermediate queries. When the complexity of the query increases there is a conceptual comprehension gap that needs to be overcome by the user.

Finally, we compared the overall performances of the users by grouping the results on the three query classes.

		SYSTEM	
		SQL	QBD*
USERS	NAIVE	87%	100%
	INTERMEDIATE	83%	99%
	EXPERT	90%	93%

Figure 10 Overall average of correctly completed queries.

Figure 10 shows the overall average of correctly completed queries for SQL and QBD* . An Analysis of Variance test (ANOVA) yielded no significant difference for expert users on accuracy between SQL and QBD* at $F(1,14) = 1.83$, $P > 0.05$. There was however a significant difference on the subject's accuracy performance between the two systems at $F(1,28) = 40.7$, $P< 0.05$ (intermediate users) and $F(1,54) = 32.4$, $P < 0.05$ (naive users).

		SYSTEM	
		SQL	QBD*
USERS	NAIVE	99	63
	INTERMEDIATE	93	56
	EXPERT	108	74

Figure 11 Overall average of completation time

Figure 11 shows the overall average of time completation scores for SQL and QBD*. An ANOVA test yielded no significant difference for naive users on completation time between SQL and QBD* at $F(1,54) = 3.6$, $P < 0.05$. There was however a significant difference on the subject's performance between the two systems at $F(1,28) = 29.5$, $P< 0.05$ (intermediate users) and $F(1,14) = 8.2$, $P< 0.05$ (expert users).

In summary, we can say that QBD* was superior to SQL in many respects:

- it offers a complete view of the database at a higher abstraction level, which has been particularly appreciated by the users;
- the syntax is extremely simple; the user does not need to remember table or attribute names, but just to choose them navigating on the schema;
- the time needed to directly manipulate objects on the screen is less than the time used for writing SQL statements;
- the error rate is reduced, in particular for simple queries (but we understand from the experiments that we have to improve the default mechanisms);
- the users find QBD* more attractive, so they are not bored by working with it.

6 CONCLUSIONS AND FUTURE WORK

This paper describes an experiment aiming at estimating the advantages (or disadvantages) of a visual approach to database querying against a traditional one. In order to do this we compared QBD*, a visual query system based on the direct manipulation of Entity-Relationship diagrams, against the well-known SQL language. The results of the experiment were largely in favor of QBD*. However, we have to note that QBD* not only adopts direct manipulation mechanisms and a diagrammatic representation of the database, but also an external data model, the Entity-Relationship model, conceptually more expressive than the relational model. This choice was done on purpose, because we believe that the model of the database information presented to the user should be close to his/her mental model of the reality of interest, and far from the database model. So, we think that user interfaces to database systems can gain from the adoption of effective external models and metaphors, expressive visual representations, friendly interaction mechanisms. We recall that the data model and its visual representation are two distinct aspects of the interface and different mappings can be established among them (see (Batini et al. 1993) and (Haber Ioannidis Livny 1994)), but it is surely a good choice to try to improve both of them.

Our future work along these lines will be the comparison of two visual query systems based on the same conceptual model, but proposing different visual representations, namely iconic and diagrammatic, and interaction mechanisms. We already have two system prototypes and are presently setting up the experiment environment.

ACKNOWLEDGEMENTS

We are deeply grateful to Carlo Zerbo and Emanuele Mioni, who assisted us in designing and realizing the experiments. Also, we wish to thank Albert Badre for his helpful comments on a previous version of this paper.

7 REFERENCES

Ahlberg, C. Williamson, C., and Shneiderman, B. (1993)- Dynamic Queries for Information Exploration: an Implementation and Evaluation - In: *Sparks of Innovation in Human-Computer Interaction*, B. Shneiderman Ed., Ablex Publ., Norwood, NJ.

Angelaccio, M., Catarci, T., and Santucci, G. (1990) - QBD*: A Fully Visual Query System - *Journal on Visual Languages and Computing*, Vol. 1, No. 2, pp.255-273.

Angelaccio, M., Catarci, T., and Santucci, G. (1990) - QBD*: A Graphical Query Language with Recursion - *IEEE Transactions on Software Engineering*, Vol.16, No 10, pp.1150-1163.

Badre, A.N. (1993) - Methodological Issues for Interface Design: a User-Centered Approach - Technical Report DI/DS - 93/01 of Dipartimento di Scienze dell'Informazione, University of Rome "La Sapienza".

Batini, C., Catarci, T., Costabile, M.F., and Levialdi, S. (1991)- Visual Query Systems - Technical Report N.04.91 of Dipartimento di Informatica e Sistemistica, University of Rome "La Sapienza".

Batini, C., Catarci, T., Costabile, M.F., and Levialdi, S. (1993) - On Visual Representations for Database Query Systems - Proc. of the Second International Conference "Interface to Real & Virtual Worlds", Montpellier, France.

Bevan, N. and Macleod, M. (1993) - Usability Assessment and Measurement - In: "*The management of Software Quality*", M. Kelly Ed., Ashgate Technical/Gower Press.

Catarci, T. and Santucci, G. (1994) - Query By Diagram: A Graphical Environment For Querying Databases - , Proc. of ACM SIGMOD Conference on Management of Data.
Catarci, T., Chang, S.K., Costabile, M.F., Levialdi, S., and S.Santucci, G.(1994) - A Visual Interface for Multiparadigmatic Access to Databases - *IEEE Transactions on Knowledge and Data Engineering,* to appear.
Chen, P.P.(1976) - The Entity-Relationship Model toward a Unified View of Data - *ACM Transactions on Data Base Systems*, Vol.1, N.1.
Codd, E.F.(1972) - Relational completeness of database sub-languages - In *Data Base Systems*, R.Rustin, Ed., Prentice Hall, Englewood Cliffs, 65-98.
Date, C.J.(1987) - *An Introduction to Database Systems* - Vol.I, Addison-Wesley Publishing Company.
Haber, M.E., Ioannidis, Y.E., and Livny, M. (1994) - Foundations of Visual Metaphors for Schema Display. *Journal of Intelligent Information Systems*, Special Issue on "Advances in Visual Information Management Systems", *Vol. 3*, N. 3, pp. 1-38.
ISO (1991)- ISO 9126: Software product evaluation - Quality characteristics and guidelines for their use.
ISO (1993) - ISO DIS 9241-11: Guidelines for specifying and measuring usability.
Macleod, M. (1992) - An Introduction to Usability Evaluation, NPL Report DITC 102/92.
Maissel, J., Macleod, M., Dillon, A., Thomas, C., Rengger, R., Maguire, M., Sweeney, M. and Corcoran, R. (1993) - *Context guidelines handbook* - Version 2.1, National Phisical Laboratory, DITC, Teddington, UK.
Miller, R.B. (1971) - Human Ease of Use Criteria and their Tradeoffs - IBM Report TR 00.2185, 12 April. Poughkeepsie, NY: IBM Corporation.
Nielsen J. (1993) *Usability Engineering*. Academic Press, San Diego, CA, 1993.
Reisner, P. (1988)- Query Languages - In *Handbook of Human-Computer Interaction*, M. Helander, Ed. Elsevier Science Publ., 257-280.
Santucci, G. and Sottile, P. A. (1993) - Query By Diagram: a Visual Environment for Querying Databases - *Software Practice and Experience*, Vol. 23, No. 3.
Shackel, B. and Richardson, D.J. (1991)- *Human Factors for Informatics Usability* - Cambridge University Press.
Shneiderman, B. (1978) - Improving the Human Factors Aspect of Data Base Interactions - *ACM Transactions on Database Systems*, 3, 4, 417-439.
Shneiderman, B. (1980)- *Software Psychology* - Winthrop, Cambridge, Mass.
Shneiderman, B. (1983) - Direct Manipulation: A Step beyond Programming Languages - *IEEE Computer*, 16, pp. 57-69.
Spaccapietra, S. (1994) User Interfaces; Who Cares?, Proc. of the 20th International Conference on Very Large Data Bases, Santiago, Chile.
Thomas, J.C. (1977) - Psychological Issues in Data Base Management - Proc. of the 3rd International Conference on Very Large Data Bases, Tokyo, Japan.

8 APPENDIX: NATURAL LANGUAGE QUERIES

In this appendix we list the natural language queries used in the experiment together with their english translation (since the experiment subjects were italian speakers, the original queries were expressed in italian).

LOW COMPLEXITY QUERIES

D1) Elenca tutti i dati delle divisioni con un budget inferiore a 200.000.000.
List all the information on the departments having a budget less than 200.000.000 liras.

D2) Elenca i dati di tutti i reparti della divisione “SECONDA”.
List all the information on the second division.

D3) Elenca nome e cognome dei dirigenti.
List names and surnames of the company managers.

D4) Elenca i dati del personale appartente al reparto Al o al reparto A2.
List all the information on employees belonging to either the A1 or the A2 Department.
D5) Elenca il personale che non sia dirigente.
List all the employees who are not managers.
D6) Elenca i nomi dei dipendenti del reparto 'AI' e sono dirigenti.
List all the employees belonging to the A1 Department who are managers.

MEDIUM COMPLEXITY QUERIES

D1) Per ogni reparto, elenca nome e cognome di tutti i dipendenti.
For each department, list names and surnames of the employees working in it.
D2) Elenca nome ed indirizzo dei dipendenti del reparto 'BI'.
List the name and address of the employees belonging to the B1 department.
D3) Elenca divisione e settore di ogni reparto.
For each department, list its area and division.
D4) Elenca nome e cognome dei dipendenti di reparti non appartenenti alla divisione 'SECONDA'.
List names and surnames of employees working in departments which do not belong to the second division.
D5) Elenca i dati dei dipendenti dei reparti della divisione 'PRIMA', che non siano dirigenti.
List all the information on the employees of departments of the first division, who are not managers.
D6) Elenca il nome, cognome e reparto dei dipendenti di tutte le divisioni del settone 'MARKETING'.
List name, surname, and department of all the employees belonging to the MARKETING area.

HIGH COMPLEXITY QUERIES

D1) Elenca le province di residenza del personale dei reparti con budget annuo superiore a 100.000.000.
List the states where employees working in departments which have a budget greater than 100.000.000 liras live.
D2) Elenca nome e cognome degli impiegati che risiedono a Milano o a Roma e possiedono almeno un appartamento.
List names and surnames of employees living in Rome or Milan and owning at least one apartment.
D3) Elenca tutte le citta' dove non sono situati appartamenti del Signor ROSSI.
List all the cities where Mr. ROSSI does not own apartments.
D4) Elenca tutte le divisioni che non hanno ne' manager donne, ne' manager con meno di 40 anni.
List all the divisions whose managers are both non female and older than 40.
D5) Elenca tutti gli impiegati che risiedono a Roma e hanno un appartamento anche a Milano e tutti gli impiegati che risiedono a Milano.
List all the employees who either live in Rome and own an apartment in Milan or live in Milan.
D6) Elenca i nomi di tutti i dirigenti con retribuzione inferiore a quella di Smith
List all the managers whose salary is less than the Smith's salary.

9 BIOGRAPHIES

Tiziana Catarci

Tiziana Catarci was born in Roma, November 6, 1961.

She was graduated in Electrical Engineering from the University of Rome "La Sapienza," Rome, Italy, on 1987. She received the PhD degree in Computer Science from the University of Roma "La Sapienza", 1992.

Since 1987 she teaches courses in Computer Science at Italian universities. From 1987 to 1990 she was research assistant at the University of Roma "La Sapienza", where she is now an assistant professor.

Her main research interest is in visual formalisms for database representation and querying. Moreover, she worked in semantic database modeling, cooperative information systems, statistical databases, methodologies for database design. Dr. Catarci has published over sixty papers, and written or edited four books.

She is member of the Association for Computing Machinery (ACM), and the Institute of Electrical and Electronics Engineers (IEEE).

Giuseppe Santucci

Giuseppe Santucci was born in Rome, Italy, on February 8, 1958. He was graduated in Electrical Engineering from the University of Rome "La Sapienza," Rome, Italy, on 1987. He is currently Assistant Professor in Computer Science at Department of Computer Science of the same University. His main research activity concerns both theoretical and practical aspects of visual query language and user interfaces. Other fields of research are data dictionaries and graphical environment. He is the co-author of several scientific papers on these topics published on international journals and conference proceedings.

6

Flexibility of visual languages for data manipulation

Y. DENNEBOUY
Swiss Federal Institute of Technology
EPFL-DI-LBD CH 1015 Lausanne
(41 21) 693 5213 Fax (41 21) 693 51 95
Yves.Dennebouy@di.epfl.ch

Abstract

Quality of visual languages for data manipulation can be defined in terms of readability, direct manipulation, power of expression, adaptability, flexibility and level of abstraction. As some papers already defined methods to evaluate some of these qualities, flexibility is till now a fuzzy concept. This paper tries to quantify flexibility of such languages. For this purpose we define of a set of errors that can occur during the definition of a query. This grid of errors is applied to several tools or prototypes.

Keywords

Visual interfaces, visual languages, databases, query languages

1. INTRODUCTION

Two paradigms have gradually emerged in the area of user interfaces for database management systems (DBMS) : visual interaction and object support. The former became achievable thanks to the availability of powerful workstations and efficient window management systems, which is a standard nowadays for application developers in general, and for CASE or DBMS vendors in particular. The second paradigm, object support, is concerned with the combined evolution of database techniques and user requirements. On the one hand, database researchers have succeeded, via the object-oriented approach, in developing an operational alternative to the relational management of flat data structures only. In this way, complex objects can be defined and manipulated. On the other hand, the database approach has entered many new application areas, with many new potential users who are normally unwilling to trade their usual view of application objects for flat representations but were obliged due to technological constraints. Both these phenomena lead us to the present situation where the support of complex objects is the standard for new interfaces and design methodologies.

Based on this evolution, and also considering that the complexity of textual languages for OO models will probably exceed the capabilities of average users, despite the SQL-like syntax, we expect that numerous visual interfaces, supporting definition and manipulation of complex objects, will be offered by CASE or DBMS vendors in the next decade. For the time being, however, an established know-how exists for data definition only. However, visual data manipulation is confined to some SQL generators which operate on the relational database and allow a query to be built using menus for selecting tables of interest and the operations to be performed on these tables. The design of visual interfaces supporting queries on objects is still an open research issue. While some of the available OO-DBMS offer visual browsing facilities and textual (SQL-like) assertional query languages, none of which supports visual query formulation. A limited number of prototypes support visual query formulation to some extent. PASTA-3 (Kuntz, 1989), QBD* (Angelaccio, 1990) and Graqula (Sockut, 1993) are among the most advanced. However, they generally fail in providing full support of the object paradigm since the relational structure of the underlying database influences the language. They also fail in providing a totally visual approach: they provide a visual formalism for underlying operators, in a procedural way of thinking, rather than visual specifications which could be termed as declarative because they do not presuppose a one-to-one mapping onto the underlying algebra. Moreover, they sofar have given very little attention to the complexity of the visual query formulation process, resulting in limited facilities for correcting the current formulation. These facilities will play a key role in future systems, where query engineering (the process where users will finally succeed in formulating a query after a number of correction steps) might become standard in the development of application programs.

This paper describes an approach which has been designed to offer a visual data manipulation interface, where the emphasis is on its visual nature, on supporting direct manipulation of complex objects and on providing for query re-formulation with minimal complications for users. A detailed description of the approach may be found in (Dennebouy, 1993). The current implementation is based on an objects+relationships data model, namely ERC+ (Parent, 1992), and the associated algebra. The database schema is displayed using ER-like diagrams (entity-relationship). Visual queries are translated into the ERC+ algebraic operators and executed on an ERC+ machine currently implemented on top of an OO-DBMS.

The paper focuses on the query formulation and re-formulation processes. Section 2 recalls the basic steps in query formulation. Section 3 analyzes the errors which may lead the user to backtrack the process to correct the current formulation. Section 4 checks how three existing prototypes support the correction process. Section 5 presents our approach. The conclusion points towards future work.

2. QUERY FORMULATION

There are two ways to extract data from a database. One way is extensional, by navigating through the database at the occurrence level, picking data of interest while flicking through.

Browsers are the tools for this. The other way is intentional, by formulating a query: asserting which properties have to be matched by objects and/or values in a database in order to be selected to be included into the resulting set of objects/values. Query formulation is normally in terms of the types in the database schema in order to define which object classes are relevant for the given query and in terms of attribute values and of links among objects in order to define which subsets of those populations are relevant. A query also defines which data from the relevant subsets has to be put into the result (typically a projection operation) and how these data have to be structured for the end result (unless the result is by definition a flat first normal form relation).

In a classical query language as SQL, we can find these different specifications expressed as SELECT-FROM-WHERE blocks: the FROM clause defines the relevant classes, the WHERE clause restricts these classes to the relevant subsets, finally the SELECT clause specifies the projected data.

In a visual environment, the definition of the relevant object classes (the FROM clause) is performed by visualizing the database schema on the screen (usually as a diagram, but also as a list in a menu) and by clicking on the desired types to lift them out from the schema into the query subschema (alternatively, by clicking on undesired types to remove them from the schema, which gradually reduces to the target query subschema). The query subschema is a subgraph of the original schema graph. It is easy to show that if the query subgraph includes a cycle, visual queries cannot be interpreted without ambiguity (Auddino ,1992). In these cases some transformation has to be done to obtain an acyclic graph. The latter is referred to hereafter as the **query frame**: the acyclic graph containing all object (and link) types relevant for the query. Unless the result is a flat Cartesian product of all objects in the frame, the graph has to be turned into a tree whose root denotes which object class is being queried.

For example, assuming the schema in figure 1, figure 2 illustrates the frame for the query "Give the information on persons, with the cars they own, for all persons who insure Ford cars that are all of the same color and either one of the Ford cars has been made after 1993 or all of them have been made before 1960" (note: this query is not meant to be semantically meaningful, but to illustrate the various issues we discuss in the paper). Since the query result will be in terms of people, the type person is the root of the query. The root type is visually denoted using bold lines.

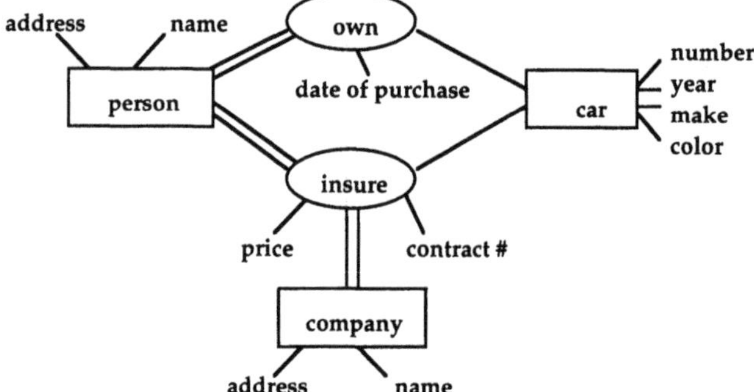

Figure 1: the example database schema.

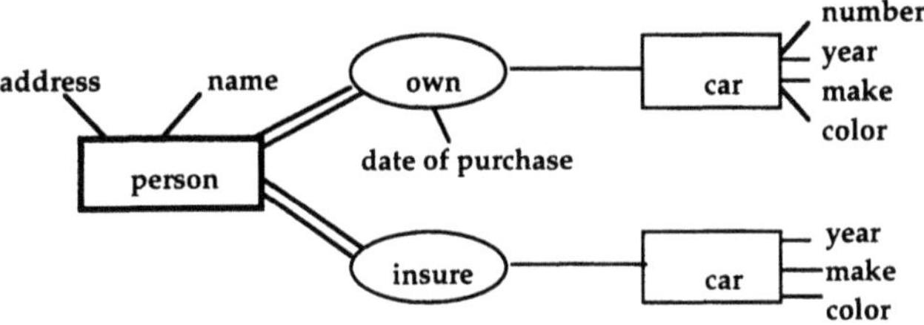

Figure 2: the frame for the example query.

The definition of the relevant subsets of the classes in the query (the WHERE clause) is expressed as conditions (predicates) on instances of the types in the frame. Only those objets that match the conditions will contribute to the result.

The definition of whose data is to be presented to the user, and of the manner in which it is to be presented (the SELECT clause) can be seen as the definition of a new, virtual object type. We will refer to this new type as the structure of the result (**query structure**, in short). The structure contains certain items (classes, links, attributes) from the frame, but not necessarily all of them. These items may be renamed. The query structure for the example query above is shown in Figure 3.

Although the condition on person in the example query could have been written as a single query, for the purpose of our discussion in sections 3 and 4, the following two predicates have been defined:

P1 that must be evaluated first, it states that the insured cars under consideration are restricted to Ford cars, it reduces the set of insured cars and does not reduce the set of persons.

P1: insure | insure.car.make = 'Ford'

And then P2,that reduces the set of persons, it states that there must be an insurance link (verifying P1) such that for all other insurance links for this person it is true that the corresponding cars have all the same color as the car in the first insurance link (i.e., all Fords of this person have the same color) and either all the cars insured by this person are made before 1960 (*forall* insure_2 ... insure_2.car.year < 1960) or one of them has been made after 1993 (*exist* insure_1 ... insure_1.car.year ≥ 1994).

P2: person | exist insure_1 forall insure_2
and (${\text{insure}_1}$.car.color = insure_2.car.color
or (insure_2.car.year < 1960,
insure_1.car.year ≥ 1994))

The overall query formulation process, with its input and output, is depicted in figure 4.

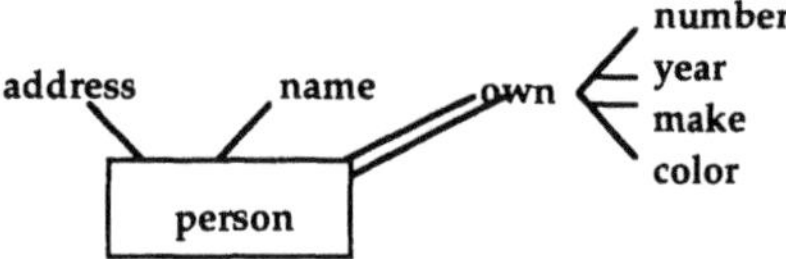

Figure 3: the query structure for the example query.

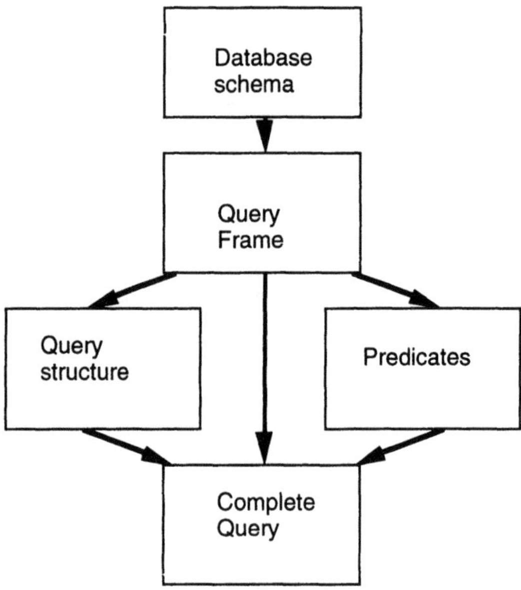

Figure 4: steps in the query formulation process.

3. ERRORS IN QUERY FORMULATION

A logical way of writing a query is to define in a sequence the three facets of the query. This is the 'methodology' provided and enforced in most of the existing tools. This sequence may not exactly correspond to the user needs. As shown in figure 4, there is no inherent ordering between the definition of the query structure and the definition of the predicates. Moreover, users can have a mental image of a query as a composition of subqueries or as a refinement of increasingly complex queries. Users can also (and will most probably) make some mistakes, which they will notice later, maybe after the first evaluation of the query.

Thus, a metric for a visual language cannot be defined by the expressive power of the underlying language only (i.e., by the set of all possible queries) (Batini, 1991). The quality of a visual language should also include a flexibility measure: 1/ to what extent the language frees users from having to follow a specific sequence in query formulation, and 2/ which facilities are provided to correct errors.

In order to help quantify the flexibility of a visual language, we list below all possible errors that the user may make during the query formulation process. Errors are performed on one of the three facets. This checklist will be confronted in the next section with the facilities provided by current prototypes. Illustrations are based on the example schema and the example query from section 1.

1 - Frame definition errors

11 - Missing objects in the frame

The user forgot to include owned cars in the frame. The frame reduces to:

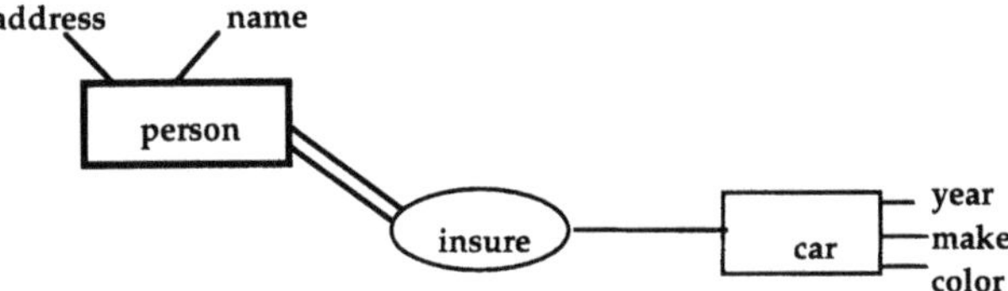

12 - Having non relevant objects in the frame

If the user forgot to take out the company, the frame will be:

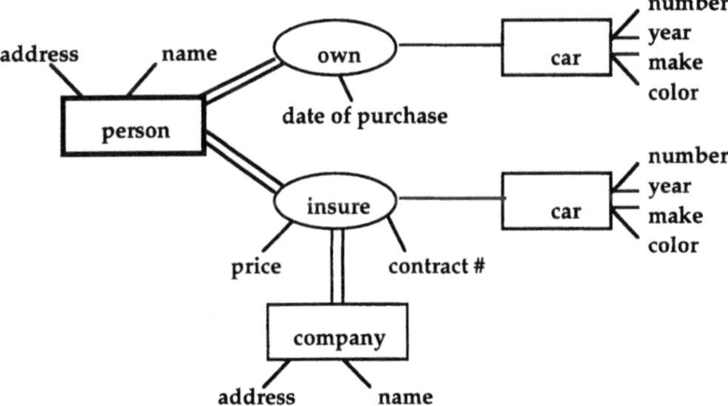

13 - Using a wrong path in the frame

The user selected the 'insure' relationship instead of the 'own' relationship:

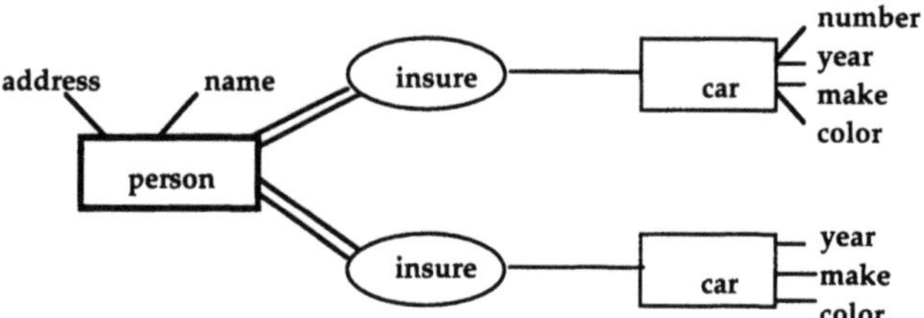

14 - Getting a wrong root object type

The user designed the frame to obtain cars instead of persons:

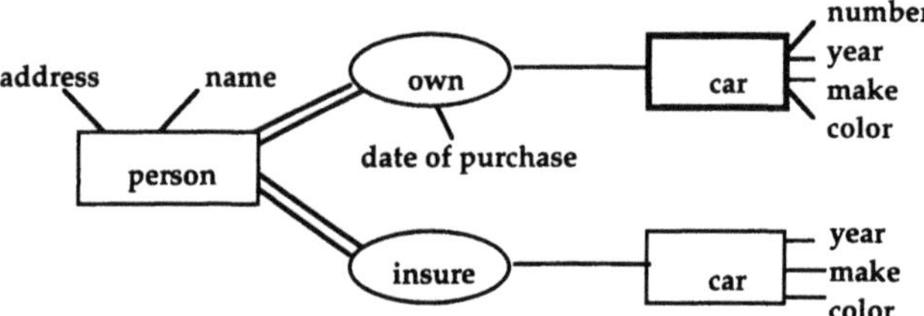

2 - Structure errors

21 - Missing attributes in the structure

The user deleted the 'address' attribute to the 'person' entity type:

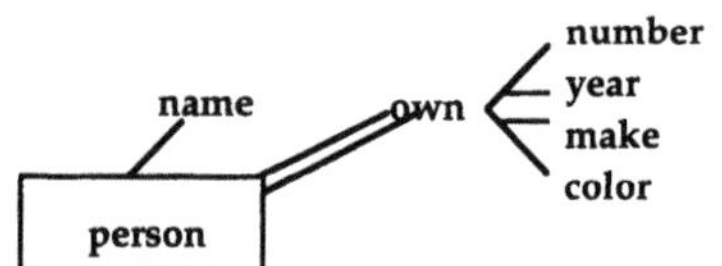

22 - Having undesired attributes in the structure

The user omitted to delete the 'insure' and 'company' attributes within the insurance information:

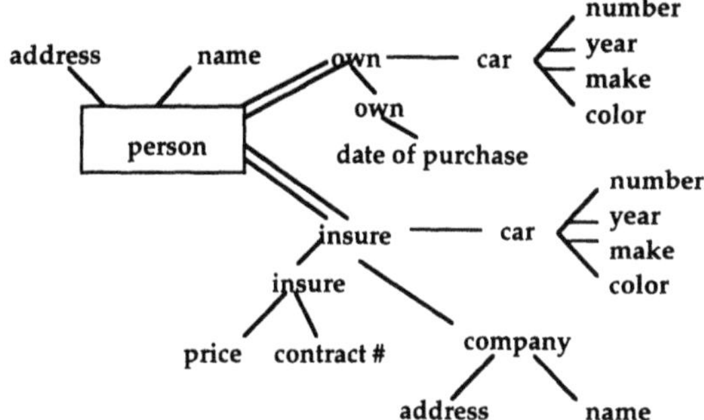

23 - Bad (re)labeling in the structure

The user erroneously renamed the car attribute as repairs:

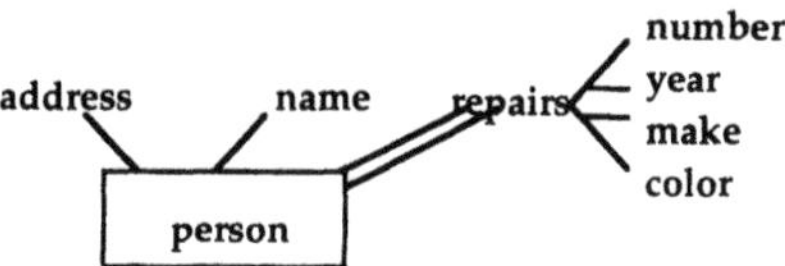

24 - Creating a predicate on wrong objects

The following predicate defined on the attribute insure, instead of the one normally defined on *person*, will keep all persons and for them their 'special' Ford car (as previously defined).

insure | forall insure_2
and (insure.car.color = insure_2.car.color,
or (insure_2.car.year < 1960,
insure.car.year ≥ 1994))

3 - Inner predicate errors

31 - Misquantified variable in a predicate

The user can make a mistake in the choice of a quantifier:

Person | *exist* insure_1 *exist* insure_2
and (insure_1.car.color = insure_2.car.color,
or (insure_2.car.year < 1960,
insure_1.car.year ≥ 1994))

32 - Wrong order in quantification

The user can make a mistake in the ordering of the quantifiers:

Person |*forall* $insure_2$ *exist* $insure_1$
and ($insure_1$.car.color = $insure_2$.car.color,
or ($insure_2$.car.year < 1960,
$insure_1$.car.year ≥ 1994))

33 - Wrong comparison type

Person |*exist* $insure_1$ *forall* $insure_2$
and ($insure_1$.car.color = $insure_2$.car.color,
or ($insure_2$.car.year = 1960,
$insure_1$.car.year ≥ 1994))

34 - Wrong value for a constant

Person |*exist* $insure_1$ *forall* $insure_2$
and ($insure_1$.car.color = $insure_2$.car.color,
or ($insure_2$.car.year = 1960,
$insure_1$.car.year ≥ 1994))

35 - Missing variables in a predicate

The user can forget one condition concerning the year of the first quantified insured car

Person |*exist* $insure_1$ *forall* $insure_2$
and ($insure_1$.car.color = $insure_2$.car.color,
$insure_2$.car.year < 1960)

36 - Introducing too many variables in a predicate

Person |*forall* $insure_2$ *exist* $insure_1$
and ($insure_1$.car.color = $insure_2$.car.color,
or ($insure_2$.car.year < 1960,
and ($insure_1$.car.year ≥ 1994,
$insure_2$.car.make = 'Ford')))

37 - Comparing two variables to each other instead of comparing each of them to a constant

Person |*forall* $insure_2$ *exist* $insure_1$
and ($insure_1$.car.color = $insure_2$.car.color,
$insure_2$.car.year = $insure_1$.car.year)

38 - Comparing two variables to a constant instead of comparing them to each other

Person |*forall* $insure_2$ exist $insure_1$
and (and ($insure_1$.car.color = 'red', $insure_2$.car.color = 'red'),
or ($insure_2$.car.year < 1960,
$insure_1$.car.year ≥ 1994))

39 - Wrong combination of logical operators

Person |*forall* $insure_2$ *exist* $insure_1$
or (*and* ($insure_1$.car.color = $insure_2$.car.color,
$insure_2$.car.year < 1960),
$insure_1$.car.year ≥ 1994)

4. EVALUATION OF SOME GRAPHICAL QUERY EDITORS

Principles

In this section we analyze three graphical tools and check how they allow the user to recover from the errors listed above. There are three ways to recover errors. The best one is to make the change directly where the error appears and to preserve the work that has already been done. The second is to backtrack in the tool to the state where the mistake occurred, correct the error and redo the steps that followed the erroneous specification. Finally, the worst case is when the user has to redo the entire query formulation from scratch.

The tools we analyze below are defined on first normal form models, either relational or ER. With first normal form models, the structure of a query is flat, and so very different from its frame. The predicates are notably easier to write. As in SQL, there is no need to define several variables on the same attribute. The use of several variables in the same table is described by the use of several copies of the same table in the frame. As we shall see in the section presenting our visual language, which is defined on a complex object's model, this trick cannot be used with non first normal form models.

As these models do not include the notion of object identity, there is no concept of root object type of a query, so error 14 will not be discussed.

QBD*

The query process in QBD* (Angelaccio, 1990) is a transformation of the database schema, performed as a sequence of several predefined steps. The query representation is unique, and many operations are non reversible. Errors leading to unwanted objects in the schema (12, 22) can always be corrected by removing these objects, but, as the original schema is no more available, errors due to the lack of some objects in the query workspace (11, 13, and 21) cannot be corrected and can lead to the complete rewriting of the query. Attributes can be renamed, so error 23 can easily be corrected. As predicates are not related to a particular object, error 24 is not relevant .

As the QBD* paper only shows simple predicates, without any universal quantification, we could not check how the quantification order is defined, so errors 31 and 32 are undetermined. If a variable is missing in a predicate, the correction may require to use another copy of a table in the query so error 35 cannot be corrected. Edition of a predicate that include all necessary variables can be done easily (33, 34, 36, 37, 38). We also cannot draw a conclusion in case of wrong combinaison of logical operator (error 39), because of the lack of examples showing a complex combination of logical operators.

In conclusion, four errors cannot be corrected, eight can be corrected, three are not relevant to the QBD* model and for the last three we do not have enough information to conclude.

PASTA-3

PASTA-3 (Kunt, 1989) offers a multiwindow environment. The objects used in a query are highlighted in the database schema (which is presented in two different windows: one for the relationships graph and one for the specialization hierarchy). PASTA–3 allows almost all possibilities of error recovery, but mainly by the use of menus. Frame definition errors (11, 12, 13) are easily corrected mainly due to the fact that database schema is still available.Structure errors that didn't implies predicates (21, 22, 23) can be easily recovered. As it is impossible to define several predicates on the same query, it requires the use of subqueries to write queries like our example query. The subquery is the selection of Ford cars, this subquery is reused in the main query. So it is quite difficult to recover from error number 24, a predicate defined on the wrong object. Conditions in the predicate can be moved to restruture the predicate, it permits correction a wrong combination of logical operator (error 39). Quantification is by default existential but maybe changed (31) and quantification order can be change in moving the first left or up the second (32), comparison type are choosen in a menu (33) and values are choosen in the set of possible value or directly typed by the user (34), condition can be added or removed to a predicate and so correct errors from 35 to 38.

In conclusion, PASTA-3 is a very flexible environment, even if most of the manipulations is made by menus instead of direct manipulation.

Graqula

Graqula (Sockut, 1993) is also a multiwindow environment. It always contains a display of the database schema. This allows the representation of the frame of the query. Errors on the definition of the frame can be corrected (11, 12, 13). Attributes' member of the structure are presented in reverse video: they can either be removed or added to the structure. This permits the correction of errors 21 and 22.

Operation to rename attributes is not explicitly described. It seems that the renaming of entity types is automatic, so we cannot give a definite answer for the correction of error 23.

The construction of complex predicates is done by making frames, which can always be removed and created. This allows correction of errors 31 and 32, with some rewriting. A comparison operator can be changed in the 'OP' row (it corrects error 33). In the same way, the user can change the value in the VALUE row to correct error 34. Adding or removing variables in a predicate seems to be easy, so errors 35 and 36 only have minor consequences.

The comparison of variables is realized by drawing a vertex between the variables: this can always be drawn or removed; the comparison to a constant can also be created or removed. Errors 37 and 38 can be corrected. A wrong combination of logical operators can also be corrected. This can sometimes be complex and lead to the introduction of new objects in the query, so error 39 can be corrected but again with some rewriting.

In conclusion, all errors can be corrected, eight easily, four with some rewriting, one is not relevant to this kind of models (relational and ER) and for another one we do not have enough information.

5. SUPER MANIPULATION TOOL

Short description

Our manipulation tool is part of a set of visual interfaces which together form a conceptual front end, called SUPER, to existing OO or relational DBMSs (Auddino, 1993). SUPER relies on a semantic data model, ERC+, supporting complex objects and object identity (Parent, 1993). The manipulation editor allows formulation of retrieval and update queries, but only the former will be discussed here. Firstly we shall briefly describe our tool and then describe more precisely the construction of predicates, which are, as we have already stated, more complicated in an NF2 model.

User interaction with the manipulation editor uses three windows. The first window contains the diagram of the database schema (figure 5). The second window, named the Working Schema window (WS), allows the user to create the query frame from parts of the database schema (figure 6). The third window contains the structure of the query.The structure of an ERC+ query is still a tree (as the frame). This make a big difference with first normal form models, in which structure is transformed in a flat join of all attributes.

A temporary structure is automatically built by the tool as soon as the root of the frame has been defined by the user. The final structure will differ from this one only if the user specifies that some attributes, which have been kept because they are involved in a predicate, have to be hidden in the result. Predicates are expressed against the structure, not against the frame, because of ergonomic reasons: 1/despite they are equivalent, the structure gives a more intuitive visual image of the resulting objects than the frame, where the resulting objects still appear as a net of components, and 2/ this allows the user to visually separate the mental task of designing the frame from the task of defining the predicates.

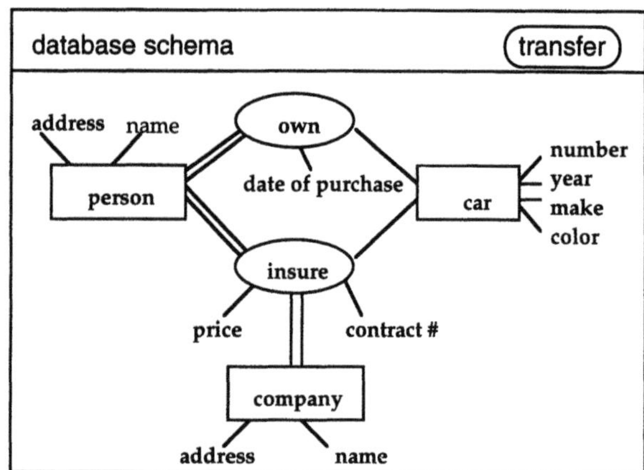

Figure 5: a SUPER database schema window.

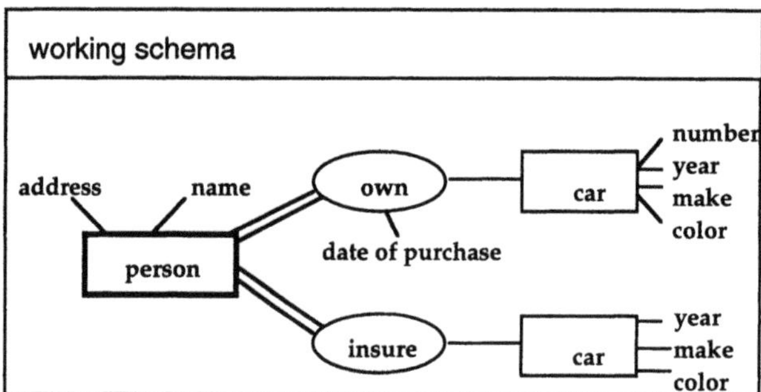

Figure 6: a SUPER working schema window.

The definition of the frame and of the structure of a query are quite easy. Attributes that do not belong to the structure are shaded (as **insure** in figure 7).

The definition of conditions is, itself, rather complex.

One variable is implicitly defined for each attribute of the structure and can be used in predicates. If the user needs to use a second variable on the same attribute, (s)he can create a variable that is shown in italic, linked to the attribute it is defined on. In our example (figure 7), the user has created, from the attribute **insure_ford**, a new variable *insure_ford1* that (s)he can use in the definition of P2.

A predicate can be attached to the root object or to one of its attributes. If attached to the object (P2 in our example) it selects instances of the object. If attached to an attribute, it selects values of the attribute in all instances of the object. For example, P1 restricts, for each person, the values of insure to those values that match the predicate. As in our example, this may be used to define nested predicates. To this purpose, a copy of the restricted attribute is shown to denote the restricted set of values: insure_ford in figure 7 denotes the result of P1. In this figure, the variable insure ranges over any of the insured cars, while variables insure_ford and $insure\_ford_1$ range over only insured Fords (which is needed in P2).

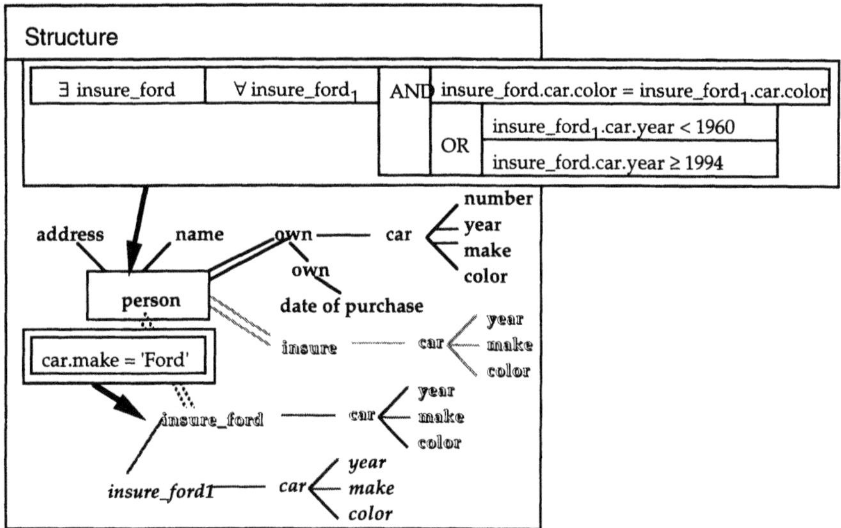

Figure 7: state of structure window corresponding to our example.

Error recovery with SUPER

We now check the way to recover the 18 errors describe above.

1 -Frame definition errors

-11 The user has forgotten owned cars in the frame. (S)he has to copy the relationship own into the working schema, where it will appear with both related object types, person and car. Then (s)he drags one of the two person types over the other one, to unify them into a single copy. The query is corrected without any loss of previous work.

-12 The compagny is still in the frame. The user only has to select in the WS the non relevant objects and delete them, using either the delete key on the keyboard or the delete command in a menu.

-13 The user selected the 'insure' relationship instead of the 'own' relationship, (s)he has to combine the two previous corrections: remove irrelevant objects, copy the relationship own and unify the two copies of the object type person.

-14 The query selects cars instead of persons, The user just has to double click on the object type person to make in become the root object type.

2 - Structure errors

-21 The result of the query does contain the address of persons. This address has not been physically removed from the structure. It appears as shaded items and a simple click toggles its state from hidden to shown (black).

-22 In the same way if the attributes 'insure' and 'compagny' are still in the result, a simple click on these desired attributes will hide them.

-23 If the attribute car has been erroneously renamed to 'repairs', the user only have to select the wrong name and type the good one, 'cars'.

-24 The predicate is linked by an arrow to the attribute insure instead of person, the user selects the arrow, drags it from insure to person and the predicate is automatically modified to keep a consistent quantification.

3 - Inner predicate errors

-31, 32, 33, 34 A bad quantifier is simply corected, quantifiers are graphic objects that react in the same way as radio buttons: double click on them switches their current value to the other value. To correct a wrong order in quantification , the user only has to drag them where (s)he wants to put them. The tool checks the correctness of the operation and, if it is possible, it makes the change. if a comparison operator is wrong, a double-click on a pops up a menu showing all operators of the domain: the user only has to choose the good one. Constants in predicates are editable text boxes.

-35 The user forgot one condition concerning the year of the first quantified insured car, (s)he gets the following predicate box:

$\exists$ insure_ford	$\forall$ insure_ford$_1$	AND	insure_ford.car.color = insure_ford$_1$.car.color
			insure_ford$_1$.car.year < 1960

To add a new variable to a predicate the user drags it to the predicate box: the variable will appear in the predicate box, after its quantification. Here, the user drags the variable year (insure_ford.car.year) in the predicate and (s)he gets:

$\exists$ insure_ford	AND	$\forall$ insure_ford$_1$	AND	insure_ford.car.color = insure_ford$_1$.car.color
				insure_ford$_1$.car.year < 1960
		insure_ford.car.year = ?		

The structure of the predicate is as the user wanted: (s)he has to drag the AND box down in the tree (the drag action is represented by the gray arrow above)

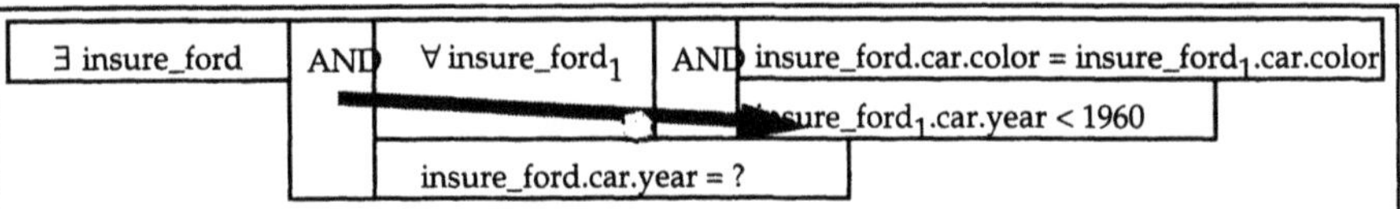

(S)he obtains the following result:

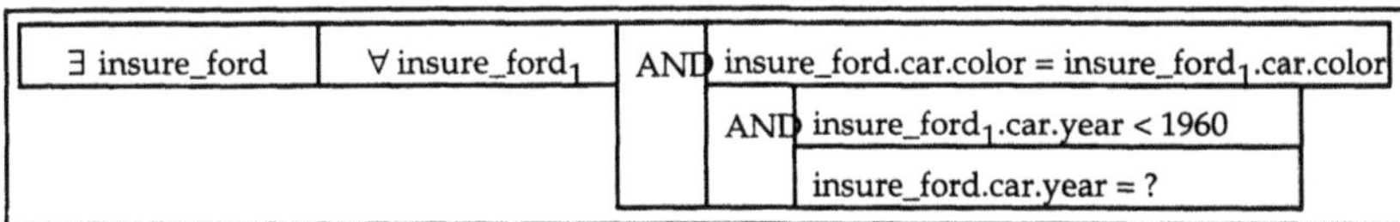

The user now has to double-click on the AND statement to make it toggle to an OR statement, which finally produces the good structure:

∃ insure_ford	∀ insure_ford$_1$	AND	insure_ford.car.color = insure_ford$_1$.car.color	
			OR	insure_ford$_1$.car.year < 1960
				insure_ford.car.year = ?

To finally get the complete predicate, the user has to change the comparison operator and introduce the value of the year as shown in correction of errors 33 and 34. This example also shows how to correct a wrong combination of logical operators (error 39).

-36 If a extra condition has been accidentally introduced in the predicate, the user only has to select the box containing this condition and delete it. The conjunction (or disjonction) is automatically removed and the user gets the good predicate.

-37 The two conditions related to the year of production of cars have been accidentally transformed into one comparing the two variables to each other:

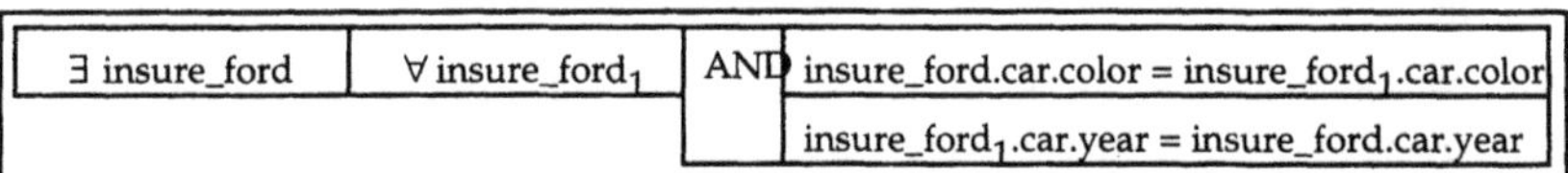

A double click on the wrong condition shows a menu, where the user can choose between all possible evolutions of the condition. In this case the proposed choices are the negation or a split of the condition:

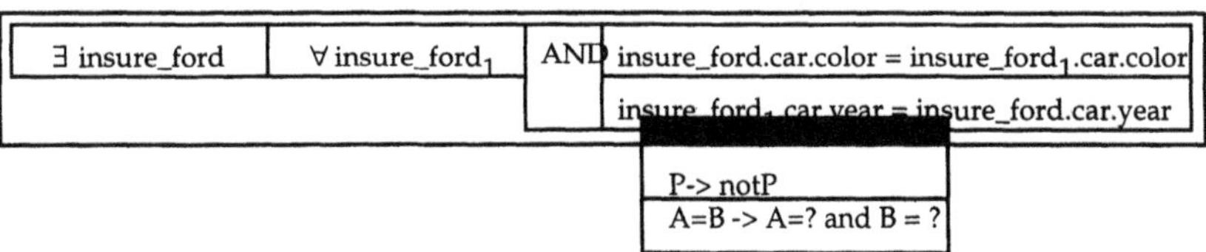

The user chooses the split and gets the following:

$\exists$ insure_ford	$\forall$ insure_$ford_1$	AND	insure_ford.car.color = insure_$ford_1$.car.color	
			AND	insure_$ford_1$.car.year = ?
				insure_ford.car.year =?

(S)he has to change the AND in OR as above, to type the values of the constants in the comparisons and to change with a pop-up menu the type of the operator.

-38 The user thought that all cars have to be red instead of beeing of the same color, (s)he wrote the following predicate:

$\exists$ insure_ford	$\forall$ insure_$ford_1$	AND	AND	insure_ford.car.color = red
				insure_$ford_1$.car.color = re
			OR	insure_$ford_1$.car.year < 1960
				insure_ford.car.year ≥ 1994

The user has to drag one comparison to the other to get the good predicate.

Conclusion

SUPER allows correcting of all the errors we listed without any loss of previous relevant work. These corrections are made in the same way the user normally writes the query, mostly by direct manipulation. Only twice a pop-up menu and twice the delete key had to be used. Pop-up menus are quasi direct manipulation and the use of the delete key is quite natural. The only possibilities to avoid the use of that key is to introduce a waste basket, which seems quite inappropriate, or to match the delete action with the action of dragging the object outside the window, which is difficult to do with scrollable windows, which are needed for large schemata.

Possible extensions

Our manipulation paradigm can be used with any other model and with other languages. We particularly have in mind the possibility of defining such a language for an object oriented model. The expressive power can also be improved by the definition of new operators, like transitive closure. This operator is not in our language for two reasons, the first is naturally safety and the second is more philosophical. As we have seen before, the structure of a query is isomorphic to its frame, there is no loss of information. The use of an operator like the transitive closure leads to information loss. It maintains departure and arrival but looses the path.

6. CONCLUSION

The importance of visual interfaces is nowadays well recognized. Despite many commercial tools and research prototypes, significant advances are still needed to extend the visual paradigm from data definition to data manipulation and from relations to objects. As far as we know, browsers are the only tools that succeeded in combining both extensions. However, they only support navigational access.

We have developed a visual language for assertional object manipulation (Dennebouy, 1993). It has been implemented as part of a conceptual front end (the SUPER prototype) to existing DBMSs. A description of the main features of our language can be found in (Dennebouy, 1995). Besides the basic functionalities, one of our aims has been to allow for easy correction of the query being formulated. The experience with SQL shows that query formulation on objects will probably be a non trivial task for users for whom visual interfaces are intended. If we compare the process of query design and the process of program writing, we know that a programmer who forgets to define a variable or a loop in his program in a high level language will not accept to rewrite the program due to this error. Neither (s)he will accept to correct the program by patching the object code at machine level language. We believe that a query designer needs to debug a query the same way (s)he wrote it.

While some evaluation criteria (expressiveness, ...) for visual languages have been discussed elsewhere (Batini, 1991), this paper focused on flexibility of these languages, mainly intended as the provision for easy re-formulation of an incorrect query. As a metric for flexibility we have proposed a list of typical errors during query formulation. We have analyzed how some visual manipulation languages, including ours, behave concerning correction of these errors. We hope that this work will help visual languages designers to take into account this main feature, flexibility.

REFERENCES

Angelaccio, M.,Catarci, T., and Santucci, G. (1990) "Query by Diagram*: A Full Visual Query System", *Journal of Visual Languages and Computing* (1) pp. 255-273.

Auddino, A., Dennebouy, Y., Dupont, Y., Fontana, E., Spaccapietra, S., and Tari, Z. (1992) Super-Visual Interaction with an Object-Based ER Model, *Lecture Notes In Computer Science* 645, pp. 340-356

Batini, C., Catarci, T., Costabile, M.F., and Levialdi S. (1991) Visual Query Systems, RAP 04.91 , Universita di Roma "La Sapienza"

Dennebouy, Y. (1993) Un langage visuel pour la manipulation de données *Ph.D. Thesis #1182*, Swiss Federal Institute of Technology .

Dennebouy, Y., Andersson, M., Auddino, A., Dupont, Y., Fontana, E., Gentile, M., and Spaccapietra S. (1995) SUPER: Visual Interfaces for Object+Relationship Data Model", *Journal Of Visual Languages and Computing* , Mars 95

Kuntz, M. and Melchert R. (1988) Pasta-3's graphical query language: Direct manipulation, cooperatives queries, full expressive power *Proceedings of the. 15th International Conference on Very Large Data Bases* pp. 97-105

Parent,C. and Spaccapietra, S. (1992) ERC+: An Object-based Entity-Relationship Approach, *Conceptual Modelling, databases and CASE: An integrated View of Information Systems Development*

Sockut, G.H., Burns, L.M., Malhotra, A, and Whang, K.Y. (1993) GRAQULA: A graphical query language for entity-relationship or relational databases, *Data & Knowledge Engineering* 11 pp. 171-202

BIOGRAPHY

Yves Dennebouy received his DEA in computer engeneering from the university of Rennes, France in 1985. After two years spent in a software compagny in Paris he joined the database lab of the Swiss Federal Institute of Technology (Lausanne) where he received his PhD in 1993. He is now first assistant and leads the interface research activity of the laboratory.

7

Design perspectives in visualising complex information

M. Chalmers
UBILAB
*Union Bank of Switzerland, Bahnhofstr. 45, 8021 Zürich, Switzerland**
chalmers@ubilab.ubs.ch

Abstract

We use an increasing number and variety of systems to present information. Many of the early visualisation systems concentrated on scientific information where dimensions were low in number, objective and orthogonal e.g. in visualising fluid flow over a turbine, or population density over a nation. Recently, however, more complex information has been the subject of spatial models, for example databases of documents, patterns of economic and financial data, and design spaces for electronic circuits. Data dimensionality may be in the thousands, and each dimension may have complex interrelationships with many others. In designing systems for interaction with such data, a variety of topics become relevant which were mostly ignored in early systems. Following on from a brief overview of my own work and some of the lessons and problems arising from it, three points of view are offered—spatial, semantic and social—on the design of spatial information systems. It should be emphasised that these three do not partition the relevant issues. Just as in the more general topic of design, they weave through each other with many interconnections. By looking from each of these perspectives, it is suggested that we need to broaden the range of topics considered relevant to the design of information visualisation systems.

Keywords

Information visualisation, information design, perception, shared use of information.

1 BACKGROUND

A number of groups have been working recently on the visualisation of sets of documents. There are many dimensions to the representation of each document: words are merely the most

*. This work was carried out at Rank Xerox Research Centre Cambridge Laboratory (formerly EuroPARC).

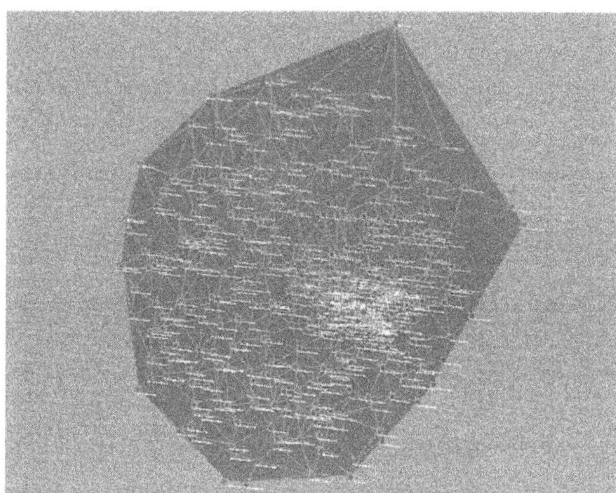

Figure 1 A view from far above an 'island' of documents constructed by Bead from just under 500 CHI and TOIS papers. A small cube and title represent each document. At this range we can see that many of the matches for the search word 'interface' (darker-coloured documents) occur in the same dense area.

commonly used in automatically generating layouts of this type of information. Apart from being an important and widespread type of information, documents are an example of the more varied and complex information which is increasingly available in these days of burgeoning networks and connectivity. The complexity of this type of information suggets that applying visualisation techniques to such information might make access and use easier.

Work on the Bead system has concentrated on producing layouts of sets of documents using a metric of similarity or 'document distance' between a pair of documents. (An example result is shown in Figure 1.) This metric is based on word co–occurrence, and is at the core of an annealing/optimisation technique based on simulated annealing. In this process the members of the set of documents iteratively push and pull on each other to create an emergent structure: a visualised model of the entire corpus. Similar documents which are far apart pull towards each other. Dissimilar documents which are too close together push away from each other. The system works to reduce these forces and energies i.e. it tries to minimise the energy of the system. As these forces gradually ease off, the model of the corpus settles into shape. Those interested in more details of this method are directed towards (Chalmers, 1992).

Being an annealing-based technique, this process and the emergent structures are related to the Kohonen maps of (Lin, 1991). Some experimentation was done with regard to the various parameters to this process, for example the similarity metric which effects (amongst other things) the visually–important tightness (or 'clumpiness') of clustering. A good deal of work was done in an effort to make the underlying algorithm more scaleable, as the simpler algorithms have high computational complexity. Bringing down the order of complexity for each iteration to $O(N \log N)$ from $O(N^2)$ helped in this regard, and early work on a linear time algorithm gave grounds for optimism. This type of technique would appear to have wider applica-

Figure 2 Dropping down closer to the landscape we can see individual documents as well as some artificial landmarks (the pole at the spatial origin, and some distant islands). Another user is visible in the space — the 'blockie' figure near the pole.

bility: by defining a distance metric and employing a similar layout/optimisation algorithm, other types of information can be laid out. Numerical optimisation can be rather a 'black art', and those looking for an introduction might try (Press, 1988).

Initially Bead worked to create a 3D 'point cloud' where spatial distances approximated document distances as closely as possible. However, as discussed in (Chalmers, 1993), the visual complexity of such structures and the difficulties in orientation and navigation led to a major change in the modelling. Rather than try to push further dimensions into the system, an attempt was made to improve the design by making a simpler model of a corpus of documents in the form of a landscape. The model went from three dimensions down to nearly two. Graphical objects representing documents are placed in a space, and the objects meshed together with polygons to make an 'island'.

In these landscapes, all the words in the documents are used to make a single layout wherein similar documents tend to be close to each other. We can browse with the mouse to get details on individual documents. We also can see global features such as patterns of density, and areas of roughness (peaks and valleys) where the layout is rough and perhaps unreliable. Word searches lead to each document being coloured one colour if it matches and another colour if it does not. In this way we can pick out individual matching documents but also see what other nearby documents might be of interest. We also see information about the search word in that we see how it is distributed across the corpus. By searching and browsing, we can build up a notion of what themes and clusters there are and gain an overall model of where to go to find out about various types of information. Inherent in the structuring algorithm is a tendency for documents which are peripheral to the main themes of the corpus to be pushed outwards to lie on the 'shoreline' of the island. The shoreline, the peaks and valleys, and the patterns of word usage and document similarity are all features which can be used to help build up familiarity with the model and to help in future navigation and retrieval tasks.

At present the patterns of word searches are the only 'higher-level' representations of subsets of the corpus which are presented, and this is a hindrance to the scaleability of the interface. A related issue here is the legibility of text, as the 3D text objects in the modelled space are illegible from a distance, and also have an implied orientation for the reader's viewpoint..

The DIVE toolkit (Fahlén, 1993) has been used to construct the shared virtual environment, and visualisation uses the DIVE Visualizer which offers a view onto a landscape which can be shared by others. Other Visualizers on the network show the same landscape and in each one one can see other people moving around the landscape and the changes in colour due to word searches being performed. Although various schemes for limiting or constraining the visiblity of such activities are feasible, at present all people in the space see all searches as in Figure 2, above.

2 SPATIAL REPRESENTATION AND PERCEPTION

Those designing information visualisation systems should give attention to work on the perception of spatial form. In presenting information spatially, we potentially gain a great benefit by employing many of our innate perceptual skills. As pointed out in ecological models of perception (Gibson, 1979), however, the traditions of psychology have de–emphasised how features like dynamism, exploration and memory combine over time to help form our perceptions of the environment around us. In designing an information display, we should support movement and exploration through the space so as to let people build up their own models of the information. By moving and searching through a complex environment, looking in detail at some parts, and in overview at others, we make sense of it and make our own decisions about how to use it and work with it.

Note that it is not enough to have an information space through which people can move. One has to give thought to what people will see from different positions and angles. Here the classic problems of levels of representation arise: cartographers speak of generalisation and specialisation of information in this regard. The information one presents in a high-level overview is not going to be the same as in a close-up view. When looking at a map of a city, one might look in detail at individual streets, buildings and parks, for example the individual squares and landes in the 'Old Town' of some city. A smaller-scale map might also show all of the city area, but the pattern and density of streets would show that the character of the city centre is old and urban even though detail like street names was mostly unavailable. Overlaid on the texture of the street pattern might be more general labels, such as names of city districts. To some extent this is the micro/macro issue discussed in (Tufte, 1990) but I would also refer here to the importance of local consistency in aiding orientation and navigation as discussed in *The Image of the City* (Lynch, 1960). The analogy or commonality between urban spatial structures and information-based spatial models will be revisited later.

With a spatial model of more abstract information one should similarly be able to see detailed descriptions of individual items when up close. As one zooms out that detail should become 'texture', while more general or abstract labels for the area become apparent. This is in contrast to the approach where at a certain level of abstraction all detail is hidden e.g. seeing only a directory name and nothing of the files in that directory. By retaining some of the lower-level information you rely less on the ability of higher-level labels to summarise everything below. One can still use dynamic techniques in combination with such labelling e.g. seeing the patterns of colour change on a map of documents as one makes a command to the effect of "all documents matching the word 'interface' now turn bright green".

Here we see an advantage of graphical layouts when compared to more traditional interfaces to information retrieval systems. One of the things that 2D and some 3D representations support is a space for relative comparisons. In many IR systems, retrieved documents (perhaps matching some keyword) are offered to the user in a ranked list i.e. relative to a query. The list, however, does not afford much information on the relations between members or the relationships with other non-matching but potentially relevant documents. The context of each document is hidden, as the internal structure of the corpus of documents is kept as a high-dimensional 'black box'. Browsing or exploring outwards from an interesting document is therefore a rather indirect and ill-framed process. One might be able to ask for 'other documents like this one' but again we have to blindly plunge our hand into some unknown part of the black box without being able to use any sense of overall setting and structure. We cannot easily use our prior experience with the corpus to build up a model of what is where i.e. use our spatial memory skills to guide future work.

For such uses of an information space, a naturalistic 3D view seems a powerful but familiar way of controlling information detail. Perspective lets us gain an overview of distant regions and detail of what is close. Note that although the view may be 3D the structure has to be such that it allows for a mostly unimpeded view i.e. either 2D (a plane) or near to it (e.g. a rolling landscape). If information structures are too 'strongly 3D' with many parts occluded by others—for example in the Cone Trees of (Robertson, 1991)—then overviews are difficult to present. It becomes difficult to maintain orientation and navigation becomes more complex.

In graphical displays, resolution is a very significant constraint. As we move through an information space and change our point of view, we continually reallocate this scarce resource to suit our information interests: things we are interested in we often move close to, while things of less interest can be further away. We should tie this in with the design of the information display. When information is distant we will have fewer pixels with which to show its character. We should tailor the display of such a distant region by suppressing some details, allowing others to become texture, and bringing in other higher-level labels or symbols to convey general properties.

The character of a local region is only one of the spatial properties proposed in *The Image of the City* as being significant for the design of complex spatial structures such as cities and, for the purposes of this paper, information spaces. Lynch also discusses other features for orientation and navigation (for 'imageability') such as how landmarks and major edges (e.g. shorelines, rivers) act as reference points for orientation, how our routes in and out of a city, and our views from them, are often the basis for our growing knowledge of the city. Some modification of these ideas to the particular technological setting may be necessary (e.g. our practice of using 'flying' viewpoints over the space rather then usually being constrained to stay on the ground and enter an area by standard routes) but many of the principles of design that Lynch espouses are general enough to be applied in this new context.

We should not forget, however, that imageability is, however, only one issue in design. We should not forget people's uses and models of the space, and how their various tasks may be varied (sometimes to the point of contradiction) and concurrent. Apart from being a legible, unfolding structure it should also have significance for people in that the model should fit and support their behaviour as they follow their various tasks and interests. Issues of structure, fit and meaning are discussed in the following section.

3 STRUCTURE AND SEMANTICS

The spatial environment of an information display benefits by having semantic structure. The design should 'make sense' somehow—although it should be borne in mind that there are many ways that it might make sense. For example, with books in a library the spatial layout usually relies on classification systems such as the Dewey Decimal. A book on a shelf is likely to be nearby to others which are similar in textual content. If we have a reference to a book and find it on the shelf then even if it is not what we want it may be a good spot to start browsing from.

Other libraries use the date of accession as the primary spatial factor but still have subject and keyword-based indices available, but it seems better for the purposes of browsing and exploration to structure a layout so that local areas have similar content or character. The graphical representations of this information should also scale up so that in overview some sense of the character is conveyed to the more distant observer. Also, this consistency will aid when trying to create concise, descriptive labels or symbols to form higher-level representations for these distant regions.

These higher level representations should themselves scale up. As we move towards handling large databases we will most likely have to consider hierarchies of representations so that we can offer manageable amounts of information to the users at each point in their work. We have to be able to support the dynamic patterns of browsing and searching that make up many information-seeking tasks (O'Day, 1993). By making available views of the information at different levels we maintain the context within which detail fits. By making higher-level abstractions reflect aggregations of lower-level detail we allow the user to work with large bodies of information. By making the transitions between levels smooth and continuous we retain context as we zoom in one some detail, and therefore maintain orientation. This suggests that the kind of low-level structuring we do to cluster items of similar character (i.e. at the 'bookshelf' level) should also happen at progressively higher levels (the entire stack, the row of stacks, the wing of the library). If consistency at these various levels is maintained then we can make sense of regions of information at any scale.

To some extent we wish the model of the information to 'feel right': to make sense for the people who work with the information so that they can more easily go about their tasks. The ways in which we structure information should therefore reflect the ways in which they structure their work, if possible. Some of the ways in which people structure information representations for their tasks have been discussed in (Russell, 1993) and (Marshall, 1994). These papers emphasise how a group of people with a particular task in mind will iteratively customise the structure of a body of information in order to find a set of organising criteria and an associated representational structure to support their work. Information can sometimes be structured to suit a path through it if the tasks involving the information have a simple order e.g. chapters and their prerequisite materials in a textbook may determine its structure just as the enforced order of check-in, customs, and passport control define the route through an airport when boarding an aeroplane.

Very little work in information retrieval has supported this type of endeavour. More often we have concentrated on much wider groups of people and more general tasks e.g. the users of a library, and the vast variety of queries they might have about the library's contents. In this case it is unlikely that there will be a standard path through the information, nor a simple spatial structure for such a path. We so rarely focus on a particular group of users and their particular needs and styles of information use, but we should consider the fact that different groups or individuals will wish to structure and use their information in their own ways. As we design spatial models for the increasing numbers of people who use information systems, we should be aware that we are building workspaces (or even 'workplaces') for them, and—in the many ways one might consider the word 'fit' to apply here—we ought to make the workplaces fit people and their work.

We might wish to have a model of the information that is essentially the same as the user's mental model. This might be feasible for one person, but perhaps only for a short period of time or for a particular task. As people use information they evolve and revise their mental model, and of course such dynamism is hard for a system to handle. An advantage of a more static type of information modelling is that constancy aids users in becoming familiar with a complex model i.e. they adapt their mental model to work with the model offered by the information system. There are of course some situations where such dynamism would be required e.g. visualising the results of a query or when trying out a new structuring scheme interactively. Still, if a large information resource changes too drastically too quickly then people can become confused and their work disrupted e.g. when a library changes its shelving layout to accommodate new stock. (Lynch and related writers such as Alexander also discuss the issue of dynamism and evolution of structure.) Slowly changing or static layouts also help people to help each other in that a shared model of information becomes a resource for mutual awareness, collaboration and sharing of duties. Some issues in social use of information are discussed in the following section.

4 SOCIAL AND SHARED USE OF INFORMATION

In the earlier sections I have often used the word 'work' rather than 'use' when discussing how people interact with information. For many people, there is an aspect of their use that is often negelcted in the design of information systems, namely that any particular interaction with an information system is merely a part of a larger task of work. The interaction is a means to an end and not an end in itself, and the users bring their own particular experience, expertise, customs and associations to their information task. One side of this issue relates to customisation for the individual or work group, as well as the attempt to design information to take advantage of our perceptual and memory skills. The other side, however pushes further on the fact that for most people work is a collaborative or social activity. In day to day work, social protocols and habits pervade our use of information.

Who gives us an item of information, who else is interested in it, who created it, who owns it, what will my boss think of it: we work with these issues as well as the 'semantic' content. These issues can change how we perceive and use information, making us adjust our perception of what is useful, significant or interesting. Social and organisational issues therefore should affect how we structure information representations. We should also be aware of how people will share information to build up social means of navigation. How often have you learnt about an article because of a personal recommendation by a colleague? How often do you consider the author's reputation, review or sales figures when you look at a book you might read? Why do people often offer a list of 'URLs they found interesting' in their WWW home pages? Social use pervades many environments where database systems are used — systems which internally enforce strict rules of non–interference of data access. A person may well still sit up and tell their neighbour about where to look for some useful data. This would be a perfectly natural thing to do in a workplace, although the technology designed to support it (e.g. a database) offers no direct and comfortable technological means of maintaining this commonplace example of everyday database use. Sometimes it seems as though there are no computer systems which, while not being CSCW systems *per se*, nevertheless are used in collaborative work.

People continually share information on how to use information systems—from '.login' files to shell scripts to good bulletin boards to read. A lot of people don't read manuals or go on courses to learn about new systems and programs. They ask people they consider to be reasonably expert how to do things or they just look around nearby to see what their neighbours do. How would we use traditional information systems to answer a question like "what's happening in low-temperature physics nowadays?" A friend of mine who works on the edge of this field tells of the many (perhaps 30) reviews of activity in LTP that are published each year. He says that he wants a system which "won't tell me what reviews have been written.. it'll tell me *the* review that was written." i.e. the one considered the best by the people who know about such things. Voting schemes and 'seals of approval' can also provide for more formal declarations of awareness or activity in a topic and opinions on the quality of an item of information (Goldberg, 1992). Such metainformation might be woven into the structuring of a spatial model, but we should also consider more informal or transient types of metainformation.

When you see someone browsing the books on the same library shelf as one you've been referred to, you can guess that the person may know something about the topic of your reference and may be able to help you. If someone writes an article or posts to a bulletin board, this is a public action that declares an interest or activity in a topic. We could take this type of information into a spatial information model but we could also offer a more direct representation. A shared information space would offer the opportunity to make visible both individuals exploring and working on particular areas of information, and also some cumulative information on their past or collective activity. We might see the 'hot topics' where people in the information space are more closely positioned or where they have left their 'footprints' behind. Ideally we should combine the direct and the indirect, as our glossy new spatial information systems will only be one of many tools used in the course of a person's work.

A great number of possibilities open up for research in this area, even though (or perhaps because) the inherent complexity and subjectivity of such issues are somewhat at odds with the tradition of scientific data analysis. However, if we accept that these issues are significant in the perception, structuring and use of complex information then we would be unwise to ignore them.

5 CONCLUSION

As we work on prototypes of spatial information systems, it becomes more apparent that a wide range of issues influence the system design. From the mathematical techniques for automatic layout and document retrieval, through to perceptual issues to semantics and levels of representation, and on to social information use and the 'organisational mind'—the range may seem daunting. Such a variety of issues was rarely if ever considered in earlier information systems but as we move to more interactive, graphical and networked systems we must take these issues on board.

One possible means to achieve this is to consider our design and research tasks as being similar to that of architects and urban designers. They have built up a tradition of creating workplaces within which they accept that people do different jobs, follow different interests, and interact in complex ways. They have to mix issues of aesthetic design, social opinion and organisational patterns while retaining a grasp on the technical and functional basics. Just as our systems will only be a small part of peoples' information activities, a building is usually seen as part of a wider urban setting where people perform their own tasks their own ways. We can learn from the design problems, examples and theory of this field. We should widen and deepen the knowledge used in our own field, and as a result we may further our efforts to create better interfaces and systems.

6 REFERENCES

Chalmers, M. and P. Chitson (1992), Bead: Explorations in information visualisation, *Proc. ACM SIGIR'92,* Copenhagen, published as a special issue of *SIGIR Forum*, ACM Press, 330–37.

Chalmers, M. (1993), Using a landscape metaphor to represent a corpus of documents, *Proc. European Conference on Spatial Information Theory*, Elba, September 1993. Published as *Spatial Information Theory*, Springer Verlag LNCS 716, A. Frank & I. Campari (eds.), 1993, 377–90.

Fahlén, L et al., (1993), A space based model for user interaction in shared synthetic environments, *Proc. ACM InterCHI'93*, 43–8.

Gibson, J.J. (1979), *The Ecological Approach to Visual Perception*, Lawrence Erlbaum.

Goldberg, D. et al. (1992), Using collaborative filtering to weave an information tapestry, *Comm. ACM* **35**(12), 61-70.

Lin, X et al. (1991), A self-organizing semantic map for information retrieval, *Proc. ACM SIGIR'91,* Chicago, published as a special issue of *SIGIR Forum*, ACM Press, 262–69.

Lynch K. (1960), *The Image of the City,* MIT Press.

O'Day, V. and R. Jeffries (1993), Orienteering in an information landscape: how information seekers get from here to there, *Proc. ACM InterCHI'93*, 438–45.

Marshall, C., F. Shipman and J. Coombs (1994) VIKI: Spatial hypertext supporting emergent structure, to appear in *Proc. ACM ECHT'94.*

Press, W.H., B.P. Flannery, S.A. Teukolsky & W.T. Vetterling (1988), *Numerical Recipes in C,* Cambridge University Press.

Roberston, G.G., J.D. MacKinlay and S.K. Card (1991) Cone trees: animated 3D visualizations of hierarchical information, *Proc. CHI'91*, ACM, New York, pp. 189–94.

Russell, D.M. et al. (1993) The cost structure of sensemaking, *Proc. ACM InterCHI'93*, 269–76.

Tufte, E. (1990) *Envisioning Information*, Graphics Press.

7 BIOGRAPHY

Matthew Chalmers obtained a B.Sc. (Hons) from Edinburgh University and then a Ph.D. in ray tracing and multiprocessor programming from the University of East Anglia. He was an intern at Xerox PARC and later joined Rank Xerox EuroPARC where his work on information visualisation began. In January 1995 he moved to Ubilab to carry on this line of work and to help set up a new group in the area of interaction with complex information.

PART THREE

Video Databases

8

Feature Based Digital Video Indexing

Arun Hampapur
Virage Inc
9605 Fcranton Road, Suite 240, San Diego,CA92121,U.S.A
Email: arun@virage.com, Phone 619-587-4080, Fax 619-587-4071
Ramesh Jain
Department of Electrical and Computer Engineering
University of California at San Diego, La Jolla, CA 92093-0407
Email: jain@ece.ucsd.edu, Phone 619-534-8639
Terry E Weymouth
Department of Electrical Engineering and Computer Science
University of Michigan, 1101 Beal Ave, Ann Arbor, MI 48109-2110
Email: weymouth@eecs.umich.edu, Phone 313-763-6985, Fax 313-763-1260

Abstract

Indexing video data is essential for providing content based access. Indexing has typically been viewed either from a manual annotation perspective or from an image sequence processing perspective. This work proposes a methodology for designing video indexing schemes which use low level *machine derivable* indices to map into the set of application specific *desired video indices*. The indexing procedure uses image sequence processing and application requirements analysis to arrive at the low level and desired indices. The mapping is created based on the domain constraints. A mapping efficacy measure is presented. Experimental results of indexing video using *image motion features* are presented.

Keywords: Digital Video, Video Indexing, Video Databases, Content based retrieval, partial index, Video Processing, Image Sequence Analysis, Video Classification, Video Production

1 INTRODUCTION

Digital Video technology promises to make video the ubiquitous mode of communication in the future. There are several technological hurdles that need to be crossed before these promises are met. One of the major hurdles is the ability to access video based on its content. This requires content based indices into the video data. The process of attaching content based labels to video is referred to as *video annotation or indexing*. This process can be performed manually by an operator who views the video. The indexing effort is directly proportional to the granularity of video access. For example, the indexing effort for video library applications which model video by its title is lesser than the indexing effort for a multimedia authoring application which indexes video based on the content and style of the shots used to compose the video. Thus as applications demand finer grain access to video, automation of the indexing process becomes essential. Given the current state of art in computer vision, pattern recognition and image processing, reliable and efficient automation is possible for low level video indices like scene changes and image motion properties etc. But most applications demand a much higher level of content based access. This paper explores the use of low level image measurements to derive higher level content based indices with the help of domain constraints.

The proposed approach begins to tackle the problem of content based access in a systematic way. This work defines the problem of video indexing and proposes a design methodology for video indexing schemes. The indexing schemes presented use low level image sequence features in a feature based classification formalism to arrive at a machine derived index. Domain constraints are used to design a mapping from low level machine derived index to the desired video index. An efficacy measure is proposed to evaluate this mapping. An example feature based indexing scheme based on the image motion feature to generate a shot framing (Bordwell, 1980) video index is presented.

The organization of the paper is as follows. A short literature survey is presented in section 2. Section 3 discusses the problem of video indexing and provides a formal definition. The design procedure for feature based video indexing is discussed in Section 4. Section 5 presents the example design for a video database to support authoring and editing applications. The mapping between the machine derived index and the desired video index is presented in section 6. The results of applying indexing scheme to cable television feed are presented in section 7. A summary of the work concludes the paper in section 8.

2 LITERATURE REVIEW

Existing work on content based video access and video indexing can be grouped into three main categories.

High Level Indexing: The work by Davis (Davis 1993, Davis 1994) is an excellent instance of high level indexing. This approach uses a set of predefined index terms for annotating video. The index terms are organized based on a high level ontological categories like *action, time ,space, etc.* Davenport et al (Davenport, 1991) have proposed a structured model for a shot. Smith et al (Smith, 1992) have proposed a video annotation system based on a layered annotation approach.

The high level indexing techniques are primarily designed from the perspective of manual indexing or annotation. The index terms used ,data structures and user interfaces are geared towards a scenario where an operator views and indexes the video. This approach is suitable for dealing with small quantities of new video and for accessing previously annotated databases. Ignoring the need for automation in video insertion is one of the main limitations of these approaches.

Low Level Indexing: These techniques provide access to video based on properties like color, texture etc. These techniques can be classified under the label of low level indexing. Ioka et al

(Ioka, 1993) have presented techniques for retrieving video sequences based on the estimation of motion vectors in video sequences and using these vectors as the key for retrieving video. Gong et al (Gong,1994) have applied color based image indexing techniques to retrieving key frames of video sequences. Nagasaka et al (Nagasaka, 1991) present video search based on object appearances. Arman et al (Arman 1994) have presented a key frame based browsing technique for video. This approach uses image moments to measure key frame similarities. The key frames are used as models of the video shots.

The driving force behind this groups of techniques is to extract data features from the video data, organize the features based on some distance metric and to use similarity based matching to retrieve the video. Their primary limitation is the lack of semantics attached to the features. Hence from the user perspective, the utility of such approaches becomes limited.

Domain Specific Indexing: A number of researchers have worked on the areas of domain specific video indexing and retrieval. One of the pioneering efforts in the area is by Swanberg et al (Swanberg, 1992, 1993). They have presented work on finite state data models for content based parsing and retrieval of news video. Smoliar et al (Smoliar, 1994) have also presented work on parsing news video.

These techniques over come the limitations of both the above categories. They use the high level structure of video to constrain the low level video feature extraction and processing. These techniques are effective in their intended domain of application. The primary limitation of these techniques is their narrow range of applicability.

Apart from the above research efforts work by Akutsu et al (Akutsu, 1992, 1994) has considered the cinematographic structure of video and the low level video feature based techniques to extract some of the cinematographic properties. The work by Akutsu et al is a very balanced approach to the problem of video indexing. How ever they have not completely utilized the structuring that exits in video information.

All the above work has viewed video in isolation and has not considered video as a component of a video database system. The proposed approach views video indexing from a video database perspective while utilizing the structure inherent in video to derive the indices. Preliminary results from this research have been reported in (Hampapur, 1995-A).

3 VIDEO INDEXING

The term indexing as used in database literature (Date, 1975), (Korth, 1986) refers to the ordering of data based on a particular attribute. This is referred to as the *search key* . For example, a telephone directory is indexed on the name attribute using *lexicographic* ordering. Video indexing serves an analogous purpose in video databases. A video index requires *video search keys* based on which the index is generated. The process of choosing search keys and designing representations for video data based on the content and the typical queries is called video data modeling. This problem has been addressed in (Hampapur, 1995-B).

The concept of a video index is illustrated below using an example. Consider a television news cast. The typical structure of a television news cast (Zettl, 1984), (Millerson, 1975) involves a segment in which the headlines are presented by the news anchor. This is followed by introduction of each individual report by the anchor followed by the actual report itself. The news concludes with a commentary on the news by the anchor. A video index into the news cast will provide *temporal intervals of video* with *associated descriptions* of the temporal interval. The following are examples of video indices into a newscast. Depending on the type of video and its content, video indices can be of many different types (Hampapur, 1995-B).

: { Temporal-Interval = News cast} with
: {Description = (date, anchor-person-name, lead-story-name, etc) }. (1)
: {Temporal-Interval =News report } with
: {Description= (story-titles, reporter-name, production-style, etc) } (2)
: { Temporal-Interval= Shots } with
: {Description= (transition-effects, cinematographic-properties, visual-properties) } (3)

With the example indices presented, the newscast video can be accessed in terms of news casts of a particular date, or news reports with a particular topic, video shots (Bordwell, 1980), (Hampapur, 1994-A), (Hampapur 1994-B), (Hampapur, 1995-C), video shots with specific cinematographic or visual properties, etc. There are many other possible video indices. The ones presented here are meant to illustrate the idea of a video index.

A feature in the context of this paper is a low level measurable property of the image sequence. Given any video, a feature based index into the video will provide *temporal intervals of video* with *associated feature based descriptions* of the temporal interval. The typical temporal intervals for a feature based index are continuous image sequences or shots. The following are some typical feature based indices.

: { Temporal-Interval=Shot } with
: { dominant-color = blue, dominant-texture = random
: motion-type = local, flow-direction= left to right, etc } (4)

A feature based index describes the video in terms of low level measurable properties of the image sequence. The feature based descriptions of video are domain independent and can be extracted from any video and are independent of the domain or type of the video.

The focus of this paper is on how to generate the desired video indices (equation 3) based on the feature based indices (equation 4) which can be automatically extracted from the video. The paper has addressed the issues of how to arrive at a mapping between feature based indices and video indices, how to quantitatively evaluate the mapping between the two sets of indices. A motion based index is used to map into a cinematraphic property based video index.

3.1 The Digital Video Model

The model used for video data depends on the purpose for which the data is being used. The design of video data models for database applications has been addressed in (Hampapur, 1995-C), (Jain 1995). Swanberg et al (Swanberg, 1992), (Swanberg 1993) model video in terms of the temporal events in the content of the video. They use a finite state machine for representing this model. Hampapur et al (Hampapur, 1995-B) have modeled video in terms of the *editing* process of video. They use the model for video segmentation. The video model used in the indexing process is based on (Hampapur, 1995-C), (Jain 1994). The structure of the model is shown in equation 5.

$$\begin{aligned} \mathcal{V} \;:&\; \text{Video Interval: } [t_b, t_e] \\ :&\; \text{Temporal Relations: } \mathcal{R} \\ :&\; \text{Feature Count: } n \\ :&\; \text{Type: } (\omega_0, \omega_1, \ldots, \omega_n) \in \Omega \\ :&\; \text{Features: } (\mathcal{F}_1, \mathcal{F}_2, \mathcal{F}_3, \ldots \mathcal{F}_n) \end{aligned} \tag{5}$$

Video Interval: t_b, t_e represent the begining and end of the temporal extent of the video respectively. All the other elements of the video model refer to this time interval.

Temporal Relation: $\mathcal{R} = ((r_1, \mathcal{V}_1), (r_2, \mathcal{V}_2), \ldots (r_k, \mathcal{V}_k))$ is a set of k temporal relationships. r_i is one of the thirteen possible relationships between time intervals listed in (Allen, 1983). Thus every video model can maintain temporal relationships to k other video models.

Feature Count: n is the number of features used to describe the video segment being modeled.

Feature Type: ω_i is the feature type for feature $\mathcal{F}_i$. The different possible types of features are discussed in (Hampapur, 1995-C), (Jain 1995).

Features: $(\mathcal{F}_1, \mathcal{F}_2, \mathcal{F}_3, \ldots \mathcal{F}_n)$ these are the different features that are used to describe the video being modeled. The actual structure of the features is discussed in (Hampapur, 1995-C), (Jain 1995). The number of features used in a video model and the type depend on the exact nature of the application. Any feature $\mathcal{F}_i$ takes on a label l where $l \in \mathcal{L}_i = (l_{i1}, l_{i2}, \ldots l_{ik})$. Thus the features are qualitative in nature and take labels form a predefined finite set.

3.2 Definition of Video Indexing

Existing literature on video indexing implicitly defines video indexing as *the process of extracting from the video data the temporal location of a feature and its value*. A similar but more explicit for of this definition is adopted in this work.

Video Indexing: Given a video data model $\mathcal{V}$ and a video interval $v = [t_b, t_e]$

$$\forall_{i=0}^{n} \mathcal{F}_i \text{ assign } l_{ji} \in \mathcal{L}_i \text{ based on } v \tag{6}$$

where n is the number of features in the video data model, $\mathcal{F}_i$ is the ith feature, $\mathcal{L}_i$ is the set of labels that P_i can take.

Video Indexing as Classification Given the above definition of indexing, the problem of indexing video data can be reformulated as a problem of classifying a particular interval of video into one of the predefined categories. This reformulation is possible since the features in the video data model take only a finite set of values. The classification problem is defined as follows. Given a video interval $v = [t_b, t_e]$ and a label set $\mathcal{L} = (l_1, l_2, \ldots, l_k)$

$$\text{Assign to } v \leftarrow l_i \text{ where } l_i \in \mathcal{L} \tag{7}$$

3.3 Definition: Partial Video Index

Let $\mathcal{I}_1$ be an index on $\mathcal{VDB}$ based on a video model $\mathcal{V}_1$ and $\mathcal{I}_2$ be another index on $\mathcal{VDB}$ based on a video model $\mathcal{V}_2$. Then $\mathcal{I}_2$ is called a partial index on $\mathcal{VDB}$ with reference to $\mathcal{I}_1$ if $\mathcal{V}_2 < \mathcal{V}_1$ where the ordering of video models is based on some linear criteria. The criteria for ordering video models is presented in section 4.1. Here $\mathcal{V}_1$ is referred to as the *complete video data model* and $\mathcal{V}_2$ is referred to as the *partial video data model.* The labels in the complete video data model are called the *complete label set* and the labels of the partial video model are called the *partial label set*

The idea of a partial index is motivated by the fact that *using machine vision techniques it is possible to assign to a video shot a **machine derived label** which covers a group of **complete labels**.* The *machine derived* label set is a partial label set with reference to the *complete label set.* For example, if the complete labels set included labels like *Human-Subject-Motion: (Left to Right, Right to Left)* the machine derived label set could be *Object-Motion: (Left-to-Right, Right-to-Left).* A machine derived label like *object-motion* will cover the label *Human-Subject-Motion* however it may also include other objects like *vehicles.*

The reason machine derived labels are at a lower level of abstraction is due to the fact that it is fairly straight forward and computationally inexpensive to design a reliable analysis technique which can extract labels like *direction of object motion* automatically. However recognizing a human figure in an arbitrary video sequence and estimating its direction of motion is currently not within the reach of most machine vision techniques. Thus using automatic analysis to derive a partial index is a feasible approach to automating the indexing procedures.

A video data record with a partial index provides lesser information about the video data than the same record with a complete video index. Since a record with partial index will have fewer features and the total number of labels among these features will be smaller than that for a complete video index. A quantitative measure of the effectiveness of a partial video index is provided in section 4.1. There are several advantages of the partial index process including *feasibility, constrained processing cost* and *ability to incorporate techniques into prototype designs.*

4 DESIGNING FEATURE BASED INDEXING SCHEMES

This section presents the detailed procedure for designing feature based indexing schemes. A schematic of the steps involved is presented in figure 1. Each of the steps in the design procedure is discussed below:

User Specification: These are the inputs to the design process. The two main inputs are the *purpose of the video database* and the *computational constraints* in terms of the amount of computational resources available. These factors dictate the complexity of the design that can be adopted, the structures associated with the video data, the physical storage to be used and several other system parameters.

Design Steps: These are the actual steps in the design process. They include the design of the video data model, feature section, feature based class design and feature based classifier design.

Data Model Design: This step typically requires the purpose of the video data base, database expertise and content expertise (knowledge about the content of the video data and the application). The design of the video data model is driven by the application. For example, the video data model for a video library will be entirely different from the data model for a database to support video editing.

Primary Feature Selection: The primary feature is defined as a measurement made directly from the video data. For example, the difference image between two consecutive frames of video is a primary feature, while the average difference pixel value is not. The computational constraints of the user along with computer vision or image processing expertise are needed to make the feature choice. Typically the initial design iterations will result in the choice of simple features like difference images, while later design iterations will result in the choice of more complex features to perform the feature based indexing.

Secondary Feature Selection: Secondary features are derived from some combination of primary and secondary features. Typical examples would be average value of the difference image, variance of the difference image, filtered difference images, etc. The choice of the secondary feature requires the use of vision expertise and the video data model.

Feature Based Model Design: This is a model similar in structure to the video data model, but the instantiation of this model is based on the automatic processing of the video data. The typical procedure for arriving at the feature based model is to design video data classes based on a qualitative classification. The qualitative classification process relies on the secondary features that are extracted.

Feature Based Classifier Design: (Duda, 1975) This step involves the actual design of the algorithms and code for the feature based classification process. This step relies on the vision and software engineering expertise available.

Design Evaluation Step: This is one of the key steps in the design process, and provides a comparison of the feature based model against the video data model. This measure of design efficacy should be linear and monotonic, i.e. if the feature based data model exactly matches the video data model the measure of goodness (called fbi efficacy) should be one and should decrease linearly to zero as the mis-match between the video data model and feature based model increases. One such measure is proposed in section 4.1.

Design Outputs: These are the outputs of the design process.

FBI Efficacy: This is a measure of goodness of the design and is a number which lies between (0,1) with 0 indicating an ineffective feature based indexing scheme, and 1 indicating a perfect feature based indexing mechanism.

Feature Extractors: These are the functions for extracting measurements from the video data. Typical examples include, difference images, flow, dominant colors, color distribution maps, texture maps, etc.

Discriminant Function: This is the function which combines the output of the various features to arrive at a feature based class for a given video interval.

The flow diagram of figure 1 shows the steps involved in designing a feature based indexing system. The next step is to apply the feature based indexing to actual data in the application domain and to evaluate the experimental performance of the system. Typically this will lead to refined user specifications and a redesign of the *indexing scheme*.

4.1 Efficacy of feature based indexing

This section presents a measure which evaluates the effectiveness of the design. The problem of evaluating the effectiveness of the feature based model as compared to the video data model can be mapped into a problem of rating the *goodness of the mapping between the classes in the feature based model and the video data model*. Let $\mathcal{V}$ be a video data model. Let $\mathcal{V}$ have a single feature $\mathcal{F}$. Let $\mathcal{L}$ be the set of labels that can be assigned to the feature $\mathcal{F}$. Let $\mathcal{V}_f$ be the feature based video model. Let $\mathcal{V}_f$ have one feature $\mathcal{F}_f$ which can take on labels from $\mathcal{L}_f$. The problem of evaluating the goodness of the mapping between $\mathcal{V}_f, \mathcal{V}$ can now be defined as the problem of evaluating the mapping between $\mathcal{L}_f, \mathcal{L}$. Figure 2 shows the range of mapping between the two sets. There are three mappings shown in the figure (top, middle, bottom). The number in the left bottom corner for each mapping indicates its ranking. The set (oval) on the left indicates the feature based index (automatically derived partial index), and the oval on the right represents the ideal or desired index. The mapping shows how the machine derived index relates to the desired or ideal index. The top mapping (figure 2) has an efficacy measure of 1.0, indicating that it is perfect. The middle (figure 2) mapping has an intermediate value for the efficacy measure, since here the feature based index provides a sub grouping on the ideal index. The bottom mapping (figure 2) is the worst, since the feature based index does not provide any information about the ideal index.

A measure which behaves in this manner is used to characterize the goodness of a feature based indexing scheme. Such a measure can be designed by ranking the mappings between two sets. A *one to one* and *onto* mapping is given the highest ranking and a mapping in which one element in the feature based index covers all elements in the ideal index receives the lowest rank. In the following derivation $Card$ stands for cardinality of a set, i.e. the number of elements in the set.

$$Card(\mathcal{L}_f) = k \tag{8}$$

$$Card(\mathcal{L}) = n \tag{9}$$

Each element in $\mathcal{L}_f$ can be treated as a subset of $\mathcal{L}$. Let S_i be a subset of $\mathcal{L}$ where

$$S_i = (l \in \mathcal{L} : l^{-1} = l_f \in \mathcal{L}_f) \tag{10}$$

$\mathcal{L}$ has k subsets where $k = Card(\mathcal{L}_f)$.

$$\bigcap_{i=0}^{i=k} S_i = \emptyset \text{ and } \bigcup_{i=0}^{i=k} S_i \neq \mathcal{L} \tag{11}$$

The sets S_i have a null intersection but don not necessarily constitute a partition of $\mathcal{L}$.

$$\text{Let } \mathcal{O} = \{l \in \mathcal{L} \ : \forall_{i=0}^{i=k} S_i \ l \notin S_i\ \} \tag{12}$$

$\mathcal{O}$ is the set of omitted labels in $\mathcal{L}$. Let $o = Card(\mathcal{O})$. Let $\mathcal{C}$ be the set of covered labels in $\mathcal{L}$. Let $c = Card(\mathcal{C})$. Now

$$\mathcal{C} = \mathcal{L} - \mathcal{O} \text{ and } Card(\mathcal{C}) \ + \ Card(\mathcal{O}) \ = \ Card(\mathcal{L}) \ \ c + o = n \tag{13}$$

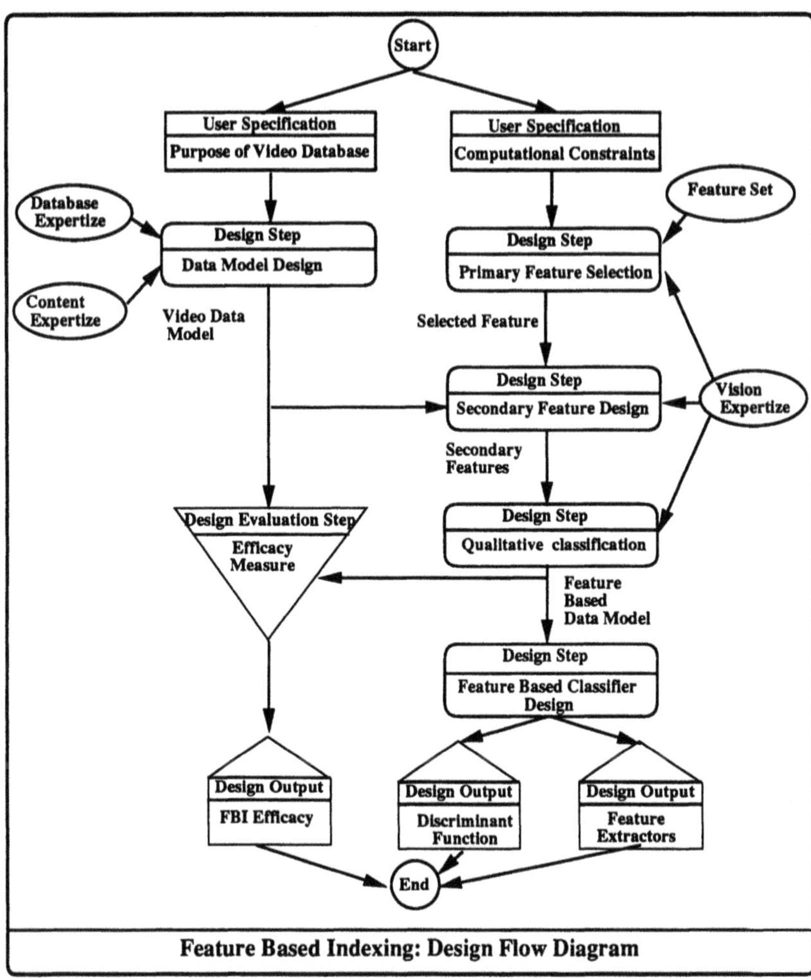

Figure 1: Feature based Indexing: Design Procedure

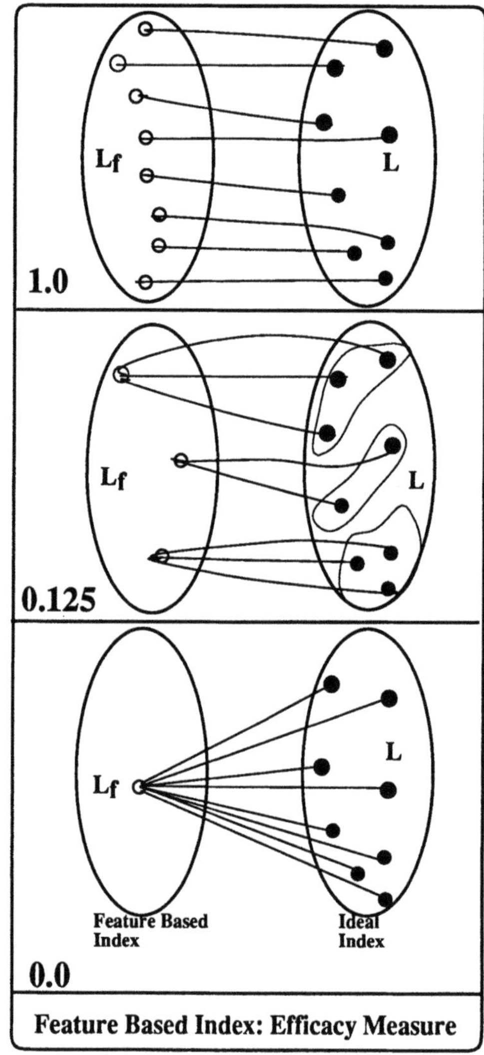

Figure 2: Feature based Indexing: Efficacy Measure

Let f be the fraction of labels covered in $\mathcal{L}$. $f = \frac{c}{n}$. f is a measure of coverage of $\mathcal{L}$ by $\mathcal{L}_f$ but does not measure the discrimination provided by the feature based data model. The measure of discrimination is the nature of the distribution of the members of C among the sets S_i. Such a measurement is provided by the variance of the cardinalities of S_i.

$$\forall_{i=0}^{i=k} H(i) = Card(S_i) \quad (14)$$

Let σ^2 be the variance of H and σ^2_{max} be the maximum variance of H.

$$\sigma^2 = \frac{\sum_{i=1}^{i=k} \left(Card(S_i) - \frac{c}{k}\right)^2}{n} \quad (15)$$

$$\sigma^2_{\text{max}} = \frac{c(k-1)}{k} \quad (16)$$

$$\text{Let } \delta = \frac{\sigma^2}{\sigma^2_{\text{max}}} \quad (17)$$

δ is a measure of the uniformity of H. $\delta = 0$ for a perfectly uniform distribution and $\delta = 1$ for a distribution in which $\mathcal{L}$ is covered by one label in $\mathcal{L}_f$. In addition to the uniformity of the distribution, for the ideal case the mapping between $\mathcal{L}_f$ and $\mathcal{L}$ is one-to-one and onto. For such a mapping $c = k$, the mean of H is a good measure for this $\mu = \frac{c}{k}$. Let ε represent the efficacy measure of the mapping.

$$\varepsilon = \frac{(1-\delta)\frac{c}{n}}{\frac{c}{k}} = \frac{k(1-\delta)}{n} \quad (18)$$

5 EXAMPLE DESIGN

This section presents an example of the design process illustrated in section 4. The example design presented here emphasizes the Feature based model design step. Further details of the design process can be found in (Hampapur, 1995-C). The presentation in this section lists the name of the step with reference to figure 4, presents a brief discussion and presents the output of the step.

User Specification: Purpose The purpose of the video database in this example is assumed to be a database to support video editing, multimedia authoring, etc, where video is typically reused from earlier footage.

Design Step: Data Model Design The system specification that can be derived from the purpose are listed below:

Access Granularity: Editing applications typically access video at the granularity of shots (continuous camera operation image sequences).

Typical Query Patterns: The typical nature of queries will include content queries and production style queries.

The video is assumed to be segmented into shots. There are a number of techniques available for segmenting video into shots (Hampapur, 1995-B) The current design example will limit queries to production style queries, specifically to shot framing queries (Zettl, 1984). This simplification is done to keep the presentation simple. The video data model is:

$$
\begin{aligned}
\mathcal{V}_{ap} \;:\;& \text{Video Interval: } \textit{Shot}\\
:\;& \text{Temporal Relations: } \emptyset\\
:\;& \text{Feature Count: } 2\\
:\;& \text{Type: } (\omega_0, \omega_1)\\
:\;& \text{Features: } (\mathcal{F}_0, \mathcal{F}_1)\\
:\;& \text{where } \mathcal{F}_0 = \text{Cinematographic Label Set}, \mathcal{F}_1 = \text{Content Labels}
\end{aligned} \tag{19}
$$

Feature	Type	Range
$\mathcal{F}_{00}$ = Framing Distance	ω_0 = Qualitative	$\mathcal{L}_{00}$ = Long, Medium, Close Up
$\mathcal{F}_{01}$ = Framing Angle	ω_1 = Qualitative	$\mathcal{L}_{01}$ = High, Eye, Low
$\mathcal{F}_{02}$ = Framing Motion	ω_2 = Qualitative	$\mathcal{L}_{02}$ = Tracking,Panning $\mathcal{L}_{02}$ = Object,Camera-Static,Null
$\mathcal{F}_{03}$ = Shot Purpose	ω_3 = Qualitative	$\mathcal{L}_{03}$ = Establishing, Zoom, $\mathcal{L}_{03}$ = Tracking, Conversation

Table 1: Complete Video Model: Features and Labels

The different features used in the above model of video are the common terminology used to describe a shot in film literature (Zettl, 1984). Thus given a video database constructed based on this model of video, it can be searched based on attributes like *shot distance, shot angle.*

Design Step: Primary Feature Selection This step relies heavily on the vision expertise available. Given the shot framing model of video the primary feature was chosen to be ***Difference Image Sequence (Jain, 1979) (Jain 1984).***

Design Step: Secondary Feature Design : This step requires a vision expertise and the study of the video production process and a study of experimental video shots. Based on all the above factors the following were chosen to be the set to secondary features.

Thresholded Difference Image Sequence: This image is generated by thresholding the difference image. The threshold is chosen to be a small value which eliminates difference pixels generated due to camera optics, digitization effects and small variations in lighting.

Area of Thresholded Difference Images: This is the number of pixels above the selected difference image threshold.

Connected Component Difference Images: The thresholded difference image is filtered and a connected component analysis is used to obtain a grouped component representation of the difference image.

Component Metrics: Different component measurements like size, shape, locations within the image etc are measured from the component image.

Design Step: Feature Based Data Model Design: Figure 3 shows a tree representation of the feature based data model used. The feature based model was designed based on an organization of the secondary features to yield a good classification of the data. The feature based data model is presented below. The process of computing the feature based model is presented in figure 4

$$\begin{aligned} \mathcal{V}_p &: \text{Video Shots: } [t_b, t_e] \\ &: \text{Temporal Relations: } \emptyset \\ &: \text{Feature Count: } 3 \\ &: \text{Type: } (\omega_0, \omega_1, \omega_2) \\ &: \text{Features: } (\mathcal{F}_0, \mathcal{F}_1, \mathcal{F}_2) \end{aligned} \tag{20}$$

Feature	Type	Range
$\mathcal{F}_0 =$ Temporal Motion Variation	$\omega_0 =$ Qualitative	$\mathcal{L}_0 =$ Homo, Hetero
$\mathcal{F}_1 =$ Cumulative Motion Magnitude	$\omega_1 =$ Qualitative	$\mathcal{L}_1 =$ Motion, Still
$\mathcal{F}_2 =$ Spatial Motion Distribution	$\omega_2 =$ Qualitative	$\mathcal{L}_2 =$ Local, Global

Table 2: Partial Video Index Features

The definition of the various labels in the feature based data model is provided below.

Homogeneous Shots (HO): A shot which has uniform motion properties along most of its temporal extent. For example, a panning shot, or a tracking shot, etc.

Heterogeneous Shots (HT): A single shot in which different temporal regions have distinct properties, or that the motion properties of the shot change over the duration of the shot. Typically such shots are called *long takes*. A long take could initially be a still close up shot, then zoom out to a medium shot, and end as a tracking long shot all within one camera take.

Motion Shots (MS): Shots which incorporate a significant amount of image motion.

Still Shots (SS): Shots which incorporate a negligible amount of image motion.

Localized Motion shots (LM): Shots in which the motion is localized to some parts of the image space of the shot. Such shots correspond to static camera moving object shots.

Global Motion Shots (GM): Shots in which the motion is significant in all portions of the image space.

Figure 4 shows the procedure used to compute the feature based index. The first step is to extract difference images from the video sequence. The difference images are thresholded

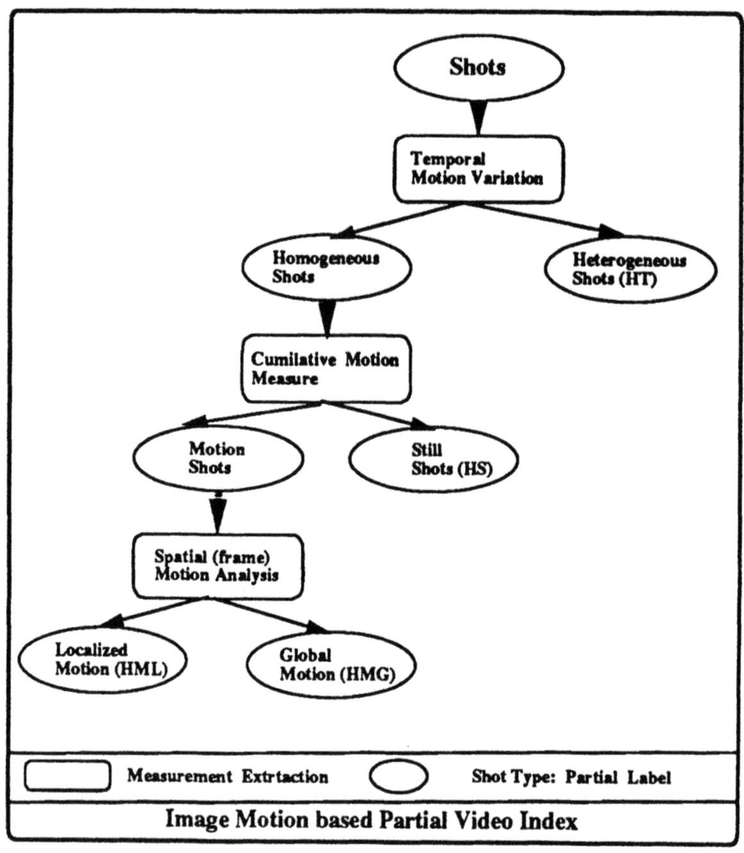

Figure 3: Difference Image based partial video data model

to eliminate noise. The thresholded difference images are grouped into components using a standard connected component labeling algorithm. The first decision in the tree (figure 3) is made based on the *variance of the total image motion area* over the length of the shot. This separates out *homogeneous* from heterogeneous shots. The grouping of *still* and *motion* shots is based on the thresholding the total motion area within a frame and using the frames to vote for the classification. The grouping into *local* and *global* motion shots is based on the *average component size* of the components in a frame.

6 MAPPING BETWEEN VIDEO MODELS

Given a partial video model $\mathcal{V}_p$ (equation 20) and a complete video model $\mathcal{V}$ (equation 19) a mapping between the two sets is necessary in order to use the partial video data model in the indexing procedure. Such a mapping between the *image motion based partial index* and the *shot framing based index* is presented in figure 5. The derivation of this mapping is based on two factors:

Partial Indexing Techniques: A thorough knowledge of the techniques used to derive the partial index and the meaning of the labels of the partial index is necessary in order to be able to create the mapping.

Video Content and Production: As the video models are domain specific it is necessary to have a good understanding of the content of the video and the techniques used to produce the video data.

Given that the application domain is *multimedia authoring and video production* the knowledge necessary to create this mapping is a knowledge of machine vision techniques (Jain-1995) and a knowledge of film production. The study of film and video production presented in (Hampapur, 1995-C) is used as a basis for arriving at this mapping. The mapping shown in figure 5 is based on the following:

HMG: Homogeneous global motion shots cover panning shots and establishment shots. Typically panning shots and establishment shots are used to provide the viewer with a panoramic view of the scene. Hence the camera is panned which causes homogeneous motion through the extent of the image.

HS: Homogeneous still shots typically cover still shots, shots of very small motion like medium shots of people talking etc.

HML: Homogeneous local motion shots cover medium shots with static camera. This is because a static camera precludes global image motion unless the objects are very close to the camera.

HT: Heterogeneous shots cover shots in which the framing parameters change over the length of the shot. For example, if a shot changes from long shot to close up, or if the camera begins motion in the middle of the shot, etc.

7 EXPERIMENTS

The feature based indexing scheme described in this paper, uses a set of low level labels derived by video processing algorithms as indicators of higher level features that are actually required by the video model. There are two factors that need to be evaluated in this approach:

Validity of Mapping: This is the problem of evaluating how faithfully does a particular machine derived label indicate or map to a desired label. This factor depends to a very great extent on the nature of the video data. Characterizing the mapping between the feature based video labels and the higher level of video features requires an extensive analysis of video data. This requires a classification of video based on different production styles and assessing the mapping for each of these production styles. This paper does not report on these experiments.

Reliability of Machine derived Index: This factor pertains to how well the low level video processing algorithms are able to extract the video classes. This is dependent on two factors, namely, the design of low level classes and the performance of the feature based classification scheme. The reliability of the feature based index can be measured in terms correctness of the labels derived by the video processing algorithms as compared to a manually assigned label set. This result can be expressed as a confusion matrix of the feature based classes. The experimental procedure and results are presented in the remainder of the section.

7.1 Procedure

The experimental procedure followed for evaluating the reliability of the machine derived index is presented in this section. A brief description of each of all of the steps involved are presented. Further discussions of some of the steps are presented in later sections.

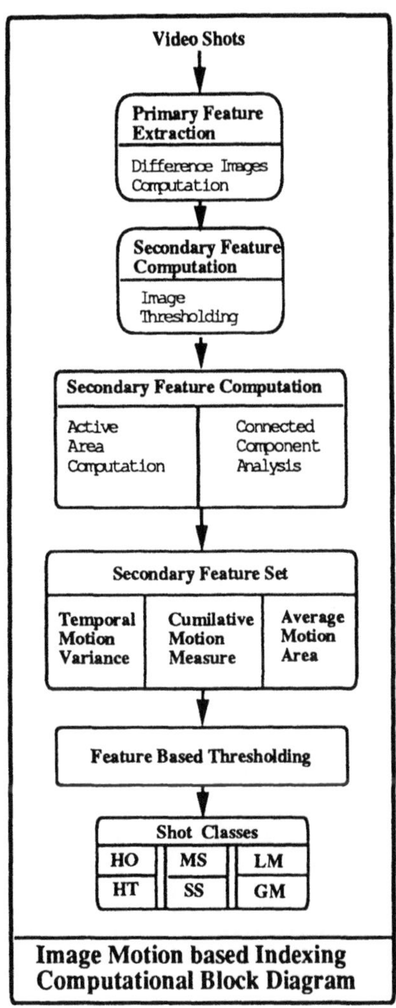

Figure 4: Image Motion based Indexing: Computational Block Diagram

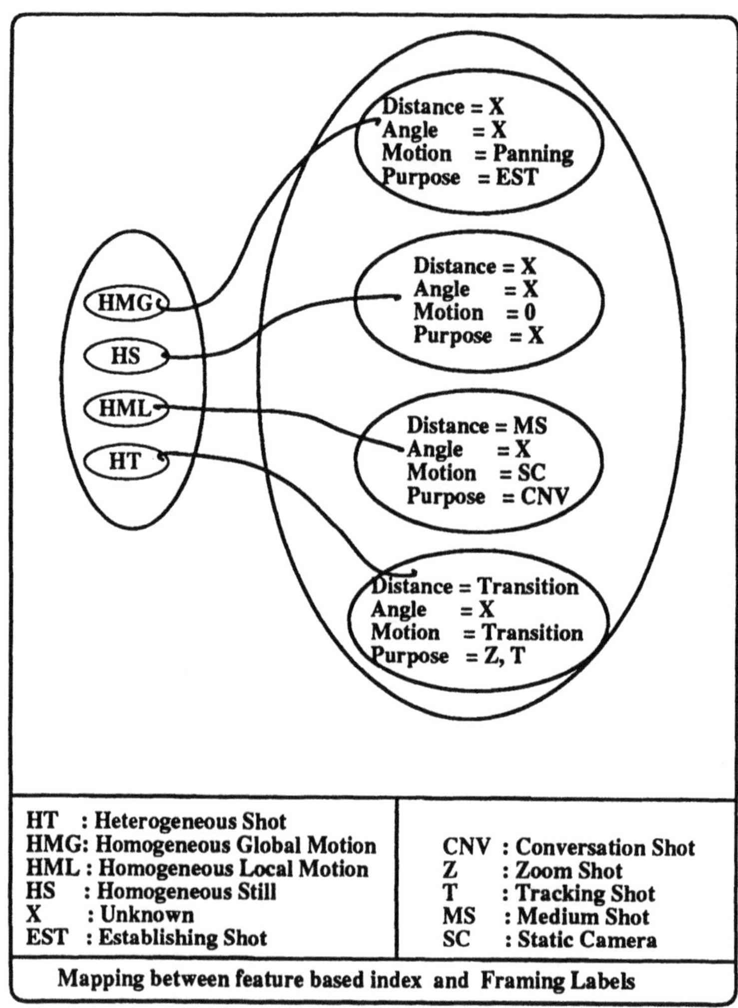

Figure 5: Mapping between machine derived features and video model features

Experimental Data: The experimental data used was taken from commercial cable television feed here in Ann Arbor, MI. The data included a wide variety of cable television programming including, news videos, comedy shows, sitcoms, music videos, commercials, sports telecasts, etc. The data is stored on a video disk.

Shot Segmentation: The video data taken from cable television was segmented into shots. The segmentation was performed using the video segmentation techniques presented in (Hampapur, 1995-C). Each shot of video is represented as a time interval (begining and ending frame numbers on the video disk).

Training Set: This is the set of shots used to tune or train the feature based indexing algorithm. The set chosen here must be representative of all the feature based classes. Further discussion of the training set is presented in section 7.2

Threshold Selection or Training: This is the process of selecting the various thresholds used by the feature based labeling algorithm. This procedure for training is presented in section 7.2

Experimental Set: This is the set of shots on which the the feature based labeling algorithms are applied. This set is chosen randomly from the set of experimental shots that is available.

Feature based labels: These are the labels that are derived by applying the feature based labeling to the experimental data set.

Manual labels: Manual labels are derived by viewing each shot manually and assigning a label. The rules for manual labeling are presented in section 7.3.

Confusion Matrix Computation: The confusion matrix is a $n \times n$ matrix. n is the number of feature based classes. The diagonal entries in the matrix indicate the percentage of shots that were correctly classified. The off-diagonal entries indicate the percentage of misclassification performed by the feature based indexing algorithm. The ideal confusion matrix would be an identity matrix.

7.2 Training

The process of training or threshold selection involves the selection of a set of shots called the *training set*, and using these shots as a basis for choosing the thresholds for the feature based indexing algorithm. The algorithm processes the video frames to extract from it the difference image between consecutive frames. The difference images pass through several computational steps and are finally converted into connected component measurements . These measurements are compared to thresholds in a sequential manner to arrive at the final classification of the shots. Training is the process of choosing these thresholds based on example data. The set of shots used for training are presented in figure 6. The training procedure for selecting the thresholds is outlined below.

1. To each shot in the training set assign a correct label (manual label) based on viewing the shot using the procedure outlined in section 7.3.

2. Run the feature based classification algorithm on all the shots in the training set and record the features.

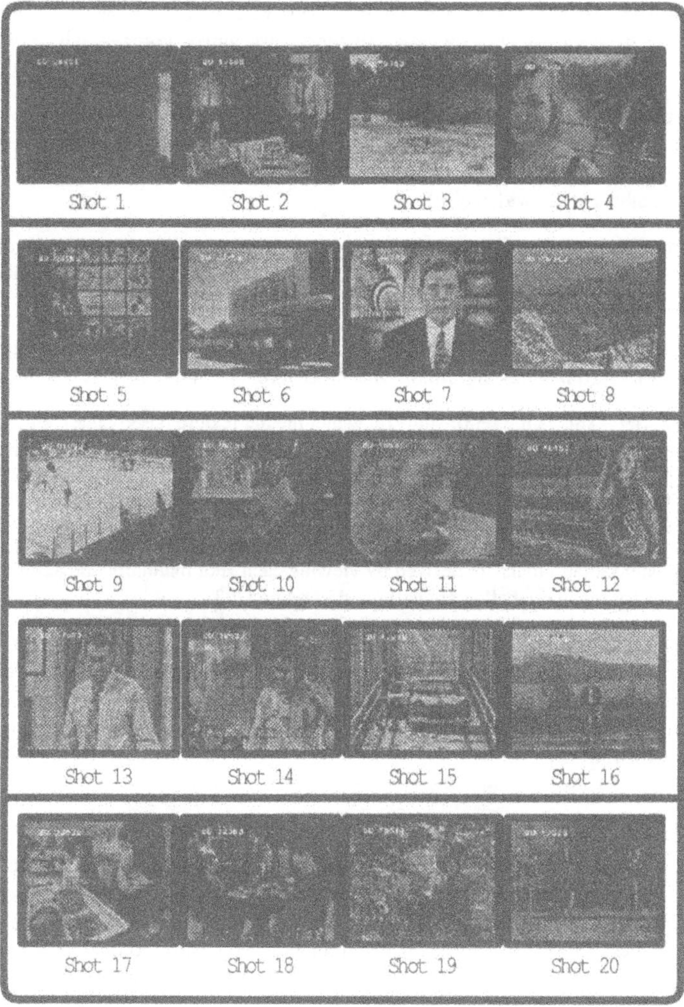

Figure 6: Training set for feature based indexing experiments

3. Choose the thresholds for each of the features which gives the best result in the training set. There are several automatic techniques for choosing these thresholds (Duda, 1975). In the experiments reported here the thresholds were manually chosen.

Figure 6 shows the first frames of each of the shots in the training set. Table 3 shows the actual cinematographic labels for each of the shots in the training set. Also shown are the manual labels assigned to each shot and the corresponding machine derived labels. The confusion matrix for the training set is presented in table 4. Given the set of shots used the confusion matrix of table 4 was the best result that could be achieved by appropriate choice of thresholds.

7.3 Ground Truth Derivation

This section presents the rules or the procedure to be followed by a human operator to label the shots with the feature based labels. The operator views each shot individually and assigns it a label based on the set of rules presented below.

Heterogeneous Shots: If the motion within the shot changes significantly over time, the shot would be termed heterogeneous. The amount of motion within the shot should be significant. Typically heterogeneous shots tend to be shots of long duration. Homogeneous shots exhibit a uniform motion behavior through the temporal extent of the shot.

Still Shots: These are shots with minimum motion in them, they typically include complete stills and conversation shots in front of a static camera, like an anchor person shot.

Local Motion Shots: These are shots where the motion is localized to different parts of the image. Typically this includes static camera shots with single and multiple moving objects.

Global Motion Shots: These are shots where the motion is distributed uniformly over the entire frame of the image. Typically, these include camera panning shots and tracking shots.

7.4 Test Set and Results

The test set for the experiments presented consists of shots taken from cable television programming. These shots were chosen at random from the experimental data set. The set consisted of seventy shots. The shot labeling algorithm was applied to all the shots and the results were recorded. Each of the shots was also assigned a manual label based on the ground truth derivation procedure presented in section 7.3. Based on these results the confusion matrix for these shots is shown in table 5.

7.5 Interpretation of Results

The results presented for the test set of shots is interpreted in this section. The interpretation presented here attempts to analyze the source of the errors. There are two main sources of error that contribute to the total error in the confusion matrix of table 5:

Operator Error: This is the error that arises due to a mislabeling of the shots by the operator. The primary reasons for this error are

Column 1	Column 2	Column 3	Column 4	Column 5	Column 6	Column 7
Shot Label	Distance	Angle	Motion	Objects	FBI Manual	FBI Machine
Shot 1	CU	Eye	SC	1 →2	HT	HoS
Shot 2	LS →MLS	Eye →High	SC	1	HT	HT
Shot 3	LS →CU	High	SC	1	HT	HT
Shot 4	MS →CU	Eye	SC	2	HT	HoS
Shot 5	MS	Eye	SC	1	HoS	HoS
Shot 6	LS	Low	SC	1	HoS	HoS
Shot 7	MS	Eye	SC	1	HoS	HoS
Shot 8	XLS	High	SC	1	HoS	HoS
Shot 9	LS	High	Panning	Multiple	HMG	HMG
Shot 10	CU →MS	X →Eye	Panning	1	HMG	HT
Shot 11	XCU	High	SC	1	HMG	HML
Shot 12	MS	High	Hand Held	1	HMG	HT
Shot 13	MS	Eye	SC	1	HML	HML
Shot 14	MS	Eye	SC	2	HML	HML
Shot 15	LS	Eye	SC	2	HML	HML
Shot 16	XLS	Eye	SC	1	HML	HoS
Shot 17	MS	High	SC	Multiple	HML	HoS
Shot 18	MS	High	SC	Multiple	HML	HML
Shot 19	MS	High	SC	Multiple	HML	HT
Shot 20	LS	Eye	SC	Multiple	HML	HML

CU: Close Up Shot. **MS:** Medium Shot. **MLS:** Medium Long Shot **LS:** Long Shot **XLS:** Extreme Long Shot **Eye:** Eye Level Shot. **High:** High Angle Shot **Low:** Low Angle Shot **SC:** Static Camera **Panning:** Camera pans	HT: Heterogeneous Shot HoS: Homogeneous Still Shot HMG: Homogeneous Motion Global HML Homogeneous Motion Local

Table 3: Manual Derived Index and Ground truth for feature based Index

Labels	Hetero	Still	Global	Local	Total
Hetero	2	2	0	0	4
Still	0	2	0	0	4
Global	2	0	1	1	4
Local	1	2	0	5	8

Labels	Hetero	Still	Global	Local
Hetero	50%	50%	0	0
Still	0	100%	0	0
Global	50%	0	25%	25%
Local	12.5%	25%	0	62.5%

Table 4: Confusion Matrix for Training Set

Labels	Hetero	Still	Global	Local	Total
Hetero	10	0	0	7	17
Still	0	12	0	3	15
Global	4	1	14	5	24
Local	2	4	0	21	27

Labels	Hetero	Still	Global	Local
Hetero	60%	0%	0	40
Still	0	80%	0	20
Global	16%	4%	60%	20%
Local	10%	15%	0	75%

Table 5: Confusion Matrix for Experimental Set

- Error in applying the classification rules to the data.
- Data items which lie close to class boundaries.
- Operator fatigue and other reasons.

In the results presented it is estimated that about 20 % of the error is due to misclassification by the operator.

Machine Classification Error: These are errors that arise due to the mislabeling of the shots by the algorithm. The primary sources of this error are:

- The different classes in the classification scheme are not separable based on the measurements being made.
- The choice of thresholds are not correct, as the training set may on be representative of the test data set.
- The features being used for classification are not appropriate for the classification task.

Specifically the confusion between the classes in table 5 arises because of the following reasons. The list presented below is itemized by the correct class name followed by the erroneous class name.

Heterogeneous →Local: The primary reason for heterogeneous motion shots being mislabeled as local motion shots is *the motion is not detected by the difference image operator* due to the fact that sequence has many areas which have similar or smooth intensity properties. This is the problem of non uniform distribution of motion information through the image.

Local →Still: The primary reason for local motion shots being classified as still shots is *the choice of thresholds for differentiating between motion and still shots.* These shots which are misclassified typically lie near the boundary between the still and motion shots.

Global →Heterogeneous: The primary reason for global motion shots being misclassified as heterogeneous shots is that *in some frames in the shot the difference image operator does not pick up the motion.* This causes a larger variance in the motion over the length of the shot causing it to be misclassified as a heterogeneous shot. The other reason for this misclassification is due to the fact that many of the shots manually labeled as global were *close up hand held camera shots* this causes the motion between frames to be jerky and hence causes the labeling as heterogeneous.

Global →Local: The primary reason for global shots being misclassified as local shots is that *the difference image operator does not pick up the motion.* In the case of the specific shot used in the experimental set were low illumination shots which caused the non response of the difference image operator.

Local →Still: The primary reason for local motion shots being misclassified as still shots is the *choice of threshold.* These shots lie close to the boundary between motion and still shots.

One of the reoccuring reasons for the error is the inadequacy of the motion measurement feature used. This problem can be remedied by using other motion meaurements like *optic flow*. However in many cases the motion information is not available through out the image, in such cases using a better motion measurement operator does not provide much gain. Other types of analysis which perform motion measurement based on large scale object structure will have to be applied. These techniques tend to be very computationally expensive.

The confusion between heterogeneous and other classes occurs mainly due to the fact that the temporal analysis of the shot is local. Using feature variations over longer temporal intervals can effectively reduce this confusion.

In summary, the results of the classification process can be improved by using more complex image analysis techniques. From the perspective of video processing algorithms this is a tradeoff that needs to be made depending on the nature of the application. Since the use of more complex image analysis techniques implies additional computational effort per frame. Given the voluminous nature of video data, a small increase in the computation per frame can result in a significant performance loss for the complete system, which could directly affect the usability of the system.

8 SUMMARY

A novel approach to feature based indexing of video is the focus of this paper. The paper presents a methodology for designing feature based indexing schemes. This method uses the *purpose of the video database* and the *computational constraints* to design an indexing scheme. The method yields a low level video feature based classification scheme, a mapping between the machine derived index and the desired index and an efficacy measure for the machine derived index. The motivations behind this approach to indexing are the limited amount of computation that can be invested per frame of video and the in-feasibility of deriving high level labels based on automatic video processing techniques. An example of image motion based video indexing was presented. This indexing scheme was implemented and tested on video data taken from cable television feed.

9 REFERENCES

Arman , Depommier and Hsu and Chiu. (1994),Content-based Browsing of Video, Proceedings Second Annual ACM MultiMedia Conference.

Allen. (1983) Maintaining Knowledge about Temporal Intervals, Communications of the ACM.

Akutsu and Tonomura and Hashimoto and Ohba. (1992) Video indexing using motion vectors, Proceedings of SPIE: Visual Communications and Image.

Akutsu and Tonomura. (1994), Video Tomography: An efficient method for camerawork extraction and motion analysis, Proceedings Second Annual ACM MultiMedia Conference.

Bordwell and Kristin. (1980), Film Art: An Introduction, Addison-Wesley Publishing Company.

Date. (1975), An Introduction to Database Systems, The Systems Programming Series, Addison-Wesley Publishing Company.

Davis. (1993), Media Streams: An Iconic Visual Language for Video Annotation, IEEE Symposium on Visual Languages.

Davis (1994), Knowledge Representation for Video, Working Notes: Workshop on Indexing and Reuse in Multimedia Systems, American Association of Artificial Intelligence.

Duda and Hart. (1973), Pattern Classification and Scene Analysis, A Wiley-Interscience Publication, John Wiley and Sons.

Davenport, Smith and Pincever. (1991), Cinematic Primitives for Multimedia, IEEE Computer Graphics & Applications.

Gong, Zhang, Low, Smoliar and Chua. (1994), Indexing and Retrieving Images based on color features, Technical Report, Institute of Systems Science, National University of Singapore.

Hampapur, Jain and Weymouth. (1994-A) Digital Video Indexing in Multimedia Systems, Prooceed ings of the Workshop on Indexing and Reuse in Multimedia Systems, American Association of Artificial Intelligence.

Hampapur, Jain and Weymouth. (1994-B) Digital Video Segmentation, Prooceedings of the ACM conference on MultiMedia.

Hampapur, Jain and Weymouth. (1995-A) Indexing in Video Databases, IS & T/SPIE Symposium on Electronic Imaging Science & Technology.

Hampapur, Jain and Weymouth. (1995-B) Production Model based Digital Video Segmentation, Journal of Multimedia Tools and Applications.

Hampapur. (1995-C), Designing Video Data Management Systems, Doctoral Thesis, The University of Michigan, Ann Arbor.

Ioka, Kurokawa. (1993) Estimation of Motion Vectors and their application to scene retrieval, Technical Report, IBM Research, Tokyo Research Laboratory.

Jain and Nagel. (1979), On the analysis of accumulative difference pictures from image sequences of real world scenes, IEEE Transactions on Pattern Analysis and Machine Intelligence, Vol 1, No 2.

Jain. (1984), Difference and Accumulative Difference Pictures in Dynamic Scene Analysis, Image and Vision Computing, Vol 2, No 2.

Jain and Hampapur. (1994), Metadata in Video Databases, Sigmod Record: Special Issue On Metadata For Digital Media.

Jain, Kasturi and Schunck. (1995) *To be published* Introduction to Machine Vision, McGraw Hill.

Konigsberg. (1989), The Complete Film Dictionary, Penguin Books.

Korth and Silberschatz. (1986), Database System Concepts, McGraw Hill Book Company.

Millerson. (9175), The technique of Television Production, Hastings House Publishers.

Nagasaka and Tanaka. (1991), Automatic Video Indexing and Full-Video Search for Object Appearances, 2nd Working Conference on Visual Database Systems.

Smith and Davenport. (1992), The Stratification System: A Design Environment for Random Access Video, Workshop on Networking and Operating System Support for Digital Audio and Video

Swanberg, Shu and Jain. (1992), Architecture of a Multimedia Information System for Content-Based Retrieval, Proceedings of the Audio Video Workshop.

Swanberg, Shu and Jain. (1993), Knowledge Guided Parsing in Video Databases, Electronic Imaging: Science and Technology.

Smoliar, Zhang and Wu. (1994) Using Frame Technology to Manage Video, Prooceedings of the Workshop on Indexing and Reuse in Multimedia Systems.

Zettl. (1984), Television Production Handbook, Wadsworth Publishing Co.

10 BIOGRAPHY

Arun Hampapur received his B.Eng in Electronics and Communication Eng from the University of Mysore, India in 1987. He received his Masters degree in Electronics and Control Eng from the Birla Institute of Technology and Science, Pilani, India in 1989. He received his M.S in Computer Eng from Louisiana State University in 1991 and Doctorate from the University of Michigan, Ann Arbor in 1995. His dissertation work is on the Design of Video

Data Management Systems. He is currently employed as Senior Software Engineer at Virage Inc, San Diego. His research interests include video databases, digital video processing, image databases, multimedia systems, computer vision, image processing and robot navigation systems.

Ramesh Jain is currently a Professor of Electrical and Computer Engineering at the University of California at San Diego. Before joining UCSD he was a Professor of Electrical Engineering and Computer Science at the University of Michigan, Ann Arbor. He has also been affiliated with Stanford University, IBM Almaden Research Labs, General Motors Research Labs, Wayne State University, University of Texas Austin. His research interests are in multimedia information systems, image databases, machine vision and intelligent systems. Ramesh is a fellow of IEEE, AAAI and Society of Photo-Optical Instrumentation Engineers. Currently he is the Editor-in-Chief of IEEE Multimedia and is on the editorial boards of Machine Vision Applications, Pattern Recognition and Image and Vision Computing. He received his Ph.D from IIT Kharagpur in 1975 and his B.E from Nagpur University in 1969.

Terry Weymouth received his dissertation in May of 1986 from the University of Massachusetts, where he was involved in computer vision research. Dr. Weymouth is an Senior Research Scientist in the Electrical Engineering and Computer Science department of the University of Michigan. He is a member of IEEE, ACM and AAAI. His research interests include video and image databases, computer vision, robot navigation, biomedical image processing and distributed collaboratory systems.

9

Dynamic Object Clustering for Video Database Manipulations

Q. LI and C.M. LEE

Department of Computer Science
Hong Kong University of Science & Technology, Hong Kong

Abstract

Extensions to the object-oriented data model are described which address the dynamic nature of video database manipulations. These extensions support the dynamic grouping of objects to form a new object or cluster, and within each cluster a set of roles may be employed and/or introduced to define the behavior and interactions of the objects. In the context of a video database system, we examine the types of video data objects that require these extensions, and consider the utility of these extended features in supporting several generic types of video database manipulations, including video classification, video editing and video production.

Keywords

Conceptual object clustering, dynamic roles, object video databases, video data manipulations

1 INTRODUCTION AND MOTIVATION

"Video data" management is emerging as one of the most important topics in multimedia database systems. Within a *video database management system (VDMS),* flexible and advanced facilities are needed to provide support in video data processing and management. Most work on video data processing has concentrated on image analysis and recognition (for video classification), image structuring and indexing (for feature representation), and spatial reasoning and image retrieval (for video access) [(Chang 1992), (Hirata, 1992), (Kato 1992), (Nagasaka 1992)]. Little has been done to provide facilities for other types of video data processing such as *video editing* and *video production*, nor has there been much effort to develop efficient video data management facilities, which we regard as integral part of the VDMS's functionality.

Object modeling and object-oriented technology is having a major impact on the development of multi-media database systems [(Masunaga 1989),(Woelk 1987)]. While many object-oriented concepts and techniques coincide with what are required by multi-media database systems, extensions are needed to adequately accommodate the new requirements of a VDMS, many of which involve domain dependent information that can be used to facilitate, e.g., more effective extraction of features from images stored in the database or used in queries (Jain 1993). In this paper, we describe an extended "object-oriented" approach of supporting effective video database manipulations based on the concept of *conceptual clustering*. In particular, we demonstrate that conventional object-oriented database facilities supplemented with dynamic conceptual clustering techniques allow a wide range of video data processing and management to be accommodated elegantly. In next section we briefly summarize the key concepts of object-oriented databases, followed in subsequent section by a review of the conceptual clustering model we have developed. Section 4 applies the various concepts and techniques which were introduced to video data processing and manipulation. Section 5 briefly describes our prototype environment and status, and finally Section 6 concludes the paper.

2 OBJECT-ORIENTED DATA MODELS

In this section, we first summarize a collection of concepts that are fundamental to object-oriented data modeling in general, and then introduce some generic types useful to describe video data objects in particular. We also illustrate some important elements in a type/class hierarchy relevant to the subject matter of the paper, and which in some cases require extensions to the current object-oriented data model facilities.

2.1 Some Basic Concepts

The most fundamental concepts of object-orientation include *object* and *class*. In an object-oriented database (OODB), the term object represents an encapsulation of instance variables constituting a state, and methods for manipulating it. Classes are used to describe object types*, as defined by their *properties* (connoting instance variables and methods); they are also used to create, destroy, or store objects through such run-time facilities as object-factory and object-warehouse (Atkinson, 1989). Objects communicate through *messages*, and the handling of messages (the translation of method names to the actual program addresses) is done at run-time and is called "late binding". For each instance variable, the set of values it may have is confined by its class type (which is called the *domain class)*; both atomic (e.g., integer, string of characters) and abstract (i.e., object) domain classes are possible in an object. Objects are uniquely distinguished with their (system-generated) object identifiers (Oids), hence the existence of an object is independent of its values.

Inheritance is a powerful mechanism used for defining specialization ("is-a") relationships between classes in an OODB. In particular, a class X may be defined as a specialization of another class Y; class X (called the subclass of Y) inherits all the properties of Y (called the superclass of X), and the user may specify additional properties for the subclass. A class may have any number of subclasses, but a subclass may have only one direct

*Here, we follow the convention of unifying classes with types as found in most OO languages (such as C++).

superclass (in the case of *single inheritance*) or any number of direct superclasses (in the case of *multiple inheritance*).When only single inheritance is supported, the classes form a strict class hierarchy (a tree). If multiple inheritance is allowed, the classes form a rooted directed acyclic graph (DAG). For simplicity, we will also call the DAG a class hierarchy.

In a class hierarchy, subclasses are allowed to refine/restrict the domain of an inherited instance variable. The domain of an instance variable inherited from multiple superclasses is hence restricted to the intersection of the instance variable domains. Further, subclasses can also have different implementations of any method defined at the superclass level (which is called "overriding"), resulting in a single method name denoting different programs (i.e., *overloading*). In the case of multiple inheritance, it is possible to have naming conflict among the inherited properties (methods and/or instance variables). One way of resolving such property naming conflicts is by means of prefixing the name of the class in which the property is locally defined. In this paper, we shall follow this convention in dealing with naming conflict resulting from multiple inheritance.

Besides the class hierarchy, another type of hierarchy typical in an OODB is the composition hierarchy. This is fundamental in capturing the "is-part-of" relationships between a parent class and its component classes. A *composite object* O can be defined as an object with a set of *abstract* instance variables (whose domain classes are non-atomic), each of which refers to one or more component objects of O. Composite objects add to the integrity features of an OODB model through the notions of existence *dependency* and component *shareability.* Following the treatment of (Kim 1989), the following four cases are pertinent to composite objects and their component objects (also called "sub-objects"):

1. **dependent and shareable**: the existence of the sub-objects is dependent on the existence of a composite object (also called "parent object"). As such, a component object can not be created if its parent object does not already exist. But the sub-objects may be shared, i.e., they can be a component of more than one parent object at the same time.
2. **dependent and exclusive:** the existence of the sub-objects is dependent on the existence of a composite/parent object, and the component objects are not sharable, i.e., they are exclusive sub-objects *owned* by one parent object.
3. **independent and shareable**: the existence of the sub-objects is not dependent on the existence of a composite/parent object; as such, the deletion of the parent object does not imply the deletion of (all) the sub-objects. Further, the sub-objects may be shared by more than one parent object at the same time.
4. **independent and exclusive:** the existence of the sub-objects is not dependent on the existence of a composite/parent object, and the component objects are not shareable, i.e., they are exclusively referenced by only one object (i.e., the parent object).

2.2 Video Data Objects

Video data objects (VDOs) are the basic type of objects involved in video database manipulations. We now introduce two important generic object types which feature in a video composition hierarchy. The first is called a Video-Frame (V-Frame). It is the fundamental type of video data object that embraces the common imagery properties (even with colors) of video data objects; it is also the elementary unit of storage of video data objects (e.g., as BLOBs - Binary Large OBjects). The second generic object type is called a Video-Program (V-Prog). It is a composite object consisting of a finite number of V-Frame objects. A V-Prog object typically defines bibliographic properties such as the title, subject, producer, and year. Aside from these two generic object types, it is convenient to think there is also an intermediate "virtual object type" called Video-Segment (V-Seg). In particular, a V-Seg object can be viewed as an object derived dynamically by grouping a sequence of V-Frame objects (the derivation of V-Seg objects using the clustering technique is discussed in Section 4). Typical properties of a V-Seg object may include "structural metadata" (e.g., the sequence of scenes of a segment represented by a sequence of frames) (Davenport, 1991), and even "content metadata" (e.g, sets of key frames depicting the major scenes in the video segment) (Rowe 1994). Figure 1 intuitively illustrates V-Prog object and its V-Frame sub-objects together with a number of V-Seg objects each of which groups several V-Frame objects. Note that the composition links from a V-Prog object to the V-Seg sub-objects are in general **dependent** and **exclusive**, whereas the links from a V-Seg object to its V-Frame sub-objects may also be **independent** and/or **shareable** (e.g., a V-Seg object may be edited/formed by including some V-Frame objects that are desirable-to-have, though not necessary-to-have).

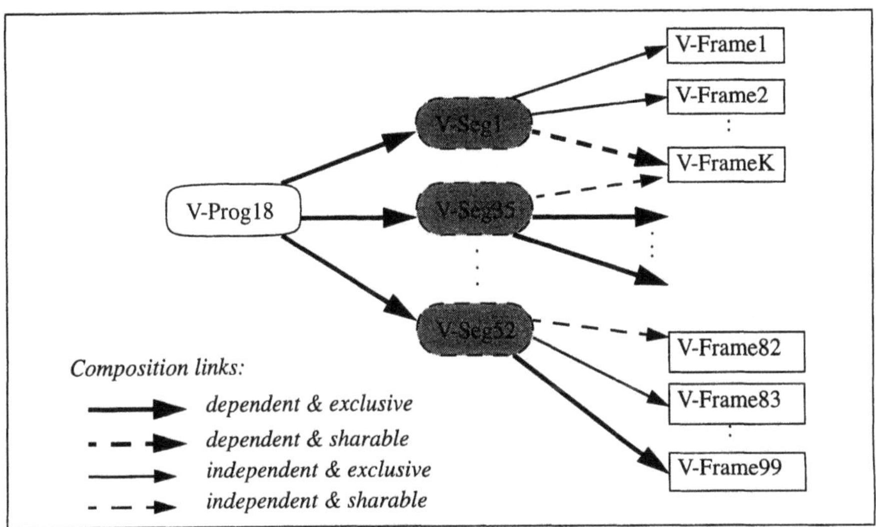

Figure 1 Example of a V-Prog Object and its Component Video Sub-objects

2.3 Exclusive/Inclusive Subclasses and Dynamic Objects

We articulate that in a video object database, an *is-a* hierarchy subclass may be exclusive or inclusive. By exclusive subclasses we mean that if there is more than one specialization stemming from a class at any level in the hierarchy, then an object at the subclass level may be of one and only one subclass. If subclasses are non-exclusive (i.e., inclusive), then an object at that level may be of more than one subclass. Figure 2 illustrates some examples of exclusive and inclusive subclasses in the *is-a* hierarchy of an object-oriented video database. Note that the most general classes are system abstract data types, which are generalized data types from which there is no instantiation, only inheritance. At this level we add the abstract type of Dynamic Object because, in future applications, objects will have dynamic behavior as well as static behavior. With the Dynamic Object we associate the functionality to add and drop attributes and methods dynamically. Cluster and role are introduced in Section 3.

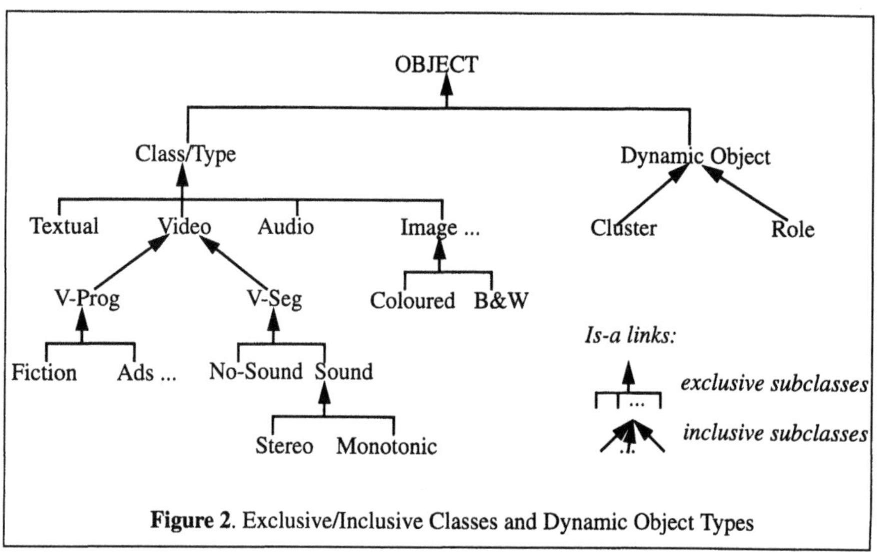

Figure 2. Exclusive/Inclusive Classes and Dynamic Object Types

The Video sub-type hierarchy inherits from the static object Class (or Type). On the other hand, an obvious specialization of the Dynamic Object type is the cluster. As already mentioned this is a type which is added on to an existing OODB model, which is a collection of existing database objects playing particular roles defined within the cluster. In next section, we introduce this "extended" facility in detail. The utility of this facility in video database manipulation is describe in Section 4.

3 DYNAMIC OBJECT CLUSTERING

The conceptual clustering model (CCM) facilitates dynamic creation, deletion, and manipulation of *ad hoc* object collections (called "clusters"), with a goal to complement the existing object class power for accommodating generic application dynamics (Li 1992). In CCM, existing objects can be dynamically grouped with newly introduced *roles* to form active or passive clusters. In this section, we review some of the basic aspects of CCM, including taxonomy and role mechanism, with examples drawn from the video database domain to show the relevance and potential utility of this new concept in supporting video database applications.

3.1 Cluster Taxonomy

From the semantic modeling point of view, a cluster acts like a "context" through which database objects take up new or relinquish existing *roles* dynamically. Roles typically imply extra properties (attributes and/or operations) for their member objects, known as "players" (which are also referred to as the constituents of the cluster). Depending on the manner of clustering and the potential interactions among the constituents, clusters are further distinguished into several kinds. In (Li 1992) a taxonomy of 12 kinds of clusters has been set up, which is based on the perspectives of derivation, uncertainty, and behavior (see Table 1).

Table 1 A Taxonomy of Dynamic Object Cluster Types

Derivation	*Adaptive*	*Infixed*	**Certainty**	*Obscure*		*Explicit*	
Deep	DAC	DIC	- - - →	ODAC*	ODIC*	EDAC*	EDIC*
Shallow	SAC	SIC	- - - →	OSAC	OSIC	ESAC	ESIC
Remarks: (1) Deep clusters are always loosely-coupled.			**behavior**	↓	↓	↓	↓
(2) Asterisked combinations constitutes the taxonomy.			*Loosely-coupled*	LOSAC*	LOSIC*	LESAC*	LESIC*
			Tightly-coupled	TOSAC*	TOSIC*	TESAC*	TESIC*

First, from the perspective of derivation, clusters can be formed by either "clustering-by-copy" or "clustering-by-reference". The former results in aggregate-like clusters (called **Deep Clusters**) in which *deep copies* of the source constituent objects are made, and subsequently become *owned* members of the clusters; the latter yields complex clusters (called **Shallow Clusters**) whose constituents are simply references/pointers (i.e., *shallow copies*) to existing source objects (of some classes), as opposed to being owned members of the clusters. Orthogonally, clusters can also be formed by applying some local changes or without any adaptations, which leads to the distinction of **adaptive** clusters and **infixed** clusters. For example, a new video segment (internally defined as a cluster) may be formed by composing several of the existing video segments and/or frames with some "special-effect" exercised on some of the segments and/or frames. We note that such special-effect adaptations are of *local scope* only, i.e., they do not carry global effect outside the cluster.

Complementary to the above perspective, a cluster can have constituent objects that are fully determined, are only partially identified, or are identified disjunctively. If a cluster's constituents are fully determined, then it is called an **explicit** cluster, else it is an **obscure** cluster. An obscure cluster may or may not become explicit at a later stage. This depends on the nature and degree of uncertainty involved.

The last perspective of cluster classification regards the behavioral interactions of the constituents. In particular, the constituent objects may (or may not), as a consequence of the clustering, exhibit new behaviors which may interact with their pre-existing behaviors (defined in their classes). If such behavioral interactions exist, the resultant cluster is called **tightly-coupled**, otherwise it is called **loosely-coupled**. For example, a previously silent video (sub)segment may be upgraded to sound video after it has been incorporated into a new video. On the other hand, a black-and-white video frame may be desired to remain in black-and-white even after it has been added into a colored video segment with other color video frames.

Combining all three perspectives, we obtain 12 possible kinds of clusters based upon *applicable*[*] combinations of the terms identified above (see Table 1). A set of associated cluster operators has been devised on a prototype, which supports the basic definition and manipulation of the clusters (Li 1992). Together, the cluster primitives and operators provide a rich set of facilities that are both semantically expressive and behaviorally powerful in modeling real-world application dynamics.

3.2 Role Facilities

As mentioned earlier, a cluster can be viewed as a context through which its constituent objects are able to play various *roles*. In a sense, therefore roles are like "threads" that link constituent objects together in forming the cluster. Examples of roles in video databases include any features relevant to the description of VDOs, which can be *descriptive* (e.g., theme-frame, break-points, etc.) as well as *active* (i.e., with operations defined, as exemplified by color, background, foreground, etc.). From the functional point of view, roles can be regarded as *virtual classes* which do not create/delete objects, but only include-in or exclude-out objects of the database. Like a class, a role has in its definition a set of attributes and methods (if active) which are applicable to any objects playing this role. But unlike a class, the objects that play a role can be heterogeneous (i.e., of different types, as opposed to homogeneous ones). Furthermore, roles can be created, deleted, or (structurally and/or behaviorally) modified dynamically.

Similar to the classes that form an *is-a* hierarchy, roles can establish a super-role/sub-role hierarchy, in which a sub-role may inherit the attributes and methods defined by the super-role. In addition, a sub-role can also define new properties and/or overwrite some of the inherited ones. For example, in a video documentary to be produced (represented as a cluster), the role called "music" defines the various music pieces used in the documentary, and its objects (i.e., the role players) are the actual audio files stored in the database. Suppose another role called "theme-music" is defined as a sub-role of the role "music", then all the properties defined by "music" become relevant and applicable to the role "theme-music", and any objects (music files) playing the sub-role (viz., theme-music) should therefore be counted as players of the super-role (viz., music) as well. Note that it is possible for the sub-role to define new properties (attributes and methods) in addition to the inherited ones, and also it may modify the definition of an inherited property from the super-role.

4 VIDEO MANIPULATIONS BASED ON CONCEPTUAL CLUSTERING

A frequent requirement in video database applications is to cluster/group existing video data objects to form dynamic collections, as exhibited by such manipulative activities as video classifications, feature extractions, and video editing and productions, the primary function of

[*]Note that some of the combinations such as **Deep** with **Loosely-coupled** are regarded as inapplicable, since it is trivially true in any case (cf. (Li 1992)).

the latter two is to tell some story (Davenport, 1991). In this section, we examine some of these activities (particularly video classification and video production) in detail, and illustrate how object-oriented modeling facilities, in general, and the conceptual clustering mechanism introduced above, in particular, can be applied to support general-purpose video manipulation operations in a video database context.

4.1 On Video Feature Representation

A fundamental task in video database manipulations is *video classification* [(Lee 1993), (Lee 1994), (Xiong 1995)]. In particular, an "intelligent" video classifier is a software component that can, ideally, classify not only the *structural* but also *semantic* contents (metadata) of a given video program in a (semi-)automated manner. We note that such a view has also been taken and supported in the Berkeley Distributed VOD project (Rowe 1994), which uses Postgres DBMS to store the index/metadata. While developing such a video classifier calls for a set of "intelligent" algorithms (see [(Lee 1993), (Lee 1994), (Xiong 1995)]), an appropriate data structure for the representation of the various features and/or semantic-indices created by the classification process must also be devised to account for the semantic contents of the classified program and its decomposed (semantically meaningful) segments. Clearly, the structure should also facilitate the search of the classified segments and frames of the video program.

We believe clusters as introduced in previous section are a good means for representing semantic features derived from the video classification process. In particular, the role part of a cluster can facilitate the representation of various semantic features, while role players refer to actual video frames. For example, given a video program (e.g., V-Prog17), a pre-processing video classification (based on a set of algorithms) may yield several segments (i.e., V-Seg objects), each consisting of a collection of video frames (i.e., V-Frame objects). Figure 3a shows three resultant V-Seg objects, plus an additional index (e.g., Prog17-Index), all represented as clusters. A sample "zoomed-in" V-Seg object (e.g., V-Seg3) with its cluster definition is shown in Figure 3b. Note that V-Seg3 is a TESAC (tightly-coupled, explicit, shallow and adaptive cluster), therefore it is possible to apply the operations defined in the cluster and/or roles (if active) to the component objects (i.e., V-Frames) directly.

While all three V-Seg objects in this particular example are at the same abstraction level, it is possible that finer-grained segments may be further decomposed and/or derived, with necessary inter-cluster operations provided [(Li 1993), (Li 1995)]. Such inter-cluster operators allow the inter-segment relationships (such as *subset, similarity, continuity, inverse,* and *dependency*) to be established, which may be utilized later in facilitating efficient access to video segments (and video frames) in the database. Further investigation on this issue is currently being carried out in our subsequent research.

4.2 On Video Editing and Production

Using clusters as primary means for describing video segments (V-Seg objects) and semantic indices is advantageous not only from the video classification (feature representation) point of view, but also in video editing and video producing applications. Below we examine how clusters can be utilized for these kinds of activities.

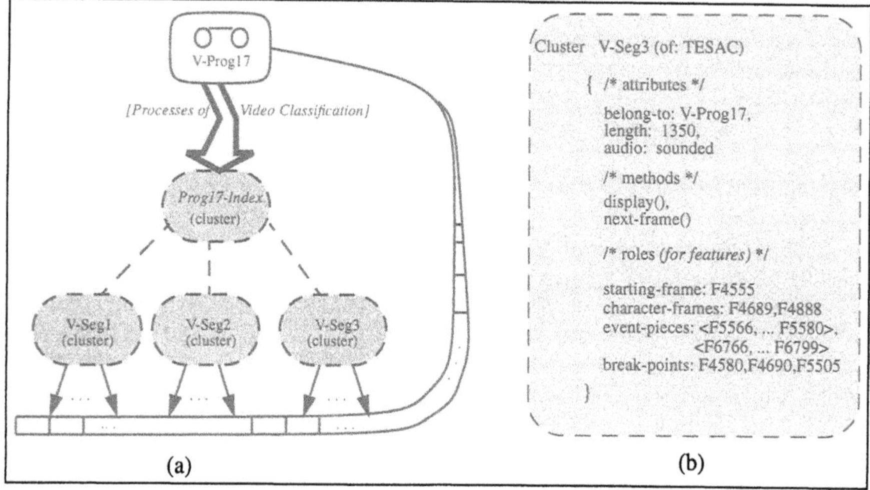

Figure 3 A Classified Video Program (a) and One of Its Segments (b)

4.2.1 Editing

With video segments being represented as clusters, an immediate advantage is that various editing operations that are defined in the clusters can be applied to the segments, and to the video frames of each of the segments. First, let us consider video editing at the video-frame level. As mentioned before, the video classification process enables video frames to be partitioned and grouped into semantically meaningful segments. Such segments can be implemented as tightly-coupled clusters which may define appropriate editing operations (through active roles) to be applied to the member frames. Suppose, for example, that in segment V-Seg3 described in Figure 3 there is a role called "monochrome", which records the frames that are non-colored (i.e., black-and-white) in the segment. Further, assume this role is an *active* one (i.e., it defines operations that are applicable to its role players, including coloring(), darkening(), lightening(), etc.). Thus, individual V-Frame objects that are players of this role may be edited to achieve the desired effect, using some (or all) of the operations defined in the role. Note that additional editing operations may also be dynamically introduced during the editing if necessary, since roles and clusters are dynamic constructs that support dynamic addition (and deletion) of attributes as well as methods (operations) (Li 1992).

At the video segment level, various editing can also be done if a higher-level cluster is created out of the classification process. This higher-level cluster would have all the resultant V-Seg objects to be its constituents. An example would be a global *video index* that describes a classified video program (e.g., *Progl7-Index* for V-Prog17 in Figure 3a). The global video index may record, among other features, such global properties as the *structure* (in terms of the component V-Seg objects), the *semantic* descriptors (e.g., title, key-words, primary-segments, action-segments, music-segments, etc.) of the video program. By defining some of the semantic descriptors as *active* roles (with appropriate operations defined or attached), individual segments that belong to such roles may be edited as needed according to the operations. For example, a pre-processing (classification) of a video documentary (Doc2) may generate an index as shown in Figure 4a, which is internally defined as a TESIC (tightly-coupled, explicit, shallow and infixed cluster). An active role (viz., music-segments) of this index cluster is shown in Figure 4b. By applying some of the operations defined for the role (e.g., Analog-On(), Stereo-On(), etc.), any segment that plays this role (within the video documentary) may be edited and modified as desired.

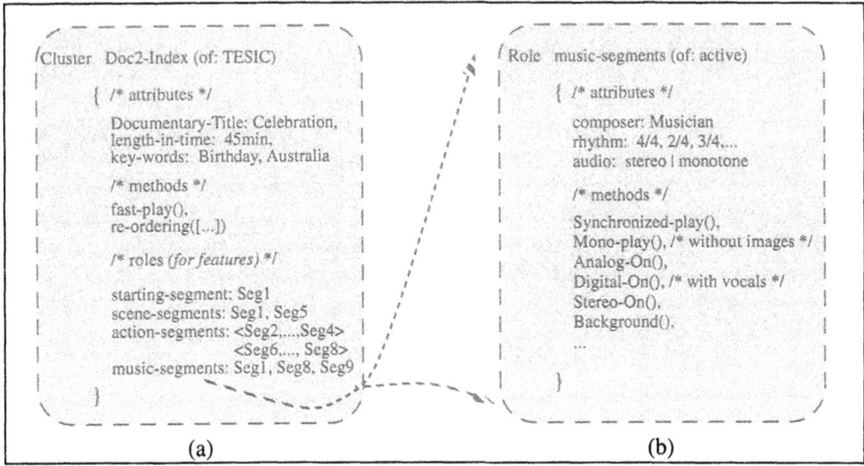

Figure 4 A Global Video Index (a) and One of Its Active Roles (b)

4.2.2 Production

To a large extent, video production can be viewed as an "inverse process" of video classification: the latter generates a set of semantic segments and indices out of existing video programs, whereas the former creates new video programs out of a collection of video segments which are pre-existing and/or newly produced. Here, our discussion focuses on those kinds of video production that make use of pre-existing video segments (and frames) in producing new video programs. Clustering techniques, again, can provide very effective means for accommodating activities in this domain.

Consider, for instance, a short video advertisement of a classic black-and-white film (e.g., "Rome Holiday") is to be produced. Suppose for the sake of entertaining, the producer would like to include tinged pictures extracted from selected segments. By defining the new advertisement (called V-Ads.RomeHoliday) as an EDAC (explicit, deep and adaptive cluster) as shown in Figure 5, it allows deep copies of selected segments to be taken out of the film (i.e., V-Prog objects) when the cluster (i.e., V-Ads.RomeHoliday) is formed. Further, local adaptation operations (e.g., *tinging()*, *fading-out()*, etc.) can be applied to the selected segments in producing the advertisement as desired. "Special effects" techniques such as quick-motion, background, and foreground may also be used, by defining roles corresponding with role players (i.e., the video segments) and role operations (which may call up existing library functions or players' methods). Note that in the cluster V-Ads.RomeHoliday, there is a special role called "sequencing", which is an active role that sets (and can reset) the playing order of the selected segment copies.

When the new video program to be produced is a long one, making actual copies of the video segments may prove to be neither feasible nor desirable. Hence, shallow-clustering techniques are usually more appropriate in such cases. For example, suppose one needs to produce an hour-long video documentary on Ronald Regan which reuses many of the existing video segments from various documentaries and perhaps even from movies in which he has starred in. Instead of creating deep copies of all the segments that constitute the final documentary, a more cost-effective procedure is to simply use shallow copies of the segments by defining the final documentary as a LESIC (loosely-coupled, explicit, shallow and infixed cluster). This avoid any impact on the video segments (due to loose-coupling), while facilitating the sharing of segments from various programs.

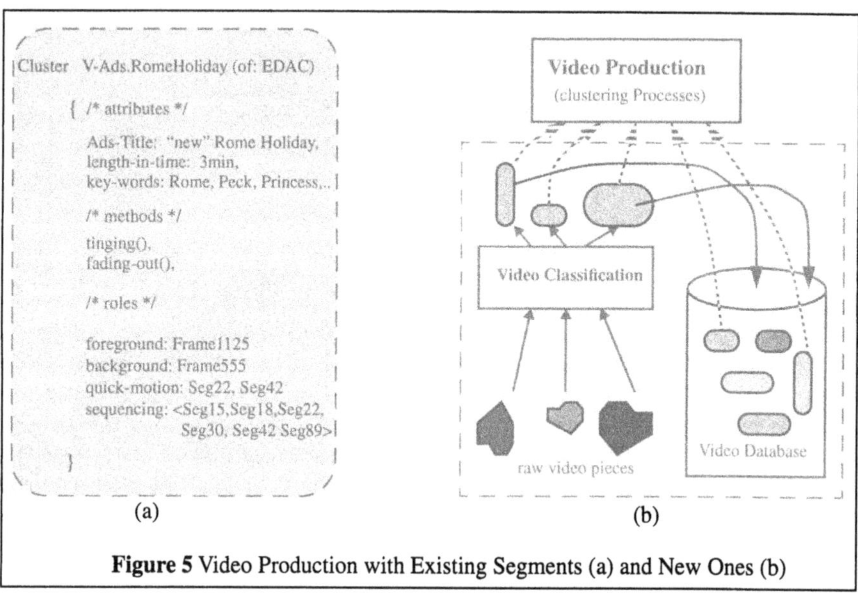

Figure 5 Video Production with Existing Segments (a) and New Ones (b)

Although the examples discussed so far have only considered video production which involves reusing only existing video segments, the same principles should also be applicable to producing video programs that involve newly taken segments, as long as they are represented and stored as clusters. The only difference is that these new video segments (raw video pieces) need to undergo pre-processing or video classification, which generates a corresponding set of classified (possibly edited) video segments (i.e., clusters). Figure 5b intuitively illustrates this situation. Note that processed segments may also be added into the database for later use.

5 SOME DESIGN AND IMPLEMENTATION ISSUES

As part of the research, an experimental prototype of VDMS is currently being developed at Hong Kong University of Science and Technology. The prototype system is being built on the platform of Macintosh Quadra series. Figure 6 illustrates the conceptual architecture of the prototype system, in which it is shown that there are two main development components on top of an object-oriented database. One is the Video Classifier Component (VCC), and the other is the Conceptual Clustering Mechanism (CCM), both are connected to the underlying database and an upper front user-interface. Note that the relationship between VCC and CCM is not always uni-directional, since an edited video segment and/or package may lead to an enhanced classification or trigger a re-classification process to be activated. On the other hand, a newly produced segment/package (through CCM) is automatically a classified video segment/package.

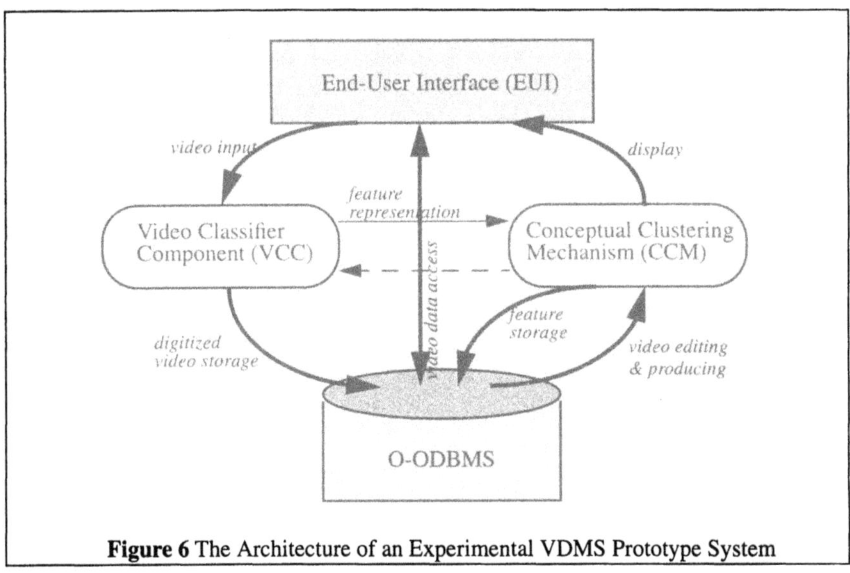

Figure 6 The Architecture of an Experimental VDMS Prototype System

5.1 Current Status

To date, the first component (i.e., VCC) of the whole system is close to be completed, and the second component (CCM) is being implemented. The system consists of a Macintosh Quadra 700, a Pioneer LD-V8000 video laserdisc player and a 24-bit color RasterOps MediaTime video board. The laserdisc player is connected to the Macintosh Quadra through a RasterOps MediaTime video board, which digitizes images from the laserdisc player and displays them at a rate of 30 frames per second (fps). For the first component, a number of sophisticated video classifiers has been devised [(Lee 1993), (Lee 1994), (Xiong 1995)] for:

(1) classifying video images into segments with similar contents, (2) assigning index terms to individual segments, and (3) combining the index terms to form a table of contents or an inverted index file.The aim here is to come up with an "intelligent" VCC that can efficiently organize, through indexing, a sequence of video images in order to enable end-users to access particular video segment and/or frame quickly. At present, our Macintosh-based system is able to read image sequences directly from a laser disc in either CLV or CAV format and provides the following functions:

1.Detects camera breaks in an image sequence (i.e., change of scene),

2.Builds a table of contents based on key frames for the entire sequence of images,

3.Allows end-users to index any segment of the image sequence using key frames,

4.Allows end-users to change the order of image sequences,

5.Allows end-users to manually select an object/pattern in a frame and track or search for that object/pattern in image sequences based on color, size or shape,

6.Groups regions in a frame automatically based on color.

Our present system is able to classify various contents of video segments that include scenes with moving objects, camera zooming and panning, complex road scenes, fade-out (special effect), noisy scenes (e.g., raining, gun flare), video with degraded quality (fluctuating in intensity) and very dark video images. Figure 7 shows some sample indices obtained from a video sequence together with the computer interface of the control panel for the laser disc player. These classified features are then to be fed into the second component (CCM) for later storage into, and future reuse from, the underlying video database (as depicted in Figure 6).

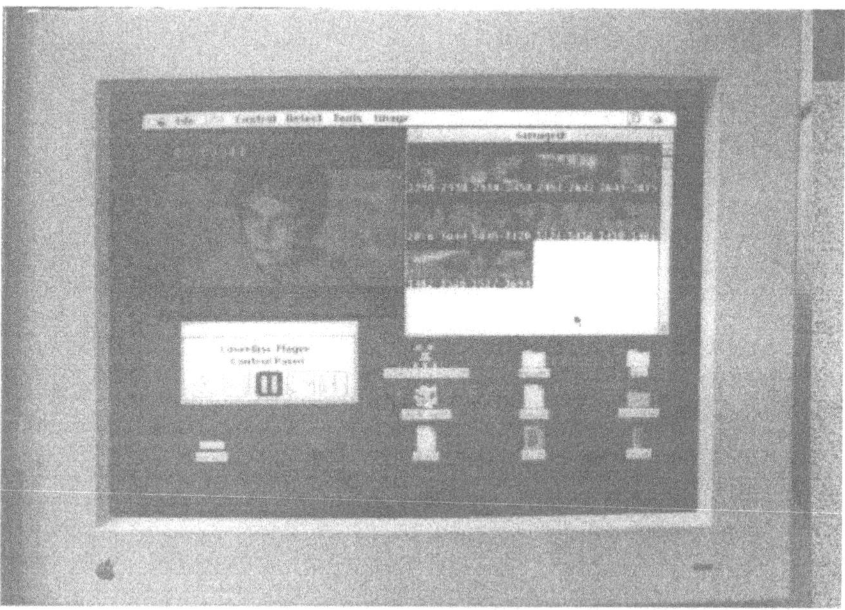

Figure 7 Screen Layout of the Intelligent Video Manipulator

6 CONCLUDING REMARKS

In this paper we have described an approach towards supporting video data management and manipulations using *extended* object-oriented technologies. In particular, conventional object-oriented concepts and features (such as composite objects, is-a hierarchy, method encapsulation, etc.) have provided suitable facilities for storing and manipulating video data objects (VDOs) to a great extent. In order to accommodate and represent dynamic VDO features that arise from video manipulation activities, necessary extensions centred around the notion of *conceptual clustering* have been introduced. Such extended facilities allow tentative, irregular, and/or evolving object collections ("clusters") to be dynamically formed, stored, and manipulated. Such clusters can further impact on, and interact with, the constituent objects (i.e., VDOs) through the functions defined by the active *roles* within the clusters. Example video manipulation activities in the domains of video classification, editing, and production have been considered, and the utility of the clustering facilities in each of the domains is discussed. Finally, we briefly described our experimental prototype environment and system, which is currently being constructed at our institute.

The research described in this paper is being continued and further improved at present. As mentioned, we are close to complete the kernel VDO object-oriented database system, and are adding the conceptual clustering mechanism on top of it. This enhanced VDO database system is then to be interfaced with the devised video classification component (VCC), the latter is also being further extended to support classifying schemes for identifying indoor and outdoor scenes, kung-fu scenes, car racing scenes, sports scenes, etc. In addition to this Mac-based prototype, we are also developing a larger scale prototype based on a persistent object storage management system (namely, EOS from AT&T Bell Lab (Biliris, 1994)) with MPEG on Sun Sparc20 workstations. Other issues of interest include the investigation of the feasibility to incorporate auditory signal processing (ASP) component into the whole system, which may provide us with an additional means for more effective (and meaningful) video data classification and manipulations (e.g., to build keyword indexes from the sound track). Finally, we plan to test and refine our system (upon completion) by applying it into several real-life environments, including TV News Room studios, university Educational Technology Centres, and possibly Telecommunication Companies.

ACKNOWLEDGEMENT

The authors thank the anonymous referees for their constructive comments and helpful suggestions that improved the presentation of this paper. This research is supported, in part, by UPGC Research Grant Council of Hong Kong under grant HKUST 611/94E, and Sino-Software Research Centre of HKUST under grant SSRC 93/94.EG16.

7 REFERENCES

Atkinson, M., F. Bancilhon, D. Dewitt, K. Dittrich, D. Maier and S. Zdonik (1989) Object-Oriented Database System Manifesto, in *Proc. of 1st Int'l Conference on Deductive, Object-Oriented Databases*, Kyoto, Japan, 40-57.

Biliris, A. and E. Panagos (1994) EOS User's Guide (Release 2.1), 600 Mountain Ave, AT&T Bell Laboratories, Murray Hill, NJ 07974, USA.

Chang, S.K. (1992)Image Information Systems: Where Do We Go From Here? in *IEEE Transactions on Knowledge and Data Engineering,* Vol. 4 No. 5, 431 - 442.

Davenport, G., T.G.A. Smith and N. Pincever (1991) Cinematic Primitives for Multimedia, in *IEEE Computer Graphics & Applications,* 67 - 74.

Hirata, K. and Kato, T. (1992) Query by Visual Example - Content based Image Retrieval, in *Lecture Notes in Computer Science,* Vol.580, Springer-Verlag.

Jain, R. (1993) NSF Workshop on Visual Information Management Systems, in *ACM SIGMOD RECORD,* Vol.22, No.3, 57-75.

Kato, T. (1992) Database Architecture for Content-based Image Retrieval, in *SPIE,* Vol.1662, Image Storage and Retrieval Systems.

Kim, W., E. Bertino and J.F. Garza. (1989) Composite Objects Revisited, in *Proc. of ACM SIGMOD Int'l Conference on Management of Data,* 337-347.

Lee, C. M., S.W. Cheng, and M.C. Ip (1993) Camera Break Detection Algorithms and Their Evaluation, *Technical Report HKUST-CS93-10,* Dept. of Computer Science, HK Univ. of Science & Technology (HKUST).

Lee, C. M. and M. C. Ip (1994) A Robust Approach for Camera Break Detection in color Video Sequence, in *Proc. IAPR Workshop on Machine Vision Application (MVA'94),* Kawasaki, Japan.

Li, Q. and J.L. Smith (1992) A Conceptual Model for Dynamic Clustering in Object Databases, in *Proc. of 18th Int'l Conference on Very Large Data Bases,* 337-347.

Li, Q. and M.S. Yuen (1993) Developing a Dynamic Mechanism for Conceptual Clustering in an Object-Oriented DBMS, *Technical Report HKUST-CS93-15,* Dept of Computer Science, HKUST.

Li, Q. (1995) Advanced Functions for Conceptual Clustering in Object Databases, *Technical Report HKUST-CS95-21,* Dept of Computer Science, HKUST.

Masunaga, Y (1989) An Object-Oriented Approach to Multimedia Database Organization and Management, in *Proc. of Int'l Symp. on DASFAA,* 190-200, Seoul, Korea.

Nagasaka, A. and Tanaka, Y (1992) Automatic Video Indexing and Full-Video Search for Object Appearances, in *Transactions of IPSJ,* Vol.33 No. 4.

Rowe, L.A., J.S. Boreczky and C.A. Eads (1994) Indexes for User Access to Large Video Databases, in *Proceedings of IS&T/SPIE Symposium on Storage and Retrieval for Image and Video Databases*, San Jose, USA.

Woelk, D. and W. Kim (1987) Multimedia Information Management in an Object-Oriented Database System, in *Proc. of 13th Int'l Conference on Very Large Data Bases, Brighton*, 319-329.

Xiong, W., C. M. Lee, and M. C. Ip (1995) Net Comparison: A Fast and Effective Method for Classifying Image Sequence, in *IS&T/SPIE Symposium on Storage and Retrieval for Image and Video Databases*, San Jose, USA.

8 BIOGRAPHY

Q. LI received the B. Eng degree from Hunan University, China in July 1982, and the M.Sc and Ph.D degrees (both in computer science) from the University of Southern California in May, 1985 and December, 1988, respectively. From 1989 - 1991, he worked at the Australian National University as a Lecturer of the Department of Computer Science. Since 1992, he has joinned the newly founded Hong Kong University of Science and Technology (HKUST), where he is now an Assistant Professor at the Computer Science Department. His research interests include object data modeling, schema evolution and object migration, object-oriented video databases, intelligent data/knowledge base systems, information sharing and integration, and interoperable database architecture. Dr. Li is a member of the IEEE Computer Society, and the Association of Computer Machinery (ACM).

John C.M. Lee received his Ph.D from University of Minnesota in1989. From 1989 to 1992 he was a research staff member of the Institute of Systems Science at the National University of Singapore. He is currently an Assistant Professor of Computer Science Department at the Hong Kong University of Science and Technology (HKUST). He received the Digital Equipment Corporation's Alpha Innovator's Award in 1993. His research interests include computer vision, image processing, pattern recognition, artificial intelligent, and robotics. Dr. Lee is a member of the IEEE Computer Society, and the Association of Computer Machinery (ACM).

10

Iconic Retrieval by Contents from Databases of Cardiological Sequences

Gianfranco Congiu[†], *Alberto Del Bimbo*[†‡], *Enrico Vicario*[†]
[†] *Dipartimento Sistemi e Informatica, Universitá di Firenze*
[‡] *Dipartimento Elettronica per l'Automazione, Universitá di Brescia*
email: congio,vicario@aguirre.ing.unifi.it, alberto@idea.ing.unibs.it

Abstract
The inherent complexity of retrieval by contents of image sequences imposes the use of appropriate techniques supporting the representation of the contents and the specification of content-oriented queries. A number of such techniques have been proposed in the literature but all of these consider images representing un-deformable rigid shapes. In this paper, the case of time-varying imaged curves is addressed with reference to a database of cineangiographic reports. Qualitative static and dynamic shape descriptors are introduced to provide a symbolic representation of the evolution of deformable shapes, and a language based on Interval Logic is presented which supports the expression of content-oriented queries. A prototype system is described which exploits these indexing and querying languages to support retrieval by contents from a database of cineangiographic reports through visual iconic interaction.

Keywords
Image Sequence Retrieval by Contents, Image Sequence Indexing, Deformable Imaged Shapes, Time-Varying Curves, Visual Iconic Querying.

1 INTRODUCTION

With the emergence of multimedia applications, a growing interest is being focused on databases of pictorial data such as images, image sequences and video. In these databases, the lack of a native structured organization and the inherent visuality of the information contents advises against the use of conventional indexing and retrieval based on textual keywords. A more effective retrieval is achieved by directly referring to the visual contents of pictorial data.

Iconic indexes, which stand for imaged objects, object features, and relationships, have been proposed in (Tanimoto 1976) to support image retrieval by contents. The use of iconic indexes naturally supports visual querying through iconic interaction as it permits the iconic expression of the distinctive features of data to be retrieved. This querying approach improves the user's involvement in the querying activity and reduces human/computer distance in the access to the database.

A number of techniques have appeared in the literature which deal with iconic indexing and visual querying of single images, taking into account different facets of the informative contents of pictorial data, such as picture color distribution (Swain 1991), object texture organization (Niblack 1993), similitude with visual sketches (Niblack 1993),(Hirata 1992),(Del Bimbo 1994), and semantic relationships between imaged objects (Chang 1984), (Chang 1987), (Chang-JVLC),(Roussoupoulos 1988), (Del Bimbo 1993).

As opposite to the large number of experiences on single images, only a few techniques have been proposed for indexing and querying of image sequences and video. Different proposals consider the sequencing of color histograms (Nagasaka 1992), hand-made annotations reflecting the occurrence of significant situations (Davis 1993), semantic networks capturing high-level spatio-temporal interactions (Walter 1992), symbolic projections capturing the temporal evolution of spatial relationships among imaged objects (Arndt 1989),(Del Bimbo 1996). Moreover, all of these attempts deal with image sequences representing rigid objects and they cannot be extended to the case of image sequences where motion includes the deformation of a time-varying shape. This is the case of image sequences of fluids, gases, or deformable solid objects, and it finds a major relevance in the context of biomedical applications.

In this paper we present an original technique for symbolic indexing and querying of the contents of image sequences representing time-varying curves. This technique relies on a formal nucleus made up of two languages which support the *concrete* description of the actual contents of data at their storage time, and the specification of *abstract* data properties expressing content-oriented queries. The two languages are related by the fact that they permit the automatic checking of abstract queries against concrete data descriptions.

The definition of the two languages used to describe data and to express queries is largely conditioned by the type of data managed in the retrieval system and by the type of user interface that this is supposed to offer. To give concreteness to the treatment, the specific case of curves deriving from medical cardiologic reports will be addressed. Qualitative static and dynamic shape descriptors are introduced to provide a symbolic representation of these type of curves, and a language is presented which supports the expression of queries on their contents. A prototype system is described which exploits these indexing and querying languages to support retrieval by contents from a database of cineangiographic reports. The user interface of this system relies on a visual language allowing physicians to compose queries on geometric and temporal properties of reports to be retrieved through iconic interaction.

2 CONCRETE DATA DESCRIPTION

A cineangiographic report consists of a sequence of images sampling the evolution of a section of the left ventricular heart wall along a complete beating period. For each individual sample, conventional edge detection and segmentation techniques partially support the automatic extraction of the contour of the ventricular wall. This extraction is usually completed through the manual marking of the contour, and through the automatic computation of its numerical representation in the form of a planar curve mapping a finite number of points of a conventional parametric axis onto a set of points of the Cartesian plan (see Fig.1).

Figure 1 Two subsequent time samples in a cineangiographic diagnostic report. Conventional diagnostic equipments represent the complete beating period through 14-28 time samples.

The numerical representation of cineangiographic reports allows for digital storage and visual display, but not for a direct access in contents-oriented retrieval operations. To overcome this problem, cineangiographic reports can be associated with symbolic representations extracting the relevant features of sample contents while leaving undefined unnecessary numerical details.

Matching the native organization of cineangiographic reports, one such representation can be accomplished through a separate description of the static contents of individual samples and of the tracking information capturing the sequence evolution.

2.1 Static Curve Description

Studies on human perceptual processing show that the observation of curves does not focus on the position of individual points but rather on their organization within continuous regions characterized by homogeneous features (Haber 1983)(Palmer 1983). This yields a two-layered knowledge model in which the overall shape of a curve is segmented in subcurves reproducing a small number of basic elementary patterns (Leyton 1982). Different sets of such basic patterns and different partitioning criteria have been proposed in the literature (Leyton 1982)(Marshall 1989).

In the *codon* approach (Richards 1984), a curve is regarded as a chain of codons:

$$curve := codon \mid curve_1 \rightarrow codon \tag{1}$$

each codon being comprised of the curve points between two subsequent minima of the bending function. The codon approach appears to be well suited for the case of cineangiographic reports as its orientation towards the characteristics of the bending function naturally matches the relation between the shape of the heart contour and the partitionment of the heart body into physiologic regions characterized by different values of internal muscular tension forces. Codon-based descriptions are also independent of either the orientation or the zooming factor that are employed during the imaging process.

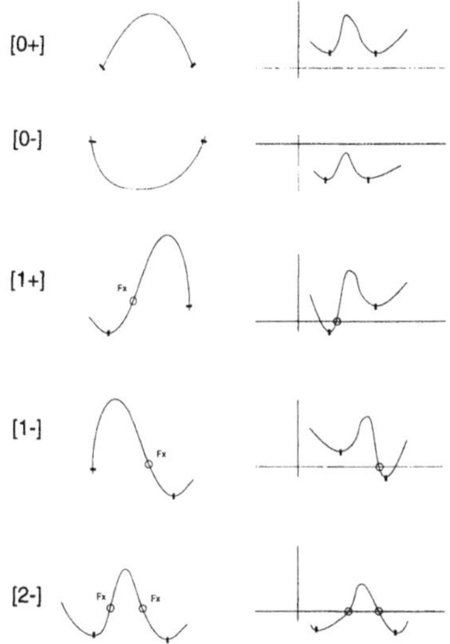

Figure 2 A codon is a sub-curve delimited by two subsequent minima of the bending function. Codons can be classified on the basis of the sign of the bending function in the extrema and of the number of flex points between them. There exists five different combinations: two with no flex points, two with one flex, and one with two flex points.

Codons can be associated with *static attributes* providing a symbolic characterization of their geometric shape. In the case of cineangiographic reports, each codon is associated with a *type* reflecting the pattern of the bending function, and with three shape attributes of *symmetry*, *bending*, and *extension*:

$$static\ attributes := type + bending + symmetry + extension \quad (2)$$

The codon *type* reflects the five possible patterns of the sign of the bending function along the codon (see Fig.2). *Symmetry* accounts for the position of the bending maximum with respect to the middle point of the codon; *bending* is a qualitative representation of the maximum value of the bending function with respect to symbolic thresholds; and *extension* captures the linear distance between the extrema of the codon.

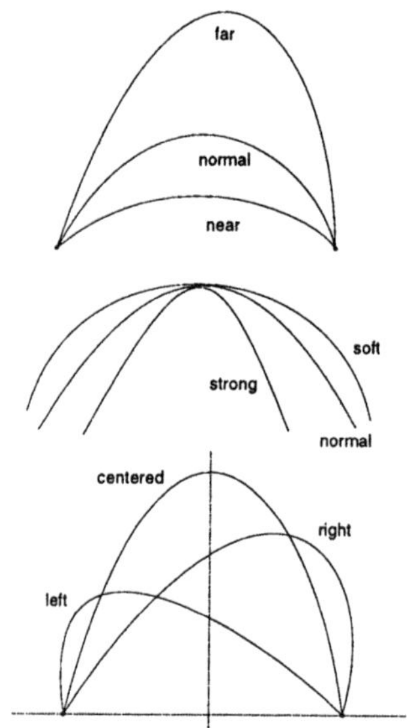

Figure 3 The three characterizing attributes of *symmetry*, *bending*, and *extension*, and their corresponding symbolic values.

2.2 Dynamic Curve Description

The static attributes of codons provide a description of geometric static features of the individual samples of a cineangiographic curve. In order to capture the temporal evolution of the overall report, codons belonging to subsequent samples are associated through a parent-child *tracking relation* (see Fig.4). The tracking relation is usually one-to-one (i.e.

each codon of sample j is biunivocally associated with a single codon of sample $n+1$). However, due to the appearance or disappearance of bending minima, cases of splitting (i.e. a codon of sample j is associated with multiple codons of sample $j+1$) or merging (i.e. multiple codons of sample j are associated with a single codon of sample $j+1$) are also possible.

To cope with merging and splitting, the tracking relation is more easily derived from the parent/child relation among codons extrema (i.e. minima of the bending function): if $\{m_k^j\}_{k=1}^{K_j}$ denotes the sequence of bending minima in the jth sample, a tracking relation for a sequence of J samples is a sequence of J relations γ_j associating minima through subsequent samples:

$$\gamma_j : \{m_k^j\}_{k=1}^{K_j} \rightarrow \{m_k^{j-1}\}_{k=1}^{K_{j-1}} \bigcup \{new\} \tag{3}$$

Specifically, $\gamma_j(m_k^j) = m_h^{j-1}$ means that the minimum m_k^j in sample j is the evolution of minimum m_h^{j-1} in sample $j-1$, and $\gamma_j(m_k^j) = new$ means that the minimum m_k^j is newly appeared in sample j. All the minima of sample $j-1$ that are not associated with any minimum of sample j are assumed to be disappeared.

Depending on the aliasing yielded by the time sampling, the association of bending minima through subsequent frames is carried out through an heuristic decision which basically consists in minimizing a cost function accounting for the curvilinear abscissa displacement between related minima (Congiu 1994). Specifically, if $dist(m_k, m_h)$ is a distance between minima belonging to subsequent frames, the tracking relations γ_j are chosen so as to minimize the sum of distances between related minima:

$$cost = \sum_{j=1}^{J} \sum_{k=1}^{K_j} dist(m_k^j, \gamma_j(m_k^j)) \tag{4}$$

Once the tracking relation has been reconstructed, the static characterization of codons (see Sect.2.1) can be refined through the introduction of two *dynamic attributes* derived from the analysis of relationships among related codons in subsequent frames:

$$dynamic\ attributes := straining + region \tag{5}$$

The *straining* attribute captures the instantaneous expansive/contractive trend of each codon, and it is derived by comparing the position of the codon with that of its parents in the tracking relation (see Fig.5). It is worth remarking that the straining attribute provides a local representation of the evolution of the curve in that it refers to the individual codons. In general, different straining trends may be exhibited by different codons of the same sample. In the cineangiographic diagnostic activity, the simultaneous presence of strongly

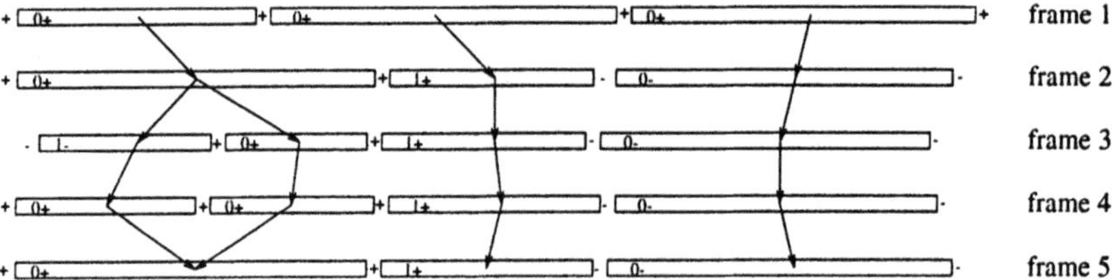

Figure 4 Codon tracking for six samples of a cineangiographic report. For each sample, the curve is represented in curvilinear abscissa and it is segmented into codons that are tracked along subsequent samples. The first codon of the first sample is tracked onto the first codon of the second sample. In turn, this is split into the first and second codon of the third sample. The first and second codon of the fourth sample are merged into the first codon of the fifth sample.

differentiated straining trends is a condition of main relevance as it points out important pathologies.

The *region* attribute is strictly related to a specific properties of the heart wall contour which is natively partitioned in three different anatomic regions, usually referred to as *anterior*, *apical* and *inferior*. Reflecting the physiologic separation between the three parts, the tracking relation identifies three disjoint sets of codons which are not connected through any merging or splitting event. This permits the automatic attribution of each part of each sample of the curve to one of the three anatomic regions. Please note that each codon of each sample is assigned to one of the three regions on the basis of a global analysis of the entire heart-beating period. For this reason, the belonging of a codon to a certain anatomical region is regarded as a dynamic attribute.

3 ABSTRACT QUERY SPECIFICATION

In retrieval by content systems, queries are expressed through an abstract characterization of the expected distinctive features of the concrete description of data in the database. In the case of time-varying curves, this characterization involves both the geometric features of the curve at individual time instants and the ordering relationships between the time intervals in which these features are maintained.

According to the organization of concrete descriptions of individual static samples (cf.

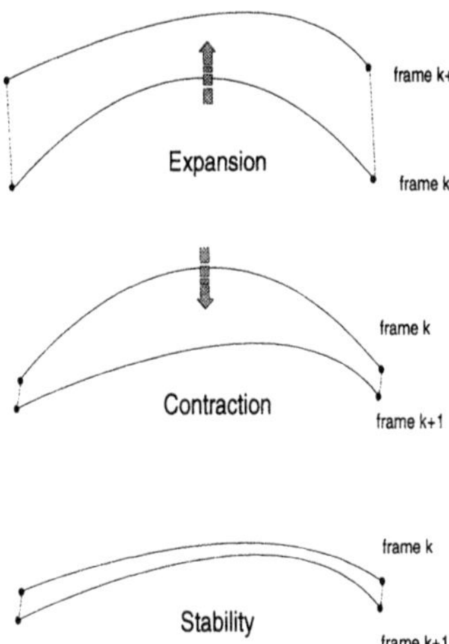

Figure 5 The *straining* attribute captures the instantaneous straining trend of an individual codon. It is assumed to be *expansive*, *stable* or *contractive* depending on the relation between the areas subtended by the codon and its successors. Each of these three conditions is further specialized by an *intensity* qualifier which may take the values *soft*, *normal* or *strong*.

Sect.2.1), geometric features can be expressed as a Boolean combination of basic propositions stating the existence of a codon with a certain set of attributes:

$$\begin{array}{l} \theta := basic \mid \neg\theta_1 \mid \theta_1 \wedge \theta_2 \\ basic := \text{``}there\ exists\ a\ codon\ with\ attributes\ p\text{''} \end{array} \tag{6}$$

where p is any possible evaluation for the static and dynamic attributes of a codon. The temporal evolution of the curve can now be described in terms of the ordering relationships between the lasting intervals in which geometric features of interest are maintained (see Fig.6). To this end, if $I(\theta)$ stands for the any interval in which the property θ is maintained, any such ordering relationship can be expressed in the form

$$\Theta := I(\theta_1) \sim I(\theta_2) \mid \neg\Theta_1 \mid \Theta_1 \wedge \Theta_2 \tag{7}$$

$\sim$ standing for any of the 13 possible ordering relationships which may occur between a couple of intervals (Allen 1983). These relationships, which are pictured in Fig.7, distinguish all the possible conditions of precedence and coincidence between any two extremes of the two intervals.

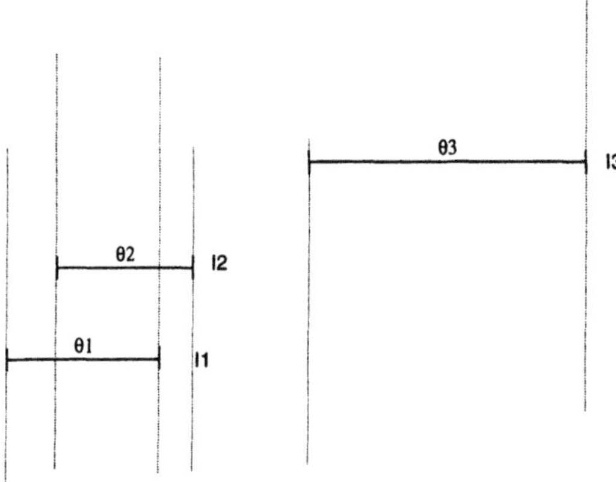

Figure 6 A temporal evolution characterized by three conditions θ_1 θ_2 and θ_3. Condition θ_1 begins first and lasts until overlapping the first part of θ_2. Condition θ_3 occurs after the end of θ_2. The overall timing is captured by the sentence $I(\theta_2) \sim_3 I(\theta_1) \wedge I(\theta_3) \sim_1 I(\theta_2)$.

4 A SYSTEM FOR VISUAL SEARCH AND RETRIEVAL

The two languages described in Sects.2 and 3 have been exploited as formal nucleus of a system for retrieval by contents of cineangiographic reports supporting medical personnel in the diagnostic analysis of cineangiographic reports *.

At storage time, a cineangiographic report is given as a sequence of raw digital images. These are reduced in numerical representation through a semi-automatic process, which includes automatic edge detection and segmentation, manual marking of the left-ventricular contour, and automatic derivation of the chain code representation and of the bending function of contours of individual samples (Baroni 1992). The numerical representation is stored in the system along with a symbolic content representation expressed according to the description format expounded in Sect.2.

In the retrieval stage, the user expresses content-oriented queries through a visual iconic interface. Specifically, the user defines the distinctive conditions which characterize se-

*The system presently runs on an IBM R6000 workstation.

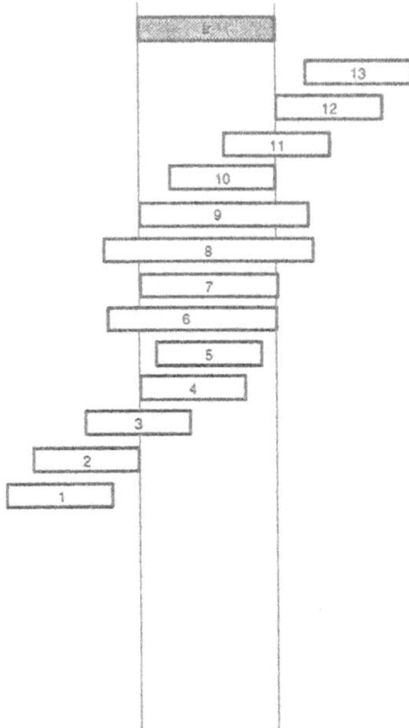

Figure 7 The 13 possible mutual positions of two intervals. Disjunctive composition of the individual positions permits the expression of relevant ordering conditions such as *after* (#13), *before* (#1), *during* (#4 ∨ #5 ∨ #10) and *overlapping* (#3 ∨ #11).

quences to be retrieved and defines the ordering relationships among the lasting intervals of each of these conditions.

Visual queries are automatically interpreted and translated into formulae of the querying language described in Sect.3. These formulae are then checked against the symbolic description of the reports stored in the database, and, finally, matching sequences are displayed on the screen.

4.1 Visual Querying

The basic graphic objects that are employed in the visual expression of queries are icons and lines. Following an approach similar to that used in (Kutty 1993), these objects are arranged on the screen to express visual queries that will be automatically interpreted by the system and translated into formulae of the querying language described in Sect.3.

Icons represent significant conditions in the evolution of a report, such as an expansive straining or the presence of a sharp bending in some of the codons of the cineangiographic curve. Multiple icons can be grouped together to express the Boolean composition of multiple events: conjunctive and disjunctive compositions are expressed by arranging icons in rows and columns, respectively, while icon crossing expresses negation (see Fig.8).

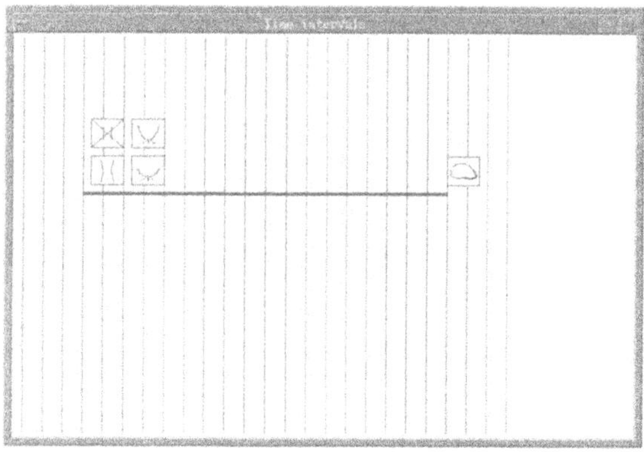

Figure 8 The horizontal line stands for the time interval in which the condition expressed by the icon arrangement on the left hand side is maintained in the region specified by the icon on the right hand side. Formally, it denotes the interval $I(\theta)$, where *theta* is expressed as *"there exists a codon with attributes p"*, with $p = (region = apical) \wedge ((straining = contractive \wedge bending = soft) \vee (\neg(straining = stasis) \wedge bending = medium))$.

Lines are used to denote the lasting time intervals in which events and event compositions occur. To this end, lines are drawn on the screen and annotated with the iconic representation of the event composition. Each line is also annotated with a special icon denoting the anatomic region in which the event composition occurs. As a particular case, lines can be annotated with any of two icons representing the two reference phases of systolic contraction and diastolic expansion of the heart beating cycle (see Fig.9). The mutual positioning of event lines on the screen defines the temporal ordering among the lasting intervals of distinctive events. To permit the expression of *don't care* conditions in the interpretation of this mutual positioning, each line is associated with one or more colors, and the mutual position between intervals which do not share any common color is ignored in the interpretation of the visual arrangement.

Once lines and icons have been placed on the screen, the system interprets their visual arrangement and translates it into a formula of the querying language described in Sect.3. This occurs through two distinct phases. First, the mutual positioning of event intervals sharing one or more grouping colors are analyzed and classified into one of the 13 possible mutual ordering relations of Fig.7. Afterwards, icon compositions associated with

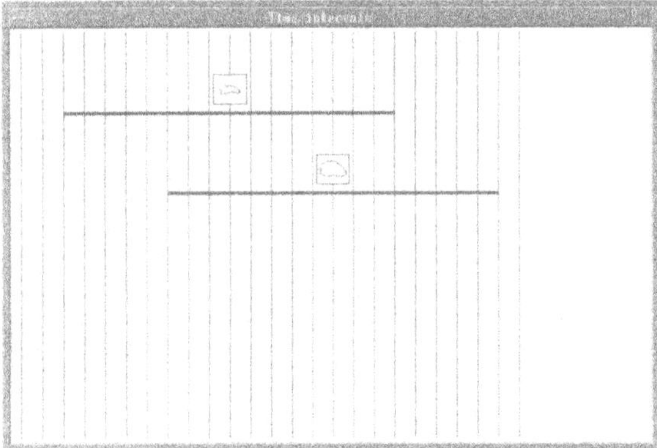

Figure 9 Two lines representing the lasting intervals of the systolic (upper line) and diastolic (lower line) physiologic phases of the heart beating period.

each interval are parsed and translated into interval formulae expressed according to the language of Sect.3.

The model-checking algorithm and the parser work together interactively. For each reduced grammar level corresponding actions are produced for matching with possible intervals coming from the symbolic representations related to image sequence stored in the database, and standing as candidates.

After decoding the textual sentence, the intervals which meet the temporal relationships recognized by the first visual parser are selected. These formulae are then checked against the concrete descriptions of the sequences in the database, and matching reports are retrieved and displayed on the screen.

4.2 An Example

For the sake of concreteness, let us consider an operation example in which the system is used to retrieve reports characterized by an outward motion in the apical region during the systolic phase. This is a pathologic behavior in that, during the systolic phase, the entire wall contour should exhibit a contractive motion.

Fig.10 reports the visual query capturing the phenomenon of interest. The upper line is annotated with the systolic icon thus denoting the time interval in which the heart should expand. The lower line is annotated with two icons representing an expansive strain (in the left hand side of the line) and the apical region (in the right hand side of the line) so as to represent a time interval in which part of the apical region exhibits an expansive motion. The two lines are associated with a common color so as to make significant the mutual positioning of the two intervals.

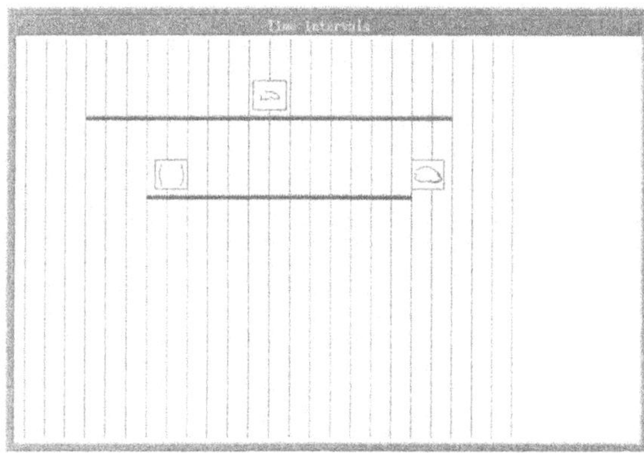

Figure 10 A visual query expressing a contractive strain in the apical region during the systolic phase: $I(\theta_1) \sim_5 I(\theta_2)$ with $\theta_1 =$ *systolic phase* and $\theta_2 =$ "*there exists a codon with attributes p* with $p = (region = apical) \wedge (strain = expansive)$.

The system interpretation of the overall arrangement produces a query statement which causes the retrieval of the reports characterized by a time interval which is contained in the systolic phase and which exhibits a contractive motion in the apical region. When retrieval is completed, reference names of retrieved reports are listed on a menu which permits selection and display on the screen of reports of specific interest for the user (Fig.11).

A more selective retrieval is obtained if the query is refined by the addition of further conditions. In particular, Fig.12 shows the query which is obtained adding the request for an inward motion in the apical region during the diastolic phase. Two further lines are added (in the bottom part of the screen), one standing for the diastolic phase and the other for the lasting interval of the contractive motion in the apical region. These two lines are associated with a common color different from that associating the previous two lines. As a result, the system interpretation will take care of the ordering between the two new lines and between the two old lines, but it will not consider the ordering between new and old lines. Again, after the interpretation of the query, retrieval is carried out and matching reports are listed and displayed on the screen. Of course, retrieved sequences are a subset of the ones found by the previous query (Fig.13).

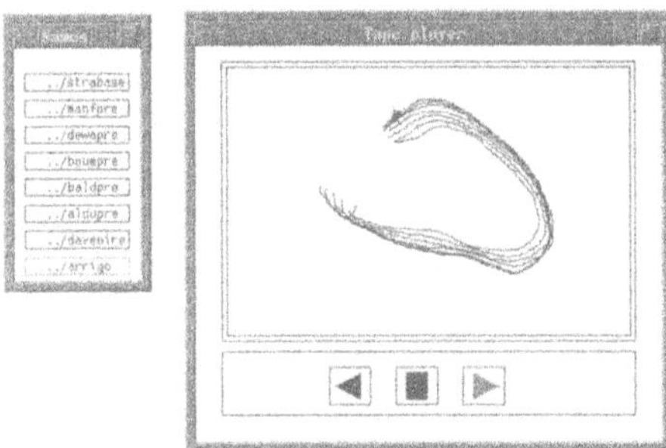

Figure 11 The list of retrieved reports (left hand side menu) permits selection and display (right hand side window) frame by frame of reports of interest.

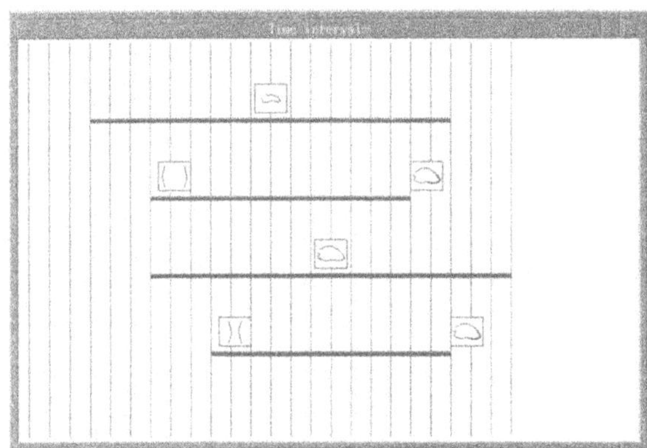

Figure 12 A refinement of the query of Fig.10. In this case, the query expresses the existence an expansive strain in the apical region during the systolic phase and a contractive strain, again in the apical region, during the diastolic phase. The textual expression of the statement is: $(I(\theta_1) \sim_5 I(\theta_2)) \wedge (I(\theta_3) \sim_5 I(\theta_4))$, where θ_1 and θ_2 are defined as in Fig.10, while θ_3 = *diastolic phase* and θ_4 = "*there exists a codon with attributes p* with $p = (\textit{region} = \textit{apical}) \wedge (\textit{strain} = \textit{contractive})$.

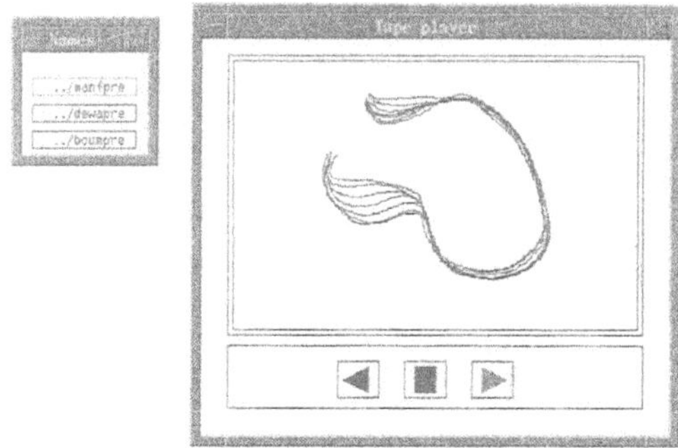

Figure 13 Retrieval result for the example query of Fig.12.

5 CONCLUSIONS

Two original languages for the concrete description and the abstract specification of the contents of images representing time-varying curves have been presented. The concrete description language supports the symbolic representation of the spatial and temporal evolution of a curve, while the abstract specification language permits the expression of properties characterizing a possible multiplicity of curves. The two languages are related by the fact that they permit abstract specifications to be automatically checked against concrete descriptions.

This automatic checking has been exploited in a retrieval system supporting visual iconic querying by contents from databases of biomedical image sequences representing cineangiographic reports. In this system, the user is allowed to compose visual queries describing distinctive features of visual data to be retrieved through the use of a two-level iconic interface. At the first level, the user arranges iconic indexes to express static geometric features occurring in the individual images of reports to be retrieved. At the second level, the temporal ordering with which static features occur is expressed by associating static indexes with time lines representing their lasting intervals.

While the treatment of this paper has been focused on the specific case of medical reports handled by the system, the use of two dual languages for the concrete description of stored data and the abstract specification of content queries can be extended to a large variety of applications concerned with retrieval by contents of image sequences containing non-rigid, time-varying curves.

REFERENCES

Allen,J.F. (1983) "Maintaining Knowledge about Temporal Intervals," *Comunications of the ACM*, Vol.26, n.11, Nov. 1983.

Arndt,T, Chang,S.K. (1989) "Image Sequence Compression by Iconic Indexing", *IEEE VL '89 Workshop on Visual Languages*, Roma, Italy, Sept.1989.

Baroni,M., Barletta,G. (1992) "Digital Curvature Estimation for Left Ventricular Shape Analysis," *Image and Vision Computing*, 1992.

Binaghi,E. (1992) "Indexing and Fuzzy Logic-Based Retrieval of Color Images," in *IFIP Transactions A-7, Visual Database Systems II*, Knuth, Wegner (Eds.), Elsevier Pub. 1992.

Chang,S.K. Liu,S.H. (1984) "Picture indexing and Abstraction Techniques for Pictorial Databases", *IEEE Transactions on Pattern Analysis and Machine Intelligence*, Vol.6, No.4, July 1984.

Chang,S.K., Shi,Q.Y., Yan,C.W. (1987) "Iconic Indexing by 2-D Strings", *IEEE Transactions on Pattern Analysis and Machine Intelligence*, Vol.9, No.3, July 1987.

Chang,S.K., Hou,T.Y. Hsu,A. (1992) "Smart Image Design for Large Image Databases", *Journal of Visual Languages and Computing*, Vol.3, No.4, Dec.1992

Congiu,G. (1994) "Rappresentazione e Ricerca Visuale di Sequenze di Immagini Cardiologiche (In Italian)," *Doctoral Thesis*, A.Del Bimbo (Adv.) Dept.Sistemi e Informatica, Univ. Firenze, Italy, July, 1994.

Davis,A. (1993) "Media Streams, an Iconic Visual language for Video Annotation," *Telektronik*, No.4, 1993, (also appeared in reduced version in *Proc.IEEE VL'93 Workshop on Visual Languages*, Bergen, Norway, Aug.1993).

Del Bimbo,A., Vicario,E., Zingoni,D. (1996) "Symbolic Representation and Visual Querying of Image Sequences Usinral Logic," accepted for publication in the *IEEE Transactions on Knowledge and Data Engineering*.

Del Bimbo,A., Campanai,M., Nesi,P. (1993) "A Three-Dimensional Iconic Environment for Image Database Querying," *IEEE Transactions on Software Engineering*, Vol.19, No.10, Oct.1993.

Del Bimbo,A., Pala,P., Santini,S. (1994) "Visual Image Retrieval by Elastic Deformation of Object Shapes," *Proc. IEEE VL'94, Int.Symp. on Visual Languages*, St.Louis, MI, Oct.1994.

Haber,R.N. (1983) "Stimulus Information and Processing Mechanism in Visual Perception," in *Human and Machine Vision*, Academic Press, New York, 1983.

Hirata,K. Kato,T. (1992) "Query by Visual Example: Content-Based Image Retrieval," In *Advances in Database Technology - EDBT'92*, A.Pirotte, C.Delobel, G.Gottlob (Eds.), Lecture Notes on Computer Science, Vol.580, Springer Verlag, Berlin, 1992.

Kutty,G., Dillon,L.K., Moser,L.E., Melliar-Smith,P.M., Ramakrisnha,Y.S. (1993) "Visual Tools for Temporal Reasoning," in *Proc. IEEE VL'93, Int.Symp. on Visual Languages*, 1993.

Lee,S. Shan,M.K., Yang,W.P. (1989) "Similarity Retrieval of Iconic Image Database," *Pattern Recognition*, Vol.22, No.6, 1989.

Leyton,M. (1982) "Shape and Casual History," in *Visual Form*, Plenum Press, 1982.

Marshall,S. (1989) "Review of Shape Coding Techniques," in *Image and Vision Computing*, Nov.1989.

Nagasaka,A., Tanaka,Y. (1992) "Automatic Video Indexing and Full Video Search for Object Appearances," in *IFIP Transactions, Visual Database Systems II*, Knuth, Wegner (Eds.), Elsevier Pub. 1992.

Niblack,W. et alii, (1993) "The QBIC Project: Querying Images by Content Using Color, Texture and Shape," Res.Report 9203, IBM Res.Div. Almaden Res.Center, Feb.1993.

Palmer,S.E. (1983) "The Psychology of Perceptual Organization,: a Transformational Approach," in *Human and Machine Vision*, Academic Press, New York, 1983.

Richards,W., D.D.Hoffman,D.D. (1984) "Codon Constraints on Closed 2D Shapes," in *Computer Vision II*, Natural Computation Group, M.I.T., Cambridge, 1984.

Roussopoulos,N., Faloutsos,C., Sellis,T. (1988) "An Efficient Pictorial Database System for PSQL", *IEEE Transactions on Software Engineering*, Vol.14, No.5, May 1988.

Swain,M.J., Gallard,D.H, (1991) "Color Indexing," *Int.Journal of Computer Vision*, Vol.7, No.1, 1991.

Tanimoto,S.L. (1976) "An Iconic/Symbolic Data Structuring Scheme," in *Pattern Recognition and Artificial Intelligence*, C.H.Chen (Ed.), New York Academic, 1976.

Walter,I.M., Sturm,R., Lockemann,P.C. (1992) "A Semantic Network Based Deductive Database System for Image Sequence Evaluation," in *IFIP Transactions, Visual Database Systems II*, Knuth, Wegner (Eds.), Elsevier Pub. 1992.

6 BIOGRAPHIES

Gianfranco Congiu was born in Firenze, Italy, in 1967. He received the doctoral degree in Electronics Engineering from the Università di Firenze, Italy, in 1994. He is currently with the Department of Sistemi e Informatica of the Università di Firenze with a grant funded by Bassilichi S.P.A., Florence, Italy. His research activities are in the field of image representation, indexing retrieval with a specific interest in databases of dynamic images.

Alberto Del Bimbo was born in Firenze, Italy, in 1952. He received the doctoral degree in Electronics Engineering from the Università di Firenze, Italy, in 1977. He was with IBM ITALIA from 1978 to 1988. He is Full Professor of Computer Systems at the University of Brescia and the University of Florence, Italy. Dr. Del Bimbo is a member of IEEE and of the International Association for Pattern Recognition (IAPR). He is in the board of the IAPR Technical Committee n. 8 (Industrial Applications) and the Vice-President of the IAPR Italian Chapter. He presently serves as Associate Editor of *Pattern Recognition* Journal and of the *Journal of Visual Languages and Computing.* His research interests and activities are in the field of image analysis, image databases, visual languages and virtual reality.

Enrico Vicario was born in Firenze, Italy, in 1965. He received the doctoral degree in Electronics Engineering and the Ph.D. in Computer Science from the Università di Firenze, Italy, in 1990 and 1994. He is currently Researcher with the Department of Sistemi e Informatica of the Università di Firenze. His research activities are in the field of software engineering, with a particular interest in visual formalisms, specification languages and validation techniques for time-dependent systems.

PANEL

11

Data models, visual representations, metaphors: how to solve the puzzle?

T. Catarci[☆], M.F. Costabile[♣], I.F. Cruz[♥], Y. Ioannidis[♦], and B. Shneiderman[♠]

[☆]*Dipartimento di Informatica e Sistemistica, Università degli Studi di Roma "La Sapienza"*
Via Salaria, 113 - 00198 Roma, Italy, e-mail: catarci@infokit.dis.uniroma1.it

[♣]*Dipartimento di Informatica, Università di Bari*
Via Orabona 4, 70126 Bari, Italy, e-mail: fcosta@ercole.ba.cnr.it

[♦]*Computer Sciences Departmen, University of Wisconsin*
1210 W. Dayton St., Madison, WI 53706, USA, e-mail: yannis@cs.wisc.edu

[♥]*Department of Electrical Engineering and Computer Science, Tufts University*
Medford, 02155 MA, USA, e-mail: isabel@cs.tufts.edu

[♠]*Department of Computer Science, University of Maryland*
College Park, MD 20742, USA, e-mail: ben@cs.umd.edu

Abstract

The need of a precise definition of the concepts of metaphor and visual representation in the database realm was widely discussed in the VDB3 Panel. Also, the issue of singling out the relationships existing between the above two concepts and the data model was addressed. An introduction by the panel organizer together with a short position statement by each panelist are reported in the following document.

Keywords

Data model, metaphor, visual representation.

1 INTRODUCTION

The need of a better interaction between users and database systems has been widely recognized and discussed. It is generally accepted that the quality of the interaction mainly depends on the interface characteristics. Thus, the crucial point is to develop good interfaces, where the word "good" is to be interpreted from the user's perspective. Now, the point is to understand which parts of this interaction belong to the interface and which to the database system.

A database is typically defined in terms of a data model, but the abstract concepts of such a model need to be expressed through a representation in order to be perceived by a user. Any representation of a model aims at stressing some basic features of the model itself, and obviously a many-to-many correspondence exists between data models and representations (visual or not). The representation should be part of the interface, while the data model should be part of the database system. On the other hand, there are data models, the so called semantic models, which convey more information to the user by offering richer mechanisms in order to structure the data contained in the database and to show more relationships among them. Also, a representation can be effective, but cannot add semantics to the data. Finally, in addition to data models and representations, a well known component of any interface to any system is the metaphor. Unfortunately, the experience in the other computer science areas does not help us very much. Indeed, most of the famous interface metaphors have been introduced for interaction purposes, i.e., in order to explain some new kind of task through well known actions performed in familiar environment. A typical example is the desktop metaphor. On the contrary, the metaphors we need in developing interfaces to database systems have to deal firstly with the problem of representing the database content, then with the interaction mechanisms.

As a consequence of the above, the basis for the design and construction of database interfaces is still largely ad hoc. We do not yet know:

- how data models, representations, and metaphors interact;
- how to model metaphors and (visual) representations formally,
- how to design metaphors and representations with confidence in both their usability and effectiveness and their adequacy to the underlying data models.
- how to construct systems to incorporate metaphors and representations efficiently and with adequate modularity to support modification and reuse.

Nevertheless, we hope this panel will give some hints on these open questions.

2 EXPLOITING METAPHORS IN DATABASE INTERFACES (by Maria F. Costabile)

Many authors agree that the metaphor is a tool for creative interface design that makes information easy to find and use, but little research on systematic use of metaphor in interface design exists. This is also true for database interfaces, even if examples of use of metaphors in this field already exist in the literature. Often, metaphors are exploited to help representing the intensional part of the database, i.e. the data schema; in such cases, the metaphor mediates between the data model and the user. However, the user might have a certain mental model of the reality of interest, which is not necessarily reflected by the metaphor used for showing the data model.

A different choice relies on avoiding the visualization of any data model. One possibility is to offer to the user a scenario where the information contained in the database is pictorially represented as a virtual reality, so that the user is no longer aware of a presence of a structured database, but he or she is interacting as in the real world. In this case there is a metaphor from the designer point of view, to bring out of the database (which is not the reality but an internal representation of it) the reality that was meant to be represented when constructing the database.

The very problem I like to point out is that, in many cases, database designers have exploited metaphors that are easily understandable by scientists, such as the table or the node-and-arc metaphor. Unfortunately, the literal meaning of such metaphors is still too far from most non-expert users. The power of the metaphor is to understand something (the target concept) in terms of something else (the source concept), therefore it is essential to know the source domain at a certain level of detail in order to benefit from the metaphor. Showing on the screen an E-R diagram (even if powerful interaction mechanisms to focus on some portion of the diagram, to scroll a large diagram, etc. are provided) does not really help many users, who are not familiar at all with such a model. If we want information systems to become as easy to manipulate as automobiles are easy to drive, or washing machine are easy to operate, we have to invent more effective metaphors that are closer to the users. This can be achieved by looking carefully at the users, the task they perform, their habits, their preferences, the things they are familiar with. Once potential metaphors have been identified, they need to be tested with users to check if they support the users' understanding of the system. Metaphors originating from a source domain that is not easily understandable by the users must be discarded. Therefore, user observation and testing are key elements for an effective metaphorical design.

3 TAILORABLE VISUALIZATIONS AND META-QUERYING (by Isabel F. Cruz)

New database applications, such as multimedia and scientific applications generate and use large amounts of textual and quantitative data that need to be comprehended by specialists in the different application domains. One possible way to help the users is to display the data in a visual form. For example, if the data is quantitative, plot charts or bar charts can provide a quick overview of the data. Only rarely do users know in advance exactly what data they want to visualize, or how they want to visualize the data. One key issue is to allow for the user to select and process just the relevant data. Powerful database query languages are therefore needed. Another key issue is related to the visualization of the data. We argue that the user should not be limited to a single visual representation (or even to a pre-specified set of visual representations of the data).

Previous research in visual query languages has focused on pre-defined visual representations of data and queries, which are suitable for specific applications, but difficult to extend and generalize. The queries themselves, although visually expressed, conform to the same pre-defined visual representations.

We have been investigating a system based on a meta-query language, DOODLE, which supports a variety of powerful visual query languages that are user-defined. The visual query languages we are investigating allow the user to give a high-level visual specification of the relevant subset of the database. Using an interactive approach, the user can then further specify new visual queries, causing the display to change accordingly, and to possibly evolve from one representation (e.g., graph) to another representation (e.g., temporal chart). We are using DOODLE in software engineering and graph drawing applications.

In the context of DOODLE, many issues pertaining to the choice of visual representations arise. We have been investigating the expressiveness of visual representations, e.g., the adequacy of a visual representation to encode a given set of database facts. With DOODLE it is also possible to express transformations between visual representations. This raises the issue whether two visual languages have the same "capacity" to express data. We are laying a formal framework that addresses these questions.

4 DESK-TOP SCHEMA MANAGERS (by Yannis Ioannidis)

As database schemas increase in complexity and the user base of database systems widens, a pressing need emerges for the development of improved techniques and tools for schema management, and primarily schema visualization. Although existing database systems and prototypes support graphical user interfaces where schemas are represented visually, most of them only provide a single hard-wired such representation, without flexibility.

What we need are Desk-Top Schema Managers that are external to the database system proper, and consist of generic code - not tied to any particular data model or visualization style. Such a system may be built following a framework that, analogously to database models and schemas, introduces visual models (formal visual representation styles) and visual schemas (actual visualizations, instantiations of the visual model). A visual metaphor can then be defined as a mapping from (the elements of) a visual model to (the elements of) a data model. Through this mapping, one is able to assign meaning to a visualization (visual schema) in terms of the underlying data schema. Moreover, both the visual and data models and the visual metaphor may be specified declaratively, so that schema visualization is not realized through code that is hardwired in a system, but is established externally in an extensible way. Thus, one may specify different visual models and corresponding visual metaphors to a data model, making it possible to visualize schemas of a given data model in different ways. Another benefit of the formalism is that one can enhance schema visualizations with user-specific annotations and aesthetic preferences, information that is unrelated to the underlying schema.

Desk-Top Schema Managers built based on the above methodology will be able to read external specifications of data and visual models and metaphors and essentially `become' managers of schemas in these models interpreted by these metaphors. Users will then be able to create, modify, and explore database schemas using any visual representation they find most appropriate. The behavior of the system will also be determined by the characteristics of the input models and metaphors, in the sense that model/metaphor-specific buttons, menu entries, etc. will only be constructed at run-time.

Opossum is a Desk-Top Schema Manager that is being developed at the Univ. of Wisconsin following the above visualization formalism. It offers the spectrum of functionality mentioned above and is currently being used by scientists in Soil Sciences, Genetics, and Biochemistry to design schemas in various models, using a variety of visual models and metaphors.

5 A NEW INTERFACE GENERATION (by Ben Shneiderman)

Our recent projects have spawned a new conception of the future of computing. These new ideas allow designers to couple the remarkable human ability at visual information processing with the increasing capacity of computers to display high resolution dynamic color images, in order to ideate a new generation of graphical and direct manipulation user interfaces.

As a first step in this direction, we have developed Visual Information Seeking principles (VIS) to support fact-finding and browsing by novices and experts. We begin with an overview, and then allow users to filter out unwanted data, zoom in on relevant items, and then get details-on-demand. The interface components are tightly coupled to give users appropriate feedback, facilitate query refinement, and prevent errors. Our contributions include dynamic query methods with continuous visual presentation of results as the query is changed (using sliders, buttons, maps), color-coded 2-D space-filling treemaps to show hierarchies in a single display (hundreds of directories and more than 3000 files can be seen at once), and the starfield display (a zoom-able 2-D display with thousands of selectable points of light).

Our work is also concentrated on the Visual Information Explorer (VIZER), a multi-year project to develop advanced software and user interfaces that will allow novice and expert users to visually explore very large databases, spreadsheets, geographic information, temporal sales data, financial reports, and medical information. VIZER's components include the filter/flow representation of boolean operations, dynamic queries that allow small changes in input variables to be shown immediately by changes in a 2- or 3- dimensional display, tree-maps that allow a space filling representation of trees with 3-5000 nodes on the screen at once, and remote visualization that allows users to browse through telepresence. Our goals include the construction of an integrated tool to support exploration, retrieval, gathering, traversal, and capture with goal-directed task-level actions for saving, printing, and sending text, numeric data, images, sound, and other structured information through highspeed distributed networks.

6 AUTHORS' BIOGRAPHIES

Tiziana Catarci

Tiziana Catarci was graduated in Electrical Engineering from the University of Rome "La Sapienza," Rome, Italy, on 1987. She received the Ph.D. degree in Computer Science from the University of Roma "La Sapienza", 1992.

Since 1987 she teaches courses in Computer Science at Italian universities. From 1987 to 1990 she was research assistant at the University of Roma "La Sapienza", where she is now an assistant professor.

Her main research interest is in visual formalisms for database representation and querying. Moreover, she worked in semantic database modeling, cooperative information systems, statistical databases, methodologies for database design. Dr. Catarci has published over sixty papers on the above topics, and written or edited four books.

She is member of the Association for Computing Machinery (ACM), and the Institute of Electrical and Electronics Engineers (IEEE).

Maria F. Costabile

Maria Francesca Costabile received her doctoral degree in Mathematics at the Universita' della Calabria in 1977. From 1989 she is associate professor at the Department of Computer Science of the University of Bari, Italy.

From 1978 to 1988 she worked at the Dipartimento di Matematica, Universita' della Calabria, Italy, first as postdoctoral fellow and later as university researcher. She has been visiting scientist in several foreign universities. Her research activity was initially in image analysis and computer vision. Her current interests include visual languages, visual interfaces, visual languages for querying databases, formal methods for human-computer interaction, user models. She has published several papers on the above topics.

She is member of the Association for Computing Machinery (ACM), the Institute of Electrical and Electronics Engineers (IEEE) and the Italian Chapter of the International Association on Pattern Recognition (IAPR).

Isabel F. Cruz

Isabel F. Cruz is an Assistant Professor in the Department of Electrical Engineering and Computer Science at Tufts University. Previously she was a Postdoc in the Department of Computer Science at Brown University. She received her Ph.D. in Computer Science from the University of Toronto in 1993.

Her research interests include databases, user interfaces, multimedia, graph drawing, visual languages, software visualization, and constraint programming.

Currently she is the co-guest editor of the special issue of the Journal of Visual Languages and Computing on Graph Visualization, the co-chair of the 1995 International Workshop on Constraints for Graphics and Visualization and of the 1995 ACM Workshop on Effective Abstractions in Multimedia, and in the program committees of several international conferences. Her research has been funded by the Government of Canada, NATO, and ARPA.

Yannis Ioannidis

Yannis Ioannidis received his Diploma degree in electrical engineering from the National Technical University of Athens, Greece, in 1982, the M.Sc. degree in applied mathematics (computer science) from Harvard University in 1983, and the Ph.D. degree in computer science from the University of California at Berkeley in 1986.

Since then, he has been on the faculty of the Computer Sciences Department of the University of Wisconsin at Madison, where he is currently an Associate Professor.

His research interests include query optimization, scientific databases, intelligent/graphical user interfaces, knowledge bases, and heterogeneous databases. He has written over 35 articles on these topics and is a co-author of a patent that is pending.

Dr. Ioannidis is the recipient of an NSF Presidential Young Investigator (PYI) award for 1991-1996. He is currently an Associate Editor of several journals and has been a member of the program committees of over twenty conferences. Dr. Ioannidis is a member of the IEEE Computer Society, the Association of Computing Machinery, and the Technical Chamber of Greece.

Ben Shneiderman

Ben Shneiderman is a Professor in the Department of Computer Science, Head of the Human-Computer Interaction Laboratory, and Member of the Institute for Systems Research, all at the University of Maryland at College Park. He has taught previously at the State University of New York and at Indiana University. He regularly teaches popular short courses and organizes an annual satellite television presentation on "User Interface Strategies" since 1987.

Dr. Shneiderman is the author of several books on HCI, in addition he edited three technical books, published more than 170 technical papers and book chapters.

Ben Shneiderman has been on the Editorial Advisory Boards of nine journals including the newly formed ACM Transactions on Computer-Human Interaction and the ACM Interactions. He edits the Ablex Publishing Co. book series on "Human-Computer Interaction." He has consulted and lectured for many organizations including Apple, AT&T, Citicorp, GE, Honeywell, IBM, Intel, Library of Congress, NASA, NCR, and university research groups.

PART FOUR

Visualization

12

The Design of 3D Metaphors for Database Visualisation

J. Boyle [1] *and P.M.D. Gray* [2]
Robert Gordon University [1], *Aberdeen University.* [2]

Schoolhill, Aberdeen AB9 1FR, UK.
tel: +44 (0)1224262000
fax: +44 (0)1224 262090
email: john@csd.abdn.ac.uk

Abstract

This paper discusses the designs behind Amaze, a graphical user interface to an object oriented database system. Amaze uses three dimensional graphics to visualise both query construction and result representation. The designs behind Amaze are introduced, and the visualisations of a prototype implementation are shown. It is felt that just as word processors have changed how people interact with document processing, so to could database visualisation alter how people interact with database systems.

Keywords

Database Visualisation, 3D Graphics, Interface Design

1 INTRODUCTION

Today user interface design for database systems is on the threshold of a paridigm shift. Designs are moving from a desktop menu based query retrieve style towards a means for exploration and visualisation of the database. The query process is thought of as being more than just a simple question and answer session. The focus is moving towards allowing users to interact with the data in a more intuitive way.

This paper outlines the designs and prototype implementation of Amaze. Amaze is a graphical user interface for an object oriented database. This GUI uses three dimensional graphics to aid the user in visualising both query construction and result representation.

It was felt by the developers that the standard desktop metaphor does not have the visualisation power required for displaying the quantity and diversity of abstract information that is needed for database visualisation. Extending the WIMP system, by embedding high performance animated three dimensional graphics, could give the enhanced expressive power whilst still keeping the familiarity and use of a menu driven environment.

2 BACKGROUND

Interfaces to Databases

Interfaces to database have developed over the last twenty years in a number of directions. However there is still no approach to a standard look and feel. QBE (Zloof 1992) was developed in 1975 for use on a character based terminal (vt100), and has since been adopted by a number of relational database manufactors as the basis of their interface designs (Access, dBase, FoxPro, Paradox, Superbase). About the same time as QBE was being developed Cupid (Macdonald & Stonebraker 1975} was proposed (a more visual approach to querying a database). These two interfaces offered a different high level approach for querying databases (Figure 1. QBE was the more powerful method, which later developed to allow updates and other data manipulation methods to be incorporated.

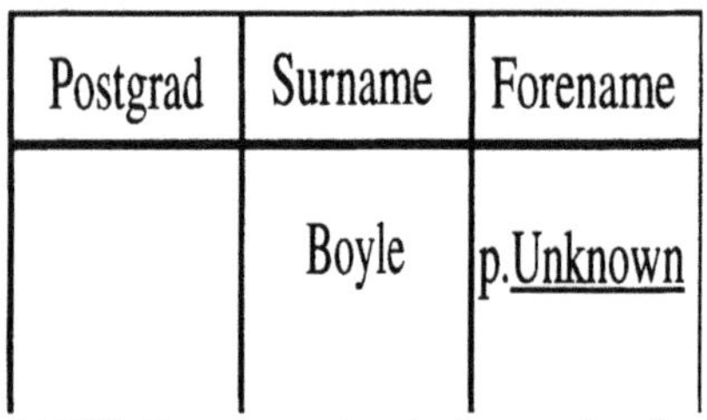

(a) QBE allows the user to enter the query by using a table as a template for the visual query

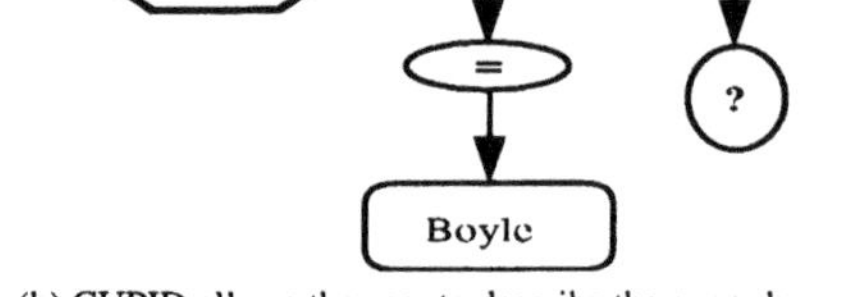

(b) CUPID allows the user to describe the query by using a simple diagram

Figure 1 Showing both the QBE and the CUPID representation for the query get the first names of any students who have the surname Boyle.

However QBE was designed before bitmap displays became prevalent and so the ideas behind its design naturally reflect this. With bitmap displays a new generation of user interfaces was born, these were able to exploit the new technology. Designs for interfaces to database systems soon made use of direct manipulation techniques e.g.Wong (1982), Fogg (1984).

Since then two families of interface to database have developed, those that use the *table* as the basis of their interaction, and those that use the *schema* (Table 1). The design methodology used largely depends on the underlying data model. The relational model lends itself more easily to the QBE/Table based visualisation, which semantic data models are more easily visualised using a schema diagram approach.

Table 1 GUIs for Database systems grouped by design style

FORM BASED	*GRAPH BASED*
QBE (Zloof, 1992)	CQL (Kari et al, 1990)
Pasta 3 (Kuntz & Melchort ,1989)	GUIDE (Wong & Kuo, 1982)
CUPID (MacDonald & Stonebraker, 1975)	OdeView (Agrawal et al, 1990)
STBE (Ozsoyoglu et al, 1989)	LID (Fogg, 1984)
SBA (Zloof & deJong, 1985)	Good (Gemis et al, 1992)
G–Whiz (Heiler & Roseenthal, 1985)	Isis (Goldman et al, 1985)
ABE (Klug, 1981)	Hy+ (Consens & Mendelzon, 1993)
Vista (Sawyer et al, 1992)	SNAP (Bryce & Hull, 1985)
OBE (Whang, 1987)	Tioga (Stonebraker et al, 1994)
GQBE (Jacobs & Walczak, 1983)	QBD (Angelaccio et al, 1990)
GRADI (Kiem and Lum, 1992)	KiView (Motro et al, 1988)

The 1990s have seen an emergence of user interfaces that use three dimensional graphics as the center of the design. This approach breaks away from the bitmap displays and offers new opportunities (in much them same way as the transition from text–terminals to bitmap displays did).

Over the last few years, people have started looking at other designs for user interfaces to databases. These designs involve using different metaphors then those found in the desktop environment. A number of information visualisers have been developed e.g. Hemmje (1993), Robertson et al (1991), Robertson et al (1993), Fairchild (1993). Recently questions have begun arising about what is the best way to portray a database to a user, and what is the best way to show a query, and how can a user see what results they have obtained – this has lead to the idea of database visualisation. The ideas have been developed further, leading to the implementation of a number of 3D interfaces to databases e.g. Mariani et al (1992), Boyle et al (1993) , Benford et al (1994), Rapleyet al (1994)

3 THE DATABASE

The interface has been developed to the P/FDM system. P/FDM (Gray etal, 1992} is an object–oriented database system based on the functional data model (FDM) (Shipman, 1981} and implemented in Prolog.

The P/FDM system (Figure 2) allows a user to access complex data through a number of user interfaces. The user doesn't need to know the mechanism through which the data is obtained or how the data is stored. The user enters the query and the results are returned.

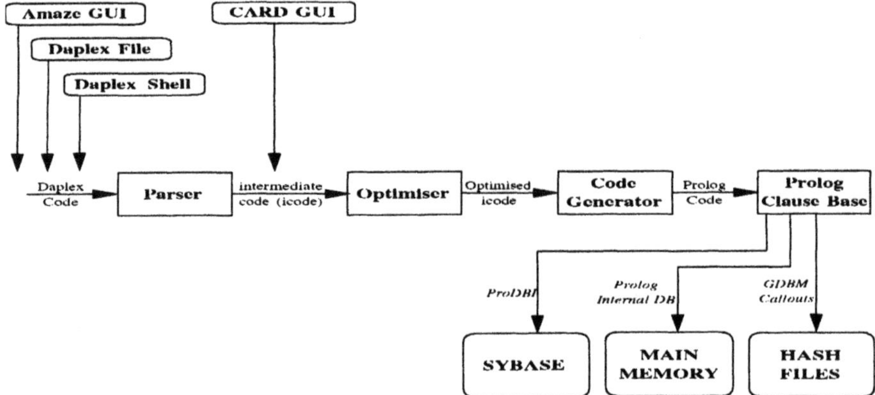

Figure 2 The Information Flow inside the P/FDM system. The user queries the database through one of the interfaces, the query is then compiled into Prolog with embedded primitive calls. The primitives access different storage schemas depending on which module the instance or function was defined.

A number of user interfaces have been developed, these vary both in complexity and ease of use:

Through the *Daplex shell* or *Daplex files* the user can write a query and then have it evaluated. At present the shell must be opened inside the Prolog environment. The user types in the query, and the system attempts to evaluate it. This offers the user a powerful mechanism through which they can query the database. Such a query language style interface is not easy to master and is difficult to use for the inexperienced. The results can only be viewed as ascii files.

The *Card* (Boyle et al, 1995) interface allows the user to graphically construct a query. The user fills in fields on *cards* to define the query, all *cards* matching other *cards* can then be viewed sequentially by the user.

The *Amaze* (Boyle et al 1993) interface allows the user to visually construct a query. This query is translated into Daplex code (actually a slightly extended version of Daplex) and then evaluated. This interface will be discussed in greater depth in the next section.

4 DESIGN OF AMAZE

The Amaze interface was developed to allow users access to the complex object–oriented database P/FDM. To do this, 3D graphics were used to visualise both the query construction and result representation processes. Both of these visualisations had to be designed and then implemented.

Query Construction

A visualisation of the conceptual schema was used as the basis of querying. The interface was designed so that the users would travel around the schema formulating the query as they moved. Each time the users arrived at an entity class they would formulate a subquery on that entity class. Each separate subquery the users formulated would be represented as a unique cube hanging beneath the relevant entity class (Figure 3).

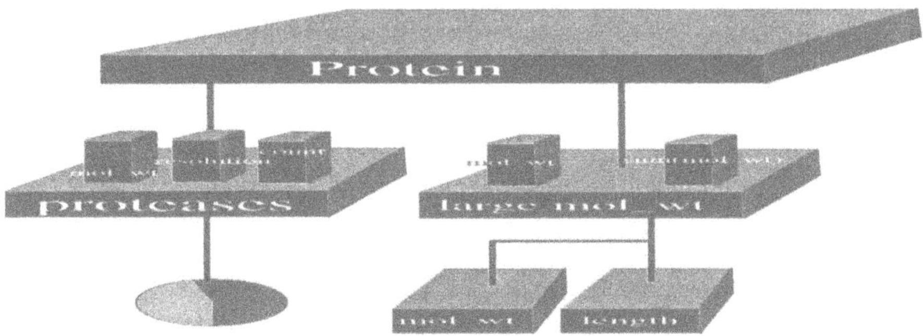

Figure 3 The design for the representation of a query on an entity class. The entity class *protein* has two subqueries attached to it: *proteases* and *large molwt.* Beneath each of the subquery box *large molwt* is the visual representation of the subquery: all instances inside the *molwt* box AND all instances inside the *length* box. Above each of the subquery boxes are those values that the users wish to know more about (either for output to file or to be used in another subquery).

Beneath each subquery would be a tree. The tree would represent the separate nodes that make up the total subquery. For example if the users wished to generate all the protein that have a high molecular weight and are of a certain length range, then the subquery *large molwt* could be generated.

The subquery would be made up of two nodes:

The molwt node. Would represent all proteins that have a molecular weight greater than 10kDa.

The length node Would represent all proteins that have a length greater than 200, but less than 10000.

The users may wish to use the results of the subquery to form the basis of another subquery (or may wish to output them to file). This would be a similar mechanism to projections in QBE (Zloof, 1975}, such projections could be represented graphically as objects on top of the relevant subquery.

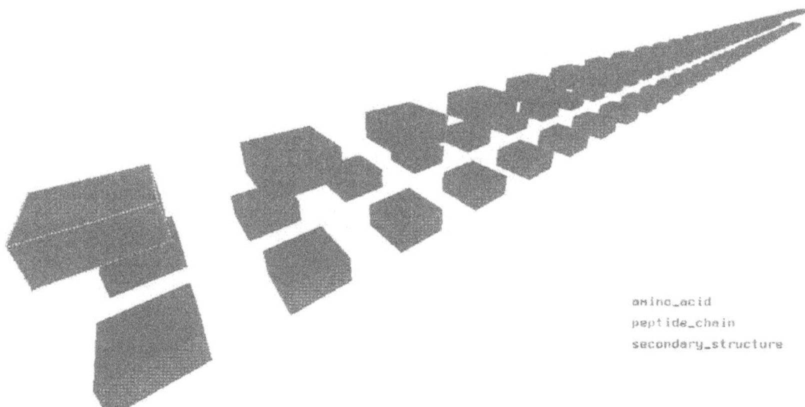

Figure 4.a: The *Maze,* each result instance is viewed as a unique cube, the cubes are clustered by entity class. A set of instances related to an instance from another class are clustered spacially It is possible to see at most two relations ahead

Figure 4.b: The *Walkthrough,* each set of results can be visualised as a corridor. The user can then walk down the corridor and can turn to see a related set of results

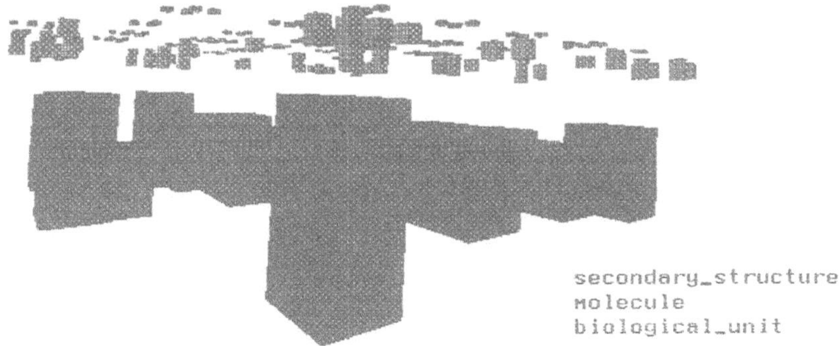

Figure 4.c: The Sea, the results are clustered by entity class, with results being further grouped into subsets to show relations between the different entity classes. The sea shows all the results – spread out in a continuous manner

Figure 4.d: The Room, the results can be placed inside a room environment. The user can either move the results around or can move their own location. To find information about a relationship the user has to walk down the corridor to the next room. the room can also be used to show other information, in this case image data is included

Result representation

Once the query has been evaluated it was felt that a mechanism for being able to visualise the results would be important.

Each resulting instance would be returned and visualised – the results would be grouped by entity class and the relationships between sets of instances would be shown spatially. This would be a generic mechanism through which the users could explore the results to find out more about the quantity of results and how they are interrelated. The users should also have the power to be able to explicitly ask for more information (in a number of visual representations) about any of these results.

Four basic designs have been implemented:

The Maze. Results are clustered by entity class. A set of instances related to an instance from another class are clustered spatially. It is possible to see at most two relations ahead (as constricted by three dimensions), if the users want to see another related set of instances they choose an instance and the other information is faded out, and the next instance set is faded in. (Figure 4.a)

Walkthrough. Each set of result instances can be visualised as a corridor. The users can then walk down the corridor and can turn to see a related set of results.(Figure 4.b)

The Sea. This is a mechanism that allows all of the results to be visualised. The *sea* of results is an expanding result set, which the users view my moving over it – as the users move into the sea more results appear. The size of each instance is proportional to the number of instances that are related to it. (Figure 4.c)

The Room. The users are placed inside a *room* with the results. The users can move their relative viewpoint in the room by selecting directional arrows that are rendered on the screen, If the users are interested in a related set of results then they can move down the corridor to the next room – placed in this room are the related set of results.(Figure 4.d)

The users can select which method they wish to see the results visualised with by selecting the corresponding button at the top of the result visualisation window. The users can change the method at any time during the querying session.

5 IMPLEMENTATION

Amaze has been implemented. While it is still being developed, it is a fully functional GUI to the underlying database. To embed the 3D graphics windows inside a menu driven system, a 'through the window' approach (as opposed to an immersion virtual reality system), with a 2D (mouse) not 6D (spaceball/bat) pointing device was used. To illustrate how Amaze can be used to answer a user's query, an example will be used.

The example query will be to the protein database (Gray et al 1990), as this is an example of a more realistic use of the database. The schema contains a description of the modelled data .

Getting all the strands in the database.
In Daplex:
for each s in sstructure
such that name(s)="S"

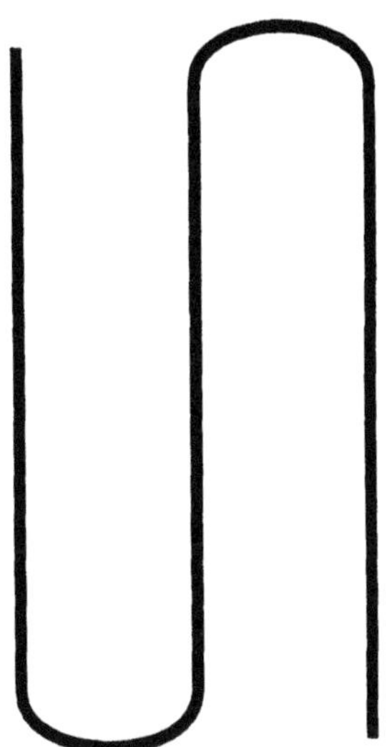

Getting all the chains that have strands in them. In Daplex:
for each s in sstructure
such that name(s)="S"
for each c in has_chain(s)

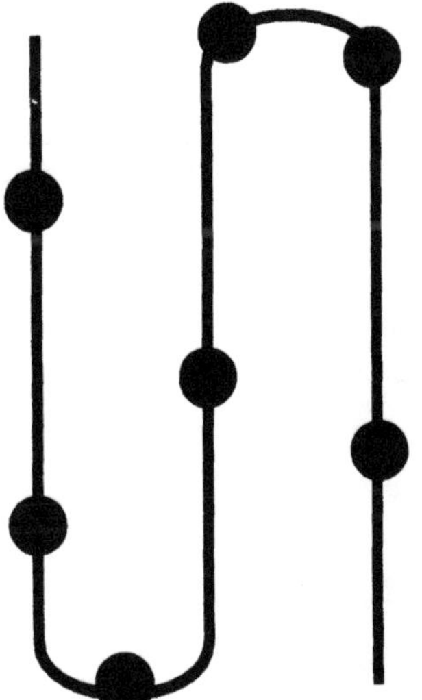

Getting all the tryptophon residues in the chain. In Daplex:
for each s in sstructure
such that name(s)="S"
for each c in has_chain(s)
for each r in res_by_name(c,"TRP")

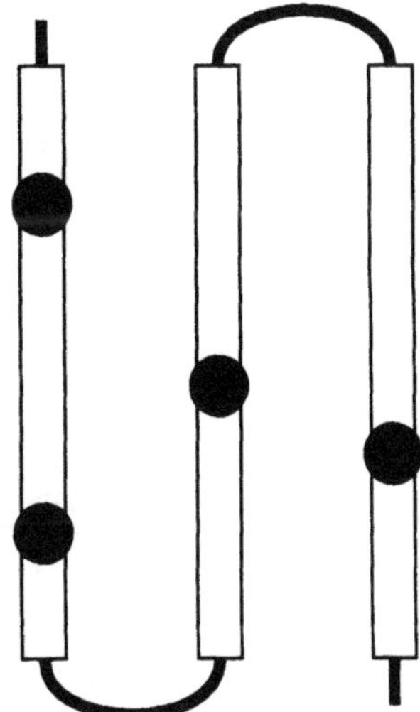

Getting all the tryptophan residues that lie in the strand regions of the chains. In Daplex:
for each s in sstructure
such that name(s)="S"
for each c in has_chain(s)
for each r in res_by_name(c,"TRP")
such that pos(r) >= start(s)
and pos(r)=< end(s)

Figure 5 Showing a possible step by step mechanism for dividing the query into subqueries

Asking the question

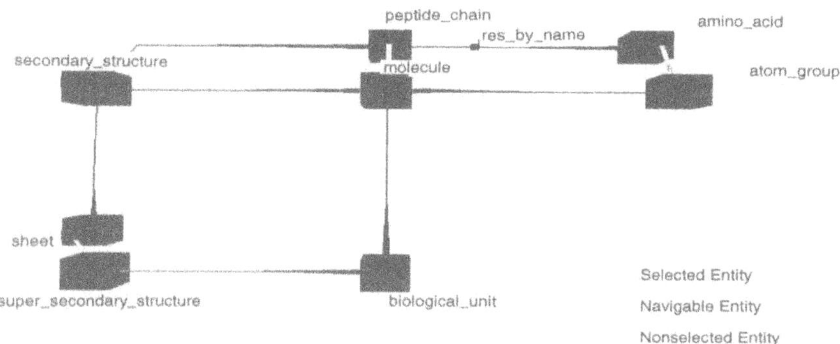

Figure 6 A subschema of the protein structure schema. A large number of the entity classes have been hidden.

If the users wish to examine all the strands of chains that contain Tryptophan (Figure 5)

The query involves navigating through three entity classes. Amaze supports the idea of subschemas – so the users doesn't have to display the whole schema if they are only interested in part of it. The subschema is defined in data files on the client side, it defines which entity classes and which scalar attributes should be shown.

Figure 6 shows a subschema of the main protein schema. The users can select the entity class *Secondary Structure* from the subschema and choose to query it. The users are presented with a dialogue box, from which they can choose to ask for all structures that have a *dssp_name* equal to "E" (extended strand) (Figure 7).

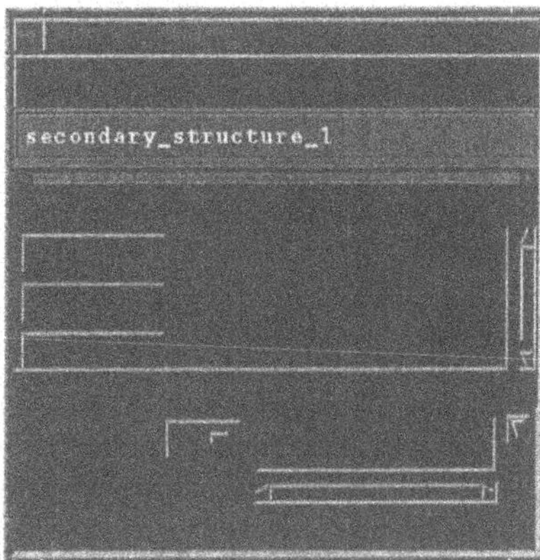

Figure 7. The user can enter the query on the entity class *secondary_structure* by filling in the dialogue box. The user has selected all the instances of *secondary_structure* that have the *dssp_name* E

The users also explicitly states that they are interested in where the strands start and stop. This is represented graphically above the subquery (Figure 8).

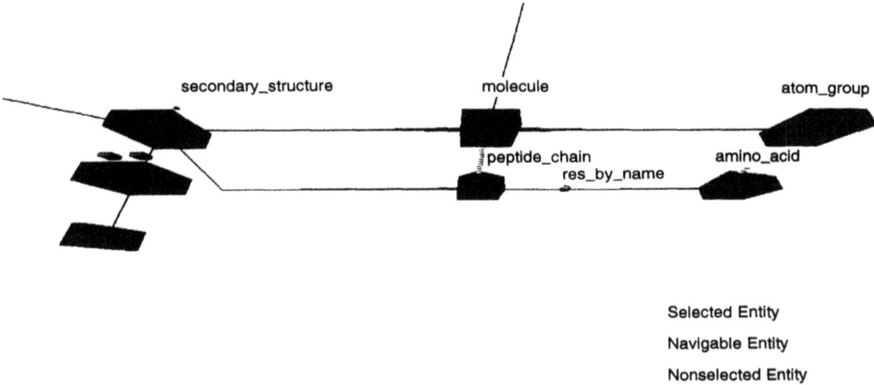

Figure 8 The subquery to *secondary_structure* is represented as a dangling cube. The users enter constraints which make up the subquery are shown as a graphical tree beneath the subquery cube (in this case all dssp_names that have a value "E". An values the users wish to export from the subquery are shown above the subquery cube – in this case the *start* and *end* values of the *secondary_structure* instances.

The users then navigate to the next entity class of interest, *peptide_chain*. selecting all of the instances of the class.

e.g.

for each s in secondary_structure such that dssp_name(s)="E"
for each c in has_chain(s)

Now the users are interested in all tryptophan amino acids. There is a two argument function between *peptide_chain* and *amino_acid*. This takes a name of an amino acid as its second argument (*res_by_name(Peptide_chain, String)*). The users can select any names for this value (if the second argument was an integer then the users could select a range of numbers).

The users then ask for all *amino_acids* that have a position inside a strand. The query (Figure 9) is shown graphically, and corresponds to the Daplex:

```
for each s in secondary_structure
  such that dssp_name(s)="E"
  for each c in has_chain(s)
        for each r in res_by_name(c,"TRP")
              such that pos(r) >= start(s) and pos(r) =< end(s)
```

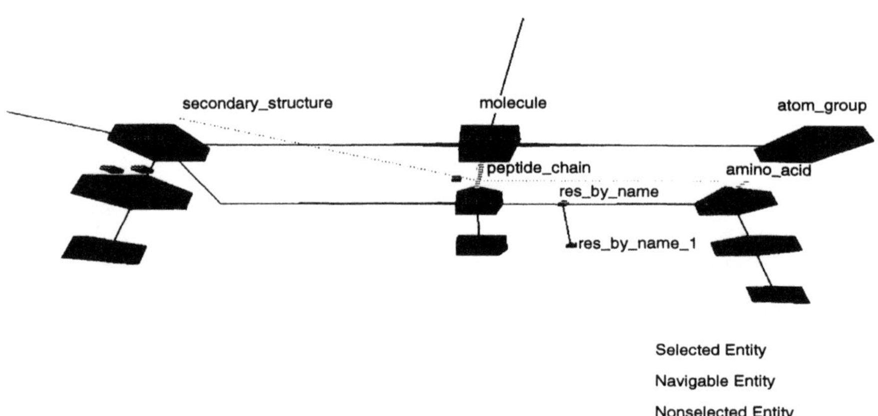

Figure 9 The whole visual representation of the query asking for 'all tryptophans that lie inside a strand'.

Viewing the results

Once the query has been formulated the users can send the query off to the database. Once the results have been returned, a visualisation of them is rendered to the screen (Figure 4). The users can then browse the results.

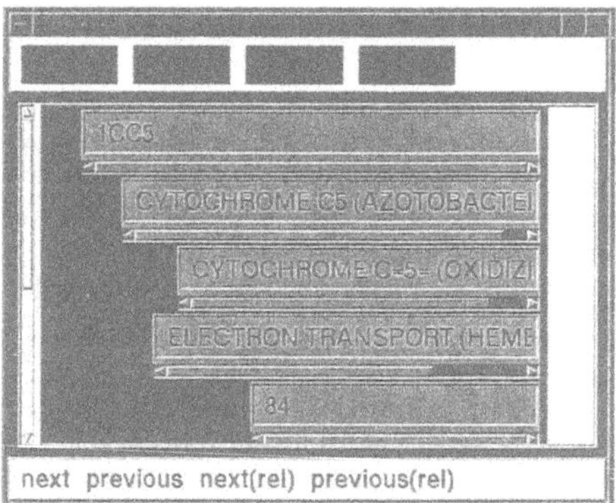

Figure 10 The browsing tool enables the users to visualise each of the token abstracts in the result maze. By using the *next* and *previous* buttons it is possible to browse the data. It is also possible to have the data visualised in alternative forms by using the top row *display action* buttons. At present the users can see the data as text (default), or for the protein data base as sequence or 3D molecule data, or for the personnel data base image data can be retrieved.}

The users can obtain more information about each result by using the browser tool (Figure 10). The browser tool has a dual purpose. It allows the users an alternative method for moving through the results (by use of the *next* and *previous* buttons) and also allows the users to visualise the results in a number of different methods (Figure 11).

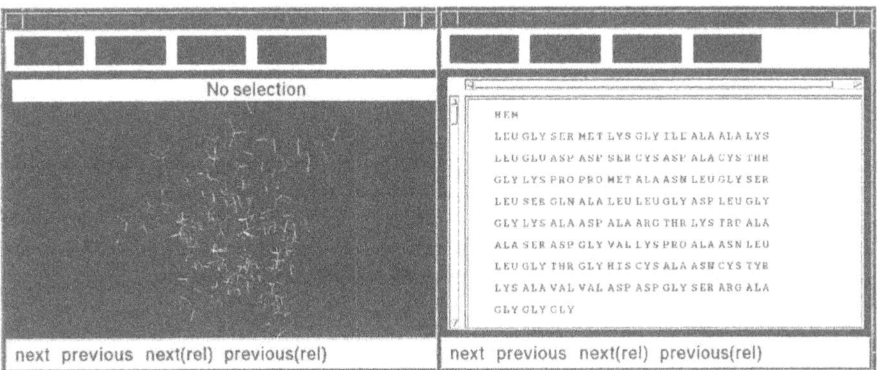

The molecule displayer allows the users to see the 3D representation of the molecule they are interested in. The displayer shows the protein Cytochrome C

The sequence displayer shows the amino acid sequence of the protein. Again the displayer shows the protein Cytochrome C

Figure 11 Amaze has been customised for biological data by defining two display actions. As well as being able to see the scalar attributes of the data, the users can also get the sequence information and the 3D protein visualisation.

6 DISCUSSION

A number of extensions are planned for Amaze – to develop it from an advanced prototype into a fully functional and reliable interface.

Improve the querying power by:

- Allow users to save and reload subqueries.
- Allow quantifiers to be used (e.g. least, most)
- Allow Daplex to be used as part of a subquery. So they can import complex Daplex (sub)queries and encorperate them visually into the main query.

Improve the result representation by:

- Allow users to actually query from inside the *result maze*. So that users can extend the query to include other entity classes. Also a mechanism for sorting the results by a scalar value will be introduced.
- Implement the other visualisations for the results.

Improve the usability by:

Distribute Amaze for evaluation/comments.

Visualise the actual query evaluation process. This has been partially done, however some mechanism to inform users approximatively how much longer the query will take to be evaluated is needed.

6 SUMMARY

The development of Amaze was driven primarily by the short comings of Card (a form based GUI for P/FDM). Amaze was designed to allow users to query large volumes of data, and to enable them to interact with the results returned from the query. The power of different visualisations was explored, both for query construction and result visualisation. Each of the two 3D visualisation have their own drawbacks, this are discussed below

6.1 The Schema

Large Schema Representation

One central question we have not attempted to provide an answer to is that of representing large schemas visually, and allowing users to navigation easily between distant entities. Amaze has a significant advantage over its two dimensional counterparts – due solely to the increased expressive power of three dimensions. More information can be portrayed to the users, and the whole schema representation can be manipulated by the users to focus in on the areas of interest.

Long distance navigation

One problem that will have to be dealt with is that of long distance navigation. Is it desirable for the users to see all the possible paths that can be navigated from one entity class to another. As the distance between the entity class grows so does the number of possible paths. Amaze can give the users all the possible paths between two entity classes – this is done by passing a meta data (Embury & Gray 1992) query to the database server which returned all the possible paths. However the most informative way to represent all the large number of possible paths has yet to be investigated.

Another approach is to have predefined paths – which the users can alter and save as they wish. These paths would be for queries the users are likely to ask at frequent intervals.

Locating the scalar attributes

With any schema representation, which shows the users the entity classes and their relationships, the users are always going to have difficulty locating the attributes they are interested in finding more information about. When the users becomes more familiar with the schema then this problem does not arise as much. A well designed schema, with well thought out classifications, will help alleviate this problem. Visualisation of the attribute values (either automatically or under some user controlled event) is also worth some investigation – as it appears feasible in the three dimensional environment.

6.2 The Result Maze

Objectcentric approach

The main application database for Amaze is one which contains protein structure information. So it is desirable to study how biochemists interact with 3D packages, however as the interfaces had been developed with flexibility and generality in mind the interfaces should be usable by all – no matter the discipline or experience. This means that the interface should not be restricted to an object centric approach (where the users stay still and the objects move), and a egocentric approach (where the users 'flys' over the data) should be investigated for the result maze. It is felt that with a large volume of data the egocentric users movement may offer a more natural mechanism for data exploration – in the very least the users should be allowed to choose between modes of movement.

Smooth animation

One of the most important aspects of 3D interface design is that of smooth unconfusing animation. The result maze does smooth the transition of 'turning the corner' by fading one dimension out and then fading the next dimension in. However this does not give a smooth feel to the transition, and is a limitation of this visual metaphor.

Better result representation

Ideas and prototypes for other ways of representing the results has been suggested previously. Building these visual representations and their behaviour still takes some time, and judging their usability will be an important next step. The visual representations of the data are still relatively primitive, and more complex representations could offer better expressive power and usability.

7 THE FUTURE OF AMAZE

Further designs will be implemented and the drawbacks of each visualisation will be considered in the next design cycle. A successor to Amaze is presently being implemented, which will address the shortcomings in the previous version, this will be developed past the prototype stage into a more robust and versatile database visualisation tool.

References

[Agrawal et al., 1990] Agrawal, R., Gehani, N., & Srinivasan, J. (1990) Ode-view: The graphical interface to ode, in *SIGMOD.*

[Angelaccio et al., 1990] Angelaccio, M., Catarci, T., & Santucci, G. (1990) *IEEE Transactions on Software Engineering 16*(10), 1150–1163.

[Benford & Mariani, 1994] Benford, S. & Mariani, J. (1994) Virtual environments for data sharing and visualisation populated information terrains in *Proceedings of Interfaces to Database Systems,* (P.Sawyer, Ed.). Springer Verlag.

[Boyle et al., 1993] Boyle, J., Fothergill, J., & Gray, P. (1993) Design of a 3d interface to a database in *Database Issues for Data Visualization,* (Lee, J. & Grinstein, G., Eds.) pp 173–183. Springer Verlag.

[Boyle et al., 1994] Boyle, J., Leishman, S., & P.Gray (1994) Wimps to 3d: design of a visual language for a database, in *Technical Report (submitted for publication).* Aberdeen University.

[Bryce & Hull, 1986] Bryce, D. & Hull, R. (1986) Snap: a graphics-based schema manager, in *Proc. Int'l Conf on Data Engineering.*

[Consens & Mendelzon, 1993] Consens, M. & Mendelzon, A. (1993) Hy+: A hygraph-based query and visualization system, in *Proceedings of the ACM-SIGMOD.*

[Cooper, 1992] (Cooper, R., Ed.) (1992) *The 1st International Workshop on Interfaces to Databases (IDS92).* Springer Verlag.

[Embury et al., 1992] Embury, S., Jiao, Z., & Gray, P. (1992) Using prolog to provide access to metadata in an object-oriented database, in *Proc. 1st Int'l Conf. on Practical Applications of Prolog.* Applied Workstations Ltd.

[Fairchild et al., 1993] Fairchild, K., Serra, L., Hern, N., Hai, L., & Leong, A. (1993) Dynamic fisheye information visualisations in *Virtual Reality Systems,* (R. Earnshaw, M. G. & H.Jones, Eds.). London Academic Press.

[Fogg, 1984] Fogg, D. (1984) Lessions from living in a database, in *SIGMOD.*

[Gemis et al., 1992] Gemis, M., Paredaens, J., & Thyssens, I. (1992) A visual database management interface based on good, In [Cooper, 1992] pp 155–175.

[Goldman et al., 1985] Goldman, K., Kanellakis, P., & Goldman, S. (1985) Isis: Interface for a semantic information system, in *SIGMOD.*

[Gray et al., 1992] Gray, P., Kulkarni, K. G., & Paton, N. W. (1992) *Object Oriented Databases - A Semantic Data Model approach,* Prentice Hall.

[Gray et al., 1990] Gray, P., Paton, N., & Fothergill, G. K. J. (1990) *Protein Engineering 3*, 235–243.

[Heiler & Roseenthal, 1985] Heiler, S. & Roseenthal, A. (1985) G-whiz, a visual interface for the functional model with recursion, in *VLDB*.

[Hemmje, 1993] Hemmje, M. (1993) Lyberworld: A 3d graphical user interface for fulltext retrieval in *Proceeding of the Workshop on Database Issues for Visualization*, (Grinstein, G., Ed.). Springer Verlag.

[Jacobs & Walczak, 1983] Jacobs, B. & Walczak, C. (1983) *IEEE Trans. on Software Engineering 9*(1), 40–57.

[Kari et al., 1990] Kari, S., Kangassalo, H., & Pösö, J. (1990) Conceptual query language - cql: A visual user interface to application databases in *Information Modelling and Knowledge Bases*, (Kangassalo, H., Ohsuga, S., & Jaakkola, H., Eds.) pp 608–623. IOS Press.

[Keim & Lum, 1992] Keim, D. & Lum, V. (1992) Gradi: A graphical database interface for a multimedia dbms, In [Cooper, 1992] pp 95–112.

[Klug, 1981] Klug, A. A. (1981) Abe: a query language for constructing aggregates by example, in *Proc. Int'l Workshop on statistical Database Management* pp 190–205.

[Kuntz & Melchort, 1989] Kuntz, M. & Melchort, R. (1989) Pasta-3's graphical query language: Direct manipulation, cooperative queries, full expressive power, in *VLDB* pp 97–105.

[MacDonald & Stonebraker, 1975] MacDonald, N. & Stonebraker, M. (1975) *ACM Transactions on Database Systems 5*, 127–131.

[Mariani & Lougher, 1992] Mariani, J. & Lougher, R. (1992) *Interacting with Computers 4*(2), 147–162.

[Motro et al., 1988] Motro, A., D'Atri, A., & Tarantino, L. (1988) Design of kiview: An object-oriented browser, in *Proc. 2nd Intl. Conf. Expert Database Systems*.

[Özsoyoğlu et al., 1989] Özsoyoğlu, G., Matos, V., & Özsoyoğlu, Z. (1989) *ACM Transactions on Database Systems 14*(4), 526–573.

[Rapley & Kennedy, 1994] Rapley, M. & Kennedy, J. (1994) Three dimensional interface for an object oriented database in *Proceedings of Interfaces to Database Systems*, (P.Sawyer, Ed.). Springer Verlag.

[Robertson et al., 1993] Robertson, G. G., Card, S. K., & Mackinlay, J. D. (1993) *Communications of the ACM 36*(4), 57–71.

[Robertson et al., 1991] Robertson, G. G., Mackinlay, J. D., & Card, S. K. (1991) Cone trees: Animated 3d visualizations of hierarchical information, in *Proceedings of ACM CHI'91 Conference on Human Factors in Computing Systems and Graphics Interface, ACM SIGCHI.* ACM-Press.

[Sawyer et al., 1992] Sawyer, P., Colebourne, A., Sommerville, I., & Mariani, J. (1992) Object-oriented database systems: A framework for user interface development, In [Cooper, 1992] pp 25–38.

[Shipman, 1981] Shipman, E. (1981) *ACM Trans. on Database Systems 6*, 140–173.

[Stonebraker et al., 1994] Stonebraker, M., Nathan, C., C.Paxson, Su, A., & Wu, J. (1994) Tioga:a database-oriented visualization tool, in *IEEE Visualization '93* pp 86–93.

[Whang, 1987] Whang, K. (1987) *ACM Trans. on Office Information Systems 5*(4), 393–427.

[Wong & Kuo, 1982] Wong, H. & Kuo, I. (1982) Guide: Graphical user interface for database exploration, in *VLDB* pp 22–32.

[Zloof, 1992] Zloof, M. (1992) Query by example, in *National Computer Conference* pp 431–437.

[Zloof & deJong, 1977] Zloof, M. & deJong, P. (1977) *Comm. ACM 20*(6), 385–396.

BIOGRAPHY

Peter Gray is a Professor in Computing Science at Aberdeen University, and is a credited author and researcher in the field of Database Management Systems.

John Boyle completed his graduate studies under the supervision of Peter Gray in 1994, it was during this period of study that most of the work discussed in this paper was carried out. He then worked briefly at EMBL in Heidelberg, and has now taken up a full-time lecturing position at Robert Gordon University in Aberdeen.

13

Issues in Visualizing Large Databases

D. A. Keim, H.-P. Kriegel
Institute for Computer Science, University of Munich
Leopoldstr. 11 B, D-80802 Munich, Germany,
phone: (+49) 89-2180-6267 (-5268), fax: (+49) 89-2180-5246,
e-mail: {keim, kriegel}@informatik.uni-muenchen.de

Abstract

In this paper, we describe our concepts to visualize very large amounts of data. Our visualization techniques which have been developed to support querying large scientific databases are designed to visualize as many data items as possible on current display devices. Even if we are able to use each pixel of the display device to visualize one data value, the number of data items that can be visualized is quite limited. Therefore, in our system we consider only those data items which are 'close' to a user-specified query. The data items are arranged according to their distance from the query. Multiple windows are used for the different attributes of the data and the distance of each of the attributes from the query is represented by color. After briefly describing the basic ideas of our visualization techniques, in this paper we focus on two specific issues which arise in connection with our visualization techniques: First, we compare the *data space* which is the amount of information available in the database to the *visualization space* which is the amount of information that can be visualized by our visualization techniques. Second, we discuss the usefulness of different color models for our distance-to-color mapping and define a new color model which produces adequate color scales.

Keywords

Visualizing Large Databases, Database Exploration, Data Mining, Visual Query Systems, Interfaces to Database Systems, Data Space and Visualization Space, Color Models

1 INTRODUCTION

The progress made in hardware technology allows today's computer systems to store very large amounts of data. The available storage space is easily filled with data which is often automatically recorded via sensors and monitoring systems. Today, even simple transactions of every day life, such as paying by credit card or using the telephone, are typically recorded by using computers. Even larger amounts of data are generated by automated test series in physics, chemistry or medicine, and satellite observation systems are expected to collect one terabyte of data every day in the near future (Frawley, Piatetsky-Shapiro, Matheus 1991). Usually, many parameters are recorded, resulting in multidimensional data with a high dimensionality. The data of all areas mentioned so far is collected because people believe that it is a potential source of valuable information providing a competitive advantage (at some point).

Finding the valuable information hidden in them, however, is a difficult task. With today's database systems and their query tools, it is only possible to view quite small portions of the data. If the data is presented textually, the amount of data which can be displayed is in the range of some one hundred data items, but this is like a drop in the ocean when dealing with data sets containing millions of data items. Having no possibility to adequately query and view the large amounts of data which have been collected because of their potential usefulness, the data becomes useless and the database becomes a data 'dump'.

For the exploration of very large databases to be successful in the near future, we believe that it is essential to make the human being an integral part of the data analysis process. It will be important to combine the best features of humans and computers. The intelligence, creativity and perceptual abilities of humans which are unmatchable need to be supported by computers which are best suited to do searching and number crunching. Some five years ago, a broader community of researchers recognized the potentials of visualization techniques to analyze and explore large amounts of data. With visualization techniques, larger amounts of data can be presented on the screen at the same time, colors allow the users to instantly recognize similarities or differences of thousands of data items, the data items may be arranged to express some relationship and so on. Over the last years, many techniques for the visualization of multidimensional data have been developed. It seems, however, that many of the techniques do not provide adequate support for the flood of data we are facing today. Since, on the other hand, the technology for generating, collecting and storing data is available, the gap between the amount of data that should be visualized and the amount of data that can be visualized is growing. Therefore, a major research challenge is to find human-oriented ways to help the user in exploring large amounts of multidimensional data.

Our work focuses on visualization techniques which use color and dense displays to visualize large multidimensional data sets. Our techniques support querying large databases by query-dependent visualizations of the data. In (Keim, Kriegel, Seidl 1994), the interactive query and visualization interface of a first prototype system is presented. Today, a complete re-implementation of the systems in C++ / MOTIF exists which runs on HP 7xx machines under X-windows. In addition to the basic technique presented in (Keim, Kriegel, Seidl 1994), the current version of the ***VisDB*** system implements several extensions and new visualization techniques which are briefly introduced in section 2 (see Keim 1994 for a detailed discussion). In this paper, we focus on two issues which arise in connection with our visualization techniques. In section 3, we compare the *data space* which is the amount of information available in the database to the *visualization space* which is the amount of information that can be visualized by our visualization techniques. In section 4, we discuss the usefulness of different color models for our distance-to-color mapping and define a new color model which produces adequate color scales. Section 5 summarizes our approach and points out some of the open problems for future work.

2 THE BASIC IDEA OF OUR VISUALIZATION TECHNIQUE

Visualization of data which have some inherent two- or three-dimensional semantics has been done even before computers could be used for visualization, and since using computers for this purpose, a lot of interesting visualization techniques have been developed by researchers working in the graphics field. Visualization of large databases which can be seen as arbitrary multidimensional data, however, is a relatively new research area. Researchers in the graphics/

visualization area are currently exploring techniques in different application domains. Examples are shape coding (Beddow 1990), worlds within worlds (Feiner, Beshers 1990), parallel coordinates (Inselberg, Dimsdale 1990), treemaps (Turo, Johnson 1992) iconic displays (Pickett, Grienstein 1988; Bergeron, Meeker, Sparr 1992), or dynamic methods as presented in (Buja et al. 1991) or (Shneiderman 1994). In most of the approaches proposed so far, the number of data items that can be visualized on the screen at the same time is quite limited (in the range of 100 to 1000 data items), but it is a declared goal to push this limit (Treinish et al. 1992). In dealing with databases consisting of millions or even billions of data items, our goal is to visualize as many data items as possible at the same time to give the user some kind of overview of the data. The obvious limit for any kind of visual representation is the resolution of current displays which is in the order of one to three million pixels, e.g. in case of our 19 inch displays with a resolution of 1024 x 1280 pixels there are about 1.3 million pixels. The basic idea of our visualization techniques is to use each pixel of the screen to give the users visual feedback about the data, allowing them to easily focus on the desired data and to understand the influence of the query parameters.

In dealing with databases consisting of millions of data items with multiple attributes (often ten and more), we had to find an adequate way of restricting the amount of data to be visualized to a number that can be displayed on the screen. In our approach, we only visualize the data items which are 'close' to a user-specified query. The 'closeness' is determined by using distance functions for each of the attributes. The distance functions are datatype and application dependent. Examples for distance functions are the numerical difference (for metric types), distance matrices (for ordinal and nominal types), lexicographical, character-wise, substring, phonetic or semantic difference (for strings) and so on. In the specification of the query, not all of the attributes have to be used. If k of the m attributes are used in the specification of the query, then the query region itself can be seen as an (m-k)-dimensional space with some extension into the other m dimensions. Attributes that are not used in the specification of the query region have basically no impact on the visualization.

Having calculated the distances for each of the attributes which are part of the query, the distances are combined into the overall distance. Important aspects such as normalizing and weighting the distances of the different attributes, the formulas used to calculate the overall distances, and the heuristics used to reduce the number of displayed data items are described in (Keim, Kriegel, Seidl 1994). The overall distances are then sorted, resulting in a one-dimensional distribution ranking the data items according to their distance with respect to the query. The basic idea for visualizing the data items is to map the value ranges of the different attributes to color and represent each data item by multiple pixels being colored according to the distance values for each of its attributes. In the following, we briefly introduce the three visualization techniques which may be used for presenting the colored pixels on the screen. A more detailed description of the techniques including several examples is given in (Keim 1994; Keim, Kriegel 1995).

Spiral Technique

The basic idea for visually displaying the data on the screen is to present the one hundred percent correct answers in the middle of the window and the approximate answers rectangular spiral-shaped around this region. To relate the visualization of the overall result to visualizations of the different selection predicates (dimensions), we generate a separate window for each selection predicate of the query and arrange them next to each other. In the separate windows, we place the pixels for each data item at the same relative position as the overall result for the data item in the overall result window. By relating corresponding regions in the different windows, the user is able to perceive data characteristics such as multidimensional clusters or correlations. Additionally, the separate windows for each of the selection predicates provide important feedback to the user, e.g. on the restrictiveness of each of the selection predicates and on single exceptional data items. An example visualization of about 70 000 three-dimensional test data items is provided in Plate 8.

Axes Technique

The axes arrangement improves the spiral technique by including some feedback on the direction of the distance into the visualization. The basic idea is to assign two dimensions to the axes and to arrange the data items according to the direction of their distance; for one dimension negative distances are arranged to the left, positive ones to the right and for the other dimension negative distances are arranged to the bottom, positive ones to the top. The partitioning of the data into four subsets provides additional information on the position of data items with respect to the axes dimensions. Since the quadrants which correspond to the four subsets are not equally filled, the number of data items which may be visualized is slightly lower. In the example visualization provided in Plate 9, the same data set is used as in Plate 8.

Grouping Technique

In the grouping arrangement all dimensions for one data item are grouped together in one area. The areas are arranged in a rectangular spiral-shape according to the overall distance of the considered data items. The coloring of the distances for the different dimensions may be the same as in the spiral and axes arrangements. The generated visualizations, however, are completely different from those of the spiral and axes arrangements. The visualizations generated by using the grouping arrangement consist of only one window with many areas visualizing all dimensions of the considered data items instead of many windows, each providing a visual representation of only one dimension. An example visualization of about 1000 six-dimensional data items is provided in Plate 10.

In trying to visualize larger amounts of data than possible with the techniques described so far, an important potential is to consider time as an additional dimension. For many applications it is natural to consider time sequences of visualizations, describing features which are changing over time. In the terminology of our system, this could be described as moving the query region along the time dimension. Most traditional systems for visualizing time series consider in each step only the data items at a certain point of time. Contrarily, with our visualization techniques we consider all data items which are 'close' to the query region including data items with differing time values as long as their overall distance with respect to the query is low enough. Our idea for visualizing larger portions of the database is to generalize the technique of generating sequences of visualizations by moving the query region. Instead of moving the query region along the time axis, the user may choose an arbitrary path through m-dimensional space. Obviously, the semantics of the derived visualizations are different. If moving the query region along some parameter, e.g. the temperature in an environmental database, the user may get insight in the corresponding distributions of the other parameters such as ozone or CO_2. The user may also choose more complicated paths through m-dimensional space, e.g. by varying two parameters such as temperature and ozone at a time. The specification of more complicated paths, however, is not straightforward and it is not clear how the user will be able to deal with the complicated semantics introduced by complex paths. An open question is which paths provide visualizations that are 'easy' to perceive and allow the user to find interesting properties of the data. Despite these open questions, generating time series of visualization holds a great potential since neither the number of data items that can be visualized nor their dimensionality is limited, and the visualizations may help the user to get important information out of the automatically generated visualization sequences.

3 DATA SPACE VERSUS VISUALIZATION SPACE

In trying to visualize very large databases, it is interesting to compare the amount of information available in the database to the amount of information that can be visualized by using current display technology. A table of a (relational) database can be seen as a set $\{e_1, ..., e_n\}$ of m-dimensional data items $[e_i = (d_{i1}, ..., d_{im})]$. The portion of m-dimensional space which is (partially) filled with data from the database is the smallest orthogonal subspace that contains all data items of the database, which can be formally expressed as

$$\prod_{j=1}^{m} \left[\operatorname*{MIN}_{i=1}^{n} \{d_{ij}\} \ , \ \operatorname*{MAX}_{i=1}^{n} \{d_{ij}\} \right]$$

If all of the domains are simple discrete domains such as integer, the size of the considered m-dimensional space may be determined by calculating the differences between the minima and maxima for each of the dimensions and computing their cross-product. In general, the size of the considered m-dimensional space may be determined by using the cardinality of each dimension, which is given by the number of possible values between its minimum and maximum. For continuous data types such as real, the cardinality can only be determined by making the domain discrete. The number of distinguishable values depends on the precision of the datatype, which itself depends on number of bits used to represent each data value.

To define our general notion of data space, we use Dom_j for the domain of dimension j and $|Dom_j|$ for the cardinality of the domain (j = 1 ... m). Analogous to the term visualization space, which denotes all visualizations, the term data space is used to denote all possible instances of databases with m dimensions and n elements. The data space can be defined as the number of all power sets with n elements in m-dimensional space:

$$Data\ Space = \left(\prod_{j=1}^{m} |Dom_j| \right)^n$$

The visualization space may be defined as the number of different visual representations that are possible on the screen. If 'Col' is the number of distinguishable colors and (X * Y) the size of the screen used, then the visualization space may be defined as:

$$Visualization\ Space = Col^{(X \times Y)}$$

Note that the number of visual representations that are pre-attentively perceptible as being different is much lower. If two visual representations which differ in just a few pixels are compared to each other, one would generally find it very difficult to find the differences, especially if the differing pixels have similar colors. Additionally, the anatomy and physiology of the human vision system restricts the number of distinguishable visual representations. Effects such as accommodation, blind spots, afterimages, lateral inhibition, and mach bands (regions near sharp transitions that are perceived brighter or darker) prevent the human vision system from perceiving visualizations as being different (Hendee, Wells 1993). Still, the remaining visualization space is very large and no visualization technique completely uses it. Visualization techniques usually have specific arrangements and colorings of the pixels which restrict the number of possible visual representations considerably. Later in this section, we derive a formula for the visualization space with regard to our visualization techniques.

Now let us compare data and visualization space. To simplify the formula for the data space, we assume that the cardinality of all domains of the data space is constant (dom). The data space can then be defined as

$$Data\ Space' = dom^{(m \times n)}.$$

Now there is an apparent similarity of the formulas for the data and visualization space. Since in general (Col << dom) and ((X*Y) << (m*n)), it is clear that any mapping of the data into the visualization space requires some kind of information reduction. To achieve a good utilization of the visualization space, it is desirable to find a surjective mapping. One possibility for a surjective mapping from the data space into the visualization space is to map the domains to colors [dom → Col] and the number of data values in the database to the number of pixels [(m*n) → (X*Y)]. In trying to use as much of the visualization space as possible, our visualization techniques use exactly this kind of mapping. The mapping of domains to colors corresponds to the normalization of data values to a fixed number of values; the mapping of the number of data values to the number of pixels corresponds to the reduction of the number of data items to those which are close to the query region.

Now let us have a closer look at the visualization space for our visualization techniques. Since certain restrictions apply in our visualizations, not all of the $Col^{(X \times Y)}$ visual representations are possible. One restriction is that in our visualizations we have a portion for the overall result representing the overall distance sorted in rising order. The sorting of this portion restricts the number of possible visual representations. The restriction can be described by the following recursive equation

$$f(Col, p) = \sum_{i=1}^{Col} f(i, p-1) \quad \text{with} \quad \begin{aligned} f(Col, 1) &= Col \\ f(1, p) &= 1 \end{aligned}$$

A numerical solution for this recurrence equation is the binomial coefficient $\binom{Col+p-1}{p}$ which can be proved by induction over (Col + p). A second restriction is that our visualization techniques use squares as sections for each of the dimensions. In general, partitioning a screen with fixed resolution $(X \times Y)$ into a fixed number of squares (m + 1) does not allow the usage of all pixels on the screen. Depending on the number of dimensions (m), the size of the squares is limited either by the X- or the Y-dimension of the screen. If the squares are assumed to be completely filled, the number of pixels in each of the squares [P(m)] can be determined as

$$P(m) = \begin{cases} \left(\frac{X}{i}\right)^2 & \text{for m-1} \in \left[i^2 - i + 1, i^2\right] \\ \left(\frac{Y}{i}\right)^2 & \text{for m-1} \in \left[i^2 - 2 \times i + 2, i^2 - i\right] \end{cases}$$

$$\underbrace{\left(1-\frac{1}{Col^{m+1}}\right)^{(P(m)-H)}}_{\text{no yellow in all sections if not a hit}} \times \underbrace{\binom{Col+P(m)-H-1}{P(m)-H}}_{\text{overall result section sorted according to color}} \times \underbrace{Col^{(m \times (P(m)-H))}}_{\text{arbitrary color of all remaining pixels which are no hits}}$$

Figure 1 Visualization Space (Spiral Technique).

A third restriction is induced by the yellow pixels that are used to denote data items inside the query region. These pixels are yellow in all m portions of the visualization. Therefore, the number of pixels that can be arbitrarily colored has to be reduced by this number (number of data items fulfilling the query: H). A last restriction is that pixels that are at the same relative position in each of the sections may not be yellow unless they are hits. We therefore have to restrict the number of possible visualizations by a factor of $\left(1-\frac{1}{Col^{m+1}}\right)^{(P(m)-H)}$

The complete formula for the number of possible visualizations in the case of the spiral technique is given in Figure 1. For the axes and grouping techniques, the arrangement and coloring of pixels is similar and therefore the corresponding formulas are analogous. The major difference in the case of the axes technique is that, in general, not all of the quadrants are completely filled. In the case of the grouping technique, the number of pixels that are used per data item is four (2 x 2) or nine (3 x 3), and therefore the visualization space is correspondingly lower.

At this point, it should be mentioned that in the above definition of data space, two databases which contain the same data items but store them in a different order are considered to be different. Although this may be true in some cases, databases are generally considered to be sets and therefore two databases with identical data items are considered to be the same, independent of the ordering of their elements. This would change the definition of data space to

$$Data\ Space'' = \binom{dom^m + n - 1}{n} = \frac{\left(dom^m + n - 1\right)!}{n! \times \left(dom^m - 1\right)!}.$$

4 THE COLOR MODEL

Visualizing the data values using color corresponds to the task of mapping a single parameter distribution to color. The advantage of color over grey scales is that the number of just noticeable differences (JNDs) is much higher (Herman, Levkowitz 1992). Finding a path through color space that maximizes the number of JNDs but, at the same time, is intuitive for the application domain is a difficult task. For our purpose of mapping the distances to color, we can restrict the task to a simpler, more solvable problem. From a perceptual point of view, brightness is the most important characteristic for distinguishing colors corresponding to a single parameter distribution. Therefore, for our purpose it is sufficient to find a color scale with a monotonically increasing (decreasing) brightness while using the full color range.

In designing the system, we experimented with different colormaps. We found that the coloration has a high impact on the intuitivity of the system. The user, for example, may implicitly connect good answers with light colors and bad answers with dark colors, or may be

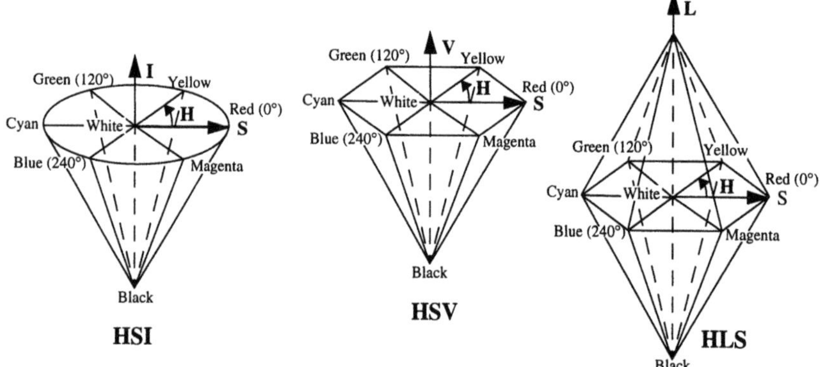

Figure 2 The HSI Color Model compared to the HSV and HLS models.

accustomed to green colors for good answers and red colors for bad answers (like the colors used for traffic lights). We tried many variations of the colormap to enhance the usefulness of our system and found experimentally that a colormap with constant saturation, a decreasing value (intensity, lightness), and a hue (color) ranging from yellow over green, blue, and red to almost black are good choices to denote the distance from the correct answers.

For generating color scales, we used a linear interpolation between a minimum and a maximum value for hue, saturation, and value (intensity, lightness) within the various color models. We first used the standard HSV and HLS color models (Foley et al. 1990). The HSV color model is best described by a single-hexcone and the HLS model by a double-hexcone (see Figure 2). Linear interpolations within these color models, however, do not provide color scales with a monotonically decreasing brightness. Figure 5 shows HSV and HLS color scales which are produced using a linear interpolation algorithm similar to the one presented in the bottom part of Figure 4. The color scales are generated using a constant saturation, a decreasing value (intensity, lightness), and a hue varying over the complete range. If the generated HSV and HLS color scales are used in conjunction with our visualization techniques, brighter colors in the visualizations do not necessarily denote lower distances. If HSV and HLS color scales are mapped to grey-scale, their non-monotonicity becomes obvious (see Figure 5)*.

Since linear interpolation within the HSV and HLS color models does not produce color scales with monotonically decreasing brightness, we developed our own color model which we call the HSI model (H: Hue, S: Saturation, I: Intensity). The HSI color model is a variation of the HSV model. In contrast to color scales generated according to the HSV model, linear interpolation within the HSI model provides color scales whose lightness ranges continuously from light to dark (see Plate 7). This is achieved by using a circular cone instead of the hexcone used in the HSV model (see Figure 2), which means that colors with constant intensity and saturation form a circle. The hue is defined as the angle α between red and the chosen color. When moving on a circle of the HSI color cone, the red, green, and blue portion of the color

* The standard mapping from color to grey-scale used by the X-windows system is a linear combination of the RGB-values [Grey(r,g,b) = 0.34*r + 0.5*g + 0.16*b] which tries to reflect the perceived brightness. Note that the X-windows mapping to grey does not correspond to the grey portion in either of the color models, which is defined as the corresponding portion of the grey axis (center of the color cones).

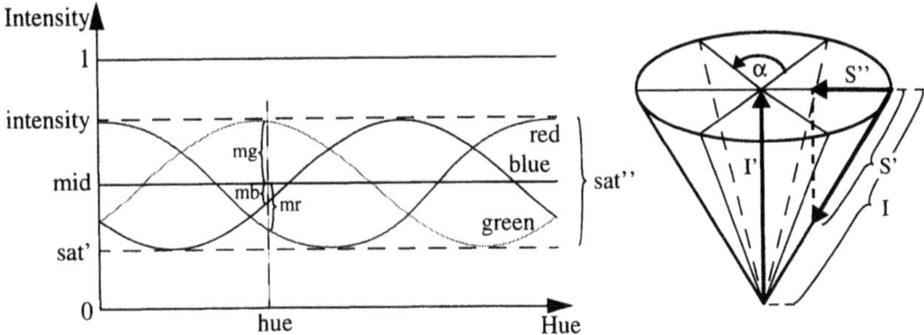

Figure 3 The HSI color model.

follow cosine-curves with phase-shifts of $\frac{2}{3}\pi$ (see Figure 3). If intensity and saturation are both equal to 1, the cosine-curves for each of the RGB-color-portions run between 0 and 1. Reducing the intensity means reducing the maximum of the cosine-curve. Reducing the saturation means lifting the minimum of the cosine-curve (sat'). In terms of the HSI color cone, the intensity is defined as the euclidean distance to the origin and the saturation as percentage of the intensity $\left(\frac{S'}{I}\right)$. In the HSV model, intensity and saturation are determined by using the maximum and minimum of (red, green, blue). In Figure 3, I and S' are marked in the HSI color cone. Since I is proportional to I' and S' proportional to S'', the HSI color cone can also be described with I' and S'' as defining axes as done in Figure 2.

The exact mathematical definition of the HSI parameters (hue, saturation, intensity) in terms of the RGB color components is rather complicated. Therefore, in the following we briefly describe the basic ideas. The intensity can be determined directly from the (red, green, blue)-components. Since the cosine-curves for red, green, and blue have phase-shifts of $\frac{2}{3}\pi$, the square sum of (mr, mg, mb) is constant and proportional to (intensity - mid)^2. The proportionality constant $\left(\frac{3}{2}\right)$ may be determined by using the special case: saturation = 1.

$$\left(mr^2 + mg^2 + mb^2\right) = const \quad \Rightarrow \quad \left(mr^2 + mg^2 + mb^2\right) = \frac{3}{2} \times (intensity - mid)^2$$

$$\Rightarrow \quad \boldsymbol{intensity} = mid + \sqrt{\frac{2}{3} \times \left(mr^2 + mg^2 + mb^2\right)}$$

To determine the saturation, we have to consider the lower limit of the cosine-curves (c.f. sat' in Figure 3). Sat' only yields values between 0 and intensity. To allow values between 0 and 1, sat' has to be normalized $\left(\frac{sat'}{intensity}\right)$. Increasing this value causes a shrinking of the amplitude of the cosine-curves which means that the equal portion of red, green, and blue and therefore the white-portion of the color increases. This is the inverse of the normal use of the term saturation. The saturation is therefore defined as

$$\boldsymbol{saturation} = 1 - \frac{sat'}{intensity} = \frac{sat''}{intensity} = \frac{2 \times (intensity - mid)}{intensity}.$$

The hue is determined by using the scalar product between the vector from the grey axis to red and the vector from the grey axis to the color-point. The point on the grey axis corresponding to a color point (red, green, blue) is calculated as $\frac{red + green + blue}{3}$. The vector from the grey axis $\left(\frac{1}{3}, \frac{1}{3}, \frac{1}{3}\right)$ to red (1, 0, 0) results in $\left(\frac{2}{3}, -\frac{1}{3}, -\frac{1}{3}\right)$, which is equivalent to (2, -1, -1) when used in the

```
...
/***************************** Constructor ***********************************/
HSI :: HSI( double h, double s, double i ): hue( h<6 ? h : h-6 ), saturation(s), intensity(i) { }

/************************** Conversion from RGB to HSI ************************/
HSI :: HSI( const RGB& c ){
    double red = c.red, green = c.green, blue = c.blue;
    double mid = (red + green + blue) / 3.0;
    double mr  = red - mid; double mg  = green - mid; double mb  = blue - mid;
    double cos_hue = (2.0 * mr - mg - mb) / sqrt((mr*mr + mg*mg + mb*mb) * 6.0);
    intensity = mid + sqrt (2.0 * (mr*mr + mg*mg + mb*mb) / 3.0);
    saturation = 2.0 * (intensity - mid) / intensity;
    hue = acos( cos_hue ) * 3.0 / M_PI;
    if (blue > green) hue = 6.0 - hue;
}

/************************** Conversion from HSI to RGB ************************/
HSI :: operator RGB(){
    if( saturation == 0.0 ) return RGB( intensity, intensity, intensity );
    double red   = value( hue + 0.0 );          //   0 Grad =   0 pi
    double green = value( hue + 4.0 );          // 240 Grad = 4/3 pi
    double blue  = value( hue + 2.0 );          // 120 Grad = 2/3 pi
    return RGB( red, green, blue );
}

double HSI :: value( double hue_phase ){
    double pure = 0.5 * (1 + cos( hue_phase * M_PI / 3.0 ) );
    return( intensity * (1.0 - saturation * (1.0 - pure)) );
}

/************************* Generation of HSIColorScales ************************/
HSIColorScale :: HSIColorScale( const HSI& from, const HSI& to )
                : foot( from ), temp(0,0,0)
                , hue_range( to.hue - from.hue )
                , sat_range( to.saturation - from.saturation )
                , int_range( to.intensity - from.intensity )
    { if( hue_range < 0.0 ) hue_range += 6.0; }

Color& HSIColorScale :: operator[]( double f ){
    temp =   HSI( hue_range * f  +  foot.hue
                , sat_range * f  +  foot.saturation
                , int_range * f  +  foot.intensity );
    return temp;
}

void main () {
    for( int i = 1; i < number; i++ ) {
        RGB rgb = HSIColorScale(MinHsi, MaxHsi) [ double(i) / (number-1) ];   ...
    }
}
```

Figure 4 Generation and conversion algorithms for HSI color scales.

scalar product. The vector from the grey axis (mid, mid, mid) to the color-point (red, green, blue) results in (mr, mg, mb). The angle α is calculated as

$$\cos\alpha = \frac{(2,-1,-1) \times (mr, mg, mb)}{|(2,-1,-1)| \times |(mr, mg, mb)|}$$

$$\Rightarrow \quad \boldsymbol{hue} = \operatorname{acos}\left(\frac{(2 \times mr - mg - mb)}{\sqrt{6} \times \sqrt{mr^2 + mg^2 + mb^2}}\right).$$

The algorithms for generating HSI color scales and for converting HSI to RGB and vice versa are presented in Figure 4. The parameters for generating the color scales presented in Figure 5 — including the HSI color scale used for the visualizations presented in Figures 6 to 8 — are:

	hue	*saturation*	*intensity*
MinHsi	1.5 (= LightGreen)	1.0	0.4
MaxHsi	1.0 (= Yellow)	1.0	1.0

Since the usefulness of colormaps varies depending on the user and the application, we allow the users to define their own colormaps and use them instead of our standard colormap.

5 SUMMARY AND CONCLUSIONS

Visualizing very large amounts of arbitrary multidimensional data is one of the big challenges that researchers in the graphics/visualization area are currently facing. The task is to efficiently find interesting data sets, i.e. hot spots, clusters of similar data or correlations between different parameters. In this paper, we presented our approach for visualizing large databases. Our techniques provide visual representations of the largest amount of data that can be displayed at one point of time on current display technology. Besides introducing our visualization techniques, we compared the *data space* which is the information contained in the database to the *visualization space* of our visualization techniques, and we defined the HSI color model which produces color scales that are adequate for our distance-to-color mapping.

Interesting topics for future research are an examination of the type of information (type of clusters, type of correlations, etc.) that is perceivable with our visualization techniques, an examination of the impact of different weighting and distance functions, and a comparison of the different visualization techniques for multidimensional data that have been proposed so far. One important step towards an in-depth examination of current visualization techniques for multidimensional data will be an integrated test data generation and evaluation tool which is currently being implemented at our institute. The tool will allow the generation of artificial data sets with given characteristics. The test data sets may be described by the distribution functions for each of the attributes, the correlations or functional dependencies between the attributes, and the clusters which again may have arbitrary characteristics. The tool may be used to evaluate one single visualization technique to find its strength and weaknesses, but it will also be helpful to compare different visualization techniques to find out which techniques are most suitable for which types of data. The goal of our future research is to improve the perception of our visualization techniques and to push their limits to be able to visualize even larger amounts of data with an even higher dimensionality.

6 REFERENCES

Beddow J., (1990) Shape Coding of Multidimensional Data on a Microcomputer Display. *Visualization '90, San Francisco, CA,* 238-246.

Bergeron R. D., Meeker L. D. and Sparr T. M., (1992) A Visualization-Based Model for a Scientific Database System, in *Focus on Scientific Visualization* (eds. Hagen H., Müller M., Nielson G.), Springer, 103-121.

Buja A., McDonald J. A., Michalak J. and Stuetzle W., (1991) Interactive Data Visualization Using Focusing and Linking. *Visualization '91, San Diego, CA,* 156-163.

Feiner S. and Beshers C., (1990) Visualizing n-Dimensional Virtual Worlds with n-Vision. *Computer Graphics,* **24 (2)**, 37-38.

Foley J. D., van Dam A., Feiner S. K. and Hughes J. F., (1990) Computer Graphics: Principles and Practice. *Addison-Wesley, Reading*, 1990.

Frawley W. J., Piatetsky-Shapiro G. and Matheus C. J., (1991) Knowledge Discovery in Databases: An Overview, in *Knowledge Discovery in Databases*, AAAI Press, Menlo Park, CA.

Herman G. T. and Levkowitz H., (1992) Color Scales for Image Data. *Computer Graphics and Applications*, **12 (1)**, 72-80.

Hendee W. R., Wells P. N. T., (1993) 'The Perception of Visual Information', *Springer.*

Inselberg A. and Dimsdale B., (1990) Parallel Coordinates: A Tool for Visualizing Multi-Dimensional Geometry. *Visualization '90, San Francisco, CA,* 361-370.

Keim D. A., (1994) Visual Support for Query Specification and Data Mining. Ph.D. Thesis, University of Munich, Shaker Publishing Company, Aachen, 1995.

Keim D. A. and Kriegel H.-P., (1995) Possibilities and Limits in Visualizing Large Amounts of Multidimensional Data, in *Perceptual Issues in Visualization* (eds. Levkowitz H., Grienstein G.), Springer.

Keim D. A., Kriegel H.-P. and Seidl T., (1994) Supporting Data Mining of Large Databases by Visual Feedback Queries. *Proceedings Int. Conference on Data Engineering, Houston, TX,* 302-313.

Pickett R. M. and Grinstein G. G., (1988) Iconographic Displays for Visualizing Multidimensional Data. *Proceedings Conference on Systems, Man and Cybernetics, Beijing and Shenyang, China.*

Shneiderman B., (1994) Dynamic Queries for Visual Information Seeking, *IEEE Software*, **11**, 70-77.

Treinish L. A., Butler D. M., Senay H., Grinstein G. G. and Bryson S. T., (1992) Grand Challenge Problems in Visualization Software. *Visualization '92, Boston, Mass.*, 366-371.

Turo D. and Johnson B., (1991) Improving the Visualization Hierarchies with Treemaps: Design Issues and Experimentation. *Visualization '92, Boston, Mass.*, 124-131.

7 BIOGRAPHY

Daniel A. Keim is a teaching and research assistant in the Institute for Computer Science at the University of Munich, Germany. His research interests include visualization of statistical data, visual support for querying databases, database support for visualization systems, interfaces to database systems, and interoperability of heterogeneous databases. Keim received his MS from the University of Dortmund in 1990 and his PhD from the University of Munich in 1994.

Hans-Peter Kriegel is a professor for database and information systems in the Institute for Computer Science at the University of Munich, Germany. His research interests are spatial database systems, particularly query processing, performance issues, and parallel operations. Data exploration and data mining in very large spatial databases led him to the area of visualization. Kriegel received his MS and PhD in 1973 and 1976, respectively, from the University of Karlsruhe, Germany.

14

Visualization of rule behaviour in active databases

Fors, T.

Department of Computer Science

University of Skövde, Box 408, 541 28 Skövde, Sweden

email: tomas@ida.his.se

Abstract

One of the characteristics of database systems is the ability to efficiently handle large amounts of information. This characteristic must apply also when rules are introduced into database systems, resulting in so-called active database systems. Hence, active database systems need to manage both a large amount of data and many rules.

One of the problems with large sets of rules is the complexity of interaction between rules. A rule that is perfectly workable by itself may in the interaction with other rules produce serious malfunctions. To prevent such situations, a rule debugger is needed, preferably a visual one.

In this paper we introduce Adela, a rule visualization tool suitable for the relational data model. We introduce a multilevel rule concept, which is important when, for example, rule visualization tools need to display how rules are related to the data model and the data instances. Three different levels within the multilevel rule concept are provided: model level, rule level, and instance level. An event/rule trace tree is introduced to display: i) the context in which rules are fired, and ii) the execution states of rules. A data trace is introduced in order to display what is happening to data instances when they are manipulated by rules. We also address issues such as scalability of rule visualization tools, and on-line rule visualization tools, which in real time show what is happening in active databases.

Keywords

Rule visualization, active databases

1 INTRODUCTION

The introduction of rules into database systems brings in the complexity of rule interaction and behaviour. Exactly what is happening in an active database at any given moment? The user does not know. In fact, there is seldom any need for the user to know. But what if something malfunctions?

Rules in an active database are executed "behind the scenes", meaning that the users of the system will not see that these rules are executed. Assume that the rule set contains some rules implemented in a fashion that will lead to a highly undesirable state if they are ever triggered and executed. Since the rule execution is done behind the scenes, the failure will be a fact without any preceding warnings. It will also be difficult to see what went wrong afterwards.

What is needed is a type of tool that can visualize rule behaviour, so that development and maintenance of active database rules is made much easier. Otherwise it will be very difficult to see the complex interactions between rules, which can hide the cause of a serious malfunction. A visualization toolkit would, if not solve this problem, then at least make it possible to prevent some failures, and if a failure does occur, make it easier to analyse the situation.

Database systems, whether they are active or not, have to efficiently manage large amounts of information. An active database system thus has to manage both a large amount of both data and many rules; a fact that may cause developers to hesitate in choosing an active database system. This can be exemplified as follows. Assume that a database system is being developed for an environment where there must not be any mistakes made by the system. There are two alternatives: Either you use an active database in which you can easily implement both data and behaviour, or you can use an ordinary passive database, for which you must implement the behaviour in all applications that use the database in question.

The active database alternative is more appealing since it is easy to update both behaviour and data, and applications will be smaller and need not be updated when some constraint changes.

Unfortunately, you will most likely be inclined to choose the passive system with all its disadvantages. Why? Simply because it is easier to understand what the system will do in a given situation. It is all there in the source code. Of course, when implementing an active system, the rules can also be checked, but only one at a time. There is no way of knowing what the system will do with all the rules interacting with each other. Diaz, Jaime, and Paton (1993) say that:

> Experiences using active rules in database systems has shown that, while such rules can be utilized beneficially in a range of applications, it is not a straightforward task to implement, debug or maintain large rule bases.

which is consistent with what Stonebraker (1993) says:

> An increasing expressiveness in rule languages is often associated with increasing complexity. As the number of rules increases, it becomes difficult to foresee the possible interactions among rules.

Some sort of debugging and explanation facility is thus important if the use of active rules is going to spread. Diaz, Jaime, and Paton (1993) mention two reasons for introducing such a facility:

- Inform the user which active rules have been fired during the execution of an operation thereby increasing the user's confidence and understanding of the system.
- To help the designer to refine and analyze interactions among rules at execution time.

The Adela project (Fors, 1994) is located within this problem area. That is, it is aimed at finding a way to visualize rules and rule behaviour. The visualization is aimed at making the context of each rule firing clear, and to make it easier to debug rule sets by making it possible to restrict the tracing to certain rules, events, or data.

The remainder of this paper is organized as follows. Section 2 contains a presentation of work done in the area of rule visualization. The DEAR rule debugger is discussed therein. In section 3, we propose the multilevel rule concept, which is a suggestion of how to define the role of rules in active database systems. We provide three different levels for the multilevel rule concept: model level, rule level, and instance level.

Section 4 describes Adela, a prototype rule visualization system that visualizes rule behaviour in a relational framework. This is followed in section 5 by a brief description of the features of Adela.

Finally, in section 6, we discuss future work in the area of rule visualization and present conclusions from the Adela project.

2 RELATED WORK

Since research within the area of rule visualization is not as yet well established, related work is very hard to find. This section contains an overview of the DEAR rule debugger (Diaz, Jaime, and Paton, 1993), the only related work found at the time of the Adela project (Fors, 1994).

2.1 DEAR

DEAR is a debugger for active rules in an object-oriented context (Diaz, Jaime, and Paton, 1993). It has been implemented on EXACT (Diaz and Jaime, 1993), which is a rule manager which supports ECA rules in the object-oriented database system ADAM (Diaz, Gray, and Paton, 1991).

A rule debugger should, according to Diaz, Jaime, and Paton (1993), provide at least three kinds of mechanisms which:

- Make explicit the context in which the active rule is fired.
- Focus the search during the debugging process.
- Automatically detect inconsistencies and potentially conflicting interactions among rules.

DEAR keeps track not only of rules, but of both rules and events. Diaz, Jaime, and Paton (1993) identifies that

> ... tracing events gives important hints to the user - the entwined event-rule cycle allows the user to know not only which rules fired, but also what caused these rules to be fired. And vice versa, when an event is awakened, such an entwined cycle permits detection of the context where the event arose.

Rules triggered at the same time, the conflict set, depend on the events raised. Therefore, to show the sequence in which rules are fired would be of little help here. A more meaningful way of keeping track of ECA rules is to show not only the rules but also the context in which these rules are fired (Diaz, Jaime, and Paton, 1993). The context can be understood as the rule's event and the conflict rule set. A drawback with only showing sequence when debugging rules, is that such a debugger will ignore the fact that a rule has to compete with other rules in order to fire. DEAR attempts to face this problem by:

- Showing the entwined cycle of rules and events. Hence, the user can ascertain which rules are awakened and the cause of the fired rules. In this way, it is also possible to detect the context in which events were triggered.
- Making explicit the conflict set of simultaneously triggered rules in the displayed tree, once the conflicts among those rules have been resolved by the rule manager. An indication of the rules participating in this conflict set is useful for focusing on a restricted number of rules where complex interactions can occur.

The debug tree can easily grow too large to analyse. Therefore, DEAR also provides a number of ways to limit the debug tree produced:

- *Spy_event.* Restrict debugging to certain events.
- *Spy_rule.* Restrict debugging to certain rules.
- *Data_spy.* Restrict debugging to certain data, i.e., a tree will be generated only if an update is detected on the data monitored.

2.2 Discussion of DEAR

The first issue concerns what actually happens to the data as the actions of rules change it. DEAR does not show that clearly. It is our opinion that any rule visualization tool should in addition to visualizing rules, also show what effects rules have on data. That is, which objects were affected, in which way, how many, etc. It should also be possible to examine these objects, i.e. browse them.

DEAR is object-oriented and therefore has some special features that come with the object-oriented paradigm. If these ideas were to be fitted to the relational model, it is likely that we would turn from an instance-oriented view to a set-oriented view. Which data does a certain rule apply to at any given moment? There is no way to be sure. The only thing we know is what data set the rule applies to.

Another issue is that of integrity constraints. It often takes several rules to form one integrity constraint. Our opinion is that a visualization tool for active systems should show the mapping from rules to constraints and from constraints to the data model itself. DEAR does not provide this. However, it is not elementary to provide such a mapping. The fact that one rule may be part of several constraints makes the mapping very complicated. How do we know when one constraint is "active"? This problem is similar to that of composite events.

In summary, the following additional requirements and issues should in general be provided or considered when a rule visualization tool is being developed.

- A rule visualization tool should show how data instances are affected as they are manipulated by rules.
- A visualization tool should provide browsing facilities for both data and rules.
- Rules should be put into data model context, and the concept of integrity constraints should be supported.

3 THE MULTILEVEL RULE CONCEPT

To visualize rule behaviour as an event/rule tree does not solve all problems. There are several open questions such as: i) what roles do rules play in the data model, and ii) how are instances of rules, events, and data related? Questions like these also need to be answered by a rule visualization tool. The *multilevel rule concept*, which was introduced by Fors (1994), is an approach which makes it possible for a rule visualization tool to answer these questions.

A rule visualization tool must be able to show how rules are related to the data model and the data instances. That is what the multilevel rule concept is about. It gives a number of abstractions and relations between these abstractions in order to easily provide the tool with necessary facilities for required visualizations.

The multilevel rule concept was developed in order to attempt to define the role of rules in active databases. This is done by introducing three basic levels, which reflect different aspects of rule behaviour: the model level, the rule level, and the instance level.

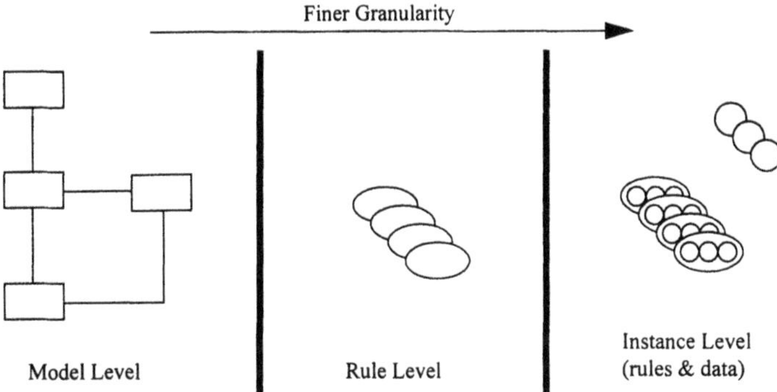

Figure 1 The multilevel rule concept.

3.1 Model level

At the model level, rules are set into a data model context, i.e. this level reflects the rule behaviour on the data model.

A constraint is intimately related to object-types or relations in the data model. For example, a constraint for referential integrity is bound to two relations in the data model. Integrity constraints are thus a part of the data model, and user expectations are governed by them. Not to show this connection would therefore be an oversight.

A constraint itself consists of one or several rules needed in order to define the behaviour needed with respect to the constraint. A constraint is in this respect much like a composite. Similar to composite events, in that several constraints may share one rule. A constraint can be seen as a "composite rule".

It is desirable to know when a constraint has been triggered. Therefore we need to keep track of which rules are triggered, so that when a rule (or rules) representing violation of a constraint is triggered, the constraint itself is triggered.

The rule-constraint problem can be outlined like this. Assume a set of rules R and a set of constraints C. For every constraint in C there are several rules in R. For any rule in R there may be more than one associated constraint, and for any constraint in C there are one or more rules and there may be rules which occur in other constraints. As rules are activated, the system has to check if any constraint is triggered as a result.

It has been mentioned that this problem is comparable to the event/composite event problem. But there is a difference: rules and constraints are concerned with database states, whereas events - in most cases - are operations on the database state. This is a complex and involved problem that will not be further analysed in this paper.

If this concept of constraints is supported within an active dbms, the only problem where the visualization tool is concerned lies in the actual visualization. But if the dbms does not support this, which is the case today, the tool itself must look after this. This is not really what a tool for rule visualization is supposed to do, so it is recommended that active database management systems are enhanced to support the multilevel rule concept.

Rule behaviour and its effects can on this level be visualized by colouring of schema symbols, sounds, text messages, and the usage of graphical symbols as messages.

3.2 Rule level

The rule level (the "middle" level) is the level on which the rule representation in DEAR could be positioned, i.e. it contains a representation of the rules themselves. Rules can be looked at from (at least) three different points of view, or sublevels. These are the constraint level, the atomic rule level, and the ECA level.

The point of having these levels is that it would be difficult to get a feeling for what is happening in the database if we were only to present animations on one single level. The motivation for each sublevel is as follows.

ECA level

As a minimum, a rule debugging environment must show what caused a rule to fire. What triggers a rule is an event, which is specified at the ECA-level.

Atomic rule level

When monitoring the entwined chain of events and rules, it is desirable to regard the whole rule as an abstraction, one single unit. So at this level, the rule level, the event, the condition, and the action parts of the rule are hidden behind the abstracted form of rule.

Constraint level

It is often the case that several rules are needed to express a constraint. It is therefore desired to be able view these rules in a higher form of abstraction, a constraint. It is the constraint that is broken down into individual rules when an active system is designed. Not to be able to see this abstraction afterwards would be an oversight.

3.3 Instance level

While the rule level keeps track of the rules in different forms of abstraction (e.g. constraints, rules as atomic entities, and the ECA parts of the rule), the instance level keeps track of the actual rule firings. To each rule firing comes a number of parameters, such as which event triggered the rule, which data is of interest, the state the data was in when the rule was fired, etc.

Why is this level needed? First, as one rule can be triggered several times in one transaction, it is needed to separate these different rule instances from each other. Second, as instances of one rule can be triggered at different times, different database states will apply to different instances. Hence it is important to reflect rule instances.

The instance level is responsible for rule visualization in respect of the database state in which each rule instance was created.

As events can be seen as objects in a system as well, it follows that they have instances in a way much like rules. The occurrence of an event generates an event instance to which a set of context parameters belong. These parameters are then passed along to the rules triggered by this event occurrence.

4 ADELA: A PROTOTYPE SYSTEM

The objective of the development of Adela (Fors, 1994) was to design and implement a rule debugger. In general, the implementation would be an animated graphical interface, which would continuously show what rules are firing, and the effects of rule firings in a set-oriented *relational* framework.

Adela is implemented as a prototype in C++, using the animation library Goofy (Ford, 1994). Goofy is built on top of another library, Polka (Stasko, 1992), which is a software system developed by John T. Stasko at the College of Computing, Georgia Institute of Technology, Atlanta. Polka provides functions for smooth animation on top of the X-Window system.

Goofy allows indirect access to Polka through a higher-level interface. With these two packages, it is easy to make sophisticated animations without having to concentrate on the low-level details that lie behind it all.

4.1 Development restrictions

Adela was developed as a prototype with a number of quite severe restrictions. The reason to these restrictions was to make it possible to produce a reasonable result within the time limits of the project.

- Adela is an application, not a database module.
- The database monitor is simulated, not actually built to interact with a real active database system.
- The main objective is to visualize rules and rule firings in a data model context. The project was therefore primarily meant to explain rules, and only secondly to provide a debugging facility.
- Adela should naturally be easy to understand and work with. However, having that as a goal would require that an acceptance test of some kind would have to be carried out. The time limits of the project (Fors, 1994) did not permit such testing to be planned. Therefore, understanding and usability is not a formal project goal.
- The only rules considered are rules that represent behavior concerned with whole objects. All other types of rules, including those with composite events, will be ignored. So the only events considered are those when an object has been updated, deleted, inserted, or retrieved.
- Assume small data model. The problem of showing large amounts of information so that it can easily be comprehended by the user is ignored.

- Deal only with whole data objects on set level. Do not bother with attributes and methods. Regard the data objects as set units, meaning that the visualization of an instance is in fact the visualization of a set of instances.

These restrictions may be seen as very crippling, making the resulting visualization seem trivial. That is true in the sense that for debugging purposes, leaving out attributes, will make the tool quite useless.

However, the Adela project, as far as it has been taken, was primarily meant to explore a way to explain active rule behaviour visually. For that purpose, attributes may be left out - even if it is true that taking them into account would enhance the way that Adela visualizes rule behaviour. Unfortunately, that was not possible to achieve within the time limits of the Adela project.

4.2 Assumptions

Adela is intended to work in a relational context, meaning (among other things) that data is set-oriented. This will impact the visualization of rule actions with respect to changes to data, i.e., all changes are sets of changes.

It is also assumed that the underlying database system will have no problems in supporting the information requirements that Adela has. If Adela is to be developed into a full-scale tool, then there might have to be changes to the database itself. The change that is most obvious is the database monitoring facility, which must take care of all communication between the visualization tool and the active database. Its duties will be of an introspective nature, in which it will monitor triggering and execution of rules, event occurrences, and the buildup of composite events. It must also support browsing of rules, events, and data. Browsing of data that have been changed by rules is also an important feature. This is not a simple task, which due to the restrictions on the objectives was not undertaken.

Due to the lack of work in the area of visualization of rule behaviour, the visualization that is suggested is based more upon reasoning than on any work already done. However, some influences have been taken from DEAR and from existing ideas of how to graphically represent data schemas. The symbols and the approaches to visualization chosen are not explicitly designed to be cognitively correct and easy to understand. They are merely intended to give an illustrative example of how rule behaviour and its effects can be visualized. As mentioned in section 4.1, understanding and usability is not a formal project goal.

4.3 Architecture

Database Monitor

In order to be able to show on screen what is happening in the active database, certain information is needed. This information should be provided by a database monitoring facility, which in the Adela prototype is a simulator of an active database.

Event Information Filter

The event information filter takes input from the database monitor and processes it into something that the graphics manager can handle. The information from the database monitor is mapped into screen objects and animation data.

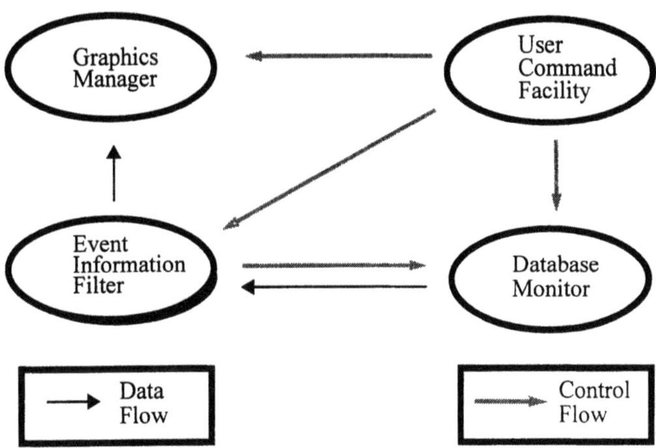

Figure 2 Architecture of the Adela system.

Graphics Manager

The graphics manager is nothing more than a slave to the event information filter. It takes input from the event information filter and takes care of the animations required.

User Command Facility

The user command facility provides the user of Adela with a number of commands to control the visualization. Due to some features of the Goofy animation library, which made it moderately difficult to add other windows than those predefined, the user command facility was not implemented. Since Adela is a prototype system intended only to show a way to visualize rules in a relational active database, the absence of this facility was seen as unimportant.

4.4 Rules

4.4.1 Events in Adela

In many systems, events can be composite. Events can therefore be put together with the use of certain operators, like conjunction and disjunction. In Adela it is unimportant how events are detected, so composite events could easily be incorporated. Whether the structure of composite events should be visualized, and more particularly whether partially detected composites should be, are open questions.

```
Event Definition
    Event identifier
    Event signal
    Object type identifier
```

Figure 3 Adela event definition.

An event consists of the following parts: an *identifier*, an *event signal*, and a binding of the *object type* involved. The event signal is a database operation, i.e., one of insert, delete, update, or retrieve. This means that the ECA style that Adela adopts conforms to the relational paradigm. The object type refers to be base relation on which the database operation operates. E.g. for the event E1, INSERT to PERSON, INSERT is the event signal and PERSON is the object type.

4.4.2 Actions in Adela

The definition of actions in Adela is similar to the event definition, except that actions are not objects themselves, i.e., do not have an identifier. Another exception is that the signal is one of insert, delete, update, retrieve, *refuse*, and *instead-of*. For the purposes of Adela, it is not necessary to express rule actions in any more detail than this.

The refuse operation is a rollback of the whole transaction (immediate-immediate coupling assumed), and the instead-of operation means that the action triggering the event is replaced by the action of the rule with the instead-of-action. This has some consequences for the model (see section 4.4.3).

Complex actions are supported in that it is possible to, for example, delete an employee and insert an unemployed as part of the same rule action. Note that for refuse, it is not possible to express a complex action. Whenever refuse is chosen as an action, it must be the only action in the action part of the rule. A similar thing goes for instead-of actions. It is not possible to express an action to be both instead-of and something else. Note that an action that is specified instead-of can naturally be complex in itself.

4.4.3 Instead-of semantics

Suppose an event initiated by a rule, user, or an application has triggered several rules, one of which has an instead-of-action. Then the action triggering the event is replaced by the action of the rule with the INSTEAD-OF in its action.

Other rules triggered by the same event will be dropped. This is because the action triggering the event is undone by the rule with the instead-of-action. If there exist rules which have been triggered by the same event and whose action parts have been executed prior to the rule with instead-of, then the changes made by those are also undone.

If one or several other rules triggered by the same event have caused cascades of rule firing, and if the rule with the instead-of-action is executed to completion, then the rule cascades made by the other rules have to be undone.

4.4.4 ECA rules in Adela

There is a problem of how to visualize the rule concept since a limitation to the objectives for Adela was that attributes would not be modeled; the rule styles of "normal" ECA rules are too complex.

This problem is solved by redefining events, conditions, and actions with respect to Adela. (See Figure 4) Rule priority is represented by a number, where low numbers are high-priority, and high numbers are low-priority.

Because the prototype implementation of Adela will not deal with attributes, the condition is highly compromised. In the Adela ECA rule, the condition is either always false, always true, or randomly true. One might ask why the condition is represented at all. There are two answers to this. The first answer is that the condition (i.e., state check) is a significant part of rule behaviour and as such must be present in a visualization of rule behaviour. The natural way to reflect the fact that a condition can be evaluated as either true or false, taking the restrictions into account, is to let the condition be randomly true.

```
Rule identifier

Priority

ADELA event:      event identifier

ADELA condition: < FALSE | TRUE | RANDOM >

ADELA action:     <list of action definitions>
```

Figure 4 The simplified ECA rule form of ADELA.

The second answer is that in debugging rules it is very cumbersome to only rely on pure chance. One might wish to control the way that rules are triggered and executed. Therefore, with respect to the condition, there has to be a possibility to overrule chance, i.e., to set the condition to always be true or always be false.

5 VISUALIZATION IN ADELA

Due to the time limits of the Adela project, a number of restrictions (section 4.1) were introduced. This means that when regarding Adela from the multilevel rule perspective, only part of the rule level is represented. If Adela is taken any further, the whole multilevel rule concept should be supported.

When visualizing rule behaviour, especially when showing the effects on data, an important question arises: just how much should be animated of the effects on data? Suggestions are:

- **Rules and object types**. Rules are connected to certain object types. This connection can be derived from i) the event definition, and ii) the action definition. If rule R1 is connected to object type 'Person', the connection should be apparent in the visualization.

- **Database operations**. When an event occurs, the animation visualizes the object type in question so that it is clear what is happening, e.g., a DELETE operation on the object type 'Person' would cause the visualization of 'Person' to change so that it is clear that somebody or something has executed a delete command on the object type in question.
- **Rule firings**. When a rule fires, it should be noticed on the object type it is connected to. If the rule itself is viewed, then it should be noticed that it has been activated. The latter is of course obvious in the event/rule trace, but that is not the point. The point is to clearly visualize the connection between the rule and the object type.

5.1 Example

The visualization as implemented in Adela (Fors, 1994) provides two animation windows, the event/rule trace view and the data trace view. The event/rule trace view visualizes the cascade of events and rules and the execution state of each rule as it is fired. The data trace view visualizes the operations of the rule actions.

Since attributes and instances are ignored in the prototype (section 4.1), the data trace view only shows operations by rules on object types. The changes to data are nevertheless animated, but the "instances" are not really instances of object types: they are to be regarded as sets of instances.

5.1.1 Graphical symbols

Event/rule trace

Events are squares which are coloured black when no rules in the branch originating from the event in question is being executed, and gray when there are rules in the branch originating from the event in question that are being executed.

Rules are ellipses that contain three circles. The circles are used to show in which stage of execution the rules are. If all circles are black, then the rule is not being executed. If the leftmost circle is gray and the other two circles are black, then the rule has just been selected for execution. If the rightmost circle is black and the two other circles are gray, then the condition has been evaluated as true. If all circles are gray, then the action of the rule is being processed.

Each node is labelled with a node identifier, which is constructed out of the name of the event/rule, tree depth level, and a count of how many times the event/rule has occurred previously in the tree. This node identifier is used to uniquely identify each event/rule instance.

The arcs between events and rules can be labelled with an 'x'. This means that the tree branch in question has been processed.

Data trace view

Rules are represented in a manner that differs from the representation of rules in the event/rule trace. Here, the execution states are not seen: rules are at all times represented by solid black ellipses. The reason for this is that the data trace view is not dealing with anything other than effects of rule action processing. Therefore to show the execution states of the rules would be to provide irrelevant and redundant information.

Object types are visualized as solid black rectangles. The connection between rules and object types as described in section 5.1 is not implemented completely. The only way rules and object types are visually connected is when the action of a rule performs an operation on an object type. The arcs that connect rules and object types are labelled with the operation.

Changes to instances of object types are visualized as small circles that are labelled with the name of the object type and the node id of the rule. The fill colour of such a circle is white, gray, or black. White circles denote unchanged data, i.e., inserted or retrieved. Gray circles denote changed data, i.e., updated, and black circles denote deleted data.

5.1.2 Visualization description

The steps described below outline the way that rule behaviour is visualized in Adela. (See also Figure 5 and Figure 6).

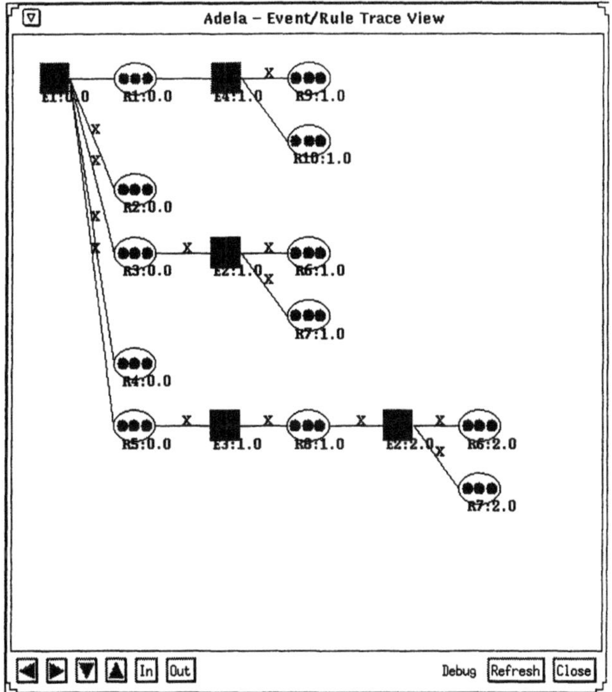

Figure 5 Event/rule trace view example.

1. The detection of an event causes an event node to appear in the event/rule trace view (Figure 5).
2. Rules triggered by an event form a conflict set, which in the event/rule trace view (Figure 5) is visualized in the form of a vertical row of rules (ellipses with circles within them). Each rule in the row is connected with an arc to the triggering event.
3. When a rule has been selected from its conflict set, it appears in the top part of the data trace view (Figure 6).

4. When the action of a rule is being processed, the object types that the action operates on are shown above the rules in the data trace view (Figure 6). The object types are connected by an arc to the rule when the operation is being performed.
5. The operations of rule actions are animated as follows: A white-colored instance symbol appears on the left/mid part of the data trace view (Figure 6) and moves to the right. It stops briefly when it reaches the space between the two grayish rectangles, where it changes color to black if it is to be deleted, and to gray if it is to be updated. This signifies the execution of the operation. After this, the instance symbol continues its movement to the right and settles in the appropriate slot (the slots are labelled deleted, updated, inserted, and retrieved).

When the processing of the action has finished, the rule object types operated on by the rule disappear. Shortly after that, the processing of the rule itself is finished, whereafter it also disappears from the data trace view (Figure 6).

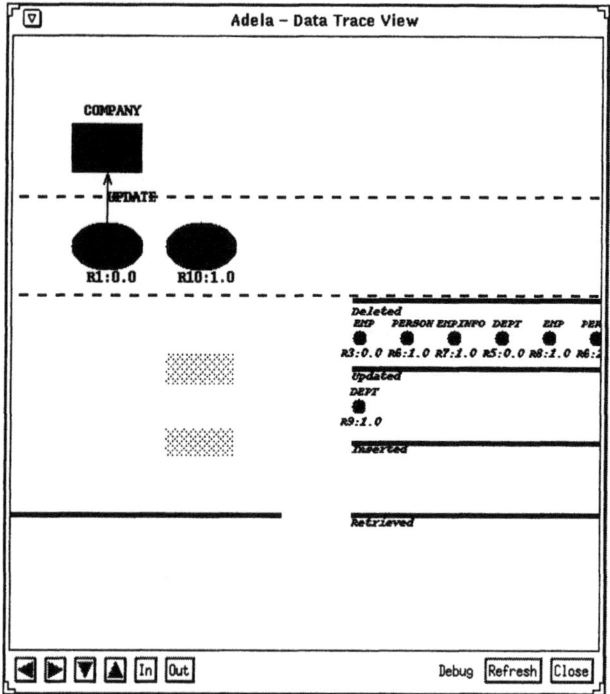

ıre 6 Data trace view example.

6 FUTURE WORK

The ideas around visualization of rule behaviour that have been presented in this paper are not enough if one tries to construct a fully-fledged rule visualization tool. The ideas of Adela have therefore to be extended.

If the Adela system is further developed, it is very important to have usability as a formal project goal. This is because Adela is meant to be a tool for understanding the rules within an active database, and to do actual debugging. As a consequence, feedback from potential users is vital.

The usability goal implies that none of the restrictions mentioned in section 4.1 must be present in the Adela system if it is further developed. In addition, issues such as these below will have to be addressed.

The multilevel rule concept

In its current state, Adela has not a very good representation of the multilevel rule concept. The model level, the rule level, and the instance level should in all their aspects be visually represented.

Database monitor

For a fully-fledged rule visualization tool, the presence of database monitoring is crucial if the tool is to be used for debugging of rule sets.

Protocol for semantics

Even though ECA rules are accepted as a basis for active databases, the semantics of these rules differ from implementation to implementation. Having a separate rule visualization tool for every type of active database is obviously a very cumbersome approach.

The alternative is to build a generic rule visualization tool which can handle all types of rule semantics. What is needed in this case is a protocol for semantics, so that it does not matter which database system is currently used; its semantics will always be reflected correctly by the rule visualization tool.

Composite events

Composite events are a natural part of an active database system and provide powerful possibilities to express when rules shall be triggered. Naturally, a fully-fledged tool for showing rule behaviour must support this feature. Since the responsibility for knowing when composite events occur lies with the dbms, the only issue here is how to visualize events versus composite events in an intuitive way.

A suggestion for how to visualize composite events is to visualize the different composite events as they are "built". The first problem lies within the database: can the event monitor in the dbms report these things? With respect to the event/rule trace tree, a composite event need not be any different from an atomic event: an event is an event. The second problem relates to scalability; vast numbers of "incomplete" composites may be generated which are ultimately irrelevant.

To enhance the debugging facilities it might be useful to provide means to visually reprioritize and suppress rules as well as rule groups, and to manipulate the rules themselves with respect to the different ECA parts.

Exactly how this is done will depend on whether Adela is meant to monitor the database, or to be a simulator. If Adela is to be a monitor, then database functionality can be used to do the actual manipulation, while Adela provides the visual interface of that manipulation. On the other hand, if Adela is only to be a simulator of rule behaviour, then a subset of the manipulation functionality in an active database must be implemented in Adela.

7 CONCLUSIONS

Visualizing rules in database systems is a new area of research, in which very little work has been carried out. In this paper we have briefly described a rule visualization tool for the relational model: Adela. This is in contrast to DEAR, which is a similar tool for the object-oriented model.

We have also introduced the multilevel rule concept, in which different aspects of rule behaviour can be captured. The multilevel rule concept results in three different levels: model level, rule level, and instance level. The purpose of the model level is to set the rules in a data model context. The purpose of the rule level is to represent the different aspects of the rules themselves. The purpose of the instance level is to represent event-, rule-, and data instances. The multilevel rule concept is important when rule visualization tools need to display how rules are related to the data model and/or the data instances.

Adela provides the user with an event/rule trace tree which makes it possible to display the context in which rules are fired. The event/rule trace tree can also display the execution states of rules, i.e. when the rule has been selected for execution, when the condition of the rule has been evaluated, and when the action of the rule is being processed. We also believe that it is important that rule visualization tools can provide a data trace. The objective of the data trace feature is to display what is happening to data instances when they are manipulated by rules.

Since visualization of rules in database systems is a fairly new research area several open questions remain. For example, it is not clear if it is feasible to use rule visualization tools for on-line monitoring of events in an active database.

The Adela prototype system with all its restrictions does not allow for large rule sets or data models. A full scale system must be able to cope with very big rule sets and data models. One way to approach this problem may be to develop a visualization which visualizes everything in such a way that patterns in the information are made clear. One possible way to do this might be to enhance the event/rule trace tree with distinctly different colours for different types of nodes and make the nodes so small that even a very large tree could easily fit within the animation window.

So it may be possible to have a visualization tool which is *scalable*. But what about *speed* and *massive information*? One of the demands on databases is that they do their job *fast* and *efficiently*. Can an on-line visualization tool be developed to match this? As the Adela prototype is implemented, there is absolutely no way it can be made to visualize in real-time. Even if it could be done - would any of the visualizations make any sense to the user? Everything would probably just be a big blur if nothing radical is done to the visualization itself in order to present sensible animations at high speed. Obviously much work lies in this.

But is it necessary to have an on-line visualization tool at all? Might it not be enough to visualize slowly, on the basis of some sort of database log? For most applications this may very well be enough. But as always, there is an exception to every rule, meaning that there will probably be applications that absolutely have to have on-line visualization of rule behaviour.

8 REFERENCES

Diaz, O. and Jaime A. (1993) EXACT: an extensible approach to active object-oriented databases. *Submitted for publication*, 1993.

Diaz, O., Jaime A. and Paton, N.W. (1993) DEAR: a debugger for active rules in an object-oriented context, *in Rules in Database Systems*, Springer-Verlag.

Diaz, O.,Gray P. and Paton, N.W. (1991) Rule management in object-oriented databases: A uniform approach, *in Proceedings of the 17th International Conference on VLDB.*

Ford, L. (1994) Goofy animation system, *Technical Report 266*, University of Exeter, UK.

Fors, T. (1994) ADELA: animated debugging and explanation of active database rules, *M.Sc. dissertation*, department of computer science, University of Skövde, Sweden.

Stasko, J.T. (1992) POLKA animation designer's package, College of computing, Georgia Insitute of Technology, Atlanta.

Stonebraker, M. (1993) The integration of rule systems and database systems, *Memorandum No. UCB/ERL M93/25*, Electronic Research Laboratory, College of Engineering, University of California, Berkely.

9 ACKNOWLEDGEMENTS

The author wishes to thank Dr Brian Lings of the University of Exeter for giving the inspiration that lead to the Adela project, and Mikael Berndtsson of the University of Skövde, who has given much help in making this paper to what it is.

10 BIOGRAPHY

Tomas Fors got his M.Sc. degree in computer science in the fall of 1994 from the University of Skövde, Sweden. He is presently working as a database consultant in Upplands Väsby, Sweden.

PART FIVE

GIS

15

Visual Map Algebra: a direct-manipulation user interface for GIS

M. J. Egenhofer and H. T. Bruns
National Center for Geographic Information and Analysis
and
Department of Spatial Information Science and Engineering
5711 Boardman Hall, University of Maine, Orono, ME 04469-5711, U.S.A., {max, tomb}@mecan1.maine.edu

Abstract

Geographic Information Systems (GISs) store, analyze, and present spatial data and information about geographic space and geographic phenomena. Virtually all aspects of a GIS have inherent spatial, graphical, and visual characteristics. While the database and analytical aspects of GIS have enjoyed considerable advancement in recent areas, a user's access to and interaction with spatial information has not. For such a highly visual system, GIS is often characterized by its distinctly non-visual user interfaces, where command-line and window-icon-menu-pointer (WIMP) user interfaces are most common, whereas visual, direct-manipulation user interfaces are rare. Direct-manipulation user interfaces based on metaphor offer increased usability for GIS. This paper extends the Geographer's Desktop, an innovative direct-manipulation environment for viewing data in a GIS, by integrating a new method for GIS Map Algebra operations. Used by planners, geographers, and other spatial scientists, Map Algebra facilitates the analysis of geographic phenomena. Historically, Map Algebra was performed manually by overlaying thematic map layers, a process that offers a rich source domain for user interface metaphors. *Visual Map Algebra* is a direct-manipulation query language that allows users to construct arbitrarily complex combinations of map layers by stacking iconic representations of thematic map layers onto an interface object called the computational platform. Users visualize such calculated map layers by moving them onto an interface object called the viewing platform that manages cartographic display parameters and is associated with a viewing window. Visual Map Algebra enables exploratory analysis by changing parameters of the overlay and immediately observing the outcome, and adding or removing map layers on the fly.

1 INTRODUCTION

Geographic Information Systems (GISs) store, analyze, and present spatial data and information about geographic space and geographic phenomena. GIS data are inherently visual, and graphical depictions of data's location—symbolized by some characteristic attribute—produce a powerful visual representation. GISs process spatial relations between spatial objects. Often, these relations are depicted visually as a fundamental and spanning set of spatial relations. While the data and processing of GIS have exhibited advanced visual characteristics, the access to these features has remained distinctly non-visual. The user interfaces for advanced GISs have so far been largely textual, and henceforth difficult to use. This paper presents the results of research to enhance the visual nature of GIS user interfaces, through the use of metaphor-based graphics and direct-manipulation. It focuses the design of a direct manipulation query language for GIS Map Algebra. This user interface was developed with an understanding of issues in two different domains: geographic information systems and human-computer interaction (HCI). GIS seeks to model spatial phenomena on a computer, whereas HCI seeks to model human behavior with a computer. A symbiosis of these disciplines brings together the necessary tools for effectively developing visual user interfaces for visual, spatial database systems. The direction here is primarily to bring HCI techniques to bear on GIS, in an effort to improve its usability. The reverse direction is conceivable, however. An understanding of how humans think and communicate about spatial phenomena is basic to human cognition, and may indeed have an impact on HCI.

Various aspects of the world can be captured in a GIS to create a model of reality. Some models consider space full of discernible objects, and measure their attributes and relations (Mark and Frank 1989). Others represent space by the continuous measurement of several different properties, or themes, over the same area (Goodchild 1992). The choice of themes and how they are combined is highly dependent on the purpose of the analysis and modeling. By treating each theme as a variable in an algebra, Tomlin (1983, 1990) has formalized the combination of themes in a Map Algebra. These combinations reveal information that was unavailable in any component theme. Spatial scientists use Map Algebra to explore relationships in the data, and gain an understanding of processes that exist in the physical world.

The techniques of Map Algebra are rooted in the history of GIS—for an overview see Chan and White (1987). The single most important concept is the *overlay* of thematic map layers. Computerized map overlay evolved from manual methods of thematic map overlay (Figure 1). Historically, map overlay was a strictly visual process, with limited analytical capabilities. Map Algebra is a completely generalized form of analytical map overlay, made possible by GIS technology. Layers of thematic data over the same geographic area are combined by some analytical operation, yielding a new thematic layer with integrated information. The analytical operations can be as simple as superimposing one layer over another, or any complex mapping expressed as a function or truth table over the values in the layers (Dorenbeck and Egenhofer, 1991).

Today, thematic map overlay in a GIS is a useful tool for market researchers, planners, social scientists, geologists, geographers, and other "spatially-aware" professionals; however, the true power of GIS Map Algebra is not fully exploited, because the implementations of GIS Map Algebra have not attained a level of usability to make the technology truly available to all that would benefit from its use.

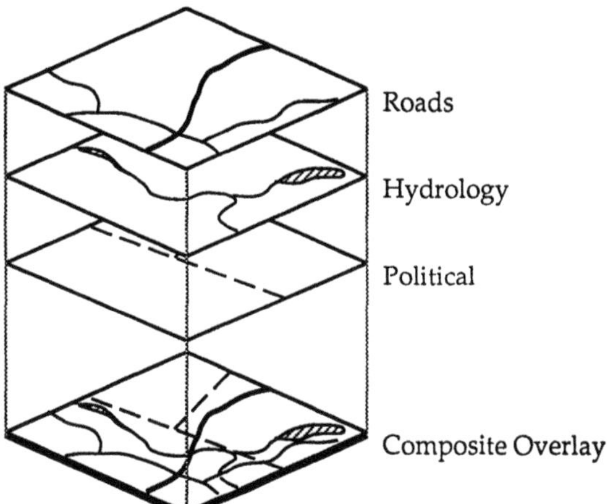

Figure 1 Thematic map overlay.

While window-icon-menu-pointer (WIMP) and flowchart user interfaces for Map Algebra do employ graphical displays, they do so only in a very limited sense. The visual characteristics of the user interface are not fully exploited, because the interaction has been restricted to manipulating user interface widgets—primarily menus and dialog boxes—to create command lines. To improve the visual interaction with spatial data, it is necessary to exploit the spatial characteristics of a user interface:

- The location of an interface object can be made as significant as its appearance.
- How the user articulates the pointing devices can have as much meaning as to what the user points.
- Tapping in on the semantics of movement and location can free the user from the difficult task of constructing command lines.

This paper presents the design of a *Visual Map Algebra*, which is high-level GIS query language that follows these guidelines. Visual Map Algebra minimizes not only the input from a keyboard, but also reduces the use of menu selections and dialog boxes, making it a truly direct-manipulation user interface. Aspects relating to the implementation of such a system, e.g., by translating Map Algebra expressions into an extended SQL syntax (Egenhofer 1991, 1994) have been discussed elsewhere. Also earlier work provides more detail about the limitations of traditional database query languages for geographic applications (Egenhofer and Kuhn 1991) and the motivation for this work (Frank 1992).

The remainder of this paper continues with a survey of different implementations of user interfaces for Map Algebra. Section 3 discusses the Geographer's Desktop as a user interface framework for interaction with geographic data. Section 4 describes the source metaphor for Visual Map Algebra and Section 5 introduces the computational platform as the user interface object where one performs Visual Map Algebra. Section 6 shows how the computational platform is integrated into the Geographer's Desktop to allow a user to perform Visual Map Algebra operations, and in Section 7 we draw our conclusions and discuss future work.

2 IMPLEMENTATIONS OF MAP ALGEBRA

There is a complex relationship between analytical software, the user, and the user's ability to create complex models, solve problems, and make decisions (Turk 1993). Users possess certain task knowledge, spatial abilities, and problem-solving skills that are brought to bear in the user's work environment (Nyerges 1993). The role of the user interface is to provide a structure consistent with this environment. User interfaces for GIS Map Algebra generally fall into the following categories: command-line user interfaces; WIMP user interfaces; and graphical user interfaces.

2.1 Command-line user interfaces for Map Algebra

With a command-line user interface, the user types in Map Algebra expressions, one at a time, at a command prompt. The syntax of the commands is highly significant, and the order of the commands is also sometimes important. Table 1 shows examples of a Map Algebra operation to create a 50 unit-wide buffer around streams in various Map Algebra command languages. Arc/Info is a full-featured, command line GIS (ESRI 1990). The software has literally thousands of commands, from which a user must select in order to find those that will fulfill any given task. MGE Grid Analysis (Intergraph 1993), Arc/Info GRID (ESRI 1992), and OSU-MAP (Sandhu *et al.* 1987) are more direct implementations of Tomlin's Map Algebra.

Table 1 Creating a buffer around streams in four different Map Algebra implementations

Map Algebra command	*GIS*
BUFFER streams streams_buf # # 50 # LINE	Arc/Info
streams_buf = EXPAND (streams, 50, LIST, 1)	Arc/Info GRID
streams_buf = FOCALPROXIMITY OF streams BY 50	MGE Grid Analyst
BUFFER streams BY 50 FOR streams_buf	OSU-MAP

Command-line systems proliferated before graphical user interfaces were available. Their syntax can be formally defined, making command interpreters and compilers relatively easy to create. Developing macros or programs is easily accomplished by grouping commands and control statements in files. However, command-line user interfaces have very poor visual and physical characteristics. Users interact only with text, which has several shortcomings: a screen full of text has a density of information that is too high for most users; typing is an interaction that is tiring and error-prone; and command-line user interfaces force users to be aware of command names and syntax. The number of commands is so great at times that a user spends more time thinking about command tools to use than thinking about the task at hand (Gould 1993).

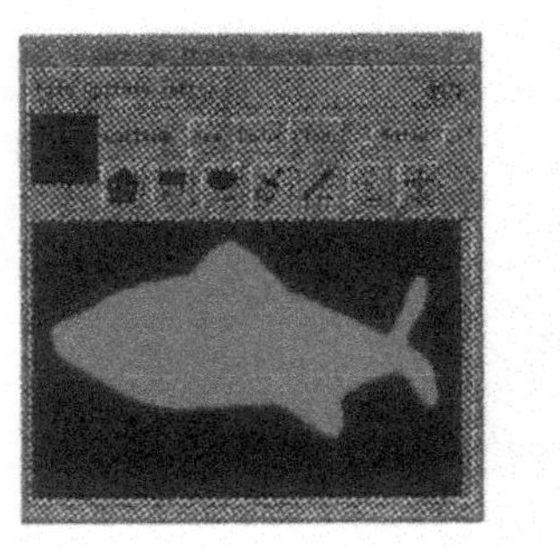

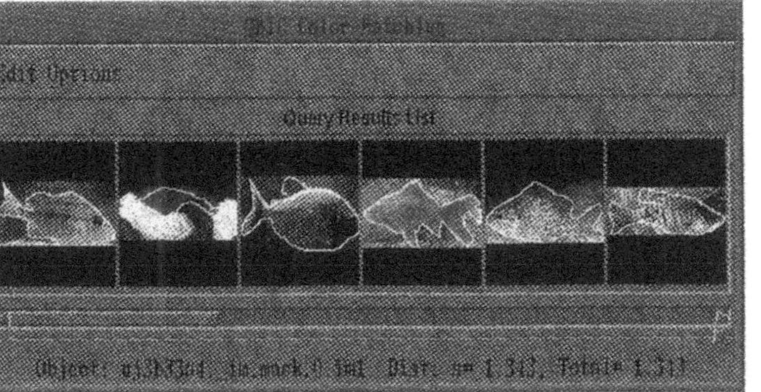

Plate 1 Example shape query. Left: freehand sketch of shape. Right: query results showing first six returned items.

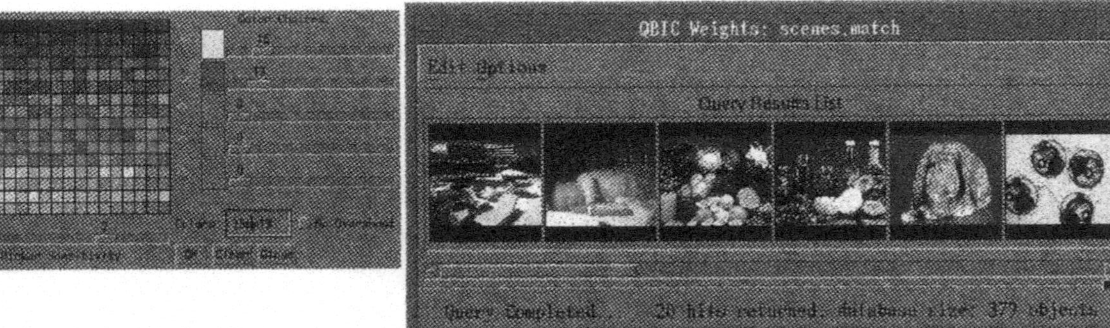

Plate 2 Example color histogram query. Left: color selection show 15% yellow, 13% blue. Right: query results showing first six returned items.

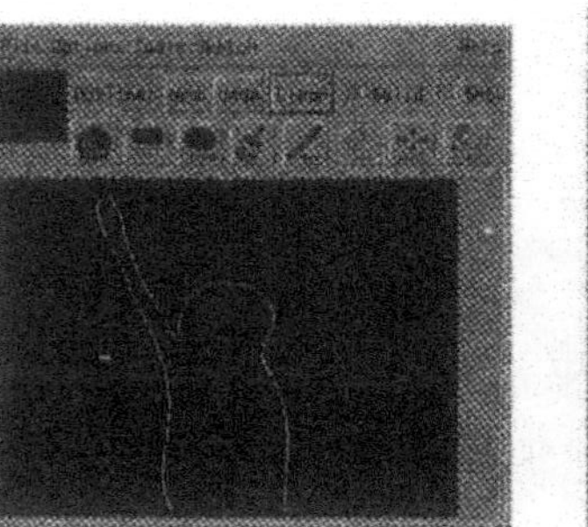

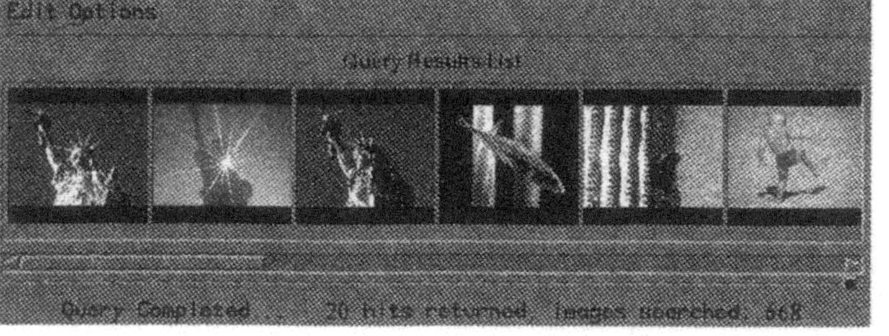

Plate 3 Example query by sketch. Left: freehand drawn sketch. Right: query results showing the first six returned items.

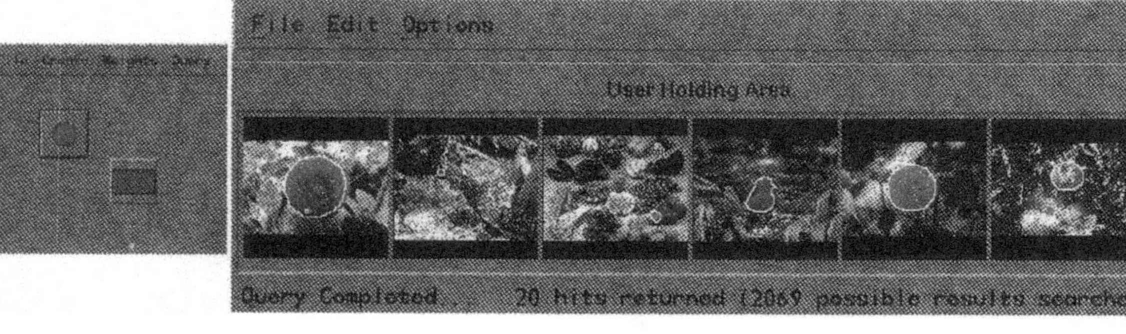

Plate 4 Example 'multi' query. Left: a visual query specification for a scene containing a red, round object (red icon) on a green background (green icon). Right: query results showing first six returned items.

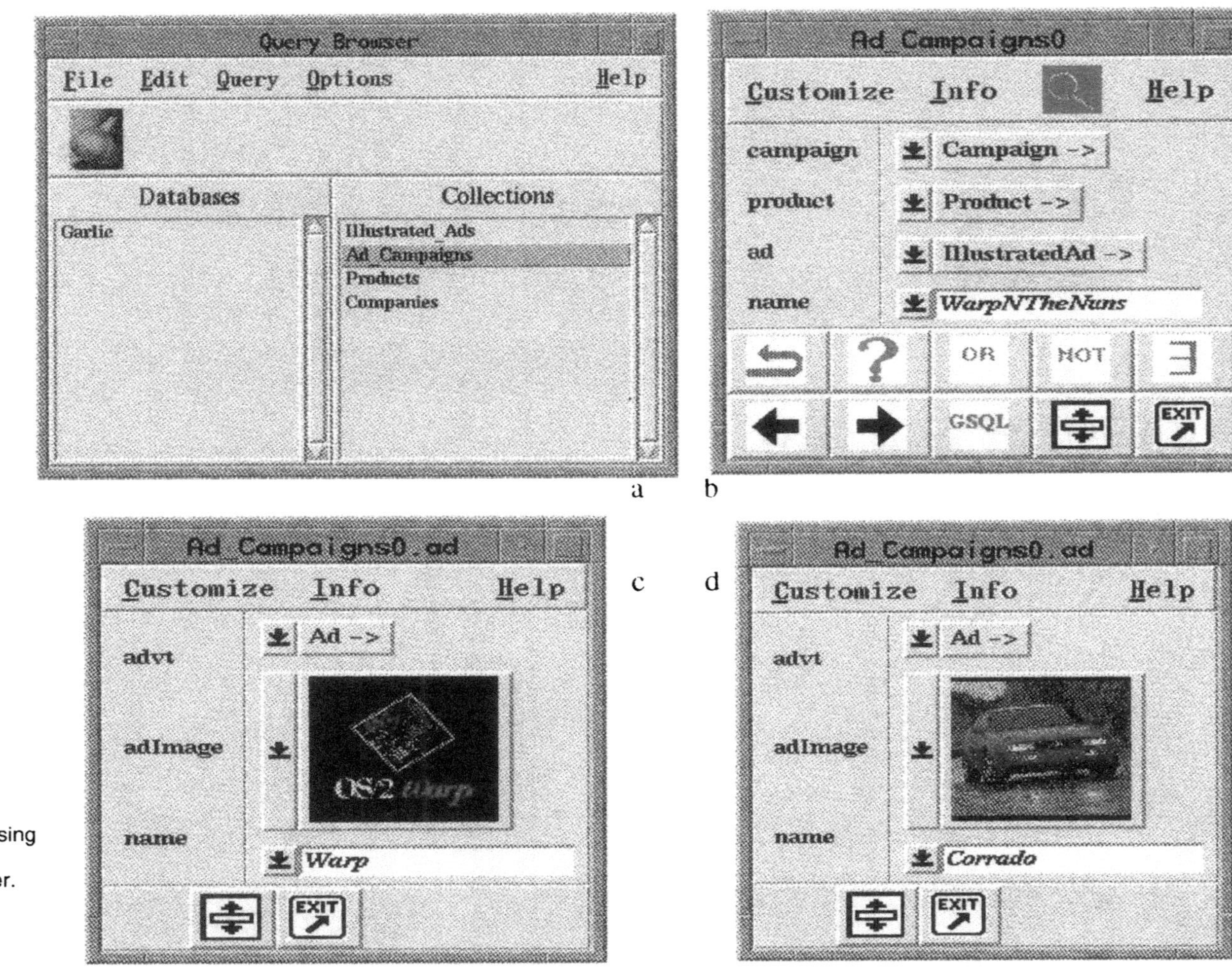

Plate 5 Browsing using the Query/Browser.

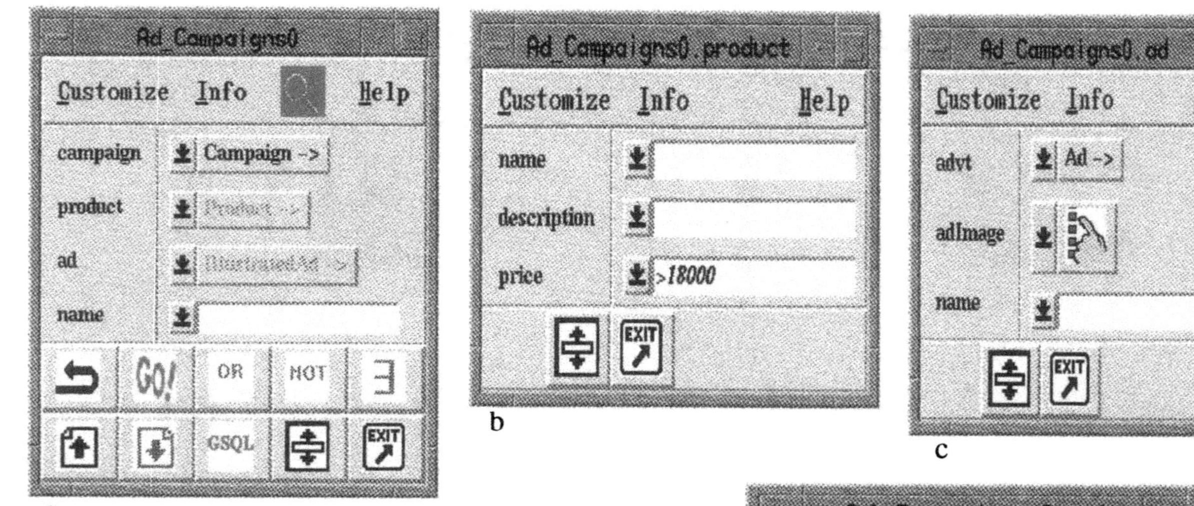

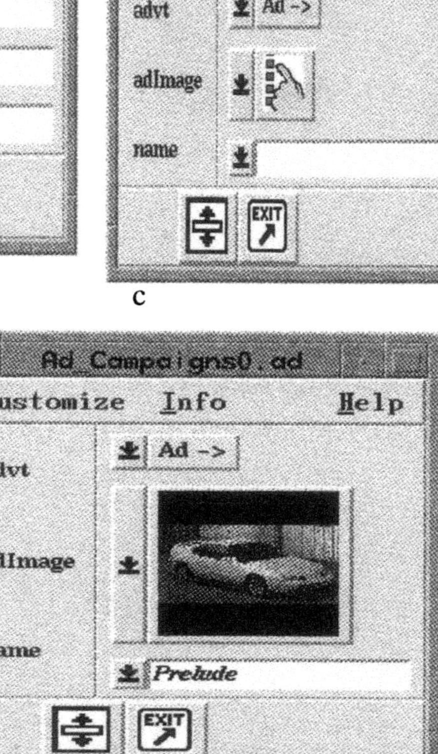

Plate 6 Querying in the Query/Browser.

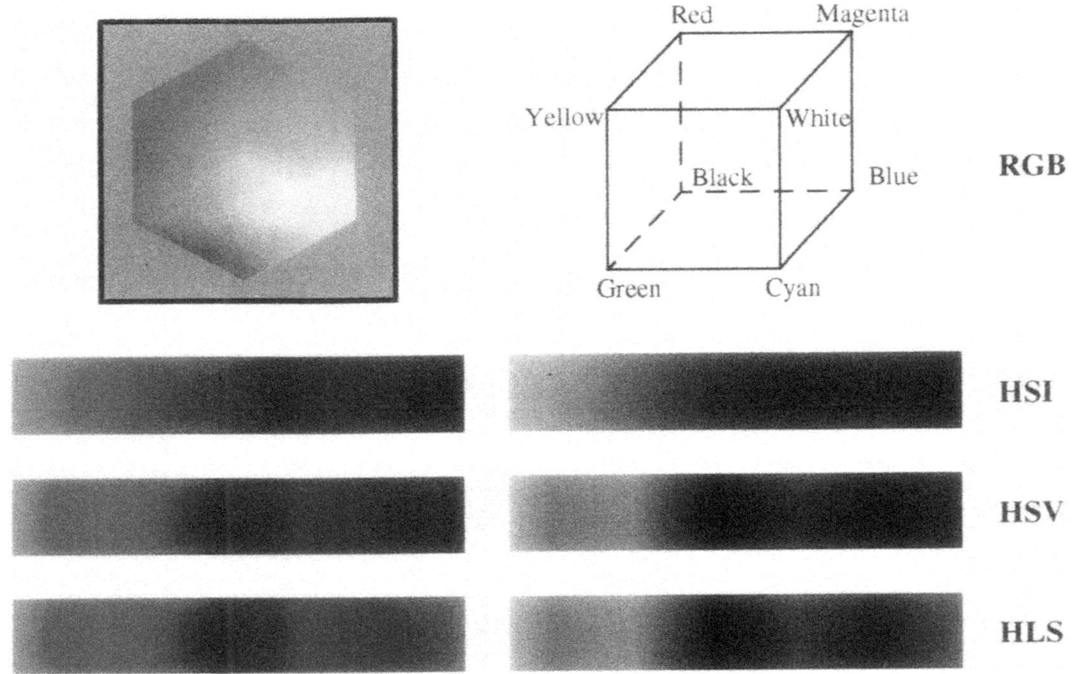

Plate 7 Color scales generated using different color models.

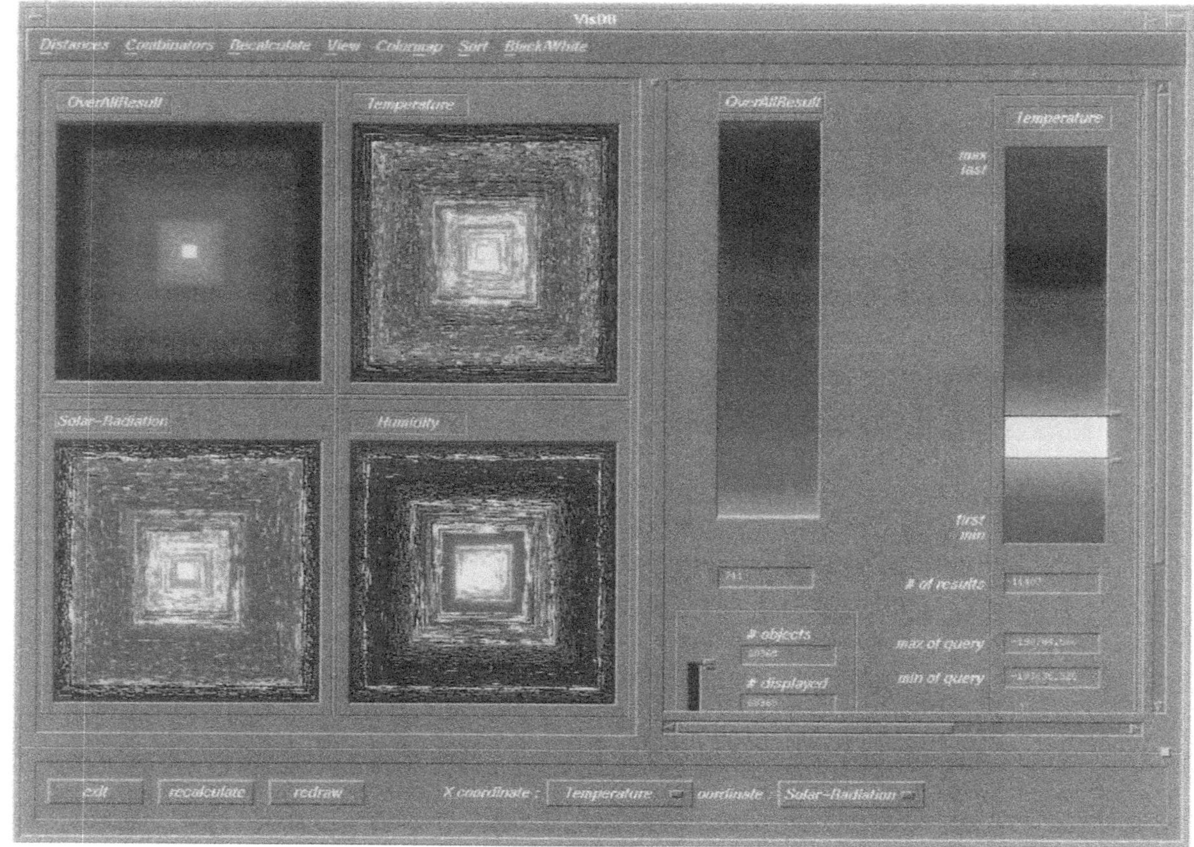

Plate 8 The Spiral Visualization Technique.

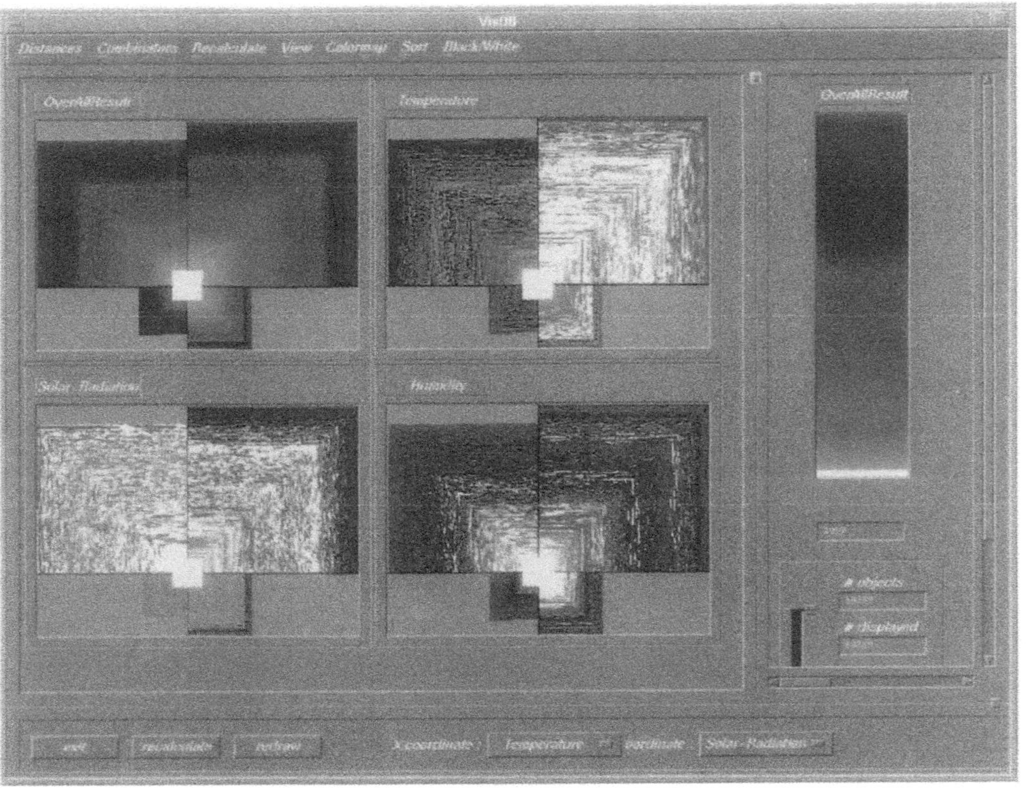

Plate 9 The Axes Visualization Technique.

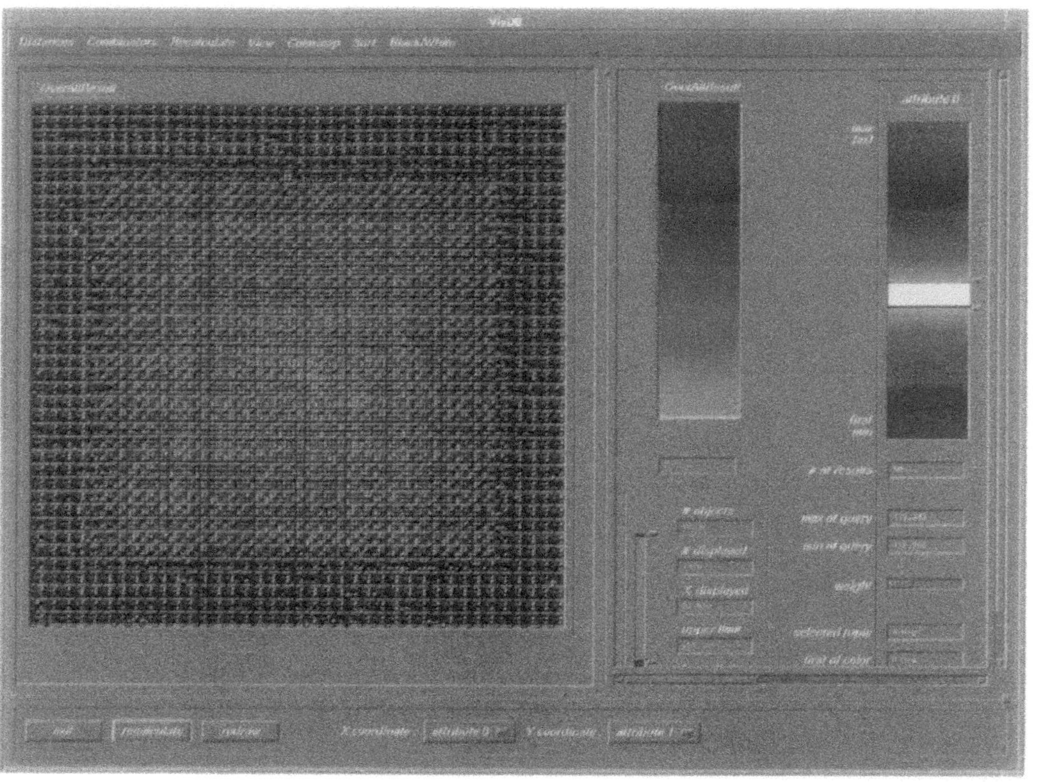

Plate 10 The Grouping Visualization Technique.

2.2 WIMP user interfaces for Map Algebra

Window user interfaces for Map Algebra offer users a variety of menus and forms with which to interact. By selecting items from menus, clicking buttons and icons, and by filling in fields in a form, a user constructs a Map Algebra expression. MGE Grid Analyst (MGGA), Intergraph's Map Algebra module, offers the user a form that is filled out to construct a Map Algebra statement (Intergraph 1993), as does Map II, a GIS for the Apple Macintosh (Pazner *et al.* 1989). With each, the user interacts with fields to select the desired functions and data, and the system generates a Map Algebra expression in another field of the form.

WIMP user interfaces have a much stronger visual component than command-line user interfaces. By viewing menus, buttons, and icons, a use is made aware of possible choices. Pointing to selections replaces remembering and typing commands. The bit-mapped graphics alone contribute to the creation of a more pleasant environment for users. While WIMP user interfaces do reduce the amount of memorization of command names a user must do, the process of mapping a task to a suite of commands remains. The user interfaces mentioned above replace typing with button pushing. Disabling certain controls at certain times can prevent the user from generating syntax errors. But command lines, and their syntax, still exist. For GIS Map Algebra, WIMP user interfaces offer little significant improvement over command-line user interfaces.

2.3 Graphical user interfaces for Map Algebra

For GIS Map Algebra, graphical user interfaces based on flowcharts are the most prevalent. Flowcharts have long been an aid in programming, and provide a means to logically structure a task in a format close to a user's mental representation (Myers 1990). Graphical flowcharts exceed command-languages in exploiting the human vision process, which is optimized for multi-dimensional data. Flowchart user interfaces have much richer visual and physical characteristics than WIMP user interfaces.

Flowcharts have been used by GIS researchers to illustrate the structure of an environmental model (Tomlin and Berry 1979; Berry 1987; Laurini and Thompson 1992; Berry 1993). Lanter and Essinger (1991) developed a flowchart user interface to run on top of Arc/Info, with which GIS data is represented by icons, and functions by lines connecting the icons. Kirby and Pazner's (1990) user interface of MAP II has both data and functions represented by icons, connected by graphical "pipes." The Erdas Imagine Model Maker (ERDAS 1993) allows users to manipulate icons for data and functions for structuring image processing operations. However, the focus of these systems is on the visualization of flowchart user interfaces, not on the interactions that underlie their creation. The placement of icons has no semantic significance to the model being constructed. These flowchart user interfaces do not eliminate the need for the user to be aware of and conform to certain command line syntax. The visual and physical characteristics inherent to GIS Map Algebra may be used to create more appropriate user interfaces.

3 THE GEOGRAPHER'S DESKTOP

Direct manipulation is an appropriate interaction style for GIS Map Algebra. Historically, the process of map overlay was a visual, tactile operation. Direct manipulation, accompanied with a visual, graphical representation of data, fosters exploratory data analysis. Exploration creates a dynamic, absorbing, and satisfying task environment. Users will become less aware of the existence of the user interface while becoming engrossed in their tasks. Direct manipulation data analysis is desirable for spatially-aware scientists performing Map Algebra in a GIS. Direct manipulation affords an empowering environment for spatially-aware scientists performing Map Algebra in a GIS.

Direct manipulation is a metaphor for touching and manipulating objects in our environment. This form of human-computer interaction became popular with full-screen text editors, like EMACS, and spreadsheets, like VISICALC, with which users could move directly to the text they wanted to edit and effect changes. Mapping movement or gesture to intent is very difficult. Mapping placement to command semantics, in a visual user interface, has more immediate, viable realizations.

The *Geographer's Desktop* (Egenhofer and Richards 1993b) is a visual, direct manipulation environment for interacting with spatial databases and viewing their content. Two fundamental, and related, metaphors form the basis of this user interface (1) thematic map layers are represented by map layer icons, providing a visual link with the source domain of the user's task and (2) the stacking of map layers is metaphorically mapped to direct manipulation in the user interface. The user sees and stacks map layer icons to express visualization and analysis functions. This is a natural mapping from the user's domain, where mylar map sheets are physically stacked on a light table to construct views. Manipulation of map layers is complemented by the *viewing platform* (Egenhofer and Richards 1993a), which is a metaphor for a light table (Figure 2). It facilitates GIS database query and visualization operations. To visualize GIS data, users place data layer icons onto the viewing platform The generation of a map view is very visual, and the placement of icons has semantic significance. The result is a tightly coupled association between the execution and evaluation of a map view and database query.

Figure 2 The Viewing Platform with a data layer on top, and another one off the platform.

3.1 Thematic map layer visualization

The icons are visualized as a perspective view of a map sheet. This perspective view gives the icons a 3D appearance, resembling actual map sheets. This metaphor is strengthened when several such icons coexist, and are stacked on top of each other (Figure 3). The visualization of the icons includes shadows, to enhance their 3D appearance.

Graphics can be placed on the icons to allude to the theme of the layer (Egenhofer and Richards 1993a). The design of the graphics depends on its contents. For some layers the graphics can be established by the system, but after some analysis, they would no longer be appropriate. It is also possible to put a graphic representation of the layer's data type on the icon (Lanter 1991). It is likely that a visualization of both theme and data type would be of use, helping the user select data layers for both viewing and analysis. Egenhofer and Richards

(1993b) divide the face of the icons into two parts, data area and map legend, to access respectively the database query and visualization parameters for each theme.

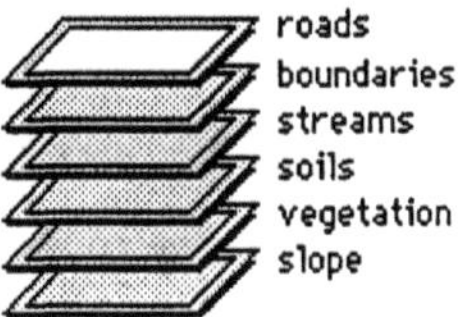

Figure 3 Stacked map layers.

3.2 Thematic map layer interaction

Data layer icons respond to standard point-and-click, drag-and-drop interactions. The user places a data layer icon on any interface object, or on the data stack. The visualization of the layer icons changes in response to a user's manipulations. Layers highlight when selected with the mouse. An outline or shadow of the layer follows the cursor when it is being moved. If there is an error or an ill-defined function, the appearance of the icon changes to alert the user.

3.3 Thematic map layer organization

Data layers can also be grouped into classes by sharing some visual characteristic, such as color or texture, or grouped spatially in different stacks on the Geographer's Desktop. Employing graphical enhancements generally increases the size of the icons, and the separation between stacked icons. The appearance of stacked icons is crucial for maintaining the map overlay metaphor of stacked thematic data maps. If the layer icons must be vertically separated to reveal added graphics, the effect of this metaphor will diminish. In the visualizations presented here, no such graphics are used, and the data layers are distinguished only by their names.

Layers can be associated in another way, by project, and stored in a map cabinet (Figure 4).

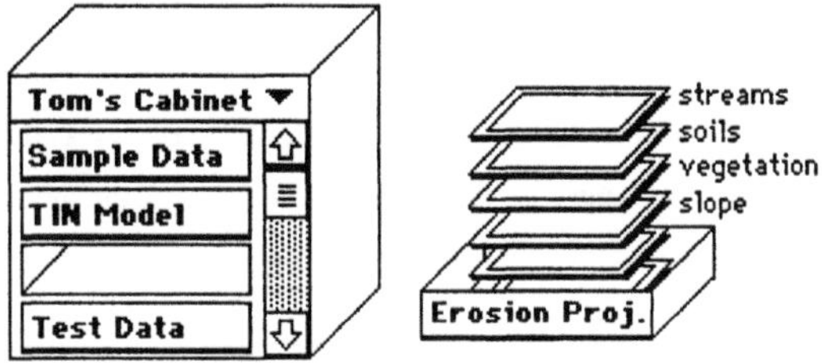

Figure 4 Map filing cabinet, with open drawer.

The user can select from the many drawers of the cabinet, opening by clicking on it with the mouse, and pulling it out. Once opened, the layers associated with that drawer appear stacked in the drawer and can be manipulated. Several drawers could be open at once, and layers can be moved between them, or multiple copies could be stored in different project drawers.

4. VISUAL MAP ALGEBRA ON THE GEOGRAPHER'S DESKTOP

The viewing platform is a highly usable user interface for visualizing thematic map layers and combining them in a particular way. Egenhofer and Richards (1993a) chose *superimposition* as the operation to combine those layers that are stacked up on the viewing platform, i.e., the top layer overrides the value of the non-empty value in the bottom layer (Table 2).

Table 2 The truth table for superimposition of layers *A* and *B* (*a* and *b* are values in the respective layers *A* and *B*)

A	*B*	*A on top of B*	*B on top of A*
empty	empty	empty	empty
a	empty	a	a
empty	b	b	b
a	b	a	b

While this combination is sufficient to do simple spatial analysis, it is far from the power Map Algebra provides with a much larger variety of analytical operations to combine map layers. For example, one may want to combine layers such that the result contains their intersection, determine the Voronoi regions, i.e., the neighborhoods around points in a layer, or create buffer zones (Table 3).

Table 3 The truth table for the intersection of layers *A* and *B* (*a* and *b* are respective values in layers *A* and *B*; *c* is the value in the resulting layer) and the formation of a 50 ft buffer around the intersection of the two layers.

<table>
<tr><th>A</th><th>B</th><th>A intersects B</th><th>50 ft-buffer (A intersects B)</th></tr>
<tr><td>empty</td><td>empty</td><td>empty</td><td rowspan="3">} c if cell is less than 50 ft
from a non-empty cell;
otherwise empty</td></tr>
<tr><td>a</td><td>empty</td><td>empty</td></tr>
<tr><td>empty</td><td>b</td><td>empty</td></tr>
<tr><td>a</td><td>b</td><td>c</td><td>c</td></tr>
</table>

While both employ the map overlay metaphor, and direct manipulation of map layer icons, the differences between these operations make it awkward to use the viewing platform for computational overlay. It might be considered also to use the viewing platform for the selection of the analytical operation to combine the layers; however, such a choice would have some serious drawbacks, because the viewing platform would now incorporate an additional functionality. Users may be confused as to what to choose—display parameters or computation formula. More importantly however, is that not every computational overlay results in something a user wants to be displayed graphically. Frequently, intermediate computational results may be constructed which in turn are used as input for the next calculation. With a viewing platform that handles the specification of the analytical formula as well as the display parameters, it would become difficult to implement intuitive mechanisms to use the result of one map overlay operation in another map overlay. To resolve these conflicts, it is necessary to introduce another concept into the Geographer's Desktop in the form of a dedicated interface object where computational map overlay will be performed.

The design goal of this extension is (1) to perform the task of computational map overlay by using some computation metaphor and (2) to integrate with the existing concepts and structure of the Geographer's Desktop, particularly the viewing platform, allowing users to exploit previously learned behavior, and allow users to elicit knowledge from the their task domain.

Three computation metaphors have been considered: (1) horizontal equations, (2) flowcharts, and (3) vertical equations. *Horizontal equations*, when read from left to right, are sentences in an abstract, mathematical language. The horizontal equation metaphor can be implemented directly with a command-line user interface when the equation language is completely defined. A language including GIS Map Algebra functions, then, creates a command-line user interface for GIS Map Algebra. Such a user interface, however, does not use visual map layers, or the visual and physical aspects of the map overlay metaphor. *Flowcharts* are a more visual computation metaphor, but they also do not employ the map overlay metaphor. Instead, they use a linking metaphor to establish connections between data and functions. A computation metaphor with which the link between data and function is accomplished with stacking is desirable.

A *vertical equation* generates expressions with operands in an arrangement similar to the stacking of layers onto the viewing platform. Making those operands thematic map layers yields a computation metaphor employing the map overlay metaphor. This is called the *addition line*, since the structure of vertical equations has its roots in the mathematical tool typically used to teach children addition, or used by adults when adding a column of numbers. This structure metaphorically evolves into the interface object for GIS Map Algebra, called the *computational platform* (Figure 5).

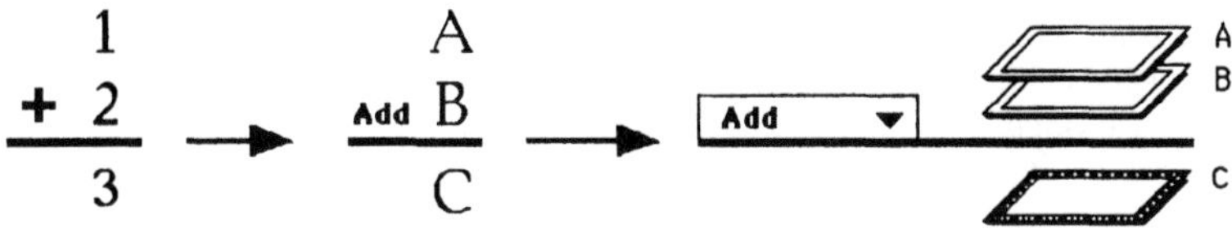

Figure 5 Evolution from addition line for numbers to computational platform for layers.

The operands are placed above a line that separates the result of the computation. The operation also appears above this line, to the left of the operands. The line that separates the "inputs" from the "output" is called the platform because the inputs are stacked on top. The platform can be thought to physically support the inputs. This is an application of the SURFACE image schema, a basic cognitive structure (Johnson 1987), where inputs are either on or off the platform. The strength of the metaphor lies in the fact that this is the same image schema used in the physical process of map overlay, as well in the viewing platform. The computational platform evolves from replacing the fixed numbers and symbols to a more generalized form, with variable names and a named operation. Finally, replacing the variable names with named icons representing thematic data layers, and by enclosing the operation within a pop-up menu, forms the final visualization of the computational platform.

5. THE COMPUTATIONAL PLATFORM

The interaction with the computational platform is consistent with the direct manipulation environment of the Geographer's Desktop. To create a complete Map Algebra expression requires several interactions: (1) creating a computational platform, (2) selecting a platform function, (3) choosing the layers to be combined, and if necessary (4) setting the parameters of the operation. To formulate a complete Map Algebra model will likely require the creation of several computational platforms, which can coexist on the Geographer's Desktop, be aggregated into a single platform, or be abstracted and represented by a new data layer icon.

5.1 Creating a computational platform

A new, empty computational platform consists of the horizontal line onto which layers will be stacked, and a pop-up menu for the selection of the platform parameters. To provide the user with guidance as to what to do with platform and layers, the computational platform features templates for input layers. These input slots have a dual purpose as they provide feedback to the user on where to put input layers and how many are needed, and they allow the user to specify, for multiple input functions, which layer is associated with which variable. Only for commutative operations, such as add and multiply, the order of the inputs on the platform can be ignored.

There are many ways to create a computational platform on the Geographer's Desktop. A platform can be created by selecting its icon from an interface tool box, or by activating a **Create Computational Platform** operation from a pull-down menu. A more natural way of making a new platform is achieved by drawing a horizontal line, much like drawing an addition line to add some numbers. This interaction can be mapped onto direct manipulations in the user interface, such that the user sketches a line representing the platform, and the system recognizes this gesture and compiles the line into a new computational platform. The sequence of creating a computational platform and assigning the layers is actually up to the user: one can first draw a platform and then stack the layers on top, or one could stack layers somewhere on the Geographer's Desktop and then draw a line underneath them.

5.2 Selecting platform function

Each computational platform is associated with one computational operation. To set the platform's operation, the platform has a popup menu, which allows the user to change its function at any time, even after the input layers have been added. The visualization of the computational platform changes dynamically, as the user walks through the function menu, to provide additional information about the function. For example, the number of empty input slots on top of the platform changes to reflect the number of inputs required by the function currently being pointed at in the menu (Figure 6). Functions that require less layers than already placed onto the platform are dimmed and disabled for selection.

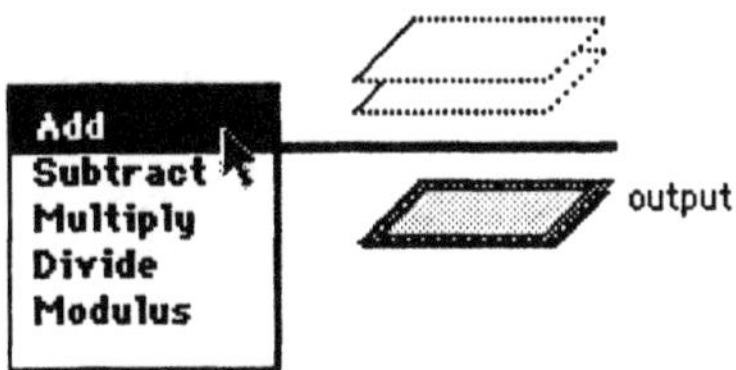

Figure 6 Platform function popup menu.

5.3 Choosing layers as platform inputs

To add a data layer to a computational platform, the user drags and drops the data layer icon onto a computational platform (Figure 7). Rather than moving the original onto the platform, this action produces a link to the original ("alias") so that the same layer can be used on different platforms at the same time. The use of links also allows changes in the original data set to be propagated through any subsequent analysis.

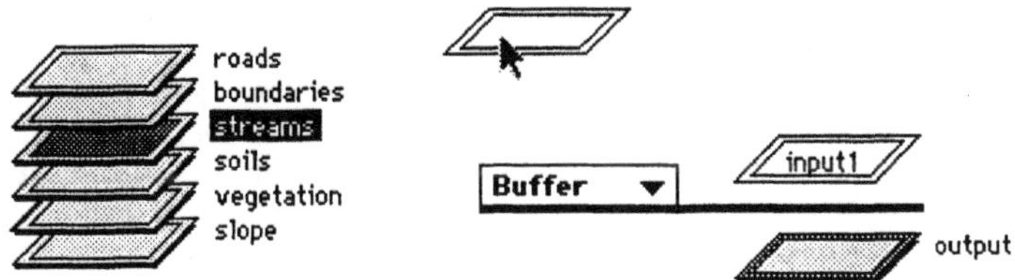

Figure 7 Adding the streams layer to buffer platform.

When a layer appears over a platform, the bottom of the platform highlights, as does the next available input slot. When the platform highlights, the user may release the layer, and it will "fall" onto the platform. For platforms with multiple inputs, the user can guide the layer outline to the desired input slot, which highlights as the layer outline intersects it. Like moving individual layers onto a computational platform, multiple layers can be selected and dragged as a group. All manipulations to drag layers onto a computational platform are reversed to correct mistakes or make changes.

While input slots guide users, they also make it difficult to support functions with an indefinite number of inputs. On the viewing platform, a user can continue to add additional data layers at will, although the resulting graphical representation may begin to look cluttered. For associative operations, this behavior is also possible on the computational platform.

Another aspect of input slots becomes clear if customized functions are considered. Such functions may integrate different algebraic operations into a single Map Overlay operation and, depending on the layers' positions in the stack, different results may be obtained; therefore, input slots must be related with specific function variables. Figure 8 shows a computational platform visualized with a custom function beneath. The names of the variables in the formula expression match those in the input slots. When the user drags a data layer icon over an input slot, the name of the corresponding variable in the formula expression would highlight, reinforcing the connection between the input and the variable.

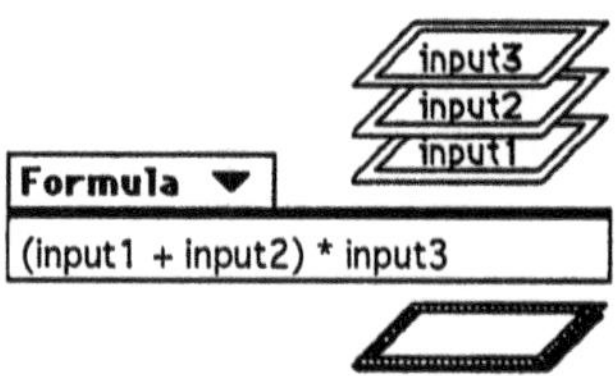

Figure 8 Custom function with labeled input slots.

5.4 Setting platform parameters

Besides the standard operations of intersection or union there are parametrized Map Algebra operations, which require a user to specify the overlay operation *and* its parameters. For example, making a buffer zone—a parametrized, unary operation—also requires the user to determine the extent of the buffer. While it could be convenient to choose from different buffer operations, each with a different extend such as 10m_Buffer, 50m_Buffer, 100m_Buffer, it is still necessary to offer a generic buffer that can be customized and modified on the fly. Unfortunately, the specification of values does not fit with the selection of an item from a menu. Some operations may have a parameter, others may have several parameters, and many have none. Since the parameters of such operations vary considerably with the function and the data model, the interaction is consequently hard to generalize. A small number of parameters can be located near or in the computational platform. For example, parameters can be placed under the popup menu (Figure 9a), but then interaction with the popup would block the parameters, and the user would be unable to see them change dynamically with the selection function. If the parameters are built into an extended platform, but the platform starts to look less and less like its metaphorical origins (Figure 9b). Alternatively, setting parameters may be relegated to a dialog box that can be accessed by double-clicking the operation.

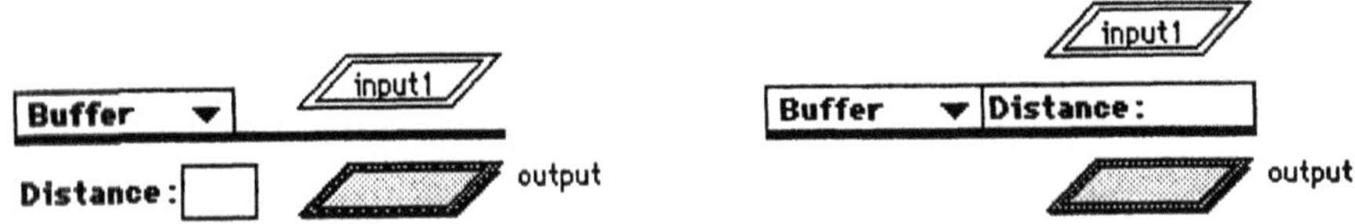

Figure 9 Platform with function parameters (a) beneath and (b) in the platform bar.

5.5 Platform nesting and aggregates

The appearance of the platform output layer icon is virtually the same as the data layer icons. This similarity affords the nesting of functions. A user interface for Map Algebra must have a mechanism allowing the output of one function to be used as the input to another. The computational platform accomplishes this by treating the output layer like any other data layer. Functions can be nested by dragging the output layer of one platform to the input slot of another. After creating and populating several computational platforms, the user has effectively created a formula or model. These platforms can be aggregated together to create a single, custom formula platform. This formula is then available in the function popup, and can be used repeatedly with other data. A simple method of creating a formula is by "example." The user proceeds with the analysis in a step-by-step fashion, creating and nesting multiple platforms. Other methods of creating a formula are possible. Expert users can create an empty formula platform, and then type in the function in the box below the platform bar. Figure 10 shows how the expression A+(B*C) is produced. The **Multiply** platform is created, and the layers B and C are placed on it. The **Add** platform is then created, and the layer A is placed on it. Finally, the output layer of the multiply platform is manipulated in the same fashion as the other data layers: dragged and dropped onto the **Add** platform.

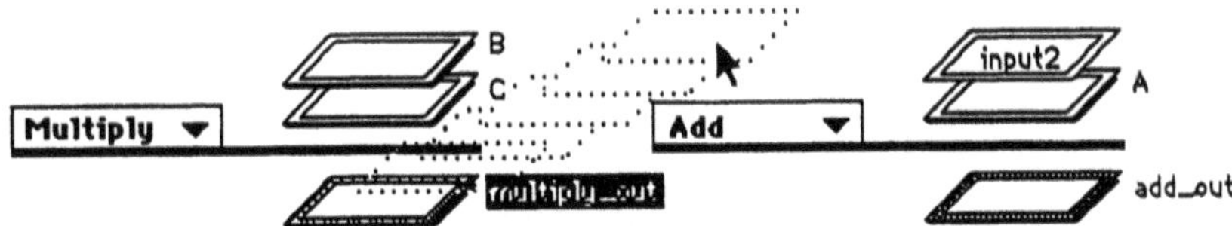

Figure 10 Using one platform's output as an input to another.

Reversely, compound layers may be expanded, either into multiple computational platforms or into atomic layers on a single platform with a complex platform function. Figure 11a shows a platform aggregate consisting of one data layer, and two platform output layers, added as inputs. Each of the platform output layers can be expanded, leaving their component layers in their place. In Figure 11b, the layer *streams_buf* has been expanded: *streams_buf* is replaced by the data layer *streams*, and the function **Multiply** becomes a formula, in which the **Buffer** operation is a part. Since the *streams_buf* layer was the output of another computational platform, which performed a buffer on streams, the computational platforms in Figures 11a and 11b are equivalent.

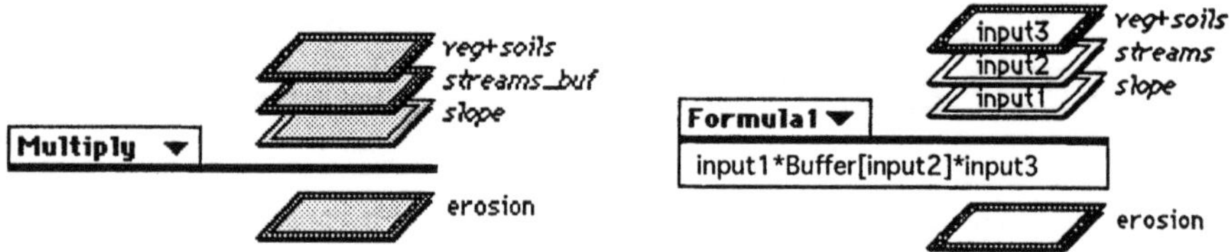

Figure 11 (a) Platform aggregate and (b) partially converted to a formula.

Figure 11b shows the platform visualized with the formula expression. The variable names illustrate the relation between the inputs and the formula. Alternatively, the names of the actual data layers can be substituted into the formula, and then the input layer names would not be needed. Figure 12a shows the same platform further expanded to the lowest possible level, showing nothing but data layer icons. Once created, the user can assign a name to the formula, which will then appear as one of the choices in the function pop-up menu, allowing it to be used again easily. In Figure 12b, the function name appears on the platform, along with brackets to show the groupings between the functional elements.

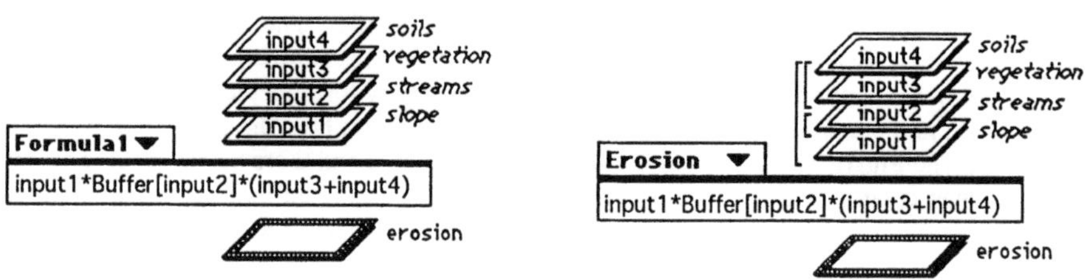

Figure 12 Platform aggregate (a) reduced to custom formula with all data layer inputs and (b) with named custom formula and functional groupings visualized.

6 INTEGRATION OF THE COMPUTATIONAL PLATFORM ON THE GEOGRAPHER'S DESKTOP

The computational platform integrates well on the Geographer's Desktop. Both the viewing platform (Egenhofer and Richards 1993a) and the computational platform (Egenhofer and Bruns 1994) are based on the direct manipulation of thematic data layers. The appearances of the viewing and computational platforms are different, driven by their respective metaphors, because their functionality are also significantly different. These interface objects can coexist on the desktop, and layers can be moved from one to the other at will. Intermediate and end results of Map Algebra expressions can be visualized by placing the respective output layers on a viewing platform, and with several viewing platforms open at the same time, users will be able to analyze visually different Map Algebra models at the same time and to compare them. If the Map Algebra model is then changed in any way, these changes propagate through the model and are immediately visualized. There is, however, some redundancy in the Visual Map Algebra, because combining several layers on the computational platform with an operation "superimpose" or "add," and placing the resulting layer onto a viewing platform is equivalent to stacking the initial layers onto the viewing platform. Since the results do not contradict each other, no interaction problems are foreseen.

Figure 13 shows a snapshot of a Geographer's Desktop. From the map layers available in the map cabinet (in the lower left corner), the user created with the Visual Map Algebra an erosion model on the computational platform in the left top, and a buffer zone around streams on the computational platform in the right top.

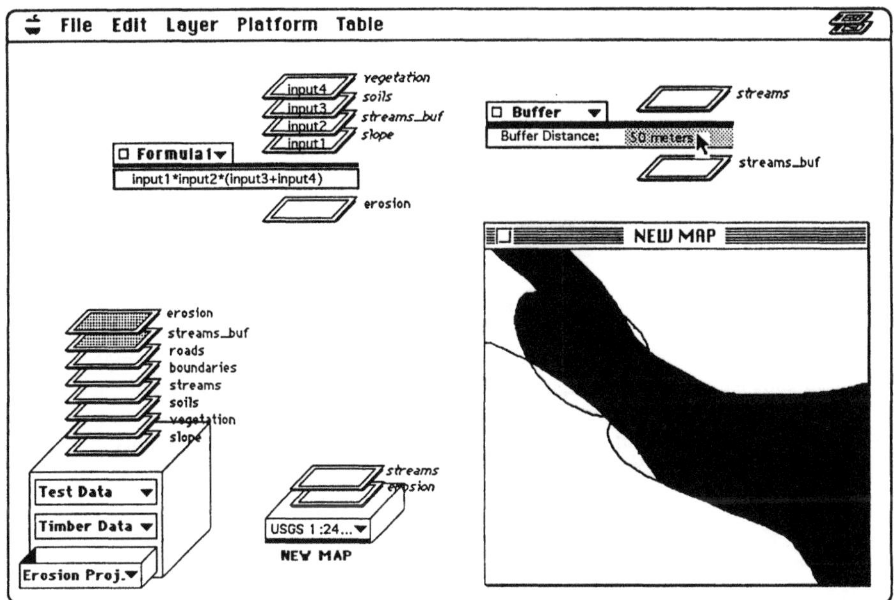

Figure 13 An erosion model created and analyzed with Visual Map Algebra on the Geographer's Desktop.

The results of the two Visual Map Algebra operations were placed on a viewing platform (bottom center) and the corresponding map view is shown in the window on the right. The user now analyzes the relationship between areas of high erosion potential and a flood zone by varying the width parameter of the stream buffer. Any change of this parameter is immediately propagated into the stream buffer layer and displayed in the viewing window.

6 CONCLUSIONS

GIS Map Algebra embodies a range of tools and techniques for spatial analysis. It is generally independent of data model, system type, or implementation. The investigation of GIS Map Algebra yields useful metaphors for user interface design. The map overlay metaphor and the addition-line metaphor formed the foundation for the design of the Visual Map Algebra. Map overlay has visual and physical components. The visual components are mapped onto the appearance and function of interface icons, and the physical component is mapped to the direct manipulation of these icons to form Map Algebra expressions.

A prototype mockup of Visual Map Algebra has been implemented on a Macintosh using Macromind Director as an animation tool. Frequent user feedback from such demonstrations was critical during its design. Several issues are subject to further investigations. Obvious steps are a prototype implementation on top of a GIS, systematic user testing, and performance comparisons with other Map Algebra implementations, or such alternatives as moveable filters (Stone *et al.* 1994). For a limited set of tasks, some analytical comparisons, using cognitive walkthrough analysis (Polson *et al.* 1992), have been made between Visual Map Algebra and a flowchart model (Bruns 1994).

Open questions for future work include:

- The integration of multiple representations into a single user interface. There are tasks like examining the lineage of a compound layer, which may be easier with a flowchart user interface than with nested computational platforms. How can the two user interfaces be integrated seamlessly?
- So far, (carto)graphic aspects have been deferred exclusively to the viewing platform, though an earlier version of layer icons integrated the data with their presentations (Egenhofer and Richards 1993b). Can one infer a reasonable graphical presentation of a compound layer from knowledge about the graphical presentation of the individual layers *and* the algebraic properties of the operation combining them?
- Can GIS operations that manipulate date be integrated with the Geographer's Desktop, without resorting to selections from pull-down menus and toolboxes?

8 ACKNOWLEDGMENTS

This work was partially supported by Intergraph Corporation and the National Science Foundation under grant number SBR-8810917 for the National Center for Geographic Information and Analysis. Max Egenhofer's work is further supported by NSF under grant IRI-9309230, Environmental Systems Research Institute, Space Imaging Inc., the Scientific Division of the North Atlantic Treaty Organization, and the Maine Mathematics and Science Alliance.

9 REFERENCES

Berry, J. (1987) Fundamental Operations in Computer-Assisted Map Analysis. *International Journal of Geographic Information Systems* **1**, 119–36.

Berry, J. (1993) Cartographic Modeling: The Analytical Capabilities of GIS, in *Environmental Modeling with GIS* (eds. M. Goodchild, B. Parks, and L. Steyaert), pp. 58–74, Oxford University Press, New York.

Bruns, H.T. (1994) *Direct Manipulation User Interfaces for GIS Map Algebra.* Master's Thesis, Department of Surveying Engineering, University of Maine, Orono, ME.

Chan, K. and White, D. (1987) Map Algebra: An Object-Oriented Implementation, in *International Geographic Information Systems (IGIS) Symposium: The Research Agenda* (eds. R. Aangeenbrug and Y. Schiffman), Arlington, VI, Vol. 2, pp. 127–50.

Dorenbeck, C. and Egenhofer, M. (1991) Algebraic Optimization of Combined Overlay Operations, in *Proceedings of Autocarto 10* (eds. D. Mark and D. White), Baltimore, MD, pp. 296–312.

Egenhofer, M. (1991) Extending SQL for Cartographic Display. *Cartography and Geographic Information Systems* **18**, 230–45.

Egenhofer, M. (1994) Spatial SQL: A Query and Presentation Language. *IEEE Transaction on Knowledge and Data Engineering* **6**, 86–95.

Egenhofer, M. and Bruns, H.T. (1994) Bringing Maps onto the Desktop: GIS User Interfaces Beyond Menus and Buttons, *International IGUG News*, Fall 1994: 8–9.

Egenhofer, M. and Kuhn, W. (1991) Visualizing Spatial Query Results: The Limitations of SQL, in *Visual Database Systems II* (eds. E. Knuth and L. Wegner), *IFIP Transactions A: Computer Science and Technology*, Vol. A-7, pp. 5–18, North-Holland, Amsterdam.

Egenhofer, M. and Richards, J. (1993a) Exploratory access to geographic data based on the map-overlay metaphor. *Journal of Visual Languages and Computing* **4**, 105–25.

Egenhofer, M. and Richards, J. (1993b) The geographer's desktop: A direct-manipulation user interface for map overlay, in *Proceedings of Autocarto 11* (eds. R. McMaster and M. Armstrong), Minneapolis, MN, pp. 63–71.

ERDAS, Inc. (1993) *Model Maker Tour Guide.* ERDAS, Inc., Atlanta, GA.

ESRI, Inc. (1990) *Understanding GIS: The Arc/Info Model*, Environmental Systems Research Institute, Inc., Redlands, CA.

ESRI, Inc. (1992) *GRID Command Reference.* Environmental Systems Research Institute, Inc., Redlands, CA.

Frank, A. (1992) Beyond Query Languages for Geographic Databases: Data Cubes and Maps, in *Geographic Database Management Systems* (eds. G. Gambosi, M. Scholl, and H.-W. Six), pp. 5–17, Springer-Verlag, New York.

Goodchild, M. (1992) Geographic data modeling, *Computers and Geoscience* **18**, 401–8.

Gould, M. (1993) Two Views of the User Interface. in *Human Factors in Geographic Information Systems.* (eds. D. Medyckyj-Scott and H. Hearnshaw), pp. 101–10, Belhaven Press, Boca Raton, FL.

Intergraph, Inc. (1993) *MGE Grid Analyst (MGGA) Reference Manual.* Intergraph, Inc., Huntsville, AL.

Johnson, M. (1987) *The Body in the Mind.* University of Chicago Press, Chicago, IL.

Kirby, C. and Pazner, M. (1990) Graphic Map Algebra. in *Proceedings of the 4th International Symposium on Spatial Data Handling*, Zurich, Switzerland, pp. 413–22.

Kuhn, W. (1992) Paradigms of GIS Use. in *Proceedings of the 5th International Symposium on Spatial Data Handling*, Charleston, SC, pp. 91–101.

Lakoff, G. and Johnson, M. (1980) *Metaphors We Live By.* University of Chicago Press, Chicago, IL.

Lanter, D. (1991) Design of Lineage-Based Meta-Data Base for GIS. *Cartography and Geographic Information Systems* **18**: 255–61.

Lanter, D. and Essinger, R. (1991) User-Centered Graphical User Interface Design for GIS. National Center for Geographic Information and Analysis, Technical Report 91-6.

Laurini, R. and Thompson, D. (1992) *Fundamentals of Spatial Information Systems*. Academic Press, New York.

Mark, D. and Frank, A. (1989) Concepts of Space and Spatial Language. in *Autocarto 9*, Baltimore, MD, pp. 538–56.

Myers, B. (1990) Taxonomies of Visual Programming and Program Visualization. *Journal of Visual Languages and Computing* **1**: 97–123.

Norman, D. (1987) Cognitive Engineering-Cognitive Science. in *Interfacing Thought—Cognitive Aspects of Human-Computer Interaction*. (ed. J. Carroll), pp. 325–36, MIT Press, Cambridge, MA.

Norman, D. (1988) *The Design of Everyday Things*. Doubleday, New York.

Nyerges, T. (1993) How do People Use Geographic Information Systems? in: *Human Factors in Geographic Information Systems*. (eds. D. Medyckyj-Scott and H. M. Hearnshaw), pp. 37–49, Belhaven Press, Boca Raton, FL.

Pazner, M., Kirby, C., and Theis, N. (1989) *Map II Map Processor Tutorial*. John Wiley & Sons, New York.

Polson, P., Lewis, C., Rieman, J., and Wharton, C. (1992) Cognitive Walkthroughs: A Method for Theory-Based Evaluation of User Interfaces. *International Journal of Man-Machine Studies* **36**, 741–73.

Sandhu, J., Amundson, S., and Marble, D. (1987) *The Map Analysis Package*. The Ohio State University, Columbus, OH.

Stone, M, Fishkin, K., and Bier, E. (1994) The Movable Filter as a User Interface Tool. in *Proceedings of ACM CHI'94 Conference on Human Factors in Computing Systems*, Boston, MA, pp. 306–12.

Tomlin, C.D. (1983) A Map Algebra. in *Proceedings of the 1983 Harvard Computer Graphics Conference*, Cambridge, MA.

Tomlin, C.D. (1990) *Geographic Information Systems and Cartographic Modeling*, Prentice-Hall, Englewood Cliffs, NJ.

Tomlin, C.D. and Berry, J. (1979) A Mathematical Structure for Cartographic Modeling in Environmental Analysis. in *Proceedings of the ACSM*, pp. 269–83.

Turk, A. (1993) The Relevance of Human Factors to Geographic Information Systems. in *Human Factors in Geographic Information Systems*. (eds. D. Medyckyj-Scott and H. Hearnshaw), pp. 1–31, Belhaven Press, Boca Raton, FL.

Weller, H. and Hartson, H. (1992) Metaphors for the Nature of Human-Computer Interaction in an Empowering Environment. *Computers in Human Behavior* **8**, 313–33.

Dr. Max J. Egenhofer

Dr. Max J. Egenhofer is the associate director of the National Center for Geographic Information and Analysis at the University of Maine, an associate professor in Spatial Information Science and Engineering, and a cooperative associate professor in Computer Science. In Summer 1993, he was a Visiting Professor at the Universita de L'Aquila, Italy. He received a Dipl.-Ing. in Surveying Engineering from the University of Stuttgart, Germany in 1986, and his Ph.D. from the University of Maine in Surveying Engineering in 1989.

Dr. Egenhofer's research interests include reasoning in geographic space, formalizations of spatial relations, user interface design for Geographic Information Systems, spatial query languages, and the design of geographic databases. His funded research includes grants from the National Science Foundation, the Advanced Research and Development Committee of the Community Management Staff, the Scientific Division of the North Atlantic Treaty Organization, Intergraph Corporation, Space Imaging, Inc., Environmental Systems Research Institute Inc, Digital Equipment Corporation, and the Maine Mathematics and Science Allience.

Tom Bruns

Tom Bruns is a Ph.D. candidate in Spatial Information Science and Engineering at the University of Maine. Prior to this he was working with GISTrans, Cambridge, MA. Tom holds an M.S. in Surveying Engineering from the University of Maine and a B.S. in Electrical Engineering from Worcester Polytechnic Institute.

16

Manipulations of Graphs with a Visual Query Language: Application to a Geographical Information System

Brossier-Wansek A.,** - Mainguenaud M.**
** France Telecom - Institut National des Télécommunications*
9 rue Charles Fourier F91011 EVRY - FRANCE
*** Cellule d'Etudes en Géographie Numérique*
16bis Av. Prieur de la Côte d'Or F94114 ARCUEIL Cedex - FRANCE
+ 33 1 60 76 47 82 (tel) + 33 1 60 77 20 06 (fax)
Email: Anne.Wansek@int-evry.fr, Michel.Mainguenaud@int-evry.fr
http://etna.int-evry.fr/BasesDeDonnees/Cigales/cigales.html

Abstract

Operators for geographical databases can be classified into two categories: thematic-oriented operators and network-oriented operators. Thematic-oriented operators are based on geometric representations (e.g., intersection, inclusion, adjacency). Network-oriented operators are based on graph manipulations whatever the geometric representation is (e.g., a transitive closure of a graph).

In this paper we present network manipulations with a visual query language for a geographical database. A query is defined with a visual expression defined with a Query-By-Example approach. The user draws a graphic representing the properties results have to verify.

Keyword

Visual query language, Graph manipulations, Geographical Information System

I INTRODUCTION

In current research toward the design of more powerful tools for urban planning and remote sensing, different research groups are simultaneously concentrating their work on Geographical Information Systems (GIS). GIS needs are very well known (Smith, 1987). Nevertheless, several problems are still open.

The need for a spatial query language has been identified. Traditionnally, operators for geographical databases are classified into two categories: thematic-oriented operators and network-oriented operators. This distinction is due to the lack of common data structures (and operators). Thematic-oriented operators are based on geometric representations (e.g., intersection, inclusion, adjacency). Network-oriented operators are based on graph manipulations whatever the geometric representation is (e.g., a transitive closure of a graph).

Visual languages are very promising. Propositions for such languages are detailed for example in (Angelaccio,1990) (Cruz, 1987) (Kim, 1988) (Kirby, 1990) (Myers, 1992) (Shu, 1988). A query

language is said to be visual whenever the semantics of a query is expressed by a drawing. It is said to be declarative whenever a query specifies the properties to be verified by the results, but not the way of obtaining them (i.e., imperative). This paper is based on the Cigales experiment. Cigales (Calcinelli, 1991) (Calcinelli, 1994) is a visual and declarative query language for GIS.
We focus, here, on the design of a visual query language to handle networks in a GIS. This issue is one of the most important to deal with when building spatial information systems. It will be increasingly true since the geographic information is now affecting non-specialist users and general applications such as tourism.

Part II presents a brief overview of the graph data model; Part III, the graph manipulation part of a visual query language for GIS; Part IV, the conclusion.

II BRIEF OVERVIEW OF THE GRAPH DATA MODEL

The user graph data model is based on graph theory (Berge, 1983) and is similar to the definition presented in (Angelaccio,1990) (Cruz, 1987). The database graph data model is based on the graph data model defined in (Langou, 1994) (Mainguenaud, 1991). Nevertheless, this data structuring is not visible from the user interface level. In this part, we present the user graph data model, its associated operators and a toy database used along this paper.

II.1 User graph data model

The user graph data model (i.e., visible from the interface level) is based on the concepts of nodes and edges. A graph is a triplet G (N, E, Ψ) where N is a set of nodes, E is a subset of the Cartesian product N x N and Ψ is an incidence function mapping E to N x N. The formal definition is presented in Figure 1.

A graph G (N, E, Ψ) is defined as follows:

$$N = \{n_1, \dots, n_p\}$$

$$E = \{ (n_i, n_j) \,/\, n_i \in N, n_j \in N \}$$

(n_i is said to be the initial node and n_j is said to be the end node for an edge (n_i, n_j))

Figure 1 - Formal definition of a graph

A node is used to model for example a town. An edge is used to model for example a link between two towns. In this paper, a graph is considered as orientated (i.e., the order, initial node / end node, is relevant). Nodes and edges are labelled. Several edges may be defined with the same initial and end nodes. We do not limit this number but we do not allow an edge (n_i, n_i). We extend the graph definition with a labelling function, ν, defined on nodes and with a labelling function, ε, defined on edges. Let $D_1, \dots, D_n$ be database domains. Figure 2 presents the complete definition of the user graph data model.

$$\nu : N \rightarrow D_i \times \dots \times D_j$$

$$\varepsilon : E \rightarrow D_k \times \dots \times D_m$$

A graph G is defined by: G (N, E, Ψ, ν, ε)

Figure 2 - Complete definition of a graph

II.2 Operators

Graph manipulations, accessible from the user interface, are divided into three classes: evaluation of paths, inclusion and intersection.
The evaluation of path is performed with a Path operator. This evaluation corresponds to the detection of acyclic paths between an origin and a destination. This path can be a direct link (i.e., a successor in a graph) or a more complex path (i.e., a transitive closure of a graph).

Three operators are defined to handle the inclusion. The first operator is an extraction of nodes in a path. The second operator is an inclusion between two sets of nodes. The third operator is an inclusion between two sets of edges.
Two operators are defined to handle the intersection. The first operator is an intersection of two sets of nodes. The second operator is an intersection of two sets of edges.

This paper deals with the Path operator. It presents the visual definition of a query involving this operator. A formal signature (taking into account constraints) of this operator is presented in (Mainguenaud, 1993a). Inclusion and intersection are handled as defined in (Calcinelli, 1991) (Calcinelli, 1994).

II.3 Toy database

To simplify the presentation, let us use the relational model extended with Abstract Data Types (Stemple, 1986) as the data model of the user interface (i.e., to model the labelling functions ν and ε). The relational model is now widely accepted (Ullman,1988), but an object-oriented data model or a semantic data model could have been used. An abstract data type,Spatial_representation_type, models spatial representations (i.e., the domain of the Spatial_representation attribute). Figure 3 presents the conceptual level of a toy database borrowed from a tourism application.

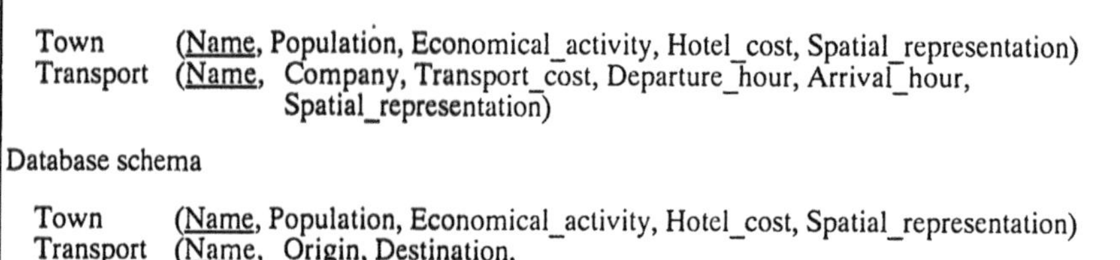
User's schema

Town (Name, Population, Economical_activity, Hotel_cost, Spatial_representation)
Transport (Name, Company, Transport_cost, Departure_hour, Arrival_hour, Spatial_representation)

Database schema

Town (Name, Population, Economical_activity, Hotel_cost, Spatial_representation)
Transport (Name, Origin, Destination, Company, Transport_cost, Departure_hour, Arrival_hour, Spatial_representation)

Figure 3 - The conceptual database

Let us define a graph G (N, E, Ψ, ν, ε) modelled with the Town and Transport relations (i.e., the nodes and the edges). The user's schema is composed of two relations (i.e., the labelling functions ν and ε). Visual queries are defined on this schema. The database schema is composed of two relations. The Town relation models the node labelling function, ν. The Transport relation represents an element of the Cartesian Product, N x N, and the edge labelling function, ε. The formal modelling of a visual query is defined on this schema. To illustrate the query language, let us define seven queries on this database (see (Boursier, 1992) for a logical benchmark to evaluate the expressive power of a query language for GIS).
Let Q_1 be the following query: "What are the direct flights with the AF company from Paris to Lausanne such as the departure time is later than 10:00 am and earlier than 3:00 pm and such as the price is less than 500 FF?". Query Q_1 requires evaluating the direct link operator. This query is a relational selection on the Transport relation.
Let Q_2 be the following query: "What are the routes from Paris to Lausanne with the AF company such as the total transport cost is less than 800 FF and the total time of inter-connection is less than 2 hours?". Query Q_2 requires the computation of a path operator in graph G with constraints on edges. This query is a transitive closure on relation Transport with two aggregate functions: the sum of the Transport_cost attribute and the sum of the differences between Departure_hour of edge i+1 and Arrival_hour of edge i.
Let Q_3 be the following query: "What are the routes from Paris to Lausanne only visiting major towns (i.e., for each town, the population is larger than 100 000 inhabitants or the economical activity is tourism)?". Query Q_3 requires a path operator with a constraint on nodes. This query is a selection on the Town relation, a join with the Transport relation and a transitive closure.

Let Q_4 be the following query: "What are the routes from Paris to Lausanne such as the total cost (hotel+transport) is less than 1000 FF?". Query Q_4 requires a path operator with constraints on nodes and edges. This query is a transitive closure on relation Transport with an aggregate function using a join on relation Town.
Let Q_5 be the following query: "What are the routes from Paris to Lausanne such as the total time of transport is less than 4 hours". Query Q_5 requires a path operator (i.e., a transitive closure on relation Transport) with a constraint involving the first and the last edges (i.e., the difference between the departure hour from Paris and the arrival hour in Lausanne is less than 4 hours).
Let Q_6 be the following query: "What are the routes from Paris to Lausanne (1) leaving Paris with the AF company; (2) and then using the train up to Lausanne or using the bus up to Lausanne?". Query Q_6 requires a path operator (i.e., a transitive closure on relation Transport) with a regular expression on edges (Cruz,, 1987).
Let Q_7 be the following query: "What are the routes from Paris to Lausanne (1) leaving Paris with the AF company; (2) then using the train or the bus such as at each stop, the cost of a hotel is less than 200 SF and (3) finally arriving to Lausanne by bus". Query Q_7 requires a path operator (i.e., a transitive closure on relation Transport) with a regular expression involving nodes and edges.

III VISUAL QUERY LANGUAGE TO MANAGE GRAPHS

The first section presents some visual query languages to manage graphs. All of them are based at the user level on the same definition of a graph. The second and third sections present the Cigales query language from the user's point of view, to solve queries using either the direct link operator (query Q_1) or the path operator (queries Q_2 up to Q_7).

III.1 Short overview

We present here a short overview of visual query languages to manage graphs. The two first one (G+ and QBD*) are designed to query a conventional database. The third one (Cigales) is designed to query a spatial database (i.e., with thematic-oriented operators).

III.1.1 G+

G+ (Cruz, 1987) is a language derived from a language called **G**. In **G**, a graphical query Q on a graph G is a set of labelled directed multi-graphs in which the node labels of Q may be either variables or constants and the edge labels are regular expression defined over n-tuples of variables and constants.
An edge which is labelled by a regular expression containing the positive closure operator (+) is drawn as a dashed edge in Q. A query is extended with a summary graph and summary operators. A summary graph tells the system how to restructure the answers before presenting them to the user. Summary operators allow to compute aggregate functions over paths and sets of paths.
The semantics of the graph query language is based on the existence of mappings known as homeomorphisms from query graphs to database graphs. Homeomorphisms formalize the idea of a subgraph of the database graph being "similar" to the query graph. A query graph represents a pattern; answering the query will require searching the database graph to find all subgraphs that are "similar" to the pattern.
Query Q_1 is represented by a graph composed of two nodes labelled Paris and Lausanne. The edge is a tuple defined with constraints on the attributes (i.e., departure_hour, arrival_hour and price).

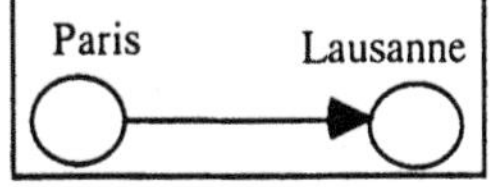

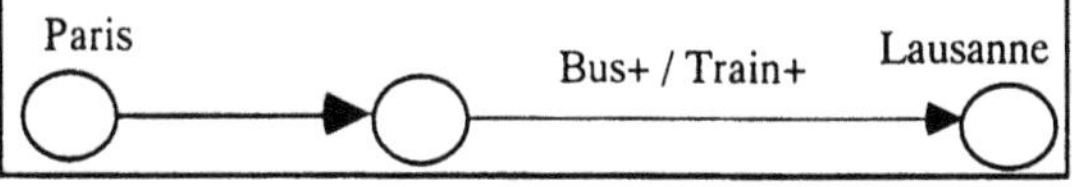

Nevertheless, the graphical visualisation of query Q_6, for example, is not very intuitive (even if the basic concept is a regular expression). A user defines a regular expression from the keyboard. A Query-By-Example philosophy should be preferable.

*III.1.2 QBD**

The goal of QBD* (Query By Diagram*) (Angelaccio, 1990) is to achieve user friendliness for a large amount of user types by means of a uniform graphical interface and a visual language. This system is based on four basic ideas: (1) to represent the intentional part of the database by means of a conceptual model (Entity-Relationship augmented by the introduction of generalization abstractions); (2) to employ a fully graphical environment as a user friendly interface with the system; (3) to study the formal properties of the graphical language by defining an isomorphic textual language; and (4) to extend the graphical constructs of the language in order to easily express a significant class of recursive queries (e.g., transitive closure).

QBD* is mainly a navigational language on ER diagrams. The operations of the relational algebra may be expressed directly by picking up symbols (entities or relationships) in the diagram and posing conditions on their attributes by means of a simple windowing mechanism. Recursive queries are also expressed by the same mechanism, the difference being the preselection of a particular icon that signals the beginning of a recursive session. In this way, the textual interaction is completely eliminated and the complexity of some query is transparent to the user.

The general structure of the query is based on the location of a distinguished concept, call the main concept (an entity or a relationship), that can be seen as the entry point of one or more subqueries. These subqueries express possible navigations from the main concept to other concepts in the schema. The subqueries can be combined by means of the usual union and intersection operators. Once the main concept has been selected, two different types of primitives are available for navigation in the schema. The first one allows the user to follow paths of concepts. The second one is used for comparing two concepts which are not directly connected to each other. Two such primitives can be arbitrarily nested.

Nevertheless, it is not clear how (1) queries involving conditions on the first and last edge are handled (query Q_5); (2) aggregate function involving nodes and/or edges are handled (Query Q_3, Q_4).

III.1.3 Cigales approach

Cigales is a visual and declarative query language for GIS based on a Query-By-Example approach. This language is visual because a query is defined by a drawing. This language is declarative because a query only defines the properties to be verified by the results. A detailed definition of the query language is presented in (Calcinelli, 1994). Cigales uses metaphores to avoid visual overload. Thus a visual query is a symbolization of a textual query.

Cigales is designed to be an upper layer of a spatial Data Base Management System (DBMS). Two metaphores, a zone and a line, represent database objects. Their semantics are defined by a Data Model Function (i.e., the definition of selection criteria applied to the labelling functions ν and ε). Five spatial operators are available at the user interface level: inclusion, intersection, adjacency, straigth line and path. Several other operators are available such as union, difference but the user is not awared of their existence. The drawing process automatically generates these operators. A query is graphically built from a combination of metaphores and operators. This query is, then, translated into a formal expression based on a functional language (Mainguenaud, 1993a), to be compiled into DBMS understandable orders. Figure 4 presents the graphical editor used to define a query. Cigales offers a unique path operator at the user-interface level. This operator stands either for the direct link operator and for the path operator. The relevant choice is performed by the user before defining the Data Model Function (Figure 5).

III.2 Direct link queries

A direct link operator requires specifying alphanumeric properties on edges of a graph (i.e., for the Transport relation in our example). The expressive power is equivalent to the From, Where, Group By and Having clauses of SQL.

A selection criterion is defined by a triplet (attribute, operator, value). An implicit conjunction is defined between triplets. Moreover, each attribute may also have a value defined as a conjunction (e.g., the departure hour is later than 10:00 am and earlier than 3:00 pm - query Q_1). The disjunction is graphically defined with the notion of page (i.e., Page 1, Page 2, ..., Page i). Each page has the same structure and allows one to define alphanumeric properties. A horizontal scrollbar allows to move from one page to another. This disjunction may be defined on one attribute (the departure hour is earlier than 10:00 am or later than 3:00 pm). It may also involve several attributes (i.e., the population is greater than 100 000 inhabitants or the activity is tourism - query Q_3). Details of other operators are presented in (Brossier-Wansek, 1994). Figure 6 presents the visualization of the Data Model Function associated with the direct link operator. This formalism is more intuitive for a non-specialist end user than SQL-like syntaxes.

III.3 Path operator

Queries Q_2, Q_3, Q_4, Q_5, Q_6 and Q_7 require computing a path operator. These queries illustrate two kinds of constraints. Queries Q_2, Q_3, Q_4 and Q_5 define constraints involving a complete path. Query Q_6 and Q_7 define constraints involving an edge-by-edge definition of a path. Therefore, the Data Model Function associated with the path operator is composed of two parts: a "Global conditions" part and a "Transportation" part.

III.3.1 Constraints on a complete path ("Global conditions")

Three kinds of constraints can be defined on a complete path. A constraint may be defined on edges (e.g., query Q_2), on nodes (e.g., query Q_3) or on both edges and nodes (e.g., query Q_4). Thus, the window defining the global conditions is divided into three parts.

Two kinds of constraints can be defined on edges. A constraint may involve a unary function (i.e., involving a unique parameter) or may involve a n-ary function (i.e., involving two or several parameters). The constraint: "the total transport cost of a travel is less than 800 FF of query Q_2" is an example of a unary function (i.e., an aggregate function on the attribute Transport_cost). The constraint: "the total time of interconnection is less than two hours of query Q_2" is an example of a n-ary function (i.e., an aggregate function involving a binary relationship between the attributes Arrival_hour and Departure_hour).
The constraint definition process involving a unary function is similar to the direct link definition process. The only difference is the addition of an aggregate function. This function is defined for each attribute depending on its type (i.e., alphanumeric, integer). Such a constraint is valid for each edge of a path (i.e., Each qualification - query Q_3) or for the entire path (i.e., total cost of a travel - query Q_2). Figure 7 presents the Data Model Function for a unary function.
The constraint definition process involving a n-ary function relies on a visual sub-language. To simplify the presentation, let us consider a binary relationship. Cigales defines a generic schema of a path. This path presents four specific edges labelled 1, i, i+1, n. The user selects attributes corresponding to these edges. The two icons modelling the retained attributes appear in the form below the schema. The user defines the aggregate function (if it is needed), the mathematical operator, the comparison operator and a value (i.e., the sum of differences between the departure hour of edge i+1 and the arrival hour of edge i is less than two hours - query Q_2 - or the difference between Arrival_hour of edge n and Departure_hour of edge 1 - Query Q_5). Figure 8 presents the Data Model Function for a n-ary function (Query Q_2).

Two kinds of constraints can be defined on nodes: a constraint may involve a unary function or a n-ary function.
The constraint definition process involving a unary function is similar to the constraint definition process involving a unary function for an edge.
The constraint definition process involving a n-ary function is similar to the constraint definition process involving a n-ary function for an edge. The only difference relies on labels associated with the generic schema of a path. They are defined on nodes instead of on edges. Figure 9 presents the Data Model Function associated with query Q_3 "What are the routes from Paris to Lausanne only visiting major towns (i.e., for each town, the population is larger than 100,000 inhabitants or the economical activity is tourism)?".

The constraints involving both edges and nodes are similar to a n-ary function (at least one attribute for an edge and one for a node). The generic schema of a path is made of four components labelled edge i, node i, edge i+1, node i+1. The philosophy of the constraint definition process is similar to the previous definitions of n-ary functions. Figure 10 presents the Data Model Function associated with query Q_4 "What are the routes from Paris to Lausanne such as the cost (hotel+transport) is less than 1000 FF?".

One can remark that results of queries involving aggregate functions can not be defined as the union of paths. As soon as a node (except the origin of the path and the destination of a path) belongs to two paths, the definition of the results as the union of paths leads to ambiguities (Mainguenaud, 1993b) since results must be graphically presented.

III.3.2 Constraints edge-by-edge ("Transportation")

This second kind of constraints requires specifying a regular expression associated with a path. This edge-by-edge definition provides a very strong expressive power. As shown in (Mendelzon, 1989), some classes of queries lead to a NP-complete problem. We restrict the expressive power to a sub-set of computable queries (Garey, 1979). This part defines the retained expressive power and presents the graphical definition of these constraints.

Required expressive power

To simplify the presentation, let us consider a unique domain called D_0. Let D_0 be $\{d_0, ..., d_n\}$. Let ν be a one-to-one node labelling function that associates with each node a distinct value drawn from domain D_0. Let ε be an edge labelling function which associates with each edge a distinct value drawn from domain D_0.
An edge-by-edge constraint is defined with a regular expression. This expression is built from a triplet (N_i, E_k, N_j) label. Let N_i be the label associated with a node n_i (a disjunction of elements of D_0). Let N_j be the label associated with a node n_j (a disjunction of elements of D_0). Let E_k be the label associated with an edge e_k defined between n_i and n_j (a disjunction of elements of D_0). Let - (the hyphen) be any value of D_0. The following rules define a query label:

(1)	(N_i, E_k, N_j) is a query label	(2)	(N_i, E_k, -) is a query label
(3)	(-, E_k, N_j) is a query label	(4)	(-, E_k, -) is a query label
(5)	(N_i, - , N_j) is a query label	(6)	(N_i, -, -) is a query label
(7)	(-,-,N_j) is a query label	(8)	(-,-,-) is a query label
(9)	If A is a query label then [A]* is a query label (the repetition)		
(10)	If A and B are query labels then $A \wedge B$ is a query label (the sequence)		
(11)	If A and B are query labels then $(A \vee B)$ is a query label (the alternative)		

An edge-by-edge constraint is built from a recursive application of properties (1) to (11). For the time, we limit the expressive power of a regular expression modelling a path. At least one of the two properties (a) or (b) must be verified:

(a) The first node label is not a hyphen (i.e., a selection criterion is defined on a key)
(b) The last node label is not a hyphen (i.e., a selection criterion is defined on a key).

Let us define a node label (N_i) or an edge label (E_k) as a disjunction of triplets (attribute operator value). Figure 11 (respectively Figure 12) presents the edge-by-edge constraint of query Q_6 (respectively query Q_7).

(Name = Paris, Company = AF, Hotel_cost < 200) $\wedge$
[(Hotel_cost < 200, Company = Train v Company = Bus, Hotel_cost < 200)]* $\wedge$
(Hotel_cost < 200, Company = Bus, Name = Lausanne)

Figure 12 - Edge-by-edge constraint of query Q_7: "What are the routes from Paris to Lausanne (1) leaving Paris with the AF company; (2) then using the train or the bus such as at each stop, the cost of a hotel is less than 200 SF and finally arriving to Lausanne by bus"

(Name = Paris, Company = AF, -) ∧
(((-,Company=Train,-) ∧ [(-,Company=Train,-)]* ∧ (-,Company=Train, Name=Lausanne) ∨
(-,Company=Train, Name=Lausanne)) ∨
((-,Company = Bus,-) ∧ [(-,Company = Bus,-)]* ∧ (-,Company = Bus, Name = Lausanne) ∨
(-,Company = Bus, Name = Lausanne)))

Figure 11 - Edge-by-edge constraint of query Q_6: "What are the routes from Paris to Lausanne (1) leaving Paris with the AF company; (2) and then using the train up to Lausanne or using the bus up to Lausanne?"

Figure 13 presents the Finite State Automaton (FSA) associated with query Q_6. The conflict on Train (or Bus) is resolved since the choice of an edge determines an end node. Figure 14 presents the FSA associated with query Q_7.

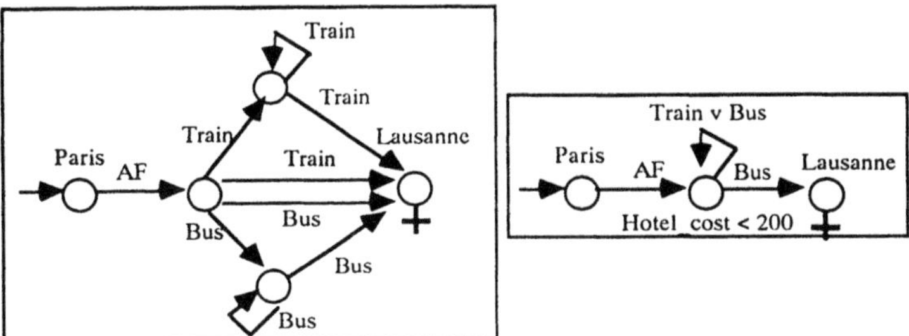

Figure 13 - FSA for query Q_6

Figure 14 - FSA for query Q_7

Graphical representation

A visual query language must provide a visual representation of a regular expression. Thus, the interface must provide a graph drawing mechanism. The objectives are (1) to draw an edge-by-edge path; (2) to specify alphanumeric properties on nodes and edges according to the user's selection criteria.

The graphical definition of an edge-by-edge constraint is provided by a graph editor. This editor adopts the same look as the main query editor. Two areas are defined. A working area is located at the bottom. This area is used to build step-by-step sub-queries. A query area, located on the top, is used to merge sub-queries and to build a final query. Two metaphores (a zone and an arrow) obey to the same Data Model Function as for Cigales. This editor takes full advantage of the context in which a regular expression is defined: a path defined between an origin and a destination. Therefore, no operator is provided since the path definition process is on. Figure 15 presents the graph editor.

The graphical edge-by-edge constraint is built step by step. A step defined in the working area corresponds to a sequence of query labels and must be validated (i.e., with a click on the validation button). The validation mechanism allows (1) the definition of the repetition factor (rule 9) and (2) the display of the graph drawing into the query area. The conjunction (rule 10) is implicit by a sequence of edges in the query area. The disjunction, while defining the $N_{i/j}$ (respectively E_k) part of a label is provided by the Data Model Function with the mechanism of pages (i.e., company = Train ∨ company = Bus - query Q_7). The disjunction in a regular expression (rule 11) is guided by the following assumption: "An end user thinks in term of disjunctive form". This disjunction is provided by a mechanism of pages for a complete path (i.e., each page represents a complete path - query Q_6).

By this way, the graphical build up of a path provides a Query-By-Example definition process. Therefore a novice user easily handles a complex selection criteria (i.e., with multiple and/or conditions - query Q_6). Moreover, the similitude between the Cigales editor and the graph editor about the query definition process facilitates the definition of a complex regular expression for a path. Figure 16 (respectively Figure 17) presents the graph editor for query Q_6 (respectively Q_7).

IV. CONCLUSION

The number of applications using a Geographical Information System (GIS) is considerable. Therefore it is of prime importance to offer a powerful and friendly interface for end-users. By end-users, we mean people who may be experts in some domains other than programming (or querying) language and who want to use a GIS to meet their particular needs. Our focus is not so much on the spatial analysis itself, but on the computational environment in which it is embedded (i.e., query language expressive power, management of visual ambiguities). Visual programming languages are very promising since they are more natural than textual query languages (i.e., extended SQL) and they offer a higher level of abstraction. The interaction with a DBMS is more complex since this level of abstraction is higher. The implementation is still going on since the design of a user interface is an iterative process. The prototype is developed using OSF/Motif (for the user interface), Yacc (for the analysis of the internal functional expression modelling a query), C programming language (for the query management) and an object-oriented DBMS, O_2 (Bancilhon, 1991), (to manage network-oriented queries) on Sun workstations.

This paper presents a brief overview of the user interface graph data model and the query definition process to manage network-oriented queries. Future work is to handle query results since several visual ambiguities may appear (Mainguenaud, 1993b) as soon as an aggregate function is involved in the query.

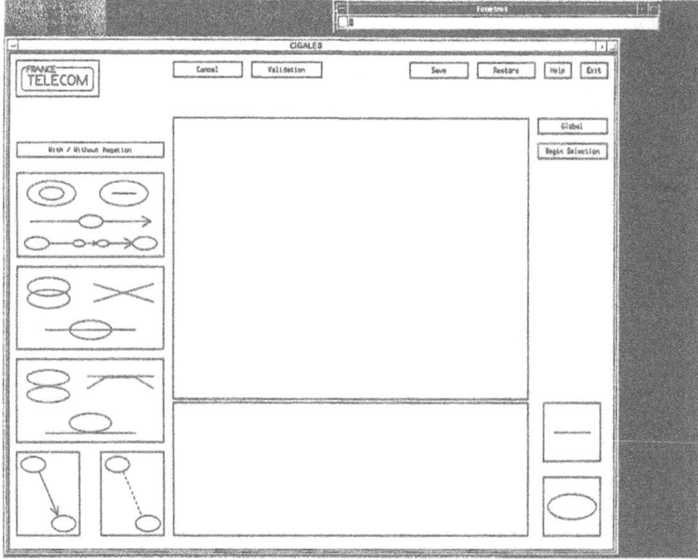

Figure 4 - The graphical editor

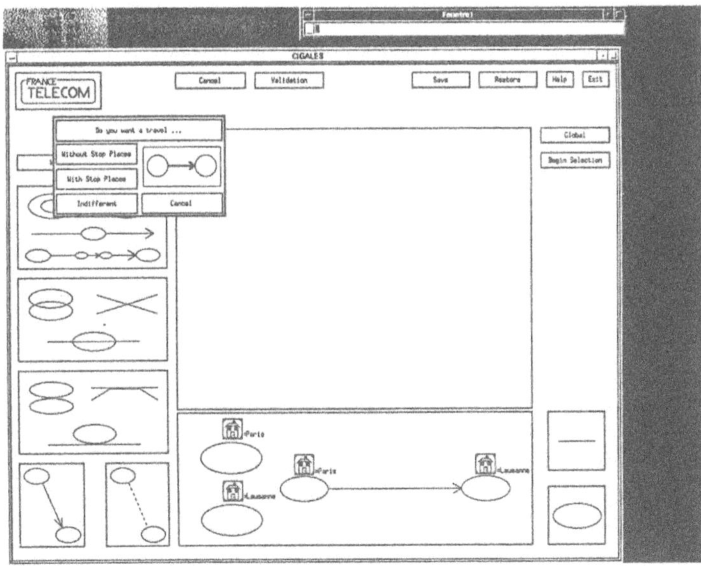

Figure 5 - Direct link or Path operator?

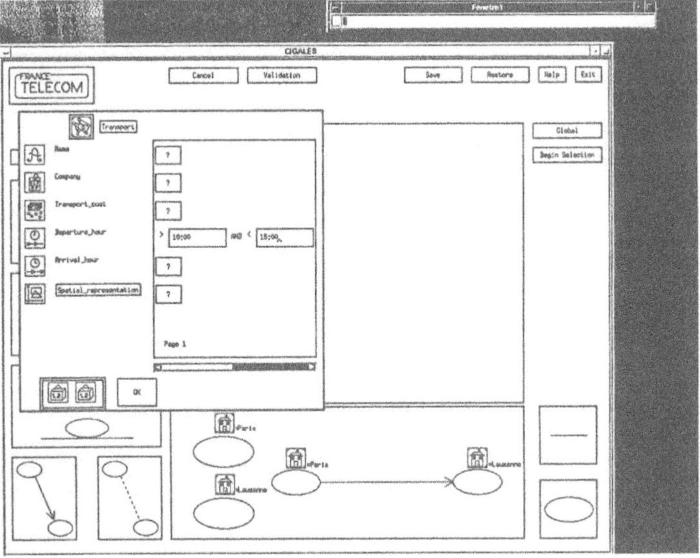

Figure 6a - The Data Model Function - conjunction
(the departure hour is later than 10:00 am and earlier than 3:00 pm - query Q_1)

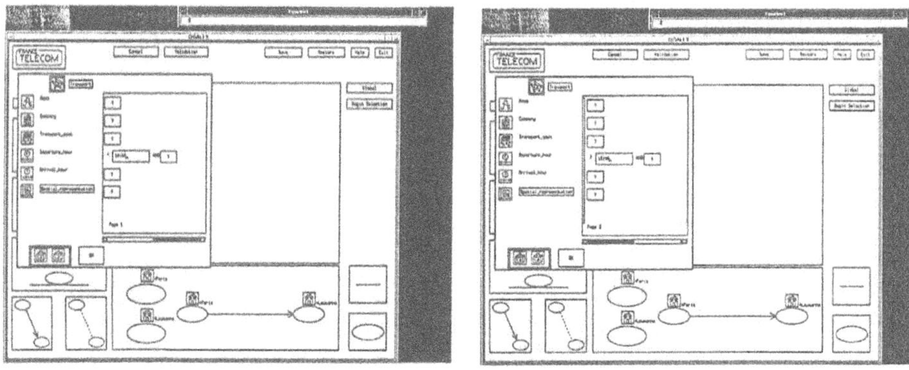

Figure 6b - The Data Model Function - disjunction
(the departure hour is earlier than 10:00 am or later than 3:00 pm)

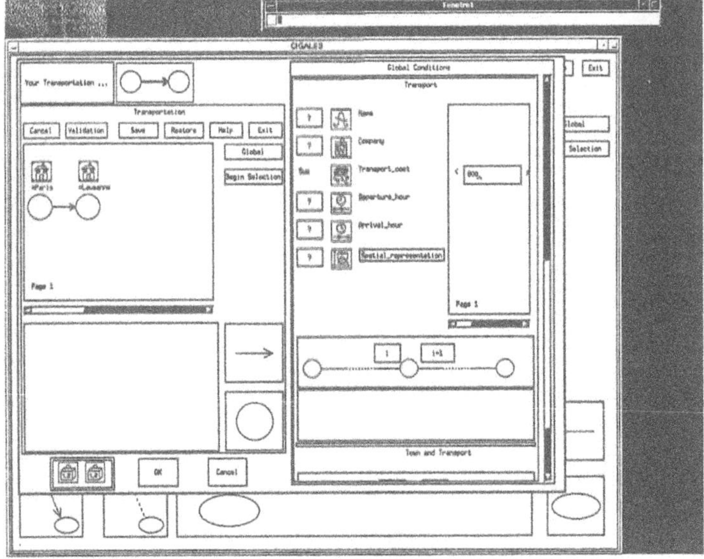

Figure 7 - The Data Model Function - a unary function
(the total cost of a travel is less than 800 units - query Q2)

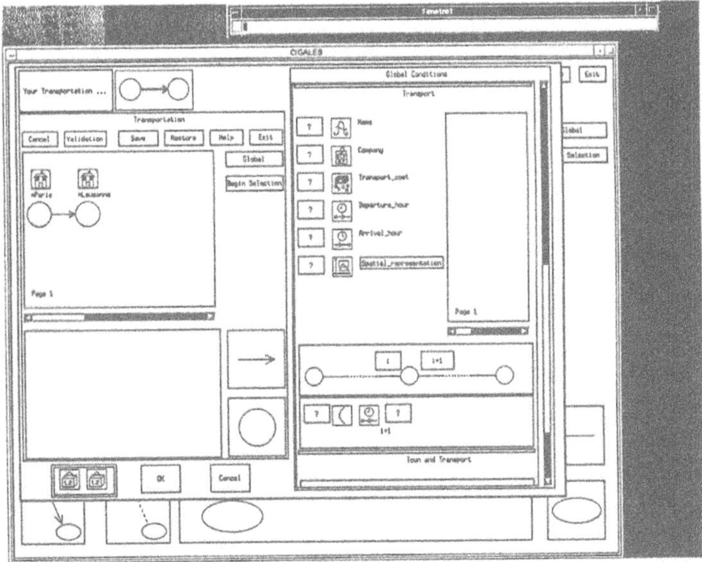

Figure 8a - Labelling of edge i+1 - departure hour of edge i+1
(the sum of differences between the departure hour of edge i+1 and the arrival hour of edge i is less than two hours - query Q2)

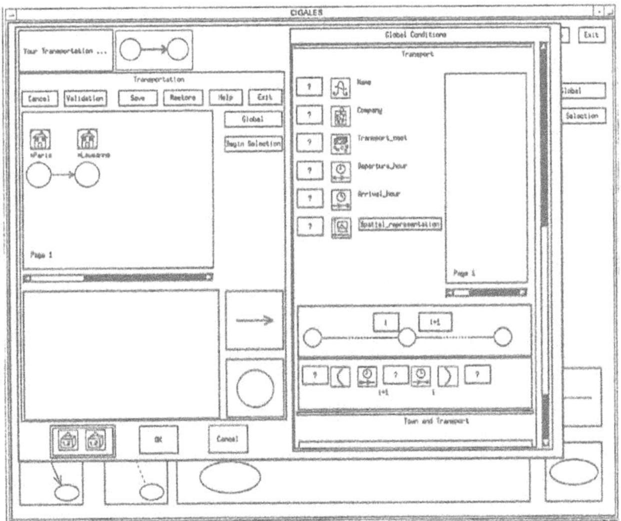

Figure 8b - Labelling of edge i - arrival hour of edge i
(the sum of differences between the departure hour of edge i+1 and the arrival hour of edge i is less than two hours - query Q2)

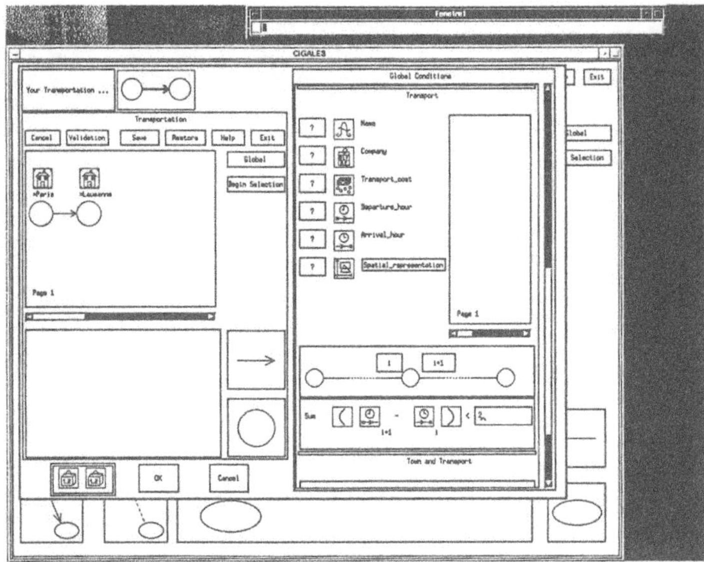

Figure 8c - Definition of an aggregate function - the sum of differences
(the sum of differences between the departure hour of edge i+1 and the arrival hour of edge i is less than two hours - query Q_2)

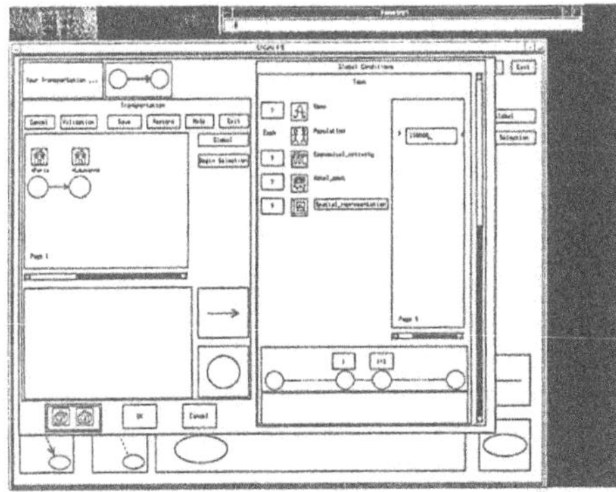

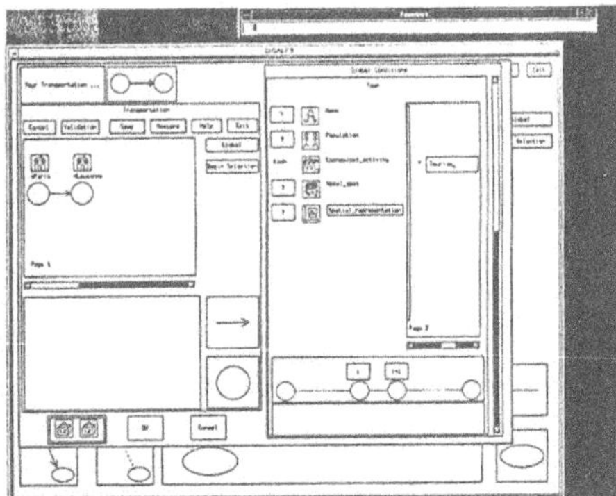

Figure 9 - Query Q_3
"What are the routes from Paris to Lausanne only visiting major towns (i.e., for each town, the population is larger than 100 000 inhabitants or the economical activity is tourism)?"

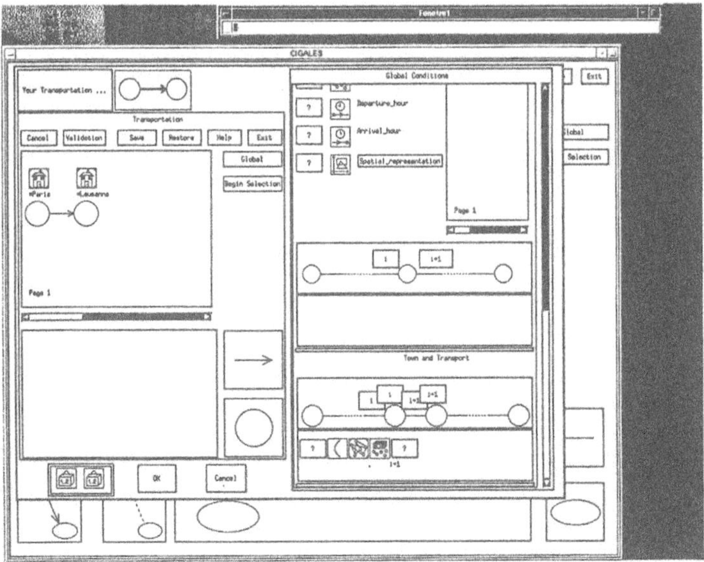

Figure 10a - Labelling of edge i+1 - Transport_cost

What are the routes from Paris to Lausanne such as the cost (hotel+transport) is less than 1000 F?

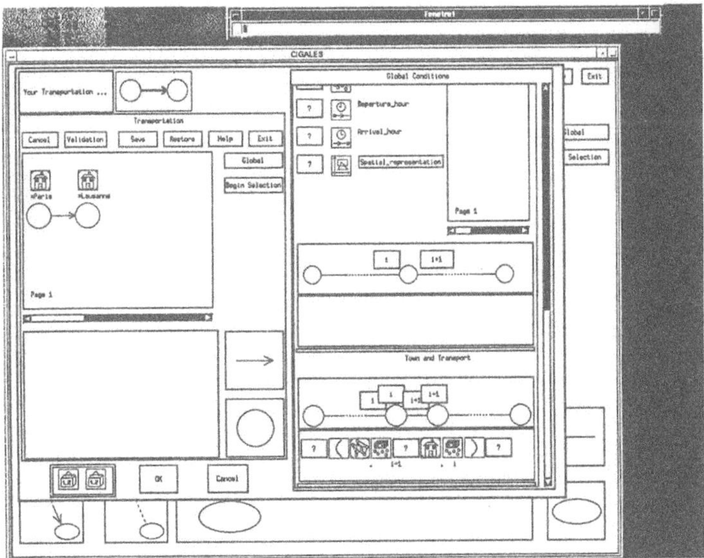

Figure 10b - Labelling of node i - Hotel_cost

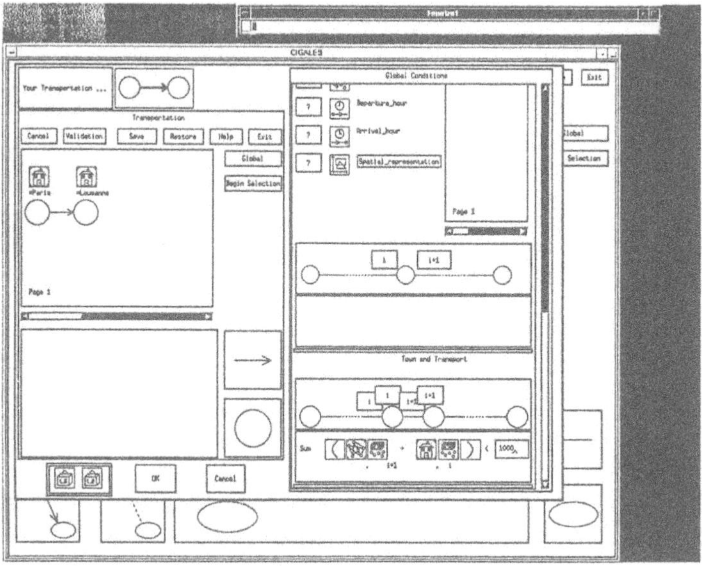

Figure 10c - Definition of an aggregate function - Sum

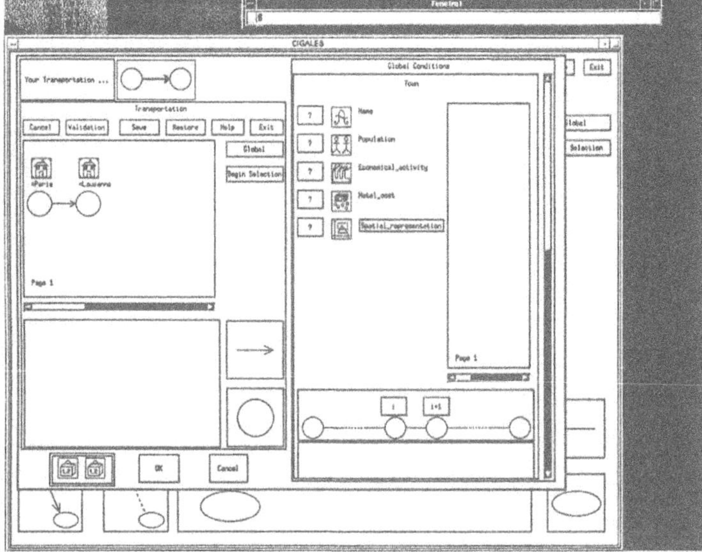

Figure 15 - The graph editor

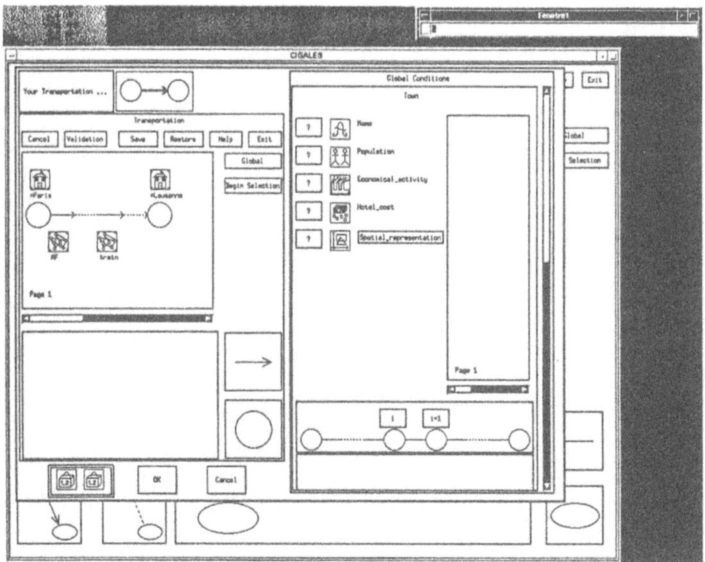

Figure 16a - Query Q6 - Page 1
"What are the routes from Paris to Lausanne (1) leaving Paris with the AF company; then using the train up to Lausanne"

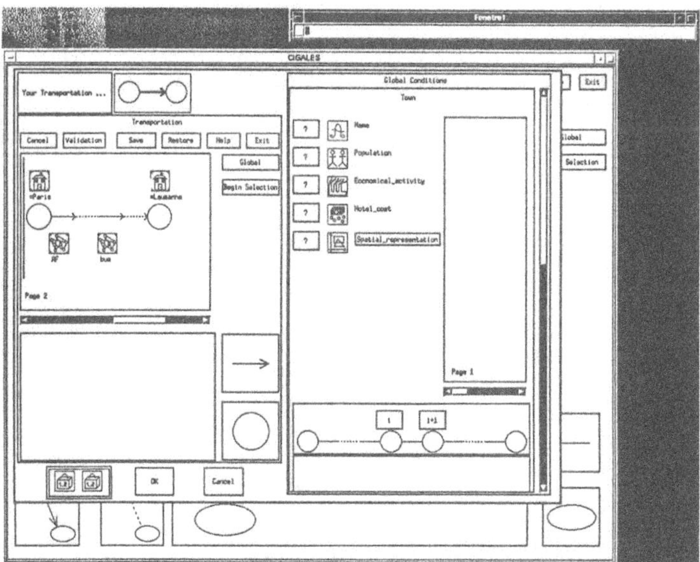

Figure 16b - Query Q6 - Page 2
"What are the routes from Paris to Lausanne (1) leaving Paris with the AF company; then using the bus up to Lausanne?"

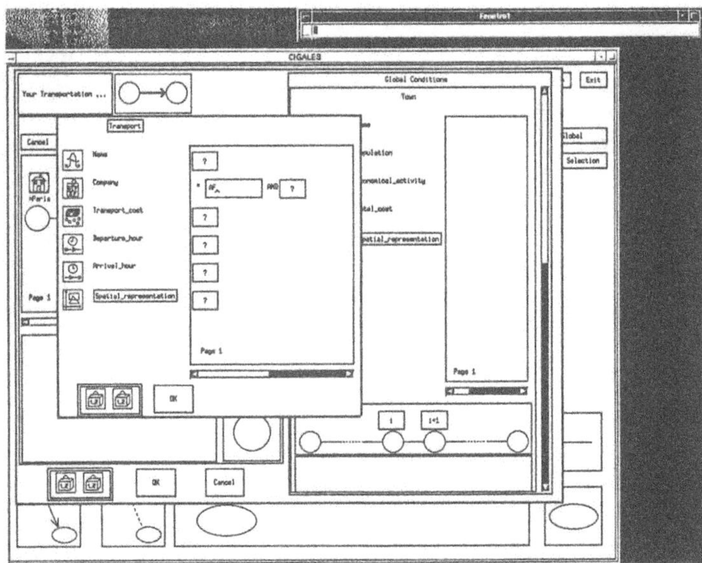

Figure 17a - Starting representation (a path from Paris to Lausanne - (Calcinelli, 1994)) What are the routes from Paris to Lausanne (1) leaving Paris with the AF company; (2) then using the train or the bus such as at each stop, the cost of a hotel is less than 200 SF and (3) finally arriving to Lausanne by bus

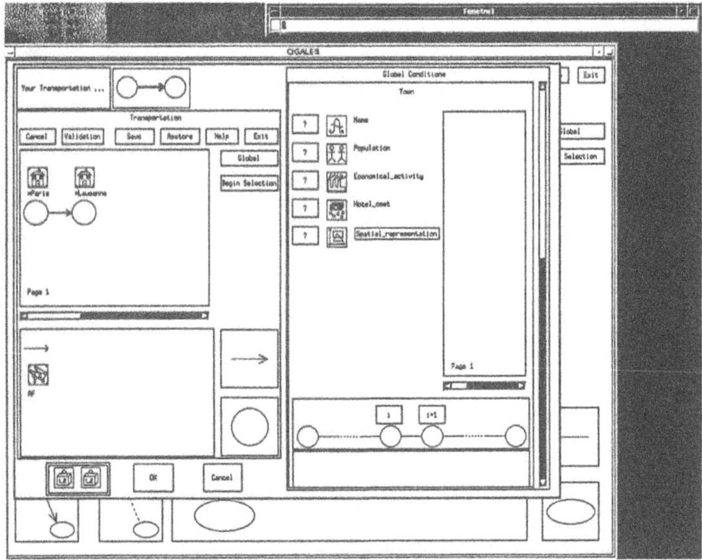

Figure 17b - The choice of an edge (labelled Company = AF)

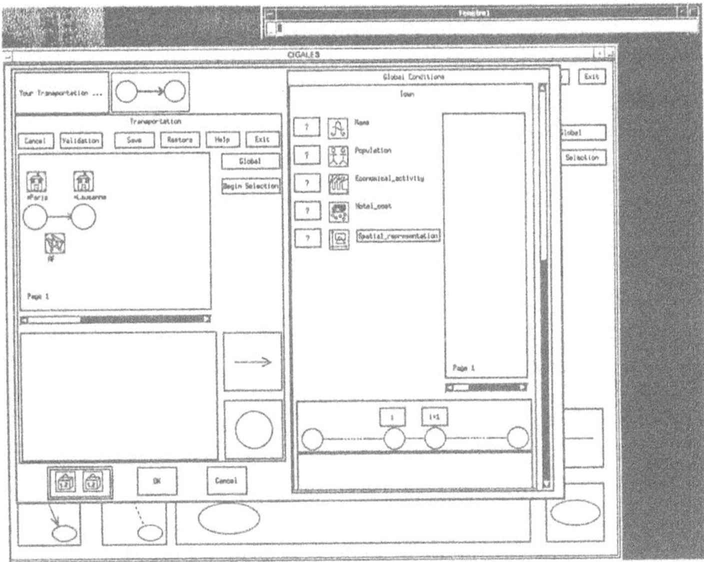

Figure 17c - After the validation (first part of the path: leaving Paris with AF)

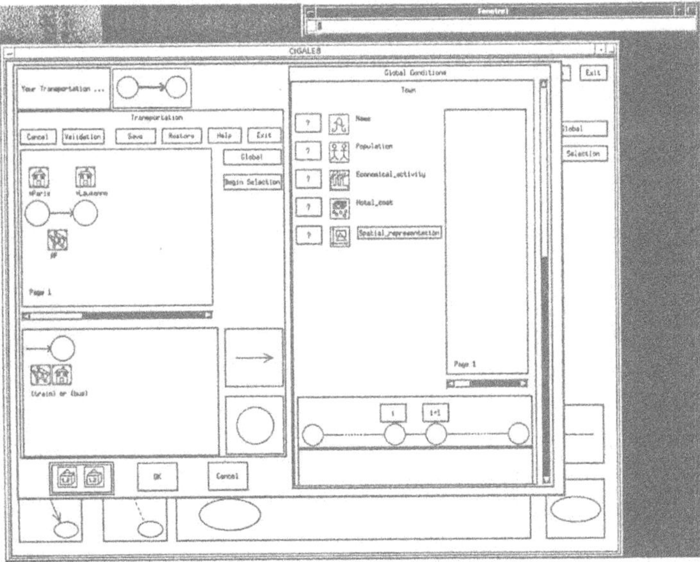

Figure 17d - The choice of an edge (labelled Company = Train/Company = Bus) and a node (labelled Hotel_cost < 200)

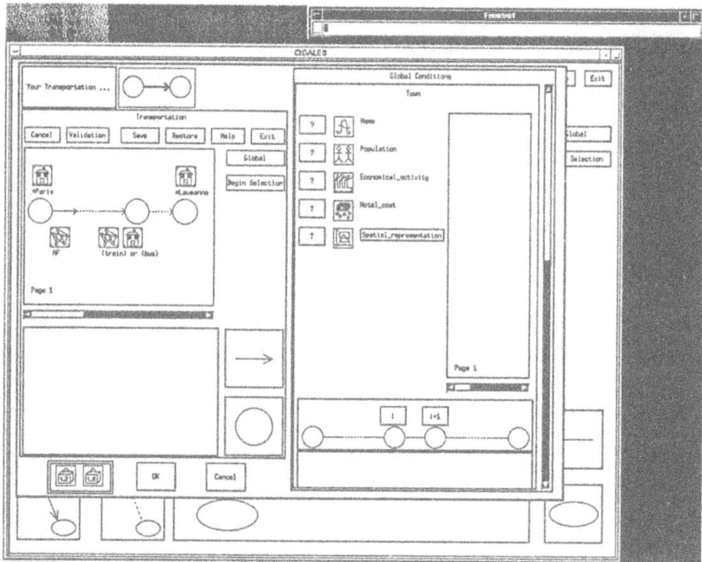

Figure 17e - After the validation with a repetition factor (dashed lines)

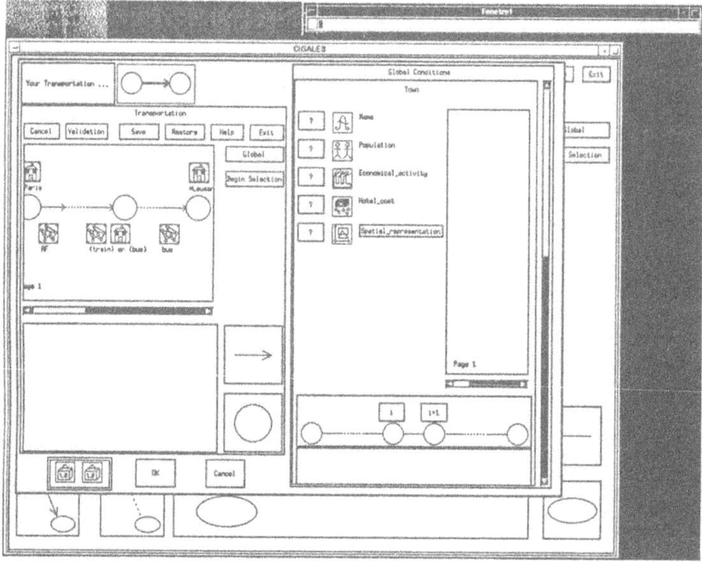

Figure 17f - After the choice of an edge (labelled Company = Bus) and the validation

REFERENCES

Angelaccio M., Catarci T. and Santucci G. (1990) QBD*: A Graphical Query Language with Recursion, *IEEE Transaction on Software Engineering*, **Vol 16 (10)**, 1150-1163.

Bancilhon F., Barbedette G., Benzaken V., Delobel C., Gamerman S., Lécluse C., Pfeffer P., Richard P. and Velez F. (1991) The Design and Implementation of O2, an Object Oriented Database System, *Proceedings of the 2nd Int. Workshop on Object-Oriented Data Base Systems*, O2 Book, Morgan Kaufmann.

Berge C. (1983) *Graphes*, Gauthier-Villars, Paris.

Boursier P. and Mainguenaud M. (1992) Spatial Query Languages: Extended SQL vs. Visual Languages vs. Hypermaps, *5th Symposium on Spatial Data Handling*, Charleston, USA.

Brossier-Wansek A. (1994) La Sémantique d'une Métaphore dans un Langage Visuel: Application à un Système d'Information Géographique, *ERGO/IA*, Biarritz, France.

Calcinelli D. and Mainguenaud M. (1991) The Management of the Ambiguities in a Graphical Query Language for Geographical Information Systems, *2nd Symposium on Large Spatial Databases*, Zurich, Switzerland, Lecture Notes in Computer Science n° 525 (LNCS).

Calcinelli D. and Mainguenaud M. (1994) CIGALES: A Visual Query Language for Geographical Information System: the User Interface, *Int. Journal of Visual Languages and Computing*, **5**, 113-132.

Cruz I.F., Mendelzon A.O. and Wood P.T. (1987) A Graphical Query Language Supporting Recursion, *Proc. SIGMOD Conference*, San-Francisco, USA.
and G+: Recursive Queries Without Recursion, *Expert Database Systems*, 645-666.

Garey M.R. and Johnson D.S. (1979) *Computers and Intractability A Guide to the Theory of NP-Completeness*, W.H. Freeman and Company, New York.

Kim H.Y. and al (1988) PICASSO: A Graphical Query Language, *Software-Practice and Experience*, Ed. J. Wiley and Sons Ltd, **Vol 18 (3)**, 169-203.

Kirby K.C. and Pazner M. (1990) Graphic Map Algebra, *4th Symposium on Spatial Data Handling*, Zürich, Switzerland.

Langou B. and Mainguenaud M. (1994) Graph Data Operations for Network Facilities in a Geographical Information System, *6th Symposium on Spatial Data Handling*, Edinburgh, UK.

Mainguenaud M. (1993a) From the User Interface to the Database Management System: Application to a Geographical Information System, *5th Int. Conference on Human Computer Interaction*, Orlando, USA.

Mainguenaud M. (1993b) The Results of Geographical Information System Queries, *IEEE/CS Visual Languages'93*, Bergen, Norway.

Mainguenaud M. and Simatic X.T. (1991) A Data Model to Deal with Multi-scaled Networks, *I.G.U.-U.G.I. Conference on Multi-scales Multi-uses*, Brno, Czechoslovakia and *Computer Environment and Urban System*, **Vol 16 (4)**, 1992, 281-288.

Mendelzon A.O. and Wood P.T. (1989) Finding Regular Paths in Graph Databases, *15th Int. Very Large Data Base Conference*, Amsterdam, The Netherlands.

Myers B.A. (Ed.) (1992) *Languages for Developing User Interfaces*, Jones and Bartlett Publishers, Boston.

Shu N.C. (1988) *Visual Programming*, Van Nostrand Reinhold Cie, New York.

Smith T.R., Menon S., Star J.L. and Ester J.E. (1987) Requirements and Principles for the Implementation and Construction of Large Scale GIS, *Int. Journal of Geographical Information System*, **Vol 1 (1)**, 13-31.

Stemple D., Sheard T. and Bunker R. (1986) Abstract Data Types in Databases: Specification, Manipulation and Access, *Int. Conference on Data Engeneering*, Los Angeles, USA.

Ullman J.D. (1988) *Principles of Database and Knowledge-base Systems*, Computer Science Press, Maryland.

BIOGRAPHY

Anne Brossier-Wansek received the Engineer degree in 1992 from the Institut National des Télécommunications (INT), a state engineer school.
She is presently working on her PhD in the CEGN and in the computer science department (database group) of the INT. Her research interets include data models and visual query languages for Geographical Information Systems and Hypertext and Hypermedia Systems.

Michel Mainguenaud received the Engineer degree from the Institut d'Informatique d'Entreprise (1985), a DEA in computer science (1985) and a PhD in computer science (1989).
He is presently an associate professor at the Institut National des Télécommunications in the computer science department (database group). His research interests are data models and query languages for multimedia databases (Geographical Information Systems -GIS- and Document Management Systems).
His main contributions are a data model and its operators to manipulate graph based data in a GIS; a visual language, Cigales, and a study on the query resolution mechanisms to address GIS databases; and a data model for multimedia hypertext like documents.

17

GISQL - A Query Language Intepreter for Geographical Information Systems

G. Costagliola, G. Tortora, M. Tucci

Dipartimento di Informatica ed Applicazioni
University of Salerno - I84081 Baronissi (SA) - ITALY
Tel. +39 - 89 - 965 333   Fax +39 - 89 - 965 382
e-mail: jentor@udsab.dia.unisa.it

M. Busillo

ITALDATA S.p.A.
Pianodardine - Avellino - ITALY

Abstract

This paper presents the definition and manipulation language GISQL for Geographical Information Systems together with its interpreter. The main characteristic of the GISQL query language is to provide the user with an homogeneous interface for querying both spatial and alphanumeric information. The homogeneous interface consists of an extended version of the well-known SQL query language. Although the information is actually stored in two different databases, the user is presented with the view of a single virtual relational database, and the GISQL interpreter is in charge of managing the actual connections to the two phisical databases. Then, a GISQL query can contain any combination of spatial and alphanumeric conditions in a single command. In order to provide the user with the view of a unique relational database, the GISQL interface makes use of the concept of virtual tables. A virtual table contains both columns to hold the values of alphanumeric attributes and columns to hold the values of graphical attributes. The alphanumeric values are directly extract from the SQL database while the graphical values are derived from the graphical database.

Keywords

Spatial data management, modeling of visual information, geographic information systems

1 INTRODUCTION

Geographical Information Systems (GIS) are based upon the integration of a DBMS with (interactive) graphical technologies for the manipulation of maps. The growing interests and applications for GIS's is raising new and complex problems in the management, storage, analysis, and visualization of geographic systems in a graphical environment. The basic functionalities of such systems can be summarized as follows:

- geographic input data coding and processing;

- DBMS organization;
- querying;
- analysis and manipulation of data;
- visualization.

The information that a GIS has to manage regards both usual features of data, traditionally represented by alphanumeric attributes, and geometrical features related with spatial shape and location. Thus, the data management in a GIS has to take into account also topological relations based on spatial attributes (e.g., connection, adjacency, overlapping, etc.). Moreover, in most cases alphanumeric and spatial information derive from different sources and are organized in disjoint and independent databases. Therefore, alphanumeric and spatial data are often not strongly integrated and different query languages are used in the same system. In fact, conventional query languages are not suited for both kind of data, or at least need more functionalities and new executing mechanisms.

This work aims to the integration of the different nature of data considered in a GIS, through the use of a unique definition and manipulation language, called GISQL, for alphanumeric and spatial data. A prototype version of an interpreter for GISQL has been implemented based on the Siemens product SICAD (SIemens Computer Aided Design) in collaboration with SNI-ASW (Siemens Nixdorf Information Systems - ASW). Our approach is based on the extension of SQL to the management of spatial data. This is mainly motivated by the fact that SQL is widely accepted and used as a standard by both application designers and users. Although this approach has already been attempted in several works, e.g., (Egenhofer 1994, Herring 1987, Ingram 1987, ISO 1990], our proposal expressly addresses the following topics:

a) Definition of topological relations among geographic entities. A given entity is considered as geographic if it is described at least by one geographically referred attribute. The use of geographic attributes requires the analysis of spatial properties, deriving from the shape and location of entities, that can involve more than a single entity. As an example, a spatial relation can be considered between a river and a house that are closer than one kilometer, or it can be interesting to consider all the cities touched by a road. In general, a *topological relation* states a link among entities based on their geographic attributes. Although a number of topological relations can be defined, we aim at reducing them in terms of elementary relations between points, lines and regions, such as adjacency, inclusion, overlapping, etc.

b) Uniform vision of alphanumeric and graphical information. Our goal is to obtain a logical organization of data based on the relational model. This corresponds to allow each table to contain any number of columns representing geographic attributes. Of course, we also have to consider new data types for the values of these attributes. We have chosen a minimal set of topological data types, including *points*, *polylines* and *regions*, to match all the description requirements for graphical entities in a two-dimensional space. Each of these types can be seen as structured. For example, a list of scalar values defines the vertex of a region, its color and filling pattern.

c) Integration of an extended DDL (Data Definition Language) and DML (Data Manipulation Language) with topological data. The extended language allows for a uniform management of alphanumeric and geographic data with the same SQL syntax. Users are not forced to learn new commands: the same commands apply to the new data types at the logical level. The existence of two distinct databases at implementation level is made transparent to the user.

d) Design and implementation of a prototype interpreter. An SQL query can be seen as a single selection and projection on a unique large table obtained as a Cartesian product of all the tables involved in the query. Of course this brute force approach is not reasonable in practice, because of its space and time inefficiency. The goal of an SQL executor is the decomposition of the query in a sequence of simple and efficient operations of projection and joining with the generation of smaller temporary tables. The same approach has been chosen to design an interpreter for GISQL. Although alphanumeric and geographic information is physically split in two different databases, one can formulate queries with arbitrary combinations of textual and topological conditions, and the interpreter is in charge of decomposing and executing them separately. It also creates virtual temporary tables used to combine the results obtained in a sequence of subqueries solutions.

The remainder of the paper is organized as follows. Section 2 presents a concise overview of some related works on spatial query languages based on extensions of SQL. A description of GISQL is given in section 3, where spatial data types, spatial operators and functions are defined and an extension of the SQL syntax and semantics is discussed. Section 4 describes the architecture of the GISQL interpreter, together with some implementation notes. Some remarks on current and future developments conclude the paper.

2 RELATED WORKS ON SPATIAL QUERY LANGUAGES BASED ON SQL

The need for spatial query language is common to all the application domains for Geographical Information Systems. In this field, the main obstacle to the diffusion of a standard language for spatial databases is the fact that languages for traditional databases already accepted as standards, like SQL, QUEL and Query-by-Example, are still lacking of capability to support spatial data manipulation. In the GIS domain, it is necessary to develop and extend spatial query languages to support spatial applications. Many efforts have been made to achieve a query language that satisfies all the needs of spatial applications and that is not too far from the currently accepted standards (ISO 1990). In particular, the wide diffusion of SQL-based applications motivates the significant commercial and research interests toward the extension of the SQL language. However, the nature of spatial data is intrinsically different from conventional one, and it is not very easy to manage them without modifying the syntax of a language conceived and suited for alphanumeric data. As an example, the tabular presentation of the results of a query typical of standard SQL is not adequate for spatial applications, which usually require graphical outputs (Egenhofer 1988).

Among the proposals of query languages extended for GIS applications and based on SQL, two recent ones are shortly illustrated in the following, to explain the characteristics and requirements of such languages. An extended analysis can be found in (Egenhofer 1992).

One of the main features of Spatial SQL (Egenhofer, 1994) is how it combines the description of a query and the graphical presentation of its solution. The approach is based on an extension of SQL to formulate queries and on the GPL (Graphical Presentation Language) tools to present graphical results. Spatial SQL supports spatial data abstraction to reflect the human conception of topological space. It provides operations, methods and relations that apply to spatial objects produced by direct manipulation devices, and introduces new domains for spatial attributes of zero, one, two and three dimensions, respectively. Spatial operations include some unary functions like *dimension*, *length*, *volume* and the binary operations *distance* and *direction*. Spatial binary relations apply to pairs of spatial attributes and return a Boolean value based on the intersections of their borders and internal parts. Typical spatial relations are *disjoint*, *meet*, *overlap*, *inside* and *covered*.

GPL provides some tools for the manipulation and graphical presentation of spatial data resulting from a query. A *visualization environment* contains the information for visually represent output data when a query is processed.

SQL3 is a project both ANSI and ISO, (ISO 1990), are working on to define a new SQL standard, including enhancements to manage spatial data for GIS applications. Many of the proposed extensions consists of object-oriented features such as inheritance, encapsulation and modularity. SQL3 allows to define subtables/supertables and abstract data types (ADTs). A subtable inherits all the columns of a parent table and can have additional columns. Users will benefit of adopting standardized sets of ADTs for different application areas. The set of basic ADTs proposed for GIS applications include:

- POINT : a position in a n-dimensional space
- NODE : a point with topological connections
- LINK : a polyline connecting two nodes and consisting of a sequence of points
- CHAIN : an ordered set of links
- POLYGON : a region enclosed in a sequence of links
- AREA : a set of polygons.

The proposed spatial functions include spatial operators which return both scalar and spatial values. The introduction of *list*, *set*, *record*, etc., data types makes SQL3 able to support functions returning structured values. Some of the spatial operators defined in SQL3 follow:

x-coordinate:	POINT → REAL
y-coordinate:	POINT → REAL
inside:	(POINT, AREA) → BOOLEAN
links_attached_to:	NODE → REAL
bounds:	LINK → POLYGON
union:	(POLYGON, POLYGON) → POLYGON
inside:	(AREA, AREA) → BOOLEAN.

Although there are many other proposals for a query language for geographic information systems based on SQL, their use and diffusion is still very small and in most cases limited to the academic environment. Most of the currently available software products for GIS applications keep alphanumeric and spatial data split into different databases that are accessed by different tools. The lacking of a general method for solving queries independently of the specific applications is one of the main obstacles to the success of such languages. In the present work we aim both at defining a new spatial query language based on extending SQL, called GISQL, and at implementing a prototype interpreter for the GISQL language independent of any particular application. To achieve this result, we have performed an abstraction step from the twofold nature of a GIS, namely from the two separated alphanumeric and spatial databases. The GISQL language considers a unique virtual database and the designed interpreter deals with this higher level abstraction. As an experimental application, we have implemented this interpreter within the SICAD environment. The GISQL language and its interpreter are described in the following sections.

3 THE GISQL LANGUAGE

The main characteristic of the GISQL query language is to provide the user with an homogeneous interface for querying both spatial and alphanumeric information. The homogeneous interface consists of an extended version of the well-known SQL query language. Although the information is actually stored in two different databases, the user is presented with the view of a single virtual relational database, and the GISQL interpreter is in charge to manage the actual connections to the two physical databases. Then, a GISQL query can then contain any combination of spatial and alphanumeric conditions in a single command.

In order to provide the user with the view of a unique relational database, the GISQL interface makes use of the concept of *virtual tables*: all the geographic information (both spatial and alphanumeric) is virtually organized in relational tables. This virtual representation is all the user needs to know about the database structure in order to use the GISQL query language. A virtual table contains both columns to hold the values of alphanumeric attributes and columns to hold the values of graphical attributes. The alphanumeric values will be directly extract from the SQL database while the graphical values must be derived from the graphical database.

Corresponding to each virtual table, there is a *physical table* consisting of the alphanumeric attributes plus a new attribute named *location* holding a pointer to a data structure (BLOB - Binary Large OBject) representing a graphical object in the graphical database (Figure 1).

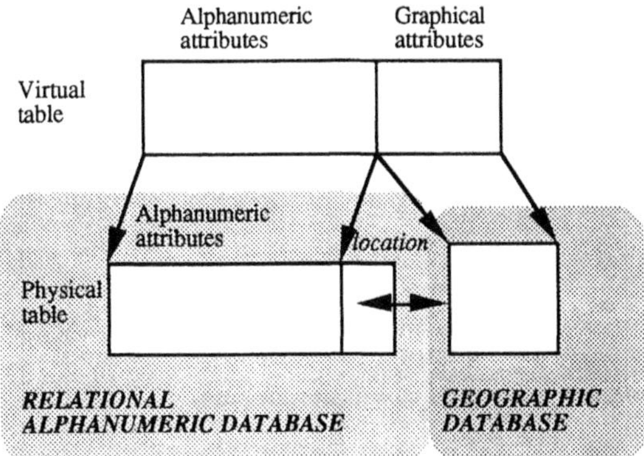

Figure 1 The correspondence between virtual and physical tables.

An entry in a graphical column of a virtual table contains the field values of geographic structured data types in the same way as an entry mm/dd/yy corresponds to the field values of the structured data type DATE. Analogously, we provide operators to extract field values from the structured data and functions to manipulate them. These operators and functions will actually operate on the BLOBs of the graphical database through SICAD procedures.

Spatial data types

The identification of a set of spatial data types and a set of operators and functions is one of the basic processes in the definition of a query languages for geographic databases.

In this section we introduce the structured spatial data types POINT, POLYLINE and REGION. Although more complex models for spatial data have been adopted in several applications, all the most frequently used spatial operators can be reduced to these three elementary types. We have chosen a minimal set of data types needed to represent geographic information in a two-dimensional space because more specific and structured types can make the syntax of a query language dependent on the particular model for spatial data. This choice is also suitable for future extensions to allow user defined data types.

For each structured type, a set of fields is defined:

POINT == (X, Y, COLOR)
where
X and Y are the x- and y- coordinates of the point,
COLOR is an optional field indicating the color of the point.

POLYLINE == (LCOORD, COLOR, MODE)
where
LCOORD is a list of coordinates,
COLOR is an optional field indicating the color of the polyline
MODE is an optional field indicating the polyline type (i.e., continue, dashed).

REGION == (LCOORD, X, Y, COLOR)
where
LCOORD is a list of coordinates,
X is the x-coordinate of a reference point inside the region,
Y is the y-coordinate of a reference point inside the region and
COLOR is an optional field indicating the filling color for the region.

The reference point is used to determine which region is referenced in a plane. As an example consider Figure 2: in (a) the referenced region is A, in (b) the referenced region is B.

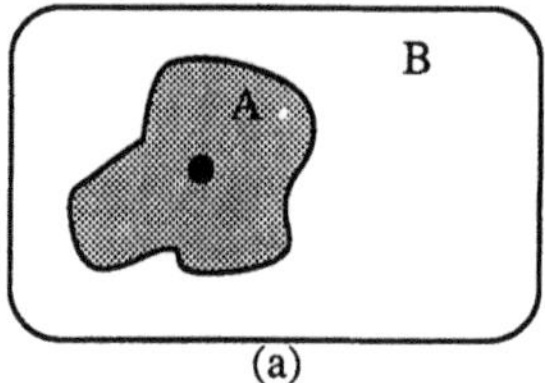

(a)

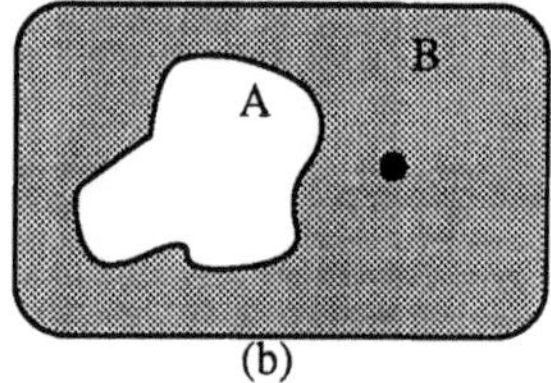

(b)

Figure 2 The use of a reference point to indicate a region.

In each type, a field corresponds to an attribute of the objects of that type.

Spatial Operators and Functions
To analyze the geometric characteristics of the objects and the topological relations among them, two types of operators need to be defined: *boolean* and *field operators*; and a set of *spatial scalar functions.*

A boolean operator verifies whether a topological relation holds between two elements, while a field operator and a spatial scalar function return the value of a graphical attribute of a particular object of type POINT, POLYLINE or REGION.

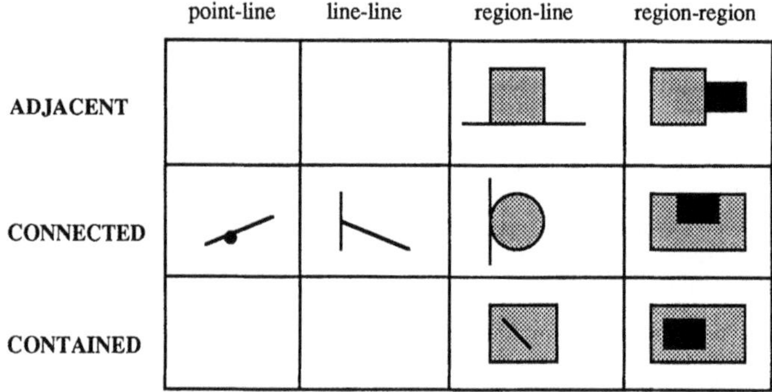

Figure 3 The spatial operators of GISQL.

The boolean operators introduced in GISQL and the possible combinations with object types are summarized in Figure 3. They are:

-ADJACENT(<*elem1*>, <*elem2*>)
true, if *elem1* is adjacent to *elem2* or vice versa

-CONNECTED(<*elem1*>, <*elem2*>)
true, if *elem1* is connected to *elem2* or vice versa

-CONTAINED(<*elem1*>, <*elem2*>)
true, if *elem1* is contained in *elem2* or vice versa.

A field operator is defined for each of the fields of the types POINT, POLYLINE and REGION defined above:

- **color_of**(<*elem_name*>)
It returns the color of the graphical element of type POINT, POLYLINE or REGION identified by *elem_name*.

- **xcoord**(<*elem_name*>)
-**ycoord**(<*elem_name*>)
They return the x- and y- coordinate, respectively, of the graphical element identified by *elem_name*. The graphical element type may be both POINT and REGION. In this last case the operators are applied to the reference point of *elem_name*.

-**lcoord**(<*elem_name*>)
It returns the list of vertices of the graphical element identified by *elem_name*. The type of may be both POLYLINE and REGION.

-**mode_of**(<*elem_name*>)
It returns the kind of line used to draw a POLYLINE.

-**set_color**(<column_name, color>)
It modifies the color of the graphical element identified by column_name

-**set_xcoord**(<column_name, value>)
-**set_ycoord**(<column_name, value>)
They modify the values of the x-coordinate and y-coordinate, respectively, of the graphical element identified by column_name

-**set_lcoord**(<column_name, list_value>)
It modifies the list of vertices of the graphical element identified by column_name

-**set_mode**(<column_name, mode>)
It modifies the kind of pen used to draw the graphical element identified by column_name.

The field operators **color_of**, **ycoord**, **xcoord**, **lcoord** and **modeof** may be used as arguments of the SELECT SQL statement to project particular attributes of a graphical object or to set conditions on the attributes of graphical data in the WHERE clause. The remaining **set_*** field operators may be used as arguments of the UPDATE statement to modify the tuples of a table.

To manipulate graphical information more easily, a number of spatial scalar functions have been defined. These, applied to graphical objects, return scalar values each indicating some properties of the objects themselves. Some examples include the length of a line, the area of a region, the distance between two objects. The following spatial scalar function have been added to GISQL:

DISTANCE(*region1*, *region2*)
DISTANCE(*region*, *polyline*)
DISTANCE(*region*, *point*)

DISTANCE(*polyline1*, *polyline2*)
DISTANCE(*polyline*, *point*)
DISTANCE(*point1*, *point2*)
AREA(*region*)
PERIMETER(*region*)
LENGTH(*polyline*).

The syntax specifications of the most characteristic parts of the GISQL language have been given by means of grammar rules.

Examples of use of the GISQL language:

Due to the introduction of the new data types, operators and functions, it is possible to define SQL-like commands which mix both alphanumeric and spatial information such that the syntax and semantics of SQL is not modified. Further, while the user is left with the view of a relational database, in fact he/she operates with two different non-homogeneous databases.

In the following, we provide a sample set of GISQL commands to show the potentiality of the GISQL language:

<u>Commands from the Description Definition Language of GISQL</u>

CREATE TABLE **ROAD**
(*name* char[15],
type char[5],
graph polyline)

This creates a table named **ROAD** with three columns:
-name a string of 15 characters to store the name of the road
-type a string of 5 characters to store the type of the road
-graph a polyline to store the graphical representation of the road.

INSERT INTO **ROAD** (*name*, *type*, *graph*)
VALUES ("Appia", "SS", ((10,4)(100, 75)(86, 50), BLUE, CONTINUOS)

This inserts into the table **ROAD** the tuple representing the "SS" type road named Appia. Its graphical representation is a BLUE, CONTINUOS polyline with coordinate vertices (10, 4)(100, 75)(86, 50).

UPDATE **ROAD**
SET *graph* = (**set_color**(*graph*, GREEN))
WHERE **ROAD**.*name* = "Appia"

This updates the table **ROAD** by modifying the color of the road named Appia from BLUE to GREEN.

DELETE FROM **ROAD**
WHERE **mode_of**(*graph*) = CONTINUOS

This deletes all the tuples from the table **ROAD** which are represented by CONTINUOS lines.

SELECT *name*, *graph*
FROM **ROAD**
WHERE **mode_of**(*graph*) = CONTINUOS.

This returns all the names of the roads drawn with a continuous line together with the corresponding road visualizations.

Commands from the Description Manipulation Language of GISQL

If a new table **STATE** is defined with attributes *NAME* of type string of characters and *GRAPH* of type region, the following query:

```
SELECT    ROAD.name, ROAD.graph
FROM      ROAD, STATE
WHERE     CONTAINED(ROAD.graph, STATE.graph)
          AND STATE.name = "Pennsylvania"
          AND LENGTH(ROAD.graph) = 100
```

returns the names and the corresponding visualizations of all the roads in Pennsylvania which are 100 miles long.

```
SELECT    min(LENGTH(graph))
FROM      ROAD
WHERE     ROAD.type = "SS"
```

This selects the minimum length among all the "SS" type roads.

```
SELECT    name, max(LENGTH(graph))
FROM      ROAD
WHERE     name <> "Appia"
GROUP BY  color_of(graph)
```

This returns all the roads with name different from "Appia" with max length grouped by the color of the roads.

```
SELECT    name, LENGTH(graph)
FROM      ROAD
WHERE     name <> "Appia"
GROUP BY  color_of(graph)
HAVING    sum(LENGTH(graph)) < 200
```

This returns all the roads with name different from "Appia" with length grouped by the color of the roads and with length less than 200 miles.

```
SELECT    name, type
FROM      ROADS
WHERE     type <> "SS"
ORDER BY  color_of(graph), type
```

This returns all the names and types of the roads which are not of "SS" type. The names and types are ordered with respect to the color and the type of the roads.

4 THE GISQL INTERPRETER

The GISQL interpreter translates a query into a set of subqueries each of which is specific either to the alphanumeric relational database or to the spatial database (Figure 4).

These queries are then solved by an appropriate module. The SQL module of Figure 4 solves alphanumeric subqueries by calling a standard SQL interpreter. The spatial module solves spatial subqueries by executing access functions to the geographic database. The set of these functions form a library that constitutes the interface with the physical spatial data.

The interpretation process consists of six phases, as shown in Figure 5. Several transformations are performed on an input query in order to separate the accesses to the alphanumeric and spatial databases. It is decomposed in elementary subqueries each containing only predicates of alphanumeric or spatial type.

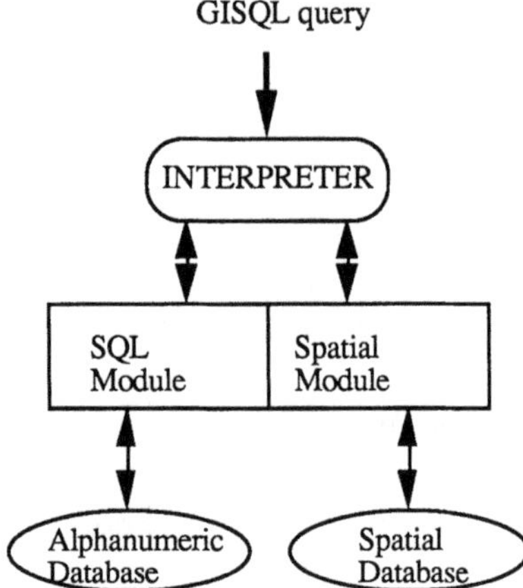

Figure 4 The schema for the GISQL System.

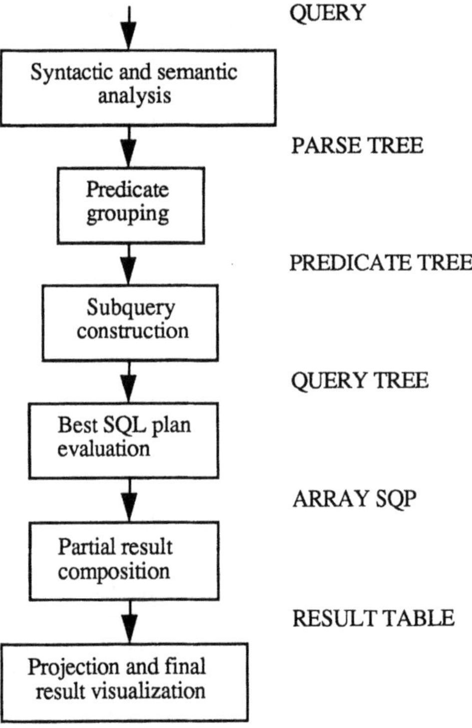

Figure 5 The interpretation process.

In the parsing phase, the query is syntactically and semantically analyzed and, after a preliminary optimization, a parse tree is created to represent the query in all the following phases. Then, the interpreter groups the predicates, in the subtree representing the *where* clause, that involve the same relation to avoid multiple readings of the same archive and possibly reducing the number of the subqueries generated in the next step. The rules to group predicates produce two types of subqueries: alphanumeric and spatial subqueries. The first type ones are solved by the SQL module; the second type ones are processed by the spatial module.

In general, the subqueries can be executed in more than one sequence, but different orders, called Sub-Query Plans (SQP), have corresponding different costs in terms of database accesses. In the optimization phase, some heuristic rules are used to select the optimal SQP. The cost estimation for an SQP is based on considerations regarding partial result propagation.

An example of heuristic rule is: "execute the alphanumeric subqueries before the graphical ones". This rule reduces the accesses to the geographical database which are usually more expensive than those to the alphanumerical database.

The last step concerns the presentation and visualization of the resulting table as specified in the *select* clause of the query. The actual visualization is a complex task involving context and zooming features (Egenhofer 1988) that are out of the scope of this work, since they depend on the particular GIS application.

5 FURTHER WORK

One of the most powerful mechanisms of SQL is the ability to specify nested queries (subqueries) within a *where* clause. This feature allows one to retrieve information by a unique complex query with any number of nesting levels. To efficiently solve nested subqueries, it is necessary to transform them into unnested ones by linearization mechanisms (Kim 1992). Our prototype interpreter for GISQL includes a solution to this problem which takes into account optimization issues and does not overload the interpreter. In fact, a linearization is accomplished by transforming the parse tree of a query before the optimization phase.

The GISQL interpreter has been implemented by using the tool YACC (Aho 1985) and the experimental prototype is under testing for possible engineering and commercial distribution. Further developments of both the language and the interpreter will probably be suggested by this testing phase. The most likely extensions presently foreseen regard user defined complex spatial data types and output presentation tools for spatial data.

6 REFERENCES

Egenhofer, M.A. (1994), SPATIAL SQL: A Query and Presentation Language, *IEEE Trans. on Knowledge and Data Engineering*, **6**, 1, 86-95.

Egenhofer, M.A. (1992), Why not SQL!, *Int. Journ. Geographical Information Systems*, **6**, 2, 71-85.

Egenhofer, M.A., Frank, A. (1988), Towards a Spatial Query Language: User Interface Consideration, *in Proceedings of 14th International Conference on Very Large Databases*, Los Angeles, 124-133.

Herring, J. (1987), TIGRIS: Topologically Integrated Geographic Information Systems, *in Proc. AUTO-CARTO 8*, Baltimore, 282-291.

Ingram, K., Phillips, W. (1987), Geographic Information Processing Using a SQL-based Query Language, *in Proc. AUTO-CARTO 8*, Baltimore, 326-335.

ISO/IEC JTC1/SC21/WG3 DBL-SEL3b (1990) Database Language SQL2, also including SQL3 extensions *ISO working draft*..

Kim, W. (1992), On Optimizing an SQL-like Nested Query, *ACM Transactions on Database Systems*, 7, 3, 443-469.

Ooi, B.C., Sacks-Davis, R., McDonnell, K.(1989), Extending a DBMS for Geographic Applications, *Proceedings IEE 5th Conference on Data Engineering*, Los Angeles, 590-597.

Aho, A.V., Sethi, R. and Ullman, J.D. (1985), *Compilers,principles, techniques and tools*, Addison Wesley.

7 BIOGRAPHIES

Gennaro Costagliola

Gennaro Costagliola received the Laurea degree in computer science from the University of Salerno, Italy, 1987 and the M.S. degree in computer science from the University of Pittsburgh, Pittsburgh, PA in 1991. Since 1993 he is a Research Associate and Teaching Assistant with the Department of Computer Science at the University of Salerno.

His research interests include visual languages, visual programming, image database indexing, picture matching on parallel architectures.

He is a member of the Association for Computing Machinery and the IEEE Computer Society.

Genoveffa Tortora

Genoveffa Tortora received the Laurea degree in computer science from the University of Salerno, Italy, 1978.

From 1978 to 1988 she was a Research Associate and Teaching Assistant of computer science at the University of Salerno. From 1989 to 1990 she was an Associate Professor, and she is currently a Professor of Computer Science at the University of Salerno.

She published more than 30 papers in international journals, books, and conference proceedings, in the area of programming Languages and software engineering.

She chaired the Fourth International Conference on Software Engineering and Knowledge Engineering that was held in Capri in June 1992 whose proceedings were published by the IEEE CS Press.

From 1991 she is Dean of the Graduate School in Computer Science at the University of Salerno.

She is a Senior Member of the IEEE Computer Society.

From 1990 she is on the board of the Ph. Doctor School in Applied Mathematics and Computer Science of the University of Naples.

Maurizio Tucci

Maurizio Tucci received the Laurea degree in computer science from the University of Salerno, Italy, 1988.

Since 1992 he is a Research Associate and Teaching Assistant with the Department of Computer Science at the University of Salerno.

His research interests include syntactical and semantic aspects of visual languages, parsing technologies for visual languages, visual geographical databases, and tool integration for software engineering.Craig Standing is a lecturer at the Department of Information Systems at Edith Cowan University and is currently working towards a Ph.D. at The University of Western Australia. He obtained his B.A.(Hons) in Geography at the University of Lancaster, UK., and his M.Sc. in Computation at the University of Manchester Institute of Science and Technology. His research interests include: visual programming languages, and systems development methodologies.

PART SIX

Visual Programming

18

Database object display definition and management with Moggetto

Pete Sawyer, Andy Colebourne, John A. Mariani and Ian Sommerville
Lancaster University
Lancaster, LA1 4YR, UK. tel. +44 1524 65201, fax +44 1524 593608,
[sawyer, andy, jam, is]@comp.lancs.ac.uk

Abstract

This paper describes a user interface framework called Moggetto for an object-oriented database system (OODB). Moggetto is proposed as an approach to the definition and management of tailorable object displays. The novelty of the approach lies in the use of embedded, inherently reconfigurable user interface components to realise object user interfaces which are modelled in the database. This obviates the need for close coupling between the OODB and the host windowing system through, for example, common language bindings and code libraries.

Keywords

User interface framework, database user interface management system, user interface components, MOG objects

1 INTRODUCTION

The object model is frequently espoused for database applications where richer semantic modelling capabilities than those offered by the traditional database models are required. Most of the older database models, exemplified by the relational model, are designed for applications where the data can be modelled using relatively few types but many instances; in other words the bulk of the data has a relatively uniform structure. Object-oriented database systems (OODBs), by contrast, are a response to the problems of supporting applications where the data is more heterogeneous. The consequent lack of uniformity of structure and semantics among the data has important repercussions for OODB user interfaces.

One of these is the mode of searching and retrieval of data. Querying via declarative query languages and form-filling is the dominant means of interacting with relational systems. With OODBs, querying alone is insufficient because a mechanism to facilitate the exploration of the interrelationships between objects is also needed. This is typically provided by a graphical browser.

A closely related issue is how the objects are visualised once they have been located by a query or by browsing. OODB objects are structurally complex compared to relational tuples. For example, they may be composed of other objects requiring a means to reveal or conceal multiple levels of composition as required. They also encapsulate behaviour in the form of methods and perhaps constraints and triggers (e.g. (Sawyer 1994)). These factors mean that the structure of the data (or a stylised representation of it) needs to be made explicit to the user. Users need visual clues to recognise objects of different types and how to interact with, or reveal new or related information about, those objects.

The provision of effective browsers and means to visualise the objects of interest are necessary for end-users of OODBs. Equally important are tools for database designers. As observed by Almarode (Almarode 1991):

"With the increased complexity of inheritance, behaviour, and complex objects in the database, building such tools for an object-oriented database management system will provide a challenge for all researchers and implementors"

Traditionally, the schema of a database is defined by hand coding using a data definition language (DDL), but attention has shifted to the use of graphical interactive tools to assist with this (e.g. (Leong 1989), (Almarode 1991)). The dynamic nature of some OODBs, where the schema can evolve without recompilation of the database, has encouraged the development of such tools.

This paper describes an OODB user interface framework called Moggetto which has been developed for the Oggetto OODB (Mariani 1992) to explore these issues. Moggetto provides:

- A run-time environment to manage the display of, and interaction with, database objects.
- A means for the interactive definition of objects' displays.
- A means for the interactive definition of the object types which constitute the database schema.
- Tools for browsing and querying.

We focus on the first three points which are novel because they have been achieved through the integration of interactive user interface components with the database schema. These are MOG objects (Colebourne 1993) which embody editing as well as end-user even handling. When integrated with the database through the framework, the information about how objects are to be displayed can be stored within the database. The major advantages of this approach are:

- A computationally rich DDL such as would be necessary if objects' user interfaces were to be defined as methods is not required. Consensus on OODB DDLs, from persistent languages to more traditional and less complete DDLs (Andrews 1987, Atkinson 1988), is currently lacking. By minimising the dependence on DDL computational completeness, Moggetto provides a generic mechanism for OODB user interface management.
- Code to manage objects' user interfaces but defined in libraries external to, and outside the control of, the database management system is not required. Storing objects' user interface definitions in the database is safer because evolution of the schema and user interface can be more easily managed and kept consistent. Similarly, the definition of new object types and their user interfaces does not require that new code libraries are generated or that they be compiled and linked with the database management system.

The remainder of this paper is structured as follows. The next section discusses the user interface tool and run-time features to be expected of an OODB and introduces the notion of an OODB user interface management system (UIMS). Section three describes the Moggetto framework in terms of an OODB UIMS. Section four describes how user interfaces are defined in Moggetto, including a description of the MOG augmented widget set and how it has been integrated with the Moggetto display manager. Section five describes object type definition in Moggetto and section six describes how Moggetto user interfaces are modelled in the database. Section seven concludes the paper.

2 DATABASE SYSTEM USER INTERFACES

In many database systems, the dominant means of user interaction is through a generic user interface where common display and interaction mechanisms are applied to every entity. In the case of relational systems, for example, every relational table can be easily mapped onto a tabular form on the user's display. Example-based user interfaces exemplify these (Özsoyoglu 1993) and many variants on the original QBE (Zloof 1975) are in existence. Tabular representation of database entities have the advantage of reducing the syntactic information which users must retain in order to interact with the database (Yen 1993). Visual query languages (Batini 1992) represent an attempt to ease the user's semantic load as well. An iconic query language, for example, will display entities according to entity-type-specific graphical icons which are deemed visually meaningful in the context of the user's application domain.

The approach of mapping every entity to a graphical representation according to a fixed set of rules has also been used for OODBs (e.g. dynamic forms (Sawyer 1988) and FO2 (Collet 1992)). To be effective where the schema and objects' structural complexity is relatively high, however, these must support browsing in addition to querying. Hence, for example, the means to follow relationships between objects and components, and types and sub/supertypes are needed.

Entity-type-specific representations are especially useful in OODBs where there are a relatively large number of different object types, each embodying different structure and semantics. Iconic representations alone are inadequate because they are atomic graphical entities and integrating navigational operations at the level of object components (e.g. expanding an attribute of a complex type) is difficult. Displays which visually distinguish the differences between object types but which allow the user to inspect and interact with the properties of which the objects are composed are needed to visualise objects.

In summary, an OODB user interface system should provide tools for the definition of objects' user interfaces and a run-time environment. Such a system may be described as an OODB User Interface Management System (UIMS).

2.1 UIMS and OODBs

It is interesting to consider user interfaces to database systems in relation to the Seeheim run-time model (Pfaff 1983) (figure 1) consisting of presentation, dialogue control and application interface components. Broadly, these components' responsibilities are as follows:

- Presentation refers to the display of the entities with which the user is interacting and the trapping of user input.
- Dialogue control manages the user interface-specific functionality (as opposed to that of the underlying application functionality). For example, triggering the display of a pull-down menu in response to a particular input event.
- The application interface forms the interface between the application and the user interface. It often takes the form of the sub-set of application entities (objects, functions) which need to be accessed by the user interface code.

Communication between these components is linear in nature so all input and output is routed between the presentation and application interface components via the dialogue controller.

For many application domains, the Seeheim model, while providing a useful conceptual decomposition of roles within the UIMS, has proven to be unsatisfactory as a run-time architecture. In particular, the strict decoupling of application and user interface functionality imposes performance problems where high levels of semantic feedback are required (the so-called bandwidth problem). This is a serious impediment to highly interactive, direct manipulation user interfaces (such as drawing packages) where every mouse movement event might require a user interface - application - user interface communication cycle. In terms of UIMS to databases, however, the granularity of communication is typically much coarser. In any case, the practicalities of the secure management of large volumes of data mean the database management system is a far more significant performance bottleneck than the user interface's run-time architecture.

Figure 1 The Seeheim model.

In a UIMS supporting graphical user interfaces to an OODB, the three Seeheim components may be broadly characterised as follows: The presentation and dialogue control components are much as described above, where the entities with which the user interacts are database objects. The application interface is the set of query operations provided by the OODB management system and through which the user interface communicates with the database. Hence, user events are mapped by the dialogue controller onto queries on the state of the database or requests to update the database's state.

DBface (King 1993) is a good example of a Seeheim-based database UIMS. Here, the display of database entities is managed by a *representational* component and the user interface functionality is managed by an *operational* component. These correspond approximately to the Seeheim presentation and dialogue control components. A novel feature of DBface is that the database acts, not only as the repository of the underlying application data, but also as the repository of the information used by the representational component to display the data.

DBface represents an attempt to provide a run-time architecture for the support of OODB user interfaces. This is broadly the same goal as Moggetto. Where Moggetto differs is in the focus of our work within the general area of OODB user interface support. We are interested in providing highly flexible, tailorable user interfaces and user interface development tools for database users.

3 THE MOGGETTO USER INTERFACE FRAMEWORK

Like DBface, Moggetto adopts a Seeheim-like architecture (figure 2). The display manager corresponds to the Seeheim presentation component, rendering objects' displays and capturing user events. The definition of objects' displays are contained in the database and consulted when a request to display an object is received. The object store interface corresponds to the Seeheim dialogue control component, maintaining a model of the state of the user interface. Valid events are mapped onto database queries and the results returned from the database are mapped onto appropriate update messages passed to the display manager to ensure that consistency is maintained between the display and the database.

Figure 3 illustrates Moggetto being used to view an Oggetto database modelling the components of a computer network. It is presented here as context for the discussion on defining and manipulating object displays which follows, not to suggest that, for example, the browser illustrated is appropriate for every OODB. Three important features of the Moggetto framework are illustrated in figure 3:

1 The background window labelled "Type hierarchy" is the top-level view of the database provided by the display manager browser. When invoked, this consults the database to construct the representation of the Oggetto inheritance hierarchy. The nodes represent

Oggetto object types; types illustrated are subtypes of the type to which they are connected immediately to their left. Object is the object type at the root of the hierarchy. Interaction with objects is through this top-level database view. For example, by selecting a node, the user is presented with the options of viewing instances of the type (see 2 below), viewing the type itself (see 3 below) or deriving a new type as a subtype of the currently selected node.

2 In the example, the user has opted to view instances of the type "SE30" and the small window labelled "Instance list" lists the instances of this type which exist in the database. Selecting one of these, as has been done to "PetesMac", causes the object to be displayed. The display of this object is managed at run-time by an object librarian which is created to collate the object's structure (type), value (instance) and display (user interface) details from the database. This information is then forwarded to the display manager for the actual rendering of the object on the screen.

3 Also displayed in figure 3 is the *type* SE30. This is actually the template used for displaying instances of the type. As the user interface of an Oggetto type may be a projection over a type, the properties displayed may be a subset of those belonging to the type. Hence, it can be thought of as a graphical visualisation of that subset of the type which is required to be made visible to users of instances of the type.

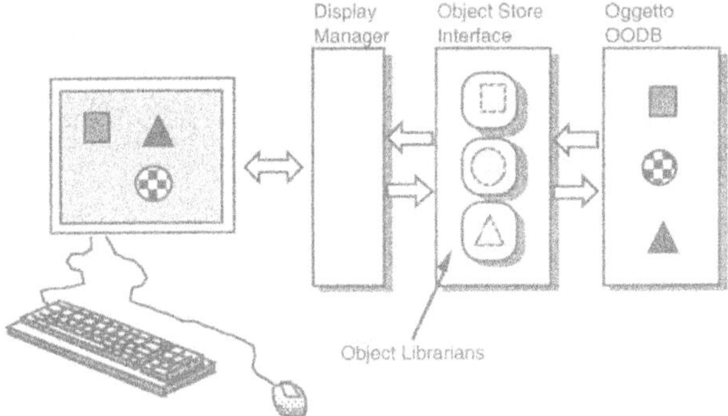

Figure 2 Moggetto's architecture.

Note that the SE30 type includes attributes of both primitive and Oggetto types, and singleton and multi-value (set) attributes. For example, "cpu" is a simple string while "pic" is a sequence of video images. The mechanisms used to visualise these are different with the value(s) of pic being mapped onto a composite user interface object incorporating a window for images' display and buttons to play and stop the sequence. Similarly, "network" is a set of instances of the Oggetto "Network" type and again, the user interface component to display this a composite one and includes a means (invoked through the button labelled "Select") to select individual values (instances of Network) for display.

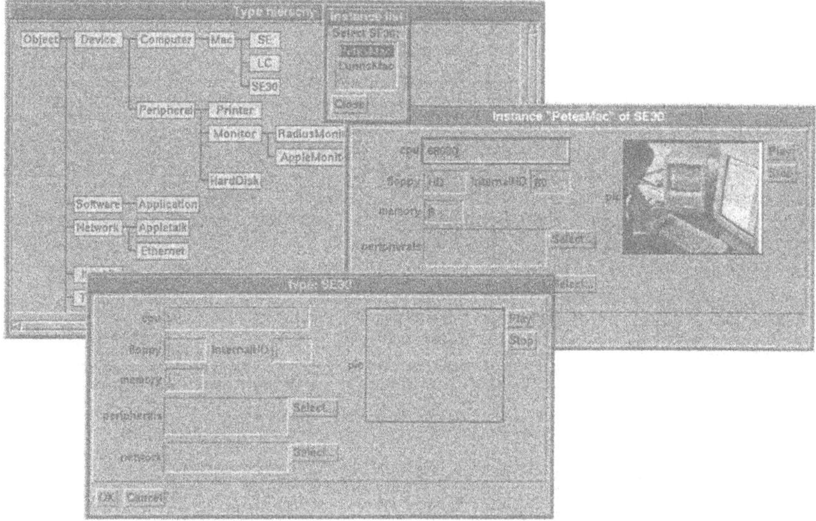

Figure 3 Moggetto in use.

4 USER INTERFACE DEFINITION

As stated above, the Moggetto framework supports the display of database objects according to the user interface definitions held by the database. We now examine how these object user interfaces may be defined.

An approach adopted by several OODBs is to provide access to a windowing system through the OODB's DDL. Each type may define its own user interface or inherit one from a super type. Inheritance is used to "bind" user interfaces to objects in exactly the same way as it is used to bind methods to object invocations (indeed, a user interface may be defined as a "display" method). Many OODBs, such as Ode (Agra90), ObjectStore (Lamb 1991) and O_2 (Deux 1991) provide bindings to general-purpose high-level programming languages, such as C or C++, permitting the direct use of windowing system libraries and toolkits. This approach has the virtue of completeness because it makes the whole range of windowing system services available, from low-level event handling through to pre-defined widget types. However, it is necessarily low-level and expensive in terms of the development effort required to exploit the windowing system.

Other OODBs use database programming languages such as GemStone's OPAL (Bretl 1989), and Kiwi's OOPS+/NAU and LOCO (Laenens 1989) which include user interface primitives as part of the language kernel. These are usually high-level abstractions over windowing system objects and functions, oriented towards the requirements of typical database user interfaces. For example, OOPS+/NAU includes primitives for defining such graphical objects as windows, text fields and buttons which may be bound to objects, views, attributes and methods.

In recent years, graphical user interface development tools have become commonplace, especially graphical user interface (GUI) builders (e.g. (Cardelli 1988)). With a GUI builder, a user interface presentation is defined by directly manipulating graphical instances (or facsimiles) of user interface components. Hence positioning, resizing, setting of components' attributes, etc. is performed by mouse selection and dragging rather than by hand-coding. This helps support the rapid incremental development of prototypes which effective user interface development demands but which textual bindings to windowing system programming interfaces support poorly. The output from a GUI builder is skeleton code which the programmer can integrate with an underlying application via call-back/event handling routines. In the OODB domain, these may be used to map user input events onto database queries and method invocations.

Moggetto has adopted this approach by integrating GUI builder facilities with the display manager. Instead of skeleton code, however, requests to instantiate database objects (*UIobjects* - see below) which store the definition of the defined display are generated (via the object store interface). The input to an object's display definition comes from the user who wishes to define its display, but also from the database. The user's input is in the form of direct manipulation of the various interactive components of which the display is composed. The database's input is in the form of schema information; information about the object type for which the user interface is being designed. For example, if an object type has a textual attribute A, then the user is permitted to associate a user interface component type such as a text field with it so that an instance of the type will be displayed using the text field to display, and allow interaction with, the value of attribute A.

The novelty of our approach is that the graphical components assembled to form the displays embody their own editing semantics and knowledge about their relationship to database object types. The user interface components used by the display manager are MOG objects (Colebourne 1993).

4.1 MOG

MOG is an *augmented widget set.* By this we mean that MOG objects add editing behaviour to the end-user behaviour embodied by normal widgets. This allows the construction of user interfaces which can be tailored or reconfigured by the user at run-time by suspending execution, editing MOG objects' presentation attributes and resuming execution with the new user interface configuration. Even where participative design (Norman 1986) methodologies are employed, end-user modifiability is a fundamental user requirement and MOG-based user interfaces support this directly (Fischer 1990):

"*End user modifiability is not a luxury, but a necessity in cases where systems do not fit a particular task, a particular style of working or a personal sense of aesthetics.*".

The MOG objects' editing mode which permits suspended-time editing is called "user config" mode. As an example of its use, a button MOG object can react to events in two ways. It will react to an end-user's mouse button press event by inverting its graphical image to provide semantic feedback and by invoking the appropriate call-back. In addition, by switching to user config mode the user can interactively resize it, change its label, change its font, reposition it, etc. (figure 4). This is done by reinterpreting user events. Normally, a button widget recognises mouse button press events and, when one is detected, simply calls the designated call-back routine (this typically forms the interface with the underlying application). In user config mode, however, this call-back routine is ignored. Instead, one of a number of different event handling routines is invoked depending on which event is detected and where on the button they occur. These event handlers implement the editing functions and are encapsulated by the MOG object and are independent of any underlying application (figure 5). When the user has finished editing the MOG object and returns it to normal end-user mode, the application can resume execution with the new user interface configuration. In addition, the changes are recorded in the application's configuration file so that they are remembered for subsequent invocations.

Of course, at run-time, the attributes which can be edited are restricted to those which do not affect the functionality of the underlying application and which only locally affect the existing user interface components' display representations.

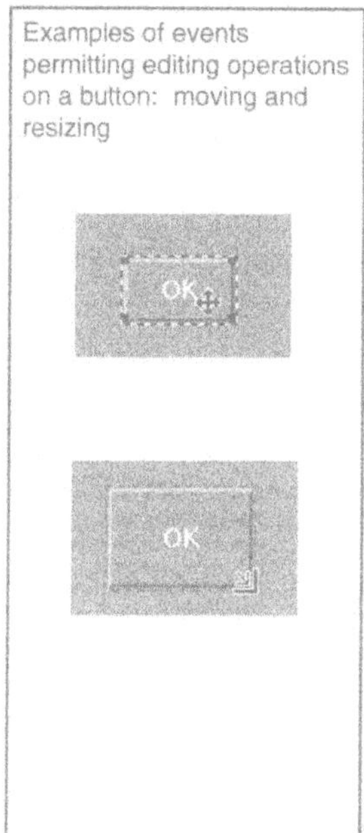

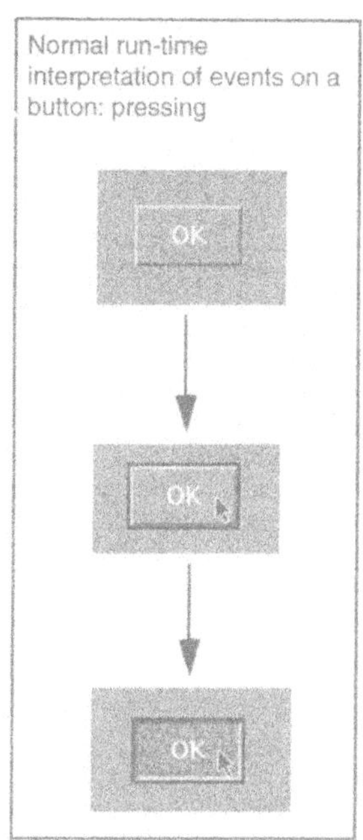

Figure 4. Examples of mouse button press events.

A MOG object is defined as a C++ object which encapsulates one or more widgets from existing widget sets such as Motif or OpenLook. The reuse of existing widget sets saves implementation effort and permits look-and-feel compatability with other applications. An encapsulated widget contains information about its resources, call-backs, recognised events, etc. and MOG augments this with operations which allow this static data to be accessed and modified. These are implemented as event handlers which forward events to the encapsulated widget when in use by an end-user but intercept and interpret as editing operations when in use by a designer (or end-user engaged in tailoring). Hence, MOG objects behave as normal widgets at run-time or as graphical editor components according to the context in which they are used. This context is determined by their mode.

In addition to performing "surface" changes whose affects are localised to the static, presentation aspects of the display, a deeper level of interactive editing can be performed on MOG objects. These include redefining a MOG object's call-back routine or creating a new MOG object and adding it to the set of MOG objects enclosed within a "container" MOG object (e.g. a subwindow such as a form). Such operations cannot be performed as suspended-time editing operations because recompilation is required and the protocol of communication between the user interface and the underlying application may be radically altered. However, the fact that MOG objects embody the necessary semantics to allow deep editing operations allows them to be easily composed to form the basic components offered to the user of a GUI builder. The mode which permits these deep editing operations is called "program" mode.

Figure 5 illustrates the basic components of a MOG object; the encapsulated widget(s), the functionality which handles the editing modes, and an event switch which redirects events to the appropriate internal event handler depending on which mode the MOG object is in.

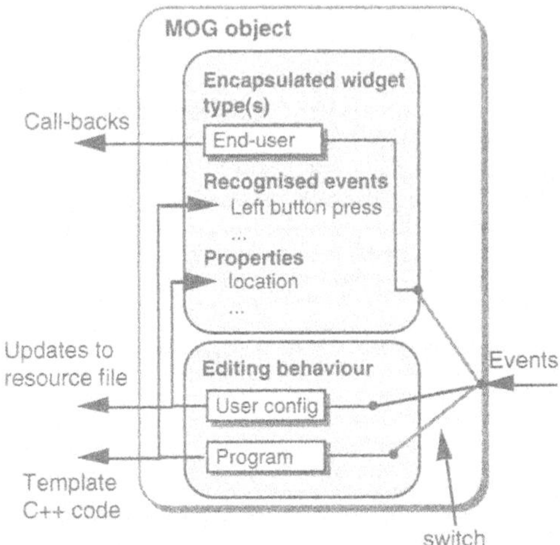

Figure 5 A MOG object.

As described above, MOG is not a GUI builder but a set of inherently tailorable user interface components. This contrasts with conventional GUI builders such as Gilt (Myers 1991), X-designer (George 1991), TeleUse (TeleSoft 1990), the NeXT interface builder and ViewCentre which are tools through which users manipulate user interface components. By embodying editing behaviour in the objects themselves any MOG-based application acquires an end-user tailoring capability without the need for a separate tool. Of course, GUI builders can be built from MOG objects (MOG can be thought of as a GUI builder-builder). A MOG-based GUI builder is simply a program where the focus is on interacting with MOG objects in edit mode(s) and which provides a means to create MOG objects of the desired types and a few other secondary functions. In effect, all other interaction is handled by the actual MOG objects of which the user interface is (being) composed. When the designer is finished, the user interface is saved by copying itself as a set of template C++ files, with the necessary MOG libraries, ready for compilation and linking with the application. Again, this is done not by the GUI builder but by the newly designed user interface itself because the top-level MOG object includes a "generate code" method.

A MOG-based GUI builder forms part of the display manager to enable Oggetto types' user interface definition. How MOG is integrated with Oggetto through the display manager is the subject of the next section.

4.2 Database object display definition with MOG

The MOG objects used by Moggetto have been adapted slightly to suit the OODB application:

- When an Oggetto object's display is first defined, instead of outputting source code which can be compiled to produce an executable user interface, it outputs requests to the database to instantiate instances of Oggetto objects which model the user interface definition (UIobjects). At run time these are read from the database and are interpreted by the display manager which remaps them onto instances of MOG objects to construct the actual object's user interface.

- When an Oggetto object's user interface is subsequently modified, instead of changes being recorded in a configuration file, the changes are recorded in the database by modifying the UIobjects.

Hence, the fact that the display is modelled in the database and interpreted at run-time by the Moggetto framework makes design and modification of Oggetto database objects' user interfaces easy to manage. In a normal MOG application, the application developer still needs to be aware of the need to write call-back routines and the details of the data structures generated by MOG. In Moggetto, this is hidden from the user because a function in the object store interface serves as the default MOG object call-back. This maps the originating user event onto the appropriate database query expression (figure 6).

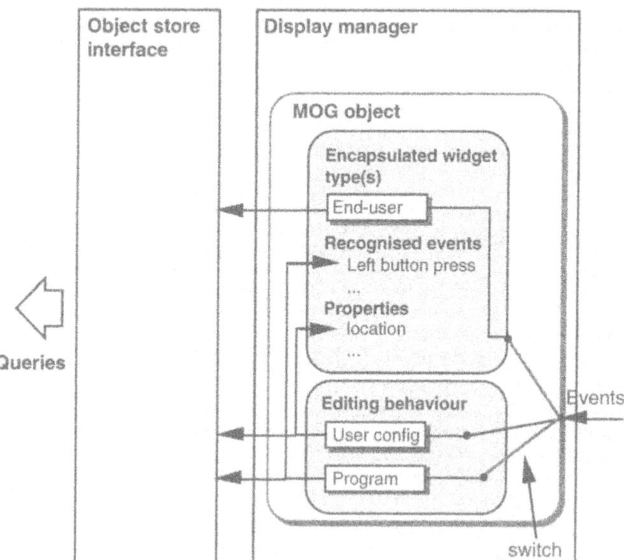

Figure 6 A MOG object integrated with the Moggetto framework.

As described above, reactive MOG objects must be associated, via UIobjects, with corresponding properties in database objects so that user events can be mapped onto the appropriate queries by the Object store interface. Failure to enforce this constraint requires that the behaviour of "unmapped" MOG objects have to be defined manually and linked with the Object store interface, breaking Moggetto's homogeneity. For example, if a database object type, who's user interface definition is encapsulated by its associated UIobject set, evolves then evolution of the user interface to track changes to the underlying object type is easily managed. This is not so where part of the user interface functionality is defined and stored outside of the Moggetto system.

5 OBJECT TYPE DEFINITION

The display manager's integral GUI builder has another function apart from the definition of displays for pre-existing object types. Its role can be reversed so that it is used as a type definition tool. Here, a new object type is added to the database schema by manipulating MOG objects to construct a graphical template from which a new object type is generated. Typically, the user will derive a new object type as a sub-type of an existing one and will be presented with the user interface defined for this supertype. To do this, the user can simply add new MOG objects, for example fields, buttons, sub-windows, etc., and, for each, specify a corresponding property of the new Oggetto object type.

Figure 7 illustrates the definition of new object type with Moggetto; the new type "LaserPrinter" is being defined as a subtype of Printer.

Here, the attributes "manufacturer" and "network" (a multi-valued attribute) have been inherited from Printer. The user has created a new text field MOG object, labelled "DPI" and is positioning it in the window which is used to represent the user interface for instances of LaserPrinter. The next step is to specify that this MOG object represents the visualisation of a new property of the LaserPrinter Oggetto class. The user is prompted to specify its name (same as the MOG object's label by default - "DPI" in this case) whether it represents an attribute or a method; if an attribute then what type, singleton or multi-valued, etc.. Properties' visibility are also specifiable. Users are permitted to define new object types where only a subset of the properties are displayed. In such projections, the properties are still defined by directly manipulating MOG objects and specifying an associated property in the new Oggetto object type, but the user specifies that the property will remain invisible when instances of the type are displayed.

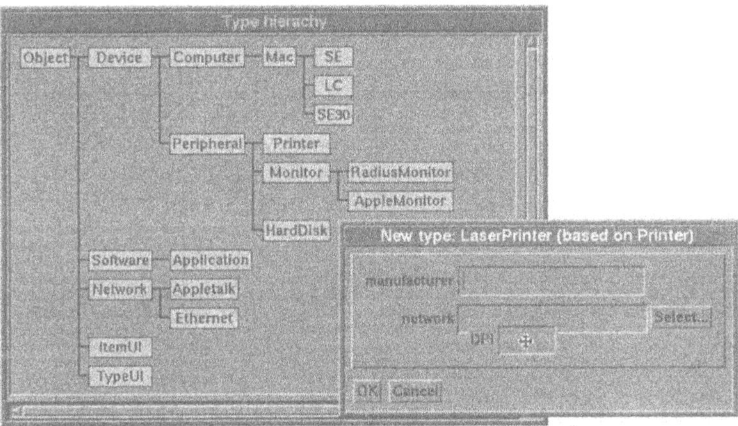

Figure 7 Definition of a new object type.

Once the new type has been defined and added to the database schema, its default display is the same as that through which the type was defined. As with any other objects' user interface, this may be subsequently redefined without affecting the underlying object type definition. This tailoring is effectively performed in MOG user config mode and where the previously described functions are performed on templates of object types' user interfaces, this shallow level of editing can be performed on actual instances of object types at run time. A change of this nature on an instance A of type X, once committed, may be made persistent and propagated to all other instances of X (if already displayed their appearance will change dynamically). Otherwise, the new user interface configuration will be local to A and forgotten when A's display is closed.

6 MODELLING THE USER INTERFACE IN THE DATABASE

The Oggetto objects' displays are modelled in the database as part of the schema. Each MOG object type has a corresponding *UIobject* type where UIobjects form a sub-hierarchy within the Moggetto type lattice explicitly defined for modelling user interface components. Every UIobject subtype corresponds to a MOG object known to the display manager and encapsulates attributes which are used to hold values of the corresponding MOG objects' visual attributes (screen co-ordinates, colour, etc.). Consider the object type Printer which has two attributes; manufacturer (a string) and network (a set of references to instances of the Oggetto type Network). These are modelled as instances of the UIobject subtypes string_field and set_of_object_field respectively (figure 8), each associated with their corresponding attribute and each corresponding to a MOG object type embodied in the display manager.

When a request is made to display an instance of Printer, the associations between Printer's attributes and its UIobjects are resolved and the UIobjects' values are collated by the object librarian which is created to manage the display of the Printer object. This display data is then passed to the display manager which dynamically creates the object display using the appropriate MOG objects which are initialised using the data from the UIobjects. For example, a text field MOG object is created to represent the attribute manufacturer with location, size, etc. as defined by the state of the string_field UIobject in figure 8.

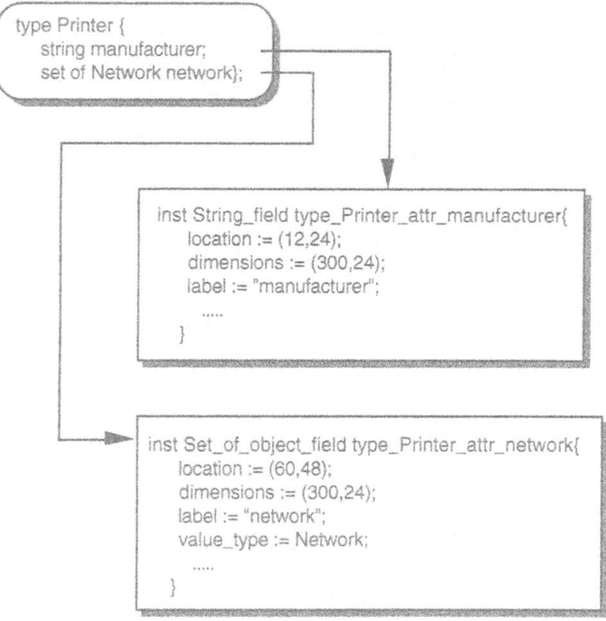

Figure 8 User interface components modelled in the database.

Subsequently, as described above, the display definition of Printer can be redefined by direct manipulation of the MOG objects of which it is composed. If, for example, the manufacturer field was enlarged and the user decided to use this new size as the default, the dimensions attribute of the string_field UIobject would be reset to the new value.

7 CONCLUSIONS

Moggetto is best viewed as a run-time framework for the direct manipulation of OODB objects on two levels; end-user interaction with the objects themselves, and object type and user interface definition by manipulation of embedded user interface components (MOG objects). It is aimed at facilitating the rapid prototyping of databases in a manner which allows the user to experiment with types and object displays without recourse to hand-coding in a data definition language. As such it has proven useful for databases such as that modelling of our department computer network.

As with King's DBface, we have adopted a variant on the Seeheim run-time architecture. While inappropriate for many user interface systems where direct manipulation of entities in a fast, reactive application is required, the architecture is very well suited to database user interface management.

MOG objects are embedded in database objects to compose their user interfaces as mappings between database object properties (attributes, methods) and instances of UIobjects. At run-time, the framework consults the UIobjects associated with a database object and dynamically constructs the object's display as a composition of the corresponding MOG objects. A user event on the display is either forwarded to the underlying database object as a query, or intercepted by the receiving MOG object and used to reconfigure the display by interpreting it as, for example, a request to relocate an attribute field.

Building database objects' user interfaces as composites of MOG objects and modelling them in the database obviates the need to store object user interfaces outside the database as code libraries. This provides all the necessary functionality to allow users to directly manipulate individual database objects. While object displays and new object types may be defined without recourse to a textual DDL, the functionality of more complex database applications would necessitate hand coding. Some problems associated with this were described at the end of section 4. These problems may be eased if the underlying OODB supports a semantically complete DDL, perhaps through bindings to other languages and programming environments, etc.. However, our intention with the development of Moggetto was to make the approach widely applicable by making minimal assumptions about these factors. Hence, we can confidently claim that the Moggetto approach is applicable to any existing OODB, requiring only that user interface components can be modelled as a separate branch of the type/class lattice.

At present, the framework incorporates simple browsing mechanisms by allowing users to interact with a graphical representation of the database schema and to traverse relationships where objects are composite (attributes of complex types). In addition we have implemented a simple object-oriented analogue of QBE and are developing ideas to graphically define more complex joins, etc. through the direct manipulation of participating object properties.

8 ACKNOWLEDGEMENTS

The authors are indebted to the UK DTI's Information Engineering Directorate and the SERC who funded the work. Additional thanks are due to the Concurrent Computer Corporation who provided useful suggestions during development and to this paper's reviewers for their comments.

9 REFERENCES

Agrawal, R., Gehani, N., Srinivisan, J. (1990) OdeView: The Graphical Interface to Ode, in *Proc. of the ACM SIGMOD International Conference on Management of Data* (eds. H. Gracia-Molina and H. Jagadish), acm Press.

Almarode, J. (1991) Issues in the Design and Implementation of a Schema Designer for an OODBMS, in *Proc. ECOOP '91*, Geneva.

Andrews, T., Harris, C. (1987) Combining Language and Database Advances in an Object-Oriented Development Environment, in *Proc OOPSLA 87.*

Atkinson, M., Morrison, R. (1988) Types, bindings and parameters in a persistent environment, in *Data Types and Persistence* (eds. M. Atkinson and R. Morrison), Springer-Verlag, Berlin.

Batini, C., Catarci, T., Costabile, M., Levialdi, S. (1992) Visual Query Systems: A Taxonomy, in*Visual Database Systems II* (eds. E. Knuth and L. Wegner), North-Holland.

Bretl, R., Maier, D., Otis, et al. (1989) The GemStone Data Management System, in *Object-Oriented Concepts, Databases, and Applications* (eds. W. Kim and F. Luchorskt), ACM Press.

Cardelli, L. (1988) Building User Interfaces by Direct Manipulation, in *Proc. ACM SIGGRAPH Symposium on User Interface Software*, Banff.

Colebourne, A., Sawyer, P., Sommerville, I. (1993) MOG user interface builder: a mechanism for integrating application and user interface, *Interacting with Computers*, **5** (3).

Collet, C., Brunel, E. (1992) Definition and Manipulation of Forms with FO2, in*Visual Database Systems II* (eds. E. Knuth and L. Wegner) North-Holland.

Deux, O. et al. (1991) The O_2 System.,*Communications of the ACM*, **34** (10).

Fischer, G., Girgensohn, A. (1990) End-User Modifiability in Design Environments, in *Proc CHI'90*, ACM Press.

George, A. (1991) X-Designer OSF/MotifGUI Builder, in *Proc European X User group Conference*, Cambridge, UK.

King, R., Noval, M. (1993) Designing Database Interfaces with DBface, *acm Transactions on Information Systems*, **11** (2).

Laenens, E., Staes, F., Vermeir, D. (1989) Browsing á la carte in Object-Oriented Databases. *The Computer Journal*, **32** (4).

Lamb, C., Landis, G., Orenstein, J., Weinreb, D. (1991) The Objectstore Database System, *Communications of the ACM*, **34** (10).

Leong, Mun-Kew, Sam, S, Narasimbalu, D. (1989) Towards a Visual Language for an Object-Oriented Database System, in,*Visual Database Systems* (ed. T.L. Kunii), North-Holland.

Mariani, J. (1992) Oggetto: An Object Oriented Database Layered on a Triple Store, *The Computer Journal*, **35** (2).

Myers, B. (1991) Separating application code from toolkits: eliminating the spaghetti of call-backs, in *Proc UIST '91.*

Norman, D. (1986) Cognitive Engineering, in*User Centred System Design* (eds. D. Norman and S Draper) Lawrence Erlbaum Associates.

Özsoyoglu, G., Wang, H. (1993) Example-Based Graphical Database Query Languages, *IEEE Computer*, **26** (5).

Pfaff, G. (1983)*User Interface Management Systems*. Springer-Verlag, Berlin.

Sawyer, P., Sommerville, I. (1988) Direct Manipulation of an Object Store, *Software Engineering Journal*, **3** (6).

Sawyer, P., Sommerville, I. (1995) MGA: rule-based specification of active object-oriented database applications, *Information and Software Technology*, (to appear).

TeleSoft (1990) *TeleUse User's Manual,* TeleSoft Inc., San Diego, Ca. USA.

Yen, M. , Scammel, R. (1993) A Human Factors Expermental Comparison of SQL and QBE, *IEEE Transactions on Software Engineering*, **91** (4).

Zloof, M.M. (1975) Query-by-Example, in: *Proc. AFIPS National Computer Conference.*

10 BIOGRAPHY

Pete Sawyer received a BSc and PhD from Lancaster University. After a period working at the Royal Signals and Radar Establishment in Malvern, he returned to Lancaster University and is currently a Lecturer in Computer Science. His research interests include HCI, Object-Oriented Database Systems and Requirements Engineering.

Andy Colebourne received a BSc from Lancaster University. Since graduating he has worked as a Research Associate in the Computing Department at Lancaster University, initially on an SERC/DTI funded research project and currently on the DTI Virtuosi project. His research interests include HCI and Virtual Reality.

John Mariani received a BSc and PhD from Strathclyde University. He is currently a Senior Lecturer in the Computing Department at Lancaster University. His research interests include Database Systems, Virtual Reality and CSCW. Dr Mariani is a chartered engineer and a member of the IEE.

Ian Sommerville received a BSc from Strathclyde University and an MSc and PhD from St. Andrews University. He is currently Professor of Software Engineering in the Computing Department at Lancaster University. His research interests include HCI, Requirements Engineering, Cooperative System Design and Safety-Critical Software. Prof. Sommerville is a chartered engineer and a member of the ACM, the British Computer Society and the IEEE Computer Society.

19

Visual construction of highly interactive applications

O. Esteban S. Chatty P. Palanque[1]
Centre d'Études de la Navigation Aérienne
7 avenue Edouard Belin
31055 TOULOUSE CEDEX
FRANCE
{esteban, chatty, palanque} @cena.dgac.fr

Abstract

This paper presents Whizz'Ed, an experimental tool for construction of highly interactive or animated applications. Whizz'Ed makes it possible to visually describe by direct manipulation the behaviour of graphical objects and their interrelations. It provides elementary bricks that encapsulate basic interactive behaviours. Whizz'Ed aims at allowing designers to build visual programs in which the control structure is described using data-flows. The flow graph can be structured in order to reuse complex behaviours, thus allowing the designer to create new reusable bricks at design time. Whizz'Ed provide designers with a visual environment that can be used for building user interfaces as well as for database visualization.

Keywords

Visual programming, user interface, visualization, graphical interaction, direct manipulation, animation.

1 INTRODUCTION

The development of highly interactive, direct manipulation (Shneiderman, 1983) interfaces is difficult because of their inherent complexity. This complexity lies in the behaviours of the graphical objects, the relationships between them and in the dynamic management of these objects. Classic interface builders such as HP Interface Architect, TeleUSE or XFaceMaker, offer a partial solution to the problem of building graphical interfaces. Such tools make it possible to create static interfaces capable to react to user's actions. But creating more dynamic, highly interactive interfaces, such as iconic interfaces or MacDraw-like drawing tools, requires more than the instantiation and parameterization of predefined interactors. To create such highly

[1] *also with LIS, University of Toulouse I*

interactive interfaces users need specialized programmers even when using high level toolkits. The challenge here consists in giving access to programming user interfaces to non-specialists in computer.science (Chang, 1987) (Williams and Rasure, 1990) by providing them with a visual programming tool for interface construction. A domain where that ease of use would be appreciated is user interface design for database systems, where ongoing research aims at providing users with simple means of representing data and interacting with them.

This paper is structured as follows. The first part describes previous work on visual systems. The second part presents Whizz'Ed, an experimental visual tool devoted to the construction of highly interactive or animated interfaces. The third part describes the implementation of our tool. We then present with a simple example showing how Whizz'Ed can be used for the design of an interactive application. The last part of the paper positions the editor according to the categorization of visual programming environments defined by Shu (1988).

2 RELATED WORK

Many studies have been carried out these last years in order to make the use of data-bases more comfortable. A new approach has been proposed based on visualization of information or data stored in traditional databases. Information are expressed with graphical representations and presented to the user in a spatial framework. Based on this approach, programming systems have been developed to offer friendly, easy to use, and understandable representations of databases. According to the literature, three main directions on visualization of databases have been exploited: the visualization of data, the visualization of data structures and the visualization of database schemas.

The visualization of data gives access to data through their graphical representations. This allows a wide range of people to manipulate these data without being trained in the use of database management systems. In order to enhance this technique, Fields and Negroponte (1977) proposed the concept of spatial data management. In spatial data management systems, the data are graphically presented in a spatial structure. Users can retrieve the information without having to know their location in the database or to learn a formal query language. They only have to go through the graphical data space using direct manipulation techniques. The View System (Friedell, Barnett and Kramlich, 1982) is such a spatial data management system. It extends the traditional systems since it generates the graphical data space dynamically according to the user's requests. SICON (Groette and Nilsson, 1988) is another tool used to navigate through a database in order to retrieve information. The information (objects) are represented by icons. Users can navigate through the set of icons. The links between objects are described by relationships such as proximity or inclusion between icons. Such systems are particularly useful for novice users with no programming knowledge.

The domain of visualization of databases schemas is still evolving. Most of progress that has been made is based on semantic database models. Hence most systems are based on semantic database model to visualize the database schemas. SNAP (Brice and Hull, 1986) is a visual editor which permits the graphical definition of the database schema. It allows the designer to navigate through the database schemas and to manipulate different entities by direct manipulation. SNAP supports the IFO model which is a formal semantic database model. SKI (King and Melville, 1984) is another visual tool for schemas browsing and/or definition. ISIS (Goldman, Goldman,

Kanellakis and Zdonik, 1985) introduces another way of visualizing database schemas. ISIS allows the user to create and manipulate entities. An entity corresponds to an object in the application environment. The new concept is the class. A class is a collection of entities of same type. ISIS allows to visualize the inheritance tree of the classes and relationships between classes as so as the attributes (data) of each class. ISIS allows users to navigate through the database at both schema and data levels. Other tools such as GUIDE (Wong and Kuo, 1982), QBD* (Angelaccio, Catarci and Santucci, 1990), PASTA-3 (Kuntz and Melchert, 1989) provide environments to visualize and manipulate database schemas in an easy way.

In the same way, the visualization of the data structures plays an essential role in giving programmers a better view of their applications. Systems for visualizing data structures provide programmers with a programming environment that enhances understanding. Kaestle (Nieper, 1983) is a graphical editor for Lisp data structures. The graphical representation of a structure is automatically generated. The graphical representations can be edited and manipulated by direct manipulation. Kaestle provides programmers with a valuable environment for the understanding of difficult structures such as circular or reentrant structures. In the same way, Brad Myers has developed a system for displaying data structures called INCENSE (Myers, 1983). INCENSE allows the programmer to design and use iconic representations in order to present data structures. INCENSE has been implemented for a Pascal-like language.

Among these different techniques of visualization, the visualization of data and data structures is close to studies on visualization of programs and program execution. These studies have been done to provide programmers with an understanding of what a program does and how it works. This step is comparable with the visualization of data-bases informations when it is used for debugging. In fact, the visualization of the variables during the execution is very similar to the visualization of the data stored in databases. In the same way, animation used to provide a dynamic description of program execution is similar to animation used to describe graphically the evolution of a data, for example in a statistical database. Systems like Balsa (Brown, 1988), Tango (Stasko, 1989) or Pastis (Müller, Winckler, Grzybek, Otte, Stoll, Equoy and Higelin, 1990) enhance visualization with adding animation. Balsa is an algorithm animation system. Pastis (Müller et al., 1990) is a program animation system based on a debugger. Tango (Stasko, 1991) is another algorithm animation system which implements a path-transition paradigm.

3 WHIZZ'ED

This section is devoted to the presentation of Whizz'Ed, a visual programming tool that allows the visual programming of highly interactive interfaces. The purpose of such a tool is to allow the creation by direct manipulation of interactive objects to build such an interface. The first part is devoted to the presentation of the conceptual model of Whizz'Ed. The second part presents the interactive editor.

3.1 The conceptual model of Whizz

The conceptual model of Whizz'Ed is based on data-flows and a set of predefined elementary components. The editor is built on top of an underlying library called Whizz (Chatty, 1992a) dedicated to the construction of highly interactive and animated interfaces. In order to explain the data-flow model of Whizz, we usually exploit a musical metaphor. In this metaphor, graphical objects are called dancers and non-graphical objects can be either instruments or tempos. Flows between these objects are made of simple pieces of data such as integers, colors, positions, etc. Referring to the musical metaphor, these pieces of data are called notes, and are produced by instruments. In order to provide communication, each object holds several input and output slots called plugs. Dancers listen to instruments and their graphical appearance (shape and visual attributes) changes according to the notes they hear. There are different kinds of instruments, some of which will be described in the next section. Among them, for instance, are instruments called rotors, each producing positions bound on a circle, thus allowing dancers connected to them to move along that circle.

Time-based behaviours are implemented by tempos that produce notes called pulses at regular time intervals. Tempos can be used to drive instruments. For each beat of a tempo, the instruments connected to it produce a note, then received by the dancers connected to them. There is no one-to-one relation between instruments and dancer as several dancers can listen to the same instrument, and one dancer can listen to several instruments at a time. Tempos can also be shared amongst instruments. This makes it possible to describe synchronized behaviours easily. For instance, in a text editor, when a user depresses one of the arrows at the ends of a scrollbar, the cursor of the scrollbar moves while the text is scrolled. These two synchronized behaviours can be obtained by connecting the text and the cursor, which are two dancers, to two instruments that describe their movements, and that are connected to the same tempo. Finally, other sources of movement than tempos can be used. Special instruments spontaneously emit the successive positions of the mouse, or the characters typed on the keyboard. Other instruments behave as active values, and can be used to communicate between Whizz constructions and other pieces of software: they are variables, that can be modified in a program, as well as instruments, that emit their new values when modified. Flows from different sources can also be combined, for instance when using several input devices at a time: Whizz has been successfully used to implement two-handed input (Chatty, 1994).

When building highly interactive or animated systems, specifying the movement of objects is not enough. It often happens that one wants to perform an action when an object has finished its movement, or when it passes a border, or even when it meets another object. Such events are generally difficult to compute beforehand, and it is much more practical to be notified when they occur. Whizz provides a number of active zones (or fields) in order to detect such events. They range from linear borders to elliptical fields or grids. They can emit events such as crossing, entering, leaving, etc. This allows for example the easy building of a maze game. Walls are built from these kind of active zones and are automatically impassable by user's actions. Similar zones can be used for building a slider to represent the interface of a thermometer. Events may also be emitted by instruments when their part is finished, or when a particular time is reached. This enables us to use the event model that has proven to be useful for interactive applications, so as to mix interaction with animation.

The underlying data-flow model of Whizz is based on two types of information propagation: streams, used for evolutions which represent a continuous phenomenon and events, used for isolated evolutions. Events are similar to those used in many graphical toolkits and represent a less structured way of communication than streams. With this stream-event model, user's actions and animation can be mixed since the model has a unique information propagation scheme. Events may also be handed to callback functions that may reconfigure the flow graph, by creating or destroying bricks, or changing connections. This allows events to change at run-time the behaviour of an object, or to fire animations.

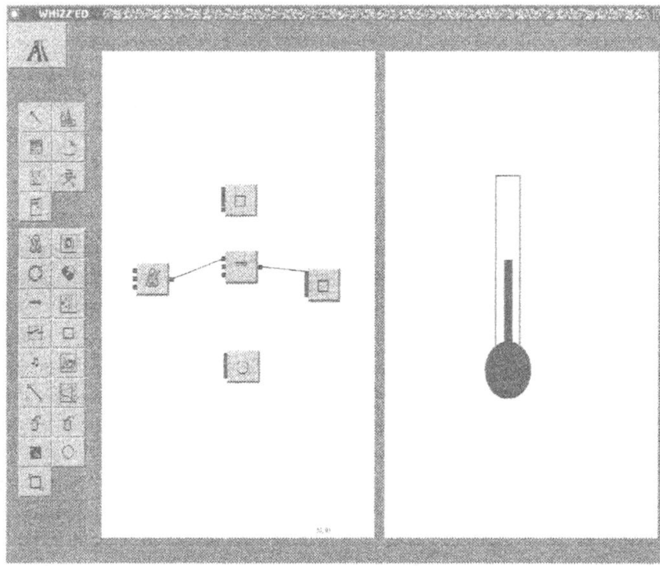

Figure 1 Animating a thermometer: the top left corner of the deformable rectangle is connected to the output of a straight trajectory. The trajectory emits positions when it receives pulses from the tempo.

Whizz'Ed provides a kit of components that can be wired together to build new components. This technique is usually called the building game metaphor. This technique is used by the Lego-Logo (Resnick, 1993) construction kit which is a rich construction environment which allows the building of creatures made with electronic bricks like sensors, motors, lights, logical-gates, flip-flops, etc. Several visual programming systems use this efficient building concept linked with a direct manipulation editor (for example see Fabrik (Ingalls, Wallace, Chow, Ludolph and Doyle, 1988)). Whizz'Ed provides a set of elementary bricks that can be dancers, instruments or tempos and makes it possible to build higher level bricks that can be seen as reusable components. When two bricks are graphically wired by the designer, these two bricks are connected and the data-flow is created.

Whizz'Ed proposes a visual language representing instruments, tempos and dancers by icons, and data-flow by lines connecting these icons. Plugs are graphically represented by small rectangles coupled with the icon representing the object. The notes are put in these plugs, and the type of the note must correspond to the type of the plug. The shapes of plugs depend on their types.

Figure 1 illustrates the conceptual model of Whizz'Ed and its user interface on a simple example of animated interface. This example describes the animation of a thermometer moving according to a predefined straight trajectory, each of its movements occurring at a given time interval. A tempo, an instrument (a glider) and two dancers (the deformable rectangle and the fixed rectangle) are represented on figure 1. Besides the icon of the tempo are three input plugs: the first one (of type date) corresponds to the interval of time between two notes it must produce, the second one (of type integer) represents the number of notes it has to produce, and the last one (of type boolean) represents its state: active or idle. On the other side of the icon, there is one output plug of type pulse allowing the tempo to send pulses to instruments. The second icon represents the glider responsible for the straight trajectory of the rectangle. The glider has three input plugs used for the calculation of the next position of the deformable rectangle. The first input plug (called Step) is designed for receiving pulses. Each time a pulse is sent through this input plug, the glider computes the next position on the straight trajectory according to the current position. The second input plug computes a position from a number representing a linear abscissa. The third input plug called "Projection" computes position by projecting given points onto the trajectory. In all cases the computed position is sent through the output plug. The two rectangles are also represented by icons featuring five input plugs and no output plug. A dancer is always a leaf of the data-flow graph, that is to say, never featuring an output plug. From top to bottom, the three first plugs of the dancer correspond to the TopLeft, BottomRight and CenterPosition of the rectangle. The two other plugs control the BorderColor and the FillColor of the rectangle.

The data-flow is graphically represented by a link between the tempo and the glider and by another between the glider and the deformable rectangle. This small visual program behaves as follows: the tempo produces a note in its output plug that is put in the input plug of the glider. The glider reacts to this note by calculating the next position of the deformable rectangle. This position is put in its output plug that is related to the input plug of the rectangle. As soon as the rectangle receives the note (the new position for its topleft corner) it changes its position on the screen. The window on the left side of figure 1 shows the visual program corresponding to the previous animated application. This program has been built using a palette that can be used through a direct manipulation style of dialogue. The right side of figure 1 shows the execution of the program described on the left side. In this window, the straight trajectory of the glider is hidden but it can be shown when editing the program. This corresponds to the internal parameters of an object, and they can be accessed interactively by double-clicking on their icon.

This simple example could be modified easily in order to describe graphically the content of a file or a database. Instead of using a brick tempo to generate sequentially the next positions of the thermometer, these positions could be computed using values read from a database or a file by a specialized brick. If the reading is synchronized by a tempo, the thermometer will show the values of a database or a file in an animated way.

3.2 The interactive editor

Whizz'Ed consists of three main parts: the palette, the editing area and the simulation area.

- The palette contains the graphical representation of the objects (cf. left side of figure 1). This part is devoted to the elementary bricks that are supplied to the designer. The chaining of these elementary bricks allows to build complex behaviours avoiding the limitations introduced by the use of complex bricks. However it is possible for the designer to build compound bricks and to declare them as elementary bricks, thus increasing the set of bricks primarily proposed. The palette is divided into three parts: the set of instruments, the set of dancers and the set of other bricks that are only used by designers to relate instruments or dancers.

- The editing area. This area allows to program highly interactive or animated interfaces using elementary bricks. The interface designer can use the palette (as in classical drawing tools) by direct manipulation, selecting an icon in the palette, dragging it to the editing area and dropping it at the desired place. Links between bricks are also built using direct manipulation, by selecting a plug of a brick and dragging and dropping it over another one. The arc is then automatically represented. The editor checks automatically that the type of the plugs are compatible. Bricks can be moved to simplify wiring. An example of the edition window is shown on the center of figure 1.
- The simulation window. This window aims at graphically representing the execution of the visual program built in the editing area. The simulating area guards against structural errors since the building of interactive objects is immediately visible and the appearance and behaviour of these objects is directly simulated. This window can be used either for debugging, rapid prototyping or simulating the program.

The elementary bricks are the foundation of the building of components of the interface. Some bricks are computational, while others provide user interface functions. The designer defines the application by directly manipulating the iconic representations of these bricks. The designer selects iconic representations of appropriate bricks, places them in the editing area and connects them to achieve the objects with the desired functionality and appearance. This reusable composite brick is immediately provided to the designer in the tools area. From this state, the designer can use the new brick as a classical elementary brick. We will not describe all elementary bricks that are provided by Whizz'Ed, but some of them will be detailed as they are used in an example in section 5 of this paper.

4 OBJECT-ORIENTED VISUAL PROGRAMMING SYSTEM

In this section, we present the implementation of Whizz'Ed. All the functionalities presented in the palette of the editor are fully implemented. This implementation has been done using the Whizz library (Chatty, 1992b). Whizz is based on C++ and exploits the Xtv library (Beaudouin-Lafon, Berteaud, Chatty, Baudel and Fekete, 1991) and the functionalities of the Net Audio Server (NCD, 1993) (cf figure 2). Xtv is designed for the development of direct manipulation applications. The current implementation of Xtv is on top of the X Window System from MIT. The Net Audio Server is a system developed by NCD™ for playing, recording and manipulating audio data over a network.

5 EXAMPLE: THE BUILDING OF AN ANIMATED SCROLLBAR BUTTON

We present in this section an example of the use of Whizz'Ed for building the behaviour of one of the buttons presented at each extremity of a scrollbar. The behaviour of such a button is the following: while the user points at it with the mouse and holds the left button down, the button blinks and the cursor of the scrollbar moves. The blinking of the button is obtained

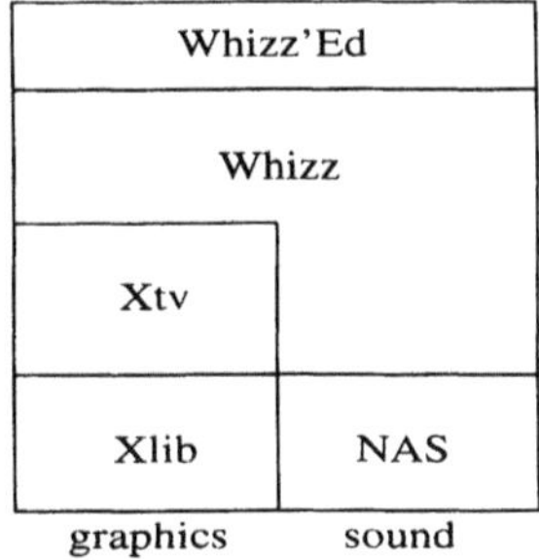

Figure 2 Implementation of Whizz'Ed.

by successively displaying it in different colors. At the beginning, the color of the button is white. When the user presses the button, it starts changing color. Moreover, in parallel with the color changing, a callback function is repeatedly called in order to move the cursor and possibly control other operations. Finally when the mouse button is released, the scrollbar button holds the current color. The behaviour of the button is relatively complicated as it combines graphical interaction such as user's actions (the click), temporal aspects (color changing) and semantic behaviour such as the callback function (for example, the text scrolling in a text processor).

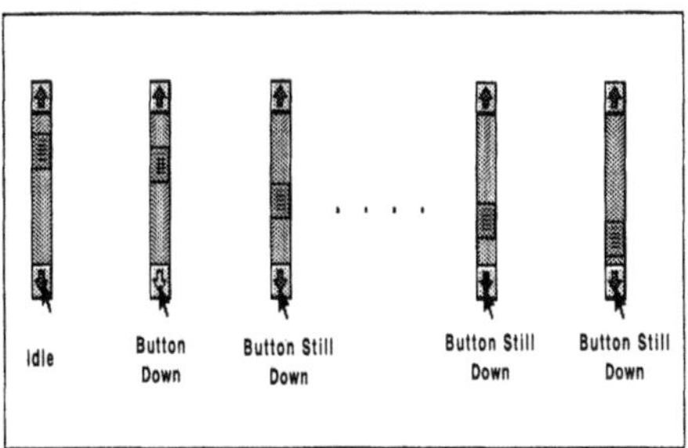

Figure 3 An example of the behaviour of the animated scrollbar button.

In spite of this relative complexity, the modelling of this behaviour is quite simple, using the conceptual model of Whizz. Figure 4 shows the behaviour of this object in terms of elementary bricks and connections. The behaviour is obtained by six elementary bricks tied together. In figure 4 only connected plugs are graphically represented as this figure corresponds to a simplified model of the behaviour of the scrollbar button done by hand. Figure 4 is organized as two high level bricks, the first one representing the detailed model of the behaviour of the animated colored scrollbar button, and the other representing the callback function related to the button. The model only describes how the connection between the two bricks is done, as the internal behaviour of the callback function is beyond the scope of this paper.

Figure 5 shows the visual program built with Whizz'Ed corresponding to the model of figure 4. First we will present the set of items (bricks and connections) of the visual program, then we will show how the behaviour of this program corresponds to the desired behaviour of the animated scrollbar button.

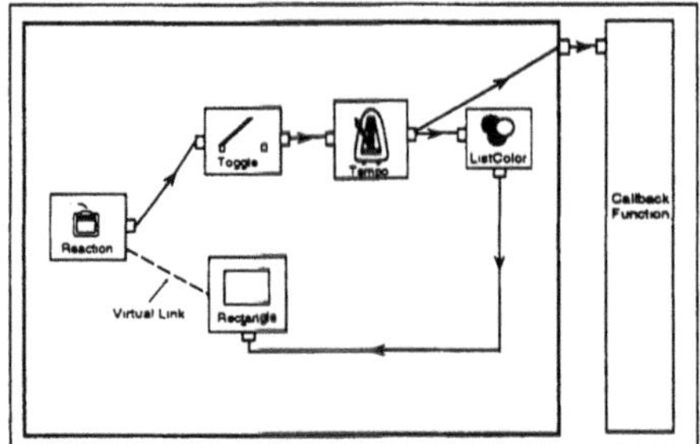

Figure 4 The informal model of the scrollbar featuring an animated button.

5.1 The items of the visual program

This section presents the set of bricks used in the construction of the visual program.

- The Reaction brick: A Reaction brick is reactive to user's actions (mouse click, mouse move, etc). It is associated with an object defined as being a sensor of the user's action and transmits this action to a connected object. These bricks are aimed at allowing user's actions to interfere with the behaviour of the system. A Reaction brick has one output plug for sending a note to the connected object when an user's action is performed on the sensor object. The designation of the sensor object is achieved by a semantic connection represented by a virtual temporary link between the reaction brick and the object which will be used as sensor.
- The Rectangle brick: Rectangles are deformable rectangles. Deformations can be achieved through the five input plugs as explained before.
- The Toggle brick: A Toggle is an integer instrument that produces alternatively ones and zeroes. It allows, for example, to start and to stop the running of another brick.
- The Tempo brick: Tempos are designed to synchronize animated actors. There is no synchronization between different tempos.
- The ListColor brick: A ListColor is a list which manages a set of colors. It features four input plugs that we will not describe in detail and one output plug. Each time it receives one event in its input plug, the ListColor emits a color note on its output plug.

5.2 The behaviour of the visual program

The visual program presented in figure 5 behaves as follows. The scrollbar button has to be reactive to mouse-down and mouse-up events. This sensitivity to user's actions is managed by the elementary Reaction brick called ButtonDn. As the button (represented by the rectangle) is directly concerned by these actions, we related the Reaction brick ButtonDn and the Rectangle brick called ScrollFrame by a virtual connection done by the drag of a invisible link between the two bricks. In order to produce the different colors that are to be integrated in the graphical representation of the scrollbar button, we add the elementary LisColor brick called ScrollColor. As the graphical representation of the scrollbar button is interested in these colors, the output plug of ScrollColor is related to the second input plug of the scrollbar button. In order to feed the input plug of ScrollColor with pulses, we introduce the elementary Tempo brick called ScrollTempo. ScrollTempo is controlled by the elementary Toggle brick called ScrollToggle. The On/Off input plug of ScrollTempo is connected to the output plug of ScrollToggle. ScrollToggle is itself commanded by ButtonDn linked to ScrollFrame. The dotted lines in the model represent the flow of events between the ButtonDn responsible for the reaction to user's actions and the graphical object where this user's action can take place (the Rectangle brick called ScrollFrame). ScrollToggle is on (allows information to cross it) as long as the button is pressed and off when the button is released. When turning to on, ScrollToggle starts ScrollTempo. As soon as the button is released, ScrollToggle, which is now off, stops the tempo.

When the user clicks on the rectangle button, the Reaction brick ButtonDn emits on its output plug a pulse towards the Toggle brick ScrollToggle. This ScrollToggle starts the Tempo brick ScrollTempo which emits pulses as long as the button is down. These pulses activate the ListColor brick ScrollColor. ScrollColor send RGB notes from its output plug to the input color plug of the Rectangle brick ScrollFrame.

In the model presented in figure 4, the Tempo is also used to realize the repetitive call of the callback function associated with the scrollbar button as long as the button is pressed ; this relation is graphically represented by the link between the Callback brick and the Tempo brick.

This animated scrollbar button can be encapsulated in a composite brick featuring a set of input and output bricks that can be directly manipulated by the visual programmer, and can be reused in other applications as the predefined elementary bricks. Since the composite brick is totally independent of the callback function, full reusability is ensured.

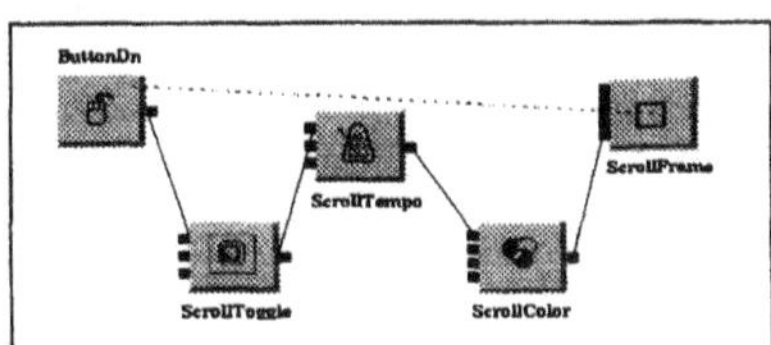

Figure 5 The visual program of the animated colored scrollbar button.

6 CLASSIFICATION INTO THE SHU CATEGORIZATION

In this section, we present how Whizz'Ed is related to the Shu (Shu, 1988) categorization. These last years, visual programming has progressed in two major directions. In one direction, graphical techniques and pointing devices are used to provide a visual environment for program construction and execution (information presentation and software understanding). In this direction, languages are designed to handle visual information, to support visual interaction and to program with visual expressions. In order to catalogue these trends, Shu proposed a categorization of the visual programming systems. She has identified two generic classes: the visual environment and the visual languages. The first class contains four subclasses:

- Visualization of data or information about data,
- Visualization of program and/or execution,
- Visualization of software design,

- Visual coaching.

The second class groups five others subclasses:

- Visual languages for handling visual information,
- Visual languages for supporting visual interactions,
- Visual languages for programming with visual expressions: Visual programming languages divided into diagrammatic systems, iconic systems and form systems.

Whizz'Ed belongs to the third subclass of the second group: the visual programming languages. It belongs more precisely to the diagrammatic systems class thanks to its data-flow model. But it can be also classed in the iconic systems class. Shu provides three criteria to assess a visual programming language. The first criterion is the level of the language. This criterion is an inverse measure of the amount of detail that a user has to give to the system in order to achieve the desired result. The second criterion is the scope of the language. This depicts the applicability of the language ranging from a general application to a specific application. The third criterion is the extent of visual expressions. This criterion is a relative measure of how much visual expressions are incorporated in the programming language.

According to these criteria, we can create the profile of the language. Whizz'Ed has a good language level thanks to its elementary bricks. The scope of Whizz'Ed is obviously restricted to the realm of user interface design. But the range of these interfaces is large from direct manipulation interfaces to animated interfaces. Moreover, Whizz'Ed uses bricks which represent visual expressions, therefore the third criterion is obviously respected.

7 CONCLUSION AND FUTURE WORK

In this paper we have presented Whizz'Ed, an experimental visual programming tool for highly interactive interfaces. Whizz'Ed allows to describe the behaviour of graphical objects in a visual way through the use of a direct manipulation editor, with a building block metaphor. A kit of elementary bricks oriented toward user graphical interaction is provided. The data-flow model ensures the dialogue between the elementary bricks, including time events and user's actions. It can be dynamically reconfigured in reaction to these events. Whizz'Ed can also be applied to databases in two main directions: the construction of visual representation of database schemas and the visual construction of interfaces to manipulate database information. In the first direction, Whizz'Ed allows designers to construct graphical representations of the schema of the database using specialized bricks. In the second direction, Whizz'Ed allows designers to visualize data using animation to represent dynamic data for example. At the moment, we are exploring directions for improving the tool. In the future, new functionalities can be added by extending the set of elementary bricks. We aim at creating a library of components to be able to define whole interfaces. For example, we need further investigations concerning the addition of sound bricks. Such an extension may be useful for multi-media interfaces. Another important next step is to create a library of functions. This library will make it possible to integrate existing domain-specific functions, by encapsulating them into bricks. We also wish to add a programming by example module to enable the design of behaviours in an easier way for end-users.

8 REFERENCES

Angelaccio, M., Catarci, T. and Santucci, G. (1990). Query by diagram*: A fully visual query system, *Journal Of Visual Languages and Computing* **1**: 255–273.

Beaudouin-Lafon, M., Berteaud, Y., Chatty, S., Baudel, T. and Fekete, J.-D. (1991). X_{TV} version 2.0 programmer's manual, *Technical report*, Laboratoire de Recherche en Informatique.

Brice, D. and Hull, R. (1986). Snap: A graphics-based schema manager, *Second IEEE International Conference on Data Engineering*.

Brown, M. H. (1988). *Algorithm Animation*, ACM Distinguished Dissertations, The MIT Press.

Chang, S. K. (1987). Visual languages: A tutorial and survey, *IEEE Software*.

Chatty, S. (1992a). Defining the behaviour of animated interfaces, *Proceedings of the IFIP WG 2.7 working conference*, North-Holland, pp. 95–109.

Chatty, S. (1992b). *La construction d'interfaces animées*, PhD thesis, Université de Paris Sud.

Chatty, S. (1994). Extending a graphical toolkit for two-handed interaction, *Proceedings of the ACM UIST*.

Fields, C. and Negroponte, N. (1977). Using new clues to find data, *Conference on Very Large DataBases*.

Friedell, M., Barnett, J. and Kramlich, D. (1982). Context-sensitive graphic presentation of information, *ACM Computer Graphics*, Vol. 16, pp. 181–188.

Goldman, K., Goldman, S., Kanellakis, P. and Zdonik, S. (1985). Isis: Interface for a semantic information system, *ACM SIGMOD International Conference on the Management of Data*.

Groette, J. and Nilsson, E. (1988). Sicon, an iconic presentation module for an E-R database, *7th ER Conference*, pp. 137–155.

Ingalls, D., Wallace, S., Chow, Y., Ludolph, F. and Doyle, K. (1988). The Fabrik programming environment, *IEEE Workshop on Visual Languages*, pp. 222–230.

King, R. and Melville, S. (1984). Ski: A semantic-knowledgeable interface, *10th VLDB Conference*, pp. 30–33.

Kuntz, M. and Melchert, R. (1989). Pasta-3's graphical query language: Direct manipulation, cooperative queries, full expressive power, *Fifteenth Conference on Very Large DataBases*.

Müller, H., Winckler, J., Grzybek, S., Otte, M., Stoll, B., Equoy, F. and Higelin, N. (1990). The program animation system PASTIS, *Technical report*, Universität Freiburg, Institut für Informatik.

Myers, B. A. (1983). Incense: A system for displaying data structures, *ACM Computer Graphics*, Vol. 17, pp. 115–125.

NCD (1993). *NCDaudio, V2.0: Overview and Programming Guide*, Network Computing Devices, Inc.

Nieper, H. (1983). Kaestle: a graphical editor for Lisp data structures, *Technical Report 347*, Computing Institute, University of Stuttgart.

Resnick, M. (1993). Behavior construction kits, *Communications of the ACM* pp. 66–71.

Shneiderman, B. (1983). Direct manipulation: a step beyond programming languages, *IEEE Computer* pp. 57–69.

Shu, N. C. (1988). *Visual Programming*, Van Nostrand Reinhold.

Stasko, J. T. (1989). *TANGO: A Framework and System for Algorithm Animation*, PhD thesis, Brown University.

Stasko, J. T. (1991). Using direct manipulation to build algorithm animations by demonstration,

Proceedings of the ACM CHI'91, Addison-Wesley, pp. 307–314.

Williams, C. S. and Rasure, J. R. (1990). A visual language for image processing, *IEEE Workshop on Visual Languages*.

Wong, H. and Kuo, I. (1982). Guide: A graphical user interface for database exploration, *Conference on Very Large DataBases*.

9 BIOGRAPHY

Olivier Esteban is a PhD student with the University of Toulouse and CENA (Centre d'Études de la Navigation Aérienne). His research interests include visual programming, human-computer interaction and construction tools for user interfaces.
Stéphane Chatty is head of the User Interface Engineering group at CENA. He is a member of the IFIP Working Group 2.7 (13.4). His current research activities include models and tools for building interactive systems, and new interaction styles, applied to air traffic control. Chatty graduated from École Polytechnique, France, and École Nationale de l'Aviation Civile, France. He received a PhD in computer science from the University of Paris-Sud.
Philippe Palanque is a lecturer at the University of Toulouse, and mainly works on formal aspects in the design of interactive systems. Palanque is a member of the IFIP Working Group 13.2. For 1995 he is co-chair of the Eurographics workshop on Design, Specification and Verification of Interactive Systems and co-editor of the book "Critical issues in User Interface Systems Engineering" to be published this year.

20

The integration of functional and visual programming for the development of a knowledge based interface

C. Standing
Department of Information Systems, Edith Cowan University
Joondalup Drive, Joondalup, Western Australia 6027
email: C.Standing@cowan.edu.au

G. G. Roy
Department of Computer Science, Murdoch University
Murdoch, Western Australia 6150 email: geoff@cs.murdoch.edu.au

Abstract

One of the requirements of a more knowledgable GIS involves the representation of knowledge related to a number of features: the data in the system; the operations that can be performed; the processing of requests; and the presentation of results. Many of the ideas presented can be generally applied to other query language driven systems.

The approach taken to the design and implementation of a prototype high-level interface to GIS is based on the functional style of programming. Functional languages appear to offer some important properties, for example: the strong and polymorphic typing and the ease with which new types can be defined; the ability to order the knowledge base within functions; and the facility to create functional hierarchies composed of compound or higher-order functions which allow high-level operations to be manipulated as units. The paper describes how a functional solution to the problems can be represented visually through the use of a graphical user interface with direct manipulation of objects/icons.

Keywords

Functional programming, visual programming, interface, GIS

1 INTRODUCTION

The development of an easy to use interface strategy for geographical information systems (GIS) is difficult due to the complexity of the systems and the range of commands available. The paper contends that certain types of information should be made use of by the interface to detect errors at an early stage of query formulation. Through the integration of functional and visual programming approaches an interface has been designed that provides the user with an unambiguous environment to formulate queries.

2 THE NEED FOR KNOWLEDGE

The particular problem that this research addresses concerns the process by which a user interacts with a GIS and how the design of such a system's interface can be developed to maximise the potential value of the GIS for that user. The approach taken by the research to the design of the user interface is one which brings this programming function much closer to the problem specification.

The research proposes that the incorporation of rules and knowledge in the interface can ensure the validity of the query to be passed to the geographical information system. This validity refers to the steps involved in the process of building the query as well as the completed query.

There are a number of problems associated with using database interfaces; namely that databases give few clues about the nature of the data, little help in indicating which operations can be strung together, and even less help in indicating which commands can be applied to which data sets. This type of information or knowledge can be embedded in the interface and hence the user can be spared time and effort in constructing a query that fails because it is syntactically or semantically incorrect.

This paper considers the interface to one particular type of database application called geographical information systems (GIS). Whilst the examples used are related to one particular commercial GIS, ARC/INFO a product of Environmental Systems Research Group, the principles we feel are readily transferable to other database applications.

Types of Knowledge

To overcome the problems stated in using database systems the user interface has to address the following objectives:

- Knowledge about the data - data availability and type are clearly defined

At present most GIS maintain limited information on the data that they store. The commercial GIS - ARC/INFO for example, can provide a list of coverage names; the names, data types, widths of attributes in a coverage; and whether it is a point, line or polygon coverage is implied by the attributes and the file extension. This is a very limited amount of information. A new user to a system may have an obstacle to overcome in simply finding out what the data represents especially if much of the data is in a coded form. For example, data may be ranked but this may not be obvious from the field name. Equally data could be in nominal form but just what the code means could be lost to a new user; a code number of 1 might signify large cities but unless this is somehow recorded in the data dictionary that information is lost to those other than those who set up the files.

- Knowledge about the operations - operations available and syntax are clearly defined

It would be useful for the user of the GIS to have access within the GIS to a clear representation of knowledge about the operations it can perform. The system should know which requests are logically feasible. Many functions in ARC/INFO, as an example, are not polymorphic; they require certain types of data. So an intersect operation takes a first argument of point, line, or polygon and a second argument of type polygon. Applying the function to two line coverage arguments would be an invalid use of the operation. It is not the intention of the research to focus on putting right just the poor design features of a particular software package but rather, in this instance, to lessen the problems associated with applying commands to the correct type of data. This is a more universal problem which has to be overcome in interface design. To solve this problem information or knowledge has to be stored in the GIS or GIS interface which represents the rules associated with each command.

- Knowledge about the sequence of processing - a query is specified in a non-procedural form

GIS are often presented as 'toolboxes', that is the user is provided with a set of available tools (perhaps expressed as commands) that enable a sequence of operations to be specified, and executed to give the required results. The effectiveness of the GIS is thus tied closely to how effectively the user can master the command language structure of the GIS. There are often long learning curves with associated significant time-costs in learning the command structure. The research is thus concerned with the processes for constructing command sequences which are required to fully utilise the powerful data processing analysis capabilities of most GIS.

- Integrated knowledge - queries are developed in such a way that are guaranteed to obey the constraints of the system both in the use of the command and the suitability of the application of the command to the type of data

It is clear there are problems in the design of GIS for the user; notably the limited knowledge represented within the systems and the time and difficulty involved in becoming a competent user because the user is effectively required to construct programs or 'macros' to perform sequences of low-level operations to carry out tasks. It is not difficult to appreciate the difficulties that the inexperienced user will get into. The required skills to become an efficient user are essentially the same as those required in writing programs in languages like FORTRAN, Pascal and C. The problems don't stop here. We also have significant problems associated with interpreting the user's *real* requirements in the formal command language. To illustrate the user's task consider this typical command sequence to produce a listing of all the schools within a 3 km radius of a particular bank:

```
RESELECT banks newbank POINT
RESELECT name = "ANZ Beldon"
BUFFER newbank bufbank # # 3 #  POLY
INTERSECT schools bufbank  schools_bufbank POINT
RESELECT schools_bufbank   new_schools_bufbank POINT
RESELECT  inside = 100
LIST new_schools_bufbank .PAT
```

Note that in this command sequence we are ignoring the fact that these commands are entered at various prompts (GIS system dependent) and that we only display the user input (to the GIS) and do not include what the GIS might display as a result.

In this command sequence the user is required to construct the commands in the correct sequence and syntactic form and to define new (intermediate) coverages or maps (eg. newbank, bufbank) along the way. The user must also be aware of the availability and type of the data so that commands can be correctly applied to the correct type of data. These are common problems in many programming tasks, especially within the procedural programming paradigm.

The above command sequence could be expressed more naturally as:

"Which schools are within a 3 km radius of the Beldon ANZ bank?"

To put this query to the GIS the user must:

- realise that the process requires the availability of the banks and schools coverages
- understand that a new coverage is required that contains just the Beldon ANZ bank
- recognise that a buffer area is required around the bank
- request an intersection of the two coverages
- select the schools that fall just within the buffer zone (inside = 100)
- list the resulting data
- determine the right sequence of steps involved
- express each command in the correct syntactic form

The knowledge that the system requires to know that the query is valid and that the data is available has to be provided within the interface or the interface has to have the capacity to collect its own knowledge, for example by interrogating the GIS database, or by requiring the user to provide some additional information. This arrangement is shown diagrammatically in Figure 1.

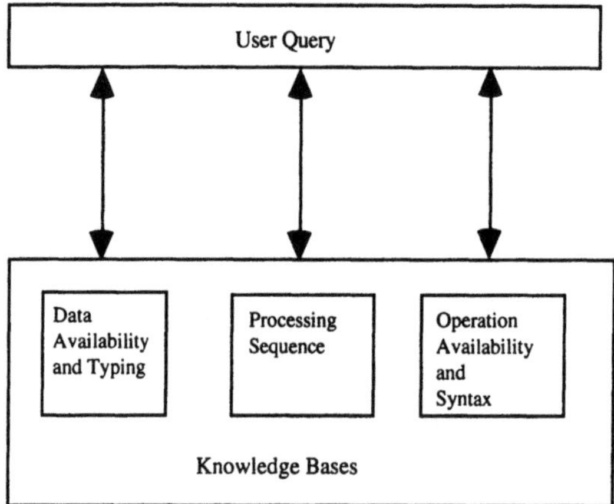

Figure 1 Knowledge incorporated within the interface.

Once we are sure that this user request conforms to the known rules and knowledge content of the GIS, then it can be formally translated into a procedural program which will provide the required results for the user.

3 FUNCTIONAL SPECIFICATIONS AND KNOWLEDGE

It is a hypothesis of the research that a functional specification along the lines as defined for standard algebraic expressions and the theory of functional analysis is a useful development method for meeting some of the objectives of the interface. This approach to problem solving is embodied in a range of programming paradigms, usually under the title of functional programming, eg. Bird and Wadler (1988), Henderson (1980) and MacLennan (1990).

What is functional programming?

As indicated by the name functions play an important role in functional programming. A function maps arguments to results. The function *half* maps an argument n to a result n/2. A program in functional programming is composed of function definitions and a sequence of function applications and therefore is rather like programming with algebraic expressions. An algebra is basically a set of values and the operations that are used on them. All functions map objects onto objects. Other functions are built using a fixed set of combining forms called functional forms. Functional forms combine existing functions or objects and return functions as a result.

Advantages of functional programming

- Referential Transparency

Better programming understanding can be achieved through programming without side effects. Imperative languages rely heavily on side effects whereas pure functional languages do not. They are not history sensitive and their computational results are merely temporary. It also means that because we are not concerned with how and when a function is called we can develop programs with more style and accuracy and which are not procedural in form. Field and Harrison (1988) explain referential transparency as:

"each expression denotes a single value which cannot be changed by evaluating the expression or by allowing different parts of the program to share the expression." (p.10).

This means that evaluating the expression changes the form of the expression but not its value. Any reference to a value is equivalent to the value itself and a reference to it from another part of the program does not change this. The problem with imperative languages such as Pascal is that global data can be used and this along with the use of the assignment statement means that a function value can change from one call to the next. It is these dynamic changes in the data, such as from true to false, that are called side-effects. It means that a function can have a different result even though the data passed as arguments are the same. Pure functional languages do not allow assignment statements as they are not concerned in the same way as imperative languages with updating a store. A functional program describes what needs to be computed not how!

- Strong Typing

The type of an object is the feature that characterises the aspect that the elements have in common. For example, red objects, blue objects, green objects have the type *colour*. Common data types used in programming are integers, characters, lists, etc.

In programming the programmer classifies data according to its type as a large number of errors can be detected by checking whether any values are wrongly used. It is this classification technique which is known as *typing* the data.

In a typed programming language, every value has an associated type. It is the type that defines how the value can be used. The numbers, both positive and negative (-1,0,1,2..) have an integer type. The values true and false are of type bool. The addition operator is defined to operate on pairs of type integer. The programmer can define a new set of values and provide a type name. The program then assures that operations use values of the correct type. Automatic type checking is seen as producing more reliable software (Reade, 1988). Strongly typed programming languages perform type checking and if this is done before evaluation then it is known as static type checking. Importantly, this allows many mistakes to be trapped early in the program development process.

- Abstraction - Higher Order Concepts

A common feature of programming is the use of abstraction techniques. Objects are classified according to similarities but they may still have many differences which are ignored for simplicity. Since the classification is made up to reflect the structure of some real world problem then it is abstract. Concepts are then combined into hierarchies that allow the problem structure to be defined.

Functional languages are often termed applicative, declarative or descriptive languages. Functional programs "can be viewed as descriptions declaring information about values rather than instructions for the computation of values or of effects" (Reade, C. 1988). With this approach we can develop solutions that allow us to describe the nature of the problem in the languages of the problem domain rather than having to be concerned with the lower level administrative features dealing with the machine architecture, a level that so many procedural languages work at.

Why a functional approach for interface design?

The method used takes a functional specification and automatically builds the procedural commands, in their correct sequence and with the correct syntax, which are sent to the GIS. An example of a functional specification using the sequence of commands shown earlier would be:

list(reselect(intersect (xdb "schools")(buffer (reselect (xdb "banks")(Name "ANZ Beldon")) 3)) inside = 100)

Although the functional query may not look especially elegant, it does express the semantics of the user query precisely and unambiguously. The GIS command sequences can be automatically constructed from this functional expression. Note with this specification the output of one function becomes the input of the next function with a function xdb that checks for the availability of the data. A system has been developed by the authors that incorporates all the rules and knowledge mentioned in a functional form taking as input a functional query as in the example just given (Standing and Roy, 1992).

We can take advantage of the properties of functional programs described.

1) In particular we can use the strong typing properties to ensure that functions are not applied to invalid data types. For example we need to ensure that a query to "list all the lengths of all points in a coverage" is detected as invalid since objects of the class "point" do not have a length attribute. In addition, we need to ensure that the data required for a function is available from the GIS database. In both these situations it is of some considerable advantage to be able to detect the problem before any attempt is made to formally execute the procedural specification.

   In a GIS there are other errors which are not picked up, but ideally should be prevented or the user warned about. A common source of error can arise from the use of an invalid statistical operation. For example requesting a mean of a set of ordinal (but still numeric) data may give meaningless results. The GIS may not be able to make this distinction, but our user interface should be aware of the problem. Providing data typing is enforced the problem of detection is greatly simplified. Thus the functional expression can be evaluated to produce a valid query, as a procedural program, before sending it to the GIS for final evaluation.

2) A function is considered to have a unique value, so that for a given set of arguments the value of the function is invariant, ie. there can be no side effects. We therefore need not

be concerned with how and when a function is evaluated, we can thus allow the reduction process to proceed with greater confidence.

3) Since we need be less concerned with how and when a function is evaluated we are freed from the burdens of a procedural style of programming.

4) If we are less concerned with how a function is evaluated (what is happening within the function) then we have a powerful abstraction technique where functions can be combined to develop higher order concepts which are nearer the language of the problem domain.

We can thus evaluate the functional expression to produce a valid query, as a procedural program, before sending it to the GIS for final evaluation.

4 VISUAL PROGRAMMING

Many of the problems of interface design discussed earlier relate to the problems of programming, that is programming in a traditional sense of being procedural and text based. Visual programming represents a departure from tradition and according to Shu (1988, p.7) is driven by the following premises:

1. Pictures are more powerful than words as a method of communicating as they can often concisely convey more meaning.
2. Pictures can help comprehension and remembering.
3. Pictures may provide an encouragement for learning to program.
4. Pictures, if designed properly can work across cultures and languages.

Our research contends that a visual style of programming development can play an important role in supporting some of the objectives of the GIS interface and in implementing the benefits of the functional strategy just described. In particular, a visual strategy has the potential to help in the following areas, data availability and type, operation options and syntax, the facility to express a query in a non-procedural form, and the use of the operation and its suitability of application to the type of data. If these objectives can be met in a visual way then validation of the program can be an inherent part of the programming process. This would then alleviate the need for the debugging stage.

At this point it is worthwhile defining the concept of visual programming as there are different interpretations of what it is. Shu (1988, p.7) takes the term *Visual Programming* to mean the "use of meaningful graphic representations in the process of programming" and she provides a useful framework for classification. However programming is a broad term that covers the language and the environment of specification; the specifications themselves; the process of validation and the display of data involved in the execution of the specification. All of these aspects of programming can have a visual representation but visual programming primarily covers the language of specification.

5 THE DESIGN FEATURES OF FVPL

The objectives of our user interface are as follows:

- data availability and type are clearly defined
- operations available and syntax are clearly defined

- a query is specified in a non-procedural form
- queries are developed in such a way that are guaranteed to obey the constraints of the system both in the use of the command and the suitability of the application of the command to the type of data

The system that has been designed as part of our research called FVPL (Functional, Visual Programming Language) considers these objectives and creates a visual programming interface that incorporates certain rules and knowledge that allows the validation of the query to be an inherent part of query formulation. An essential design feature of the interface needed to meet our objectives is that it must be easy to work with and incorporate the relevant knowledge and rules.

A number of graphical interfaces to GIS have been developed but many just concentrate on the presentation of data, for example ArcView, a product of Environmental Systems Research Institute (ESRI). CIGALES (Mainguenaud and Portier, 1990) is a graphical, query language for GIS that uses icons to represent data and operations but it uses little information about the data or operations to provide validation during the query building process. Graphic Map Algebra (Kirby and Pazner, 1990) uses a flowcharting structure with icons that represent map layers and operations to build up a picture of the query being developed. Once specified the graphic query is executed and errors reported. This approach has some similar attributes to our own but differs in two main ways: the validation of the query is not an inherent feature of the process of building a query; and because of its reliance on a flowcharting style the query is built up in a procedural manner rather than in a functional form as we propose.

What we are proposing are that icons and options on menus can be used to represent functions and data or maps so that their availability is not an issue. An operation icon can be opened to present a schema that requires certain inputs in order that constraints can be satisfied and data types matched. Schemas, representing the detailed functions, can be combined to create a visual, functional specification. The query can be constructed in a number of ways so users are relieved of the procedural burden of typical GIS command languages. As the query is built the constraints on the operations and data are embedded in the process and have to be met since each schema would have place holders for arguments (coverages, parameters, etc) that would have to be of the correct type. If a coverage of the wrong type, or a schema that resulted in a coverage of the wrong type was placed in a place holder then the inserted object would be highlighted to denote a mismatch and rejected. An example icon, representing a line coverage, is given below (figure 2 (a)). The rectangle with the lines inside is a peg that denotes the type of the icon or data. The symbol of a scrolled map denotes a map coverage. By this method, the data availability and its type becomes clear.

The icon shown in figure 2 (b) represents a table of data that is not directly part of a coverage. An icon can also represent an operation, such as an Intersect operation (figure 2 (c)). This is a polymorphic map type, as depending on the arguments the result of the function can be a polygon, line or point type.

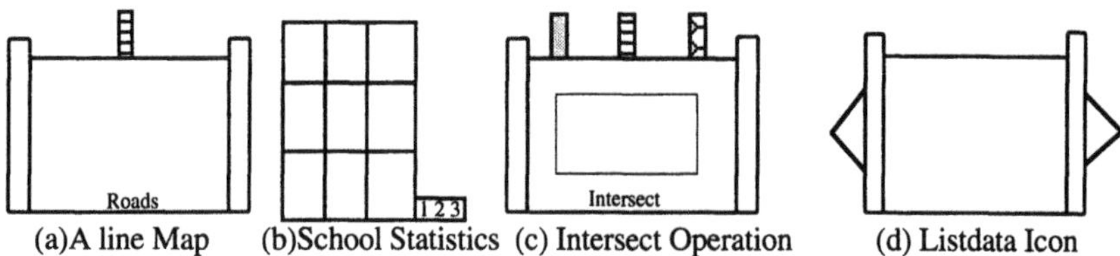

(a)A line Map (b)School Statistics (c) Intersect Operation (d) Listdata Icon

Figure 2 Examples of icons used within the system.

This system relies on a well defined set of types used in geographical information systems such as maps, a sub-type being points, lines, polygons; character data and numeric data. Numeric data could be ranked, nominal or ratio and would be metadata on the attributes of a file. While the types that have been specified in the system are suitable to illustrate the objectives, other types could be introduced if necessary to improve the validation of the query. The ListData Icon (figure 2(d)) shows the output (to the screen) type. This function takes a map or table value as an argument and converts it to a printable representation, rather like the show function that appears in most functional programming languages.

A schema represents an exploded operation or function. The function has one or more arguments, of certain types. These arguments can be data, operations or attributes. The schema can be collapsed back into an icon, and will have a completed or incomplete state, which signals whether all the arguments or sub-arguments have been completed. The schema can be seen as a form which is usually completed by dropping icons into placeholders. The schema in figure 3 is for the *Intersection* operation, which takes a line, point, or polygon coverage and overlays this with a polygon coverage. The resulting type is the same as the type of the first argument.

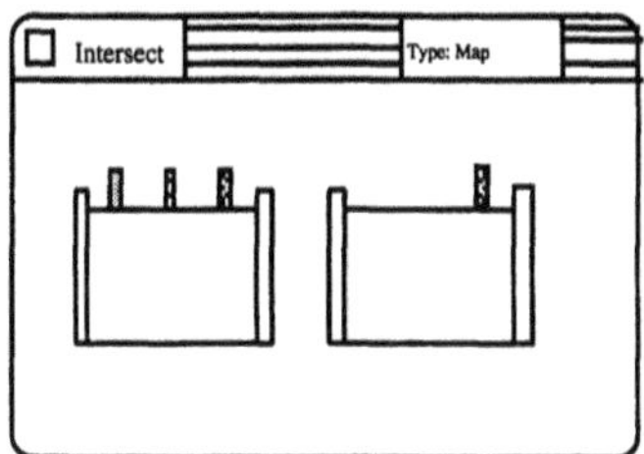

Figure 3 An exploded icon displays a schema that shows the arguments needed.

A different type of operation could take a table, operation or coverage as an argument and therefore would be a polymorphic function. An example of this type of placeholder would be *ListData* shown in figure 4 (a).

By making the data types a visual part of the system they are unambiguously defined. The user can see and therefore decide which type of argument a function requires and whether this is available. For example the roads icon (figure 4 (b)) is clearly the wrong type of argument for the polygon placeholder (figure 4 (c)).To attach an icon to a schema, the icon has to be dragged and dropped in the placeholder in the appropriate schema or similarly a schema is dragged and dropped in the placeholder. If there is a type mismatch the icon or schema will not be accepted by the placeholder.

In addition to selecting coverages as arguments some operations take attributes. Take the *mean* function: this requires a coverage or map type but also an attribute of that coverage. The attribute has an associated data type that is represented by an icon that appears in a pop-up window. Calculating the mean only has meaning when applied to certain types of data, for example it may be meaningless to find the mean of some nominal data or even an internal identification attribute for a feature. Often this function would lack meaning when applied to ranked data. For this example the mean can only be applied to ratio data.

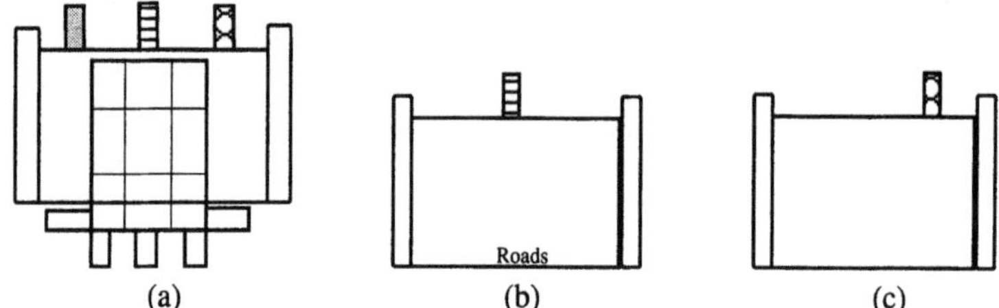

Figure 4 Type matching. (a) is a polymorphic type placeholder. (b) is a line icon and (c) is a polygon type placeholder

Figure 5 shows a pop-up window on the right with the attributes of the map type placed in the placeholder opened up. In this window the attributes are represented by names and icons which again visually signify the type. The icon has to be matched with the attribute placeholder in the schema. In this case the operator and a value have to be included which must comply with the attribute type.

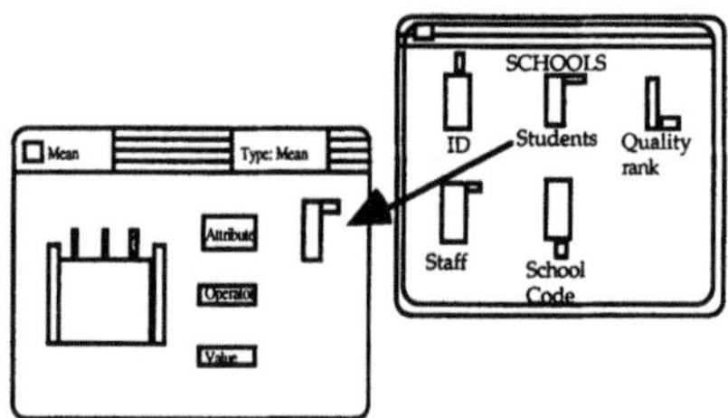

Figure 5 The mean schema and pop-up attribute window from which attribute icons can be dragged and dropped.

Any empty (no arguments completed) function is shown in figure 6(a). If it is partially completed the schema has an outline 6(b) and if all the arguments have been input then it is highlighted by the thick, dark border around the icon 6(c).

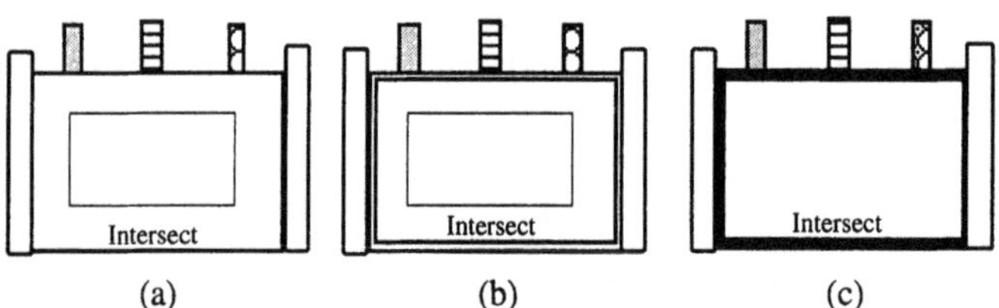

Figure 6 Icons shown in various states. (a) An icon with no arguments completed. (b) An icon with some arguments completed. (c) An icon with all arguments completed.

One of the objectives of the interface was for the process to be non-procedural. The following examples show the process of building a query and how the order of query construction becomes less important. The query in figure 7 in natural language form could be expressed as *List the schools within a three kilometre radius of Beldon ANZ Bank*. Although this may seem a simple request it does involve a number of steps:

a) Taking out the Beldon ANZ Bank from the Banks coverage;
b) Buffering that bank to three kilometres;
c) Intersecting the buffered bank and the schools coverages;
d) Reselecting those schools within the buffered zone;
e) Listing the school names.

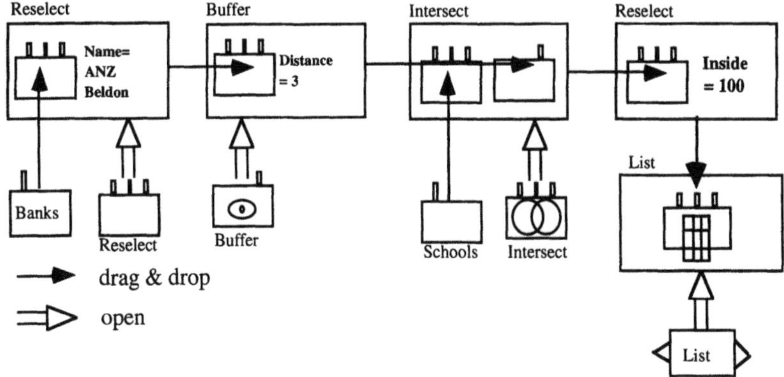

Figure 7 An example of a query being built up illustrating the drag and drop method.

The graphical, functional specification would be built up in this example by opening the *reselect* icon to present the *reselect* schema. The *banks* coverage would be dropped in the *reselect* place holder and the selection criteria added (by keyboard entry). This schema would form an object that could be placed in the *buffer* schema once opened along with the *distance* argument , which again would form an object to be dropped in the *intersect* schema as well as the *schools* coverage. The *intersect* schema would be placed in the *reselect* schema with added text input which as a whole could be placed into the *list* schema. The order in which the query is constructed is not important; the user could actually work backwards from the *list* operation and explode the icons that represent operations, for example *intersect*, and then complete the schema when required. Figures 8 and 9 show the first stage of the query being completed but this time showing the schemas closed to icons which are then dragged and dropped in the placeholders instead of schemas being dragged and dropped.

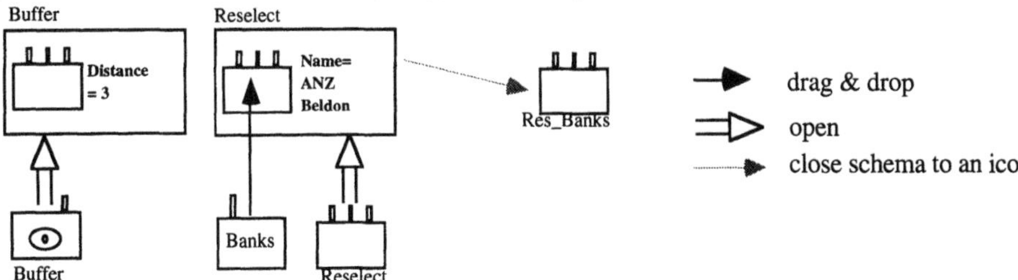

Figure 8 Open buffer icon to schema and complete reselect.

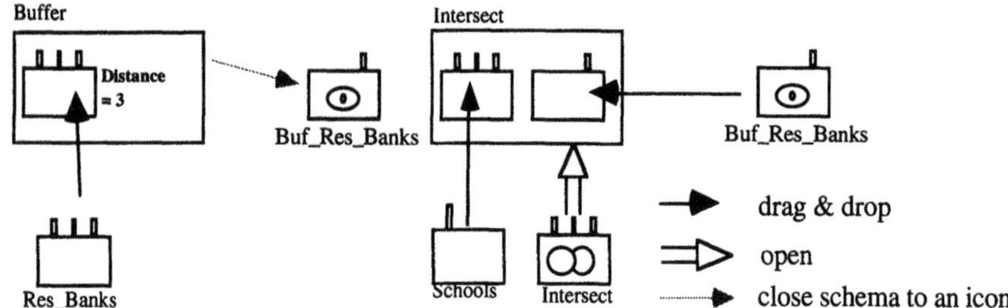

Figure 9 Complete buffer schema and close to an icon and complete intersect schema.

The completed, exploded functional specification is shown in figure 10. A query can be exploded by double clicking on the icon within a schema. The query can still be edited in this mode by dragging and dropping icons and schemas.

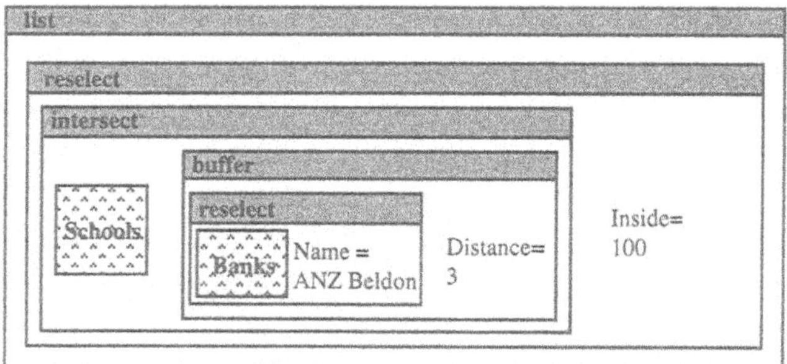

Figure 10 An explosion of a query showing the higher order nature of the approach.

The graphical interface involves validating functions as the overall query is being constructed. It is clear whether the constraints are met as each schema is completed. Once the query has been fully specified the user knows that it is a valid query. The graphical specification can be translated to a text based functional specification which can then be reduced to create the procedural sequence of commands to be passed onto the GIS. This functional, graphical user interface would appear to satisfy all of the objectives (Standing and Roy, 1992b).

6 SUMMARY

The paper started with outlining the objectives of the interface in terms of the knowledge content. Through the tight integration of the visual and functional strategies described the data availability and type are clearly defined by the use of icons with distinguishing features. If data is unavailable then no icon is shown. Similarly, the operations available in the system have an iconic representation. The set of operations is extensible since the user can create reusable higher-order functions. The syntax of the language is clearly defined by using placeholders into which only certain types may be dropped. The user has the freedom to construct queries in any order. The screen can be seen as a work area where the query can be pieced together. The query constructed at the interface level is guaranteed not to fail as all the testing of the query is carried out within the interface so the user is provided with feedback before any command is passed to the GIS. This means we do not have to rely on the GIS to report errors or bad commands, and more importantly we have a good chance of detecting operations which might be considered invalid on certain types of data before an invalid (and possibly undetected) result is produced.

7 REFERENCES

Bird, R. and Wadler, P. (1988) *Introduction to Functional Programming.* Prentice Hall.

Field, A.J. and Harrison, P.G. (1988) Functional Programming. Addison-Wesley.

Henderson, P. (1980) *Functional Programming: Application and Implementation.* Prentice-Hall.

Kirby, K. and Pazner, M. (1990) *Graphic Map Algebra.* Proceedings of the Fourth International Symposium on Spatial Data handling, Zurich, Switzerland.

MacLennan, B. J. (1990) *Functional Programming: Practice and Theory.* Addison-Wesley.

Mainguenaud, M. and Portier, M. (1990) *CIGALES: A graphical query language for geographical information systems.* Proceedings of the Fourth International Symposium on Spatial Data handling, Zurich, Switzerland.

Reade, C. (1989) Elements of Functional Programming. Addison-Wesley.

Shu, N. C. (1988) *Visual Programming.* Van Nostrand Reinhold Company, New York.

Standing, C. and Roy, G. G. (1992) *The requirements of a high-level interface to Geographical Information Systems.* Proceedings of the Fourth Annual Colloquium of the Spatial Information Research Centre, University of Otago, Dunedin, New Zealand.

Standing, C. and Roy, G. G. (1992b) *User interface design for Geographical Information Systems.* Proceedings of the Third Annual Research Conference of the Computer Science Department, University of Western Australia, Perth, W.A.

8 BIOGRAPHIES

Geoffrey Roy

Geoffrey Roy is Professor of Computer Science at Murdoch Univeristy, Western Australia. He worked for a number of years in the areas of expert systems and the design of user interfaces in CAD environments. Areas of application have included regional planning, building design, menu system design and use of codes of practice in design. A current research project involves the development of visual, functional programming languages.

Craig Standing

Craig Standing is a lecturer at the Department of Information Systems at Edith Cowan University and is currently working towards a Ph.D. at The University of Western Australia. He obtained his B.A.(Hons) in Geography at the University of Lancaster, UK., and his M.Sc. in Computation at the University of Manchester Institute of Science and Technology. His research interests include: visual programming languages, and systems development methodologies.

PART SEVEN

Text and Hypermedia

21

Visual interface for textual information retrieval systems

A. Veerasamy, S. Hudson and S. Navathe
Georgia Institute of Technology
College of Computing, 801, Atlantic Drive
Georgia Institute of Technology,
Atlanta, Georgia 30332-0280, USA.
Email: {veerasam, hudson, sham}@cc.gatech.edu

Abstract

A prototype user interface implementation for text information retrieval system is described. Using a visualization scheme, the interface provides visual feedback to the user about how the query words influence the ranking of retrieved documents. The interface also helps the user in constructing complex structured queries by simple drag-and-drop operations. An intuitive model where the user classifies the information provided to him/her as being positive and negative aids him/her in supplying rich relevance feedback information to the system. Our prototype interface has been built on top of INQUERY [Callan *et al.*, 1992]. Preliminary experience with the interface shows it to be a valuable tool in aiding the interactive search process between the user and the system. To test the effectiveness of the interface, we plan to conduct studies on users with real information need searching a large corpus of articles.

Keywords

Visualization of results, visual query languages, query processing, information retrieval

1 USER INTERFACE ISSUES FOR INFORMATION RETRIEVAL SYSTEMS

User Interface issues and interaction techniques for full text information retrieval systems have in general received much less attention than system issues like document representation and retrieval algorithms. We have developed an interface that facilitates the user in visually constructing powerful queries for ranked output retrieval systems. The interface includes a scheme for visualizing the query results in a form that enables the user to see the relationships between the query results and the query. While a majority of online library catalog systems use a boolean model of retrieval, a vast majority of existing experimental information retrieval systems retrieve a ranked set of documents in decreasing order of relevance in response to a free-form textual query. In ranked output systems, the documents and the queries are modeled by a set of weighted index terms. The index term weighting function for the documents primarily takes into consideration

- the frequency of occurrence of the index term in the document,
- the number of documents in the corpus containing that index term.

The effectiveness of a retrieval system is measured by two metrics: recall (the ratio of the number of relevant documents retrieved to the total number of relevant documents in the corpus) and precision (the ratio of the number of relevant documents retrieved to the total number of documents retrieved). The reader is referred to [Belkin and Croft, 1987, Rijsbergen, 1979, Salton and McGill, 1983] for a comprehensive description of evaluation metrics of information retrieval systems, document representation and retrieval techniques.

While processing a free-form textual query, most ranked output Information Retrieval systems automatically extract index terms from the query and weight them. The weighted query index terms are then matched against the weighted index terms of documents to retrieve a ranked set of documents in decreasing order of relevance. Each document is weighted, the higher the weight of a document, the more likely it is to be relevant to the query. Most of the existing library information systems (On-line Public Access Catalogs, OPAC) follow a boolean retrieval model. In this model, the documents retrieved in response to a boolean query are not ranked. If a document satisfies the boolean query specification, it is retrieved. Compared to boolean systems, ranked output systems are a significant improvement since the query can be in a free-form text as opposed to a strict boolean syntax. Also, the retrieved documents are ranked, thereby placing the more useful documents at the top of the list. This is a particularly useful feature since it has been shown that users of boolean systems spend a considerable effort in reducing the size of the result set [Spink, 1993]. On the other hand, ranked output systems introduce a new problem: For a naive user, the logic behind the ranking of documents in response to a query is not as apparent and straightforward as a boolean system. The interface we have developed is aimed at alleviating this problem. It helps the user in understanding how the system computed the ranking of retrieved documents by visualizing the relationship between query terms and the results of the query.

The interface also aids the user in formulating complex structured queries by graphically manipulating objects on the screen. A simple mechanism of classifying any information on the screen into positive and negative instances lends itself to easy formulation of structured queries. The interface is built using Tcl/Tk [Ousterhout, 1994] on top of INQUERY [Callan *et al.*, 1992], a ranked output retrieval system based on Bayesian inference networks. The interface supports two types of feedback:

- feedback from the user to the system and

- feedback from the system to the user.

It is interesting to note that the term "feedback" in the field of Information Retrieval typically refers to user's feedback to the system, while in the field of Human Computer Interfaces, "feedback" usually refers to the system's feedback to the user. The user's feedback to the system and the different levels of granularity at which the feedback can be provided is discussed in section 3. The system's feedback to the user and the visualization technique is discussed in section 4.

2 RELATED WORK

Numerous studies on user interaction with online library access catalog systems with a boolean retrieval model have been conducted [Spink, 1993, Spink and Saracevic, 1992, Dalrymple, 1990, Fidel, 1991a, Fidel, 1991b, Fidel, 1991c]. Spink [Spink, 1993] studies the different forms of user feedback during a retrieval session. Of the total number of feedback actions by the user, 45% were aimed at adjusting the size of the retrieved set of documents, and about 40% were related to relevancy of documents. Fidel [Fidel, 1991a, Fidel, 1991b, Fidel, 1991c] discusses the issue of user interaction by studying the process of search term selection and searching styles in online library access catalogs. Dalrymple [Dalrymple, 1990] looks at the feedback process from a user-centered perspective. Bates [Bates, 1990] describes a boolean retrieval system which integrates an online thesaurus. None of the above studies involve a ranked output system supporting free-form textual queries. All of the systems deal with boolean retrieval model only. We believe that there is a significant difference in the way users interact with a boolean system and a ranked output system. The reader is referred to [Harman, 1992] and [Hancock-Beaulieu, 1992] for a comparative discussion of boolean systems and ranked output systems. While building our interface, we have borrowed valuable ideas from the studies mentioned above. In particular, the need to integrate an on-line thesaurus with the search interface in an easy-to-use fashion and a simple interaction scheme to include words from documents into the query have been influenced by the results of above-mentioned studies.

Walker and Beaulieu [Walker, 1987, Hancock-Beaulieu, 1992] describe their OKAPI system which is a ranked output retrieval system for library catalogs. Similarly, Fox [Fox *et al.*, 1993] describes their MARIAN sysem which is also a ranked output system for library catalogs based on the vector-space model. While OKAPI has facilities for relevance feedback and query expansion using a thesaurus, it largely lacks any means of providing system feedback to the user about how the ranking was computed. The interface we have developed integrates relevance feedback information from the user as well as feedback from the system illustrating the relationship between query results and query words.

A number of visualization schemes for information retrieval systems have also been proposed. The perspective wall [Card *et al.*, 1991] describes a visualization scheme which supports browsing of documents. While such a system will not handle qualitative document classifications such as library subject catalogs, it is very useful for visualizing documents based on data which is linear in nature (like date of publication). Other visualization schemes such as [Korfhage, 1991, Spoerri, 1994, Hemmje *et al.*, 1994] have facilities for viewing a large document space. But visualizing the document space along more than 3 - 4 dimensions simultaneously becomes very cumbersome using the above systems. Also, most of them do not provide support for querying with relevance feedback and none of them provide support for query expansion using a thesaurus. The visualization scheme in our interface can gracefully handle much higher number of query word dimensions.

2.1 NOVELTY OF OUR APPROACH

The novelty of our system is in integrating a diverse set of interaction features in a seamless fashion into a single system thereby facilitating the interactive and iterative nature of the information seeking process. The following features are integrated in our system:

- Using a visualization scheme, the interface provides visual feedback to the user about how the query words influence the ranking of retrieved documents.
- By simple drag-and-drop operations of objects on the screen, the interface facilitates a naive end-user in constructing complex structured queries and in providing relevance feedback. This feedback is utilized by the system in a manner described later.
- The interface integrates an online thesaurus which provides words related to the query that can be used by the user to expand the original query.

Belkin and his group's work [Belkin *et al.*, 1993, Belkin *et al.*, 1991] on user interfaces for information retrieval systems [Henninger and Belkin, 1994] elucidates the issues in user interface and interaction techniques for full text retrieval systems. Belkin [Belkin *et al.*, 1991] mentions that

> This type of analysis led to another important conclusion, namely that information systems for end users must support a variety of goals and tasks, but through some common interface or seamless access mechanism to a variety of relevant information sources and system functionalities.

Our interface takes a step in that direction by integrating different pieces of information with a visualization scheme and simple interaction techniques.

3 INTERACTIVE CONSTRUCTION OF QUERIES

Searching a database for information is a highly interactive process with the user constantly refining the query after examining the results of previous iteration until he/she is either satisfied with the results or is frustrated with the process and gives up. In existing information retrieval systems, the interaction proceeds by the user providing feedback on which of the retrieved documents are relevant to his/her information need. The system uses this information to modify the original query resulting in an improved ranking of retrieved documents. It has also been shown by Spink [Spink and Saracevic, 1992] that during iterative query reformulation, users tend to expand the query using search terms from various sources such as a thesaurus, previously retrieved documents and user's background knowledge. Expanding the query with terms from such sources can contribute to retrieval of more relevant documents in the next iteration.

Our interface encourages the interaction between the user and the system by providing the user with simple interaction technique to let him/her supply relevance feedback at different levels of granularity: whole documents, document portions, phrases and individual words. Almost any information appearing on the screen can be used for feedback. This is achieved by simple "drag-and-drop"ping the feedback object into either a "Positive Objects" window colored green or a "Negative Objects" window colored red. This scheme provides a simple abstraction to the user for classifying any type of information without having to worry about what action to take for what type of information. A typical user session along with the response of the interface for every user action is described below using an example (please refer to Figure 1). The database being queried contains a collection of titles, authors and abstracts of thousands of CACM articles.

- The user types in his free form textual query in the query window. In the example shown in figure 1, the query is "image audio and text data compression".
- As every query word is typed in, the system consults an on-line thesaurus and displays words and phrases related to the query word in an adjacent window.
- At any point during the session the user can drag-and-drop any of the related words/phrases into the positive and negative windows. Internally the system expands the query by treating the positive words/phrases as synonyms of the corresponding query word. The negative words/phrases are included in the query with a NOT operator. For example, if for a query word "bank", the phrase "financial institution" is classified as positive and "river bed" is classified as negative, the corresponding internal query would be "#SYNONYM(bank #2[1](financial institution)) #NOT(#2(river bed))". The end-result of this classification is a possible improvement in the precision measure since documents containing the phrase "river bed" will be weighted lower than other documents, and a possible improvement in the recall measure since documents containing the phrase "financial institution" are also retrieved. The interface facilitates construction of such structured queries by simple drag-and-drop operations. In the example in figure 1, three words related to the query word "compression", namely, "compaction, "shortening" and "condensation" have been classified as positive. Internally the systems treats these three words as synonyms of "compression".

[1] #2 is the proximity operator in INQUERY specifying that the words should appear within a distance of 2 within each other

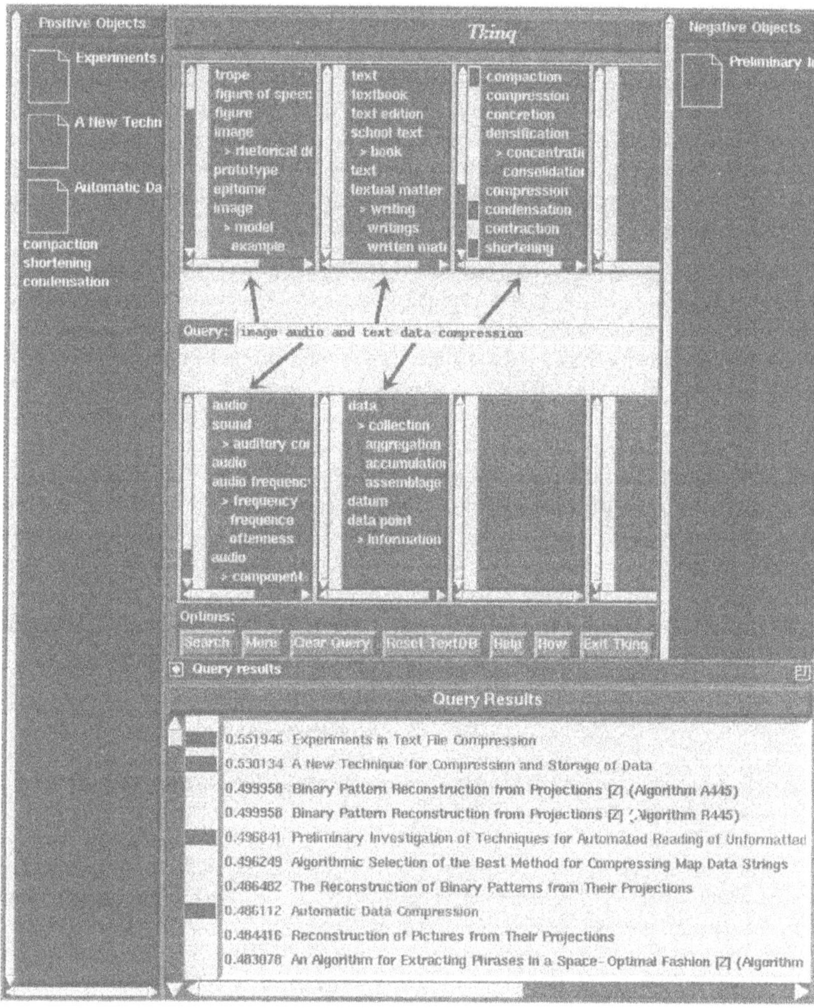

Figure 1: Sample querying session. The window titled "Positive object" is colored green and the window title "Negative Objects" is colored red. When a document is classified as positive/negative, the title of that document in the "Query results" window is also colored green/red.

- After the user types in the query, the system evaluates the query and displays the titles of top-ranked documents in the "Query Results" window.

- The user examines the query result. Double-clicking any title with the mouse will bring up the full document.

- The user can classify any document as being relevant or non-relevant by drag-and-drop'ing the document into positive and negative windows. In the example in figure 1, the user has classified three documents titled "Experiments in text file compression", "A new technique for compression and storage of data" and "Automatic data compression" as positive. The document titled "Preliminary investigation of techniques for automated reading of unformatted text" has been classified as negative. Internally, the systems extracts 4 - 6 high frequency words from the positive documents and adds it to the query thereby expanding the query. This results in the retrieval of documents similar to the positive documents.

- The user can also highlight a portion of a document and drag-and-drop it into the positive and negative windows. The words in the highlighted document portion are used to expand the query in the next iteration.

- During the next iteration, the reformulated query with the relevance feedback information is processed by the system resulting in an improved ranking of documents.

The positive and negative windows for feedback are aimed at mimicking the user's view that some information is in line with the information need and some not. After an object has been classified as positive (or negative), the system always colors the object green (or red) whenever the object is displayed, thereby reinforcing the user with the fact that the object is being used for relevance feedback. While arguing for the use of direct manipulation techniques for Information Retrieval, Mitev [Mitev, 1989] mentions that

> "Parts of document(s), individual word(s), sentences or groups of word(s) displayed could be used directly as something to be input for another search. This could be done, for example, by pointing and 'picking' them on the screen and carrying them across another area of the screen. The user would not have to input them again."

This is precisely what has been accomplished in our interface. In their retrieval system, Campbell [Campbell and Sanderson,] uses a cut-and-paste mechanism for relevance feedback by letting the user add portions of retrieved documents back into the query window.

This section dealt with the interaction technique to let the user provide relevance feedback information to the system. The next section deals with visual feedback from the system on how the query results were computed.

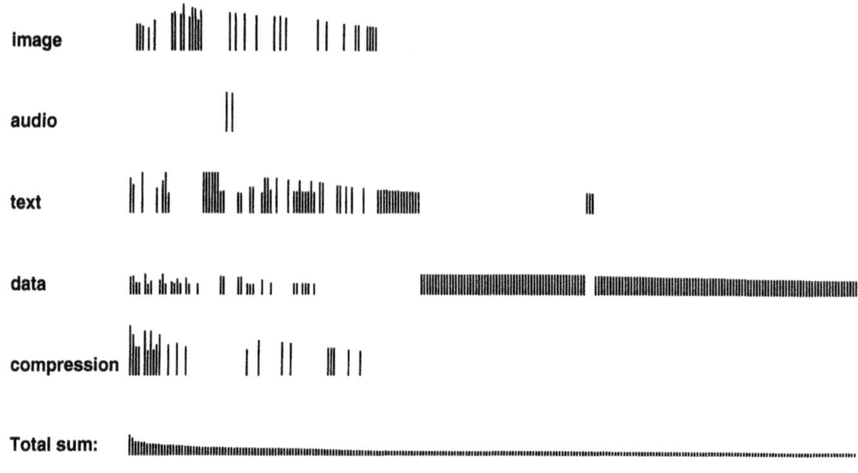

Figure 2: Visualization of results for the base query.

4 VISUALIZATION OF QUERY RESULTS

While systems with a boolean retrieval model retrieve an unordered set of documents in response to a query, ranked output information retrieval systems retrieve a ranked set of documents. While the reason for retrieving a document is fairly clear in the case of a boolean system, the reason why a document is assigned a specific rank is not apparent in the case of a ranked output system. Without knowing how the system computed the ranking of documents, the user will have to treat the retrieval mechanism as a black box. We stand to gain a lot by keeping the user more informed about the retrieval process of the system. If the user has more information about how the ranking was computed, he/she will be in a better position to reformulate the query for the next iteration. He/she can take into account the deficiencies of the system in adjusting his/her query. It will also help in reinforcing the right mental model.

In our interface, we keep the user informed about the retrieval mechanism by providing visual feedback about how the query results are related to the query words. This is done by a visualization scheme as shown in the figure 2. The visualization reveals the extent to which each query word was responsible for retrieving the set of documents. The visualization consists of a set of histograms, one for every query word (except stop words) typed in by the user, and one histogram for the total query (labeled "Total sum"). All the histograms are placed one below the other with the "Total sum" histogram appearing at the bottom and the query-word-histograms appearing in the order in which query words were typed in. Each histogram consists of a set of vertical bars, one bar for each retrieved document. For the top ranked document, a vertical bar is drawn in the leftmost position (i.e, lowest X coordinate position) in the "Total sum" histogram. The height of the bar is

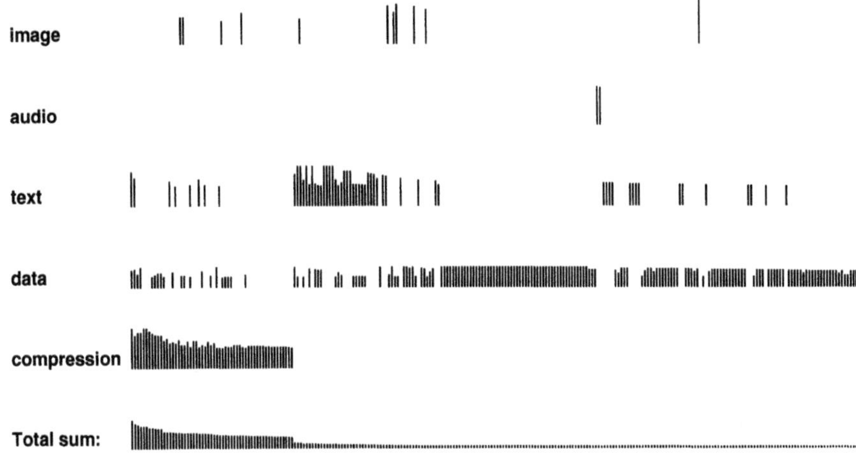

Figure 3: Visualization of results for query with feedback information.

proportional to the weight of the document. (Note that each document is given a weight. The higher the document weight, the more likely it is to be relevant to the query.) For the same document, vertical bars in the same X-coordinate position are also drawn in the query-word-histograms. The height of the vertical bar in any given query-word-histogram is proportional to the weight of the query word in that document. It represents the contribution of the query word in retrieving that document. If the query word does not appear in the document, thereby getting a weight of zero, a bar of zero height is drawn which shows up as an empty space in that X-coordinate position. The second ranked document occupies the next higher X-coordinate to the right and so on upto a maximum of top 200 documents.

The visualization shown in Figure 2 corresponds to the base query with no feedback information from the user. We can see that all but two of the top 200 documents have nothing to do with audio. Almost all of the second half of the 200 documents were retrieved because they contained the query word "data". More significantly, only about 10% of the documents have anything to do with compression – which is the crux of the query. This illustrates that the query should be expanded with more words related to "compression". In fact, the decision to classify the three synonyms of "compression" (as shown in figure 1) was made after examining the distribution of "compression" in the visualization. Figure 3 shows the distribution of query terms in the query result for the revised query in the second iteration with all the feedback information. We can see that almost all the documents about "compression" have been ranked at the very top. Also there are more documents retrieved due to "compression" because of the synonyms and the positively classified documents. Our experience with this visualization scheme has shown it to be very useful in identifying differents facets of the query.

5 CONCLUSION & FUTURE WORK

A prototype interface for a ranked output information retrieval system has been implemented. The interface facilitates the inherently interactive nature of the information seeking process. Drag-and-drop operations form the basis of interaction encouraging the user to provide feedback information to the system and helps in the dialog between the user and the system. Almost any information on the screen can be used by the user to provide feedback information. An online thesaurus, WordNet [Miller *et al.*, 1990], is integrated with the interface to form a single system.

The interface also supports a visualization scheme which illustrates how the query results are related to the query words. Visualizing the results of the query keeps the user more informed on how the system computed the ranking of documents. With this information, the user is better equipped to reformulate the query for the next iteration. It is our opinion that integrating all of the above features in a seamless interface leads to an interplay between different items that is much more beneficial than the sum of the individual items in isolation.

In demonstrating the system to the reference librarians at Georgia Tech and in observing casual users of the system, we believe that the features we have implemented in this system contributes to enhancing the end-user's interaction with the system. As a result, the system is better able to assess the user's need and the user has a better understanding of the system's inference. However we cannot categorically conclude the effectiveness and the utility of the interface without conducting formal user-studies.

In future, we plan to test the effectiveness of the interface by conducting two studies: One with users having real information needs searching a traditional library database and another with volunteers searching the TREC [TRE, 1994] document collection with supplied search statements. Since all the relevant documents for the supplied search statements in the TREC collection are known, recall and precision of searches performed with our interface can be compared against other systems.

6 ACKNOWLEDGMENTS

We are thankful to Dr. Bruce Croft for letting us use the INQUERY retrieval system. Many thanks to Dr. Marti Hearst whose Tcl/Tk code for the SMART system was helpful as a spring board for us to write the interface. Support in part by ARPA Grant No. F33615-93-1-1338 under the Intelligent Integration of Information Program is appreciated.

References

[Bates, 1990] Marcia J. Bates. Design for a subject search interface and online thesaurus for a very large records management database. In *Proceedings of the 53rd Annual*

Meeting of the American Society for Information Science, pages 20–8, 1990.

[Belkin and Croft, 1987] Nick Belkin and W.B. Croft. Retrieval techniques. In E. Martha, editor, *Annual Review of Information Science Technology*, pages 110–45. Elsevier Science Publishers, 1987.

[Belkin *et al.*, 1991] N.J. Belkin, P.G. Marchetti, M. Albrecht, L. Fusco, S. Skogvold, H. Stokke, and G. Troina. User interfaces for information systems. *Journal of Information Science*, 17:327–44, 1991.

[Belkin *et al.*, 1993] N.J. Belkin, P.G. Marchetti, and C. Cool. Braque: Design of an interface to support user interaction in information retrieval. *Information Processing and Management*, 29(3):325–44, 1993.

[Callan *et al.*, 1992] J.P. Callan, W.B. Croft, and S.M. Harding. The inquery retrieval system. In *Third International Conference on Database and Expert Systems Applications*, September 1992.

[Campbell and Sanderson,] I. Campbell and M. Sanderson. Personal communication. University of Glasgow.

[Card *et al.*, 1991] S. Card, G. Robertson, and J. Mackinlay. The information visualizer, an information workspace. In *Proceedings of CHI 91 Human Factors in Computer Systems.*, 1991.

[Dalrymple, 1990] P.W. Dalrymple. Retrieval by reformulation in two library catalogs: toward a cognitive model of searching behaviour. *Journal of the American Society for Information Science*, 41(4):272–81, 1990.

[Fidel, 1991a] Raya Fidel. Searcher's selection of search keys: I. the selection routine. *Journal of the American Society for Information Science*, 42(7):490–500, 1991.

[Fidel, 1991b] Raya Fidel. Searcher's selection of search keys: II. controlled vocabulary or free-text searching. *Journal of the American Society for Information Science*, 42(7):501–14, 1991.

[Fidel, 1991c] Raya Fidel. Searcher's selection of search keys: III. searching styles. *Journal of the American Society for Information Science*, 42(7):515–27, 1991.

[Fox *et al.*, 1993] Edward A. Fox, Robert K. France, Eskinder Sahle, Amjad Daoud, and Ben E. Cline. Development of a modern OPAC: From REVTOLC to MARIAN. In Robert Khorfhage, Edie Rasmussen, and Peter Willett, editors, *Proceedings of sixteenth ACM SIGIR conference*, pages 248–59. ACM SIGIR. June-July 1993.

[Hancock-Beaulieu, 1992] Micheline Hancock-Beaulieu. User friendliness and human-computer interaction in online library catalogues. *Program*, 26(1):29–37, January 1992.

[Harman, 1992] Donna Harman. User-friendly systems instead of user-friendly front-ends. *Journal of American Society for Information Science*, 43(2):164–74, 1992.

[Hemmje *et al.*, 1994] Matthias Hemmje, Clemens Kunkel, and Alexander Willet. Lyberworld – a visualization user interface supporting full text retrieval. In *Proceedings of the 17th Annual International Conference on Research and Development in Information Retrieval*, pages 249–59, 1994.

[Henninger and Belkin, 1994] Scott Henninger and Nick Belkin. Tutorial on interface issues and interaction strategies for information retrieval systems. In *Human Factors in Computing Systems CHI 94 Conference Companion*, pages 387–8, 1994.

[Korfhage, 1991] Robert Korfhage. To see, or not to see – is that the query? In *Proceedings of the 14th Annual International ACM/SIGIR conference on Research and Development in Information Retrieval*, pages 134–41, 1991.

[Miller *et al.*, 1990] George A. Miller, Richard Beckwith, Christiane Fellbaum, Derek Gross, and Katherine J. Miller. Introduction to WordNet: An on-line lexical database. *Journal of Lexicography*, 3(4):235–44, 1990.

[Mitev, 1989] Nathalie N. Mitev. Ease of interaction and retrieval in online catalogues: contributions of human-computer interaction research. In Charles R. Hildreth, editor, *The online catalogue*, chapter 8, pages 142–76. Library Association Publishing, London, 1989.

[Ousterhout, 1994] John K. Ousterhout. *Tcl and the Tk Toolkit.* Addison-Wesley, 1994.

[Rijsbergen, 1979] Keith Van Rijsbergen. *Information Retrieval.* Butterworths, London, second edition, 1979.

[Salton and McGill, 1983] Gerard Salton and Michael J. McGill. *Introduction to Modern Information Retrieval.* McGraw-Hill Book Company, New York, 1983.

[Spink and Saracevic, 1992] Amanda Spink and Tefko Saracevic. Sources and use of search terms in online searching. In *Proceedings of the 55th Annual Meeting of the American Society for Information Science*, pages 249–55, 1992.

[Spink, 1993] Amanda Spink. Interaction with information retrieval systems: Reflections of feedback. In *Proceedings of the Annual Meeting of the American Society for Information Science*, pages 115–21, 1993.

[Spoerri, 1994] Anslem Spoerri. Infocrystal: A visual tool for information retrieval and management. In *Human Factors in Computing Systems CHI 94 Conference Companion*, pages 11–2, 1994.

[TRE, 1994] In D.K. Harman, editor, *The Second Text REtrieval Conference (TREC-2).* NIST Special Publication, March 1994.

[Walker, 1987] Stephen Walker. Okapi: Evaluating and enhancing an experimental online catalog. *Library Trends*, Spring:631–45, 1987.

7 BIOGRAPHY

Aravindan Veerasamy is a PhD student in the College of Computing at Georgia Tech. He earned his B.E. in computer science at College of Engineering, Guindy, India. For his PhD, he is investigating research issues related to user interface design for Information Retrieval systems. His research interests include human information seeking behaviour, document databases and user interfaces.

Scott Hudson is an associate professor in the College of Computing at Georgia Tech and a member of the Graphics, Visualization, and Usability Center. His research interests include a wide range of topics in user interface software. He was previously an Assistant Professor of Computer Science at the University of Arizona. He earned his Ph.D. in computer science at the University of Colorado in 1986. He has regularly served on program committees for the SIGCHI and UIST conferences, and served as Program Chair for UIST '90 and Symposium Chair for UIST '93. He currently serves as an Associate Editor for ACM Transactions on Computer Human Interaction.

Shamkant Navathe is a professor in the College of Computing, at Georgia Tech. His research interests include data modelling, database design and integration, intelligent information retrieval, engineering database applications and federated databases. He has co-authored (with R. Elmasri) a widely used database textbook "Fundamentals of Database Systems" and another book (with C. Batini and S. Ceri) entitled: "Conceptual Database Design: An Entity Relationship Approach." He is the general co-chair of the 1996 VLDB Conference at Bombay India.

22

An ODA/Dexter hyperdocument system with automated link definition

M. Worring, R. Buitenhuis, A.W.M. Smeulders
Department of Computer Systems, University of Amsterdam
Kruislaan 403, 1098 SJ Amsterdam, The Netherlands
Tel +31 20 525 7521, Fax +31 20 525 7490
e-mail worring@fwi.uva.nl

Abstract

In this contribution we consider the construction and storage of hyperdocuments; converting scanned paper documents into hypertext. Hyperlink generation is automated by analyzing the image of the document. A number of document analysis tools are described. For the hyperlink detection the main contribution of this paper is the automated construction of links between the text and picture labels. The storage and retrieval of documents is based on the recently developed Dexter Hypertext Reference Model [4] in conjunction with the well known Open Document Architecture [1]. The symbiosis of these two standards leads to a solid base for data structures and data manipulation. Some practical results of hyperlink acquisition are presented.

Keywords

Hypertext, dexter, document analysis, OCR, ODA, picture labels, icon detection

1 INTRODUCTION

Due to increased storage capacity and network performance the storage and distribution of large collections of scanned paper documents has become feasible. Document information systems are usually constructed by "image enabling" a standard DBMS. Retrieval of the scanned documents is then on the basis of predefined identification labels only and the functionality added to the database system is limited to the display of the document.

A document can contain text and/or pictures and graphics and it would be far more appropriate to retrieve the different document parts on the basis of their content; for example full text retrieval of documents on the basis of user specified keywords or the selection of all graphical pictures containing a specific visual icon. At this point it should be noted that we only have an image of the document. In order to allow for the above type of queries we need to analyze the image to find the corresponding text and detect visual icons in the pictures. The first step in this analysis is to classify automatically different parts of the image as text blocks, photos, tables etc. Blocks classified as text can then be passed through an Optical Character Recognition (OCR) program to retrieve the ASCII text conveyed by the image of the text block. Apart from revealing the content of the document, the text analysis also leads to significant data reduction as ASCII codes are far more compact than the corresponding image data.

The appropriate data structure for storing the structure of the document is the Open Document Architecture (ODA) [1]. This data structure considers both the geometric and the logical structure of the document.

Documents can now be retrieved on the basis of the content of the different blocks or on the geometric and logical structure of the document. However, browsing through a large collection of blocks does not only require to consider the content of individual blocks but also their relations. Retrieval then becomes "jumping" from one document part to related document parts. This requires a hypertext system, providing item-to-item (hyper)links, where each item can be a piece of text, a picture, or a picture detail.

Most hypertext systems contain text-text or text-picture links only. However, links between text and picture details are very important as well. For example in patent applications or manuals, labels in the picture identify components which are described in the accompanying text. Such links are particularly convenient in complicated documents with a large number of numeric labels where finding a specific label by visual inspection is a laborious task. Furthermore, in pictures with a legend (for example tourist maps) links between a specific legend item and the positions of this item in the map are of great importance for quick browsing.

Construction of hyperdocuments from scanned documents by interactive definition of relational links is a tedious task. However, many links can be generated automatically. For example in [5] and [8], automatic text-text link definition is performed by using OCR. In [6] a system is presented where links between words in the text and the corresponding pictures as a whole are detected. The linkage types used in the references are limited. Especially the links with picture details are missing. In this contribution we consider a system for hypertext construction from documents which aids the user in the generation of all of the above mentioned linkage types.

Due to the inherent complexity of a hyperdocument system with such a complicated linkage structure it is important to carefully consider the data structures for storing the hyperdocument. We therefore base our system on the Dexter Hypertext Reference Model [4] which is a recently defined model for both describing current hypertext systems as well as a useful tool in the design of hypertext systems. In fact the model is a superset of the functionality of commonly available hypertext systems.

The reference model deals with the structure of links in a hypertext system only. It explicitly avoids defining the structure within the documents which has to be described by other models. As noted before, ODA provides a convenient way of structuring the contents of the documents. As will be shown later the ODA structure is easily incorporated into a Dexter Hypertext System. It also provides a proper basis for the document analysis.

This paper is organized as follows. First an introduction to document structure as defined in ODA is given and the set of modules for analyzing the document and its contents are introduced (section 2). Then in section 3, different types of links are analyzed and methods for finding them, based on the document analysis modules, are presented. In section 4 we consider the incorporation of the ODA model into the Dexter Model. Finally, we show results of automated link generation in section 5.

2 DOCUMENT STRUCTURE AND ANALYSIS

In this section we introduce the Open Document Architecture, which will be used later for the storage of documents and in the document analysis phase.

2.1 The Open Document Architecture

The Open Document Architecture [1] is an international standard for the representation of structured documents. It is designed to provide a standard for storing, editing and interchange of documents. In ODA two different types of structures are distinguished. First, the *geometric structure* which gives the structure of the document the way it is presented and the *logical structure* giving meaning to the different parts of the document. The smallest components considered are the basic geometric or logical objects. Such an object can, for example, be a piece of text or a picture. A geometric and logical object are connected via their content. The geometric object describes at which position the object is located, in case of text the fontsize used etc. The logical object describes the meaning of the object, for example the piece of text being a header or a paragraph.

Basic components can be grouped in frames. A section frame, for example, contains several paragraphs and headers for subsections. The ODA structure further defines pages and combines them into page-sets.

The geometric and logical structure of a document can both be described as trees where the basic objects are the leaves of the tree and the intermediate nodes are either frames or pages. For a given document the trees define the *specific geometric structure* and the *specific logical structure*, derived as instantiations of the generic geometric structure and the generic logical structure descriptions for the class of documents considered. In figure 1 an example document is shown with in figure 2 the corresponding geometric and logical structure tree.

2.2 Document Analysis Tools

The construction of hyperdocuments from paper originals requires a number of modules, which are indicated in figure 3 and described here.

First, the document is *scanned* converting it into a digital image. We only consider binary scanning where each pixel in the digital image indicates whether it is part of the foreground or the background. Pixels identified as foreground will contain the characters, lines in graphical pictures etc, whereas the background will contain all "white space" in the document. This configuration of black and white pixels implicitly contains the document structure. The aim of *document structure analysis* is to extract the structure of the document from its digital image. To be precise, we aim to find the specific geometric and logical tree corresponding to the original paper document. From there, the analysis continues by analyzing the content of the text blocks using OCR, keyword search (in the text) and label search in (text and/or picture). We will first discuss how to extract the implicit ODA trees.

Various methods for document structure analysis are known in literature (e.g. [9]). Our method is a bottom-up method based on the bounding boxes of connected components in the image rather than the run-length coding of the image as used in the reference. In

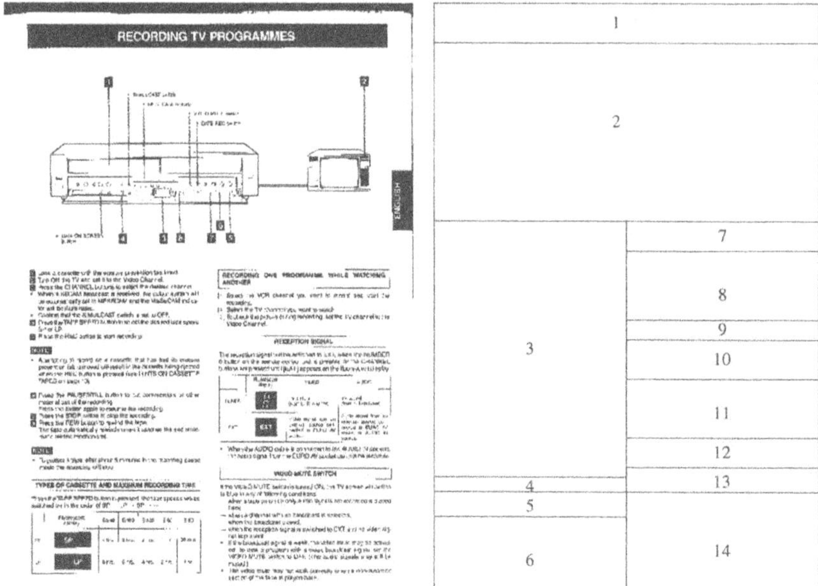

Figure 1 *An example of a structured document and the geometric blocks corresponding to the coherent parts of the document.*

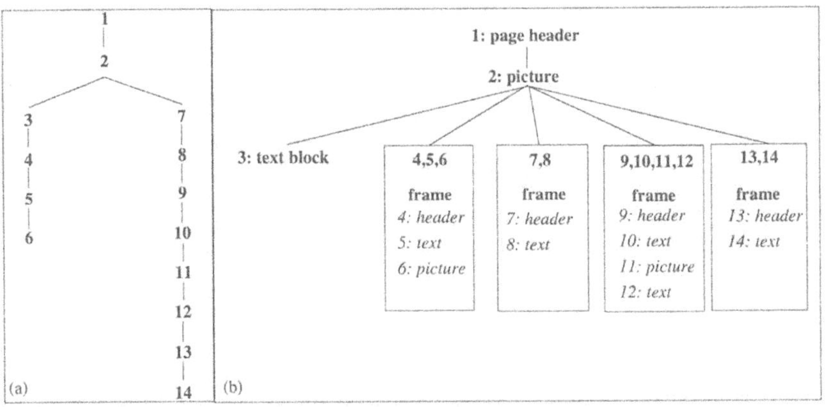

Figure 2 *The specific geometric tree corresponding to the example in figure 1 (a) and its corresponding specific logical tree (b).*

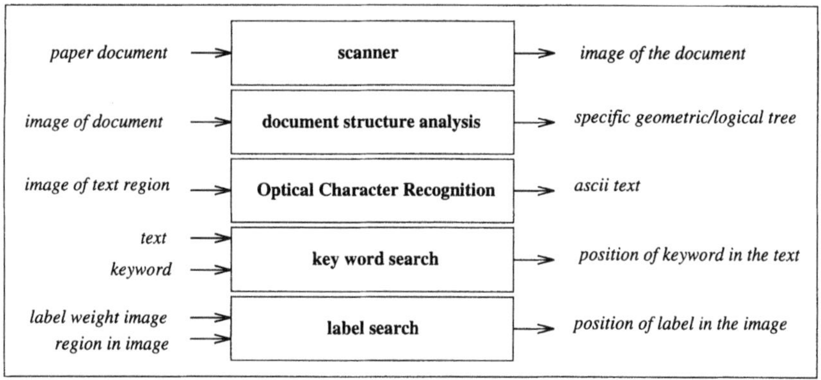

Figure 3 *Overview of the different modules which are needed to perform automated hypertext construction.*

the first step, objects in the image are extracted where an object is classified as being text, a picture, or a vertical/horizontal line in the image based on simple properties of the bounding box and the pixels within the box. From there, single characters and word fragments are combined into lines of text which are subsequently merged into paragraphs. These text blocks together with the picture blocks generate the specific geometric tree. As the method is very general it gives good results for a large class of documents with simple block structure. Given the specific geometric structure the logical structure can be created manually or using a number of rules for tree transformation as used in [9]. The latter method is useful for newspaper type of documents and is specifically aimed at establishing the reading order of the document. When the document structure is too complicated to handle, we use manual zoning and let the user define the trees interactively.

When documents have a complicated, but generic, structure as is the case in manuals of a specific company or patent applications in a particular domain one can use a method which exploits generic ODA structures [2]. This is a powerful top-down method in which a number of generic ODA trees in a hierarchical fashion are matched to a given document. This method is not included in the current prototype system.

Any of the above methods leads to a tree structure where some blocks are classified as picture blocks and some are classified as text blocks. The text blocks are sent to the *OCR* Module. This module takes a digital image of a text region, recognizes the individual characters, and returns the text in ASCII form. This step also involves lexical analysis to improve the quality of character recognition on the basis of the local context.

Having retrieved the text in a document in ASCII form we can search for specific words in the text. This *keyword search* returns the position of the given keyword in the text.

The final module in the system deals with blocks in the image of the document classified as pictures. To be precise, given a digital image of a detail l present in the picture block, we seek to find the position(s) at which this particular detail is found. This *detail detection* is done using the Enigma-system [3]. This is a system in which the user defines a binary template by extracting it as part of an example picture. From there, the user can edit the template and assign weights to different parts of the template. Positive weights indicate the importance of an object pixel to be present, whereas a negative part indicates the importance of some background pixel. Finally, the value 0 indicates a "don't care" region. A number of alternative strategies for automatic weight assignment are available where for example one can put more emphasis on pixels located on the centerline of the object (or the background) then to the contour of the template. This is to allow for some noise in the object boundaries.

Using fuzzy mathematical morphology the template is searched for in the picture and at each position a confidence value $\text{conf}(l) \in [-100, 100]$ is derived indicating the correspondence of the template specification and the local pixel configuration. The value $\text{conf}(l)$ can be interpreted as the (weighted) percentage of points in the local configuration in the picture which are of the same value as the template (which only contains the values 0 and 1) [10]. Local positive maxima of this confidence field are the candidate positions for the detail in the picture. In practice a threshold t on the confidence is applied to limit the number of candidates. For more complex picture details one can decompose the detail into several parts, locating them separately in the picture. Candidates found this way are combined to find the full detail subject to a set of strict topological relations (left-of, above etc) specified by the user.

The set of tools described above and summarized in figure 3 form the basis for the automated hypertext construction.

3 LINKS

In the previous section we considered the structure of the document and the contents of individual blocks. The essence of hypertext generation is creating links between these pieces of information. In order to propose hyperlinks to add to the hypertext we first consider the different types of links one encounters in a document and from there introduce methods, based on the modules described in the previous section, to find the various links.

3.1 Types of links

Commonly known links are *<text>*-*<text>* links. They link words in one document to related words in another document (part). This can be the same word found in both of the documents, or the two words can be different, but then they must have a semantic relation. The latter type of links will not be considered here, but methods for detecting them can be found in [7].

In a document with pictures it is important to define *<picture>* - *<text>* links, where the picture can either be a photograph or graphics. Here the link can either be to the picture itself or to its caption.

The third class of links we consider are links between parts of a picture and the text. To be more precise we define *<picture label>* - *<text>* links where the picture label can be one of the following three types:

1. <generic text label>: Label with a generic shape containing a character string.
2. <plain text label>: Isolated character string in the picture.

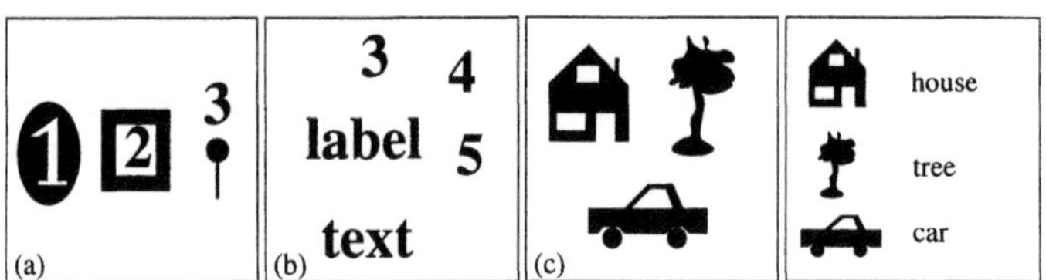

Figure 4 *Examples of picture labels. (a) Generic text labels, (b) plain text labels (c) icon labels and (d) labels in a legend.*

3. <icon label>: Label distinguished by its shape only.

In figure 4 some example picture labels are shown.

When considering links between a picture label and the text the above classes lead to 3x3 possible combinations. However, in general documents not all of them will occur. First, and most important, observation is that generic text and icon labels seldom occur in the text when there are no labels of corresponding type present in the picture. Furthermore, icon labels in the picture which have no label in the text are only useful if a semantic description of the label is present. This is the case only when a legend with <icon label>-<string> pairs is present in the paper document.

3.2 Automated link definition

We first consider <text>-<text> links. A simple automatic link definition is on the basis of user defined *keywords*. In the output of the OCR-system the keywords are detected and links between keywords detected in different document parts are suggested.

Specific logical parts of the document like the *index*, the *contents page*, and *footnotes* provide the information to define the keyword to search for automatically, based again on the OCR-result. The specific logical class also defines the region in which the keywords are to be found. For example in the case of a footnote we have to restrict the search to the page on which it is located as very often the numbering of footnotes is reset at every page. Furthermore, when analyzing the index we already know at which page to find the keyword.

Automatic <picture>-<text> links are found by locating the caption of the picture and then using the OCR result of the caption to find the general picture indication like figure.*nn*. This keyword, including its sequence number *nn*, is searched for in the text and a link is suggested.

The final class of links to analyze are the <picture label>-<text> links. The methods to find those are all based on the modules as described earlier. They differ in the order of applying the modules and the region of the image of the documents to which the modules are applied.

As concerns the number of steps in automatic link definition the easiest of the links to find is the <icon label>-<icon label> link. In this case the following steps are performed:

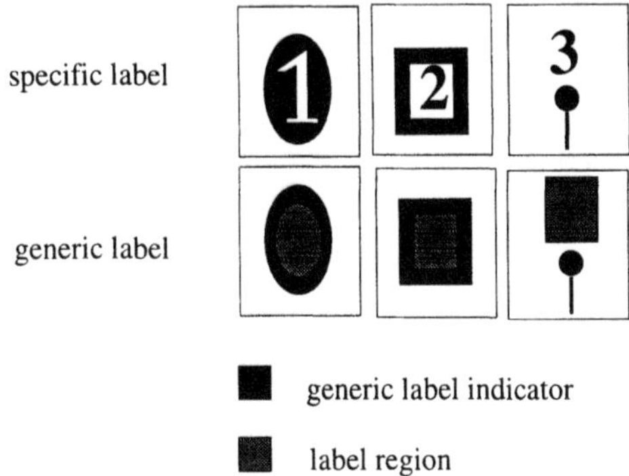

Figure 5 *In the top part of the figure some specific labels are shown. In the lower part of the figure the generic part of the label is indicated as well as the part of the label which encloses the label identifier (the label region).*

1. Label definition: the user interactively creates a label by using either the label in the image or the label in the image of the text.
2. Label search: the label is searched for in the corresponding text or picture.

The second case we consider is the case where a generic text label is present in both the picture and the text. For such a label we have to distinguish the generic part of the label, which is the same for all labels, and the label region in which the text is located which is different for each instantiation of the generic label. In the construction of a weight function for label detection the label region is set to "don't care" values. The difference between the generic part of a label and its label region is illustrated in figure 5.

As sometimes the labels in the text and the picture are of different size we treat the two sets of labels separately. For both sets we go through the following steps:

1. *Label definition* specification of the generic part of the label and the label region.
2. *Label search* in text and picture
3. *OCR* of the label region in each detected label.
4. *Link definition* on the basis of the output of the OCR-module.

In many documents the generic label is used in the picture only and in the corresponding text the character string contained in the label region is used. In this case a keyword search with the recognized contents of the label region is performed.

Doing a search for plain text labels in the picture is a difficult task as the character strings in the picture do not have any generic part identifying them as labels. In the case of numerals, assuming they are all defined in the same font, we define an example template for all 10 symbols. This is feasible if many numeric labels are present in the picture which is for example the case in technical drawings. In principle this could be done for the 26 characters as well, but often interactive location of the string will prove to be faster and more accurate. The method leads to the following steps:

1. *Label definition*
2. *Label search* in the picture
3. *Numeral grouping* of detected numerals which are close together and either oriented in a horizontal or vertical fashion.
4. *OCR* of the label in the picture
5. *Keyword search* in the text

The final links to find are the ones for which there is a legend attached to the picture. In that case the following analysis method is used:

1. *Legend analysis* to detect the icon label, description pairs
2. *Label search* in the picture
3. *OCR* of icon description to identify corresponding text string
4. *Keyword search* in the text

Note that in all cases where OCR is performed on a piece of text we have a validation of the label detection in the sense that if the OCR module does not recognize the text we presumably have detected a wrong label.

With the above techniques hyperlinks can be suggested. After confirmation by the user they are added to the hypertext. Proceeding in this manner a complete hypertext document is created. In the next section we consider the storage and the retrieval of such documents.

4 AN ODA/DEXTER HYPERDOCUMENT

We designed a simple browsing and storage system using the data structures of the recently developed Dexter Hypertext Reference Model; a standard for comparison and design of hypertext systems [4] in which we incorporated the ODA structures. In figure 6 an overview of the data structure with embedded ODA is given.

The basic items in a Dexter system are the *atoms*, where an atom can for example be a picture, a piece of text (or even a video) etc. These atoms can be combined into *composites*, which in turn might be part of another composite. The only restriction is that no composite can contain itself either directly or transitively.

Links in Dexter are between atoms and/or composites. The atoms, composites, and their relations are part of the *storage layer* of Dexter. This storage layer does not have any knowledge of the structure and meaning of the different components and this is one of the most important aspects of the Dexter model. The structure and meaning of the components is defined in the within-component layer. In this layer we can put the ODA-specific knowledge. The interface between the two layers is by means of *anchors*. Every atom or composite component can have a series of anchors defining a specific part of its contents. Each anchor has an ID which is unique within the scope of the component

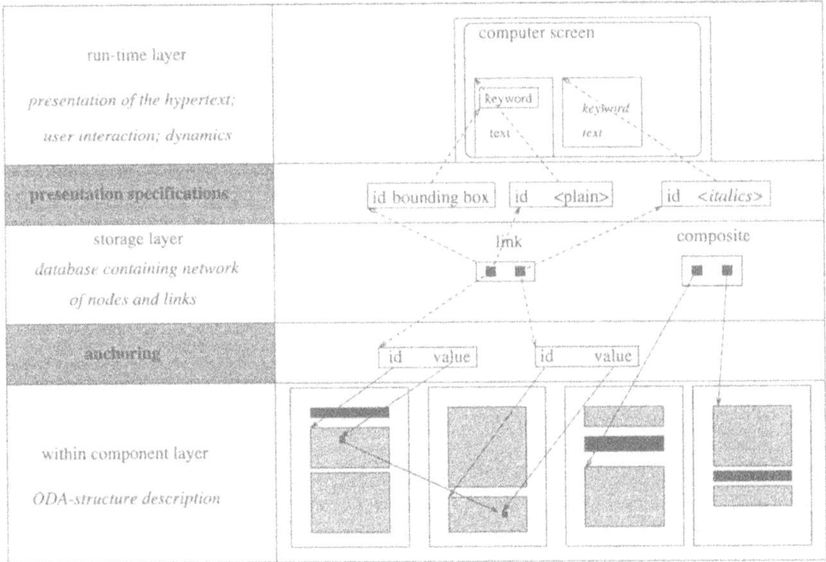

Figure 6 *Incorporation of ODA into the Dexter model.*

in which it is defined. It also has an associated value. This value can have an arbitrary interpretation like the (x, y)-position within the image of the document, or a pointer to some word in the text. This interpretation can be done by the within-component layer only. However, the storage layer can uniquely address the anchor by giving the component ID and the anchor ID. In this way the document structure analysis module can for example adjust the found position of a label, without notifying the storage layer. The latter still refers to the same anchor.

Each *link* between (parts of) components is described by two *specifiers* one for the beginning and one for the endpoint of the link. If needed one can also use multiway links by using more specifiers. Each specifier contains the following elements:

- ComponentSpec : specification of the component to link to.
- AnchorID: when the endpoint is not the component but located within its content.
- Direction: either TO, FROM, BIDIRECT, or NONE.
- PresentationSpec: what should be done if the "specifier" is activated?

Each component also has its own *presentation specification* telling how it should be presented to the user. The hypertext system has to make its final decision on the basis of the link used to arrive at the component and the the presentation specification of the component itself. A component can further have an arbitrary set of *attribute-value pairs* in which component information can be stored.

Considering the previous description it is relatively easy to define a ODA hyperdocument within the Dexter data structures. Page-sets, pages and frames are mapped directly to composites in Dexter, whereas the basic geometric/logical objects are the atoms. Specific object information is stored by making use of attributes.

It should be noted that in general it is sufficient to store the logical tree only. For example a section which is divided over two pages should be presented to the user as one composite component.

The automatically derived linkages as discussed in the previous section are stored by making use of anchors, where the anchor-value is an index into a text if the endpoint is a word and it points to a bounding box in the image if it is a (generic) text label or an icon label.

5 RESULTS

In this section we show some results of the method of hyperlink acquisition for generic text labels and icon labels. The example documents are both manuals; one for a VCR and one for a television (in dutch).

The result for the VCR manual is shown in figure 7. In this example the generic part of the text label was defined interactively in both the image of the VCR as well as in the image of the corresponding text region. From there, the labels were searched for in both images. In both cases all genuine labels were found as the top candidates using the label search module. The label region of each label found was sent to the OCR-module and on the basis of this result the linkages between the picture and the corresponding text were defined. The corresponding Dexter data structure for the link indicated is shown in figure 8.

For the second example we defined an icon label in the picture shown in figure 9 and used it to find the label in the associated text. Again the labels to be found were returned as the top candidates by the label search module.

6 CONCLUSION

In this paper we described a prototype system which starts of with a paper document and goes through a number of steps to generate the underlying hypertext conveyed by the document. First, the document is scanned leading to a digital binary image of the document. Then the structure of the document is analyzed. The Open Document Architecture makes a distinction between the geometric and logical structure of the document. This is precisely what is used in the document analysis step, first the geometric structure is found by looking at the way the document is presented and this result is used to generate the logical structure in which each block in the image of the document is given a meaning. Text blocks are then analyzed using OCR which in turn is the basis for finding keywords in the text. In the picture blocks one can automatically find picture details by using a sophisticated form of template matching. We have analyzed the various types of links one can encounter in general documents and for all generic links we have designed algorithms for hyperlink suggestion based on the limited set of modules described in the paper.

Hyperdocuments can have a very complicated structure. Both in their geometric and

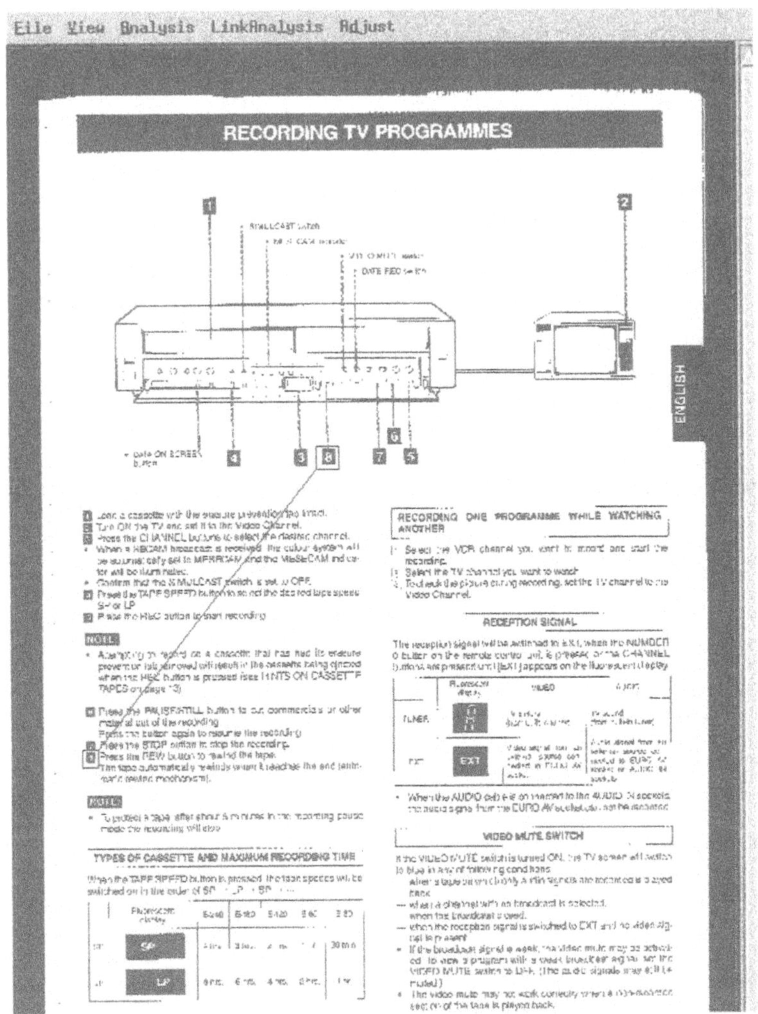

Figure 7 *Example of a document containing generic text labels in both the picture and the text. The link between the instantiations corresponding to the textual label 8 is indicated.*

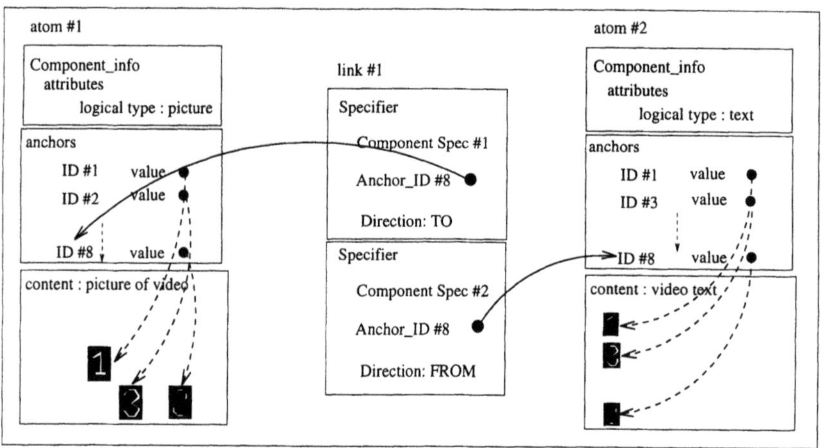

Figure 8 *Example of a link in the Dexter structure for the example given in figure 7*

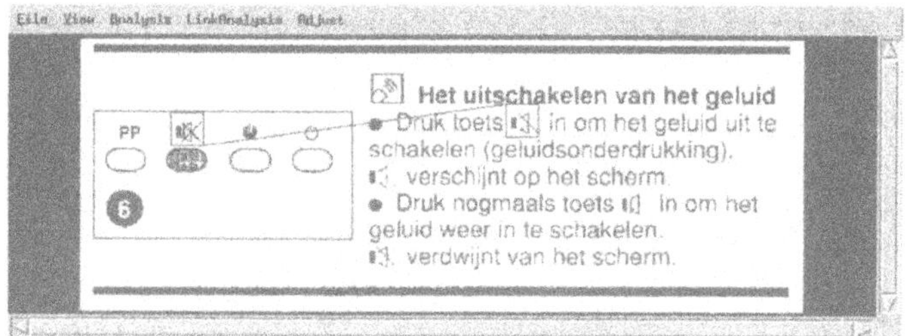

Figure 9 *Example of an icon label found in the image and linked to the same icon label found on the second line of the text. This specific line of text (in Dutch) states "push button* <icon>*".*

logical structure as well as in the structure of hyperlinks. We have therefore designed data structures combining the ODA-structure, which is the most convenient way of describing the structure of a document, with the Dexter Reference model being the appropriate model for the structure of the hyperlinks.

Although we only showed a limited set of examples of automatic hyperlinks between picture details and the text they indeed are very promising. Current research is devoted to a more elaborate evaluation of the automated linkage methods.

Acknowledgment

We thank Theo Gevers for providing us with the Enigma system.

REFERENCES

I.R. Campbell-Grant. Introducing ODA. *Computer Standards & Interfaces*, 11:149–157, 1991.

A. Dengel. From paper to office document standard representation. *IEEE Computer*, 25(7):63–67, 1992.

T. Gevers and A.W.M. Smeulders. Indexing of images by pictorial information. In *Proceedings of Visual Database Systems II, Budapest*, pages 93–100, 1991.

F. Halasz and M. Schwartz. The Dexter hypertext reference model. *Communications of the ACM*, 37(2):30–39, 1994.

A. Myka and U. Güntzer. Using electronic facsimiles of documents for automatic reconstruction of underlying hypertext structures. In *Second International Conference on Document Analysis and Recognition, Tsukuba Science City, Japan*, pages 528–532, 1993.

G. Nagy, S. Seth, and M. Viswanathan. A prototype document image analysis system for technical journals. *IEEE computer*, 25(7):10–22, 1992.

K. Parsaye, M. Chignell, S. Khosahfian, and H. Wong. *Intelligent databases; object-oriented, deductive hypermedia technologies*. Wiley, 1989.

S. Satoh, A. Takasu, and E. Katsura. A collaborative approach supporting method between document processing and hypertext construction. In *Second International Conference on Document Analysis and Recognition, Tsukuba Science City, Japan*, pages 533–536, 1993.

S. Tsujimoto and H. Asada. Major components of a complete text reading system. *Proceedings of the IEEE*, 80(7):1133–1149, 1992.

R. Boomgaard van den. Threshold logic and mathematical morphology. In *Proceedings of the 5th International Conference on Image Analysis and Processing, Positano, Italy*, pages 111–118, 1989.

7 BIOGRAPHY

Marcel Worring received his M.Sc. degree in computer science (with honors) from the Free University Amsterdam in 1988 and his Ph.D. degree from the University of Amsterdam in 1993. Currently he holds a post-doc position at the University of Amsterdam on document image analysis and model based video analysis.

Rene Buitenhuis was a Masters student at the University of Amsterdam and designed and implemented part of the described prototype system.

Arnold W.M. Smeulders is professor of Computer Science on Multi Media Information Systems. He has been in image processing since 1977 when he completed his MSc in physics from Delft University of Technology. His current interest is in image databases and intelligent interactive image analysis systems, as well as method- and system engineering aspects of image processing especially for documents and geographical information.

23

Navigation and Coordination Primitives for Multidimensional Visual Browsers*

Allison Woodruff, Alan Su, Michael Stonebraker, Caroline Paxson, Jolly Chen, and Alexander Aiken
Department of Electrical Engineering and Computer Sciences
University of California at Berkeley
Berkeley, CA 94720 USA
email: tioga@postgres.berkeley.edu

Peter Wisnovsky and Cimarron Taylor†
Illustra Information Technologies, Inc.
1111 Broadway, Suite 2000
Oakland, CA 94607 USA

Abstract

This paper describes extensions to the Tioga flight-simulator browsing protocol presented by Stonebraker et al. (1993a). These extensions allow users to navigate a multidimensional data space using sophisticated zooming capabilities. This design also allows users to move easily between different multidimensional spaces. Tunneling between different data spaces is shown to be a substantial generalization of hyperlinks in a hypermedia system. Finally, our design provides for the coordination of multiple browsers. This preserves context and allows users to explore multiple paths simultaneously.

In concert, these extensions incorporate the functionality of many information management paradigms as well as introducing new constructs. These powerful mechanisms for relating data provide users with great flexibility. For example, users can create magnifying glasses which show an enhanced view of the underlying data.

Keywords

Data browsing, hypermedia, magnifying glasses, user interfaces, visual databases, visual programming, wormholes, zooming.

---

* Supported in part by CNRI grant #M1717 and by NSF grant #FD94-00773.
† Presently with Automation Consultants Group, 650 California Street, 26th Floor, San Francisco, CA 94108.

1 INTRODUCTION

The design of user interfaces for database systems is an area in need of more attention (Stonebraker et al., 1993c). Existing database user interfaces are often unfriendly and difficult for nonexperts to use. Common database interfaces include textual programming languages or forms-based interfaces oriented towards business applications.

In Stonebraker et al. (1993a), we presented Tioga, a new paradigm for user interaction with a database management system (DBMS). Tioga is motivated by the needs of scientific DBMS users in the SEQUOIA 2000 project (Stonebraker and Dozier, 1992; Stonebraker et al. 1993b). Tioga uses the **boxes and arrows** notation popularized by scientific visualization systems such as AVS (Upson et al., 1989), Data Explorer (Lucas et al., 1992), and Khoros (Rasure and Young, 1992). Tioga improves upon these systems by providing sophisticated data management using the POSTGRES DBMS (Stonebraker and Kemnitz, 1991). In the Tioga programming model, boxes represent user-defined database queries or browsers, and edges between boxes represent flow of data. Although a limited number of boxes has currently been implemented, additional boxes may be programmed by users. Nonexperts build visual programs called **recipes** by interactively connecting boxes together using a graphical user interface. Current recipes include a photographic 35mm slide library and a geoindexing system. The underlying data manager is able to optimize and efficiently execute recipes.

The purpose of a recipe is to specify the data to be visualized, access the data through a database management system, and then locate the data in a multidimensional browser display. Figure 1 shows a typical recipe as constructed by a user. The recipe includes two browsers, viewer1 and viewer2, to display the data generated by the recipe. The default Tioga browsing paradigm allows users to visualize data results in a multidimensional space. Users navigate through their data using a flight-simulator interface. (Additional browsers may be implemented by advanced users.) Figure 2 shows a browser displaying objects in a latitude/longitude viewing space that contains California. One object, a digitized 35mm slide, has been selected and displayed.

In the default Tioga browser, the user chooses two dimensions to be displayed on the screen. Remaining dimensions appear as **sliders** which restrict the objects in the display to those which have values matching the constraints indicated by the sliders. The original navigational interface allows the user to pan over the two dimensions of the display or to zoom by enlarging a certain portion of the display. Clearly, more sophisticated navigation is desirable.

In Stonebraker et al. (1993a), we explored the basic constructs of Tioga and provided a query execution model. Chen et al. (1993) expanded the Tioga model to interface to foreign systems and provided a notion of transactions for the Tioga environment. Woodruff et al. (1994) introduced mechanisms to support navigation in multidimensional space.

In this companion paper, we extend these ideas and present three mechanisms which can be combined to support both novel, powerful constructs and constructs of proven worth. These extensions include:

- *enhanced detail*. Our system must be able to provide enhanced detail as a result of a zoom operation. For example, the Kodak PhotoCD representation for digital images supports five different resolution formats, ranging from a full size 2K by

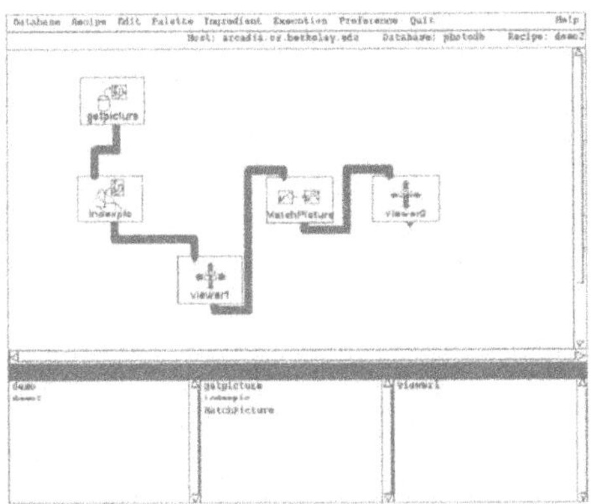

Figure 1
A Tioga Boxes and Arrows Diagram.

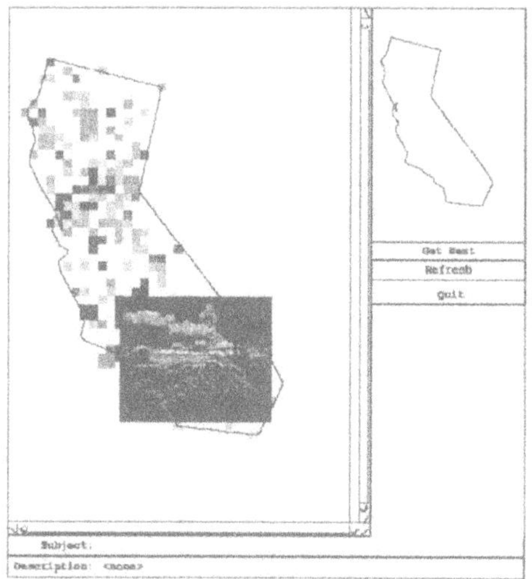

Figure 2
Data Displayed in the Tioga Browser.

3K by 8-bit color image to a 128 by 192 by 8-bit abstract (Eastman, 1992). A user would like the ability to see abstracts on the screen and then zoom in to view the images at a higher resolution. A similar feature was provided by SDMS (Herot, 1980), but it was hard-coded into that execution engine. Hence, retargeting SDMS required a considerable amount of customization.

- *movement to different multidimensional spaces.* Enhanced detail implies a change in perspective within a multidimensional space. Users also want the ability to switch to a new multidimensional space. For example, a user could zoom in on a map of Berkeley to find the Computer Science building. Additional levels of detail could yield documents corresponding to Computer Science technical reports. These documents should be displayed in a different context than the latitude/longitude coordinates appropriate for the map of Berkeley. When a document is being viewed, a further zoom could yield the image of the author or the layout geometry of his or her office. Again, a different multidimensional space should be used.
- *coordination of multiple browsers.* Our system must support multiple levels of detail in the same display. For example, it should be possible to place a magnifying glass on a portion of the display and have a zoom operation performed only for the objects under the glass. The remaining objects in the display should serve as a context for the magnified data and should not change. Because the objects in the magnifying glass are shown with enhanced detail, this function is considerably more complex than simply changing the number of pixels used for display. For example, support for magnifying glasses requires that browsers be allowed to share windows.

In the rest of this paper, we explore our design in detail. Specifically, in Section 2 we define a zoom capability that allows enhanced detail. We proceed in Section 3 to define wormholes that allow users to change multidimensional spaces. We turn in Sections 4 and 5 to our design for coordination of multiple browsers. We present the execution model in Section 6. In Section 7 we discuss potential applications, and in Section 8 we summarize our findings.

2 SHOWING ENHANCED DETAIL

To eliminate clutter in the display and to orient the user, data should have different representations when seen from different distances in multidimensional space. Intuitively, we wish to extend Tioga with the possibility of **zooming** into data to display more detail about screen objects. Our notion of zooming is semantic in that it involves changing the data objects being displayed, as opposed to simple graphical zooming. To support this functionality, we are extending the original Tioga browsing protocol.

In our design, data objects can have different abstracts that are produced by separate recipes. An **elevation map** relates these recipes to each other by specifying which recipes are valid at what distance (elevation) from the object. The elevation map is used to control the invocation of

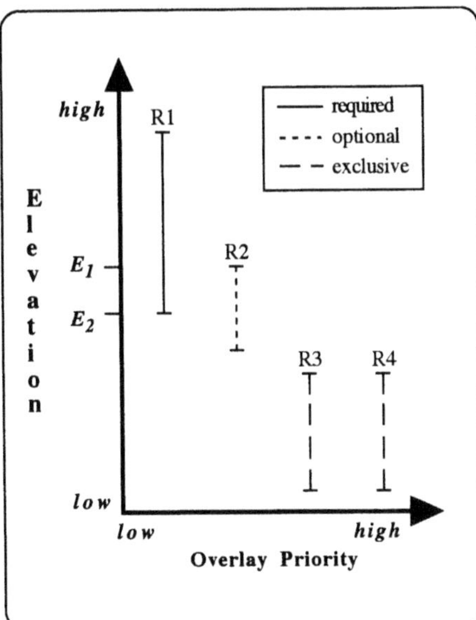

Figure 3
An Example Elevation Map.

different recipes as the user zooms in and out through the data space. Therefore, if the user zooms into the elevation range of a different recipe, the recipe providing input to the browser is changed.

Figure 3 shows an elevation map containing four recipes, R1 ("State outline"), R2 ("Census tracts"), R3 ("Rivers"), and R4 ("Highways"). R1 produces output for the browser at high elevations. When the user zooms to elevation E_1, R1 and R2 are both valid. Further inward at E_2, R1 stops output and only R2 may display data. Further zooming can display output from recipes R3 and R4.

To support this behavior, we begin by associating with any browser in any recipe an elevation range over which the browser displays data from this recipe. A browser is associated with a multidimensional coordinate system as noted above. In this presentation, we assume N dimensions which we denote $A_1, \ldots, A_N$. We add an N + 1st dimension, designated **elevation**, which is used to indicate the user's perspective. This does not represent a physical elevation, but is rather a logical representation of a user's viewing distance from the N-dimensional space.

The original Tioga implementation displays two user-selected dimensions, A_X and A_Y, on the screen. In this browser, the user can change the range of these dimensions by resizing the window. The range is adjusted proportionally to the change in window size. Note that resizing the window has no effect on elevation, as Figure 4 illustrates. Assume that the user's initial position in a displayed dimension is $ELEV_I$ with viewing angle θ_I, as shown in $TRIANGLE_I$. Adjusting the window size while remaining at a constant elevation is analogous to changing the user's viewing angle, as shown in $TRIANGLE_W$.

In our new design, the user is also allowed to adjust the elevation of a browser. When the user zooms to $ELEV_Z$, θ_I remains constant, resulting in $TRIANGLE_Z$. Because $TRIANGLE_I$ and $TRIANGLE_Z$ are similar, $RANGE_Z$ can be recalculated as follows:

$$RANGE_Z = RANGE_I * (ELEV_Z / ELEV_I)$$

Adjusting the window size or zooming may select the same range for display. However, the two operations may have very different results. Adjusting the window size does not change the recipe

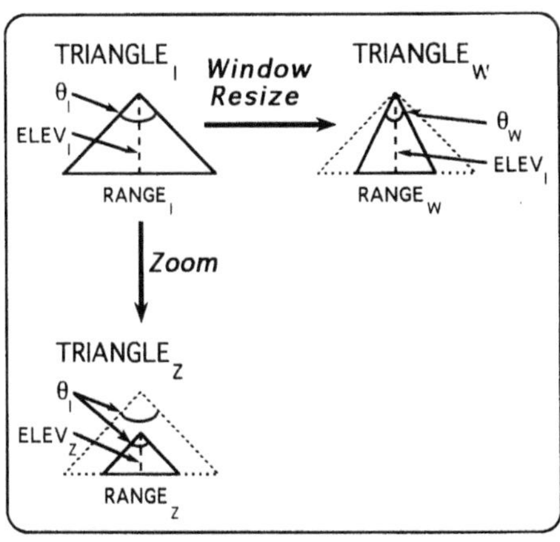

Figure 4
Changing Viewing Angle and Elevation.

providing input to the browser. Conversely, zooming may place the user in the elevation range of a different recipe. In this case, the recipe providing input to the browser is changed as specified by the elevation map.

The data provided by each recipe must be supplied to the browser in a common, multidimensional coordinate system. When more than one recipe at a given elevation may provide output to the browser, the elevation map also specifies the overlay priority of the recipes, which is shown on the horizontal axis. When conflicts occur in allocation of display space, objects from recipes with higher priority are visible on the screen in preference to those from recipes with lower priority.

In addition to specifying the elevations at which recipes are to be invoked and their overlay priority, the elevation map also contains a collection of semantic restrictions on the display of recipe output. Each recipe in an elevation map can be:

- *required*. In this case, recipe output must be displayed if the browser is at an elevation within the elevation range.
- *optional*. In this case, when the user enters the elevation range of the recipe, he or she is prompted as to whether the output from this recipe should be visible. This behavior occurs if the user zooms into the elevation range from above or zooms out from below. At any given elevation range, a mechanism allows users to turn on or off optional recipes valid at the current elevation. Using this interface, a user can change his or her mind about seeing (or not seeing) the objects from optional recipes.
- *exclusive*. A user can specify a radio button behavior for recipes that are valid at common elevations. With this behavior, at most one of the recipes can be activated, and the user is presented with a menu of radio buttons to indicate which one.

These semantics are illustrated in Figure 3. At higher elevations, R1 displays the outline of California. Upon zooming to E_1, the user has the option to see also the census tracts in the state as output by R2. At the next transition point, E_2, the outline of the state is no longer visible and the census tracts are optionally visible. Further zooming shows either the rivers or the highways of California (as generated by R3 and R4), but not both.

Previous work has identified the merits of zooming capabilities (Gorlick and Quilici, 1994; Perlin and Fox, 1993). We contribute a dynamic, visual mechanism for specifying the behavior of objects when viewed from different distances. Elevation maps allow a user to define easily the semantics of the zoom operation, assuming that all recipes produce data in the same multidimensional space. We now turn to a mechanism for changing from one multidimensional space to another.

3 CHANGING MULTIDIMENSIONAL SPACES

Enhanced detail implies a change in perspective within a multidimensional space. Users also want the ability to move to related multidimensional data spaces for new perspectives on the data, a functionality similar to that provided by hyperlinks (Conklin, 1987). Consider the following example in which Tioga presents information about the residents of Berkeley. Initially, the application displays a map of Berkeley. Zooming inward gives more detail about geographic objects, culminating with the outline of each individual residence. At this point, the user may invoke a new type of browser, defined for each residence, that displays an image of the people living there. Requesting detail on the residence therefore causes a different multidimensional space to be explored.

When a user changes to a new multidimensional space, objects have a spatial relationship that is unrelated to the relationship in effect on the near side. This behavior should be distinguished from a zoom operation where the same spatial relationship is present before and after the zoom. Therefore, we denote this operation of changing from one multidimensional space to another as **tunneling** through a **wormhole**, to differentiate it from zooming. A wormhole is a connector between two disparate data spaces, and tunneling is the process of travelling through a wormhole.

To construct a wormhole, the user must specify the following information:

- *the wormhole location.* We associate the wormhole with objects displayed by some recipe in some browser. Hence, the location is indicated by the three-tuple: (recipe name, browser name, query).
- *the new application that should be run on the other side of the wormhole.*
- *a **tag** associated with the wormhole.* Because there may be multiple wormholes for a given object in a given recipe, we require the tag field to allow a user to specify which wormhole should be followed.

In practice, a user-interface gesture indicates the user's desire to tunnel through a wormhole. The user then chooses a wormhole from the list of tags associated with the object(s) selected. At this point, a new application is invoked taking the object(s) selected as a parameter(s). In the example given above, the object identifier of the house would be passed to the new application to allow it to display only the people living there. It is also possible to define the wormhole over a collection of object identifiers. Specifically, we allow an arbitrary function to identify the objects for which the wormhole is defined. One such function could be:

```
retrieve (House.oid)
where House.architect = "Wright"
```

in which case the wormhole would be defined only for houses designed by Wright.

4 SLAVING AND CLONING BROWSERS

It is difficult for users zooming and tunneling in single browsers to explore multiple paths simultaneously. Additionally, when users are zooming and tunneling in multidimensional space, it is difficult for them to maintain a sense of context. A related problem may be observed in traditional systems such as graphics packages, help systems, and hypermedia systems. In many of these systems, users must repeatedly zoom in and out or backtrack. Somewhat more sophisticated systems provide limited browser coordination in overview-detail browser pairs (Plaisant et al., 1995). In the next two sections, we introduce mechanisms for browser coordination which support simultaneous exploration of multiple paths through multidimensional space and display context to the user.

Browsers in the same recipe can be independent of each other. In this case, movement in one browser does not affect the others. This behavior is appropriate when the browsers are displaying independent objects.

On the other hand, one browser can be constrained to another in a master/slave relationship. In this case, whenever the user changes the master's position in N-dimensional space, the slave's position in M-dimensional space automatically changes as well. More specifically, during the recipe definitions, the user defines a function, `LOC_CALC`, that translates requests in the master into requests to the slave:

```
LOC_CALC(N-space-region) → M-space-region
```

When the master is moved to REGION_1, the slave will be instructed by Tioga to move to `LOC_CALC(REGION`$_1$`)`. Both browsers must recalculate their visible rectangles and issue commands to retrieve the objects which will be displayed. Further, when the master changes elevation, the slave must automatically change elevation at the same time. Usually, slaved browsers will be constrained to have the same elevation as their master; however, we allow the user to specify optionally a second function, `ELEV_CALC`:

```
ELEV_CALC (elevation) → elevation
```

In this way, the slaved browser can be constrained to operate at a second elevation that is a function, `ELEV_CALC`, of the elevation of the master.

There are four interesting ways in which slaved browsers may be constrained:

- *Slaved browsers may display data from different regions in a multidimensional space.* For example, a user may need to examine all areas 5 miles north of a pipeline to ensure that a toxin carried by the pipeline has not affected these areas. In Tioga, the pipeline could be viewed in one browser. A second browser could be slaved with a function LOC_CALC that mapped an N-space-point to a new point 5 miles north.
- *Slaved browsers may display the same data seen from different elevations.* For example, the slave could show a detailed representation of what is seen in the display of the master. In effect, the slave would show the data of the first browser through a magnifying glass.
- *Slaved browsers may display different data from the same points in a multidimensional space.* For example, one browser could show color-coded precipitation data for an area while its slave displayed temperature data for the same area.
- *Slaved browsers may display related data in different multidimensional viewing spaces.* For example, a master browser could show a map of California while a slaved browser displayed a list of all seismographic sensor stations located in the area shown in the master browser. As the user looked at different parts of California, the slaved browser would automatically adjust the list of stations.

The four examples above assume the existence of two browsers in the same recipe. If only one browser exists, it may be more convenient to **clone** it rather than to place explicitly a new browser in the recipe graph. Cloned browsers can be slaved or independent. The examples above demonstrate possible uses for slaved clones. For instance, to display the same data at different levels of detail, the user could clone and slave a viewer to act as the magnifying glass.

Independent clones are appropriate in other situations. For example, it is easy for a user to become disoriented when navigating in a multidimensional space. Hence, the user would like to mark the position of something of interest and return to it at a later time. Cloning a browser allows one browser to remain stationary at the object of interest while the second one continues to browse the multidimensional space.

To support this functionality, we propose the following design. The original browser becomes the **originator** and the new browser becomes the **clone**. The originator and the clone have exactly the same elevation map. During the cloning operation, the user must specify if the clone is to be slaved to the originator, and if so must specify LOC_CALC and ELEV_CALC.

If the originator and the clone are independent (i.e. not slaved), then the second browser is initially assigned the same elevation and spatial location in multidimensional space as the first browser. The joystick of either browser can be moved arbitrarily, and the displays of the two browsers will typically diverge. As a result, cloning subsumes bookmarking features found in other systems.

If the clone is slaved to the originator, then the clone is constrained to operate at an elevation and location offset relative to the originator; these offsets are determined by LOC_CALC and ELEV_CALC. In this case, the slaved browser operates at an elevation of

```
ELEV_CALC (elevation of originator)
```

and at a location given by

```
LOC_CALC (N-space-region of originator)
```

If LOC_CALC is the identity function, and ELEV_CALC specifies a zoom, then the clone will provide an automatic magnifying glass, without requiring the user to perform the zoom manually.

Using slaving and cloning, a variety of offset displays and magnifying glass effects can be constructed. The next section describes mechanisms that allow two browsers to share the same screen area, thereby permitting a true magnifying glass effect to be implemented.

5 SHARING WINDOWS

We would like to allow the user to place one browser inside another. For example, the user could place a **magnifying glass** browser inside another browser displaying a map of California. This is analogous to reading a map of California with the aid of a physical magnifying glass. Adding this functionality to Tioga allows users to combine the usefulness of effects such as Magic Lenses (Bier et al., 1993) with the strength of a DBMS. To provide this functionality, we require that browsers be allowed to share their windows. If two browsers share the same multidimensional space, then it is permissible for them to share a browser window. Note that since a clone and its originator automatically share the same multidimensional space, they are able by definition to share a window.

When two browsers are declared to share a window, they are referred to as the **outer** browser and the **inner** browser. Each browser has separate slider bars that determine the content of its display. The outer browser uses the complete window to display its objects. The inner browser magnifies a portion of the data shown in the outer browser. The display of the inner browser is then overlaid on the display of the outer one, thereby creating a single composite display which can be rendered on the screen by the window manager.

To create this composite, Tioga finds the center of the inner browser's current viewing region, and then locates this point in the outer browser's window. Next, Tioga positions the inner browser's viewing region at this location within the outer browser. There are three cases of interest:

- *case 1*: the inner viewing region is completely inside the outer viewing region. In this case, the two regions are overlaid and displayed.
- *case 2:* the inner viewing region is completely disjoint from the outer viewing region. In this case, the inner viewing region cannot be seen, and only the outer viewing region is visible.
- *case 3:* the inner viewing region overlaps the outer viewing region. In this case, Tioga must clip the inner viewing region and then overlay the two displays as above.

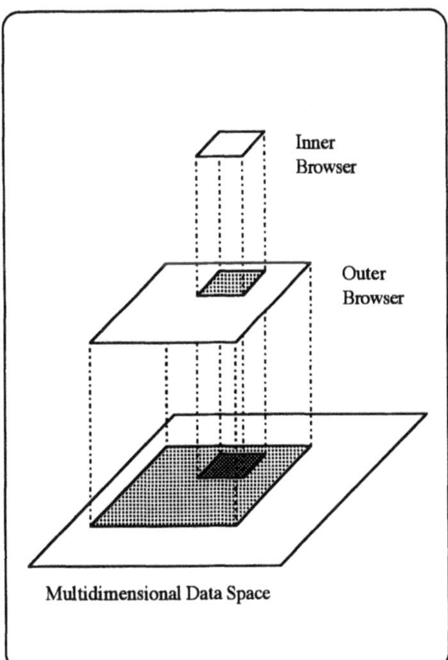

Figure 5
Viewing Regions of Nested Browsers.

These behaviors can be illustrated in the following examples. The user can clone a browser and run both the originator and the clone in a common window. A zoom operation on the inner browser will allow the user to observe a magnifying glass effect, whereby one browser is providing a detailed blowup of the region displayed by the other. Figure 5 shows a magnifying glass (the inner browser) positioned above a window (the outer browser) which is in turn positioned above a map (the multidimensional space).

Consider the case in which the inner and outer browsers are independent. In this situation, the position and elevation of each browser can be changed independently. Moving the inner browser will change its position above the map, and therefore, its contents. Because it moves independently, moving it will also change its position relative to the outer browser. This will allow the user to magnify various areas of the map. If the user moves the magnifying glass completely out of the region displayed by the outer browser, then case 2 above applies and the detail will not be shown. If the magnifying glass is partly outside this region, then case 3 above applies and only a portion of the inner browser will be displayed. Similarly, if the user moves the outer browser, the content of the inner browser will not automatically change, although its position relative to the outer browser will change.

To achieve different behavior, we can slave the clone to the originator. Since the inner browser is slaved to the outer browser, moving the outer browser will change the area displayed in both browsers. However, the position of the magnifying glass within the outer browser will remain constant. Moreover, if the user zooms the outer browser to blow up the map of interest, say to a map of a specific county, then the magnifying glass will also zoom.

The definitions presented above may be recursively extended so that an inner browser may in turn serve as an outer browser. This allows an arbitrary number of browsers to share a window, with a pairwise inner-outer relationship between them. Thus, a hierarchical collection of browsers can be defined. For example, a user may choose to have a magnifying glass on top of another magnifying glass, providing even more detail.

6 EXECUTION MODEL

The original Tioga executor considered the execution of single recipes. However, zooming requires that multiple recipes execute concurrently to supply data to a browser. We have extended our design to include an abstract manager which controls the execution of recipes and coordinates their communication with browsers.

In a naive implementation of zooming, all browsers in a recipe would be displayed when the user zoomed to the elevation at which the recipe became valid. However, different recipes in an elevation map may contain different types and numbers of browsers. Therefore, the naive implementation would result in arbitrary browsers appearing and disappearing as the user adjusted elevation. To provide a more intuitive semantics, we introduce the notion of a **base** recipe which defines the visual environment which the user can explore. The visual environment is made up of one or more browsers which appear in the base recipe. Each of these browsers is associated with an elevation map that specifies which recipes may provide data to it.

Execution begins when a base recipe is passed to the abstract manager. The abstract manager examines the elevation maps of all browsers in the base recipe to determine the set of all recipes which may be accessed through the visual environment. The abstract manager then starts an executor for each of these recipes, as well as a process for each browser in the base recipe. The abstract manager establishes communication channels between executors and browsers. These are distinct from the dataflow edges which exist in the recipe graphs. At any given time, a browser has a communication channel to every recipe in its elevation map which is currently active (i.e. valid at the current elevation). The browser uses these channels to request data from the executors. When the user adjusts elevation, the abstract manager updates the communication channels between the browsers and executors, adding and deleting connections as appropriate.

Since abstracts allow movement in a single multidimensional space, the appearance of new browsers might be disorienting. However, since tunneling by definition involves viewing a new multidimensional space, we allow the recipe invoked by a wormhole to serve as a base recipe and start a new visual environment. The invocation is similar to a fork operation; both the original browser and the new browser continue to exist as independent processes, each with a base recipe.

7 APPLICATIONS

In the preceding sections, we have defined semantics for zooming, tunneling, and the coordination of multiple browsers. The resulting model unites constructs which have proved useful in many types of information management systems.

For example, the reader can readily observe that wormholes are a substantial generalization of hyperlinks in a hypermedia system. A traditional hyperlink is a wormhole in which there is a prespecified object or collection of objects on each side of the hole. Wormholes allow a run-time specified set of objects to be on each side. Further, classical hypermedia systems only provide a two-dimensional display space composed of the X and Y screen dimensions. The Tioga paradigm extends such systems by supporting the display of objects in user-specified dimensions.

Similarly, abstracts generalize the notion of layers as used in many Geographic Information Systems (GISs). In many such systems, data is stored in separate layers representing categories such as species distribution, land use, or political boundaries. Layers may be viewed independently or displayed together in one window. Abstracts provide a mechanism for the application developer to define the levels at which each layer will be visible. Further, while some GISs support browsing in 2 or 3 dimensions representing the physical dimensions of the Earth, they do not incorporate browsing in arbitrary multidimensional spaces. Such browsers could be used to provide additional data. For example, selecting a city might offer the option to tunnel to a browser containing people objects displayed according to the dimensions age, income, and consumption of a product.

Scientific visualization systems could also take advantage of the constructs supported in the Tioga model. Many existing scientific visualization systems provide users the option of browsing through data in multidimensional space. However, many scientists would like to perform data lineage queries in which they trace the history of the operations that have been performed on their data. Slaved browsers could be used to simultaneously display different versions of data. In this case, navigation in one browser would cause the slaved browser to automatically display the corresponding data.

The model presented in this paper incorporates multiple concepts of proven worth. This model can be used both to enhance existing systems and to create new information management applications.

8 CONCLUSIONS

In this paper we have detailed mechanisms that support navigation in multidimensional space. We first outlined a zoom capability that allows users to view data at different levels of detail. We next introduced the concept of wormholes. Tunneling through a wormhole allows users to view their data in the context of a new multidimensional viewing space. We then proposed mechanisms for linking browsers together as well as for creating new browsers. We detailed the behavior of multiple browsers sharing a portion of the screen. The resulting data management and browsing model is a generalization of many existing systems. In combination, the ideas presented not only add functionality to existing paradigms but support new constructs such as magnifying glasses as well. We are currently extending the original Tioga system to support the features discussed in this paper.

9 REFERENCES

Bier, E., Stone, M., Pier, K., Buxton, W., and DeRose, T. (1993) Toolglass and Magic Lenses: The See-Through Interface. Proceedings of SIGGRAPH 93, Anaheim, California.

Chen, J., et al. (1993) Extending a Graphical Query Language to Support Updates, Foreign Systems, and Transactions. SEQUOIA 2000 Technical Report 93/38, University of California at Berkeley.

Conklin, J. (1987) Hypertext: An Introduction and Survey. *Computer*, 20:9, pp. 17-41.

Eastman Kodak Company (1992) Programmer's Guide for UNIX Systems. *Kodak PhotoCD Access Developer Toolkit.*

Gorlick, M. and Quilici, A. (1994) Visual Programming-in-the-Large versus Visual Programming-in-the-Small. Proceedings of the 1994 IEEE Symposium on Visual Languages, St. Louis, Missouri.

Herot, C. (1980) Spatial Management of Data. *ACM Transactions on Database Systems,* 5:4, pp. 493-513.

Lucas, B. et al. (1992) An Architecture for a Scientific Visualization System. Proceedings of the 1992 IEEE Visualization Conference, Boston, Massachusetts.

Perlin, K. and Fox, D. (1993) Pad: An Alternative Approach to the Computer Interface. Proceedings of SIGGRAPH 93, Anaheim, California.

Plaisant, C., Carr, D., and Shneiderman, S. (1995) Image-Browser Taxonomy and Guidelines for Designers. *IEEE Software*, 12:2, pp. 21-32.

Rasure, J. and Young, M. (1992) An Open Environment for Image Processing Software Development. Proceedings of the 1992 SPIE Symposium on Electronic Image Processing.

Stonebraker, M. and Kemnitz, G. (1991) The POSTGRES Next-Generation Database Management System. *Communications of the ACM*, 4:10, pp. 78-92.

Stonebraker, M. and Dozier, J. (1992) SEQUOIA 2000: Large Capacity Object Servers to Support Global Change Research. SEQUOIA 2000 Technical Report 91/1, University of California at Berkeley.

Stonebraker, M., Chen, J., Nathan, N., Paxson, C., and Wu, J. (1993a) Tioga: Providing Data Management for Scientific Visualization Applications. Proceedings of the 1993 VLDB Conference, Dublin, Ireland.

Stonebraker, M., et al. (1993b) The SEQUOIA 2000 Architecture and Implementation Strategy, SEQUOIA 2000 Technical Report 93/23, University of California at Berkeley.

Stonebraker, M., et al. (1993c) DBMS Research at a Crossroads: The Vienna Update. Proceedings of the 1993 VLDB Conference, Dublin, Ireland.

Upson, C., et al. (1989) The Application Visualization System. *IEEE Computer Graphics and Applications*, 9:4, pp. 32-40.

Woodruff, A., Wisnovsky, P., Taylor, C., Stonebraker, M., Paxson, C., Chen, J., and Aiken, A. (1994) Zooming and Tunneling in Tioga: Supporting Navigation in Multidimensional Space. Proceedings of the IEEE Symposium on Visual Languages, St. Louis, Missouri.

10 BIOGRAPHIES

Allison Woodruff is a Ph.D. student in Computer Science at the University of California at Berkeley. She received the Bachelors degree in English from California State University, Chico in 1987. She received the Masters degree in Linguistics in 1989 and the Masters degree in Computer Science in 1993 from the University of California, Davis. She has worked as a student assistant and as a geographic information systems analyst at the California Department of Water Resources. Her research interests include user interfaces for databases and implementation issues for visual languages.

Alan Su is a Bachelors degree candidate majoring in Electrical Engineering and Computer Science at the University of California at Berkeley. He plans to enroll in the Computer Science Ph.D. program at the University of California at San Diego in the Fall of 1996.

Michael Stonebraker is a professor of Electrical Engineering and Computer Sciences at the University of California at Berkeley, where he has been employed since 1971. He was one of the principal architects of the INGRES relational database management system which was developed during the period 1973-77. Subsequently, he constructed Distributed INGRES, one of the first working distributed database systems. Then, he turned his attention to developing a next generation DBMS, POSTGRES, that can effectively manage not only data but also objects and rules as well. POSTGRES formed one of the cornerstones of the SEQUOIA 2000 project, the DEC flagship research project of the 1990s for which Dr. Stonebraker has served as co-project director. SEQUOIA 2000 is striving to build a new computer environment for Earth science researchers and encompasses networking, storage, DBMS, and visualization activities. Currently, he is focusing on the DBMS support for visualization environments and on next-generation distributed DBMSs.

Dr. Stonebraker is a founder of INGRES Corp (now the INGRES Products Division of ASK Computer Systems), the founder of Illustra Information Technologies, Inc., a past chairman of the ACM Special Interest Group on Management of Data, and the author of many papers on DBMS technology. He lectures widely, has been the keynote speaker at several recent conferences, and was the winner of the first ACM SIGMOD innovations award in 1992.

Caroline Paxson is a Ph.D. student in Art History at the University of California at Berkeley. She received the Bachelors degree in German Literature from Harvard. She received the Masters degree in Computer Science from the University of California at Berkeley in 1993.

Jolly Chen is a doctoral candidate in Computer Science at the University of California at Berkeley. He received the Bachelors degree in Computer Science and Masters degree in Electrical Engineering and Computer Science from the Massachusetts Institute of Technology in 1990. His research interests include query optimization and user interfaces for databases. Jolly Chen is a student member of ACM.

Alexander Aiken received his Bachelors degree in Computer Science and Music from Bowling Green State University in 1983 and his Ph.D. from Cornell University in 1988. He was a Research Staff Member at the IBM Almaden Research Center before joining the Berkeley faculty in 1993.

Peter Wisnovsky has worked in the database industry for the last six years, for the Sharebase Corporation (formerly Britton-Lee) and Illustra Information Technologies, the leader in object-relational database technology. At Illustra he has worked on the Object Knowledge database visualization system and its visual programming language development environment, the Project Editor. He is currently working on interface technology at Illustra. He received the Bachelors degree in Computer Science from Princeton in 1989.

Cimarron Taylor is Chief Scientist at Automation Consultants Group. While at the University of California at Berkeley from 1987 to 1990, he contributed to the query executor, access methods and transaction system of POSTGRES. After graduating, he went to Scopus Technology where he turned Scopus's workflow prototype into a commercial product. He joined Illustra when it was founded in 1992 to build client software tools. He developed and implemented the compilation algorithms in the Object Knowledge Toolkit to translate visual programs into Illustra's dialect of SQL3. He is now responsible for the information architecture of ACG's manufacturing enterprise automation system.

PART EIGHT

Data Models and Data Structures

24

An automatic visual database interface

E. Pichat
Université Claude Bernard - Lyon 1
Bâtiment 710 43 boulevard du 11 novembre 1918
France 69622 Villeurbanne Cedex
Tel. 72 44 83 70 Fax 72 44 83 64 e-mail: pichat@ligia.univ-lyon1.fr

D. Saker
Nat Systèmes
100 rue La Fayette France 75010 Paris
Tel. (1) 40 22 95 94 Fax (1) 40 22 95 92

Abstract

Today's relational and object-oriented databases come with very powerful declarative query languages like SQL. However, such languages are still not adapted to the needs of the occasional user because of their syntax requirements and because they do not facilitate the understanding of the database semantics, navigation within tables and the formulation of queries.

This paper proposes an especially assisting visual interface for database query. This is possible with a powerful and easy-to-understand database scheme representation, the *normalized semantic graph (NSG)* which is underlain by the *Universal Relation with Inclusions* (*URI*) data model, and by making NSG more explicit by automatic generation. First the interface displays the set of the relational schemes and a set of basic links in background: it is the *relation-to-relation NSG*, a kind of restriction of NSG. Displaying links with tables makes it easier for the user to understand the database scheme and to find his way about tables. Secondly the interface calculates and displays the possible join-links of a table designated by the user. This is the *evolving query graph*. As it evolves with the designated node, the user progressively specifies his query: he only has to select the attributes to project, precise selection conditions and click on the desired join-links to obtain the *query graph*, which is translated in SQL.

This interface by-passes syntactic specifications and assists the user as closely as possible in his declaration. The paper also shows how to generate all the possible links between relations implied by the NSG as well as how to complete them with compatible attributes. In this way, the *complete query graph* is obtained. But to avoid drowning the user in a mass of information, only those links of the complete query graph which are contiguous to the node designated by the user are displayed.

A prototype is available in the GraphTalk® environment.

Keywords

Data model, universal relation with inclusion, normalized semantic graph, common attribute, compatible attribute, inclusion dependency, complete query graph, evolving query graph

1 INTRODUCTION

DBMS are today popular applications. But unfortunately, users are still reduced to asking predefined questions or to making the effort of using data manipulation languages such as SQL. Although SQL is a declarative and much easier language to use than, say, network and hierarchical model query languages, it still remains a difficult language to learn for the non-expert user [Reisner 81] and does not sufficiently enhance productivity. To formulate a query, the user is expected to know the theory underlying the data model, remember the database scheme learn, specify join conditions and force the syntax of the query language.

Considering the limited number of tables, attributes and syntactic units likely to be involved in querying a database and the advantages accruing from the graphical representation of the conceptual data scheme, visual query interfaces represent an interesting alternative to formal query expressions. This is even more so with the emergence of new techniques of Man-Machine interaction (direct manipulation, WYSIWYG and object-action dialog) that are more effective from the dual point of view of learning and use.

The table in Figure 1 provides a quick summary of the evolution of graphical interfaces aimed at assisting users in database query. The assistance provided by CUPID is very limited because the user is still expected to link the different components and maintain coherence with the data scheme himself. CUPID has served as model for many interfaces, such as LAGRIF [Lakhal 86] and IQL [Ramos 91]. ISIS represents an important step forward in the effort to assist users in query formulation: before ISIS, join paths were not made explicit to the user and syntactically correct but semantically incorrect queries were possible. Its graphical conceptual scheme, based on the semantic model SDM, generates a graphical representation of classes of objects grouped together under several trees using two types of relationship: superclass/subclass and aggregation. GLAD also represents a major step forward since it visualizes a unique graphical conceptual scheme of the database which it uses as query medium. In addition, its implementation with an object-oriented language testifies to the blessings accruing from the object paradigm in the implementation of Man-Machine dialog. The first interfaces to implement direct manipulation [Schneiderman 83] [Nanard 90] appeared in the 90s. The all-graphical approach to the specification of complex selection conditions in Pasta-3 and other interfaces such as IQL, is only justified as a component of a graphical toolbox and cannot be a substitute to the formal representation of statements. Visual interfaces also facilitate the querying of object-oriented DBMS with their inheritance and composition links. CANDID, CQL and SUPER permit the modeling of complex data. OHQL authorizes declarative queries formulated with methods and navigation operations drawn from the hypertext approach.

The user interface proposed in this paper implements the enhancements described above:

- it is descriptive in so far it provides a concise and complete visualization of the data scheme (only one medium is necessary);
- it uses the same medium both for the description of the data scheme and for the representation of the formulated query: the semantic assistance given to the user cannot be more complete;
- it is interactive: the formulation of a query is made by simply designating the nodes and arcs of the displayed semantic graph and the syntactic units through the technique of direct manipulation;
- it accepts both complex [Fallouh 94] and normalized data although because of problems of space, we will restrain ourselves here to only normalized data.

Our interface introduces three enhancements:

First, it uses a more powerful and canonical data model than the usual semantic models. In Section 2, we introduce the *Universal Relation with Inclusions* model adopted in URITalk interface, especially its graphical representation, the *normalized semantic graph*.

The only available running joins at the present state of development of DBMS and data manipulation languages concern two tables as elementary join conditions. The second advantage of the query interface presented here is that it does not only display relation-to-relation links of the normalized semantic graph but also helps the user in the formulation of queries by being able to visualize all the possible binary semantic links. Section 3 is devoted to the construction of the *complete query graph* from the normalized semantic graph. However, the complete query graph cannot be displayed because of the large number of links.

Query interface \ Visualization of	tables	join symbol	conceptual schemes	query graph	one conceptual scheme	conceptual scheme support query
SQL [IBM 81] [Melton 93]	no					
QBE [Zloof 77]	yes	no				
CUPID [McDonald 75]		yes		yes		
RU [Ullman 89]			no			
ISIS [Goldman 85]			yes	no		
Pasta-3 [Kuntz 90]				yes	no	no
GLAD [WU 84] [WU 89]					yes	yes
CANDID [Trepied 89]						
CQL [Kari 90]						
SUPER [Auddino 91]						
OHQL [Andonoff 92]						
URITalk [Saker 93]						

Figure 1 Evolution of query interfaces.

Section 4 presents a partial graph of the complete query graph which is used as query medium: the *evolving query graph* that continues to change with every progress the user makes in the specification of his query.

Finally, Section 5 shows how the URITalk interface assists the user in formulating queries involving selection-projection-joins on the evolving query graph. Thus the *query graph* is obtained.

2 THE URI DATA MODEL AND THE NSGraph

2.1 The Universal Relation with Inclusions

Relational DBMS and relational query languages are based on the relational data model [Codd 70] [Ullman 89]. The *Universal Relation* (UR) assumption provides a rigorous procedure for constructing the different relations of a database. The *functional dependencies* (FD) $\underline{L}$ R, where L (the *left side*) and R (the *right side* or functionally determined attributes side) are sets of attributes that belong to the UR **R**(U), permit the decomposition of the U into a set of relational structures $\mathbf{R}_i(\underline{K_1}\ \underline{K_2} \ldots \underline{K_n}$ Remainder) in refined third normal form [Maier 83] through the normalization process. K_1, K_2 ..., K_n are a set of keys of $\mathbf{R}_i$ and Remainder the subset of the set of the attributes of $\mathbf{R}_i$ that do not belong to any of the keys. Let be X^+ the *closure* of the attribute set X (X^+ is the set of the attributes functionally determined by X). Then each relation closure U_i^+ and the number of keys per relation are invariants of the normalized relational database scheme. The introduction of *join components* (JC), assimilable to FDs without right side, for the purpose of preserving data, increases the descriptive power of the model.

However data modeling remains unsatisfactory with respect to Entity-Relationship, for example. Inclusion dependencies make up for this shortcoming: an *inclusion dependency* (ID) [Casanova 84] [Lafaye 1982] [Mannila 86] [Mitchell 83] noted:

$$A_1 \ldots A_k \subseteq_\alpha B_1 \ldots B_k$$

where A_i and B_i are attributes and α names the ID and distinguishes it from the set inclusion, is verified on the Universal Relation **R** if and only if the projections of any instance R of **R** on the right and left sides of the ID verify the set inclusion:

$$R[A_1 \ldots A_k] \subseteq R[B_1 \ldots B_k].$$

The ***Universal Relation with Inclusions*** (***URI***) is the Universal Relation data model extended to the IDs [Pichat 90]. URI comes with a normalization process extended to IDs [Pichat 89]. The above-mentioned results obtained for the normalized form of UR are valid for URI.

The set of normalized relational structures is partitioned with the concept of ***Partial Universal Relation*** (PUR). Two normalized structures, $\mathbf{R}_i$ and $\mathbf{R}_j$, belong to one and the same PUR if and only if there is a sequence of normalized relational structures $\mathbf{R}_i, \ldots \mathbf{R}_k, \mathbf{R}_1, \ldots, \mathbf{R}_j$ such that for any pair $\{\mathbf{R}_k, \mathbf{R}_1\}$ of adjacent relational structures in the sequence, their closures U_k^+ and U_1^+ have at least one attribute in common. The PURs also partition the set U of the attributes of **R**.

2.2 The Normalized Semantic Graph

The ***normalized semantic graph*** (***NSG***) is the URI graphical representation of a database scheme. It is made up of a set of nodes and a set of hyperarcs (see Appendix 1):

- the nodes are PURs. Each PUR can, in turn, be represented with a directed graph without circuits:
  - its nodes are the normalized relational structures $\mathbf{R}_i(\underline{K}_1\ \underline{K}_2 \ldots \underline{K}_n$ Remainder);
  - the arc $(\mathbf{R}_i, \mathbf{R}_j)$ exists if and only if
    - the closure U_i^+ at the origin includes the closure U_j^+ at the extremity,
    - it cannot be obtained through the transitivity of the other arcs,
    - its origin and its extremity have at least one attribute in common: $U_i \cap U_j \neq \phi$.

    These closure inclusion arcs are termed ***common attribute arcs***; they represent monovalued functions,
- the hyperarcs represent the normalized inclusion dependencies. They are termed ***inclusion hyperarcs between PURs*** because they are graphically represented from a set of (initial) PURs to another set of (terminal) PURs (see 3.2-a below).

Example: The figure in Appendix 1 shows the NSG of the "the Program Committee's treatment of submitted papers" [Heuser 93], itself part of the classical example "Preparation of an IFIP conference" [Olle 82]. Each paper, identified by its title, may concern a number of different conference topics and be co-authored by several persons. Each referee has one address, is competent in several topics and cannot receive more than one paper at a time. As soon as a paper is read, the referee writes his report and the paper is considered to have changed from the table of distributed papers to the table of papers that have been evaluated. All the papers are judged together. The NSG in Appendix 1 has five nodes (PUR) and six IDs. Three of the nodes are made of only one relation each (**JudgedPaper**, **Evaluation** and **Distribution**). The two other PURs (RECEIVED PAPERS and REFEREES) contain two relations each (**Author** and **PaperTopic**, on the one hand, and **RefereeTopic** and **Referee**, on the other). REFEREES contains the common attribute arc (**RefereeTopic, Referee**) showing that the closure of the **RefereeTopic** relation includes the closure of the **Referee** relation, that is a tuple of the **RefereeTopic** relation identifies one and only one tuple of the **Referee** relation. We also notice that the **RefereeTopic, PaperTopic** and **Author** relations are join components. With the exception of the relation **Referee** which has two keys (RefereeName and RefereeNickName), all relations have a unique key.

The underlying principle of semantic models is to provide concepts that are powerful enough to yield the closest possible specification of a real-world situation. The URI model is more powerful than most Entity-Relationship models because of its underlying UR assumption and IDs [Andraws 91]. It provides the framework for bringing together OO data model composition and inheritance, relational database key and referential dependency, and most Entity-Relationship model extensions. It is used in this article to calculate (and visualize) the semantic relationships between tables based on common attributes and IDs.

3 FROM NSG TO COMPLETE QUERY GRAPH

In this section we examine more closely the idea floated and experimented upon by [Wu 86] concerning the formulation of queries: instead of using a pure relational database scheme (or set of relations without links), we construct a query medium defined by the data semantics.

Of course URITalk vizualizes the explicit binary links of NSG (its common attribute arcs) and the inclusion arcs between relations easily deduced from its inclusion arcs $L \subseteq_{\alpha} R$ between PURs (case of two PURs having either only one relation intersecting L or R, or a relation functionally equivalent to L or R). The graph thus obtained is called the ***relation-to-relation NSG***: it is a kind of partial graph of the NSG, but a graph between relations and consisting only of arcs of the NSG, making it easier to identify relations to be joined.

An area in which URITalk innovates is that it completes the relation-to-relation NSG with edges:

- which are common attributes not represented by common attribute arcs, or
- which are implicit because they are represented in NSG by n-ary IDs with n>2 or binary IDs concerning more than two relations, or
- which result from compatibility, or
- which are transitive links (for instance, Appendix 3, the two inclusion arcs JudgedPaper $\subseteq_7$ Paper).

We examine in this section how to construct the ***complete query graph*** (with all the possible table-to-table relationships) from the basic relation-to-relation NSG. The expression of join conditions for users becomes simply a matter of selecting the appropriate links. In the next section, we will see that the complete query graph is not visualized in its wholeness, but through the evolving query graph.

3.1 Common attribute edges

We have seen in 2.2 that the NSG visualizes common attribute arcs. However it does not visualize all the possible joins implied by common attributes. For instance the **Author** and **PaperTopic** relations of Figure 2-a have the common attribute Paper. Yet, the many-many relationship between them resulting from the common attribute is not visually represented on the semantic graph. The common attribute edge between **Author** and **PaperTopic** (see Figure 2-b) is the medium of the natural join between the two relations and is part of the complete query graph.

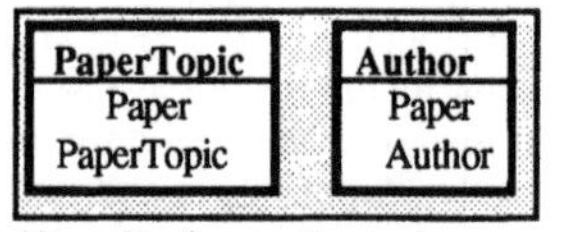

(a) *Normalized semantic graph (extracted from the NSG in Appendix 1)*

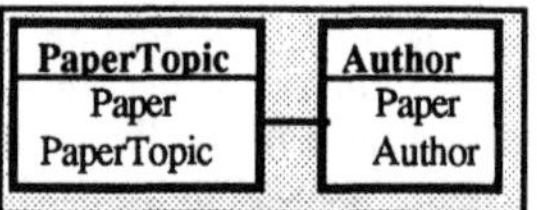

(b) *Normalized semantic graph with common attribute edge*

Figure 2 Common attribute edge.

3.2 Representation of an inclusion hyperarc with relation-to-relation arcs

We will explain this representation in three steps:

a) From an inclusion arc on the UR to an inclusion hyperarc between PURs

Generally speaking, IDs are defined on the UR (see Figure 3-a). However, given that an attribute cannot belong to more than one PUR, it is easier to understand the representation of an ID between semantic graph PURs. For example, the inclusion dependency:

TestPilot Prototype $\subseteq_1$ Driver Car

is easier to visualize in Figure 3-b than in Figure 3-a. An ID L $\subseteq_\alpha$ R will be represented by a hyperarc whose origins are PURs having an intersection that is not empty with L, and whose extremities are PURs having an intersection not empty with R. Let us emphasize that a PUR can be both origin and extremity of a hyperarc.

b) From an inclusion hyperarc between PURs to an inclusion hyperarc between relations

Because relational DBMS do not implement the PUR concept, we need to represent IDs between relations to be able to use the links resulting from the IDs as possible join paths between relations.

Figure 3-c illustrates this representation in the form of an inclusion hyperarc between relations. Each ID between PUR: L $\subseteq_\alpha$ R (from the set of the source PURs of α $\mathbf{P}_{URl}$ to the set of the terminal PURs of α $\mathbf{P}_{URr}$) can be represented by an ***inclusion hyperarc between relations***, from the relations $\mathbf{R}_{lk}(U_{lk})$ belonging to a PUR $\mathbf{P}_{URl}$ and having the not empty intersection ($U_{lk} \cap L$) with L, to the relations $\mathbf{R}_{rm}(U_{rm})$ belonging to a PUR $\mathbf{P}_{URr}$ and having the not empty intersection ($U_{rm} \cap R$) with R. In this way we obtain a NSG represented with only relations $\mathbf{R}_i(\underline{K}_1\ \underline{K}_2 \ldots \underline{K}_n$ Remainder) defined Section 2 and each hyperarc is a common attribute arc or an inclusion hyperarc defined between relations. We shall be using the term ***NSG between relations*** to designate this representation of NSG in the rest of this paper.

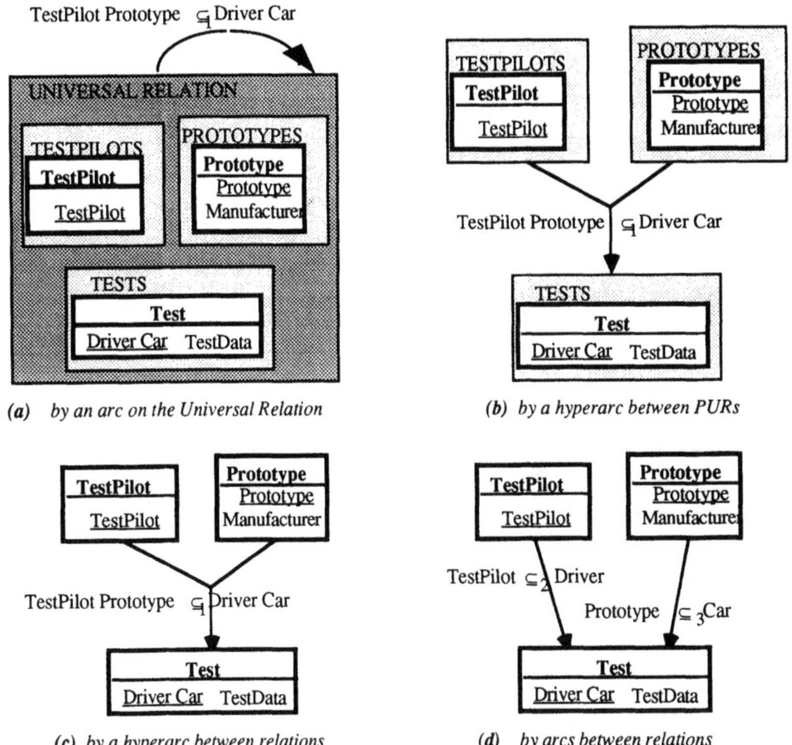

Figure 3 ID representations.

c) From an inclusion hyperarc between relations to a set of relation-to-relation inclusion arcs

If the representation of an ID by a hyperarc between relations is semantically equivalent to its definition between PURs, it does not bring out the relation-to-relation connections implied and so does not assist the user. Before specifying them, let us introduce the notations we shall be using: given an ID $L \subseteq_\alpha R$ and L' a sub-sequence of L, $\Pi_\alpha(G')$ refers to the subset of R corresponding to the subset L'. In the same way, $\Pi_{-\alpha}(R')$ is the sub-sequence of L corresponding through α to the sub-sequence R' of R. For example, given the ID ABCEF $\subseteq_1$ HIJKM, and the set X = BCFIMN, we then obtain:

$$X \cap L = BCF \text{ et } \Pi_1(X \cap L) = IJM,$$
$$X \cap R = IM \text{ et } \Pi_{-1}(X \cap R) = BF.$$

Any ID $L \subseteq_\alpha R$ from the PUR $\mathbf{P}_{URl}(U_l)$ to the PUR $\mathbf{P}_{URr}(U_j)$, or hyperarc from the relations $\mathbf{R}_{lk}(U_{lk})$ to the relations $\mathbf{R}_{rm}(U_{rm})$, is represented for querying by the set of relation-to-relation inclusion arcs obtained by:

For all relation $\mathbf{R}_{lk}(U_{lk})$ of $\mathbf{P}_{URl}(U_l)$ such that $(L \cap U_{lk}) \neq \phi$ do

For all relation $\mathbf{R}_{rm}(U_{rm})$ of $\mathbf{P}_{URr}(U_r)$ such that $(R \cap U_{rm}) \neq \phi$ do

If $R' = \Pi_\alpha[L \cap U_{lk}] \cap U_{rm} \neq \phi$ then

Create the inclusion arc $\Pi_{-\alpha}(R') \subseteq_{\alpha lkrm} R'$ of $\mathbf{R}_{lk}(U_{lk})$ to $\mathbf{R}_{rm}(U_{rm})$.

For example, the ID of Figures 3-a, b and c is represented by the two relation-to-relation inclusion arcs shown in Figure 3-d.

The representation of an ID by a set of relation-to-relation inclusion arcs is enough for querying tables but it degrades the semantics of the original ID. This is why updating operations entails checking data consistency by calculating joins in addition to checking relation-to-relation inclusion arcs [Fallouh 91].

3.3 Edges of compatible attributes

The concept of ID $A \subseteq_\alpha B$ generalizes the concept of common attribute. We can go ahead and generalize the inclusion dependency: two attributes are said to be *compatible* if their domains (or the set of all possible values) are not disjoint and if they are "semantically close". For example, knowing that sometimes workers decide to go on further studies and that students are sometimes engaged in paid employments, we can say that StudentName and EmployeeName are compatible. On the contrary, the attributes PersonName and PlaceOfBirth are, *a priori*, not compatible even if it is possible for someone to be known as Paris. However, if we are working on the etymology of names, then PersonName and PlaceOfBirth will be compatible attributes.

A *compatibility relation* Ai ⇔ Aj defined on all the attributes of the database scheme is an *equivalence relation.* Such a relation therefore defines a partition of the attributes of the database scheme into equivalence classes or *compatibility classes.*

There may be several compatibility relations on the attributes. It is also possible to define a compatibility relation between the compatibility classes, that is, create more encompassing compatibility classes from the basic compatibility classes. Consider for example the following relations:

$\mathbf{R}_1$(<u>Person</u> Name Passion)
$\mathbf{R}_2$(Person Occupation)
$\mathbf{R}_3$(<u>Student</u> Job Hobby)
$\mathbf{R}_4$(Secretary Duty)
$\mathbf{R}_5$(<u>CivilServant</u> Function).

All the attributes of these relations can be partitioned into four compatibility classes:

C_1 = {Person, Student, CivilServant, Secretary}
C_2 = {Hobby, Passion}
C_3 = {Occupation, Job, Duty, Function}
C_4 = {Name}.

If we take the ID Student $\subseteq_1$ Person, CivilServant $\subseteq_2$ Person, Secretary $\subseteq_3$ Person, the class C_1 of compatible attributes coincides with the set of all the attributes of the same rank in an ID. Generally speaking, the common attribute relation defined on all occurrences of the attributes of a database scheme is more discriminating than the inclusion relation between attributes, which in turn is more discriminating than the attribute compatibility relation, which is also more discriminating than the relation ensuing from the fact that two attributes are of the same type (see Figure 4-a). For the class C_2, a passion, for example music, can be a hobby, etc. Compatibility classes C_2 and C_3 can be grouped together in a second-order class to give a compatibility class C_{23} comprising the join possibilities defined by C_2 and C_3. The visual interface may be consulted in the restricted compatibility relation or in the extended form.

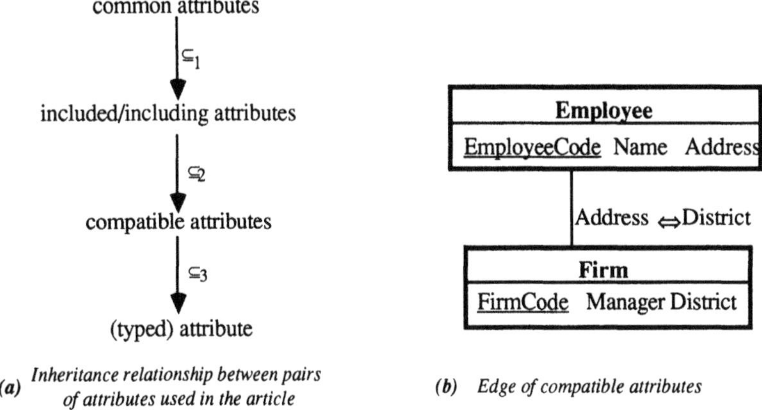

(a) Inheritance relationship between pairs of attributes used in the article *(b) Edge of compatible attributes*

Figure 4 Compatible attributes.

An edge of compatible attributes links two tables with compatible attributes: such an edge visualizes a possible join between the two tables. For example, Figure 4-b shows the edge of compatible attributes (Address ⇔ District) for retrieving the names of employees who come from the same town as a certain firm.

4 EVOLVING QUERY AND QUERY GRAPHS

The complete query graph developed in the preceding section will in complex cases be like a spider's web. That is why URITalk displays only a partial graph, the *evolving query graph.*

4.1 Links contiguous to a node in the evolving query graph

The nodes of the evolving query graph are those of the relation-to-relation NSG, and its arcs are those of the relation-to-relation NSG plus, for a node designated by the user, the contiguous links of the complete query graph. The mechanism of navigating through and displaying new links in the evolving query graph is simple. The user moves from one node to another by pointing to the destination node. For a given designated node, the ***evolving query graph*** visualizes, with the relation-to-relation NSG as background, the complete query graph links that have this node as one of their extremities. The user selects some of these links with the result that they become incorporated in the ***query graph***. Thereafter, he designates another node of the evolving query graph: the contiguous links of the complete query graph are in turn displayed whereas the contiguous links of the first node not belonging to the relation-to-relation NSG or to the query graph disappear from the query window (see the illustration in 5.3).

4.2 Extension of the query graph to autojoins, nested joins and group operators

The query graph greatly facilitates the user's task of specifying the joins of different tables. However, the definition of the join of a table by using the same table (*autojoin*) requires the duplication of the table [Ramos 91] and the creation of links between the two [Wong 76]. The formulation of a sub-query or a query linked to another query by UNION, INTERSECT or

MINUS group operator is done in an auxiliary window for duplicating evolving query graph and query graph.

Figure 5 shows the different graphs considered in the article.

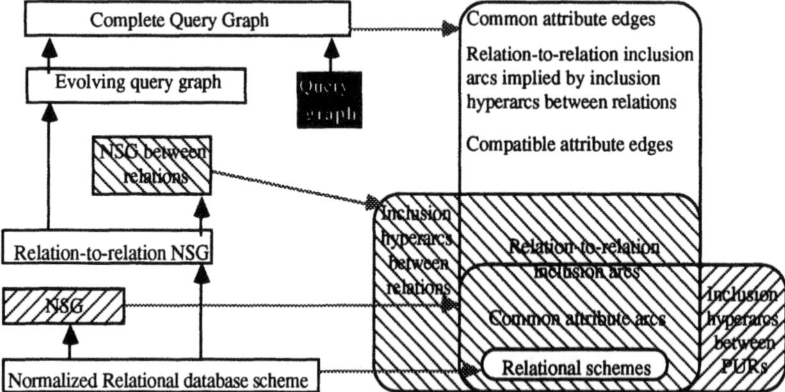

Figure 5 The different graphs considered in the article, ordered by the partial subgraph relation ↑, their nodes and links.

5 DESCRIPTION OF URITalk INTERFACE

The URITalk interface facilitates the formal and visual conception of the database scheme as well as the graphical querying of the database. It was developed in the object-oriented environment GraphTalk® [Jeulin 88] for software engineering workshop development.

5.1 The conception of the database scheme

The conception of the database scheme from functional dependencies, join components and inclusion dependencies is done with the help of the LACSI package [Roche 90]. The software package has two modules:

- a specification interface for entering and modifying FDs and JCs in a "Functional-Dependencies" window, and IDs in an "InclusionDependencies" window,
- a normalization module for fine-tuning the normalization (extended to ID) of the specification. It produces a NSG (for example, the figure in Appendix 1)

Each relation is an object represented by a rectangle named after the relation. The relation rectangle (see Figure 6) has a pull-down menu for performing the following tasks:

- *displaying* or *hide*-ing the rectangles representing keys and attributes of the relation that do not belong to a key,
- *contiguity* for searching for links that are contiguous to the relation (this operation can also be carried out by double-clicking above the relation icon),
- *rename*-ing the relation.

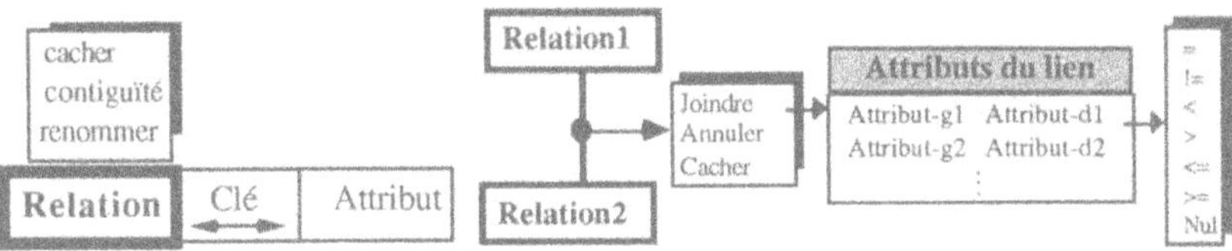

Figure 6 Relation icon. **Figure 7** Link icon.

Each ID link also has a pull-down menu which, aside from permitting the management of the graphical representation, facilitates the definition of a join condition on all the pairs of attributes of the same rank associated with the link. The "Null" option of the comparator menu, selected for a line in the list, enables the exclusion of a pair of attributes of the join condition. The "Undo" item is for undoing the join operation associated with a link. Finally, the "Hide" item in the menu hides a link that belongs to the evolving query graph without belonging to the relation-to-relation NSG. This has the effect of augmenting the readability of the scheme.

5.2 The graphical query screen

The interface has one main window:

- the **query window**, which displays three superimposed graphs with different shades:
  . the *relation-to-relation NSG* is bright and fixed, in the background to guide the user,
  . the *evolving query graph* is less bright, contains in addition to the first graph (the same nodes and arcs) all the binary links between a node selected for query and the other nodes,
  . the *query graph* under development, which is in reverse video.

  The window has a selection bar which, in addition to the traditional *File* and *Edit* menus, contains:
  1. the *Query* menu, used for choosing the type of query to be made on the query graph (default query, insert, modify, delete). To make an insert operation, the user simply designates the appropriate relation and the corresponding edit window is displayed. In the same vein, to delete or update, the user simply designates the relation concerned and enters a selection condition. The menu has the following three sub-menus:
     . Condition: for specifying a condition in WHERE or HAVING clauses or UPDATE or DELETE commands in a new query window,
     . Set operator: for formulating queries involving the three operators,
     . Execute: generates the SQL code and, if it is coupled with a DBMS, executes the query thus generated.
  2. the *Help* menu.

  The interface comes with three other windows:

- the **attribute window** for displaying all the attributes of the database scheme,
- the **SQL code window** for displaying the corresponding SQL code of the visual query formulated,
- the **result window** for displaying the result of the executed query.

5.3 Illustration

Let us use the NSG in Appendix 1 to show how to formulate the following query: "find the addresses of possible readers of the papers written by John". The user will proceed thus:

The initial screen contains the relation-to-relation NSG (Appendix 2).

The user designates the projected attributes: **RefereeName** in either **RefereeTopic** or **Referee** (see Appendix 4), RefereeAddress in the relation **Referee**. To establish the selection condition Author = 'John', the user carries out the following actions:

- double-clicks on the attribute Author of the **Author** relation and the pull-down menu associated with this attribute is displayed,
- chooses the *Selection* option in the menu,
- (implicit) chooses the comparator "=",
- (implicit) chooses the option "value to be entered",
- enters the value 'John' in the open edit box.

In order to formulate the join predicates, assuming the user has selected the **RefereeTopic** relation, the user double-clicks above its icon. The system will, in response, display the contiguous links with **RefereeTopic** (that have not yet been displayed) of the complete query graph, in this case the two inclusion arcs:

Evaluation.EvalRefereeName $\subseteq_2$ **RefereeTopic**.RefereeName,
Distribution.DisRefereeName $\subseteq_4$ **RefereeTopic**.RefereeName.

Double-clicking on the common attribute arc RefereeName from **RefereeTopic** to **Referee**, causes it to belong to the query graph, that is, specifies the natural join predicate:

Referee.RefereeName = **RefereeTopic**.RefereeName.

In the same vein, double-clicking on the arc of the ID PaperTopic $\subseteq_6$ RefereeTopic specifies the equijoin condition:

PaperTopic.PaperTopic = **RefereeTopic**.RefereeTopic.

Next the user selects the **PaperTopic** relation (see Appendix 5) and the **RefereeTopic** relation is unselected and IDs 2 and 4 not belonging to relation-to-relation NSG disappear. The contiguous links with **PaperTopic** of the complete query graph appear: IDs 3, 5, and 7, the common attribute edge between **PaperTopic** and **Author**. Double-clicking on the last line specifies the natural join of **PaperTopic** and **Author**. The query graph appears in bold on the display.

6 CONCLUSION

The normalized semantic graph of the URI model is a bold attempt to assist the user in database designing and querying: it is automatically constructed and represents much of the database semantics in a condensed and evocative visual form. However, it graphically details only part of the common attributes. It also represents ID in a condensed form (between PURs) but, *a priori*, not in a relation-to-relation representation. It does not use transitive arcs and compatibility edges. For being of the greatest assistance possible to the user in the formulation of a query, so that he only has to select already displayed links, we showed how to obtain the complete query graph made up of all the possible join links between tables. Yet the URITalk interface remains user-friendly despite the large number of possible joins because it displays them only when necessary, at the request of the user.

Further work is necessary

- to see if the relation-to-relation NSG cannot be enriched and made to draw more from the NSG without losing its evocativeness, if the complete query graph cannot shed some of its transitive arcs without losing its power or if it can be partially implemented by extended inheritance,

- to validate the usability of URITalk interface such as [Cartaci 95],
- to extend to more complex queries [Klein 95] but always constructed from the normalized semantic graph.

In conclusion, we would like to emphasize that an interface such as the one proposed in the present paper is also a prototyping tool. It also can be used to compare the hypertext approach [Conklin 87] [Nielsen 90] with declarative approaches in matters of database querying as well as to enhance database administration.

We thank Claude Boksenbaum, Thérèse Libourel and Uzoma Chukwu for their attentive comments.

7 REFERENCES

Andonoff E., Mendiboure C., Morin C., Rougier V., Zurfluh G. (1992) Une interface graphique pour l'interrogation d'une base de données orientée objet. *VIIIème Journées Bases de Données Avancées*, Tregastel, INRIA Ed, 258-276.

Andraws A., Pichat E. (1991) EAPlus ou l'introduction de rôles dans le modèle Entité-Association. *Journées Bases de Données Avancées*, Lyon, INRIA Ed, 93-111.

Atzeni P., Chan E. P. F. (1987) Independent database schemes under functional and inclusion dependencies. *Proceedings of the 13th VLDB Conference*, Brighton, 159-166.

Auddino A., Dennebouy Y., Dupont Y., Fontana E., Spaccapietra S., Tari Z. (1992) SUPER : A Comprehensive Approach to DBMS Visual User Interfaces. *Actes du 1er séminaire sur les BD 91*, Alger, 341-364.

Cartaci T., Santucci G. (1995) Diagrammatic Vs Textual Query Languages: A Comparative Experiment, in *Proceedings of the 3rd IFIP 2.6 Conference on Visual Database Systems* (ed. S. Spaccapietra and R. Jain), Chapman & Hall.

Casanova M. A., Fagin R., Papadimitriou C. H. (1984) Inclusion dependencies and their interaction with functional dependencies. *Journal of Computer and System Sciences*, **28**, 29-59.

Codd E. F. (1970) A relational model of data for large shared data banks. *Comm. ACM*, **13**, 6, 377-387.

Conklin J. (1987) Hypertext : An Introduction and Survey. *Computer*, September, 16-41.

Fallouh F., Pichat E., Saker D. (1991) Le contrôle de l'intégrité référentielle et de dépendances d'inclusion. *Actes de congrés INFORSID*, Paris, 273-291.

Fallouh F. (1994) Données complexes et Relation Universelle avec Inclusions : une aide à la conception et à l'interrogation des bases de données. *Thèse de Doctorat*, Université Lyon 1.

Goldman K.J., Goldman S.A., Kanellakis P.C., Zdonik S.B. (1985) ISIS: Interface for a Semantic Information System. *ACM*, 0-89791, 328-342.

Heuser C.A., Peres E.M., Richter G. (1993) Towards a complete conceptual model: Petri nets and Entity-Relationship diagrams. *Information Systems*, **18**, 5, 275-298.

IBM (1981) SQL/Data System: Concepts and Facilities. GH-24-5013-0, IBM corporation, White Plains, NY.

Kari S., Kangassalo H., Pösö J. (1990) Conceptual Query Language - CQL: a visual user interface to application data bases. IOS Press, Amsterdam, 608-623.

Klein H.- J., Krämer D. (1995) NQS - A Graphical Query System for Data Models with Binary Relationship Types, in *Proceedings of the 3rd IFIP 2.6 Conference on Visual Database Systems* (ed. S. Spaccapietra and R. Jain), Chapman & Hall.

Kuntz M. (1990) Description et évaluation de Pasta-3, une interface graphique manipulation directe aux bases de données avancées. *Journées Bases de Données Avancées*, Montpellier, INRIA Ed, 123-140.

Lafaye M.-C. (1982) Outil d'aide à la conception des bases de données relationnelles ou réseau (Multigraphe de projection). *Thèse de 3ème cycle Informatique*, Université de Rennes I.

Lakhal L. (1986) Contribution à l'étude des interfaces pour non-informaticien dans la manipulation directe aux bases de données avancées. *Thèse de doctorat*, Université de Nice.

Maier D. (1983) The theory of Relational Databases. Computer Science Press, Potomac, Md.

Mannila H., Räihä K.-J. (1986) Inclusion dependencies in database design. *Int. Conf. In Data Engineering*, Los Angeles, 713-718.

McDonald N.H. (1975) CUPID : a graphics oriented facility for support of non-programmer interactions with a data base. Memorandum M563, University of California, Berkeley.

Melton J., Simon A. (1993) Understanding the new SQL; A complete guide. Morgan Kaufmann.

Mitchell J.C. (1983) The Implication problem for functional and inclusion dependencies. *Information and control*, **56**, 154-173.

Nanard J. (1990) La manipulation directe en interface homme-machine. *Thèse de doctorat d'Etat*, Université Sciences et Techniques du Languedoc, Montpellier.

Nielsen J. (1990) The art of navigating through HYPERTEXT. *Communications of the ACM*, **33**, 3, 297-310.

Olle T.W., Sol H.G., Verrijn-Stuart A.A. (ed.) (1982) Information systems design methodologies. A comparative Review. *Proceedings of the IFIP WG 8.1 Working Conference*, Noordwijkirhout, the Netherlands, 10-14 May, North-Holland.

Pichat E., Bodin R. (1990) Ingénierie des données. Masson.

Pichat E., Roche A. (1989) Extension de la normalisation aux dépendances d'inclusions. *Actes du Congrès INFORSID 89*, Nancy, 57-77.

Ramos H. (1991) IQL : Interface Graphique Paramétrable pour les requêtes relationnelles. *Actes du 1er séminaire sur les BD 91*, Alger, 365-385.

Jeulin P. (1988) GraphTalk : environnement objets de développement et d'utilisation d'ateliers de génie logiciel. Rank Xerox France, 1988.

Reisner P. (1981) Human factors studies of DataBase Query Languages, a survey and assessment. *Computing Surveys*, **13**, 1, 1981.

Roche A. (1990) Définition et réalisation d'un logiciel d'aide à la conception de systemes d'information. *Thèse de Doctorat*, Université de Montpellier II.

Saker D. (1993) L'interrogation des bases de données relationnelles assistée par le Graphe Sémantique Normalisé. *Thèse de Doctorat*, Université Lyon 1.

Schneiderman B. (1983) Direct manipulation, a step beyond programming language. *IEEE computer*, **16**, 8.

Trepied C., Schneider M. (1989) Candid : un modèle sémantique et un langage d'interrogation gaphique pour l'utilisateur final. *INFORSID 89*, Nancy, 183-201.

Ullman J. D. (1989) Principles of Database and Knowledge-Base Systems. Volume I & II, Computer Science Press.

Wong E. , Youssefi K. (1976) Decomposition strategy for query processing. *ACM Trans. on Database Systems*, **1**, 3, 223-241.

Wu C. T. (1986) A New Graphics User Interface for Accessing a Database. *Proceedings Conference on Advanced Computer Graphics*, Tokyo, Springer Verlag, 203-218.

Wu C. T., Hsiao D. K. (1989) Implementation of visual database interface using an object-oriented langage. *Visual Database Systems*, T. L. Kunii (Editor), Elsevier, IFIP, 105-125.

Zloof M. (1977) Query By Example : a database language. *IBM systems journal*, **16**, 1977, 324-343.

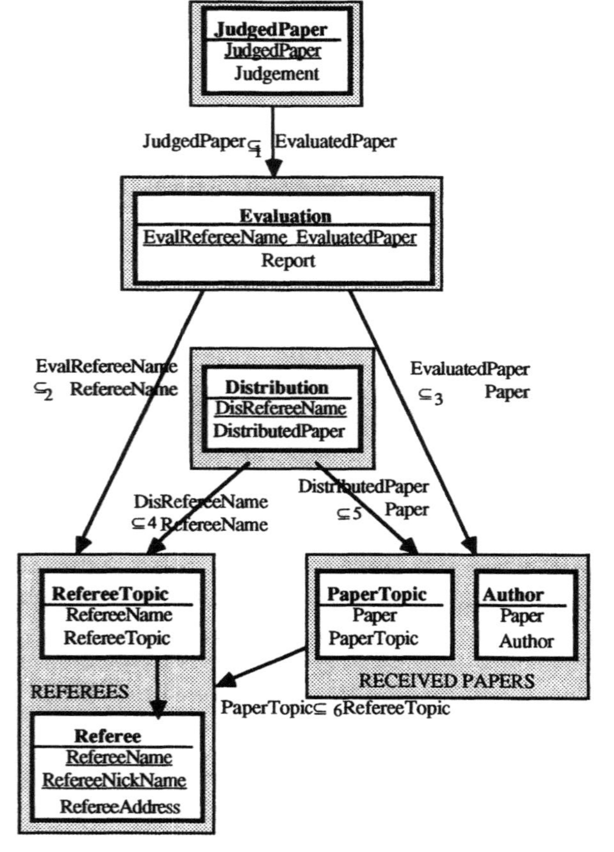

Appendix 1 Normalized Semantic Graph.

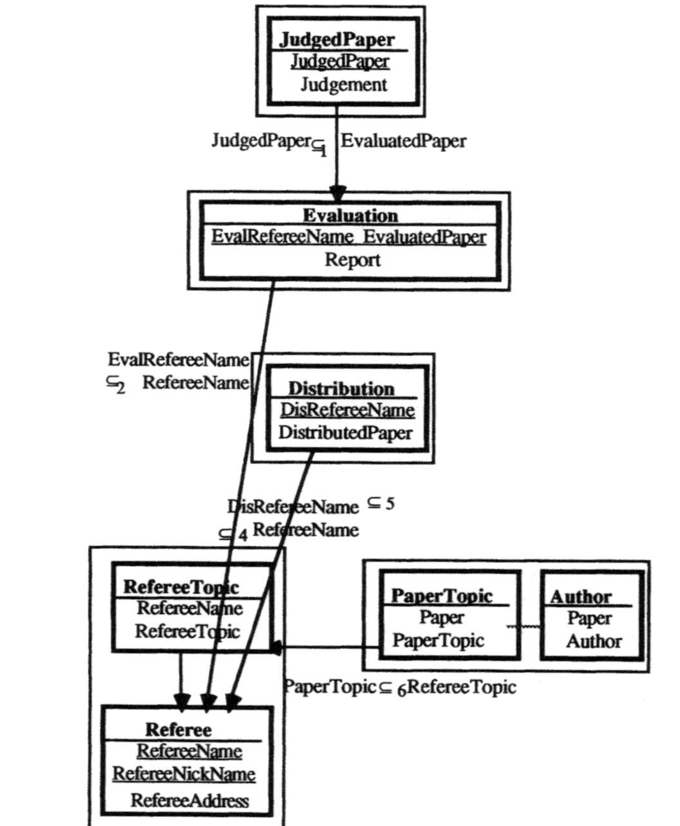

Appendix 2 Relation-to-relation NSG.

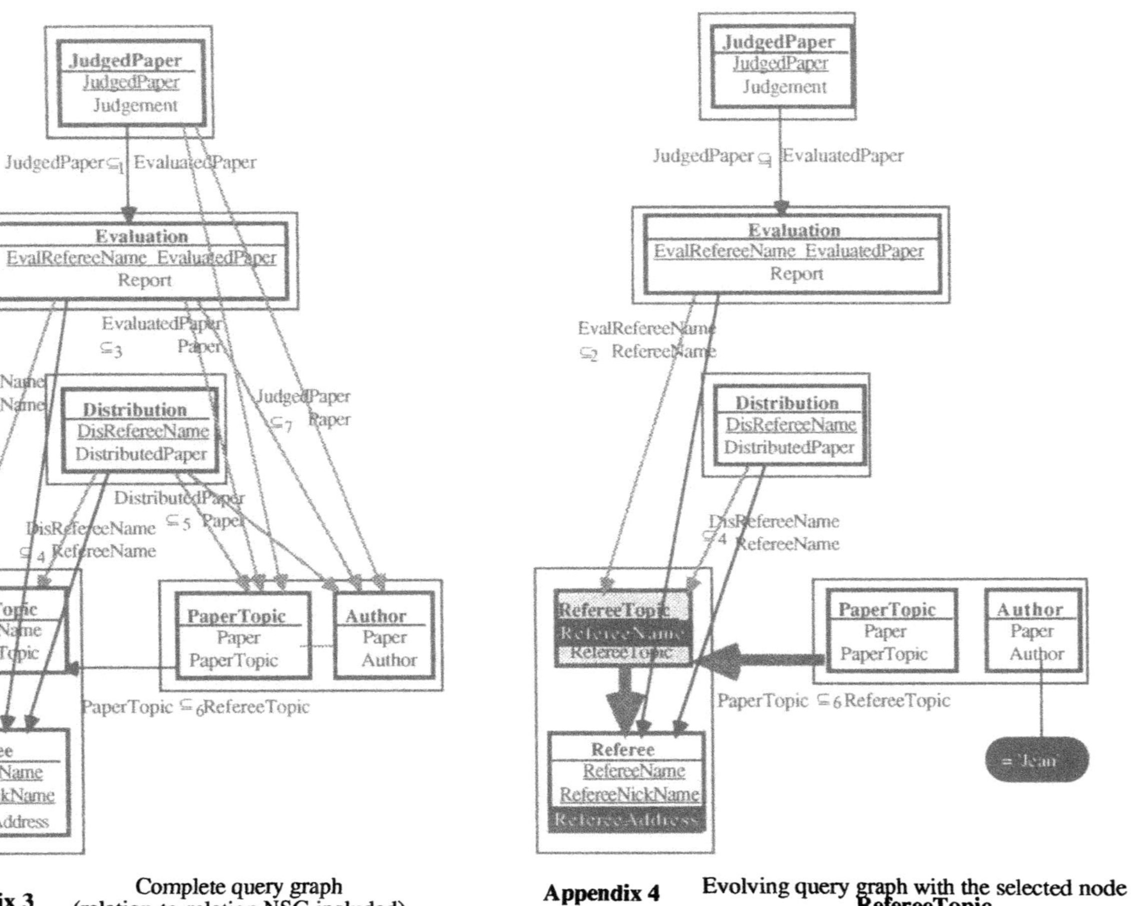

Appendix 3 Complete query graph (relation-to-relation NSG included).

Appendix 4 Evolving query graph with the selected node **RefereeTopic.**

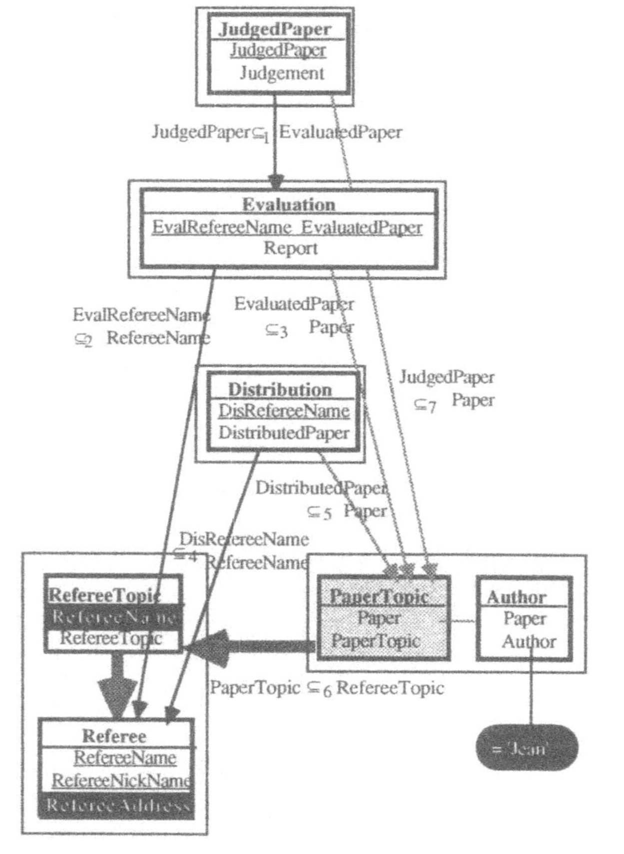

Appendix 5 Evolving query graph with the selected node **PaperTopic.**

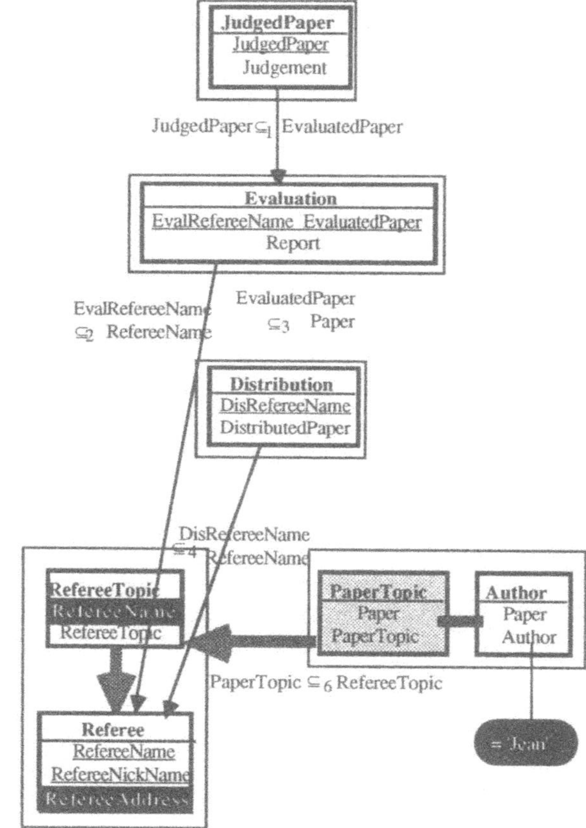

Appendix 6 Query graph (and relation-to-relation NSG).

Etienne Pichat

Etienne Pichat received the Engineer Diploma in 1963 from the Ecole Centrale des Arts et Manufactures, Paris and the D. Sc Degree in 1970 from the IMAG Institute, University of Grenoble. He is currently a professor of Computer Science at Lyon 1-Claude Bernard University. He has published papers and books in finite order sets, databases and data models.

Dib Saker

Dib Saker received the Engineer Diploma in 1987 from ISSAT, Damas and the Ph.D. degree in Computer Science from Lyon 1 University in 1992. Currently he is a member of the technical staff at Nat Systems, Paris. His main research interests are in database interfaces and distributed databases.

25

NQS - a graphical query system for data models with binary relationship types

H.-J. Klein[1], *D. Krämer*[2]
[1]*Institut für Informatik und Praktische Mathematik*
[2]*Rechenzentrum der Universität*
Universität Kiel, Olshausenstr. 40, 24098 Kiel, Germany

Abstract

A graphical query system for data models with binary relationship types is described in which queries can be formulated as annotated graphs. The concepts of the underlying descriptive query language allow to represent even complex queries in a graphical form that is easy to understand. Identifiers with local scope and the possibility to build queries in a step by step manner help to avoid problems sometimes mentioned in connection with the formulation of complex queries in descriptive query languages. Query formulation is supported by comfortable operations on graphs and by an efficient layout algorithm.

Keywords

Entity-Relationship data model, graphical user interface, visual query language, query graphs, schema layout algorithm

1 INTRODUCTION

There are numerous proposals in the literature for query interfaces applying graphics with the intention to make the interactive access to databases more comfortable for the expert and less difficult for the casual user. Among the first such proposals are QbE (Zloof (1975)), CUPID (Mc Donald (1975)), and TIMBER (Stonebraker (1982)) for the relational data model. Most graphical query systems, however, have been developed for data models which allow to model relationships between objects explicitly by named relationship types. The explicit representation of relationship types allows to visualize schemas in diagrammatic form such that complex schemas are better to understand than relational schemas where relationships are modelled by identical values in attributes having the same domain. For the basic Entity-Relationship (ER) data model and extensions of the model, graphical query systems have been described for example in Wong (1982), Zhang (1983), Elmasri (1985), Burns (1988), Kuntz (1989), and Angelaccio (1990); proposals for other data models can be found in King (1984), Mark (1989), Lam (1990), and ACM (1992).

The term 'graphical' is used for a wide spectrum of query interfaces with quite different characteristics. On one side of this spectrum there are 'procedural' facilities which allow to browse through databases at the level of schema/state diagrams by typing in commands or by using the mouse (e.g.: Burns (1988), Rogers (1988)). On the other side there are 'descriptive' query systems and proposals of 'descriptive' query languages which allow to specify queries more or less completely as annotated graphs derived from schema diagrams (e.g.: Bryce (1986), Kim (1988), Czejdo (1990), Lam (1990), Mohan (1993)). Grouped between these two classes of query interfaces there are facilities where queries are formulated as a combination of some portion of the schema diagram (eventually with modifications) and text at different locations of the screen (e.g.: Wong (1982), Burns (1988)). Further remarks on the use of the term 'graphical' in connection with query interfaces can be found in Kuntz (1989).

For many graphical query interfaces, there is no underlying query language given; thus, query semantics has to be defined procedurally based on the graphical operations of the interface. In NQS the result of each graphical query specification accepted by the system is an annotated query graph which corresponds uniquely (up to equivalence) to a textual query of the query language NQL (Network Query Language, Klein (1989)). Since semantics of NQL is formally defined, formal semantics is provided for the interface, too. The reference to a textual query language does not mean that the graphical specification of a query in NQS is guided by its textual counterpart (as, for example, in Lam (1990)) or that the user has to memorize the exact syntax of NQL. Query graphs may rather be constructed under guidance of NQS in any reasonable order.

NQL has been proposed as a high level descriptive query language for the CODASYL data model. However, the language can be used as query language for all data models with simple object types and binary relationship types because it does not refer to special features of the CODASYL data model such as the restriction of binary relationships to 1 to n relationships or the ordering of members in (CODASYL) sets.

In descriptive languages, queries are formulated with the help of predicates on the level of database schemas. This kind of query formulation may be characterized as 'logical' navigation in order to distinguish it from navigation on the level of objects in procedural languages. Predicates on the level of database schemas must allow to address all kinds of relationships between objects. For data models with explicit relationship types this means that predicate forms have to be available for explicit relationships as well as for value-based relationships and combinations of both kinds of relationships.

There are a number of descriptive languages proposed for the ER data model and other data models with explicit relationship types (e.g.: Deheneffe (1976), Markowitz (1983), Subieta (1987), Mohan (1993)). The main difference between NQL and these proposals is the form in which language constructs are adapted to the idea of logical navigation. Complex relationships between objects can be addressed in NQL by Boolean expressions over paths with relationship types and object types as elements. There are no variables referencing objects or values of objects in the language but the identifiers of object types are used with local scope instead. This use of identifiers conforms well to the idea of logical navigation. Predicate forms provided for the different kinds of relationships allow to express quantification in such a way that queries often look like English sentences (there is some similarity in this regard with ILL (Lacroix (1977)), a domain-oriented query language for the relational data model). Complex queries can be formulated in a series of steps with seperation of the specification of the target list from parts where quantifiers are needed.

The concepts underlying NQL make this language a suitable candidate as reference language for a query interface with queries represented completely as graphs and with emphasis on both the readability of query specifications and the ease of interpretation. The features of this interface help to avoid problems with the formulation of complex queries in descriptive languages reported in Welty (1981) and Hansen (1987).

A query graph is generated in NQS by modification of a diagram which is automatically produced from the textual description of a given schema. Among the possible modifications are the addition of new nodes and edges as well as the deletion of existing ones. In order not to upset the user by layouts changing drastically, NQS keeps the relative positioning of object types in the initial diagram during all stages of query formulation.

The rest of the paper is organized as follows. In the next section, a brief description of the visualization of schemas and query graphs in NQS is given. The third section demonstrates with several examples how queries are specified in NQS and how query graphs have to be interpreted. Some comments on experiences with NQS follow. The final section contains some technical details of the system and describes future directions of its development.

2 Drawing of Schema Diagrams and Query Graphs

The specification of queries as annotated graphs derived from schema diagrams should be fully supported by the query system. This especially means that a user has not to deal with the placement or rearrangement of graphical objects. A second demand is that during query formulation the layout of schema components must not change drastically, i.e. familiarity with the visual representation of the schema (relative positioning) has to be preserved. A third feature is the readability of query graphs. The number of different types of graphical symbols should not be too large. Last but not least efficiency has to be guaranteed during all steps of query formulation.

There are a number of layout algorithms for schema diagrams (see Tamassia (1988), Paulisch (1993)). In NQS we make use of the efficient embedding algorithm for planar graphs given in Chiba (1985). This algorithm is based on an algorithm of Booth (1976) which improved the planarity testing algorithm of Lempel (1967) by introducing a data structure called a PQ-tree and by employing an efficient st-numbering algorithm (Even (1976)). It is easy to implement and the PQ-tree data structure has the nice property to allow a simple realization of high-level functions for the generation of different embeddings. Thus, the algorithm is very attractive for the interactive manipulation of schema layouts. Such a layout manipulation under user control may become advantageous in NQS especially after the insertion of new schema elements.

Graph algorithms can be applied to schema diagrams for data models with binary relationship types in a straightforward manner by identifying object types with the nodes of a graph and relationship types with its edges. Schema diagrams considered as graphs in this way are often seperable graphs with many biconnected blocks (e.g.: the diagram in

Figure 1 has 5 blocks). The algorithm of Chiba (1985) supposes graphs to be nonseperable. However, it is not difficult to extend this algorithm such that it can be applied in a single step to seperable graphs without loss of efficiency (linear time complexity).

Schema diagrams are also often nonplanar. When running into situations which are in conflict with planarity, an appropriate alteration of the PQ-tree data structure allows to continue with the algorithm such that it is possible to find embeddings of nonplanar graphs, too. The result of the embedding algorithm modified so far is an ordered adjacency list for each node together with an extended st-numbering and information on the connectedness of the graph.

Given this result, different algorithms can be used to generate an appropriate drawing of the schema diagram. What has to be considered is that nodes of a schema diagram may be quite different in size if information like attributes or conditions is shown within the node and not hidden in pop-up's. In NQS, a simple algorithm produces the diagram in a tree-like manner with depth-first recursion controlled by the extended st-numbering. If there are crossing edges because of nonplanarity, they are drawn in such a way that no misleading layout results.

Our layout algorithm takes as input the textual description of a complete CODASYL database schema or of an ER schema which can be generated interactively. Figure 1 presents a schema diagram drawn by this algorithm. The algorithm can also be applied to draw query graphs in a way which preserves visual familiarity with the schema diagram: the drawing of a query graph is done in the same manner as the drawing of the schema diagram with missing nodes having no size, i.e. consuming no place. Additional nodes produced by duplication of existing nodes or by the insertion of user-defined object types (see below) are placed next to their source node.

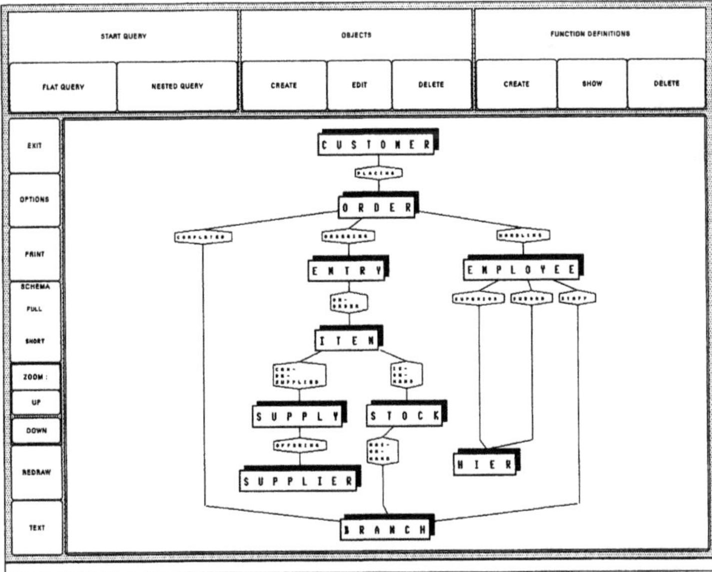

Figure 1 NQS interface with a schema diagram drawn by the embedding algorithm

3 QUERY FORMULATION

Query formulation in NQS means transformation of a given schema diagram into a query graph by use of graphical functions and by entering some text, if necessary. A graph is accepted by the system as a correct query graph if it represents a query of the textual query language NQL. Query graphs are also used for the specification of user-defined object types and for the definition of function expressions. The transformation of query graphs into NQL queries can be formally specified in a straightforward manner with the help of functions which map nodes and edges to the corresponding textual terms.

As in schema diagrams, nodes in query graphs represent object types or relationship types. Nodes representing object types, however, are further distinguished whether they represent so-called *selected elements* or *path elements.* Selected elements of a query are those object types which are addressed in the target list of the query, whose attribute values are restricted by conditions, and/or which are quantified. All other object types are called path elements since they are only necessary for the specification of paths between selected elements. In order to characterize their role graphically, nodes representing path elements are always drawn by NQS without attributes and smaller in size than nodes representing selected elements.

Query formulation may start with the diagram of an original schema, i.e. a diagram which has been generated from the textual description of a schema, or it may start with the diagram of a modified version of such a schema. Schemas can be modified by the addition of user-defined object types and their relationship types (see below). At first, the user specifies that portion of the diagram which is relevant for the intended querying. This specification is done in two steps. In the first step, object types have to be marked as selected elements by pointing with the mouse at their representation. When selecting these elements a user can take advantage of the following completion method applied by NQS: for each pair of selected elements, NQS adds the shortest path connecting them in the schema diagram; if there are several shortest paths for such a pair, all these paths are added. A path can be given by a single relationship type or by an alternating sequence of relationship types and object types.

This completion method is of a purely syntactic nature and has always a unique result. For data models with different kinds of relationship types other completion methods could be of interest (Ioannidis (1994)). As a result of this first step, NQS generates a diagram with all nodes which have been marked shown as selected elements and with all other nodes shown as path elements.

In the second step of the specification, the user must delete those paths which are not addressed in the query. If additional paths are needed or if elements not selected in the first step shall be added, this can be done in the ADD-mode where the system presents the initial diagram again. Sometimes nodes must be marked in order to add paths needed in the query and not for the purpose of determining them as selected elements. Therefore it is possible in a further mode to change selected elements into path elements and vice versa.

As a consequence of this proceeding, it is always guaranteed that there are no incomplete paths in the diagram. Paths not shown in the diagram, on the other hand, have nothing to do with the meaning of the query. What has to be taken into account in these steps is that in the final query graph all path elements must have exactly two neighbours. This is a necessary condition for paths to represent exactly one (complex) relationship type between two selected elements.

3.1 Flat queries

Flat NQL queries allow to express simple conditions on attribute values and relationships between objects of those types which are used in the target list of the query. In simple cases, conditions for relationships result immediately from the paths in the query graph taken over from the schema diagram: objects of the database state qualify for the answer if they are connected in accordance with the paths in the query graph. Thus, the result of this type of query corresponds to a set of (not necessarily connected) subgraphs from the database state if states are considered as graphs with objects as nodes and relationships as edges.

The graphical representation of flat queries in NQS shows simple comparison expressions for attribute values as part of the graphical representation of selected elements and explicit relationships which have to be present between qualifying objects as paths. In Figure 2, objects of the two selected object types ORDER and BRANCH qualify for the answer if their attribute values are as specified and if they are connected in accordance with the path between them in the graph.

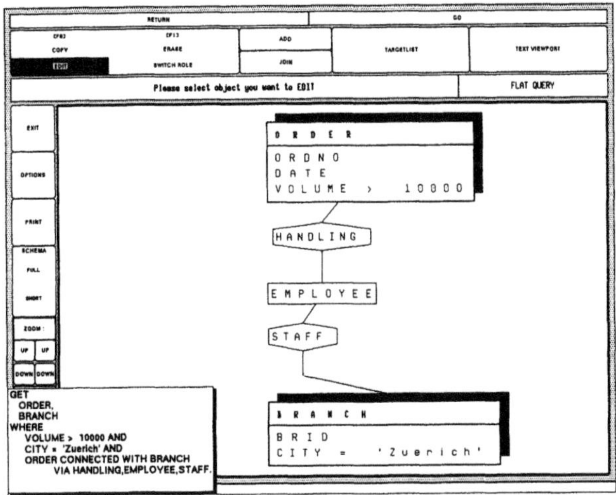

Figure 2 *Get the data of each branch in Zuerich handling orders with volume greater than 10000 together with the data of these orders.*

In flat queries it is also possible to compare values of objects of different type. To insert such a condition into the query graph, a user marks two attributes of different object types and chooses a comparison operator. The system draws an edge between the attributes and labels the edge with the comparison operator. Figure 3 shows a query graph for a flat query with a simple path and with both forms of comparison expressions.

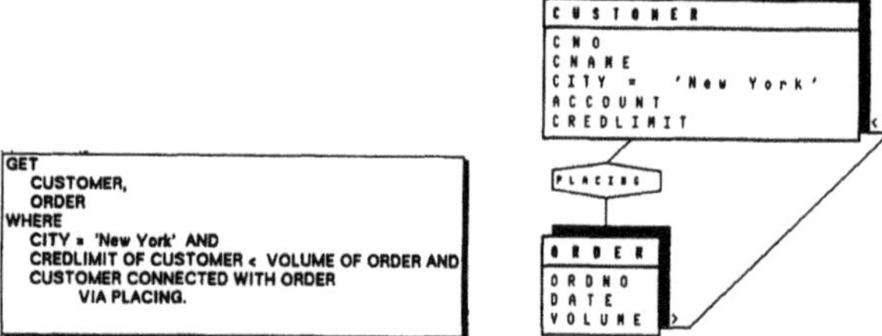

Figure 3 *Get the data of all customers from New York who have placed orders with volume greater than their credit limit together with the data of these orders.*

Predicates represented by paths in query graphs are connected by the conjunctive operator AND to predicates specified by comparison expressions in selected elements. This is a natural way to interpret query graphs. If predicates shall be connected otherwise, a corresponding Boolean expression has to be specified textually in the so-called *text viewport.* An expression in this viewport is connected by AND to the expression represented by the query graph itself. To make textual input short and comfortable, the system allows to mark paths automatically and to use the generated marks in Boolean expressions.

For flat queries, textual specification of Boolean (and arithmetic) expressions in a seperated viewport has been prefered to graphical representation for two reasons. The first reason is that the graphical representation of Boolean expressions tends to overload the query graph. The second reason is that in general there is no distinguished location where to pin a Boolean (or arithmetic) expression in the query graph (for nested queries there is always such a location).

As shown in Figures 2 and 3, a user can ask the system for the textual formulation corresponding to a graphical specification. This facility proved to be very helpful not only for the novice user but also for the expert to check whether the query graph represents the meaning of the intended query.

3.2 Nested queries

Semantics of flat NQL queries can be specified by quantifier-free formulas if there are predicate forms not only for comparison expressions but also for paths (Klein (1989)). More complex queries can be formulated in NQL by nesting quantified subexpressions to arbitrary depth. Compared with calculus-like languages, e.g. the relational tuple calculus, there is a different concept with respect to variables. Object types are not referenced by variables but their identifiers are used instead exclusively. The scope of these identifiers is restricted to the upper level of the where-clause following it in the query. Besides SOME and EVERY (ALL) there are further 'quantifiers' like NO, ONLY, AT LEAST n, etc. in the language. Quantifiers are attached directly to identifiers. This leads to more natural language like formulations. The target list of a nested query refers to exactly one object type. The idea here is to split complex queries into a sequence of definitions determining named subsets of object sets of the database state (cf. the 'data-context' in NUL (Deheneffe (1976))) and a final flat query in which these subsets can be referenced like ordinary object types.

The local scope of identifiers and the possibility to build queries in a step by step fashion help to overcome 'linguistic complexity problems' mentioned in Hansen (1987) in connection with the formulation of complex queries in descriptive query languages. As in procedural languages, it is possible to interpret parts of query specifications without having to grasp the complete specification.

Let us first consider nested queries without predicates for value-based relationships. Because of the restriction that only a single object type can be referenced in the targetlist of a nested query and because of the restricted scope of identifiers, such a query can always be represented by a query graph with the following properties: there is one distinguished node, the target node; there are no cycles in the graph apart from those cycles which exist between two selected elements because of distinct paths connecting them; if such paths exist, they do not have common elements and they do not have selected elements as members; with the exception of these cycles, the graph is a tree with the target node as root.

Because of this tree property, all paths in a nested query graph have a unique direction into which they have to be read. Thus, there is no ambiguity with respect to the interpretation of quantification.

Target nodes in nested query graphs are marked by placing GET in front of the identifier. The graph in Figure 4 shows two selected elements, ORDER and BRANCH, which are connected by two paths. For each qualifying object of type ORDER, the

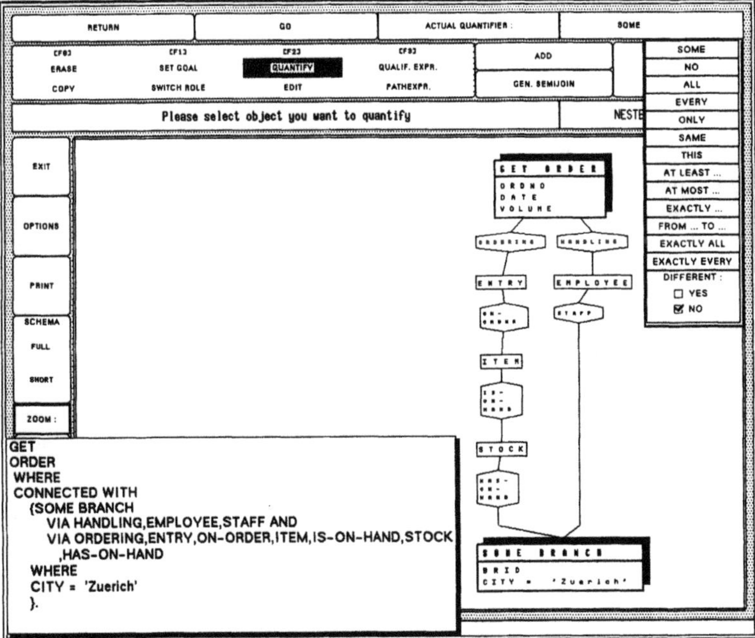

Figure 4 *Get the data of all orders handled by some employee of a branch in Zuerich such that an item is ordered in the order which is on hand in this branch.*

following must hold: there is an object of type BRANCH with 'Zuerich' as value in the attribute CITY such that the ORDER object is connected with this BRANCH object as specified by the paths in the graph.

If two or more paths shall represent alternative connections between objects or if there are more complicated conditions on paths, a Boolean expression can be specified with path marks as operands. The marks are generated automatically by the system. The expression is placed into an extra field in the representation of the object type to which the paths are directed.

If there are object types which are addressed more than once in a query, these object types must be replicated in an appropriate number as nodes in the query graph. This corresponds to the independence of different occurrences of object identifiers in a nested textual query. Duplication of nodes is done by use of a function key. Figure 5 gives an example for this concept.

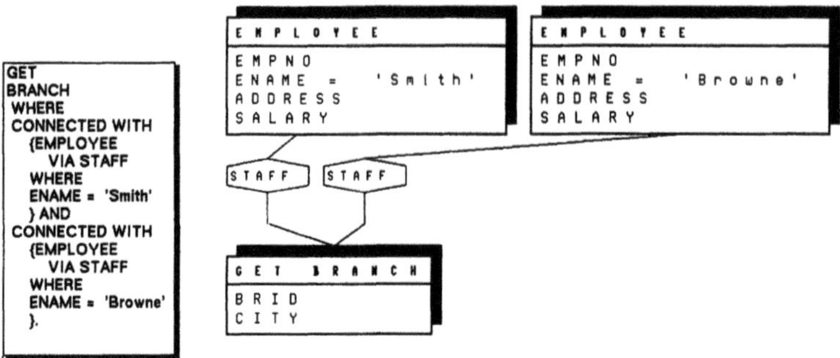

Figure 5 *Get the data of all branches with an employee named Smith as well as with an employee named Browne on the staff.*

If no quantifier is specified as for the two occurrences of the object type EMPLOYEE in the query of Figure 5, then SOME is implicit.

To refer back to an object type in a query, the keyword SAME (or THIS) can be used like an ordinary quantifier. The natural restriction is that the occurrence of an object type with this keyword is a leaf in the query tree.

Predicates for value-based relationships are called *generalized semijoins* since in these predicates all quantifiers and comparison operators can be used. They are represented in a query graph as follows: the representation of the object type for which the predicate must hold is extended by an extra field containing the comparison expression of the predicate. Each operand whose attributes originate in another object type is connected to the representation of that object type. Figure 6 shows an example.

In the query of Figure 6 there is no condition given concerning paths via explicit relationships between objects of type CUSTOMER and BRANCH. The next example demonstrates how such conditions can be specified by simply combining the corresponding edge with a path. If there are several paths involved, they are drawn seperately. Boolean expressions are handled as described above. Since simple edges and edges combined with

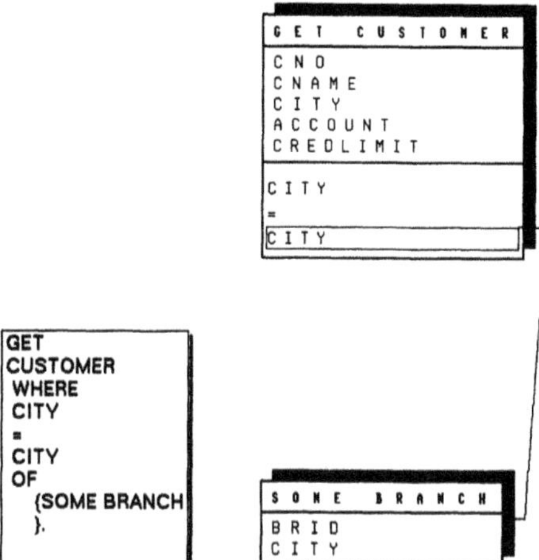

Figure 6 *Get the data of all customers who live in a city where some branch is located.*

a path in the representation of a generalized semijoin predicate have a unique direction, the property that all paths in query graphs are directed away from the target node is preserved.

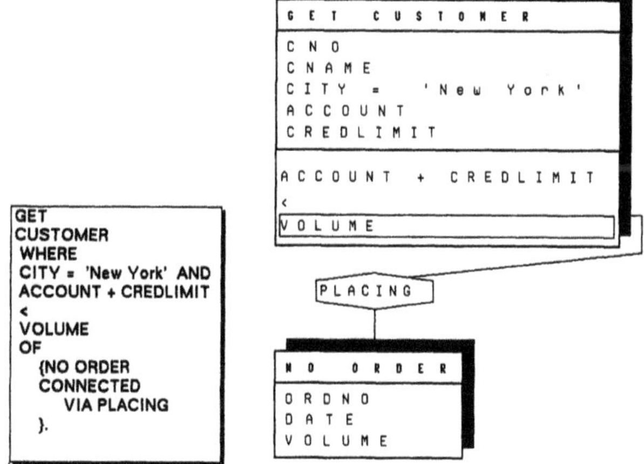

Figure 7 *Get the data of all customers from New York who have placed no order with volume greater than the sum of their account and their credit limit.*

Both operands in the comparison expression of a generalized semijoin predicate may refer to object types which are different from the object type the predicate belongs to. An example is given in Figure 8.

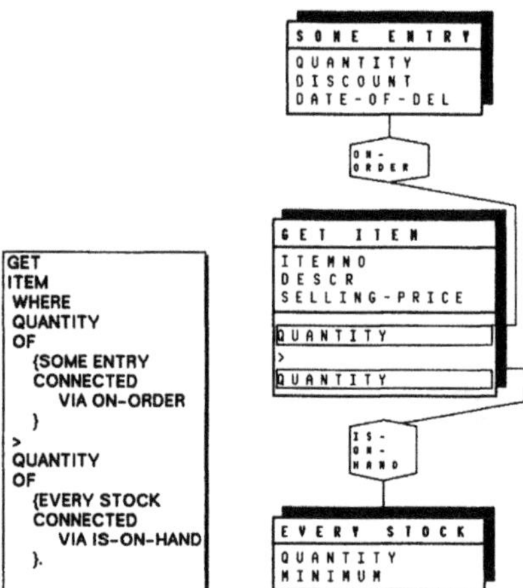

Figure 8 *Get the data of all items with an entry in which the item is ordered with quantity greater than the quantity which is on hand of the item in each stock.*

3.3 User-defined object types and function expressions

For each object type of the schema under consideration it is possible to specify an arbitrary number of nested queries and to give a unique identifier to each of them. After the completion of such a definition, the schema diagram is extended by the representation of the new object type with the identifier just introduced. This object type inherits all attributes and relationship types from the object type to which the nested query refers. It is drawn next to it and can be used for query specification or further definitions of new object types in the same way as any object type of the original schema. The specification of a new object type can be edited at any time. Updates producing cycles in a set of definitions are rejected by the system.

With the help of such definitions, a user can decompose query formulation into several steps and produce a special view of a database conforming to his/her needs. Figure 9 shows a query with user-defined object types.

The query graph of Figure 9 contains a simple Boolean expression as part of an additional field in the representation of the object type ITEM. In nested queries, Boolean expressions are uniquely attached to object types. Therefore NQS offers no viewport for Boolean expressions as in the case of flat queries. Conditions which can be used in a Boolean expression for an object type are marked by the system on request.

There are two types of function expressions in NQL called free and context-related. The current implementation of NQS restricts the use of function expressions to free function expressions. The specification of these expressions is done in a way similar to the definition of new object types. The only difference is that an aggregate function has to be specified which is applied either to an object set (NUMBER OF) or to values of arithmetic expressions with operands taken from the 'root' object type (SUM, AVG, ...). The identifiers of function expressions can be used like constants in queries.

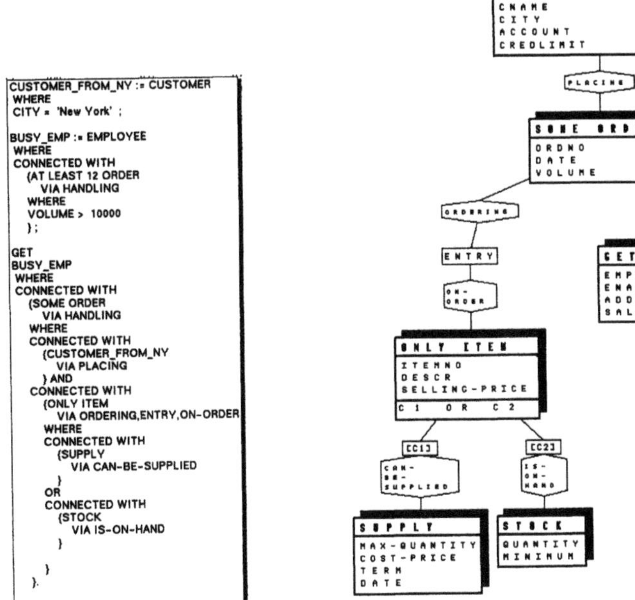

Figure 9 *Get the data of all busy employees who work on some order of a New York customer requesting in this order only items which can be supplied or which are on hand.*

4 Experiences

In the design phase of NQS we experimented with graphical representations for Boolean expressions in order to get an interface with a minimum of text entry. However, since the query language allows comparison expressions and predicates involving paths to be combined in Boolean expressions, graphical representations for more complex expressions often showed to be in conflict with the readability of query graphs. In order to keep the number of different concepts small, we therefore decided in favour of the textual specification of all Boolean expressions which are not simple conjunctions.

Our experience with the usability of NQS results from a large number of sessions where we gathered qualitative data from user comments and user performance. Several users, among them colleagues, students who had completed a course on database systems, and programmers with no database experience, took part in a test where some flat and nested queries had to be formulated with help restricted to the interaction with the system. These users were not familiar with the query language NQL.

The first step in query formulation with NQS is to decide whether a given query can be specified as a flat query or as a nested query (or both). To come to a decision on the basis of the given formulation was not difficult for most users. The specification of flat queries also proved not to be a hard problem. Some argumentation, however, was necessary with regard to our decision for a text viewport since there were test queries for which a complete graphical representation is attractive.

Difficulties with nested queries showed to be strongly dependent upon the given formulation of a query in natural language. Our observations in this point were the following: if a given query formulation had a nested structure free from complex self-references of objects, then query specification was done in a step by step manner without problems. Quantification in particular was not considered a difficult concept. In case of more complicated formulations several attempts were sometimes necessary to find the nested structure of a correct specification. As an example consider the query in Figure 4: 'Get the data of all orders handled by some employee of a branch in Zuerich such that an item is ordered in the order which is on hand in this branch.' Figure 4 shows a simple graph for this query: take ORDER and BRANCH as selected elements and connect these elements via ITEM and EMPLOYEE, resp.; add the appropriate selection condition to BRANCH. Most users, however, tried to specify the query by duplicating the object types BRANCH or ORDER and by using SAME (THIS) as 'quantification' (there is a solution in this way by duplication of ORDER).

In order to check whether the generated query graph represented what they intended to specify, users always looked at the textual query formulation produced by NQS on demand. They had no difficulties to understand these NQL queries in connection with the query graph and to compare them with the given formulation of the query in natural language. As a consequence of this control and because NQS accepts only query graphs which correspond to syntactically correct NQL queries, final solutions were without mistakes in most cases.

5 Final Remarks

NQS has been implemented in Pascal on Apollo workstations using Domain Dialogue and GMR2D. At each stage of query formulation, the user may ask the system for information about the graphical objects on the screen (e.g.: data types of attributes, specification of user defined object types). For the specification of the target list, arithmetic expressions, predicates etc., pop-up windows and pull-down menues are provided. In the current version, not all features of NQL are realized, among them the transitive closure of path expressions and context-related function expressions. The size of the system without interpreters for NQL and with a restricted facility for the presentation of query results is about 32000 lines of code (1.4 MB).

Not every diagram produced by the layout algorithm of NQS will be to the pleasure of the user. Moreover, the building of views by the specification and insertion of object definitions and the duplication of schema elements in query graphs may result in unfavourable layouts. Therefore we work on a facility which offers operations at different levels to permit the change of layouts. On a higher level, there shall be operations based on the information about the connectedness of the graph including those operations given in Chiba (1985) for finding all the embeddings of a planar graph (permutation and flip over of components); on a lower level, some simple rearrangement operations may be allowed. This proceeding seems to be more promising than to permit the user only to drag graphical objects arbitrarily over the screen.

NQL is not a complete language in the sense of a full calculus language because of the restrictions concerning the scope of identifiers and the form of target lists. In many query languages with descriptive features, completeness is achieved by set operations, i.e. procedural constructs (e.g.: Czejdo (1990), Angelaccio (1990)). For adding expressive power, we intend to go another way and to generalize the restricted view concept of the language such that complex object types can be specified by an extended form of nested queries.

Currently, a new version of NQS is under construction using an X11 based graphical toolkit. NQS is developed into a query interface for an extended version of the ER data model comprising subtypes, aggregation, and attributes for relationship types.

6 REFERENCES

ACM (1992) Special Issue: Advanced User Interfaces for Database Systems. *ACM SIGMOD RECORD*, **21 (1)**

Angelaccio M., Catarci T., and Santucci G. (1990) QBD* : A Graphical Query Language with Recursion. *IEEE Trans. on Software Engineering*, **16 (10)**, 1150-1163

Booth K.S. and Lueker G.S. (1976) Testing the Consecutive Ones Property, Interval Graphs, and Planarity Using PQ-Tree Algorithms. *Journal of Computer and System Sciences*, **13**, 335-379

Bryce D. and Hull R. (1986) SNAP: A Graphics-based Schema Manager, in *Proc. IEEE Int. Conf. on Data Eng.*, Los Angeles, 151-164

Burns L.M., Archibald J.L., and Malhotra A. (1988) A Graphical Entity-Relationship Database Browser, in *Proc. 21st Annual Hawaii Int. Conf. on System Sciences, Software Track vol. II*, 694-704

Chiba N., Nishizeki T., Abe S., and Ozawa T. (1985) A Linear Algorithm for Embedding Planar Graphs Using PQ-Trees. *Journal of Computer and System Sciences*, **30**, 54-76

Czejdo B., Elmasri R., Rusinkiewicz M., and Embley D.W. (1990) A Graphical Data Manipulation Language for an Extended Entity-Relationship Model. *IEEE Computer*, **23**, 26-36

Deheneffe C. and Hennebert H. (1976) NUL: a Navigational User's Language for a Network Structured Data Base, in *Proc. ACM SIGMOD*, Washington, 135-142

Elmasri R.A. and Larson J.A. (1985) A Graphical Query Facility for ER Databases, in *Proc. 4th Int. Conf. on the Entity-Relationship Approach*, Chicago, 236-245

Even S. and Tarjan R.E. (1976) Computing an st-numbering. *Theoretical Computer Science*, **2**, 339-344

Hansen G.W. and Hansen J.V. (1987) Procedural and Non-procedural Query Languages Revisited: a Comparison of Relational Algebra and Relational Calculus. *International Journal of Man-Machine Studies*, **26**, 683-694

Ioannidis Y.E. and Lashkari Y. (1994) Incomplete Path Expressions and their Disambiguation. *ACM-SIGMOD RECORD*, **23 (2)**, 138-149

Kim H.-J., Korth H.F., and Silberschatz A. (1988) PICASSO: A Graphical Query Language. *Software-Practice and Experience*, **18 (3)**, 169-203

King R. and Melville S. (1984) Ski: A Semantics-Knowledgeable Interface, in *Proc. 10th VLDB*, Singapore, 30-33

Klein H.-J. (1989) Pragmatics and Semantics of NQL, a Descriptive Query Language for Network Databases. *Information Systems*, **14 (1)**, 29-45

Kuntz M. and Melchert R. (1989) PASTA-3's Graphical Query Language: Direct Manipulation, Cooperative Queries, Full Expressive Power, in *Proc. 15th VLDB*, Amsterdam, 97-105

Lacroix M. and Pirotte A. (1977) Domain-oriented Relational Languages, in *Proc. 3rd VLDB*, Tokyo, 370-378

Lam H., Chen H.M., Ty F.S., Qiu J., and Su S.Y.W. (1990) A Graphical Interface for an Object-Oriented Query Language, in *Proc. 14th IEEE COMPSAC*, Chicago, 231-237

Lempel A., Even S., and Cederbaum I. (1967) An Algorithm for Planarity Testing of Graphs, in *Theory of Graphs* (ed. P. Rosenstiel), Gordon&Breach, New York, 215-232,

Mark L. (1989) A Graphical Query Language for the Binary Relationship Model. *Information Systems*, **14 (3)**, 231-246

Markowitz V.M. and Raz Y. (1983) ERROL: an Entity-Relationship Role Oriented Query Language, in *Entity-Relationship Approach to Software Engineering* (P.A. Ng et al., eds.), North-Holland, 329-346

Mc Donald N. and Stonebraker M. (1975) CUPID - The Friendly Query Language, in *Proc. ACM Pacific 75 Conf.*, San Francisco, 127-131

Mohan L. and Kashyap R.L. (1993) A Visual Query Language for Graphical Interaction With Schema-Intensive Databases. *IEEE Trans. on Knowledge and Data Engineering*, **5 (5)**, 843-858

Paulisch F.N. (1993) The Design of an Extendible Graph Editor. *Lecture Notes in Computer Science*, **704**, Springer Verlag

Rogers T.R. and Cattell R.G.G. (1988) Entity-Relationship Database User Interfaces, in *Proc. 6th Int. Conf. Entity-Relationship Approach* (ed. S.T. March), New York, Elsevier, 353-365

Stonebraker M. and Kalash J. (1982) TIMBER: A Sophisticated Relation Browser, in *Proc. 8th VLDB*, Mexico City, 1-10

Subieta K. (1987) Denotational Semantics of Query Languages. *Information Systems*, **12 (1)**, 69-82

Tamassia R., Di Battista G., and Batini C. (1988) Automatic Graph Drawings and Readability of Diagrams. *IEEE Trans. on Systems, Man, and Cybernetics*, **18 (1)**, 61-79

Tarjan R. (1972) Depth-first Search and Linear Graph Algorithms. *SIAM Journal of Computing*, **1 (2)**, 146-160

Welty C. and Stemple D.W. (1981) Human Factors Comparison of a Procedural and a Nonprocedural Query Language. *ACM Trans. on Database Systems*, **6 (4)**, 626-649

Wong H.K.T. and Kuo I. (1982) GUIDE: Graphical User Interface for Database Exploration, in *Proc. 8th VLDB*, Mexico City, 22-32

Zhang Z.-Q. and Mendelzon A.O. (1983) A Graphical Query Language for Entity-Relationship Databases, in *Entity-Relationship Approach to Software Engineering* (C.G. Davis et al., eds.), 441-448

Zloof M.M. (1975) Query by Example, in *AFIPS Conf. Proc., National Computer Conf. 44*, Anaheim, 431-438

7 BIOGRAPHY

Hans-Joachim Klein is a member of the database group in the computer science department of the university of Kiel. He received the Diploma in computer science from the university of Saarbrücken and the Dr. rer. nat. degree from the university of Kiel. His research interests include query languages, graphical interfaces, and incomplete information.

Dirk Krämer is a member of the database group in the computing center of the university of Kiel. He received the Diploma in computer science from the university of Kiel. His research interests include visual query languages and distributed databases.

26

Query Processing Methods for Connectivity Search in Visual Databases Using R+-tree

Myeong-A Kang and Ki-Joune Li
Department of Computer Science
Pusan National University
Kumjeong-Ku, Pusan, Korea 609-735
e-mail : {makang, lik}@spatios.cs.pusan.ac.kr
fax : +82 51 510 2208

Abstract

Recently, spatial database systems have been developed and widely used in many applications, including visual database systems. However, the efficient query processing in visual database systems becomes a crucial problem, due to their large volume of data. It is furthermore difficult to reuse conventional query processing techniques for visual database systems, since types of queries used in visual databases differs from the existing ones in conventional database systems. New query processing methods are therefore required. In visual database systems, it is important to represent semantic information which include topological relationship of visual objects. One of the types of queries most frequently used to represent topological relationship in visual database systems is connectivity search. In this paper, we propose several spatial query processing methods for connectivity, using R^+-tree as the underlying indexing method without any topological data. We introduce the concept of θ-partial R^+-tree and its construction algorithm, which describes any kind of spatial query processing procedure depending on the specification of θ-condition. Two query processing methods for connectivity are derived from θ-partial R^+-tree construction. We analyze the performance of our methods by simulation. It proves that our methods for connectivity search significantly reduce the number of disk accesses as well as CPU time.

1 INTRODUCTION

Spatial database systems have been developed and widely used in many applications, including visual database systems [1]. However, due to their large volume of data, the efficient query processing in spatial database systems becomes a crucial problem. And since types of queries used in spatial databases differs from the existing ones in conventional database systems [13], it is difficult to reuse conventional query processing techniques for spatial database systems. New query processing methods are therefore required.

The types of spatial queries demanded in these applications are diverse. They can be roughly divided into two categories: geometric queries and topological queries. Until now, only a small set of queries has been rigorously studied for their processing [2]. Moreover, most of the proposed spatial query processing techniques are for only geometric purposes, such like distance, intersection or containment [14]. These methods are generally based on position data of spatial objects. In addition to geometry, topological information - for example, the shortest path between two given spatial objects- plays an important role in spatial databases. But only a few researches have been done for topological query processing [2][3][4].

Among the topological queries, the *query about connectivity* is the most basic, but complex and expensive one [1]. It is a kind of spatial query which asks to find out the paths between two given spatial objects. For example, one may ask to visualize all cities reachable from a given city via railroads. In this case, the connectivities between the given city and others are to be verified. Another example of query about connectivity is the shortest path query between two objects. In order to process such a query, we first have to find out all paths between the objects, that is, the connectivity of two objects. In a similar way, processing query about connectivity, therefore constitutes a major part of spatial or visual database systems.

In general, processing query for connectivity is very complex, expensive and difficult to implement. The major difficulty lies in disk access time. Since query processing for connectivity requires a great number of disk accesses, it spends a considerable amount of response time. In this paper, we propose several query processing methods for connectivity, focusing our efforts on the reduction of disk access frequency. We use filtering and refinement procedure for the query processing, which significantly remove unnecessary disk accesses. Compared with other approaches [7][8], no additional information is needed for the query processing, except R^+-tree as the indexing tree of objects. It allows us to maintain database more dynamically. A generalized concept of filtering R^+-tree, *θ-partial* R^+*-tree*, is introduced in this paper to formalize and extend our methods.

The organization of this paper is as follows. In Section 2, an overall procedure of query for connectivity is presented. We introduce the concept of θ-partial R^+-tree that can be built from R^+-tree for efficient query processing in section 3. We also show how θ-partial R^+-tree can be used generally and adaptively in spatial query processing. In Section 4, we apply θ-partial tree to query processing for connectivity. We propose two methods; a simple one and an improved one. In Section 5, we present results of our experiments to compare the performance of the methods. And we conclude our paper in section 6.

2 QUERY PROCESSING FOR CONNECTIVITY

When analyzing visual information, we often need topological relationship between visual objects in database. Connectivity between two objects is one of the most frequently inquired relationship. For example, as shows Figure 1, suppose that we want to know if the buildings in area *A* be supplied with electricity, when transform substation *T* is crashed. In order to answer to this question, we must find out possible paths from power plant *P* to *A* via power distribution network, that is, the connectivity of distribution network between power plant and its consumers in area *A*. If there exist connected paths, we can find an alternative among them, such like, the shortest path.

The difficulties lie in the size of data volume. In order to process query for connectivity, a great number of disk accesses and a large amount of computation may be often needed due to its large volume of data. Figure 2 illustrates an example of such a case.

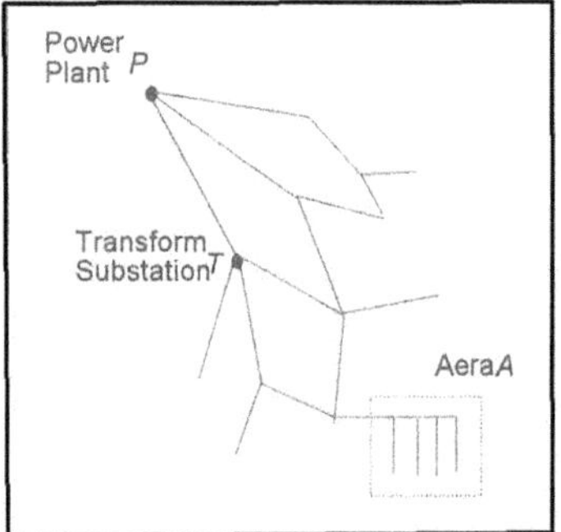

Figure 1 Example of Connectivity.

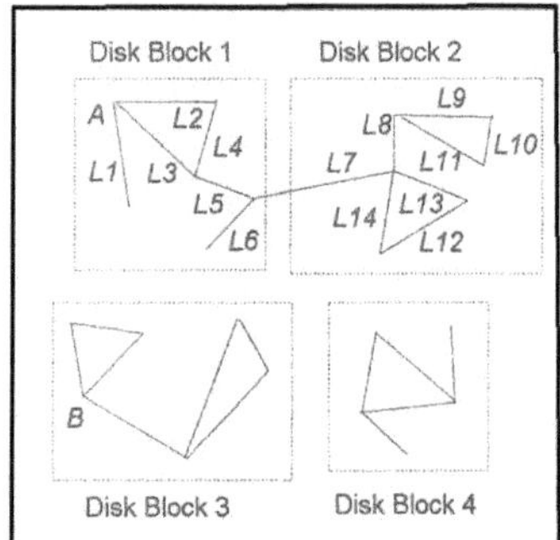

Figure 2 Storing Segments on Disk.

In Figure 2, in order to find the connected path between *A* and *B*, we must scan at least three disk blocks containing line segments which are directly or indirectly connected with *A* or *B*. That is, in order to find line segments *{L1, L2, L3}*, which are directly connected with A, we read disk block 1. On disk block 1, we can also find out line segments *{L4, L5}* connected *{L1, L2, L3}*, i.e.. But to find out line segments *{L6,L7}*, which are connected with *{L4, L5}*, we must read disk block 2 in turn. In a similar way, we read block 3. As the number of line segments grows, the number of disk accesses required may also increase in a considerable way. In an extreme case, we must scan all disk blocks to find connected paths.

Another problem we meet in query processing is that we can not guaranty that all neighbor line segments be stored in the same disk block. For example, if we store line segments on disk blocks by the order of insertion, *L2* and *L3* are no longer in the same block. Furthermore, we do not know where *L3* is stored. It means that we must scan all blocks to find line segments directly connected with *A*. In such a case, the number of disk accesses can exceeds the number of disk blocks actually used.

Very little attention has been paid on the query processing methods for connectivity except some recent researches such as [3]. The simplest method to find connectivity between two objects may be graph traversal algorithms or Dijkstra's single-source all-pairs algorithm[5]. But it has a number of serious problems. The most serious problem among them is that this method do not takes into account I/O costs. Even though the complexity by depth-first search is *O(e)*, it merely explains CPU time, and our concern is rather I/O cost than CPU time.

Another possible approach is transitive closure algorithm [6]. By computing transitive closure of visual objects, we can easily find connectivity of two objects. But this approach has an important drawback, that computing and maintaining transitive closure cost too much CPU and I/O time. For example, when a visual object is inserted, the transitive closure of the objects must be recomputed, which makes this method far from being dynamic.

Several graph traversal algorithms were proposed by [3] to find connectivity or shortest path on a massive graph, which is too large to fit in main memory and must be stored on disk. They use branch and bounding searching algorithms to prune the search space. These methods seem very attractive, since we may apply them to the query processing for connectivity. But even though this method may reduce I/O cost, their I/O cost is still unknown, and in worst case where the heuristics do not perform well, the number of disk accesses could increase by considerable amount.

The methods mentioned above are primarily based on only topological property. They represent the relationship between objects as a graph, and by using their topological properties, they try to find connectivity between objects. But by exploiting geometric information as well as topological one, we can significantly improve the performance of method. This is the basic concept of our methods.

In section 3 and 4, we present how connectivity search query can be efficiently performed, by using only geometric information. First, our approach does not require any additional topological information as above methods, and uses only geometric information and spatial access method such as R^+-tree which is a primitive requirement in any kind of visual database systems [9][10][11]. Therefore, storage can be reduced and information redundancy of object can be prevented. Second, the methods presented in this paper are dynamic at frequent insertion or deletion. Third, we significantly reduce I/O time by using θ-partial R^+-tree which will be proposed in this paper. It can be built from R^+-tree and is a formal notation of filtering and refinement spatial query processing methods. This notation helps us to describe and implement spatial query processing with ease, which are, in general complicated and diverse in visual database.

3 θ-PARTIAL R^+- TREE

The simplest method to find connectivity between objects in visual databases is to load all visual objects in main memory and process without any disk access. But it is practically impossible to keep all objects in main memory due to the large volume of visual data, and it is, thus inevitable to store visual objects in disk storage. The goal of query optimization for connectivity should be rather to reduce disk I/O frequency.

Our approach is to extend and generalize the spatial join query processing method appeared in [9]. According to this method, spatial query processing uses R^+-tree for its spatial access method and is divided into two steps; filtering step and refinement step. Each step of this method is explained below;

i. Filtering step : find all objects whose MBR* satisfy the query condition.
ii. Refinement step : for these objects, check if they really fulfill the query condition.

The performance of query processing is primarily determined by filtering. The more objects are filtered out, the better is the performance. But the filtering in query processing for connectivity search is very complicated, and we need its formal notation. In this section, we try to formalize filtering process by θ-partial tree.

Definition 1 : *Partial Tree*
Suppose that T is a tree and R is its root node. T_P is a partial tree of T if and only if

1. the root node of T_P, R_P is identical to R ;
2. when $C(R)$ is the set of child nodes of R, $C(R_P) \subseteq C(R)$;
3. each subtree of T_P is a partial tree of a subtree of T ;

An example of partial tree is illustrated by Figure 3. A partial tree T_P is derived from T such that their root nodes are identical and internal nodes on each level in T_P is a subset of T on corresponding level. We now define θ-partial tree which is a key concept of our paper.

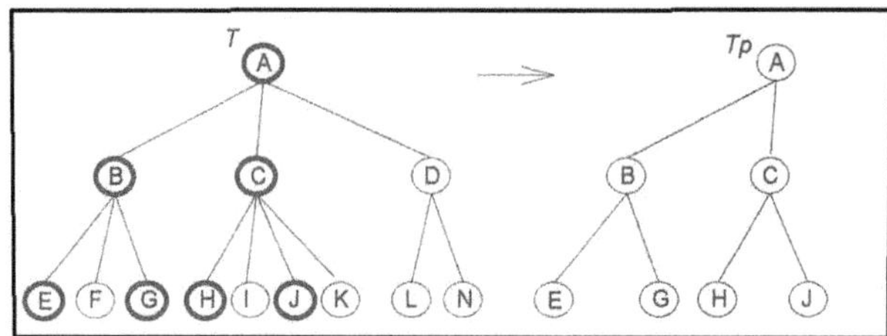

Figure 3 Example of Partial Tree.

Definition 2. θ-*Partial Tree* and θ-*Partial R^+-Tree*
Let T be a tree. Then T_θ is a θ-partial tree if and only if

1. T_θ is a partial tree of T ;
2. on each level of T_θ, the set of sibling nodes satisfies condition θ ;

And when T is a R^+-tree, we call its θ-partial tree as θ-partial R^+-tree.

In order to construct a θ-partial tree from a given tree, we must examine if selected nodes on each level satisfy the condition given by θ. Figure 4 shows an example of θ-partial tree where θ is given as follows ;

* Two terminologies, *MBR*(Minimal Bounding Rectangle) and *node* in R^+-tree are interchangeable in this paper for the reason of convenience, even though their meanings are slightly different.

$\theta: N = \{n \mid n \in sibling(T,i), \sum_{n \in N} n.data \leq 20\}$,

where *sibling(T,i)* is the set of all sibling nodes of T on level i.

It should be noted that when building a θ-partial tree, selection of sibling nodes on each level is not affected by nodes on upper levels, except that their parents have been already selected.

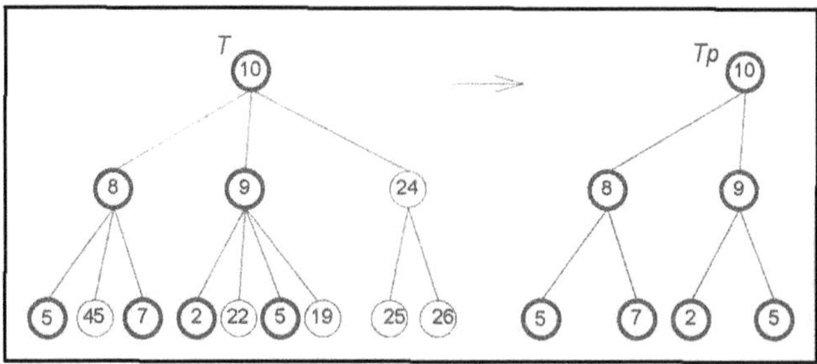

Figure 4 Example of θ-partial tree.

Now, we see how θ-partial tree can be used for spatial query processing. Suppose that a set of visual objects and its R$^+$-tree T are given as Figure 5(a) and we specify condition θ as

θ: *N(i)* = { n | n is a node on level i and MBR(n) intersect with region W }.

It means that we want to find visual object which intersects with a given searching area W. Then we can derive a θ-partial tree from T as shown by Figure 5(b).

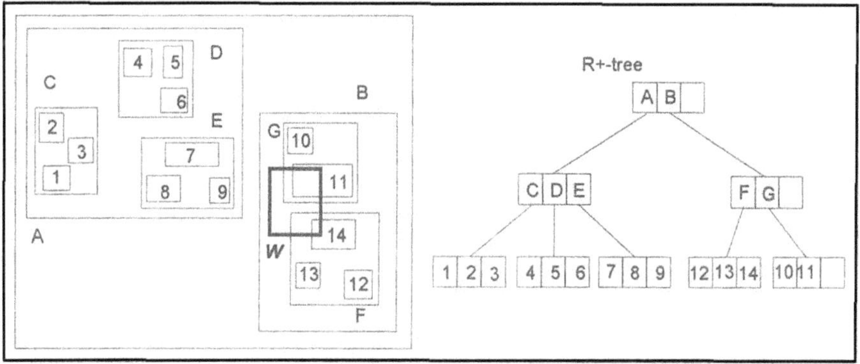

Figure 5(a) R$^+$-tree of a set of visual objects.

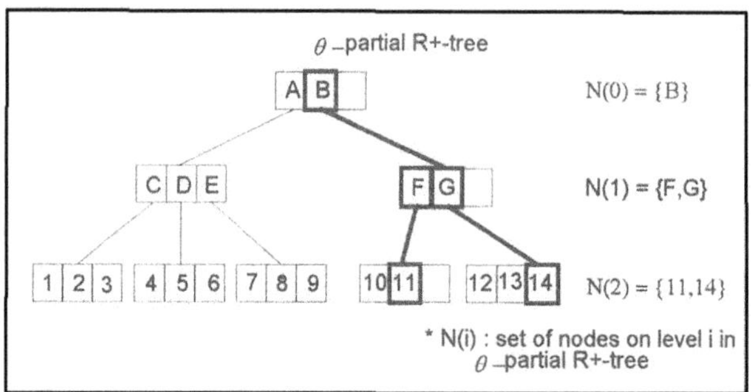

Figure 5(b) θ-partial R⁺-tree.

In Figure 5(b), we find that the nodes in the θ-partial R⁺-tree, which are $\{B,F,G,11,14\}$, are same as the MBRs that we select during filtering step. In fact, the construction of a θ-partial R⁺-tree is identical to filtering process using R⁺-tree. And according to the type of θ, we can describe any kind of spatial query process using R⁺-tree. Construction of a θ-partial R⁺-tree is therefore a generalized process of filtering step. A generalized algorithm for constructing θ-partial R⁺-tree is shown by *Algorithm 1*.

```
Procedure BuildθPartialR+-tree(R : root node of R+-tree,θ : filtering condition)
    Np(0) ← {R};                // Np(i) is set of selected nodes in level i //
    for level i from 0 to d     // d is height of R //

        N ← ∪_{n∈Np(i-1)} children(n);   // N is set of all sibling nodes on a level //

        Np(i) ← { n | n ∈ N and satisfies condition θ };    // statement 1-1 //
    end For
    return Np(d);               // return MBR of candidate objects //
End Procedure
```

Algorithm 1 Build θ-partial R⁺-tree.

We now explain how to use this algorithm to find connectivity in visual database in the next section.

4 TWO QUERY PROCESSING METHODS FOR CONNECTIVITY

In order to apply θ-partial R⁺-tree algorithm mentioned in the previous section to connectivity search query, we define θ-condition as follows;

$$\theta: N = \{m_a, m_b\} \cup \{n \mid n \in sibling(R,i)\ and\ for\ \exists\, x \in N, n\ is\ connected\ with\ x\} \quad \text{- (eq. 1)}$$

where m_a, m_b are respectively MBRs of query objects A, and B on level i.

This condition implies that the set of nodes satisfying θ, includes MBRs of given query objects *A* and *B*, and MBRs which are connected with *A* and *B* in direct or indirect way. In fact, the set of nodes, *N* in θ condition is a connected component. It is obvious that if two given objects are connected, them their MBR on each level in R^+-tree are also connected. Based on the definition of θ-condition, we can write a brief algorithm of query processing for connectivity search as *Algorithm 2*.

```
procedure ConnectivitySearch ( R : R+-tree, A, B : query objects )
    // find connectivity between A and B //
    define θ as N in (eq.1);
    CandidateMBRSet ← BuildθPartialR+-tree(R,θ);
    FilteredObjects ← all objects in the nodes of CandidateMBRSet;
    Objects ← Refinement(FilteredObjects, A, B);
End Procedure
```

Algorithm 2 Query Processing Algorithm for Connectivity Search.

This algorithm consists of two steps; filtering step by BuildθPartialR$^+$-tree and refinement step. However, the major part of this algorithm is obviously filtering step, since it dominantly determines the performance of the query processing. Refinement step fulfills the connect condition with filtered objects by existing algorithm or similar filtering algorithm, it takes a little processing time. It suffices to define θ condition as connectivity for this step and BuildθPartialR$^+$-tree function performs the filtering.

4.1 A Simple Method for Connectivity using *θ*-Partial R$^+$-tree

In order to complete BuildθPartialR$^+$-tree function, we have to precise how to find the set of nodes *N*, satisfying θ-condition on each level in a θ-partial R$^+$-tree. In other words, we should find connected component on each level *i*, which corresponds to *Np*(*i*) in *Algorithm 1*. In the two subsequent sections, we will see how *Np*(*i*) can be found in efficient way, that is, how to perform *statement 1-1* in *Algorithm 1*, when θ-condition is given as (eq.1). *Algorithm 3* illustrates a simple method to perform this statement.

```
Procedure SearchConnectedComponent1(M : set of MBRs, A and B : object, i : level)
   // M is the set of MBRs whose parents are connected //
   m_a ← MBR(A, i), m_b ← MBR(B, i);        // find MBRs of A and B on level i //
   Mp ← {m_a};                              // Mp : set of candidates //
   while(there is no change on Mp)
        Mp ← Mp U { m | m ∈ M - Mp and m is directly connected with Mp};
                                  // statement 3-1 //
   end while
   if m_b ∉ Mp, then return Fail; // m_a and m_b are in different connected component //
end procedure
```

Algorithm 3 Finding Connected Component on Level *i* : Simple Method.

For example, a set of line segments and its R$^+$-tree are given as Figure 6, and we will see how *Algorithm 2* and *3* perform query processing for connectivity.

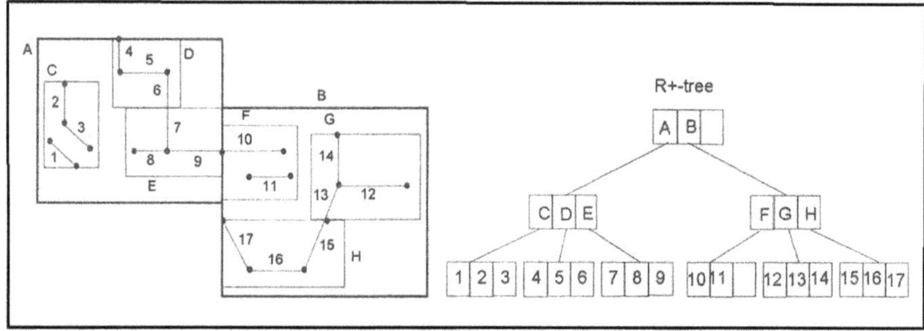

Figure 6 Line Segments and it's R$^+$-tree.

Suppose that a connectivity query is given as *'Is line 14 connected with line 16 ?'*. In *SearchConnectedComponent1* algorithm, *Mp* is $\{B\}$ on root level, and becomes $\{H,G\}$ on the next level, since G is the MBR containing line 14, and H is the only MBR which is connected with G. Thus, refinement step only has to check lines in H and G. In this case, the number of disk accesses is at most four times, that is, one disk access for root node, node B, node G, node H, respectively. However, this filtering step requires slightly more CPU time. Figure 7 demonstrates detail procedure of the filtering step, that is BuildθPartialR$^+$-tree.

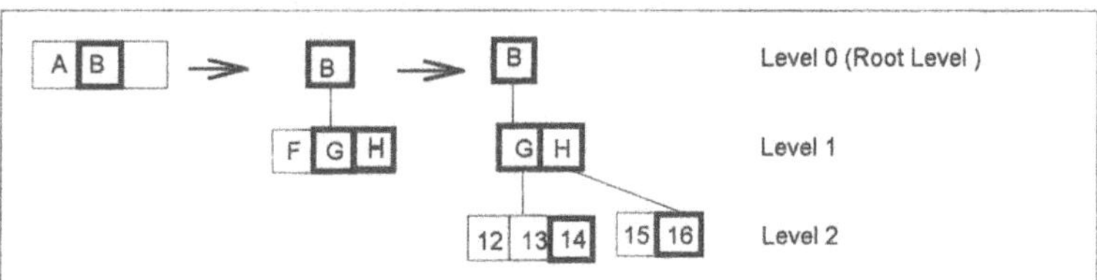

Figure 7 the procedure of processing given above query.

Another query example is *'Is line 12 connected with line 1 ?'*. Then algorithm *SearchConnectedComponent1* finds MBRs of line 12 and line 1 on root level. That is, $\{A,B\}$ is taken on root level as connected component which is *Mp* in Algorithm 3. These nodes practically consist of nodes θ-partial R$^+$-tree on root level. On the next level, the connected component *Mp* containing the MBR of line 12, becomes $\{H,G\}$, which does not include the MBR of line 1. It means that line 12 and 1 are not connected. It is therefore not necessary to continue any process in the algorithm, and we can get its answer that two line objects 12 and 1 are not connected. In this case, the number of disk accesses is 3; one for root node, one for node B and one for node C. It implies that we can economize a lot of disk accesses and CPU time, when the query objects are disconnected. In this case, the height of θ-partial R$^+$-tree may differs from the original R$^+$-tree. In general, it can occur when the query objects are disconnected. That is, it becomes unnecessary to continue to buid θ-partial R$^+$-tree, if it is proved that the MBRs of the objects are not connected.

However, *Algorithm 3* has room for improvement. In this algorithm, concrete processing method of *statement 3-1* is not described. The simplest method we can implement is to load all child nodes on main memory, whose parent nodes belong to the connected component, and process them. However, it significantly degrades the performance of this algorithm due to unnecessary disk accesses and computation. We will see an improved algorithm which avoids from such a problem in the next section.

4.2 An Improved Method

Let us consider an example illustrated by Figure 8. Suppose that we have to find the connectivity between *a* and *e*, which are MBRs on leaf level of query objects. *Algorithm 3*, *SearchConnectedComponent1*, needs no less than 26 comparisons, that is, 8 comparisons to extend the connected component, *Mp* from {*e*} to {*e*,*d*}, and 7 for *Mp*={*e*, *d*, *b*}, and so on. However we can considerably reduce the number of comparisons and disk accesses by our improved method.

When we carefully look at the placements of MBRs in Figure 8. we can find that it is unnecessary to examine *C* and its child nodes. It is because no child node of *B* is connected with *C*. Therefore, we can remove unnecessary comparisons and corresponding disk accesses by using the following property;

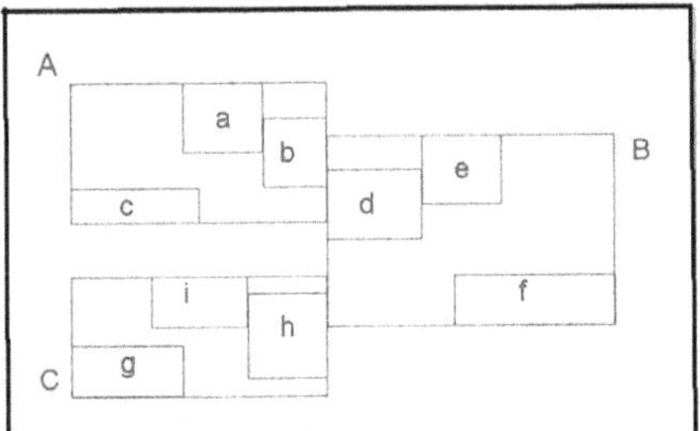

Figure 8 Removing Unnecessary Disk Accesses and Comparisons.

Property 1

Let M and M' be two different nodes on a same level in R^+-tree. If there exists no child node of M which is connected with M', then there is no couple of child nodes (m,m') which are connected, where m and m' are in M and M' respectively.

In Figure 8, we can see that any child node of *B* is not connected with *C* and consequently with any child node of *C*, according to the property. It implies that we can avoid disk access for node *C* and comparisons with child nodes of *C*. We will analyze the improvement of performance in section 5.

Algorithm 4 describes the improved procedure by using the property mentioned above. Before loading a node, this algorithm checks if it fulfills the property. The major differences between *Algorithm 3* and *4* are that we inserted condition for property 1 and we explicitly specified when a node is to be loaded. This algorithm allows to load only the nodes which are relevant. For example, if we find the connectivity of *e* and *a* on leaf level in Figure 8, *Algorithm 4* will be executed as follows;

Initially, the input parameters of *Algorithm 4* are *P*={*A*,*B*,*C*}, and *A*=*e*, *B*=*a*.
Then the following processes of execution are;

step 1. Load *B* node and set *M*, *Mp* as {*d*,*e*,*f*} and {*e*,*d*} respectively.
step 2. Check *C* if it fulfills property 1. fails.
step 3. Check *A* if it fulfills property 1, succeeds.
step 3-1. Load *A*, and find connected node with *Mp* among child nodes of *B*.
step 3-2. Update *Mp* as *Mp* U {*b*,*a*}.
step 4. check if a is in *Mp*. Succeeds and terminate algorithm.

In this case, we see that *C* is never loaded and its child nodes are not compared, whereas an additional disk access and computation for its child nodes are required by *Algorithm 3*. We will compare the performances of these algorithms in section 5.

```
Procedure SearchConnectedComponent2(P: set of MBR, A and B : object, i : level)
   // P is set of parents which forms a connected component on level i-1 //
   p_a ← MBR(A, i-1),  p_b ← MBR(B, i-1);   // find MBRs of A and B on level i-1 //
   m_a ← MBR(A, i),    m_b ← MBR(B, i);     // find MBRs of A and B on level i //
   load(p_a),   load(p_b);
   M ← {child nodes of p_a };
   Mp ← {m_a } U { m | m ∈ M, and m is connected with m' ∈ Mp };
   for each p in P
      if p is connected with at least one node in Mp, // property 1 //
         load(p);
         M ← {child nodes of p };
         while(there is no change on Mp)
            Mp ← Mp U { m | m ∈ M - Mp,  m is directly connected with Mp }
         end while
      end if
   end for
   if m_b ∉ Mp, then return Fail;  // m_a and m_b are in different connected component //
end procedure
```

Algorithm 4 Improved Method for Finding Connected Component on Level *i*.

5 PERFORMANCE

In order to analyze the performance of query processing for connectivity using θ-partial R^+-tree, we must consider three measures; filtering rate, number of disk accesses and CPU time. It is obvious that reducing the number of disk accesses is crucial in spatial query processing. The results of our experiments have shown that we can not ignore the CPU time needed for query processing of connectivity as well as disk I/O time. The filtering rate, which can be defined as the rate of candidate objects over total objects, tells about how many unnecessary objects are removed by filtering process. Small filtering rate implies that the number of objects which are o be verified on refinement step is small. The more objects are removed, the less becomes the filtering rate.

These three measures are, however correlated. For example, as filtering rate increase, the number of candidate objects increases and the amount of CPU time for refinement step may increase at the same time.

We simulated the performance of the two methods *Algorithm 3* and *4* proposed in section 4, with 10000 segment objects, which were clustered into 100 regions, and R^+-tree built from the objects. In reality, the distribution of objects is clustered rather than uniform [15][16]. We varied the relative size of objects over the size of total area from 0.0005 to 0.002. In order to find out connectivity between two objects, we also generated 100 couples of query objects. The query objects were also distributed around clusters. The simulation was performed on Sparc workstation under Unix system. We observed CPU time, number of disk accesses and filtering rate.

Table 1 Filtering Rate

Relative size	*0.0005*	*0.001*	*0.0015*	*0.002*
Average number of R^+-tree leaf nodes	424	433	465	467
Average number of leaf nods in θ-partial R^+-tree	47	212	244	366
Average filtering rate	0.110	0.313	0.524	0.784
Average number of internal nodes referenced in θ-partial R^+-tree	15.5	19.5	21.0	19.5
Average probability(filtering rate=0)	0.825	0.685	0.475	0.215

Table 1 shows the filtering rates of the methods proposed in the previous section, depending on the different relative sizes. When the relative size is large, the probability that two objects are connected is strong, and the number of objects in a connected component is also large. And it should be also noted that while their checking processes of θ condition in the two methods are different as explained in the previous section, the numbers of filtered nodes are identical. In table 1, we can observe that the number of leaf nodes in R^+-tree slightly differ depending on relative size. It is due to the handling policy of overlapping MBR in R^+-tree construction algorithm.

We find that the filtering efficiency is excellent, when the relative size is very small (=0.0005). Even though we count the CPU time and the numbers of disk accesses during filtering phase, which are eventually identical to the numbers of references on internal nodes in R^+-tree, listed on fourth row, the overhead of filtering phases is not comparable with the benefits of our methods, which are reduction of total CPU time and disk accesses required.

But as the relative size grows, the filtering efficiency becomes worse. It is because our checking process is to find out connected components and when the relative size increase, the number of nodes in a connected component also increase. When the relative size is 0.0005, the filtering rate is about 0.1. It implies that the number of objects which are to be verified for refinement step, reduces by 1/10. When we consider the CPU time to process refinement whose complexity is $O(n^2)$, we gain CPU cost by 100 times.

The last row in Table 1 means the probability that the filtering process detects that query objects are not connected and stops processing by returning *NotConnected*. In this case, no more disk accesses or CPU time become useless and the query processing performance is improved by considerable amount.

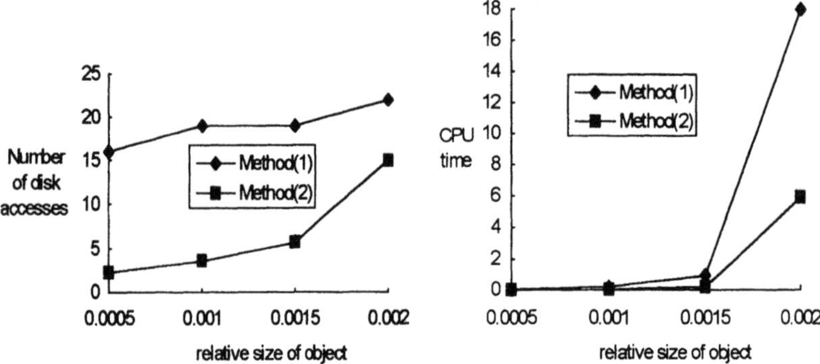

Figure 9 Number of Disk Accesses. **Figure 10** CPU time.

We compared the two methods proposed in section 4, by means of number of disk accesses and CPU time needed by filtering. Figure 9 shows the numbers of disk accesses of the methods depending on relative size. *Algorithm 3* requires more disk accesses than *Algorithm 4*, as we already mentioned. However, the difference between the methods decreases, as increases the relative size.

Figure 10 shows CPU time for the two methods. We find a difference between the methods. For small objects, the performances of the methods slightly differ. But for large objects, we observe a great difference between the two methods.

6 CONCLUSION

To processing topological query in visual databases is in general very complicated and expensive. In this paper, we have proposed several spatial query processing methods for connectivity, using geometric data and R^+-tree tree as the underlying indexing method, without any topological data. Our approach was inspired by filtering and refinement spatial query processing strategy. The goal is to minimize the number of disk accesses and CPU time for query processing, and on the same time to speed up the filtering process. To achieve these goals, we propose

i. A general spatial query processing method for filtering using θ-partial R^+-tree. We can employ this procedure for any kind of spatial query, by specifying θ condition and its checking method.

ii. Two checking methods when θ condition is connectivity. These methods speed up the filtering process by minimizing the number of disk accesses and CPU time.

We compared the performances of the proposed methods by simulation. The results of simulation showed that the second method gives better performance than the first. When the size of objects is small, the second method is excellent. And both of the methods considerably reduce the number of objects to be verified during refinement step.

The connectivity query is a fundamental one in visual databases. Other types of queries can be derived from it. For example, the shortest path search query is an application of connectivity query. Further work could focus on the topics such like upstream, downstream, and shortest path query processing method based on connectivity. These are intensively required in many real applications of visual database systems.

Another focus of our researches includes the generalization of θ-partial R^+-tree to other types of query which requires complex and expensive processing. Also parallelization of θ-partial R^+-tree with use of parallel R-trees [12] could be one of research focus.

Acknowledgement

I would like to thank T. Sellis for giving me R^+-tree source program.

7 REFERENCES

[1] Laurini,R. and Thompson,D. (1992) *Fundamentals of Spatial Information Systems. A*cademic press, 470 pages.

[2] Guenther,O. and Buchmann,A. (1990) Research Issues in Spatial Databases. *SIGMOD Record.* Vol.19 No.4, pp.61-68.

[3] Agrawal,R. and Jagadish,H.V. (1994) Algorithms for Searching Massive Graphs. *IEEE Trans. Knowledge and Data Engineering* Vol.6 No.2, pp.225-238.

[4] Jagadish,H.V. (1990) On Indexing Line Segments. *Proc. 16th VLDB Conf.* , pp.614-625.

[5] Aho,A.V., Hopcroft,J.E. and Ullman,J.D. (1983) *The Design and Analysis of Computer Algorithms.* Addison-Wesley, 680 pages.

[6] Ioannidis,Y.E and Ramakrishnan,R. (1987) Efficient Transitive Closure Algorithms. *Proc. 14th VLDB* , pp.507-518.

[7] Brinkhoff,T., Kriegel,H.P. and Seeger,B. (1993) Efficient Processing of Spatial Joins Using R-trees. *Proc. SIGMOD'93*, pp.237-246.

[8] Orenstein,J. (1986) Spatial Query Processing in an Object-Oriented Database System. *Proc. SIGMOD'86*, pp.326-333.

[9] Sellis,T., Roussopoulos,N. and Faloutsos,C. (1987) The R+-tree: A Dynamic Index for Multidimensional Objects. *Proc. VLDB* , pp. 507-518.

[10] Guttman,A. (1984) R-trees: A Dynamic Index Structure for Spatial Searching. *Proc. SIGMOD'84*, pp.47-57.

[11] Beckmann,N., Kriegel,H.P., Schneider,R. and Seeger.B. (1990) The R*-tree: An Efficient and Robust Access method for Points and Rectangles. *Proc. SIGMOD'90*, pp.322-331.

[12] Kamel,I. and Faloutsos,C. (1992) Parallel R-tree. *Proc. SIGMOD'92*, pp.195-204.

[13] Graefe,G. (1993) Query Evaluation Techniques for Large Databases. *ACM Computing Surveys*, Vol.25 No2, pp.73-170.

[14] Lu,W. and Han,J. (1992) Distance-Associated Join Indices for Spatial Range Search. *Proc. ICDE'92*, pp.284-292.

[15] Hoel,E.G. and Samet,H. (1992) A Qualitive Comparison Study of Data Structures for Large Line Segment Databases. *Proc. SIGMOD'92*, pp.205-214.

[16] Faloutsos,C. and Kamel,I. (1994) Beyond Uniformity and Independence : Analysis of R-tree Using the Concept of Fractal Demension. *Proc. PODS'94*, pp.4-13.

8 BIOGRAPHY

Myeong-A Kang received the B.S. degree in computer science from Pusan National University, South Korea, in 1994. She is currently a graduate student in department of computer science at Pusan National University.

Ki-Joune Li received the B.S. and M.S. degrees in computer science from Seoul National University, South Korea, and Ph.D from INSA, France, in 1992. He is currently in department of computer science at Pusan National University, South Korea. His current research interests include spatial information systems, hypermedia and object-oriented software engineering .

INDEX OF CONTRIBUTORS

KEYWORD INDEX

GPSR Compliance
The European Union's (EU) General Product Safety Regulation (GPSR) is a set of rules that requires consumer products to be safe and our obligations to ensure this.

If you have any concerns about our products, you can contact us on

ProductSafety@springernature.com

In case Publisher is established outside the EU, the EU authorized representative is:

Springer Nature Customer Service Center GmbH
Europaplatz 3
69115 Heidelberg, Germany

www.ingramcontent.com/pod-product-compliance
Ingram Content Group UK Ltd.
Pitfield, Milton Keynes, MK11 3LW, UK
UKHW020152250726
13967UKWH00003B/1013
* 9 7 8 1 4 7 5 7 6 9 3 6 4 *